Hillebert

Adopting: Sound Choices, Strong Families

As I finished reading Pat Johnston's new book—*Adopting Sound Choices, Strong Families*—I felt as if I had just found "Adoptipedia." Johnston leaves no rock unturned as she takes readers through a journey which begins long before people even know or realize that they may have an adoption journey. She examines every single issue mentioned in adoption literature; I found each page filled with valuable information for those individuals considering adoption. This well integrated piece of work is a "must read" for anyone thinking about adopting; it should be mandatory reading for all professionals who work within the adoption arena. Johnston illuminates issues well beyond those typically addressed in pre-adoptive training. This will become a handbook for those exploring adoption and for those working with them. I highly recommend this book!

Gregory C. Keck , Ph.D.,
Founder/Director of the Attachment & Bonding Center of Ohio
co-author of *Adopting the Hurt Child* and *Parenting the Hurt Child*

The world of adoption has changed dramatically over the last few years, making this update to Pat Johnston's previous books an essential tool. *Adopting: Sound Choices, Strong Families* will become one of the classic resources for the adoption community.

Mark T. McDermott, Esq.
Adoptive Parent, Adoption Attorney
Past president of the American Academy of Adoption Attorneys

Pat Johnston has the unique ability to understand the feelings of a person struggling with infertility and has once again shown why she is the authority on infertility and adoption resources. *Adopting: Sound Choices, Strong Families* is a wonderful tool that will help many people trying to make the transition from the emotional burdens of infertility to adoption. I would recommend this book for my infertility patients, regardless of where they are in the treatment process

Jeffrey L. Deaton, M.D.
Reproductive Endocrinologist
Premier Fertility Center, North Carolina

Touched both personally and professionally by adoption for over three decades, Pat Johnston brings to her newest work, *Adopting: Sound Choices, Strong Families*, wise direction and thorough advice gained from such incredible life experiences. With solid insight, Pat guides her readers through the early stages of exploring and learning about adoption through to preparation for a child's arrival and the early months that follow, touching the emotional, relational and practical aspects of the journey. She fills each and every chapter with valuable information for families considering adoption and for the professionals that guide them in their journey of family building. This book will be a great addition to any agency's pre-adoption suggested reading. I highly recommend this tremendous resource!

Jayne Schooler
author and adoption educator
author/co-author of *The Whole Life Adoption Book* and
Telling the Truth to Your Adopted and Foster Child.

I have been recommending Pat Johnston's Adopting after Infertility for 15 years. In truth, I have almost insisted that prospective adopting parents read what I have considered to be the adoption Bible.

I didn't think it was possible to improve upon Adopting after Infertility, but Pat has done it again. Adopting: Sound Choices, Strong Families has incorporated the wisdom of her prior books and expanded to include updated material and current adoption professionals' thinking on virtually every imaginable aspect of adoption.

This is the quintessential book for those considering adoption and those who are already adoptive families. It is also a must-read for those facing any genetic or gestational loss, as she guides singles and couples through the grief process, helping them to make wise and considered family building choices.Thorough and clear, this book is simply excellent. I will be buying it, gifting it, loaning it and reading it for many years to come.

Carole LieberWilkins, M.A.
Marriage and Family Therapist

Pat Johnston's book *Adopting: Sound Choices, Strong Families* is a thoughtfully written book that addresses a myriad of unique issues likely to be encountered by families preparing to embark on their adoption journey. Richly illustrated by poignant and sometimes humorous vignettes it delves into the complex aspects of adoptive parenting in a style that is compassionate and child focused. Married couples, same gender couples and singles hoping to build their family through adoption will find Pat's practical "how-tos" and sound advice invaluable. This comprehensive book is my number one choice for families and professionals seeking to broaden their knowledge of adoption.

Jane M. Page, LCSW
Clinical Director of Adoption
The Cradle, Evanston Illinois

Having placed my son for adoption almost a decade ago, only through *Adopting: Sound Choices, Strong Families* have I come to know and respect the dragons faced by my sons adoptive parents. Underlying this book is a great how-to guide for communication in marriages, whether the issue faced is infertility or who cleans what when! Through Pat Johnstons insight, expertise, and personal experience in the fields of adoption and infertility, she brings knowledge and understanding to a diverse audience of readers from infertile couples and singles, to their children, to supportive family members and friends, to parents considering placement and birthparents who stand on the other side of the adoption process, to the media and general public. Certainly, a "must read

Courtney Lewis
Birthmother and Adoption Advocate

I couldn't be more thrilled with Pat Johnston's latest book *Adopting: Sound Choices, Strong Families.* There is a tremendous need for such a comprehensive work addressing all family compositions and every avenue of adoption. Her chapters on attachment and transitioning are extremely relevant and applicable and should be required reading for any family considering adoption (as well as those formed by birth). Pat's voice educates and entertains simultaneously. Her new book is a must read for adoption workers, families and those who support them.

Kathie G. Stocker
Adoption Social Worker, Adoptive Parent
NACAC state rep and board member of
NorthwestAdoptive Families Association (NAFA)

ADOPTING:
Sound Choices, Strong Families

Patricia Irwin Johnston

Perspectives Press, Inc.
Indianapolis, Indiana

Perspectives Press, Inc.
P.O. Box 90318
Indianapolis, IN 46290-0318
USA
(317) 872-3055
www.perspectivespress.com

Book and cover designed by Bookwrights
Manufactured in the United States of America
Hardcover ISBN-13 978-0-944934-34-0

Library of Congress Cataloging-in-Publication Data

Johnston, Patricia Irwin.
    Adopting: sound choices, strong families / by Patricia Irwin Johnston.
       p. cm.
    Includes bibliographical references and index.
    ISBN-13: 978-0-944934-34-0
    1. Adoption.   I. Title.
HV875.J677 2007
362.734--dc22
                              2007033077

Dedication

To Dave, Joel, Erica, Lindsey, and Mary Jane, and to Baby Girl Marchetti—the much anticipated granddaughter who will be born between the time this book goes to press in October 2007 and the time you hold it in your hands—she will become the first member of yet another generation of our multiracial, multi-ethnic, birth and adoption expanded family.

Table of Contents

Introduction   11

**Part One
Acknowledging and Unraveling
Challenges to Family Building**

Chapter 1: Beware the Dragon   18

Chapter 2: Confronting Dragons   30

Chapter 3: The Plan   42

**Part Two
Life Inside Adoption: An Overview**

Chapter 4: The Culture of Adoption   83

Chapter 5: As a Family Grows   104

Chapter 6: Special Issues along the Way   137

Chapter 7: Ethics: Assuring a Firm Foundation   160

**Part Three
Embracing Adoption and Making Sound Choices**

Chapter 8: The Plan, Revisited   202

Chapter 9: Which Child?   226

Chapter 10: Openness   257

Chapter 11: Finding Your Path and a Guide   271

Chapter 12: Approval (and Preparation!)   312

Part Four
The Real Thing

Chapter 13: Anticipation   339

Chapter 14: Planning for a Happy Homecoming   397

Chapter 15: Adjustments in the First Year Together   429

Chapter 16: Adoption in the Big Wide World   482

An After Thought   508

Acknowledgments   510

Endnotes   511

Index   517

Introduction(s)

Readers often skip introductions. That's too bad, because introductions set a tone for a book and offer important information that helps a reader to understand just where an author's ideas come from. With this introduction, I will introduce you to myself as the author of this and several other books, and help you to understand how my personal evolution as one who has been living in adoption for over 40 years and working both as a hyperactive volunteer and as a paid professional for 30-plus of those has developed and driven the philosophy that undergirds this book. What's more, this introduction offers you a look at the framework for what this book proposes to do for you, the reader.

The Author

Like all of the books I have written, *Adopting: Sound Choices, Strong Families* does not pretend to be objective. In fact, it is very opinionated! That's part of who I am—the very well-read, well-informed, well-connected, experienced, outspoken, get-to-work-and-pull-others-with-you, drag-it-out-from-under-the-rug-and-shake-it, and highly-opinionated part—which explains why I am one of those love her/hate her people in the infertility and adoption worlds. I am a true *consumer advocate*!

When Dave's and my first child was a newborn in 1975, the state of Indiana tried to eliminate the form of adoption—independent—which had brought him to our home. I lobbied furiously in our legislature, and, to the chagrin of the good old boys who had brought the bill to committee, "that cute young woman with the baby" defeated them. An *adoption advocate* was born.

Three years later, having moved to a new city, Dave and I met another newcomer couple who was struggling with infertility. We became fast friends, and the woman (Carol, a nurse) and I decided to write a book about it. Instead we stumbled upon Barbara Eck Menning's then-new book *Infertility: A Guide for the Childless Couple* and the fledgling organization which she had founded: Resolve, Inc. *Infertility advocates and patient educators* emerged; and for several years Carol and I were embroiled in chapter founding and growth, publicity, and then being part of a group that "made over" the national organization. Our book was never written, but Carol Perrott and I remain good friends. She has three grown sons, one adopted by her and two born to her. Dave (himself adopted as a baby) and I adopted three babies—all now young adults.

Adopting: Sound Choices, Strong Families is my fourth book on infertility-related decision making. First there was *An Adoptor's Advocate* in 1984. Our youngest child (in our first open adoption) had just been placed with us. It was the first book to look at adoption in the context of infertility; the first to identify multiple losses attached to the infertility experience, and I'm proud to say that it influenced a different approach to counseling infertile couples. I continued to be active in Resolve, and eventually became the co-chairman (with my friend Dr. Gary Gross) and then chairman of its national board of directors, leaving the board in 1992.

Then there was *Adopting after Infertility* in 1992. To the multiple-loss concept, it added a uniquely practical decision-making model that helped it to become a standard that many professionals have required that their clients read.

Friends who were physicians, nurses and counselors in infertility practices encouraged me to adapt *Adopting after Infertility*'s decision-making model to their patients. I hoped that Carol's and my third partner in founding a Resolve chapter in Indiana, William R. "Bud" Keye, Jr., MD, would be ready to work on that with me, but he was very busy writing and editing academic materials, and in the political practice world of infertility through The American Society for Reproductive Medicine (where he was one of the founders of a psychological special interest group that pulled mental health professionals into the ASRM fold. Eventually he became president of ASRM). I went on to write *Taking Charge of Infertility* alone in 1996, but collaborated with Dr. Keye by writing a couple of chapters for medical texts that he has edited over the years.

Our experience with our third child taught me even more. Lindsey had arrived in 1984, not a newborn, but as a bounced-from-foster-home-to-foster-home, two-and-a-half-month-old sad sack. Ensuing discussions with my own parents-in-law about their adopted children's arrivals, each at six months of age, from U.S. baby nurseries of the 1940s made clear that ours was not an unusual experience, but a normative one that was almost never spoken about! It drove me to read stacks of research-based books and interview multiple attachment professionals and discuss arrivals with hundreds of families and resulted in a fifth book, *Launching a Baby's Adoption* (1997). This book was focused on the things that adoption workers had never told new adopting parents, not because they were "hiding these things," but because they didn't know! It offered practical issues of attachment in adopted infants, rather than older children (which was the focus of every single one of the other attaching in adoption books at the time). A *child advocate* had emerged.

My most recent book, *Adoption Is a Family Affair* (2001) was a collaboration between myself and the members of three adoption chat boards that I have moderated for INCIID (The International Council for Infertility

Information Dissemination) for several years. The revolving members of these pre-adoptive and newly adoptive parent groups had shared a single concern over and over and over: what can we do to help our families and friends "get" adoption. Together we pooled questions, comments and anecdotes, and I then pulled together this book which deals with almost any sort of adoption for almost any sort of family and offered the royalties to benefit INCIID. I had become an *adoption mentor* for a new generation of advocates.

The Book

Sure, there were things about *Adopting after Infertility* that needed updating. Since 1992 there had been a number of new written resources developed and some of the older ones had gone out of print. Since I have an educational and experiential background as a teacher and school librarian, those changes were important to me. Layers of education and information needed to be changed.

Even more importantly, one of the most important resources for adopting families—one whose board I had served on twice and believed in so strongly that I repeatedly referred to it in that earlier book—had shocked the adoption community by going out of business in a sudden financial tornado in 2000. Adoptive Families of America, based in Minnesota, had grown and thrived for over 30 years. It had been the most visible not-for-profit "umbrella organization" for local adoptive parent support groups, developing training tools for those groups, serving as a frequently quoted voice of sanity and correction in the media, offering several highly successful national conferences for adoptive parents (as opposed to the primarily professional conferences offered by several other good organizations), and had turned its venerable meaty newsprint magazine *Ours: The Magazine of Adoptive Families*, into the glossy newsstand-available *Adoptive Families*. Now AFA was gone, leaving only the still-wonderful magazine, purchased by a for-profit corporation. A layer of consumer education and protection was gone and there had been no real replacement.

In addition, I felt it was important to try to broaden the audience for this book. I had deliberately addressed the first two books to infertile couples like Dave and me (whether primarily or secondarily fertility impaired). But over the years it has become clear to me (because non-infertile consumers have told me) that anyone who comes to adoption through any barrier to their being able to give birth to a child without the permission and cooperation of an outsider (probably a paid outsider) faces similar losses and must make similar decisions. Same-sex couples, single parents, or heterosexual partners who are infertile all face dragons in trying to build families. Today I think of all of these folks as "family challenged." So, while infertility has informed the base of my personal understanding of coming into adoption, I believe that the struggle itself embraces all of the family challenged, those for whom adoption has become the only route to parenthood, and that the emotional impact of the striving itself should be clearly addressed, examined and puzzled out before parenthood begins.

A relatively early non-academic user of the Internet (email and usergroups in 1995, URL purchased in 1996, a website in 1998), I had watched the worldwide web grow and change for over a decade. The problem with the Internet and adoption now is that the Internet has passed the point where it is a genuinely useful source of accurate information. The unregulated Internet has allowed for the proliferation of one-on-one personal scams (including a burgeoning adoption version of the ubiquitous Nigerian scam[1]), has made it easy for fraudulent or incompetent businesses to set up shop and lure clients/customers, and has pulled prospective adopters away from the legal and consumer protections in place when using resources relatively close to home. It is not at all unusual for a prospective international adopter living in one state to use a homestudy agency there, a marketing entity located in another state, a "partner of a placement agency" in yet another state, a placement agency in a fourth state, and a facilitator in another country connected to the orphanages there. Multiple levels of placement providers like this create two distinct problems:

1. Every layer of service adds to the overall cost of the adoption (which is why we see the range of costs for adoption of similar children from the same area of the world range from the low thousands to the mid tens of thousands of dollars).

2. Every layer of service adds to the risk that someone along the line will either drop an important bureaucratic ball, deprive you accidentally or on purpose of information that is important to your decision making and future parenting, or do something not quite ethical or ride roughshod over a law or policy here or abroad to put not just *your* adoption, but future adoptions by others at risk.

So, while *Adopting: Sound Choices, Strong Families*, like the earlier *Adopting after Infertility* and *Launching a Baby's Adoption* which it replaces, remains primarily a guide to making good decisions about adoption rather than a how-to guide, and while this book retains many of the tools and the familiar vignettes that worked well for readers in those books, it has also been scrubbed and polished to make it current. New tools have been added and new questions asked, and I've stripped away any doubt of where I fall on the side of an issue of controversy.

The book has been designed to move with its readers through four stages, from early exploration and learning to communicate, through examining tough stuff and making clear choices (pro or con), to commitment, and finally through adoption expectancy and the first months after the arrival of a child in your family. At each stage common myths and stereotypes will be clarified with facts. You will be asked to examine parts of yourself

which you may not like and to make decisions in the context of a well-connected, communicative partnership (if you have one) rather than based on general feelings, which can be fed by fear and false information.

Part One doesn't assume that you are "into" adoption at all. It assumes instead that while some readers have picked this book up with great enthusiasm, many readers are feeling ambivalent about adoption, some may have even been dragged into reading this book and learning more about adoption, and that a few have even been delivered an ultimatum: Go at least this far with me in exploring adoption options, or else! In this first section the concept of exploring adoption as a challenge to family building is examined, placed in the context of how our cumulative experiences with crisis and loss contribute to how we communicate, how we make decisions, and how we live out the consequences of our decisions. In this section the goal is to help readers to regain some sense of control over their lives, to offer some practical tools for making all kinds of future decisions, and, by its end, to help each reader decide whether he or she can genuinely open up enough to the idea of adoption as a positive way to build a family to learn more about what life inside adoption is really like. Some folks will stop here.

The second section will introduce those who are open, but still unsure, to the central issues that are an ongoing part of adoptive family life. Here's where we'll talk about the possibility of attachment challenges, address as fact that adoption comes with an added layer of issues that last a lifetime, begin to honestly think about the reality that children in adoption will always have two families, and discuss adoption as a "walking around in the world" issue for both parents and kids. The goal here is to lay bare as many of adoption's important differences as possible, so that by the end of this section you will know whether or not adoption is a viable option for you. It is not a good option for everyone, and determining that it is not a good one for you right here and now is a good thing. For readers who feel able to take on those challenges in exchange for the opportunity to parent, this section will ready them for the third section.

Commitment questions form Part Three's core. This is the place where we'll talk about making solid, well-informed decisions about the nuts and bolts of moving into adoptive family life. How flexible can you realistically be to choices of race and ethnicity, age, and abilities in your child? What should you know about birthfamilies and their role in your becoming parents and in your future life with your child? Will you adopt openly or confidentially, domestically or internationally? How do you choose the professionals who will assist you in building a family through adoption? What can you expect in a homestudy?

Finally, Part Four, titled "The Real Thing!" offers parents-to-be and new parents support and highly practical information about allowing themselves first to feel expectant, bringing their families and friends aboard with them as they wait, and letting them know what they should realistically expect from both themselves and their child emotionally and physically during the first several months after a placement. The focus of the last part of this section is primarily, but not exclusively, devoted to issues of adopting an infant through pre-school aged child.

My hope is that what I've learned can help you learn what you need to know to make the best possible decisions about your journey to family building.

Pat Johnston
Indianapolis, August, 2007

PART ONE

Acknowledging and Unraveling Challenges to Family Building

CHAPTER 1

Beware the Dragon

> Once upon a time there lived a princess so beautiful both inside and out that every man in her parents' realm longed to marry her. After many months of grueling challenges, a noble, kind, and handsome prince won her hand, and they were married.
>
> As they left the palace of her parents to make their own way in the world, the young people were given the blessings of the monarchs, who presented them with a carefully drawn map. On it were plotted the roads and the rivers, the mountains and the mansions, the forests and the fields, the towns and the trading posts of their known world. It was a beautiful map, complete in every way—for as far as it went, that is.
>
> All around the edge of the map, beyond the blue of the wide sea and the purple of the impenetrable mountains, were printed warnings in bold red ink, "DANGER! Here there be dragons!"

Most of us spent many childhood days curled in warm laps listening as a parent read even more sexist versions of stories much like this one. Surrounding us was the firm shape of a parent who kept us safe and secure. The fairy tales gave way to more realistic stories, but the themes remained substantially the same: for those who are good, noble and true, for those who try their best, the dangerous unknown is only a fairy tale. Those who try hard will succeed.

And so, like the fairy tale princes and princesses of our childhoods, our expectations about love and family building were idealistic and simplistic. Two people fall in love. They commit to one another. They establish a firm foundation on which to build a secure home. They have children.

In biology class, in family living, in health and sex education there were drawings and diagrams, and warnings about the dangers of premarital sex. These classes offered several messages for Gen Xers and Millennials who are reading this, my third infertility/adoption decision-making book. The first message was about the demons of sexually transmitted diseases, and in particular AIDS. The second was the one familiar to earlier generations:

our bodies are time bombs set to go off. If we engage in sex, we will get pregnant! Beware of *that* dragon, for sure!

Social studies sent a third message to those of us who did not find a partner with whom to parent as well as to those of us who were not heterosexual. It was that growing tolerance in society would soon open family building opportunities for us as well.

Ah, and then there was the comforting final message: People of the second and third birth control generations, you have as long as you want to become parents! Go ahead and delay marriage and parenthood. Get all of your financial, educational and career ducks in a row; take time finding just the right partner before parenting. There's *always* time.

You listened, and here you are—young-marrieds or married-agains, without a partner or with a same gender partner—facing a dragon guarding the entrance to parenthood.

When this dragon rears its head, many tend first to play ostrich, burying their heads in the sand and pretending not to see. For months and even years we may deny the possibility of a problem. We just haven't met the right person, we tell ourselves. Or, when we have and we are trying to conceive it's, well . . . We're under so much stress at work. Our timing is off. The travel schedule has gotten in the way. Looking back now and remembering your own denial, you may wonder why it took so long for you to realize that you needed help, why you wasted so much time with the wrong partner, the wrong doctor, why you refused to acknowledge that there was a problem brewing here.

The answer is not so difficult. You were afraid. Somewhere in the back of your mind you sensed that a dragon was lurking there. You hoped to avoid the crisis of facing the dragon by ignoring it.

The Chinese—an ancient and philosophically sophisticated culture—write not with a sound-based alphabet, but with complex word pictures. Interestingly, in Chinese, the written expression of the concept of *crisis* is said to be drawn by putting together the characters for two other words: *danger* and *opportunity*.

危機

Because we sense danger in the face of any crisis, we often put off facing its reality. And so it was with singles, with gay couples, with fertility impaired heterosexual couples. To acknowledge a barrier to becoming a parent was to face imminent danger. Though at first we might not have been able to clearly identify precisely what it was that we feared, our subconscious sensed the possibility of loss or disappointment ahead and insulated us from pain through denial.

Losses Accompanying Challenged Family Building

- Control over many aspects of life
- Individual genetic continuity, linking past and future
- The joint conception of a child with a beloved life partner
- The physical satisfactions of pregnancy and birth
- The emotional gratifications of pregnancy and birth
- The opportunity to parent

Do you remember that childhood friend who moved away when you were four? The special toy lost irretrievably on the plane to Grandma's? The cat that ran away? The math test you failed? The first love who dumped you unceremoniously? The college which turned you down? Getting laid off from that great job? Every day we experience losses and disappointments. Some of them are painful, etching themselves on our memories, changing who we consider ourselves to be. Others pass by nearly unnoticed because we have become so accustomed to dealing with them—keys misplaced for a couple of frustrating hours, another lottery ticket with the wrong numbers, forgetting an appointment, missing your train. But every loss—the large and the small—is one of the lessons which contribute to the development of a unique and very personal pattern for how each of us copes with disappointment and loss, a pattern which becomes so familiar, so automatic, that one rarely even recognizes that it has begun and is going on again.

Do you recall, for instance, having found yourself in a situation like the following[1] . . .

After having spent a day shopping, you arrive at home with your house key in your pocket and your arms loaded with packages only to hear the insistent ringing of your telephone on the other side of the door.

Almost since the invention of the telephone at the dawn of the 20th century, people who have one have had a terrible time allowing a phone to go unanswered, so as a typical person, you struggle with the packages you are juggling in order to fish out a key and then rush inside to answer the phone.

As you put the receiver to your ear, you hear yourself saying, "Hello? Hello?" to a dial tone (*denial*). You're *surprised* to hear that dial tone, and yet, after ten rings, you knew of course that enough time had passed between the last ring and your picking up the phone . . .

You begin a litany of "if onlys" (*bargaining*). "If only I'd had my key out and ready." "If only they'd let it ring one more time."

Feeling frustrated and disappointed about the lost call, you begin to vent a little *anger* at somebody. . . . "Doggone it! Why are people so impatient? They should have let it ring!" Or, perhaps, "Darn it, won't I ever learn to keep my keys in my hand!?"

You look at the packages strewn in your foyer and, subconsciously you begin a familiar process—your personal process—for coping with (*accepting/resolving*) a loss.

Remember, all of us have been experiencing losses since infancy. There was the babysitter who talked on the telephone despite your cries for a diaper change or a bottle. The goldfish from the fair died and Daddy helped bury it in the backyard. Your best friend moved clear across the country when his mom was transferred. That really cute girl said no when you asked her to the eighth grade dance. You failed an all important math test. Your favorite uncle died. A lover left.

There are many ways of coping with loss, and after years of experiencing losses large and small, each of us develops a personal pattern for doing so. Some people are more comfortable than others in accepting loss as normal and natural—as a part of their fate. They may shrug this lost phone call off with an "Oh well, if it is important, they'll call back" and go about the business of putting away the groceries. Others feel more comfortable with a substitution. Such a person may pick up the phone and call a friend. "Hi, did you just call? No? Yeah, well, I missed a call just as I got in from shopping and I thought it might have been you. . . . So what're ya doin'?" Still others cope with loss more aggressively by seeking to avoid future losses of a similar kind and assuming as much control as possible over every situation. If this is what you most commonly do, your reaction to an accumulation of lost phone calls may inspire you to explore the option of adding voice mail or caller ID to your phone service or send you out shopping for an answering machine.

Those whose family building is challenged by infertility or their marital status or their sexual orientation experience multiple losses, each with its own degree of significance. Taking the time right now to determine how it is that you (and your partner, if you have one) cope with loss is an important step toward deciding what family building alternative is right for you. But first you must acknowledge the series of losses built into your experience. Over many years of thinking about it, reading about it, talking with hundreds of couples about it, I have come to see six distinct areas of significant loss[2], many of which encompass several other related losses. The following sections address each of those areas.

The Loss of Control

Perhaps most clearly and immediately felt by those who experience family building challenges is the loss of control over numerous aspects of their lives.

Today's adults, who came to sexual maturity and selected partners after the birth control revolution precipitated by the wide availability of the birth control pill in the mid sixties, have always had the distinct expectation that they would be able to *control their family planning.* Unfortunately, because infertility was not discussed as they grew up, this expectation included not just the expectation that they would be able to avoid pregnancy when they so desired, but that they would be able to achieve pregnancy when they so desired. Losing control of a part of life which one's peers take so completely for granted is devastating and, for many people, precipitates a humiliating blow to self esteem.

Treating infertility demands that couples give up even more control. *Control of their sexual privacy and spontaneity,* for example, is forfeited to a medical team which asks them to chart their intercourse, supply semen samples, appear within hours after intercourse for a post-coital test, etc. *Control of their calendars* is given over to treatment.

Couples often comment that with infertility they feel that they have lost *control of every aspect of their lives.* What type or size car to buy depends on whether or not it will be carrying children. Accepting a new job or a promotion can become dependent on how travel impacts the treatment program, whether or not the new company has excellent health care benefits which cover infertility treatments, as well as whether or not the new employee's coverage for infertility treatment would be excluded because it was defined by the insurance company as a pre-existing condition. Continuing education may be put on hold when a woman expects that any day she will become pregnant, so that finishing a term might be difficult or impossible. Whether to buy a house in the suburbs with sidewalks for Big Wheels and excellent schools, or a condo in the city close to work and cultural events is controlled by infertility. Social calendars may be driven by the menstrual cycle. Even the most private of decisions—how much time to spend in a hot tub, how much coffee to drink, how many miles to run each week, whether to buy briefs or boxer shorts—can be controlled by the infertility experience.

Singles and gay couples, most already feeling the sting of discrimination, have often compensated for much of the rest of their feelings of being "out of control" by taking careful control of as many aspects of their lives as they can. They may have planned and lived out successful careers, own beautifully designed homes in carefully chosen communities, yet they know that the dragon which guards the door to family building is outside their control.

To many individuals for whom being in control is an important part of their ability to feel confident and competent, challenged family building represents a devastating loss, but this is not its only loss.

The Loss of Genetic Continuity

Potentially, challenged fertility means the loss of our individual genetic continuity—our expectation that we will continue the genes of our families in an unbroken blood line from some distant past into a promising future. For those raised in blood-is-thicker-than-water cultures, this loss is significant enough to be avoided at all costs. While some extended families are entirely comfortable with the idea of adopting in order to carry a family into the future, others believe strongly that the family blood line cannot be grafted onto. Why we feel this way is not as important as is the fact that we acknowledge that we do. When the potential for this loss is felt powerfully—sometimes re-enforced by repeated conceptions which end in miscarriage—alternatives such as donor insemination which allow a woman to use her own eggs and to be pregnant, or traditional surrogacy which provides a man with the opportunity to carry on his genetic material, or gestational surrogacy which allow both partners to use their own genetic material can sometimes be more attractive than traditional adoption. However, as we'll discuss later, for individuals for whom loss of genetic continuity is central and powerful, pursuing family building alternatives which allow the other partner to retain genetic continuity at the loss of one's own can be devastating to the relationship.

The Loss of a Jointly Conceived Child

Our earliest dreams about parenting included the expectation of our parenting a jointly conceived child. Gay and lesbian partners perhaps face this loss earlier than heterosexuals do. In choosing a life partner all of us do at least a little fantasizing about what our children might be like. Will he have her intellect and his sense of humor? Grandpa's red hair and Aunt Wilma's athletic prowess? Gosh, think of the medical expenses if she inherits both her mother's crossed eye and her father's terrible overbite! This child who represents the blending of both the best and the worst of our most intimate selves also represents for many a kind of ultimate bonding of partner to partner. In giving our genes to one another for blending, we offer our most vulnerable, intimate and valuable sense of ourselves—a gift that is perhaps the most precious we can offer. How more vulnerable can we be to another, how much more trusting, than to agree to give 23 of our unique chromosomes in exchange for 23 of our partner's to make a new 46 chromosome human being? Losing that dream and so feeling forced to consider alternatives such as donor insemination, hiring a surrogate mother, adopting, etc. can be painful indeed for those for whom this expectation was particularly important.

Pregnancy and Birth—Lost Physical and Emotional Expectations

Another challenging loss to deal with is that of the physical satisfaction of successful pregnancy and birth experiences. Though many people see the loss of a pregnancy as belonging entirely to women, this is not so. True enough, the physical changes and challenges of pregnancy and birth are experienced by women alone, but producing a child, as any counselor of pregnant teens will verify, is the ultimate rite of passage for both men and women—the final mark of having reached adulthood. You're grown up now, and your parents aren't in charge anymore. Beyond that, the physical ability to impregnate a woman or to carry and birth a child represents the ultimate expression of maleness or femaleness—our bodies at work doing what they were built to do. For many people, losing such capacities challenges their feelings about their maturity or their sexuality or both—about their competence as adult men and women. It is their own discomfort with, and fear of, this loss which generates from outsiders the tasteless humor which relates infertility to sexuality in comments such as, "Do you need a little help there? Happy to offer my services!" or "Let me show you how it's done." or "Hey, all Steve has to do is look at me and I'm pregnant—must be in the water!"

Some do succeed in becoming pregnant—sometimes over and over again—but these pregnancies result in repeated miscarriages and neonatal deaths. Trying to block out the unhelpful platitudes from well-meaning others ("Perhaps it was God's will." . . . "Don't worry, there will be another." . . . "At least you know that you can get pregnant!") can be a struggle like no other.

And there's more. Over the last several decades, a substantial element of our society, fearful of the impact of massive changes in family structure (and there certainly have been some), has mystified the experience of birth to an exaggerated extent. In search of the perfect "bonding" experience, couples carefully choose specific kinds of childbirth preparation—they attend classes together, read books, practice breathing, and so on. They expect to experience a magical closeness in spousal relationships, an irreplaceable wonder in sharing the birth experience, an expected instant eye-to-eye bonding between parents and child (a kind of magical superglue without which many fear that families will disintegrate). Hospitals marketing to the expectations of these couples, compete with one another to provide birthing rooms with the perfect equipment (birthing beds, chairs, tanks), the perfect atmosphere (music, guests allowed, champagne afterwards), and the perfect preparation (Lamaze classes, classes for siblings-to-be).

This set of expectations about the emotional gratifications of a shared pregnancy, prepared childbirth, and breast-feeding experience, though far too often unrealistic, is widely held. To risk losing such an experience is much more significant to today's would-be parents than it would have been to their parents and grandparents—whose mothers gave birth anes-thetized in sterile operating rooms while fathers paced in waiting rooms outside, who often didn't see and hold their children until hours after their births, who bottle fed formula to their infants—and, who bonded with their kids!

The Loss of the Parenting Experience

Finally, to be permanently family-challenged threatens the opportu-nity to parent, which is a major developmental goal for most adults. The psychologist Eric Erickson identified a series of developmental milestones humans work toward throughout their life span. In adulthood, Erickson wrote, the major goals are regenerativity and parenting. To be infertile, single and partnerless, or homosexual on the surface threatens our ability to achieve that goal, so that for many, challenged family-building represents a devastating blow.

Erickson and others have clearly demonstrated that it is possible for individuals to achieve this developmental goal and to satisfy the need for nurturing without becoming parents. Many adults find other ways of re-directing or rechanneling their need to nurture—through interaction with nieces and nephews and family friends; by choosing work which brings them in frequent contact with children; by volunteering as religious class teachers, scout leaders, or for a group such as Big Brothers/Big Sisters; by substituting pets for children; by becoming active in non-child centered volunteer work; by nurturing the earth through nature hobbies such as gardening, etc. This is not to imply that lists of possible redirections like these are seen as equivalent substitutions, or as realistic direct replace-ments for the lifelong experience of parenting a child jointly conceived and birthed with a much loved partner. While some adults can and do actively choose to meet their developmental needs to nurture without becoming parents, for those who have made the choice to become parents and have then been thwarted by family building challenges, the choice to redirect that energy is difficult.

For readers of this book—people who are considering adopting—reac-tions about this particular loss (parenting) are the most important of all. Adoption provides the opportunity to avoid this loss and this one alone. Singles and couples who adopt will become parents, but in doing so they will give up even more control to the process of adoption: they will forfeit their genetic continuity, they will lose the jointly conceived child of their dreams, and they will be deprived of the emotional and physical expecta-tions of pregnancy.

It is these potential and realized losses which tore at your gut during those days or weeks or months when you tried to deny the challenges you faced. These losses were the danger lurking in the crisis, and they were difficult to face. Now you are asking yourself to examine adoption—one of the potential opportunities which is a part of the crisis. Facing your feelings about infertility's losses can help you to decide if adoption is right for you.

So unless the loss of the opportunity to parent strikes you as the one loss you would most like to prevent—the one you would find most devastating—adoption may not be for you. The truth is that adoption is not a good choice for everybody!

Addressing the Crisis of Challenged Family Building

When I was a child we had a toy—a child-sized plastic figure with a clownish face filled with air and weighted on the bottom with beans or sand. Its purpose was to be punched, and to rise from the blow grinning, waiting to be punched again.

It has often seemed to me that as my husband and I experienced infertility we were like a pair of those punching bag toys placed on a conveyor belt moving through a system punctuated by swing arm gates. As we moved along that conveyor belt from doctor to lab to bed, to doctor to hospital to bed, to doctor to pharmacy to bed, to doctor to counselor to agency to attorney, and on and on, we found that the belt began to speed out of control (rather like the conveyor belt in the candy factory where Lucy and Ethel scrambled to fill boxes that rushed by).

Grinning madly (stiff upper lip, and all that) we were knocked askew by alternating swing arm gates—the doctor, the lab, the hospital, etc.—and sent separately reeling to cope with new information, new alternatives. Occasionally in swinging upright again from a blow we would bump against each other and provide one another with a momentary steadiness. But each time we were hit again, we went our own separate ways—alone.

There are several ways that people commonly deal with crisis, but victimhood is the least helpful. Spending significant amounts of time allowing yourself to become the victim of the crisis, floundering in a sea of despair as you are overwhelmed by waves of decisions that must be made is often undergirded by a sense of damaged self esteem. Infertile heterosexual couples, gay or lesbian couples, partnerless adults may all harbor the fear that family building challenges are a punishment of some sort or a message that they wouldn't be good parents anyway. Some fertility-impaired people react by believing that they are somehow less competent than they were before infertility was discovered. If their reproductive systems aren't working, they somehow illogically reason, then maybe they shouldn't trust their judgment, either. (Maybe Uncle Charlie was right; we're just trying too hard. Perhaps Mom's manicurist's cousin's doctor in Podunk is better than the reproductive endocrinologist at the medical center. Maybe my neighbor who thinks adoption is a sad substitute for real parenting because nobody could ever really love somebody else's reject isn't so far off base!)

Feeling neither confident nor competent, victims become unwilling and unable to make decisions. They begin to abdicate more and more control to others, losing their power. The partnerless may date desperately or not date at all, putting aside any thoughts that time is passing quickly. Infertile people may move robotically from treatment to treatment, never looking at alternatives such as adoption or collaborative reproduction. Caught up in the panic of the situation, such people tend to make decisions only when they *must* be made, struggling forward from crisis to crisis.

Those who allow themselves to become victims drift into a childless future they do not want because they haven't been able to make the decisions that might have helped them consider choices available to them. Victims will fall into a dropped-into-their-laps adoption because someone they saw as competent told them it was the next logical step, and, unprepared for the challenging differences in adoptive parenting, will struggle for years with a feeling that things aren't quite right, that this didn't work either.

I worry about victims, because when one operates by crisis management there is little opportunity for reflection. Victims stumble forward on that conveyor belt carried by a panicky momentum much like that we felt as out-of-control young runners about to skin our knees again. I worry because family-challenged people operating in such a mode tend to act out of desperation. With self-conscious laughter, they tell you that they would do anything to have a baby—even drink poison! Sadly, many really would. They sense that the surrogacy service or the adoption lawyer made it just a little *too* easy (and yet too expensive) for them to skip ahead of more "traditional" clients. They beg for one more cycle of a drug their doctor has decided isn't working. They borrow money for yet another in a long string of unsuccessful IVF attempts. They get involved with an adoption facilitator whose promises they know seem unrealistically promising in comparison to other sources. They risk it all on a not-quite-legal adoption. They juggle two or more potential adoptions or an adoption and a high risk pregnancy at the same time. Obsessively driven toward the goal of bringing a baby home to a waiting nursery, they have thought very little beyond arrival day.

I worry about these would-be parents, because by allowing themselves to become victims of the challenge to their family building dreams, by allowing themselves to avoid thinking about the ramifications of their crisis management style, they almost guarantee that they won't effectively deal with their losses. And, that years later those losses will reappear as reopened wounds when new and different losses set a grief reaction in motion—for example, losses of jobs, divorce, death of a parent or close friend or spouse, their adopted child's recognition of loss as a part of his adoption experience.

I worry because the self-absorption of people operating as victims won't allow them to feel compassion for others—for birthparents, for people dealing with secondary infertility, for the confused and panicked parents of quads or quints conceived on fertility drugs or in IVF cycles, for couples dealing with an untimely pregnancy, for pregnant infertiles who can't find a place to "fit in" anymore. For one who has experienced reproductive loss or challenged family building to have lost compassion for those experiencing other types of family-related challenges is particularly ironic.

I worry because for victims there is no joy in living.

There comes a time to stop—to recognize that one has not been in charge and to step off the conveyor belt, regain balance, and look around for a better way. My hope is that the process for decision making offered in the next chapters of this book can become a tool to help couples and singles make that pause for reexamination happen, offering them practical ways to regain control of their lives again, helping them to look far enough beyond the danger represented by the dragon to see the opportunity lying just ahead.

Many significant beginnings and endings in our lives are marked by rituals that publicly mark the transition and invite the support—either in celebration or in mourning—of others. Weddings, funerals, christenings, baby showers, bar mitzvahs, graduations, going-away parties are examples of transitional rituals. Psychologists and sociologists are increasingly noting that transitions which are not accompanied by ritual—divorce, loss of a job, miscarriage, private changes of direction—are often harder to make, since they lack support.

Many family-challenged people are finding it important to create and participate in private or public rituals which acknowledge the progress of their lives. Infertility support groups across the county have put together periodically repeated mourning ceremonies for miscarried or unconceived children. Such ceremonies offer the opportunity for couples and their supportive family and friends to experience a release similar to that in a traditional funeral service.

> Several years ago Bonnie and Lawrence Baron of San Diego wrote about their personally composed ceremony in which they formally ended treatment and moved on. Their ceremony was firmly rooted in their Judaic tradition and included elements of several ceremonies and prayers, as well as some nonreligious readings and music.
>
> Mike and Jean Carter of North Carolina, authors of *Sweet Grapes: How to Stop Being Infertile and Start Living Again* (Perspectives Press, Inc., 1989, rev. 1998), note in their book and in their presentations the formal way in which they marked their choice to live a childfree lifestyle.
>
> Wendy and Rob Williams of Ontario, Canada, created a poignant and very personal ceremony for saying goodbye to the child whose

adoption was not completed because his birthmother changed her mind several weeks after placement.

In many ways the structure of the decision making format which will follow encourages the opportunity for using or developing rituals, whether formal or informal. You may wish to explore with your partner the idea of participating in appropriate transitional rituals yourselves as you mark your journey.

In "The Picnic," one of the wonderful short stories in her collection *The Miracle Seekers: An Anthology of Infertility*,[3] Mary Martin Mason tells the story of Jill and Dan, frozen in time and unable to move beyond the miscarriage of Gerald, the baby they had waited for so long. In an awkward attempt to help, Dan takes Jill on a picnic along the raw Rhode Island shore. With her sketch pads and charcoal in hand, Jill makes her way to an ancient cemetery to do some rubbings. Dan finds her later, weeping over a one hundred year old tombstone that bears the names of a couple and their five sons—each of whom was named Josephus, each of whom died in infancy.

Here, Jill comes to see that what is preventing her from moving on is the fact that no one—not her mother-in-law, not her friends, not her husband—has allowed her to experience her grief openly, to mourn the loss of her son, to say goodbye in a formal way to the baby who was not to be. And so, together, Dan and Jill say goodbye to Gerald by burying a baby rattle which Jill has brought with them in the earth above the babies Josephus.

All significant endings and beginnings are indeed crises, fraught with the fear that is a part of facing the unknown. The Chinese concept of crisis consisting of both danger and opportunity is an important one for us to keep in mind as we do the hard work of making good decisions. Many years ago I clipped from a church bulletin a wonderful quote that speaks to this. It was attributed to Merle Shain.

"There are only two ways to approach life—as a victim or as a gallant fighter—and you must decide if you want to act or react . . . a lot of people forget that."

But not you, the reader of this book! You'll remember and *decide*!

CHAPTER 2

Confronting
Dragons

With the map in hand, the prince and the princess set off into the world. On the first day they traveled through a deep forest. The prince, intent upon reaching the other side as quickly as possible, hacked away at the underbrush with his sword. Meanwhile, the princess, following behind, examined the lovely flowers and moss beneath the trees and frequently noted a bird fluttering by or a small animal scurrying across the path. The prince became impatient with her dawdling. She, on the other hand, found it difficult to understand why he was in so big a hurry on this honeymoon trip.

On the second day the couple faced a mountain range. Each assessed the situation and offered an opinion for dealing with the obstacle. The prince saw the quickest route as straight over the top and suggested that they abandon unnecessary gear and climb the rocks. The princess, on the other hand, was intensely curious about what they would find in the valley created by the stream that skirted the mountain. She suggested that they take the time to go around the mountain rather than risk injury by going over it.

They entered a small cave to rest, reflect and make a decision. As they sat on the stones at the entrance to the cave, each suddenly sensed that they were not alone. The prince felt a looming, ominous presence and the princess the warm glow of a fire. They turned together to face . . . a dragon! Oh dear, now what?

Forgive the fact that these anecdotes about the prince and the princess drip with stereotypes! The decision to allow them to do so was deliberate. After all, those stereotypes were a part of the fairy tales of childhood and in many ways contribute to our expectations about adulthood, no matter how hard we are working to eliminate them. Reminder: I am well aware that much of the material in these first three chapters may seem

30

weighted toward the family building challenges brought on by infertility in heterosexual couples. However, my own experience and the confirmation of many social workers in the adoption field has led me to believe strongly that most of the information shared here is also applicable to singles and same-sex couples facing family building challenges. I've worked hard to be inclusive. Please don't think that examining the issue of loss in adoption can be skipped in deciding whether or not to build or expand your family through adoption. For all whom it touches, adoption is a blend of gain and loss, happiness and pain.

Who's Infertile Here?

Often it is difficult for couples themselves—let alone outsiders—to understand the significance of the fact that infertility is a couples issue. While in about 30% of cases both partners are subfertile (infertile when paired with an equally infertile partner, but fertile when paired with a normally fertile or super fertile partner), in the majority of cases of infertility one partner's reproductive system is flawed and the other partner is fertile enough to reproduce given a more fertile partner. This dilemma is the root of much angst on the part of less fertile partners—particularly for those who personally feel a strong reaction to the idea of losing their genetic continuity or the pregnancy/birth experience. Such people, while grieving, may test their spouse's commitment to them by suggesting divorce, by insisting on plunging into the use of donor gametes, and so on—suggesting these not necessarily because they sincerely want them, but instead to create challenges which dare the spouse to bail out.

In truth, fertile partners of infertile people most often see themselves as infertile as well. Having made the commitment to a person they chose as a life and parenting partner, fertile partners, too, grieve the loss of their dreams and expectations. Even when they recognize immediately that they retain the option of expressing their fertility with a different reproductive partner (surrogate, semen donor, egg donor), fertile partners of infertile people must seriously address all of infertility's losses, recognizing that in choosing an option which will prevent themselves from losing genetic continuity, the emotional and physical gratifications of a pregnancy experience and the parenting experience, they will still give up a dreamed for, jointly conceived child.

Concerned about their spouses' battered self esteem, the majority of fertile partners indeed choose to render themselves infertile, too, electing to become childfree or to adopt when they come to understand how important this loss of fertility is to their partner. And the majority of infertile people fail to recognize the significance of such a decision and such a sacrifice, which, when acknowledged, might be the greatest self esteem restorer of all.

That year was the worst of Jeanine's life. After many years of encouraging infertility testing and treatments, she and Alan were hit with a bombshell: the most recent surgery had not only failed, but her tubes were ruined forever. IVF was not an option. In those years it was still very experimental and rare. Adoption was an option they had already talked about and agreed to pursue, but it would be a long time, they knew, before they became parents that way. Though Jeanine really wanted to be a parent, she also wanted to be able to give her husband a child—not so much for the pregnancy experience, but because they had dreamed so long about their funny blended baby.

Jeanine descended into a dark depression that lasted months and months. As she slowly emerged, the sky was brightened by encouraging news about adoption. They threw themselves into that process and were thrilled beyond belief when their child arrived a couple of years after that final diagnosis.

As engrossed as they were in parenting, as delighted as Jeanine was to mother this particular child and not another, a piece of her continued to mourn. She mourned for her body, which didn't work the way it was supposed to. She felt ugly, unattractive, defective. She felt guilty that her husband felt he had to stick with her. Nothing Alan could say seemed to make it any better.

Until one day over five years after the end of treatment when Jeanine and Alan were thinking about a second child, she attended a conference and heard a male therapist talk about how men grieve differently from women—often silently. She went home and talked at length with Alan, a man who finds it hard to share his feelings.

The conversation was startling. No message could ever have been more self esteem enhancing or more important to their marriage. Alan told Jeanine how carefully he had thought through all of her offers and threats of divorce from years before and how frightening they had been for him. What he wanted, he told her (once again, and for the thousandth time—but this time she heard) was not fertility, but Jeanine. For him, the thought of losing Jeanine as his wife had been more terrifying than the thought of losing his fertility.

"I've wondered many times," says Jeanine, "why I couldn't have understood that earlier. We both wanted our fertility, and we wanted it together, but beneath it all what we each wanted most was the other, and in our badly communicated grief we could have lost it all."

What is most important here? Sometimes we forget that it was the partnership that came first and the love we felt for each other that led us to decide to try to add children to our family of two. Vision tends to blur when you're bobbling along on that out-of-control conveyor belt. Get off! Recommit to one another before deciding how to proceed.

Coping with the Stress of Infertility and other Family Building Challenges

No, you haven't been trying too hard. With rare exceptions, stress does not produce infertility. Family building challenges *of all kinds* do, however, produce stress. Though it is medically defined as a disease, and though it often produces an emotional reaction very similar to that expressed by sufferers of chronic illness, infertility creates none of the outward signs of illness which would prompt outsiders to offer support or sympathy. Other kinds of frustrated family building are similarly invisible. Furthermore, with the exception of single women trying to conceive with donated gametes, family building challenges affect a couple, not an individual.

Leaping into adoption will not circumvent or solve the stress which is a part of challenged family building. The related issues are too significant to bypass. Over a lifetime, addressing these issues head on will prove to have been a valuable part of the process of moving on.

Clear and direct communication is vital to healthy relationships. The stress of any kind of crisis makes this communication much more difficult. Searching for ways to reduce stress for oneself and for one another can be an important part of reinforcing the relationship.

Begin by treating your bodies more kindly. Many readers are still in treatment, so they are being poked, prodded, medicated and forced to perform under the glare of spotlights. But even those who are not in treatment are likely feeling pressured about making good decisions about family building. Try some of the following suggestions for coping with stress:

- Keep regular hours and have regular sit-down meals. This is a particular challenge for people who do not have children, since they tend to have developed habits which include eating on the run and sleeping whenever they get around to it.
- Cut down on caffeine, salt, alcohol, and sweets, since they tend to make your already overworked nervous system work even harder.
- Become aware of your breathing. Learn to control it with deep breathing exercises in order to manage stress.
- Begin some form of regular exercise that will relieve tension in order to keep your body and mind tuned.

Other stress relievers are psychological. For example:

- Reduce the minor irritations in your life that tend to accumulate and cause stress. Oil that squeaky door, clean that dirty window next to your desk, straighten your messy underwear drawer. Even better, rather than work on your own minor irritants, surprise your partner by working on his or hers!

- Give yourself a few minutes absolutely alone each day during which you allow yourself to regroup.
- Go easy on yourself. Accept your feelings as legitimate and refuse to allow others to make you feel guilty for feeling the pain and the disappointment of your fertility impairment.
- Know your limitations and work to avoid people and tasks that irritate you.
- Treat yourself to something special—a manicure or a massage, a new book you've wanted to read, a weekend away with your spouse.
- Share with your spouse as much as possible (though remembering the Twenty Minute Rule, which we'll discuss in the next section). Work at keeping the two of you a family with your own traditions. This is especially important during the holidays, when stress can be magnified by the tendency of others to ignore your pain.
- Prod your sense of humor. Try to be silly about some things, and, wherever possible, try to find silliness in the things that irk you most. Laugh as often as you can find a good reason to, and create some of those reasons. Avoid melodrama in your T.V. or movie viewing and watch some sitcoms you might usually avoid.
- Tell people that things are bothering you rather than gunnysacking them until you explode. Let them know how they can help you rather than expect them to read your mind.

Communicating

For committed partners, one of the most confusing and frustrating parts of battling a challenge to family building is coming to recognize and deal with the fact that partners do not see the struggle in exactly the same way. An important part of who we are and how adaptable or flexible we are able to be is simply inborn. Some people are just inherently more adaptable than others. The issues of adaptability will become even more important for you to consider when we begin to discuss issues of parenting in adoption, but adaptability is part of why we react to challenges, changes—and losses—as we do.

Our environments and experiences contribute greatly to who we are, too. Because each of us is an individual, brought up in separate homes with different families, our backgrounds have taught us different ways of reacting. We probably attended different schools and houses of worship. Most often we lived at least part of our lives in disparate geographic locations. Growing up, our experiences of place in the family, of friendship, with the people who taught and guided us, with the material we read, the television we viewed and the music we listened to—the combination of our experiences—made us unique individuals, with separate needs and expectations.

Most of us understand the impact of such differences only after they are called to our attention, preferring instead to assume that surely two people who have chosen one another with whom to spend their lives and form a family would agree on the most primal of issues and needs.

Though as a society we are acknowledging that there is no one "male" way to look at things and one "female" way to react to things, it remains true that in general the experiences of men and women have caused them to view challenges differently. In general, men tend to look for logical answers, women to feel things from the heart. Men tend to be less inclined to share their innermost fears, women spill it all for many to see and hear. There are, of course, many exceptions to this "general rule" of gender-specific reaction, and that's a good thing. But whether the differences between us are gender-based or personality-based, the odds are good that most of us who live in partnerships—heterosexual or homosexual—will not be living with a partner whose reactions to things "match" our own.

Deborah Tannen is a linguist who has spent many years focusing on how people communicate in diverse cultures. One of her studies focused on the differences in communication between men and women—who experience, even when raised in the same location, different cultures. In her excellent book *You Just Don't Understand: Women and Men in Conversation*, Tannen points out that in our closest relationships we look for confirmation and reassurance. "When those closest to us respond to events differently than we do, when they seem to see the same scene as part of a different play, when they say things that we could not imagine saying in the same circumstances, the ground on which we stand seems to tremble and our footing is suddenly unsure. Being able to understand why this happens—why and how our partners and friends, though like us in many ways are different in others—is a crucial step toward feeling that our feet are planted firmly on the ground."[1]

Tannen observes that men tend to operate in a world they view as having a hierarchical social order in which they are either one-up or one-down. Through a lens where life is viewed as a contest—a struggle to avoid failure and preserve independence—men tend to see conversations as negotiations, where the goal is to retain the upper hand and protect oneself from another's attempt to push one around. Women, on the other hand, view life as a community, and struggle to preserve intimacy and connectedness and to avoid isolation.

When sharing their problems with one another, observes Tannen, women tend to look for and offer reassurance and understanding—intimacy. Men in conversations with other men, on the other hand, often jockey for position in a competitive kind of problem solving. As a result, when men and women communicate with one another about problems, often women complain that men just "order them around, tell them what to do" which they often interpret as dismissing their problems as unimportant. Men, on the other hand, assume that when a woman shares a problem she's looking for an answer to it, so they are confused when their advice is not welcome.[2]

If the observations of Tannen and others regarding the differences between women and men, both in their style of communicating and in their expectations from communication, are correct, they offer some interesting applications to communicating about infertility and about choosing the option of adoption. Consider, for example, the physical and emotional losses of the pregnancy experience. Tannen's theory would suggest that men who feel this loss strongly do so because they experience humiliation in being "one down" from other men—and therefore less a man, while women for whom this loss is particularly painful react more strongly to the pain of losing the intimacy of the connection to a partner and to a child. Certainly many couples have observed retrospectively that they felt out of sync with one another during phases of the infertility experience when, faced with sudden bad news, husbands began to problem solve and look beyond the loss to a next step while their wives were wishing for the comfort of mutually mourning the disappointment.

Couples in treatment as well as those who are pursuing adoption often complain that one or the other partner seems obsessed with the process to the exclusion of everything else in life while the other partner is able to compartmentalize it. Merle Bombardieri, a Massachusetts-based therapist who served for a time as clinical director at Resolve, Inc. and devoted a significant percentage of her private practice to infertility, offered a helpful prescription for such couples.

> The Twenty Minute Rule is a compromise tactic that acknowledges the diverging needs for talking about the struggle in family building. Using it, couples adopt a routine that requires that only twenty minutes a day be spent discussing family-building related issues. The twenty minutes are mutually agreed upon and preset. They don't get dropped into the middle of one partner's Monday night football game or the other partner's absorption in a good book. The timing chosen takes into account when during the day each partner is likely to be the least stressed, the most relaxed and thus receptive to what the other partner has to say.
>
> During this twenty minutes, both partners agree that each will give undivided attention to listening to and reacting to what the other partner is feeling a need to communicate. The twenty minutes should not be spent with one partner listening from behind a newspaper to a

monologue from the other, but instead should involve a willingness to engage one another in conversation and dialogue, with the goal being to communicate and work together to make decisions.

The Twenty Minute Rule creates a win-win situation, by offering the partner who most needs communicative interchange the guarantee of a particular time each day during which s/he won't be ignored, rebuffed or rejected but instead will be attentively listened and responded to, and by offering the less verbal partner protection from a sense of being "ambushed" by giving him or her the opportunity to prepare carefully for what otherwise might be a painful and resented intrusion.

Most of us have not been taught good communication skills. In confronting the dragon, good communication is imperative. Now may be an ideal time to commit to enhancing communication skills. There are many ways to accomplish this. You should begin with a promise to one another to be honest, direct, and clear and to be respectful of one another's pain, fears and need for privacy. Using Bombardieri's Twenty Minute Rule and using it to deal with family-building challenges in bite-sized pieces may be another useful step. Then you may choose to read some books on communication suggested at the end of this chapter.

On this list is Mike and Jean Carter's *Sweet Grapes: How to Stop Being Infertile and Start Living Again* (Perspectives Press, rev. 1998). Yes, I know. You'd decided not to read it because you thought it was about childfree living, and you'd already dismissed that option. Well, it is about childfree living, in that Mike and Jean have chosen a childfree lifestyle and joyfully put their family building challenges behind them. But more than that, the Carters offer the only organized material on communicating and decision making in infertility that has been written not by a woman, but by a man and a woman, together. Their insights will be helpful to anyone making any decision which is colored by family building challenges. Mike writes about his early approaches to their infertility:

> It took me a long time to learn that I really wasn't helping. Both of my strategies—silence and problem solving—were actually ways of keeping problems at arm's length. At that distance, I didn't have to feel them. I didn't have to be a part of the hurt and confusion that come with tough issues.
>
> Infertility changed all that.[3]

Dealing with Family and Friends

Parenthood challenges aren't easy. In fact, that may be the understatement of the century. Infertility is very hard work—work from which there seem to be no evenings and weekends off, no vacation, not even a real end to the job in sight much of the time. I well remember the period of time when nearly anything and everything could remind me of the loss I was feeling and move me in the span of an instant to fury, to terror, or to tears. Singles and same-gender couples face even bigger difficulties. Far too often the "traditional world" not only fails to understand and support their interest in parenting but actively discourages it.

But, then, it isn't easy to be the friend or relative of people dealing with family building challenges either, and, having come out the other side of this long dark tunnel, I feel a responsibility to play devil's advocate on behalf of the people whose lives touch yours. Infertile people tend to be moody, swinging in two-week cycles of anticipatory hope followed by crashing despair. The family-challenged tend to find events that make other people feel excited and celebratory—events like baby showers, a christening or a bris, Mother's Day and Father's Day, little kids' birthday parties, culturally child centered holidays such as Christmas, Chanukah, Easter, Halloween—uncomfortable and even unpleasant.

Those absorbed in a course of testing and treatment can often be pretty inwardly focused. Calendars which record a daily basal body temperature and are punctuated with doctor's appointments, days to begin and end medication, a schedule for intercourse, lab dates, etc., don't leave much room for social engagements and just plain fun. Those who are immersed in an adoption waiting period are often irritable and tense, feeling completely "on hold" as they wait for "The Call." Sometimes it seems as if the family-challenged are the rain on everybody else's parade, the sore spot that must be nursed and treated gingerly by the family at the expense of their own ability to be spontaneously joyful.

But let's face facts. How much did you know about infertility or about adoption before you faced it yourself? Not much, I'll bet. Your friends and family are at that point now. Unless you educate them, you can't expect them to understand your frustrations. They have, after all, been exposed to the very same cultural expectations as you have, and, if you'll remember, you were somewhat surprised by what faced you as a family-challenged person at first.

You probably tended to deny those challenges for a while because the idea was frightening. Well, it frightens your mom, too. She had been expecting to be a grandma. So she says the first thing that comes to her mind, "Relax, honey, you're probably trying too hard."

You may have been a little embarrassed by the infertility at first when you didn't understand how common it was. You might yourself have felt that it was somewhat sexual in nature and expressed a little nervous humor about it. Is that what your brother is feeling when he cracks, "Hey, Bub, ya need a little advice on how it's done?" Before you were educated about infertility, you, too, were likely to believe some of those old myths that have now come to be oh so much more than annoying:

Take a vacation.
Have a glass of wine before bedtime.
Try my doctor.
Adopt—then you'll get pregnant!
It's probably all part of God's plan.
If you really wanted a child you'd . . .

Before you had settled into an acceptance that you would be making family building decisions as a single person—back then, when you were still figuring that you would find the right partner—just how sensitive were you to the challenges of trying to build a family as a single person? How deeply had you thought about whether singles or gays and lesbians faced closed or open doors at medical clinics or at adoption agencies? And, heterosexual couples, how many of you had really considered that singles or that same-sex couples could be facing challenges similar to your own?

Come on, admit it, you've all been guilty of insensitivity, too—back then, before these issues became so personal, you, too, were frightened about changes of heart in adoption, about how much it cost, about who "qualified."

What changed *you*? Learning about these things. And that is also the answer for your friends and family. Since you've probably learned from experience that the information they are likely to stumble across in the daily newspaper (that important medical journal) or in an interview on a television talk show is incorrect or misinformed, if you want them to truly understand the facts and feelings behind infertility, family building, and adoption, you'll have to educate them yourselves.

There are many ways for you to do this without hurting feelings, coming on too strong, or badgering. Here are some suggestions you may find helpful: whether you are in treatment or actively pursuing adoption

- Subscribe to a newsletter or magazine for your family member or friend (see Resources)
- Give them a copy of my booklet *Understanding Infertility: Insights for Family and Friends* or Resolve's brochure for friends and family, or *How Can I Help?* from Merle Bombardieri and Diane Clapp.
- If you are exploring adoption, give them my book *Adoption Is a Family Affair: What Relatives and Friends Must Know.*
- Take these significant others with you to an agency's information night, to a support group meeting, or to a symposium. There will be more on the topic of bringing family and friends on board about adoption in Part Four of this book.

In the back of the booklet *Understanding Infertility: Insights for Family and Friends,* I provide a list of twelve suggestions for loved ones to follow in order to provide support for an infertile couple. They apply to others with family challenges as well. I'd like to suggest that there are things that your family should expect from you too:

1. Information. People can't be sensitive toward something they don't understand. Each time that you diplomatically point out a painful error that a friend, a family member, a medical person, a member of the clergy has made in referring to you or to your particular family challenge, you increase the likelihood that this person's sensitivity level will be raised to the point of her being unlikely to repeat such errors.

2. Sensitivity. Just as you expect that your family members should be sensitive to your pain, you must realize that your situation may be painful to them too. Parents, in particular, often tend to feel guilty that they may have done something to contribute to a medical problem. As well, they shared your assumptions that grandchildren would be born who shared the family genes. Just as you mourn the potential loss of your genetic children, so do they. They will, however, feel guilty about publicly mourning such a loss, realizing that you may interpret their mourning to mean that you have failed them. Mourners need one another. Be sensitive and open to each other's pain. Understand how very difficult it will be for your friends and family to enjoy their own pregnancies if you have not given them permission to do so.

3. Patience. Your friends and family are at least one step behind you in learning about and dealing with the impact of your family challenges. You will have spent a great deal of private time making decisions before you announce them publicly. Be prepared for the fact that when you announce your decisions, particularly controversial ones, your family has not yet had the time to adjust to them as you have. They may react with shock, with fear, even with revulsion. Gay and lesbian readers have likely already experienced reactions like these in revealing their homosexuality. People close to you must be given time to adjust, and you must support them in this adjustment, just as you wish them to support you in your decision. Beyond this, it is important to accept that people who have not been where you are cannot be expected to fully understand your experience.

4. Openness. Quietly taking note of each mistake, each carelessly hurtful remark, each uncomfortable reaction from family members and friends, and socking them away in the gunnysack to be dumped into the middle of Thanksgiving dinner is not fair. No one can be expected to change his behavior if he is not made aware that his behavior is causing pain. Use private moments to sensitize your loved ones.

5. Clarity. As you work to sensitize and inform, keep your discussions simple, brief, and factual whenever possible. Most listeners, not absorbed in the daily challenges facing you, are unable to absorb or deal with the heaviness of your situation all at once.

6. Responsiveness. Sometimes the people who love you can be a bit more objective about your situation than can you. Once you have educated a friend about the options you are considering, you should be able to assume that she will no longer offer advice unless she has thought it over carefully and is prepared to accept a negative reaction to it. Consider that sometimes educated friends offering opinions may in fact be right. Blinded by your own obsession with your challenges, you may need to take a step away in order to see clearly. Give some thought, at least, to the opinions of the informed people who love you.

Having now played devil's advocate on behalf of those insensitive others, I want to back up here and re-advocate for you too. It's perfectly fine to avoid baby showers and child-centered holiday celebrations. In fact, that is often the healthiest thing you can do in finding ways to regain a measure of control. The challenge is in avoiding the painful situation in a way that does not cause you additional pain or embarrassment, and which produces as little discomfort as possible for the friends and family members involved. Here are some ways to do this:

- Create a conflict in your schedule. Miss Manners reminds us that you are under no obligation to explain what it is, just offer your regrets and don't allow yourself to be sucked into explanations. This works particularly well for showers and christenings, etc., but is more difficult to do for holidays. Consider allowing yourself the privilege of leaving town altogether for the holidays, offering your family the exciting news that you've arranged a special getaway weekend for yourself without mentioning your holiday discomfort at all.

- Enlist the help of a sensitive friend or family member who will serve as your advocate with persistently snoopy and insensitive others. Ask this person to have a quiet heart-to-heart with the potentially offended or offensive host or the guest of honor, enlisting that next person to become part of your sensitivity team as well.

Finally, understand that some people will never respond well. No matter how carefully you try to educate them, no matter how many copies of great articles and all the right books that you pass out, a few people in your sphere of intimacy are likely to remain insensitive. Don't continue to beat yourself up about this by trying over and over again. The best method for coping with these few, no matter how closely they are related to you, is by avoiding them.

CHAPTER 3

The Plan

Faced with the dragon and the need to get around him, our prince and princess knew that they would need a plan of action. It appeared that it would be just the two of them against that enormous obstacle. They retreated to give it some thought.

There were options. Of course, they could always give up—throwing themselves on the dragon's mercy, hoping that they wouldn't become his dinner. They could go back and get reinforcements. They could marshal their courage and risk going straight through. They could look for a way around the dragon.

The prince and the princess were not without resources. They were bright and talented individuals, each with valuable strengths. In order to develop their plan of action, they thought carefully about those strengths and weaknesses, they talked about how to use them to their best advantage, and, after considerable time, they had developed a plan.

Having learned to communicate effectively, you can put what you've learned to practical use in decision making. To manage a business one develops a business plan. In order to conquer a dragon you must develop a battle plan. Looking at adoption and deciding whether it feels right for you lends itself well to similar strategic planning.

No matter what kind of decision needs to be made, the process is pretty much the same. Decision making involves gathering information, examining short and long term implications, prioritizing needs and desires, choosing among alternatives, allocating budgeted resources, and committing to a course of action. Of course when the problem is small, these steps are most often taken subconsciously. When the problem is a large one, sometimes the weight of it causes us to freeze (there's that danger reaction we spoke about earlier) and we may need to force ourselves to be particularly aware of this danger.[1] I've found that the family-challenged often need such a nudge.

Humans have a tendency to look back on decisions made earlier and to wonder if they made the right ones. "If onlys" are a common part of our looking backward with 20/20 hindsight. The goal of good decision making is to be able to look back on carefully made decisions with confidence, knowing that at the time and under the circumstances we made the very best possible choices. Because family challenges will always be a significant part of the people each of you are and become, it is important that you feel comfortable and confident about the decisions you make along the way.

For most readers of this book the facts are these: once upon a time you decided to have a baby, and you expected that to be a relatively simple feat. But then you met the dragon, and that earlier decision to have a baby was complicated by an entirely new set of facts. In light of those facts, you have been placed in the position of needing to make that decision to become parents all over again—perhaps several times. Do you still want to be a parent if it means that the child you parent will not be genetically connected to you? Do you still want to be parents if it will take years more to accomplish? Do you want to parent enough that you are willing to submit to having others determine whether you are fit to do so? Do you still want to be parents?

The process described here can help you decide, but first, a word of caution. This process is a skeletal format for decision making rather than a road map. Because adoption options change frequently, it would be impossible to formulate all of the questions for every contingency likely to arise during the course of your family planning process. Instead, what I hope to do is show you how to go about predicting the questions you need to have answered, gathering the data you need, following a process for evaluating that data, communicating directly with your partner about these issues, and then deciding together on a course of action.

My plan involves eight distinct steps:

1. Engaging in a period of private personal reflection.
2. Sharing your discoveries about yourself with your partner, if you have one, or with a trusted, educated family member or friend if you are single.
3. Discussing ways to blend your separate needs and wishes in order to select a consensus or compromise course of action.
4. Inventorying personal resources—time, money, emotional energy, and physical capacity.
5. Gathering information about the options you find of interest.
6. Building a detailed plan for pursuing that course of action—developing strategies, assigning tasks, allocating resources, setting a time for evaluation.
7. Pursuing the course of action.
8. Evaluating and adjusting the plan as needed.

While what follows will be a time consuming process—ideally it will take a number of weeks because it is a "set-up round"—many users have found that once they have worked through this process once, subsequent opportunities to use the process for other decisions they make in the context of family life take far less time and energy. Each of you will spend several hours separately doing some personal homework (reflection) and then follow that with some sharing, with the goal of having a long retreat weekend where you will use the data you have already gathered to create a personal plan (step six above).

Dealing with an Impasse

Before we even begin the process of decision making, let's directly address what I know to be a couple's greatest fear: *"What if we can't agree?"* What if it feels as if your needs and desires are in such direct conflict that there is no route to compromise and consensus?

For many couples it is this very fear that prevents them from communicating directly with one another and leads them to drift aimlessly through too many years of, well, just waiting. But, waiting for what? What can happen without movement? A miracle, likely, and those miracles are few and far between. The underlying fear is that without clear agreement the partnership itself is in jeopardy, and for some people this fear tends to lead them to acquiesce to options with which they are not really comfortable.

So here's what to do with an impasse. If at any point during the decision making process you find yourselves stalemated, or if you realize that your needs appear to be in direct conflict, so that together you are unable to see a route to compromise, there are at least three important things that you should do.

First, pause to catch your breaths and recall some of the important things we've already covered. You are each unique individuals with different backgrounds and influences which have contributed to those differences in needs and feelings. You cannot feel identically. You chose one another to be life partners because you shared values and dreams, and because there were things about each of you that complemented or balanced the other's strengths and weaknesses. You are committed to one another and to finding a solution to the problem you face together.

Second, give yourselves some time and space. The issues you are dealing with are profound, emotional, and life changing. One or the other of you may find that something in the decision making process triggers a visceral and wrenching reaction which is, purely and simply, grief. Working through a grief reaction cannot be rushed. The most important thing the two of you can do if either or both of you feels temporarily overcome by the confusion or negativism of grief is to postpone further discussion and planning for an agreed upon length of time—usually several weeks, though it can take months. During that time try to give yourselves a total time out from exploring family building, feeling confident that on some future date that you have mutually agreed upon, you will examine once again whether it is time to pursue the need to make clear decisions about the future.

Third, consider the value of arranging some sessions with a mediator or counselor—an objective and emotionally uninvolved professional who can help you to sort things out, advocating for each of you as well as for the process, pointing out flawed thinking and offering observations which neither of you have considered. Finding such a counselor is not always easy. Many human service and mental health professionals are not well informed about infertility or adoption issues. You may wish to start with someone known to you already—a counselor you have seen or heard good things about or your clergyperson. If you do not know of such a resource or if you find those known to you to be unfamiliar with, or insensitive to, the unique characteristics of this experience, ask your doctor or the closest infertility or adoption support group for a referral.

A Word for Singles

Throughout this book, in places much of the writing may seem to be oriented toward, and pertain mostly to, couples. This is simply because the overwhelming majority of people who explore adoption do so as couples. However, you, dear single reader, should not feel left out. Those who adopt as single people can, and do, make wonderful parents for the children whom they adopt. That said, I do hope you can be patient with me about how difficult it is to write for such a varied audience! I believe that the process offered here, while it is sometimes described in language that does not feel inclusive of singles, can work well for singles, too. There are many places in the book where I have added some special thoughts and advice just for you!

Perhaps the best advice I can offer you, though (and you'll find this advice echoed in Chapter 15 by Cynthia VN Peck, 30 year adoptive parent of eight children), is that you should not depend on friends or relatives who aren't living your life, yet who have strong opinions about how you should live it. Of course, you certainly may have a family member or longtime best friend who can just be there to listen and who is neutral—someone perhaps who has experienced the world of adoption herself, or whom you have been successful in educating on the unique issues involved in adoption. However, if you find you need help sorting out your feelings and your options, just as couples sometimes need help to "mediate" their disagreements, singles will often find it helpful to use an objective but adoption-literate professional with whom to "bounce around" ideas and impressions as they are going through the process. This might be a very close, well informed and highly sensitive friend, or it might be a therapist, counselor, clergyperson, or life coach.

So, be patient with the process and know that you will find much of the material that follows useful to a single person as you explore your options.

And so, let's begin.

Reflecting

Step one, a period of self reflection, should be done independently. Find a quiet spot (away from your partner, if you have one, or if you are single, by turning off home and cell phone ringers and letting the machine pick up) where, all at one time or on several different occasions spread out over days, you can spend a significant amount of time privately examining the six potential losses which accompany the experience of being family-challenged and your feelings about them:

Where and when to do this is a matter of personal choice. While some couples have done this separately but at the same time as a first step during a retreat weekend (which will be fully discussed later in this chapter) and then shared the results immediately with one another, most who've talked to me after using the process have found it much more helpful for each partner to accomplish this step days or weeks before their retreat, at a time personally chosen and unknown to their partner, and then to give themselves at least a few days afterwards to ruminate further upon their self discoveries before sharing them with their spouse. Consider these options and decide together which you feel would be most useful in your situation.

During reflection the task at hand is yours and yours alone. Without trying to predict how your partner (if you have one) might personally react to these losses or react to your feelings about these losses and their alternatives, think seriously about those six potential losses and try hard to determine how you might rank them as to their importance to you and to you alone. If you are single, be especially careful to avoid any worry or concern about what other people in your life—family members, friends, co-workers—might be thinking or feeling about your various options or about how you are handling this decision making process.

Potential Losses for the Family-Challenged

- Loss of control
- Loss of individual genetic continuity
- Loss of a jointly conceived child
- Loss of the physical expectations of the pregnancy experience itself and of feeling the power to impregnate
- Loss of the emotional expectations that come with a shared pregnancy, birth, breastfeeding experience
- Loss of the opportunity to parent

Without considering at all the physical realities of your fertility status or your family building challenges, ask yourself, "If I had the power to avoid personally experiencing one or more of these losses, which would I want most to avoid?"

Try ranking the losses from one to six (the first is the most significant loss, the sixth is the least significant loss). Then assign a weight to each loss on a scale of zero to three such as

0   Experiencing the finality of this loss would mean little or nothing to me

1   This loss, if final, would bother me somewhat, but other losses are more important to avoid

2   This loss is relatively important for me to avoid

3   Experiencing this loss would be very painful for me

You may be wondering why, if you've already ranked the losses from most important to least important, you would need also to give a weight to each of those losses. This step is an important part of fully understanding the depth of feeling you (and your partner) experience about every one of these loss issues so that you can creatively work on compromise and consensus plans for your family.

As you are asked to give weight to your reactions to the potential losses you ranked, do you find yourself feeling equally or almost equally strongly about more than one of those losses? Or do you find yourself ranking only one loss high on the scale in terms of both its impact on you and its importance to you? As you think about your expectations while growing up about family building and being a parent, about the messages you received from your own family about connectedness and parenting, you may be surprised to discover how deeply you feel about some of these losses.

It is imperative that you be honest with yourself in completing this step. Again, do not try to guess how you think your partner will rank and weight each loss. Don't consider at this point how what you already know about your own relative fertility or your partner's will impact your choices and rankings. Simply be gut-honest here in ranking and weighting how you feel about these potential losses.

When you complete this step you will feel clearer about your own needs, your own values, and your own dreams and how they have been challenged by the barriers that challenge you in family building. You will be able to think more clearly about the four general groups of choices open to couples who are dealing with a fertility impairment. You may also feel frightened and sad. That's to be expected. Take a deep breath; don't try to bury those feelings. The thinking that comes to you now will help you make carefully considered choices.

I'll show you how this process can help you work together as partners a couple of pages from now. For singles, this section will be equally helpful.

Personally Pondering Adoption[2]

During your time of personal reflection, ask yourself these questions:

In light of what you've learned about yourself and your reactions to the potential losses which those who are family-challenged face, how important do you feel it is for you to learn more about further treatment options which would help you to conceive and birth a child genetically related to you? Now, while you are reflecting alone, think about the options available through collaborative reproduction—using the donated gametes of another person, or hiring a surrogate to carry a child conceived with your gametes or your partner's (or the sperm and/or eggs of family members). If you have a partner, what about using your partner's gametes but not your own with donors or a surrogate? Do these seem important to explore given what you've identified about your own expectations, needs, and dreams?

What about traditional adoption—independent or agency, infant or older child, domestic or international? What do you actually know about these? At this point, do you believe that it is possible to love, nurture, and parent a child not genetically related to you? Was adoption a part of your extended family? Did you ever have a childhood friend who was adopted? As an adult, do you know many or few adoptive families? Where have you gotten your current adoption information—from friends and colleagues? from the media? from the Internet? How have these things colored your general impression of adoption as a way that families are formed? How open are you to the idea that what you think you know about adoption may be inaccurate or even entirely wrong?

Are you interested in either collaborative reproduction (certainly a form of adoption) or traditional adoption as an alternative to not becoming a parent at all?

And finally, what about the option of not parenting at all in a permanent way? Given what you now know about yourself, are you willing to learn more about, and discuss with your partner, the idea of electing to follow a childfree lifestyle and meeting your needs for regenerativity in other ways?

Sharing with a Partner

The next step in making a good decision about your family plans is to share your new-found self knowledge with your partner. Some singles may feel ready to move on at this stage, while some may find it useful to do this next step with the help of an objective other—possibly a counselor. This discussion will take a minimum of two hours, and sets the stage and tone for the biggest step: the Retreat Weekend.

Hand your partner a sheet of paper on which you have listed only your own ranking and weighting of the potential losses you face. Examine one another's lists and then compare them.

Of course it would be ideal if you found that your lists were identical. How much easier making your next choices would be! But, as you will understand from our having discussed the many factors which make individuals so different when responding to the same crisis, you will likely find that your lists differ. So before you panic about how different your lists may look, let me share an example using a much simpler situation of how this ranking and weighting system might work outside of adoption decision making.

Suppose that my husband Dave and I have come to realize that neither of us is enjoying the meals we prepare at home much because we've never really talked about vegetables before. Think how much nicer dinner would be, each of us thinks, if I didn't have to eat vegetables I don't like or if I could eat more of the vegetables I love. Below is a table which shows how Dave and I might rank the appeal of certain vegetables against one another.

Vegetable	Pat's Ranking	Dave's Ranking
broccoli	2	4
corn on the cob	5	1
peas	3	2
potatoes	1	5
beets	6	6
carrots	4	3

Now, looking at this list which has only been ranked, one thing is entirely clear: Dave and I feel the same about only one vegetable on the list, and we don't appear to feel similarly about any of the others. How on earth, then, will we plan our menus? It looks hopeless.

But when Dave and I also assign weights to our feelings about each of these individual vegetables on a scale of 0 to 3 (0 means we can't stand the vegetable, 3 means we love it), we have a great deal more information.

Pat's List		Vegetable	Dave's List	
Ranked	Weighted		Ranked	Weighted
2	3	Broccoli	4	2
5	1	corn on the cob	1	3
3	2	Peas	2	2
1	3	potatoes	5	1
6	0	beets	6	0
4	3	carrots	3	2

This ranked and weighted list gives us a lot more information with which to work. What we find is that Dave and I will eliminate beets from our household menu. (Actually, each of us would have liked to have been able to give beets a –3. I don't think any of our three kids ever even had the opportunity to taste beets until they were grown.)

Because corn is Dave's favorite vegetable, I serve it fairly frequently, and because potatoes are mine, he eats them more often than he would on his own. What's more, a conversation about our dramatically different feelings about these two vegetables tells us even more. For me, the problem with corn on the cob is those little things that get stuck in my teeth and the oh-so-necessary butter sliding down my chin (but, he reminds me, I can cut the kernels off the cob and avoid this). For him it isn't potatoes in general that he dislikes; it's mostly roasted or baked potatoes (and since he actually likes mashed potatoes and French fries, we can serve potatoes this way). But the broccoli and the peas and the carrots (he prefers them raw, so they are often sticks or shredded into salads) are more in the middle for each of us. We each like them, so at home we eat these three vegetables fairly often—more often than either of us gets to eat our favorite vegetable from this list. When we go out to eat, each of us tends to choose that favorite vegetable that we don't get enough of at home.

Of course, ranking and weighting the losses that come with challenging family building is significantly more important to planning your future than is ranking and weighting your feelings about vegetables. Be prepared for the discussion about the differences in your lists which follows, having looked at one another's ranking and weighting, to be a little difficult.

If your lists are ranked and weighted similarly, you may move quickly from this step to examining specific family planning alternatives. If your lists are quite different, your goal will be to search for areas of agreement as you seek to compromise and build consensus about where you will be going together. Expect this discussion to produce deep feelings in each of you.

Often couples discover that what seems like a clear solution to one partner in reality enhances the other's pain. Let's consider some quick examples of situations like this.

> Miguel's low sperm count makes his impregnating Sondra unlikely. Sondra, however, seems to be normally fertile. To Sondra a clear, quick, cheap, private solution to the problem is donor insemination (D.I.)—she even suggests that perhaps Miguel's brother would be willing to be the donor so that at least the baby would share Miguel's genes. She is shocked and even angry to hear that Miguel doesn't immediately agree to this solution, which, to her way of thinking, even respects Miguel's genetic pool. Sondra has not taken into consideration how important his own ability to impregnate his wife is to Miguel. She isn't thinking at all about how competitive Miguel and his brother have always been. She's not respecting the anti-DI teachings of the Catholic faith in which

he, but not she, was raised. If Miguel is to seriously consider this option for building their family, Sondra will need to give him time and space to sort out his feelings, to mourn his significant loss and will need to be respectful of his ultimate decision—which may be that this option is rejected and another compromise route to parenthood needs to be selected.

Bill and Sharon want a family, but Sharon's endometriosis has not responded to treatment. Bill has had it with trying. He's ready to adopt and doesn't understand why Sharon is resisting. Sharon's endometriosis is incredibly painful. Besides being a reproductive problem, it is taking over other aspects of her life as well. While Bill is focused on putting the infertility behind them, Sharon can't yet see beyond solving the medical problem which could continue to consume her. It's too early for Sharon to consider adoption. The endometriosis needs to be managed first.

And sometimes, in going through a process like this, possible options that hadn't been considered before pop to the surface—and even work their way to the top of the list!

Sam, who is single, would love to be a parent, but he has known several "poorly adjusted" adopted people in the past, and he just can't bring himself to risk adopting one of the waiting children that seem to be most "available" to singles and same-gender couples. But the pull toward parenthood is strong; Sam decides to see a counselor, who helps him sort through these issues and see that there is at least one other option. What about using a surrogate? His genes, fewer barriers between himself and the child, more control. That works for Sam! Now he needs to learn about choosing the right surrogacy agency.

Your personal answers won't necessarily come easily, and at this stage it is likely to be unreasonable to expect that you will see only one path of choice. In fact, it's a good thing if you are flexible enough to see more than one alternative open to you. You will need to do a great deal of talking, questioning, and sharing. If each of you feels able to keep an open mind during these early explorations and is willing to try to reject nothing out of hand, if each of you is able to hear about options, to try them on and wear them for a while, to explore them with your partner before deciding whether or not this is an option you care to pursue together, you are ready for the next steps in the decision-making process—assessing your personal resources and then gathering information about all the alternatives which you have not agreed to dismiss.

Resources to Be Inventoried

Financial Resources include salaries and other income, savings and capital investments, and the sources from which you might borrow. Life and disability insurance can be important financial resources for parents. Elements of your employee benefits package are a part of your financial resources, including life and medical insurance, adoption expense reimbursements, availability of parenting leave, on-site daycare, and more. Assessing financial resources realistically includes looking at how the expenditure of resources on family building will impact your future ability to raise and educate the children who come into your family.

Emotional Resources are not concrete. They cannot be objectively measured. Emotional resources are affected by ethical, religious, and moral responses to an issue and can be assessed only through honest self examination (and discussion between partners). Emotional resources are expended on worries, tension, frustrations, disappointments, etc. They include patience and adaptability, and a variety of other personality traits. They are affected both positively and negatively by self esteem issues, general mental health, and reaction to loss. The crisis of family building can "use up" this resource. Would-be parents who have adequate outside support from family, friends, professionals or a group often find that their emotional resources are increased or replenished as a result.

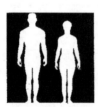

Physical Resources are calculated by looking at the realities of your general health, your genetic health risks and benefits, your current age, and, in the case of treatment for infertility, the prognosis for success in treatment. You must assess what impact these factors have on your ability to manage other aspects of your daily life and your ability to parent a child not just now, but ten years from now, 20 years from now. Your normal physical energy level and your reaction to physical discomfort and a challenged routine can be factors, too.

Time must be assessed from both day-to-day and long term perspectives. Examine temporal benefits or restrictions which accompany your job (availability of flex time, medical leave, parental leave). Consider age as it applies both to options currently open to you and to your future parenting abilities.

Taking Inventory

In creating a logistical plan for any purpose, an early step is to assess the resources available to be budgeted and expended in order to achieve a series of goals and objectives. Planning an assault on the dragon which guards the door to family building is no different.

Resources at your disposal for this battle are all available in limited quantities and are for the most part nonrenewable, so they must be budgeted. Those resources are money, emotional energy, physical capacity and time. I have found it helpful to use some visual symbols to represent each of these resources.

Pulling together and discussing this inventory will take a large chunk of your retreat weekend. The question you will ask of yourselves and each other as you consider each step in putting together your personal plan will be, "How much of each of these limited resources—how much time, how much money, how much emotional energy, how much of my body's capacity—am I willing to risk on this step?"

In order to plan thoroughly, then, you will need to have gathered some practical, concrete information about each of your resources before your retreat. Gather raw data right now, but this is not the time for discussion. You will discuss the issues brought up in the sections which follow during the early stages of your strategic planning retreat.

Financial resources

Gather the raw data of your finances. If you are partners, please do this together. Perhaps you are already using software that helps you keep track of your finances, but if not, take the time to develop some sort of spread sheet that will help you understand your monetary situation. An income/expense report demonstrating your current spending patterns over the last two years or more will give you information with which to consider altering your budget. You'll need to know how much money you have in savings and investments, what the limits and balances are on your credit cards, the interest rates and the balances on your home mortgage and car loans (if you have these), and other basic financial information. List the accessibility you have to borrowing—from a home equity line of credit, life insurance, 401Ks, family members, and so on. Later in this process (probably during your retreat weekend), after you have gathered as much information as possible about all of the adoption options open to you, you'll use this information to ask yourselves a number of financially-situated questions. Can you afford to adopt? The information you have gathered from meetings and seminars in your community, or the large city near you, should have provided you with a general idea of how much public agency, private agency (domestic or international), and independent adoption costs in your part of the world (and these costs do vary significantly geographically). You will also want to consider how much of your credit, savings you have set aside for emergency purposes, or assets and investments you have for your future retirement, you are willing to use or borrow against for your family building.

Emotional resources

Energy and emotions are not concrete. They cannot be objectively measured. Only through self examination and careful discussion with your partner can you assess the extent of this resource. Singles and couples who have adequate outside support often find that their emotional reserves are increased as a result. This support may come from family and friends, from medical and mental health professionals, or from members of a support group.

The extent of your personal emotional resources and the support available to you should directly drive your choices. For example, of all routes to creating a family, those which require you to "put yourself out there"—advertising your interest in adopting, installing a separate phone line and being available to answer it 24/7, becoming the primary emotional support system of a pregnant woman who is not receiving counseling from a trained, licensed, mental health professional—will not only create a steady and significant drain on your emotional reserves, but will also open you to of the possibility of experiencing a change of heart. Some would-be parents find that being this intensely involved in the process rebuilds their lost sense of control; others find the risk too much to bear.

Physical resources

Depending on whether you are considering the collaborative reproduction adoptions or the adoption of a child with no genetic links to you, you must consider your physical resources in slightly different ways. How is your general health? If you are considering using donated eggs or adopting an embryo, how is your reproductive health and what are your odds for success with these procedures?

How much physical capacity do you have? How is your energy level? If you will be adopting a toddler, for example, are you in good enough physical shape already to begin lifting 40 pounds multiple times a day without getting yourself in better shape first? The younger the child at arrival, the more your sleep schedule will be dramatically changed by the child's waking and sleeping patterns as he adapts to new surroundings.

Are you at genetic risk for any problems that could shorten your life? Agencies often ask that people who have been treated for cancer wait until the five year non-recurrence mark before applying to adopt. Women considering making an adoption plan have the right to make choices about adopting couples, and some will use health and fitness as criteria as they read through profiles.

Do you have chronic health problems or physical disabilities which would interfere with your ability to parent effectively? If so, even agencies with no general health-related restrictions will expect that you have a realistic plan in place for obtaining support in caring for your child. Beginning to build that plan before you even select a service provider is an important part of the process of readying yourselves for parenting.

Some countries establish physical qualifications for international adopters. For example, as I write in 2007, China has recently announced that it will set health related limits on those who wish to adopt its children. These restrictions include those who are on certain kinds of medications such as anti-depressants, anxiety medications, etc., and those whose body mass index is higher than a level to be set by the Chinese government. Other countries could follow suit, or these restrictions could be dropped at any time.

These are all health and physical capability questions that *will* come up in an adoption assessment and can influence your adoptions both domestically or internationally.

Time

Temporal resources involve both *current, day-to-day* time and cumulative, *future* time. In the present, you need to be realistic about the amount of time you have to devote to issues that are relative to various routes to adopting and parenting. For example:

If you were to adopt internationally, many countries now expect that you will travel there once or even twice, staying for several days or for as long as several weeks to accomplish the acceptance of a referral, a transition in care, and the finalization of an adoption. Are you able to take this time from your job? And (back to finances) can you afford to do so?

Adopting a child who has experienced institutional delays in an orphanage, who has been prenatally exposed to harmful substances, or who has been neglected or abused in prior placements will require a parent to make substantial investments of time when it comes to ongoing testing, treatment, and therapy. Are you able to have flexibility of time for such appointments?

Infants and toddlers are particularly "labor intensive" when it comes to the amount of active time and attention they require from their parents. Are you prepared to go from 0–60 in five seconds after placement?

Promoting attachment with a child who has attachment challenges (and every child adopted beyond the newborn stage comes to you with attachment challenges—more on this later) needs several weeks nested at home with his new parent before going off to school or daycare. Is parenting leave available to you? For how long, and can you afford to take it if it is not a paid leave?

Now comes what I believe is probably the hardest time-related issue: cumulative time and your age(s). Most of us don't like thinking about how the consequences of our decisions to delay parenting, or the number of years spent in pursuing unproductive treatment or hoping that we would find a suitable parenting partner have affected our future, but we must. You may need to stop here for a while and give yourselves time to recharge before seriously plunging into considerations about how to budget time as it relates to age, and how that is going to impact your parenting options and decisions.

How old are you now? What about your future? No matter how youthful you (and your partner) look and feel now, be realistic about where you are likely to be not just in ten years, but in twenty years. Think about not just your own needs, but the needs of the children you want to parent. Research is demonstrating that more and more of today's young adults are spending a longer span of time in a late adolescence—a period of time up to about age 30 when they remain emotionally, and to a slightly lesser extent financially, dependent on their parents.

The only way to be entirely realistic about how your ages factor into whether or not adoption is right for you right now is to examine not just your own health, but to take a closer look at your genetic history. How healthy, fit, and active are your aunts, uncles, cousins, and siblings who are ten years older than you are now? How about twenty years older? Now think a little like an actuary might. . . . What is not just the longevity record, but the health and fitness record within your family as people age? How old and how able were your grandparents and their siblings when they died, and what was the state of their health when they were 15 years older than you are now? What about your parents, aunts and uncles, siblings, and cousins?

Think about the ages of older members of your family when they began to need the help of a younger generation. Is it fair to a child who has already experienced so many losses related to family before landing softly in your loving arms that he becomes the main "worrier," if not caretaker to his parent, at an age when his peers may be finishing their educations or just starting their own families? How can you plan to avoid this situation, or should you? Certainly some practical steps that include getting long term care insurance and careful financial planning can help.

To be realistic about age as a factor in what approach to adoption is reasonable for you, one has to look carefully at finances in many ways. You may have amassed a very nice investment portfolio and savings account while delaying parenthood, but money is far from the most important need of a child who has been orphaned. Can you, will you, likely be around for the child you would like to parent until he reaches true independence?

If you are parenting with a much younger partner, you may feel that you have that covered financially . . . but what about the additional emotional and physical stress that single parenting will bring to that widowed partner? Some prospective adopters have much older children from this or earlier relationships. They may assume, inappropriately, that those older siblings can and will want to step up in a worst case scenario of your dying and leaving a still-dependent child. How fair is this to either the older or younger children in your family? Are there ways to avoid this and still add a young child to your family now?

In looking at your choices, you are going to need to consider whether you have passed a personal point of no return in planning to parent a child from birth. That does not necessarily mean that you can't adopt at all. Future chapters will provide more information (and more hard questions!) about these options.

Taking inventory has been a preliminary process. You will use the data you have gathered and talked about together here in making the very specific decisions to come in Part Three of this book.

Educating Yourselves and One Another

Having agreed on whether or not to rule out certain options, and having taken stock of your resources, you must obtain as much background information about each option which remains open to you as you possibly can. This will take some time. So that you can both feel confident that the final decision is mutually satisfying, *both members of a couple should take responsibility for participating in the information-gathering process*. Most find this an empowering experience, allowing them to regain an important measure of control. If your partner will not agree to take responsibility for some of this information gathering, stop the process and ask him or her to join you in some counseling sessions to determine what is causing the impasse.

Further discussion about getting accurate information will be shared in the very practical Part Three of this book. The following is provided as an overview.

Published Materials

Information is available in a variety of genres. Books, CDs and tapes, DVDs, fact sheets, magazine and professional journal articles are important sources of information and should be considered one of your most important resources. For a nominal fee your local library can obtain nearly anything they do not shelve through the interlibrary loan program.

The Internet

The Internet, too, is a valuable source of information, but it is important to keep in mind when using web sites as a primary source of information that information on personal websites has not been vetted by anyone as a published book or newspaper has, and that the websites of service providers are, basically, designed as advertisements. Internet information, then, while in many cases more up-to-date than a book can be, must be fact checked by comparing it with numerous other sources for accuracy.

Meetings and Symposia

Face-to-face education is equally important. Today adoption is a competitive business, so that most agencies, both private agencies and the public agencies which represent the children in State care, offer periodic free, open-to-the-public informational meetings which can provide you with a no-obligation opportunity to learn about parental qualifications, ages and races and abilities of children available through a particular agency, programs and countries represented, costs, philosophies, and more. You will often find these advertised in local newspapers or you can simply make a series of calls to area agencies using the telephone book. Monthly meetings of infertility and adoptive parent support groups are good sources of more objective information, and will offer you the opportunity to connect with families who have used the providers you are considering. Locate such groups, as well as educational opportunities, through contact with infertility medical providers, adoption agencies, and through the Child Welfare Information Gateway site on the Internet (see Resources).

In most large cities you can find periodic day-long adoption conferences which offer a menu of presentations by social service, legal, counseling, and medical professionals. Sometimes these are sponsored by an infertility or adoption support group or by a single agency, and sometimes a coalition of groups or service providers pull these together for their community. If you live in a smaller city, it is almost always well worth your time and expense to travel to a larger city within your state or region to attend such a large event, where, most often, several providers are represented both as session leaders and in the conference area where tables and booths allow for one-on-one conversations. Keep your eyes and ears open for these special events, or ask groups and agencies to keep you on mailing lists for such events they may publicize. Since these are often annual or biennial events, you may find that your own timing doesn't match that of the group. Don't despair! Frequently the sessions have been audio-taped and are available for borrowing or for purchase. Contact local infertility support or adoptive parents' support groups about these opportunities.

I often speak to people who are reluctant to reach out to an advocacy group. The excuse most often reported is, "We're feeling fine. We don't want a support group." While I understand that many people do not wish to seek the support component of such groups, these groups offer much more than support. These are the real experts in a field—those whose personal experience with it have taught them how important it is to be well informed. Volunteer leaders of mutual support groups have made it their business to gather as much data as possible and to keep track of the frequent changes in your community and beyond. Additionally, these groups are becoming more and more involved in legislative advocacy work on behalf of their constituents. I believe that families exploring adoption do themselves a serious disservice if they do not take advantage of the educational and referral and advocacy opportunities available through volunteer run advocacy and support organizations. More about that later.

Setting Up a Retreat Weekend

After you have had ample opportunity for self reflection and information gathering—including, for most readers, finishing this book (though this process can be used preliminarily)—it will be time to build a plan. Setting aside a weekend for the purpose of making some careful decisions and formulating a battle plan is a worthwhile investment in your family's future. Logistics require your willingness and commitment to give undivided attention to planning your assault on the dragon. You will need a minimum of 48 hours for this phase of your planning process.

Your time will be most constructively spent without the interruptions of normal routines. Many people who have used this process have found it useful to plan a weekend away from home—camping, in a hotel, in a friend's borrowed vacation home, etc. If your finances do not allow for escape, or if you feel that the pull of an escape location might distract you from the task at hand, your retreat can be equally successful conducted from home base. Just be sure that you tell your family and friends that you have plans for the weekend, hide your cars (so that no one will know that you are home), unplug your doorbell (so that you won't be tempted to answer the door to friends who drop in unexpectedly), kennel your pets, turn off your phone's ringer, and use an answering machine (with the screening feature turned off) to take messages for you. Turn cell phones all the way off, and leave the email and instant messaging features off on the laptop you may decide to take with you for making notes and doing some research. Yeah, I know it's hard to go "unplugged." That's why that telephone anecdote in Chapter One still works in explaining the concept of loss.

Whether you are staying at home or leaving for your retreat, free yourselves of all normal weekend "must-do's." Change the laundry, shopping, cleaning, and lawn care schedules for the week—or better yet, reward yourselves by hiring these jobs out for this once. Give careful thought to meal planning for the weekend. If you will be staying at home, do all necessary shopping in advance and be sure to plan one or more meals out—you'll need the break. Plan to include time in the 48 hour retreat weekend for exercise and/or entertainment. Plan some walks or a jog together, take in a carefully chosen escapist movie or play or a concert.

If the location offers complete privacy, so that neither of you will be exposed to the observation of others if emotions rise to the surface, some of the talking you will do during the retreat weekend can easily be done while you are sitting on the bank of a river fishing, walking through a woods, lying on a quiet beach. Holding such intimate conversation in busy public places—city beaches, park benches, while walking down busy downtown streets or through a weekend art fair—is not recommended.

You will need paper and pencils, perhaps a laptop, and summaries of books, tapes and articles that each of you has already read and wishes to share with the other, staples to ward off the munchies, and perhaps some music CDs that you mutually agree are stress-relieving without being sleep-inducing. I also urge you to take with you a completely open mind when it comes to adopting through collaborative reproduction or the style of "traditional" adoption you might pursue, the kind of child you might adopt, and from where. Working through this process allows you to make those decisions from a well-informed position rather than from a heart tainted by fear or misinformation.

This decision making process will be hard work—physically and emotionally draining. Take breaks as often as either of you feels a need.

Building the Plan

Setting Goals

The purpose of the Retreat Weekend is to create a concrete plan for managing your family building challenges—a plan that will allow you to reassert control over as many aspects as possible of your family planning, a plan that will take into account your dreams and desires while realistically addressing your limitations, and a plan that you feel completely confident directing your energy toward pursuing. Using the information you have gathered, you will make long lists, transfer them to charts (some couples have found index cards helpful) and then during the course of several hours, you will add options and delete options as you discuss them.

Strategic planning—for battle, for business, for personal lives—presumes the setting of goals, the success of which can be measured in some fashion and which will be periodically re-evaluated. Broad general *goals* (example goal: An exciting birthday for Belinda), are achieved through a variety of possible *objectives* (example objectives: Party at home on Sunday the 24th; dinner at La Tour; friends pitch in on "the perfect gift;"). Objectives are reached through the completion of highly detailed *strategies* (example strategies: Call caterers to find out how much a catered home party would cost; arrange for florist to deliver flowers; design and have invitations printed and mailed). In light of the success or failure of various objectives explored and strategies attempted, goals are evaluated and reaffirmed or restructured.

The first step in creating your personal plan for defeating the dragon of challenged family building is to decide together on your major goal. For some readers ongoing infertility treatment and medically-assisted alternatives will be part of this mix the first time you apply this planning process, so I will use some of these options in the examples which follow. You will already have begun talking and thinking about your ranking and weighting of losses, and this will lead you to the task of determining through negotiation and compromise what you, as a single, or the two of you as lifetime partners identify as your major goal.

Do you need to regain control? Do you want a pregnancy? Do you want to parent? What is number one?

Having identified your major goal, it's important to at least talk about all of the objectives that could help you to reach that goal. Brainstorm and be as expansive as possible. You can always delete objectives later.

For example, if a main goal is to regain control, some of your objectives might be

1. To become better informed about treatment alternatives.
2. To set a time table for continuing treatment.
3. To find other parts of your lives in which you CAN feel a full sense of control.
4. (Continue to add your own possible objectives)

If a primary goal is to become parents, the first time through this process your list of objectives might include a need to list and then rank and weight several alternative methods in addition to adoption for achieving this goal, such as

1. Becoming pregnant with a child genetically related to you both.
2. Using donor insemination or adoptive embryo transfer, or contracting with a surrogate.
3. Adopting.

Beneath each of these objectives, brainstorm a list of all of the strategies you can think of that would assist you in reaching this objective. During this stage you should list every imaginable strategy—even those that may seem initially unrealistic. For example, under the goal of becoming parents, and the objective of parenting a genetically related child, you might list

1. Continuing standard treatments with a local gynecologist/ urologist.
2. Pursuing treatment with a nearby fertility specialist (reproductive endocrinologist or andrologist).
3. Finding the clinic most renowned in the world for expertise in our problem area(s) and traveling to this clinic for treatment.
4. (Add as many others as you can possibly imagine)

If you are working on a medical treatment plan, you should know how many treatment alternatives there are for your medical problem(s) and list them all. Beyond that, for future discussion, how many non-medical alternatives are you willing to explore? List them all in a chart or on index cards, and include the symbols for each of your four limited resources (time, money, physical capacity and energy, emotional reserves) so that you can begin to allocate those resources.

What are the advantages and disadvantages of each alternative? Do you have the resources available to pursue all of these options one at a time (it is never a good idea to pursue multiple options at once—more about that later)? Try to regain as much objectivity about your situation as you possibly can. Now is the time to get real. Above, I provided a sampling of questions about resources for you to consider in formulating your discussion, but my lists are far from exhaustive. Your own lists should be!

After you have thoroughly brainstormed and created what seems like an exhaustive list of options, you will begin to delete those strategies that simply don't appeal or won't work for you. For example, you may feel that some strategies are morally, ethically, or religiously offensive to either or both of you. Some strategies may demand more of certain resources than you are willing or able to expend. You may be unwilling or unable to travel for treatment, unable to afford certain routes to adoption, or feel constrained by your ages from certain alternatives.

With a more realistic list of alternatives to consider it is important to constantly evaluate your reactions and your willingness to compromise, expect total openness and honesty from one another, and consider questions such as

1. Is this decision being considered after having thoroughly dealt with the loss of our assumed child?
2. What effects will the choice for this alternative have on our feelings about ourselves, on our moral or religious convictions, on our self esteem?
3. What effects will this alternative choice have on the feelings of my spouse?
4. What effects will this alternative choice have on my feelings about my spouse, or his or her feelings about me? In other words, how will this affect our relationship with one another?
5. (If the alternative under consideration is not childfree living) What effects will the choice of parenting by this alternative have on the relationship each of us will have as parents to the child who will join our family in this way?
6. What effects will our choice of this alternative have on our relationship with family and intimate friends, and how do we each feel about this?

Strategizing

Your finished plan will probably include more than one alternative, each listed in prioritized order. Your first choice is your first objective; your second choice is your second objective, etc. The planning process presumes that because each objective is time consuming, you will want to accomplish some of the tasks of each objective concurrently. For example, if adoption is one choice, but not the first choice, you still need to begin to explore some specifics such as how long the wait is on the list of an agency you would like to work with. Perhaps the wait is long enough that you feel it wise to get on the list now, while you are still working on medical treatment.

Your strategies, then, will be very specific, and each of you will want to take responsibility for pursuing some of them (e.g. writing necessary letters and making phone calls, reading books and articles).

A word of caution . . . Conveyor belt couples may find it tempting to race from medical treatment directly to another option. Deciding to end treatment is a big step. Resolve to give yourself space for reflection and re-evaluation between the end of treatment and the aggressive pursuit of either gamete or traditional adoption.

Applying Resources

In this process you will reconsider the resources you have inventoried in a much more detailed fashion. For example, how much time can be expended? You will need to look at time from several angles: near term and long term. Near term, for example, if travel is involved for this treatment option or this adoption route, can you take time from your work or are you willing to have the need for time off impact negatively on your job? For how long could you be away? In pursuing an international adoption, would you be able to travel to and live in another country for several weeks? How will taking time to pursue one alternative affect the availability of other possible alternatives? Thinking long term about time brings your ages into consideration. Have you realistically evaluated the impact of your ages on the likelihood of success in treatment at this time and weighed that against the impact of unsuccessful treatment on your ability to pursue another route such as egg donation or an adoption?

Consider the emotional energy involved in each option being considered. How much are you willing to spend on this alternative? No matter which partner is in treatment, the stress of treatment is felt by both partners. No matter how physically or emotionally strong one partner feels after facing a disappointing change of mind in an adoption, the other may feel depleted and unable to go on. Can you come up with a mutually agreeable level of comfort beyond which point one partner has the absolute right to call, "Stop!"?

Barbara and Rusty spent their retreat weekend ensconced in the lake cabin of Barbara's parents. For three days they reflected, shuffled index cards, debated pros and cons, cried as they realized that some dreams were being let go, and built a plan for themselves.

They wanted a child to parent, and they weren't getting any younger. At 33 and 38, they were beginning to watch their oldest friends emerge from the stresses of caring for very young children and find time for adult pleasures again. Their insurance plan had covered only the basic parts of their treatment. Now that they were involved in assisted reproductive technologies, they found themselves with ever mounting balances on their bank cards. Already they had had to cash in an investment bond that had been earmarked for the down payment on the larger home they would need in a few years when they did become parents. Rusty had been a loving and supportive partner of Barb's wish to become pregnant, but he was wearing thin. The drugs of each cycle of GIFT made Barbara moody, strident and sick. She produced eggs, all right, but only a couple each month, despite the high doses of hormones. They had never had a positive pregnancy test. Rusty was running out of energy and patience. He needed to move on. After the retreat weekend, Barbara knew that she did too. They would stop GIFT and put their energies into adoption. Barbara would tell her doctor at her next appointment the following week.

The appointment went differently than she had expected. She tried to tell the doctor about their decision to stop treatment, but he had just come back from a professional meeting with exciting ideas about new things to try. The pump might be the answer—wearing a device which would constantly pump the appropriate levels of medication through a shunt in Barbara's arm might help induce better quality ovulation. He was so excited that it was hard for Barb not to get caught up in his enthusiasm. She went home having promised to talk to Rusty about it and get back to him.

But Rusty was full of his own enthusiasm. Part of his "home-work" after the retreat weekend had been to make calls to two agencies, an adoption attorney, and a consulting service in town to gather preliminary information. On his second call, to an agency facilitating open adoptions, the workers had been excited to hear from him—did Barbara believe that?! It seemed that they were working with a birth-mother who was Jewish. Five months pregnant, she wanted her child to be placed with Jewish parents, and, frankly, they had only two resumes on file, neither of which had intrigued this birthmother. She had asked Rusty to bring Barbara in for an interview in the next few days.

"Remember what we decided, Barbara? No more 'medical may-bes.' It's time to invest in a surer thing!" Rusty pleaded. And, you know, for the first time, Barbara didn't even hesitate. Their weekend of hard work had paid off. Both of them knew where they were headed now.

Time/Age

If you are considering adoption as opposed to collaborative reproduction, you will have learned from your conferencing and reading that some private agencies do have age and length of partnership requirements, some countries impose such requirements on international adopters, and in programs where birthparents select adopting parents for their babies, some have strong feelings about age as well. If the answers to the questions which follow produce a feeling that perhaps it is too late to begin with a baby, don't reject adoption before carefully examining the idea of adopting an older child. Consider as well that adopting without an agency is an alternative to agency adoption and may, if carefully explored and pursued, neutralize some age restrictions . . . but should they?

Borrowing Genetic Material—
Special Issues

This is a book aimed primarily at those considering adopting children unrelated to either of them as an alternative route to parenthood after experiencing a family challenge such as infertility. Therefore, the rest of the book has been designed to lead readers considering this option step by step in exploring the many issues necessary to making an informed choice about adoption as a method of family building.

Many couples, however, after following the decision making process outlined here, will wish to pursue an alternative form of adoption: the conception of a child using the genetic material of someone from outside the partnership. This may mean using the sperm of a more fertile male either known or unknown to you in the process referred to as donor insemination. It may mean taking advantage of advancing technology which allows for the harvesting of ova from a more fertile woman, fertilizing it in vitro with the sperm of the husband in the infertile couple and reimplanting it in the infertile wife in a process most often called egg donation. Some programs offer the service of combining donor insemination and egg donation by borrowing the genetic material of both another man and another woman and having the resulting in-vitro-fertilized embryo transferred to the infertile wife for gestation and delivery, a process properly labeled a customized form of embryo adoption. It could mean arranging to use a surrogate mother. Traditionally (and the practice goes back to Biblical times) a surrogate has been inseminated with the sperm of the husband in an infertile couple and has then given birth to a baby which she agrees to allow the infertile wife to adopt. Now a surrogate (also called a gestational carrier) may also agree to carry and deliver an embryo genetically unrelated to her—either conceived in vitro from the ova and sperm of an infertile couple or an embryo which will be adopted by the intended parent(s).

Some of the material in the rest of this book will remain helpful to those readers—especially the material on parenting issues and talking to children about their genetic parents and about adoption in general. The resources at the end of this section also refer couples considering quasi-adoption options to several books and websites which can help in making the decision. This group of alternatives, however, far too often remains shrouded in shame and secrecy, myth and misconception. It is unfortunately the case that the majority of physicians practicing in this field continue to deny the important reality that these alternatives are not medicines that cure infertility, but are alternative choices that result in forms of adoption. There continue to be practices that do not offer the kind of pre-procedure education and post-procedure support that can help families deal with the practical realities these forms of family building bring to their homes.

This is a lengthy way of saying that I feel that I would be remiss if I did not offer some specific suggestions for couples considering these alternatives. In making final choices about using donor gametes, you must keep in mind that you are making a choice with the potential to throw the relationship into disequilibrium. Make sure you have discussed and made decisions about the following factors:

1. Each partner must deal with the loss of the couple's assumed child. Make no decisions until each of you has had time to bury the child you would have created together.

2. Have you both acknowledged this as an alternative choice rather than as a medical treatment? This does not cure the infertility of the partner not genetically related to the child, though it does end the childlessness.

3. Have you discussed the ongoing impact of the fertile partner's gain in choosing this option (genetic connection) on the self esteem of the infertile partner (who experiences the permanent loss of genetic continuity and connection)? How might this affect the balance in the parenting relationship? Have you agreed on how to deal with this both now and in the future?

4. Are you certain that the decision has been made positively, rather than conceded to by a guilty-feeling infertile partner?

5. Will you tell others? Will you tell the child? If yes, have you discussed how and when? If no, have you thoroughly examined the ongoing burden on relationships of maintaining such a weighty secret?

In many cities, infertility and single parent support groups, referral to a well qualified mental health professional running private groups, or doing one-on-one counseling can be a helpful resource for would-be parents exploring quasi-adoption options.

Evaluation

Good planning calls for periodic evaluation. In fact, all goals and objectives should carry with them a projected completion date. Time, of course, is budgeted as a resource, built into the plan in such ways as your having decided to pursue three months' worth of a particular therapy before re-evaluating whether to continue or pursue another course of action, or your planning to place an ad directed at birthparents in five issues of a national newspaper or on six websites before evaluating whether to renew or revise it.

Your overall plan should carry the expectation for periodic evaluation too. I recommend that part of your commitment to one another and to your jointly made plan should include scheduled promises to meet over dinner to discuss progress at least quarterly until your goal has been reached and, in the event that your initial goals have not been met, to plan another retreat weekend to be held one year following your first. At this time you can evaluate your progress, adjust your goals and objectives if necessary, and develop new strategies.

"We'll still be stuck a year from now?" I hear you exclaiming. No. If your plan has been made carefully and takes into account the limitations of your resources, the odds are that you will be successful or at least well on the road to success and you will not need to rework your plan. All good planning, however, contains a contingency measure for reevaluation and reexamination of the goals within at least a year if needed.

Following Your Plan

Even people facing what seem, on the surface, to be similar family building challenges may make entirely different decisions about how to proceed based on their individual and jointly shared values. Let me share with you examples of people who have already worked through the decision making process outlined here . . .

Darlene's dreams since childhood had included a brood of children. She married her college sweetheart right out of school without their having thoroughly discussed those future plans. She divorced him ten years later when it became clear that he just did not want children and she realized that her biological clock was ticking away. Because Darlene was a devout and conservative Catholic, the divorce was a difficult enough decision to make. She waited ten more years, hoping that the right second partner would come her way, at which point she might consider having the first marriage religiously annulled. When that didn't happen, Darlene, now in her 40s, looked more carefully at single parenthood. Though she would have loved a genetic connection to her child and the pregnancy experience, her religious convictions led her to decide that donor insemination was not for her. She examined domestic adoption, and realized that her single status made her adoption of a newborn more complicated. So she began to look at adopting an older child. Adopting from a public agency (the child welfare system) was Darlene's first choice, but she soon learned that for those who dream of young children (infants and toddlers) that route involved fostering the child first while the little one's birthparents were being offered the opportunity for rehabilitation and parent education. This felt too emotionally risky for Darlene. Then she heard about the single sister of a long-time friend who had recently adopted from Russia. The world suddenly opened for her. Within ten months Darlene made the first of two trips to a small orphanage in a remote part of the former Soviet Union, where her 4-year-old son waited to meet her and to be brought back home six weeks later to an extended family of similar aged cousins and a house full of pets and love.

Carmaine and Randy had been stymied by Carmaine's premature ovarian failure. Both wanted desperately to parent, but Randy found the idea of adoption particularly difficult because of his myth-filled but firmly held convictions (not shared by Carmaine, who was ready to adopt) that bonding could be achieved only through genetic connection. Since Carmaine could not ovulate, they could see no hope, and their relationship became increasingly pressured by their blaming of one another for their joint failure to become parents. Almost serendipitously they approached their pastor just as he had recently met just the right counselor—a woman well versed in infertility issues, who, after spending several sessions with them working through their reactions to their individual and joint losses and allowing them to mourn those lost expectations, opened windows not even seen before: surrogacy and embryo adoption. They seriously considered both, found medical and legal advisors to answer their questions about each, and finally decide to pursue adopting an embryo. This option allowed the two of them to experience the pregnancy and birth together.

Sara and Matt are the owners and operators of a family farm. Together they were clear about their major interest—to become parents. They had pursued all of the least invasive medical treatments they could to try to prod Sara's stubbornly uncooperative ovaries. She responded best to a cycle of Pergonal—expensive for this uninsured couple with limited financial resources. The reproductive endocrinologist working with them at a major medical center saw another promising treatment and provided them with a great deal of literature, encouraging statistics of success for couples who tried three cycles at the center's clinic, and a promise to work them into the waiting list quickly. Their doctor was convincing. It was tempting, and, frankly, they had trouble letting this very nice doctor down, but they really didn't see how they could afford up to three cycles of this procedure. Sara and Matt more or less disappeared from the clinic—not formally ending treatment, but just not coming back. Through their church, they learned of a young woman in another community who was parenting one child alone and was pregnant again. Within months they were the parents of her two children—a toddler and a newborn—in an open adoption. The birth-mother's employee insurance plan covered all medical expenses of the birth, the local department of social services provided their homestudy (not possible in all locales), and their total expenses involved minimal legal fees of an attorney specializing in family law who was also a member of their congregation. Sara and Matt's family was completed just before I wrote *Adopting after Infertility*. Their youngest child is now working with them on the family farm and the older child has just given them their first grandchild.

Logan and Marshall had been partners for seventeen years and had seen the world change a great deal for gay partners in that time. They had chosen to move to a state in which they could be seen legally as life partners with the same rights and responsibilities as married heterosexuals. That made them feel braver about the idea of parenting too. Logan had long before chosen a career as a pediatric nurse to meet some of his needs to nurture the young, but now he lived in a city where the local social services department actively recruited gay parents for their foster-adopt program. He saw the opportunity to nurture a child or children whose special medical needs he already understood, and brought with them the medical and other subsidies that would allow him to leave his job and be a full-time parent for a while. He laid the plan out for Marshall on a retreat weekend, and his partner was wowed by the opportunity this presented for the two of them. Logan and Marshall have since adopted two of their former foster children, prepared another to return to his birth grandmother, and continue to foster, now having added older kids to their resume of specialized parenting skills.

Jocelyn and Mary considered the losses of their family building challenges and identified what they each wanted most from their original decision to become parents. For Mary, the need was to experience a pregnancy as well as to be a parent, yet she also mourned the loss of sharing a pregnancy and then a child with Jocelyn. For Jocie, on the other hand, individual continuity was just not important. Her dreams were of parenting—reading bedtime stories, coaching athletic teams. For this couple the carefully discussed choice to use donor insemination was an attractive one—offering them each the opportunity to achieve their dreams and avoid the losses most painful to each. If this option were successful for them, each of them would win what she wanted most. Both, however, agreed that their highest priority was shared parenthood, so that, should D.I. prove unsuccessful, Jocelyn and Mary were ready to embrace adoption as an equally attractive way to build a family. They began to gather information about international adoption just in case. The D.I. worked, and they used the same donor a second time. Their family building is complete.

Mark and Amy, on the other hand, acknowledged different needs. The grandchild of Holocaust victims and survivors, Mark mourned deeply his inability to provide another generation for his family. He was willing to go to dramatic lengths to improve his sperm count and to enhance his chances of impregnating his wife. Amy, too, wanted a genetic connection, and initially saw clearly that she could have it, if only she could convince Mark to agree to D.I. Their physician endorsed this choice, reminding Mark that no one need ever know that Amy's child is not his by blood. With the help of a skilled facilitator, their communication led each to see that for Mark to accede to such a demand from Amy would create a win-lose situation in the balance of their relationship and could impair his ability to relate positively to the child to whom Amy would give birth. The child would serve as a daily reminder that Mark had lost what both wanted most—genetic continuity—while Amy had achieved it. Additionally, for this couple, the interest in parenting is simply not strong enough in the face of their powerful interest in genetic linkage for either to consider that there could be a win-win after loss-loss in the compromise option of adoption. After careful reflection and a reaffirmation of their primary commitment to one another and to their marriage, this couple decided that their interest in a jointly conceived child was strong enough for them to spend significant amounts of time, money and energy researching and seeking out the clinics in the world with the highest rate of success in treating Mark's problem. After having pursued surgery, medications, and several courses of IVF without achieving a pregnancy, this couple chose to embrace a childfree lifestyle.

Each of these families considers themselves successful in resolving their issues and making family building decisions. Their carefully considered choices were right for the two of them. Each was ultimately nurtured by a caring, helpful professional who helped them to identify their personal needs, limitations and values, and was able to feel personal success reflected in their joy. There could be more Mark and Amys, Carmaine and Randys, Sara and Matts, and Jocelyn and Marys and fewer drifting, disappointed infertile people if all of the professionals working with family challenged people would make it a part of their practice to link services, and to provide a full spectrum of information and care for their patients and clients.

Infertility support groups, both face-to-face and online, can help you find a caring medical professional. Later in this book, we will talk about the qualities and qualifications to look for in selecting the right adoption professionals for you.

No one said that managing your family-building challenges would be easy. In making all of your decisions, setting all of your goals, following all of the strategies that will allow you to meet your objectives, be certain that the decisions you make now are made together and with enough care that you will remain comfortable with them ten, twenty, or thirty years into the future. It is always easy to look back and say "if only . . ." When decisions are made carefully, however, and with complete knowledge and full communication between partners, they can last for a lifetime.

Helen Keller, a woman intimately familiar with profound loss, may have said it best,

> "When one door of happiness closes, another opens. But often we spend so much time looking at the closed doors that we cannot see the doors that have opened for us. We must all find these doors, and, if we do, we will make ourselves and our lives as beautiful as God intended."

Some who are reading this book may well find it helpful to stop after reading this chapter and spend time using the process described here to look more carefully at other options that have piqued your interest or to deal with complications that the process has brought to the surface. If, having done that, you find that you wish to explore adoption more deeply, examining how it "lives" over the long term, and using the planning process to make specific choices about who and when and how and where to adopt, the sections and chapter which follow will be waiting for you as a resource.

Resources to Accompany Chapters in Part One

Grief and Loss

Boss, Pauline. *Ambiguous Loss: Learning to Live with Unresolved Grief* (Cambridge: Harvard University Press, 1999)

Kubler-Ross, Elisabeth and David Kessler. *On Grief and Grieving: Finding the Meaning of Grief Through the Five Stages of Loss* (New York: Scribner, 2007)

Kushner Harold S. *When Bad Things Happen to Good People* (New York: Shocken Books, 1981)

Levine, Stephen. *Unattended Sorrow: Recovering from Loss and Reviving the Heart* (Emmaus, PA: Rodale, 2005)

Sterns, Ann Kaiser. *Living through Personal Crisis* (New York: Ballantine Books, 1984)

Communication

Carter Jean W. and Michael Carter. *Sweet Grapes: How to Stop Being Infertile and Start Living Again* (Indianapolis: Perspectives Press, Inc., 1998 revised edition)

Chapman, Gary. *The Five Love Languages: How to Express Heartfelt Commitment to Your Mate* (Chicago, IL: Northfield Publishing, 1995)

Gottman John M. and Nan Silver. *The Seven Principles for Making Marriage Work* (Orion, 2004)

Hendrix, Harville PhD and Helen Hunt Atria, PhD. *Receiving Love: Transform Your Relationship by Letting Yourself Be Loved* Reprint edition (October 4, 2005) (There is also a companion *Receiving Love Workbook: A Unique Twelve-Week Course for Couples and Singles*)

Tannen, Deborah. *You Just Don't Understand: Women and Men in Conversation* (New York: Harper Paperbacks, July, 2001)

Decision Making

Covey, Stephen R. *The 7 Habits of Highly Effective People* (New York: Simon & Shuster, 1989)

Dawson, Roger. *The Confident Decision Maker: How to Make the Right Business and Personal Decisions Every Time* (New York: William Morrow & Co., 1993)

Freeman, Dr. Arthur and Rose DeWolf. *Woulda, Coulda, Shoulda: Overcoming Regrets, Mistakes and Missed Opportunities* (New York: HarperCollins, 1989)

Johnston, Spencer MD *Yes or No: The Guide to Better Decisions* (New York: HarperCollins, 1992)

Rubin, Theodore Isaac MD *Overcoming Indecisiveness* (New York: Harper & Row, 1985)

Schlossberg, Nancy K. and Susan Porter Robinson *Going to Plan B: How You Can Cope, Regroup, and Start Your Life on a New Path* (New York: Fireside, 1996)

Infertility

American Society for Reproductive Medicine
1209 Montgomery Highway
Birmingham, AL 35216-2809
phone: 205-978-5000
email: asrm@asrm.org
www.asrm.org/

American Fertility Association
666 Fifth Avenue Suite 278
New York, NY 10103
phone: 888-917-3777
email: info@theafa.org
www.theafa.org

INCIID: International Council on Infertility Information Dissemination
P.O. Box 6836
Arlington, VA 22206
phone: 703-379-9178
email: INCIIDinfo@inciid.org
www.inciid.org

Infertility Awareness Association of Canada
2100 Marlowe Avenue, Suite 350
Montreal, QC H4A 3L5
Phone: 514-484-2891
Toll Free: 1-800-263-2929
email: info@iaac.ca
www.iaac.ca

Resolve, Inc. The National Infertility Association
7910 Woodmont Avenue, Suite 1350
Bethesda, MD 20814
Phone: 301-652-8585
www.resolveinc.org

Jaffe, Janet and David Diamond and Martha Diamond. *Unsung Lullabies: Understanding and Coping with Infertility* by (St Martin's, 2005)

Johnston, Patricia Irwin. *Taking Charge of Infertility* (Indianapolis: Perspectives Press, 1994)

Single Parenthood

Choosing Single Motherhood www.choosingsinglemotherhood.com

Mattes, Jane. *Single Mothers by Choice: A Guidebook for Single Women Who Are Considering or Have Chosen Motherhood* (Three Rivers Press, 1994)

Morrissette, Mikki. *Choosing Single Motherhood: The Thinking Woman's Guide* (Be-Mondo Publishing, 2006)

Peck, Cynthia Van Norden and Wendy Wilkinson. *Parents at Last: Celebrating Adoption and the New Pathways to Parenthood* (New York: Clarkson Potter, 1998

Varon, Lee. *Adopting On Your Own: The Complete Guide to Adoption for Single Parents* by (New York: Farrar, Strauss, Giroux, 2000)

Gay/Lesbian Parenthood

Families Like Mine www.familieslikemine.com/

2 Moms, 2 Dads www.2moms2dads.com/

Lev, Arlene Istar. *The Complete Lesbian and Gay Parenting Guide.* (Berkley Trade, 2004)

Brill, Stephanie. *The New Essential Guide to Lesbian Conception, Pregnancy, and Birth.* (Alyson Books, 2006)

McGarry, Kevin. *Fatherhood for Gay Men: An Emotional and Practical Guide to Becoming a Gay Dad* by (Harrington Park Press, 2003)

Sember, Brette McWhorter. *Gay & Lesbian Parenting Choices: From Adopting or Using a Surrogate to Choosing the Perfect Father* (Career Press, 2006)

Clunis, D.Merilee and G. Dorsey Green. *The Lesbian Parenting Book: A Guide to Creating Families and Raising Children* (Emeryville, CA: Seal Press, 2003)

Collaborative Reproduction

OPTS: The Organization of Parents through Surrogacy
P.O. Box 611
Gurnee, IL 60031
Phone: 847-782-0224
Email: bzager@msn.com
www.opts.com

Donor Conception Network www.dcnetwork.org

Cooper, Susan L. and Ellen S. Glazer. *Choosing Assisted Reproduction.* (Indianapolis: Perspectives Press, Inc., 1998)

Menichiello, Michael. *A Gay Couple's Journey Through Surrogacy—Intended Fathers.* (Binghamton, NY: Haworth Press, 2006)

Glazer, Ellen Sarasohn and Evelina Weidman Sterling. *Having Your Baby Through Egg Donation.* (Indianapolis: Perspectives Press, Inc., 2005).

Dutton, Gail. *A Matter of Trust—The Guide to Gestational Surrogacy* (Irvine CA: Clouds Publishing, 1997)

Ragone, Helena. *Surrogate Motherhood—Conception in the Heart* (Boulder, CO: Westview Press, 1994)

Vercollone, Carol Frost Heidi Moss, and Robert Moss *Helping the Stork: The Choices and Challenges of Donor Insemination.* (New York: Wiley, 1997)

Childfree Living

www.child-free.com/

Happily Childfree www.happilychildfree.com

No Kidding www.nokidding.net

Safer, Jeanne. *Beyond Motherhood: Choosing a Life Without Children.* (New York: Pocket, 2003)

Carter, Jean W. and Michael Carter *Sweet Grapes: How to Stop Being Infertile and Start Living Again.*(Indianapolis: Perspectives Press, Inc., 1998 revised edition)

Adoption

Detailed "how-to" resources will follow each subsequent section of this book. The following is the only other "should we" book of which I am aware:

Adamec, Christine. *Is Adoption for You: The Information You Need to Make the Right Choice.* (New York: Wiley, 1998)

PART TWO

Life Inside Adoption, an Overview

Adoption doesn't happen in isolation. It lasts a lifetime, and it directly influences several generations of two families' (birth and adoptive) lives and relationships both forward and backward. Though adoptive family life has more in common with the lives of families connected strictly by genes than one might think, the differences in adoption are significant. It's not, then, in either a would-be parent's or a child's best interests for the adults to dive into the how-tos of adoption without having thoroughly considered the unique elements of adoptive family life over the long term—in other words, how living in adoption might feel.

I want to introduce this section of *Adopting: Sound Choices, Strong Families* by acknowledging a unique segment of this book's audience. While this is not a book aimed at people who have *already* adopted a child (they've made their decisions about whether adoption is a good option for them), some readers of this book are indeed *already parents*. Some of you are experiencing secondary infertility after having successfully given birth to one or more children. You are exploring adoption because you want to expand your family and have been challenged in attempting to do it "the usual way." Others are in partnerships in which at least one of you has one or more genetically connected children from an earlier relationship. You want to "share" a child who feels equally connected to each of you, and you are exploring adoption as a route to that kind of family expansion. These families know parenting in general. What they do not clearly understand—any more than the childless who are reading this book—is how adoption and adoptive relationships are different—different to those living the relationships, different to the world outside. The chapters in Part Two will introduce both childless readers and those already parenting children to the most significant issues within adoptive families and relationships—the issues which form adoption's unique culture.

But first, some quick statistics which may reassure you that you indeed do want to read on.

While there is a generally accepted informed estimate that there are approximately 120,000 adoptions completed by U.S. families both domestically and internationally each year, no one is keeping full and careful track of all adoption statistics in the U.S.—not the federal government and not the states. While where children come from and how they are adopted fluctuates, that figure of 120,000 adoptions per year has been fairly stable over several decades, after a high in adoptions of about 170,000 in 1970.

Immigration statistics for intercountry adoptees are easiest to come by and are accurate, so we know that over the last decade 15–22,000 children (these numbers vary from year to year, and have been rising) have been brought here from other countries by U.S. citizen families. (Part Three will include a comparison of which countries have been sending how many children over a comparative length of time). Singles adopt from some countries outside the U.S. Few openly gay/lesbian couples do, however.

Foster care statistics, which *are* required of the states, further tell us that 50–60,000 more children have moved from the U.S. foster care system into the permanency of adoption over each of the last several years. For example, the AFCARS (Adoption and Foster Care Analysis and Reporting System) report for fiscal year 2004 tells us that there were 517,000 children in U.S. foster care, that the permanency goals for 25% of those children was adoption, and 52,000 children actually exited care to adoption. These children varied in age from infants to teens, with a mean age of 10.9 years, and the mean time spent in care was 30 months. These children—46% of whom were white, 29% African-American and 17% Hispanic—were adopted one at a time or in sibling groups. We also know from reported statistics that about one third of children adopted from foster care were adopted by single parents, and that in many states gay/lesbian couples are welcomed as foster/adoptive parents.

Exact statistics of the number of children (mostly newborns of various races) who are adopted through private agencies or independently (using an agency only for a homestudy) are very hard to come by, but educated guesstimates put that figure at an additional 50–60,000 placements each year. Gay and lesbian couples, unmarried partners, and singles are often successful in adopting independently when they find it difficult to qualify with private agencies.

The statistics for kinship placements outside the public fostering system (step-parent adoptions, voluntary trans-generational adoptions within a family that don't require an agency) are elusive and aren't included in the 120,000 total adoptions estimate.

It will probably be surprising to most readers that a growing number of U.S.-born children are being placed outside of the United States, mostly in Europe and Canada. Hague requirements will begin to tell us how many, but as I write, pre-Hague-implementation in 2007, we don't know how many children fit this profile. We know about them only anecdotally and the guesses are that the number is under 1000 each year. A few of these children are older kids with special needs, but most of them are healthy infants and many of them children of color. Most are placed by adoption attorneys and a handful of private agencies.

And then there is the collection of commonly held myths about who is even eligible to adopt. Let's clear those up right away . . .

Who Can Adopt

Myth: Only childless, heterosexual married couples adopt.

Fact: Let's be honest. It is usually easiest and fastest for same-race, heterosexual married couples to adopt. But adoptive parents can and do include heterosexuals, homosexuals[1], married couples, long term partners,[2] the widowed, singles,[3] and people with and without children born to them. The keys to success for nontraditional families include flexibility about the who and the where (some states and some countries are more open to "difference" than others), and a willingness to self-advocate.

Myth: Adoption is for white people.

Fact: Very often agencies and attorneys do a poor job of recruiting people of color as adoptive parents. The result is that there appear to be proportionately more white people adopting. The truth is, however, that there are proportionately more children of color to adopt than there are white children in need of adoption. All service providers—agencies and attorneys—should enthusiastically welcome people of color as adoptive parents for the many babies and children of color born to their birthparent clients, and if you run into one who doesn't seem to be enthusiastic about you, run—don't walk—to another service provider! While race matching is not the only factor in an adoption, service providers do consider placing children in racially matching families to be ideal. In fact, families of color are a "hot commodity" these days and most ethical service providers would bend over backwards to work with more of them!

Myth: You have to make a lot of money to adopt.

Fact: Bottom line is that prospective families are asked to demonstrate that they earn enough money to support a family, and that they manage whatever money they have wisely. Some paths to adoption are more expensive than others, but the bottom line is that virtually any functional and motivated parent-to-be who can demonstrate that s/he earns enough to support self and a child can find a service provider who will happily work with him or her.

Myth: I'm not old enough, or I am too old to adopt.

Fact: Adoptive parents must have reached legal adulthood. There is no legally set upper age limit for domestic adoption. Some agencies and some countries do, however, set upper or lower age limits for adoptive parents or guidelines about the distance in age between one or both parents and the children they wish to adopt. In voluntary placements, birthparents may influence the upper or lower age limits of the parents who will adopt their children.

Myth: Only Christians can adopt.

Fact: While some agencies are religiously based and privately funded, and thus can set religious requirements for their clients, all public agencies and many private agencies are secular and so do place children with people of all religions, as well as with atheists and agnostics. Independent adoptions are also a good source of adoption for these people.

Costs

Myth: Adoption is incredibly expensive!

Fact: Costs of adoption vary dramatically within the type of adoption and between service providers. Costs can be influenced by how an agency is funded, where the children come from, and the kinds of services provided to would-be parents. Realistically, the costs of an ethical adoption can range from almost nothing to upwards of $40,000, and these costs are predictable, so you need not be caught unaware.

For example, public agencies are funded by the individual states. This almost always means that not only will there be low to no fees at all, but that the children represented may be eligible for some sort of ongoing subsidy—a payment to their adoptive family to help meet their future needs.

Furthermore, there are resources available in many cases to help cover the pregnancy and adoption process and adoptive parenting-related expenses in any form of adoption. Some agencies set their fees proportionate to clients' incomes rather than as flat fees or actual costs of services. A growing number of employers now offer adoption reimbursement benefits of a few thousand dollars, and currently the federal government allows a several thousand dollar tax credit for non-recurring adoption expenses. Also there are a very small number of grants available from houses of worship and from foundations.

Myth: Adoption is buying a child.

Fact: Parents who adopt are not paying *for a child*. Adoption is not about how much a child "costs." Rather, fees charged are for *services* provided by the agency for the adoptive parent and usually are collected only once that service has been provided.

Myth: Adoptive parents pay for everything.

Fact: It is true that in non-public agency adoptions, fees collected from adoptive parents form the major source of funding for the counseling and medical services provided for expectant parents. Adopting a child through a public agency (often through foster care), however, can be virtually without cost, and costs for foster care and birthparent services are covered by public monies collected from all taxpayers.

Myth: Legal fees are overwhelming.

Fact: When adoptions are done completely through a public or private agency, and not independently, legal fees are sometimes included in agency fees, or, at most, involve very few billable hours from an attorney. Independent adoptions handled by attorneys do produce higher legal fees, as the attorneys often take on much of the work usually done by agencies.

Homes

Myth: Adoptive parents must own their own homes.

Fact: Not true. Many adoptive families rent. Agency workers are looking for homes to be clean and safe, not luxurious.

Myth: There must be a separate bedroom for every child.

Fact: Children of similar ages and the same gender may share bedrooms unless one of them has been identified as having emotional problems which could be a danger to the other child.

The case, statistically, is that most family-challenged readers of this book are likely to be able to adopt.

So there you have it; some of the most misunderstood factoids in adoption, clarified and corrected. If, at the end of Part Two, you are feeling confident about finding the resources and the support to make adoption's culture and its special issues a part of your family life, Part Three will offer you practical tools for making decisions about what kind of child, what style of adoption, and what adoption service providers are right for you.

CHAPTER 4

The Culture of Adoption

Adoption has its own "culture" based on core issues that make it different from families connected by birth. Choosing to build or expand your family by adoption will require that you be able to comfortably embrace this culture as a part of who you will become. For adults making adoption decisions—adopting parents and birthparents—it's only a slight exaggeration to compare embracing adoption to converting to a new religion or deciding to live your life in a country other than the one you were raised in. In fact, the following essay by *Sesame Street* writer Emily Perl Kingsley, the mother of a child with a disability, comes pretty close to describing the differences between parenting through adoption and parenting through birth.

Welcome to Holland
by Emily Perl Kingsley

I am often asked to describe the experience of raising a child with a disability; to try to help people who have not shared that unique experience to understand it, to imagine how it would feel. It's like this . . .

When you're going to have a baby, it's like planning a fabulous vacation trip to Italy. You buy a bunch of guide books and make your wonderful plans. The Coliseum. The Michelangelo David. The gondolas in Venice. You may learn some handy phrases in Italian. It's all very exciting.

After months of eager anticipation, the day finally arrives. You pack your bags and off you go. Several hours later, the plane lands. The stewardess comes in and says, "Welcome to Holland."

"Holland?!?" you say. "What do you mean Holland?? I signed up for Italy! I'm supposed to be in Italy. All my life I've dreamed of going to Italy."

But there's been a change in the flight plan. They've landed in Holland and there you must stay.

The important thing is that they haven't taken you to a horrible, disgusting, filthy place, full of pestilence, famine and disease. It's just a different place.

So you must go out and buy new guide books. And you must learn a whole new language. And you will meet a whole new group of people you would never have met.

Holland's just a different place. It's slower-paced than Italy, less flashy than Italy. But after you've been there for a while and you catch your breath, you look around . . . and you begin to notice that Holland has windmills . . . and Holland has tulips. Holland even has Rembrandts.

But everyone you know is busy coming and going from Italy . . . and they're all bragging about what a wonderful time they had there. And for the rest of your life, you will say "Yes, that's where I was supposed to go. That's what I had planned."

And the pain of that will never, ever, ever, *ever* go away . . . because the loss of that dream is a very, very significant loss.

But . . . if you spend your life mourning the fact that you didn't get to Italy, you may never be free to enjoy the very special, the very lovely things . . . about Holland.[4]

This chapter will examine the elements which color the culture of adoption, making it different from families built by birth. The goal is to help you sort out whether you will be able to embrace that culture and help your child do so, too.

Exploring and Acknowledging our Motivations for Adopting

On the surface, when one is challenged in giving birth to a child, the motivation for adopting might seem clear: the desire to be a parent. But just wanting to be a parent is rarely the only reason that anyone, including the family-challenged, chooses to adopt. As we look at adoption's impact on a family over a lifetime, it makes sense for us to explore and then keep in mind how our motivations drive our decisions. So let's begin with a general list of what motivates families to adopt. Later, in Part Three, we'll include similar lists of motivations that influence people's decisions to choose particular types of and places for adoption.

In the thirty or so years that I've been reading books about adoption and the dozen years that I've been browsing the Internet reading essays, articles, and now blogs, I've gathered quite a laundry list of motivations for adopting a child. They include the following reasons (in random order).

- Because we have fertility problems and cannot conceive a (first, or second, or third, etc.) child together.
- Because one of us is infertile, and it seems more "balanced" for neither of us to be genetically related to the child we parent together.
- Because I'm single and my family would be upset about a pregnancy without marriage, and I want to be a parent.
- Because we are gay and can't make a baby together.
- Because there are genetic problems that put us (me) at too high a risk of giving birth to a child with devastating problems.
- Because my biological clock is ticking, and I don't have time for fertility treatments.
- Because, though we want to parent, we believe in zero population growth and would rather adopt a child than reproduce ourselves.
- Because we want to choose the gender of our next child.
- Because we really don't want to go through a pregnancy.
- Because we are called to make a difference in the world, even if only one child at a time.
- Because we can assure that one child stops "waiting" or drifting in the foster care system.
- Because we can save one child from poverty or neglect in a country currently in the news as in crisis through war or famine.
- Because we are drawn to a particular culture or ethnicity and want to make it a part of our lives.
- Because we know others who have adopted, and feel good about their families.
- Because we are a new couple, past childbearing years, who want to "share" a parenting experience.
- Because we'd like an "instant family" and can adopt siblings.
- _____
- _____
- _____

I'm sure that as you read this list you probably saw some motivations that match your own. But you may also have discovered that there are some personal motivations of your own which were not on the list. Add them. Then keep your list nearby as you think through the issues raised in Parts Two and Three of this book.

Building a Sense of Entitlement

In his book *You're Our Child: The Adoption Experience*, Jerome Smith offered his theory of entitlement in adoptive families. Dr. Smith (whom I consider to be my first "academically-oriented and research-informed mentor" in adoption) observed that families built by adoption need to engage in the life-long process of building a sense of vested rightfulness between parents and children (and I would add between siblings and with extended family members)—each coming to believe that they deserve and belong to one another.

Entitlement, says Smith, is a multi-step process worked on both consciously and unconsciously over and over. Those steps include

- recognizing and dealing with the losses which brought all of the members of an adoption triad—birthparents, adoptive parents, and child—together
- recognizing and accepting that adoption is different from building a family by birth
- learning to handle reflections of a widely accepted societal view of adoption as a second best alternative for all involved.

Dr. Smith's book dealt with what are called *traditional adopters*—couples who choose to adopt as an alternative to being childless because some medical problem (primary or secondary infertility, genetic issues) or personal challenge makes their giving birth unwise or impossible. But it is clear to me that all families built by adoption, including those labeled *preferential adopters* (because nothing prevents them from giving birth, and indeed many have one or more children by birth, but whose motivation to adopt has to do with a sense of mission, or a world view) have entitlement issues on which to work. Indeed, after you've had a chance to think about this concept for a while, you'll probably join me in thinking that families connected by birth sometimes have "entitlement" issues too, but that's a subject of another book.

People touched by adoption work on entitlement and refine it throughout their lifetimes. What's important is recognizing that this is so and being committed to doing the work, making it conscious, because, as Smith writes, a poorly developing sense of entitlement is at the root of many family problems: poor communication, super-parent syndrome, inconsistent discipline, over-permissiveness, over-protectiveness, obsessive fear of the birthfamily, and more.

It is also important to understand that entitlement building and attachment building, while different, are inextricably interwoven, so that problems in attachment can contribute to problems in building a sense of entitlement and vice versa. We'll talk about attachment—the claiming process, the effects of earlier experiences, parent-child interactions and responsiveness to one another, the impact of psychological mismatching and more—in depth in a later chapter. Entitlement, though, is a separate goal—the key to successful adoption. This story may help you understand the importance of entitlement:

> My mother- and father-in-law, Perry and Helen, raised two children whom they adopted after many years of infertility and several pregnancy losses. Each child was about six months old at placement, and they were two years apart in age. This family consistently acknowledged adoption. From early childhood adoption was part of the conversation. Perry and Helen—both college educated—were warm, gentle, loving parents who raised their children in a lovely Midwestern community, involved themselves as volunteers in school and extra-curricular activities, and offered their children many "advantages."
>
> Their son, Dave, who was the older of the two, was always comfortable with the adoption. Close to his parents, and particularly to his father, he never questioned their connectedness, and, while predictably annoyed as a kid with his parents' conservative parenting style, experienced it as consistent. Quiet and smart, with a wry sense of humor, Dave was like his father in many ways. He grew to adulthood with an entirely confident sense of self.
>
> Their daughter, MJ, always felt "different." MJ had some learning differences which made school a challenge, found that her interests and talents were a little "foreign" to the other members of her family, and didn't "look like" anyone at home. Her mother, very talented in most domestic arts, found a disinterested pupil and partner in her much loved daughter. Spunky and inclined to rebel, MJ's refusal to "go with the flow" of Perry and Helen's parenting style made discipline a challenge. As a result, it was inconsistent, as her parents tended to experiment now and again. As an adult, this daughter continued to search for the answer to who she is.
>
> As they prepared to sell the home in which the children grew up, Perry and Helen asked Dave and MJ if there was anything in particular that they wanted as a remembrance from home. Perry had already divvied up a number of his family's heirlooms—a Civil War sword, some books and papers, his father's railroad watch, etc. Helen, on the other hand, had not. MJ made her list of china, crystal, silver, etc. and it was sent. Dave, not a "things" person by nature, had a shorter list—mementoes only.
>
> Two things stood out as memories from home. A set of sleigh bells from his maternal grandparents' farm hung in their hall. From as far back as he could remember until he left for college, every Christmas Eve, after the children were tucked into bed, his father had taken those sleigh bells down from the wall and climbed to the roof of their house, where he

rang them and called out, "Ho, ho, ho!" What a wonderful memory. Dave wanted to pass it on to his children. The second item was a somewhat rustic sideboard in the dining room. It had been brought to the Midwest from Pennsylvania by his mother's great-grandparents in a covered wagon. He asked only for these two items.

The answer from his mother was a shock. "I'm sorry, David, but those belonged to my family. It didn't occur to me that you'd want them, so I've already given those things to your cousin, Bob; he's my only living relative."

He's my only living relative? Perry and Helen were wonderful, loving parents, their children well raised and the family fully attached to one another. But the two of them and each of their children had quite different experiences in building a sense of entitlement. Perry had thoroughly accomplished each step, and, in his relationship with his son and with his daughter, had passed it on. But someplace deep inside, Helen had some unfinished business about genetic connection. She loved her children, but she wasn't completely entitled, and so for her, neither were they.

In its time, it was a predictable situation. The steps to building a sense of entitlement aren't necessarily going to be easy, but with good education and support, which wasn't a part of adoption in the 1940s and 50s, they are doable. Most importantly, they must be done. Entitlement-building is adoption's central task.

In the next section of this book, as we lay out and ask readers to work through the controversial and unsettling issues that are unavoidably a part of finding a child, having parental rights to that child legally transferred to you, and then parenting that child, the question underneath it all is still *Is adoption for you?* But in order to answer that question you need to have a sense of how committed you are to building a healthy sense of entitlement with your child—resolving and successfully incorporating your challenges in building a family into your positive sense of self, accepting and acknowledging as consistently as possible that adoption is different from parenting by birth, and helping yourself and your family learn to respond to society's feeling that adoption is a second-best alternative. Adoption has been a wonderful way to expand families for millions of family-challenged (and unchallenged) people! Examining the steps in building a sense of entitlement will help you in making the decision about whether adoption is the right choice for you.

Loss, Revisited: A First Step in Entitlement Building

As parents experiencing challenged family building, yours are not the only losses in adoption. Indeed, adoption is based upon loss. Birthparents experience losses, adoptive parents experience losses, people who have been adopted experience losses in adoption, and even siblings born to the family which also includes adopted children experience losses. Of course all of these people touched by adoption also experience significant gains in the process of being adoption-touched, but we focus on loss here because loss left untouched and unresolved tends to fester, like a wound, impacting most other facets of our lives. Loss, then, is a core issue in adoption.

As we discussed in Part One, for the fertility challenged, the process of resolving their losses can be the one step most likely to be ignored or denied by couples preparing to adopt. We'd rather bury it. We'd rather substitute for it. We prefer to believe that the very act of becoming a parent will erase all of the losses related to being fertility-challenged. We want the losses to go away. In fact, many of us actively proclaim that we don't see loss here at all. Sometimes the most unlikely people are the very ones who deny infertility's impact on them until years later, when, like a moth in the darkest closet, it has had time to nibble away at the fabric of families.

> Juliette was a family therapist who was delighted to discover that a Resolve chapter was coming to her town. Resolve had not existed when she was dealing with infertility—two nearly-grown adopted children ago. She volunteered to serve as a support group leader and was accepted at once. What qualifications!
>
> But half way through the ten week cycle of the group, Juliette, like a carefully mended piece of china soaking in sudsy hot water, came unglued. In helping others deal with their active grief over infertility's losses, she realized that she had never even identified them for herself. Was that why she harbored these unwelcome thoughts about her lack of connection with her daughter? Was it less an issue of a lack of psychological fit than a nagging feeling that her much-wanted birth child would have been different, more compliant, more like her mother?

Building a sense of entitlement is not unique to traditional adopters like Juliette. Fertile people who choose to expand their families by adoption are called preferential adopters, and these families, too, need to develop a sense of entitlement. It's tempting for preferential adopters to ignore loss completely unless forced to address it. Rarely do they expect any loss as they begin the process of adoption. Most often these are folks who have already experienced genetic connection, a jointly conceived child, the pregnancy and birth experiences. Their motivations for adopting don't come out of deprivation. They are, most often, feeling pretty good about themselves. Indeed, they have almost always come to adoption not for a healthy, same-race newborn, but to parent children who usually wait a long time for a family—children who linger to older ages in orphanages in other countries, children whose race, age or special medical, emotional or cognitive needs bounced them from foster home to foster home in this country. What are these parents losing?

Gains and Losses for Those Touched by Adoption

	Adoptive Parents	Birthparents	Adoptees
+	• Child • Siblings for other children • Meet new people • Knowledge of child's history • Receive and impart love • Int: good life in U.S. • Feel good about decision • Open adoption prevents "taking" a child from biological families • Different culture to appreciate and learn about • Get on with life • Enriched by differences • Education	• Good home for child • Child raised with siblings • Meet new people • Play role in child's life • Receive and impart love • Feel good about child's new life in U.S. • Feel good about decision • Depending on the culture, stigma of having a child could disappear for birth mom • Get on with Life • Chooses parents	• Family • Siblings • Meet new people (community) • Birth connection (if open) • Receive and impart love • Good life in U.S. • Wanted child—feels good about decision • Different culture • Birthparent chooses
–	• Birth (fantasy child) • Birthing a child like everybody else—not first choice • Self-esteem • Control • Genetic Connection • Time—loss of a child's first months of life • Privacy • Loss of feeling like every other family	• Child • Raising your child like everyone else—not first choice • Self-esteem • Control • Genetic connection/continuity • Time • Privacy • Lose option of knowing where child goes in a closed adoption • Birth father is supposed to disappear because U.S. immigration says if father is present, child is no longer an orphan	• Ability to grow up in a birth family • Feeling different—may feel rejected by birth parents • Self-esteem • Control • Genetic connection • First year of life • Privacy • Culture

This helpful grid was developed by Jane Page, LCSW, Clinical Director of Adoption at The Cradle 2049 Ridge Avenue, Evanston, Il 60201. Please contact The Cradle for permission to use elsewhere.

The loss step for preferential adopters is the necessity to clearly identify and acknowledge their motivations for adopting and how those motivations may affect their parenting and perhaps their children's feelings about their own losses. They need to be realistic in facing that their lack of genetic connection and the pregnancy and birth experiences with this particular child do indeed have meaning, both for them and for the children they adopt.

That lack of genetic connection may well make it more difficult for them to "connect" with a child whose personality or interests or abilities and talents may be so different from others in the family. Rarely does such a child feel "grateful" to those who have added him to their family. The special needs of these children may well change forever—and not in a good way—the connections and culture that the core original family already shared. Parents will have gone through a preparation process in readying themselves to adopt, but far too often these people, already successful at parenting, do not "get" that the expectations they have about parenting which come from the experience of raising a child born to them aren't accurate when it comes to adopting a child.

> Jock and Belinda were change-the-world people. Active in their community in environmental issues, a community food bank and politics, they decided six years after having given birth to the second of two healthy girls that it just made sense from every viewpoint for them not to "try again" for a boy, but to adopt one, instead. They began attending a local adoptive parent support group's meetings and felt an immediate connection with several large, multi-racial families who were making differences in the lives of some very special kids. We can do that, they decided, and they signed up to foster. They took the required classes and fostered a couple of emergency care babies before they were sent to birth relatives, and soon decided that adopting an older child made more sense to them.
>
> Along came Jeremy, 5 years old, bi-racial, abused in both his birth home and in a former foster family. Jock and Belinda took him in and the family experienced a real honeymoon period of many months. During this time, Jeremy told them about two older brothers, whom he knew to exist but hadn't seen in years. Jock and Belinda did some digging and discovered that indeed these brothers lived together in a foster home in another county in the state, and that in fact there was also a younger sister whom Jeremy had not even known existed, who was in care in yet a third county, in a neighboring state.
>
> Three over-loaded social workers in three different jurisdictions made contact with one another about these "lost siblings" and the fresh-faced adoptive family who wanted to bring them together. The one who had the older boys on her caseload raised some red flags. Both

of these boys had been sexually abused by a stepfather, and one had begun to show predatory characteristics. She worried some about his placement in a home with girls close to his age where the parents did not have skills and experience as therapeutic foster parents. Still, his current placement was in jeopardy. She needed to find a new placement for him. The second boy was placed with him and was doing well in this placement, but agency policy was to try to keep siblings together. Yes, said the caseworker for the toddler aged girl, and this was an opportunity to bring all of these siblings together! And so they did.

Subsidies were transferred, counseling records were sent to Jock and Belinda's caseworker. The little girl moved first, after two weekend visits from her new family. She seemed to settle right in. Two months later (about 18 months after Jeremy's initial placement and three months after the finalization of his adoption), the older brothers arrived. The younger of the two didn't want to be there—he had attached well to his last foster parents. The oldest brother seemed to sit back and observe.

"No need to jump right into therapy," the caseworker opined. "Let's get everybody settled in, and then, if there seems to be a need for some counseling, we'll work on finding someone." Weeks later the oldest boy assaulted his baby sister. He was immediately removed from the home. Genuine chaos ensued, as all of the siblings and the ill-prepared and shell-shocked parents struggled to understand what had happened and what it meant for each of them and all of them together in this family.

Within weeks the oldest boy was moved into long-term residential treatment, the middle boy was returned to the prior foster home where he had been doing well (though now he worried about his permanence there), and Jock and Belinda, now less optimistic and idealistic, returned to parenting two older daughters, a boy, and a toddler girl. A sense of wariness settled over the home as everyone seemed to be waiting for "something to happen." Whatever that "something" was didn't happen, but nobody really talked about what *had* happened, either. It sat there, an elephant in the living room that everyone moved cautiously around.

This family needed immediate and intense support and post-adoption services, but they didn't get it. A collection of sudden changes both positive and traumatic, of additions and subtractions of family members had resulted in traumas for everyone, some worse than others. Every member of the family had had expectations about how this process would work, and not a single individual family member's expectations had been met. The structure of this family had changed, yes, but so had its culture, and the changes wrought by the process of both adoption and disruption could not heal themselves. The lesson here? Expectations must be realistic, but even more so, families must be prepared to advocate for their adoption-related needs with the professionals who helped to form their new constellation. Going to court does not necessarily mean that agency assistance and/or intervention should not be sought out and expected.

Everyone understands that birthparents experience loss in adoption, but there's little support for those losses. Indeed, as we'll discuss in a later section, few people outside the adoption community even attempt to "get" the plight of birthparents, who will forever be parents, but not "real" parents because they've "given their children away." They will often be shamed (though the speaker rarely sees it as shaming) for having made such a sacrifice, because "how could anyone ever give up their very own flesh and blood?" Their unresolved losses color future relationships with both adults and children.

> The amazing poet and birthparent advocate Maryanne Cohen, herself a birthmother in the time of completely confidential adoptions, a time when girls were "sent away" to give birth in secrecy and told to "forget" and get on with their lives, refers in some of her eloquent work to the son who was adopted as a "ghost" in her family, haunting them all, glimpsed by her subsequent children in her parenting.

Adoptees, too—including the overwhelming majority who are happy, well-adjusted, and firmly attached to their adoptive parents and siblings—experience losses in adoption, though they experience them unpredictably and often in silence. Because parents have, for the most part, accomplished this step in building a sense of entitlement long before their children have the cognitive maturity necessary to recognize it, let alone process it, they have often "forgotten about" losses for their children until the issue just suddenly appears. The story which follows illustrates this very concept.

> My daughter, Erica, had the same teachers (who job shared) in both fourth and fifth grades. An intelligent, athletic, confident kid, Erica was enjoyed by most of her teachers. These two were special for her, as she was she for them.
>
> Erica, a child with a sunny disposition, came home from fifth grade one day in a funk. She didn't want to talk to me, and she disappeared into her room to do homework. At dinner she was quiet, still not willing to "let it out." This went on for several days, until, fortuitously, it was time for my end-of-grading-period conference with her teachers.
>
> The teacher, Ms. XYZ, began our meeting with a list of Erica's achievements—academically, on the playground, with her peers. I lapped it up, of course. It's always great to hear good things about your child. But then Ms. XYZ summed up her praise with a stunner: "Erica is such a wonderful girl," she said. "Why, I told her just the other day,

'Erica, you tell your parents that if they ever decide to give you away, they should give you to me.' "

Knocked me for a loop, it did. I simply had no response. And I realized that it had similarly knocked Erica for a loop. This 10-year-old with a lot of adoption information had a firm grasp on the story that her birthmother had "planned an adoption for her." However, she had only recently acquired the cognitive skills necessary to recognize and begin to process an important introduction to her adoption-related losses, which had been triggered by this teacher's off-hand comment meant to be a compliment. What loss, you ask? In order for Erica to be in this family who loved her and where she felt safe and secure, someone had had to "give her away." What did that mean?

There was a lot to be talked about with my little girl over the next weeks and months. (And there was something to be talked about with the teacher too, but I needed to calm myself and organize my thoughts first.)

And then there are the other siblings—children born to the parents who raise them, step-siblings, other children who were adopted—who all can experience loss in adoption (whether related to their own adoptions, or not!)

Ossie and Antonia sandwiched Altin, age 4, between the two daughters born to them. Maxine was 8 and Libby 3 when Altin came from an orphanage in Siberia. Altin had arrived with known special needs: he had a skeletal problem in need of surgical intervention. Indeed, this was one of the features that had drawn his parents' attention to him. Ossie is a physician in a large orthopedic surgical practice. He knew that he could solve Altin's medical problems.

The problem became that this family felt so confident about the solutions to those surgical problems that they paid scant attention to their social worker's attempts to help them understand the extent of Altin's social deficits. Altin had been left at the hospital at birth and spent his first months there having the first of several surgeries. He then went to a baby home, where he remained for two more years (longer than usual because his physical needs were more "baby like") before being transferred to the orphanage from which he finally went home.

Altin had no concept at all of family life. Indeed, Altin was always happier and more cooperative at the hospital around one of his several surgeries than he was at home. His mother felt rejected by this behavior. Maxine and Libby found themselves ignored in the face of Altin's demanding behavior. The beloved nanny who had been with the family since Maxine's birth was unwilling to cope and left after six months. It took two more for Antonia to find a good replacement.

Six years after placement, Altin's orthopedic problems had been managed successfully, everyone had learned to set boundaries around his frequent tantruming, the childcare issues were under control, and Maxine was in therapy. She had been cutting herself.

Maxine's desperate cry for help was about her losses! She had completely lost a primary attachment figure (the nanny) and found another (her mother) slipping away from her to care for a needy brother. Because Altin and Libby were closer in age, they seemed to get attention together, while she was expected to "grow up."

But, hey, you don't want to hear this story! I know that. So why do I keep sharing the difficult ones? Because it's always better to be prepared for the worst so that you can celebrate the best. Had Ossie and Antonia really heard, they would probably still have adopted Altin. But had they really heard what the educators tried to help them understand in those classes, and had they really read those books suggested by their caseworkers, they could have, should have probably would have made more careful preparations and taken advantage of interventions.

So, indeed, recognizing, surfacing, and resolving loss is an important part of building a strong sense of entitlement for each adoptive family member in every adoptive family. As a matter of fact, the work of H. David Kirk, discussed next, demonstrates the value of acknowledging one another's losses in building the empathy that draws adoptive families closer together.

Second Step: Adoption Is Different— Shared Fate and Entitlement

Another element in building a sense of entitlement is coming to understand and accept that adoption is not the same as having genetic connections. Indeed, adoptive relationships are different in significant and unavoidable ways: some are legal, some are relational, some are obvious and out there, some are just under the surface of consciousness. Acknowledging these differences consistently, says Dr. Jerome Smith, is an important part of feeling "entitled" within a family.

H. David Kirk is a Canadian sociologist and adoptive parent who made a long, influential, and highly respected career, beginning in the 1950s, in studying adoption's impact on the people whom it touches from a sociological (pertaining to human behavior in social settings and relationships) perspective rather than a psychological (related to mental processing and behavior) perspective. Dr. Kirk's work provided, to a substantial extent, the academic, research-based underpinnings that supported adoption consumer groups from the 1970s and on to push against traditionalism, and which led to a completely changed face for adoption practice and philosophy by the dawn of 21st Century.

That research began by Kirk's following a large number of adoption-built families in both Ontario and California, in a study that encompassed the entire growing up years of their children. Kirk then presented his Shared Fate Theory and created an "Aha!" moment for many of adoption's thinkers, movers, and shakers. First laid out in the 1964 book *Shared Fate* (revised 1984, Ben Simon Publications, Brentwood Bay, BC) and expanded in the 1981 offering *Adoptive Kinship: A Modern Institution in Need of Reform* (Butterworth's, Toronto), Kirk's theory, condensed and simplified, is this:

> All of us come to adulthood expecting to fill certain roles, but every social role also carries with it a set of societally-imposed expectations about how that role should work and be filled. When people assume a role without being able to assume with it all of the expectations about that role, they experience what Kirk calls a *role handicap.*
>
> The first societal expectation about the roles of *parent* and *child* and *brother* and *sister* presume that these people are genetically related to one another through the process of conception and birth. People touched by adoption, then—birthparents, adoptive parents, adoptees—all experience role handicaps because they don't share that expected genetic connection. Indeed, both sets of parents are role handicapped—birthparents because they are parents without children to nurture; adoptive parents because they are nurturing and legal parents but have not given birth, and have no genetic resemblance or connection to their children. Adoptees are role handicapped because they will be, throughout life, the children of two sets of parents, and, while unrelated by blood to the nurturing parents who are their psychological and legal parents, they are often virtual social strangers to the parents who provided their genes and whom they resemble in so many ways.

When the Shared Fate theory was first introduced, sociologists, including Kirk in earlier work with other populations, had long observed that people and families who experience any kind of handicap (the preferred terms today are *disability* or *challenge*) tend to deal with it in one of two ways: they either accept and *acknowledge the differences* that the challenge creates for them and look for ways around or through it, or they deny or *reject the differences*, trying to pretend that they don't exist. Sociological research had repeatedly demonstrated that those families dealing with physical or mental or emotional handicaps who consistently accept/acknowledge difference are usually more successful at helping their children deal productively with their disabilities over the long term.

> Kirk's Shared Fate theory, supported by his observations of hundreds of families over an extended period of time, noted that when adoptive parents consistently accept/acknowledge the differences that adoption brings to their lives (he calls this practicing A.D. behavior)

> they are not only more successful in resolving those differences, they
> also eventually develop closer relationships because they are able to
> empathize with one another about the losses each has experienced
> in living a role handicap and thus are inclined to communicate more
> intimately.

Now, I want you to think carefully about Kirk's position here and to validate it for yourself through your observations of adoption-touched families. Many adoption-built families tend to practice R.D. (rejection of difference) behavior most of the time. They try as hard as they possibly can—on the surface at least—to pretend that their families are "just like" families built by birth. They read little about adoption. They don't attend continuing education opportunities. They tend to distance themselves as soon as possible and in every possible way from the agencies and intermediaries who facilitated their adoptions. They don't belong to adoptive parents' groups, face-to-face or online. They have a hard time understanding why others whose lives touch theirs need even to know that adoption was how their family was formed.

Why would this be? Let me explain it a little differently than Dr. Kirk did. Families who "match" (the child arrives as a newborn in a racially matching family) are families for whom denial of difference is easy. For many of these families, this denial is a continuation of the loss reaction brought about by their family challenges. By denying the differences in adoptive family relationships, one can try to deny the discomfort of the losses of the pregnancy experience as a sign of manhood/womanhood, of genetic continuity and connection, etc. and can play ostrich about whether adoption will ever be seen as being "sad" by the child they love so much. Many adults choose to adopt inracially—domestically or through a handful of countries in the world where they are able to find children who will physically resemble them—specifically because they do not want to stand out as different among genetic families.

Families who adopt older children or children of a different racial or ethnic background than their own attend seminars, read books, subscribe to magazines, and join parent groups in much higher proportionate numbers than those who adopt same race infants. The reason for this is clear. Every time such a family goes out into the public marketplace, enrolls a child at school, etc., it is obvious that their family has been expanded by adoption. The differences in their families are evident to society at large, so they couldn't reject difference if they wanted to (and some want to). That doesn't mean, however, that all of these families plug themselves into the adoption community, offering themselves and their children the opportunities which help to normalize adoption. Some of them practice R.D. behavior, too!

Birthparents and adoptees have tended to practice R.D. behavior too. Birthparents hoped to be able to end the pain of the many losses they had suffered in the experience of an unplanned pregnancy and selecting adoption by burying it rather than by actively resolving their feelings of grief and loss. Adoptees often were afraid to "hurt" the adoptive parents they loved so much by asking questions or expressing interest in their families of origin. This "stuffing" of legitimate feelings because social cues from outside the family (and sometimes from inside) seem to indicate that such thoughts and reactions are inappropriate can be an emotionally stunting experience.

Today, in many places—though far from universally—the parent preparation process for prospective adopters, and the support and facilitation process for people considering making an adoption plan, is more supportive, more informative, and more empowering of client choice than it was in the past. This has encouraged more straightforward communication between clients and social work professionals, which has resulted in less victimization, more confidence in decisions made, and thus less of a need to deny adoption's realities. And today, as more and more families are engaging in varying degrees of openness with birthfamilies, the percentage of families who are able to reject or deny difference in any consistent way is plummeting.

But rejection of adoption's differences will always be tempting. There isn't one of us who hasn't observed, even when our losses have been carefully resolved and we believe that we don't want to parent any other children than the ones we adopted, that life would be easier—for us, for our children, for their birthfamilies—if these children had only been born to us.

> Judy and Ross privately adopted two daughters as newborns and then firmly "put the infertility and adoption issues away" in their family. They didn't belong to a parents' group, subscribed to no newsletters or magazines, and had read virtually nothing about adoption. Didn't need to, you see—Judy and Ross were both college professors. They knew what they needed to know.
>
> The girls asked questions and they were answered in a straightforward way (just the facts, please). There wasn't much ongoing discussion. Judy thought that everything was going so well, in fact, that she was delighted to accommodate when asked by a friendly neighbor (one of the few who even knew the family had been formed through adoption) to participate on a panel at an adoption conference. Why not, she thought, and she decided to attend the day's events herself—a first experience—though her panel was to be held last.
>
> Judy listened to the how-to sessions led by attorneys and social workers. She popped into a session on "Getting Ready for Adoption" and was interested in the nurse who taught infant care classes for adoptive parents-to-be. Things had changed some. She decided to attend a panel populated by birthparents to be held right before her own

session. Listening to their stories brought her not just to tears, but to great, gulping sobs. She fled the conference, missing her own panel. The box of "adoption and infertility issues" had fallen out of the closet where it had been so carefully stored.

David Brodzinsky, a now retired Rutgers University professor and researcher who also maintained a clinical practice with adoption-expanded families for many years, noted that some families tend to go overboard in acknowledging difference, in essence making adoption the major focus of the family. He has added yet another term to the alphabet soup to describe these families. He calls this coping pattern *insistence of difference* behavior (I.D.) and sees it as just as harmful to families built by adoption as is rejection of difference. A challenge, then, of healthy adoptive parenting, and one of the things we are going to discuss at length in another chapter, is the need to learn how to balance ourselves on the tightrope of acknowledging differences without overemphasizing them.[5]

Judy, mentioned above, had a wake-up call after that conference and began to read. Perhaps this explained her younger daughter's rebellious nature. She certainly wasn't like anyone else in the family. But Judy still had trouble thinking of her family as "different"—that is until her younger daughter began experimenting with drugs and became addicted to meth.

How humiliated Ross and Judy were. To save her life they put the teen in rehab, and the family was brought into therapy. Of course, the addiction was not "their problem," it was probably genetically programmed. Their "own child" would most certainly not have tried drugs, but Judy and Ross attended sessions anyway because, hard as she was to parent, they loved their youngest daughter "like their own" and wanted the best for her.

How "entitled" does this sound to you?

Nearly all of us adoptive parents waver back and forth in practicing A.D. and R.D. behavior, and this is not unhealthy (though I.D. behavior is unhealthy!). When our children first arrive, and we circle the wagons and concentrate on the business of claiming one another and falling in love with each other, it is almost essential that we spend some significant time in consistent R.D. behavior. And, truth be told, families built by adoption have more in common than they have differences with families built by birth. Therefore, in helping our children build a healthy sense of self esteem, it is important that we help them feel that they really belong to us. It is, however, a balancing act—with the goal being to acknowledge differences as consistently as possible, which opens the door to honest communication between family members who need to work out these issues. This honesty creates empathy between parents and children, forging closer relationships between them.

Society's Reactions—A Third Step in Entitlement Building

One of the primary reasons why we'd prefer to pretend that adoption isn't an "issue" in our lives is that we get such mixed messages about adoption from the world at large. Those whose lives have not been directly touched by adoption just don't get it. Birthparents, adoptive parents, and adoptees are repeatedly exposed to a set of mixed messages that may be best summed up like this . . .

Adoption is a second-best alternative for all involved because it means that birthparents don't live up to their real responsibilities ("How could anyone ever give up their own flesh and blood?"), children live in second-best families ("Do you know anything about his real parents?"), and adopters still cling to the hope of having a child of their own ("Now that you've adopted, you'll get pregnant. They always do.").

Yet, adoption is family building "the easy way"—just ask your co-worker; and even though your kids will never know "real" mother love, aren't they "lucky" that someone as "good" as you was willing to take them in? I mean, really, adoptees wouldn't search if they really loved and were grateful to their adoptive parents, now would they? No wonder that it's common knowledge that adoptees are less healthy emotionally than other people.

The result of this stereotyping and misinformation? Another task in developing a sense of entitlement to our places in our family: accepting that the rest of the world doesn't get it and doing our best to help them change their views.

These stereotyped assumptions are difficult to ignore. From the day your child arrives, the questions from those closest to you (let alone from strangers who somehow learn about the adoption) will include prying questions about how much you know about your child's birthfamily, whether or not you intend to tell him he was adopted, your future family plans (now you'll get pregnant, is there any medical reason why you couldn't get pregnant?), how much the adoption cost, and more.

But why not just accept that this is the way it is and move on? Must we become activists? I'm sorry, but yes. We must, each to the extent that we can stretch ourselves to do so. Widely promoting understanding of adoption issues is important for all of us touched by adoption, but most of all it is important for our children—the children who have been adopted as well as the children who are waiting for adoption.

Your children will eventually be exposed to these misunderstandings, too. For a large chunk of their growing up years, these little concrete-thinkers are going to hear these messages and not know what to do with them. If their parents seem to be accepting these points of view, if they neither challenge them directly nor talk about them in the privacy of family, how can children be expected to think differently about adoption? Not only must we become activists in order to help society comprehend the roots of adoption issues so that people become tolerant of, empathic toward, and sensitive about the issues (not to mention more embracing of the people who live it) we must also become activists in order to help our children feel first rate and "entitled" to their places in their families.

In a later chapter we'll spend some time looking at ways that we can begin to promote understanding of adoption issues and advocate for changed thinking. Right now, though, in the context of understanding en-titlement building as a core issue in adoption while you are still trying to decide whether or not to commit to adoption, a more important task is to acknowledge that such feelings exist, and to determine whether or not you could be willing and able to deal with these reactions to the family you are considering building by adoption.

Are you willing to become prepared to comfortably and confidently deal with the teacher who feels that adopted children by nature have "prob-lems," with the school yard observations about the "realness" of your fam-ily, with the myth-filled made-for-T.V. movies and sitcoms that your family will innocently stumble into? Of course, I'm not suggesting that you will ever reach a level of such comfort with insensitivity that you won't mind it! Actually, the fact that you embrace adoption as a positive option and are its advocate should mean that you will always be offended by such stupidity, but, if adoption is for you, you will need to be willing to learn coping skills and teach them to your child.

In a later chapter we will discuss ways to practice reactions to such interference. Most adopters find that with time, response and reaction get easier and less bothersome. This is true in part because in living adoption you become part of a specialized learning curve. Spokane, Washington therapist Jim Mahoney, in his wonderful trainings on adoption (he hasn't written a book, but there are excellent tapes available from several NACAC conferences), talks about the adult learning model as applied to adoption.

> Adults go through several steps in learning about any difficult issue, says Jim. They begin with *unconscious incompetence*—just plain not knowing that they don't know much about an issue. Gradually, they become *consciously incompetent*—understanding how much they don't know and feeling anxious about it. Tentatively they move toward *conscious competence*—working hard to deal with the realities of an issue on a conscious level every day. And the ultimate goal is to achieve the stage of *unconscious competence*, where one has learned so well that he no longer needs to consciously think about what he is doing. In order to demonstrate how this works, Jim uses an anecdote about learning to drive a car.
>
> Jim suggests that you think about yourself as a teenager, eager to learn to drive. First you expected to be able to jump right in and do it (unconscious incompetence). Then, behind the wheel in driver's ed

you realized that driving wasn't as easy as it looked (conscious incompetence). As the class progressed, you learned to think carefully about every stop sign, every turn, every signal, every highway access and you were rarely distracted while driving (conscious competence). Finally, driving became so habitual and easy for you, that you have reached a stage of unconscious competence, where you get in the car, turn on the ignition and drive.

As you learn more and more about adoption, you and those who care about you will move from unconscious incompetence to unconscious competence.

I want to make clear that though these issues will come up from time to time in adoptive family life, they are not a relentless, ongoing battle for most adoption-expanded families, whose daily lives are, for the most part, filled with the normalcy of being ordinary. Yes, it is true that adoption for you as parents may have been a second choice to your original expectations about family building, yet a task central to adoption for you, as well as for your child, is your ability to move beyond society's constantly humming message that adoption is second choice and second rate. You need to come to a place within yourself where you firmly believe that adoption is *first* best for all of the members of your extended adoptive family—those related to anyone and everyone genetically or by the adoption formula of love and law, which includes your biological family, step relatives, and birth relatives of the adopted ones.

To help you see that entitlement does usually work quite well, let me continue the story with which we began this chapter:

> Since the article "Getting Real" in which the Perry and Helen story was first written down in the 1992 book *Adopting after Infertility*, the story above has come full circle. Several years later, Dave and I were invited to the wedding of his cousin Bob's daughter—the first wedding in this next generation of the family. We were delighted to be there, and were pleased to be seated in what seemed to be a place of honor behind the family of the bride at the church and then to find ourselves at the bride's parents' table at the reception. As introductions began, we listened as Bob's wife introduced her large extended family of many brothers and sisters and their children. Then Bob rose, and looking around the room, he chuckled that his family introductions would be shorter. He had been an only child, and his parents had been dead for many years. He put his arm around Dave's shoulder, tears welled in his eyes, and he said, "I'd like you to meet my cousin, Dave Johnston, and this is his wife, Pat. Dave and his sister Mary Jane are my only living relatives."
>
> Bob never knew the story of Dave's request for the sleigh bells and the table which were bequeathed to him instead. But Bob's feeling of

family entitlement was secure. He, like his cousin, was buoyed by the family he had loved his whole life—no matter how those connections began.

Just a couple of months after Bob died tragically in 2004, our older daughter was married. My large family and the groom's were there en masse. And so was Bob's widow and his oldest son (who was still recovering from a terrible motorcycle accident)—there to stand with Dave to welcome new members to the very small clan which is their family. It was the right thing to do, to represent Bob for Dave, because they all "got it."

Building a sense of entitlement to one another is a part of the claiming and bonding process for all of those in adoption-expanded families. It's about believing, with all of one's being, that despite loss, despite difference, you are OK—that you are deserving, that you belong, that, together, the family and each of its members is whole and strong. We are **real families**.

Resources

Entitlement: Loss and Difference

Brodzinsky, David M., Marshall Schechter and Robin Henig. *Being Adopted: The Lifelong Search for Self.* (New York: Anchor, 1993)

Brodzinsky, David M. and Marshall Schechter eds. *The Psychology of Adoption.* (New York: Oxford University Press USA, 1993)

Brodzinsky, David M. and Jesus Palacios, eds. *Psychological Issues in Adoption: Research and Practice.* (New York: Praeger Publishers, 2005)

Kirk, H. David. *Shared Fate: A Theory and Method of Adoptive Relationships* (Vancouver, BC: Ben-Simon Publications, 1964, rev. 1984)

Kirk, H. David, *Adoptive Kinship: A Modern Institution in Need of Reform* (Vancouver, BC: Ben-Simon Publications, 1985)

Smith, Jerome. *You're Our Child: The Adoption Experience.* (Washington, DC: Villard Books 1981 rev. 1987)

Entitlement: Family, Friends, the Rest of the World

Johnston, Patricia Irwin. *Adoption Is a Family Affair! What Relatives and Friends Must Know.* (Indianapolis: Perspectives Press, Inc., 2001)

CHAPTER 5

As a Family Grows

"But *can* I attach with a child who isn't related to me genetically?"

There it is! The *big* question—probably the fear that is most common among people who are reluctant to adopt. Let me start at the end, rather than at the beginning, in order to dispel this greatest fear. Yes, most people can and do form strong attachments to people to whom they are not genetically connected.

Despite the mythology which remains out there, today, in the first decade of the 21st century, most attachment experts agree with Michael Lamb, PhD, former chief of the National Institute for Child Health and Development's Section on Social and Emotional Development, who flatly states that there is no compelling body of evidence to support the widely held misbelief in a sensitive period immediately after birth when bonding must occur or the opportunity will be lost forever. Even Klaus and Kennell, the researchers whose work on attachment sensitivity revolutionized the way births were handled in hospitals in the last third of the 20th century, later worked to dispel the misapplication of their early research on this. But there remains a great deal of general misinformation among members of the media, among some nurses and teachers, and among the public at large. It is possible that you will find dispelling these myths and correcting this kind of misinformation among the challenges you face as an adoption-built family.

We understand now that there are many factors which contribute to attachments or lack of them between parents and children. Attachments can, and indeed usually do, begin for mothers and fathers during pregnancy— including during the psychological pregnancies of adoptive parents which we'll talk about later. The work of Canadian psychiatrist Thomas Verny has taught us that babies are more aware during gestation than had been previously thought, and that a birthmother's psychological state during her pregnancy makes such changes in her own chemical balance that it can influence a baby's personality.

But attachment is not exclusively a genetic connection. Normal infants are able to form attachments with any caregiver open to attaching with them. Attachments can be, and often are, transferred from one set of caretakers to another. Over a lifespan, attachments between people change, so that the attachment relationship between parent and infant is different than that between parent and toddler or parent and teenager. And we form attachments with many kinds of people in our lives, all of which follow similar models.

What all this means, bottom line, for families built by adoption, is that it is possible for families to build secure attachments to one another at any time, and that it is probable that well-prepared, well-supported, well-informed parents and their children will do just that. That out of the way, let's spend some time learning about how attachment works.

Attachment: A Primer

Falling in love with your spouse was a kind of attachment experience. Remembering that experience can help you to understand many of the factors in the attachment experience between parents and children. Despite the mythology perpetuated by books and movies, hardly anyone falls in love in the eyes-meeting-across-a-crowded-room fashion of "Some Enchanted Evening" from the musical *South Pacific*. Yes, sexual attraction can be immediate and powerful, but falling in love, attaching in a lifelong commitment? Not likely.

Falling in love is an interactive experience. Certain things about another person attract you to that person until, through a process of intimate interaction which includes your meeting one another's basic needs, you feel a connection of some importance and make a commitment. The process of being in love needs nurturing. The ongoing give-and-take between lovers changes over time and affects the quality of their attachments to one another. On a much more primal level, this is what happens between parents and children.

My first teacher of attachment issues was now-retired pediatrician and therapist Vera Fahlberg, MD, who spent her career working with children and their families experiencing attachment problems, and training professionals about how to prevent attachment difficulties and to facilitate transfers of attachment where necessary. In her books *Residential Treatment: A Tapestry of Many Therapies* (Perspectives Press, Inc., 1990, now out of print) and *A Child's Journey through Placement* (Perspectives Press, Inc., 1991, 1994, 1998) and in her popular trainings, Dr. Fahlberg discussed the reciprocity exchange between parents and

Myth: You can't really love a child who was adopted as much as a child born to you.

Fact: Adopted children and adoptive parents can bond just as securely with each other as do children born to their parents. Some of our closest connections are often to people not genetically related to us.

children which leads to the child's development of trust, security, and attachment.

The Arousal-Relaxation Cycle[1]

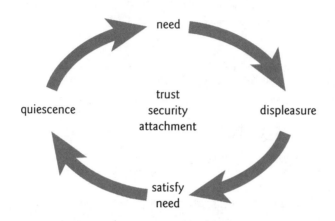

This reciprocal exchange between parent-figure and baby is known as the arousal-relaxation cycle, and in normal relationships it goes like this: Baby displays displeasure, discomfort, frustration, or tension and discharges that tension by crying, squirming, and getting red-faced. His caregiver responds to the signs of displeasure by picking him up, cuddling him with soothing words, changing his diaper, feeding him, or attempting in other ways to figure out what it is that has caused the displeasure. During this care-giving, an adult who is promoting attachment will deliberately appeal to all of Baby's senses: smiling and gazing, speaking or singing, patting and cuddling him. In response, most of the time Baby feels satisfied when his need has been met and relaxes, rewarding his care-giver with interactive smiles, gurgles, and/or his acceptance of and involvement in cuddling.

Over time, as parents and babies become familiar with one another's moods, personalities, and behaviors, an interactive relationship develops. They begin to do what many infancy specialists refer to as a kind of dance together—each partner responsible for part of the interaction. When this dance cycle between one child and one caregiver is successfully and gracefully repeated over and over—several times a day, dozens of times a week, hundreds of times a month—the child learns to trust and to feel secure that this specific caregiver will meet his needs. Attachment begins to develop. Similarly, as parent and growing child interact with one another, a positive interaction cycle develops—parent initiating interaction, child responding favorably—building self worth and self esteem in both parties, and enhancing attachment.

Without the successful repetition of this arousal-relaxation cycle occurring thousands of times in the first year of life, babies do not have the opportunity to learn to trust others and to build successful attachments. When children do not learn to trust at an early age, they experience the world as an unsafe place, which of course challenges their ability to learn attachment later. Still, when previously unattached children eventually do receive quality care from attachment-informed, well-supported, and dependable parents they can and do develop secure attachments. For any child who has been securely attached once, with competent assistance, that attachment can be successfully transferred to another parenting figure.

Health affects attachment. Children who are ill or who are in pain are in a constant state of unrelieved tension. This includes babies who are born prematurely, babies who are born drug-exposed, and babies who tend toward hyperactivity—all are at risk for attachment challenges. Since their pleas for help often cannot result in alleviation of their discomfort, these babies may not learn to trust their caregivers' ability to help them.

Timing is an important factor. It is important to take into account the relative value of time for children. When one is 25, a year is only 4% of a total life, but to a 5-year-old, a year in foster care is 20% of his life. We seem to be able to recognize the likelihood of trauma in that 5-year-old, but a month spent in foster care is too often written off as inconsequential in infants, despite the fact that when that child who started out in foster care is 2 months old at placement, he will have spent half his life in foster care. Recovering from a change which has entirely disrupted the life a person has known for such a significant portion of it can take time and lots of support. Traumatized attachments between apparently healthy babies and new parents in adoption are not as rare as adoption workers believe.

Adaptability of personality is impossible to measure. Some people just naturally seem to "go with the flow" while others fight the very suggestion of change. You probably know what I mean—it's that half empty glass point of view as opposed to the glass half full perspective. Children prone to be poor at adapting are at much higher risk for attachment challenges caused by multiple changes in care, substantial differences in routine, or poor transitions than are relaxed and happy-go-lucky children. And of course no social worker and no would-be parent can possibly predict by looking at a newborn, or by reading skeletal information on an orphanage profile of a toddler, which is naturally less adaptable—and thus at higher risk for an attachment challenge—than another.

Some children available for adoption are not known or acknowledged to be at risk. Caseworkers do not always realize at placement that a baby is hyperactive or that he has spent his gestational period in an alcohol bath. Even worse, sometimes professionals do know these things but either dismiss them as non-problematic or don't share them with unsuspecting parents at all. Why they don't share such knowledge varies. In some cases it is because they really are uneducated in this area and have no idea that it is significant. Sometimes it is because they fear that negative information which they don't understand to be of particular importance may spoil a match or may hinder the new parents' ability to give of themselves unreservedly to their new children. Very occasionally there is a deliberate intent to defraud. But parents have a right to full disclosure and must conscientiously advocate for it.

Parents Lead the Dance

Ideally, all new parents will have learned the steps to the dance of attachment from their own experience of having had a healthy attachment with their own parents. But not all of us have had healthy childhoods and adulthoods. We may have experienced abuse, trauma, or neglect ourselves. We may have suffered great losses and not resolved them. And these risks are there for all new parents, not just adoptive parents.

Attachment problems do occur in birth families. Children can be "difficult" or unhealthy. Life circumstances can create incredible pressure and stress. A parent may be physically or mentally ill, or have problems with substance addiction. She may have been a victim of untreated childhood trauma or other issues that resulted in her own attachment weaknesses or challenges. When the child of such a parent is adopted after spending time in such a first parent's care, this child will not likely have learned the steps to the dance of attachment.

An important part of parents' abilities to lead the dance of attachment, then, is dependent on how attachment-ready they themselves are. Have they resolved past traumas and losses? Do they feel confident and entitled to parent? Have they been well prepared?

For adoptive parents, most of these issues should come up during the parent preparation process. Social workers should be assessing your attachment history and your attachment skills. They should be exploring with you the losses we've referred to before. They should be providing you with a great deal of information about what challenges you might expect in adopting a child of the age, the nationality, the health and social backgrounds, etc. of the one you are hoping to parent. Just in case not enough time is spent with you on these issues, more tools will be offered in Part Four of this book.

Attachment with Babies and Toddlers

Babies are wonderful little creatures. They are warm and soft; they smell nice and feel good. They are vulnerable and totally dependent. They are pretty hard to resist. In fact, they are made that way on purpose. Babies get their basic needs for food, care, and love met because they are so irresistible. Their cries alert their caretakers to their need for attention and, given that attention, they respond with smiles and coos which caregivers experience as rewards. Very early in their lives, babies recognize the shape and configuration of the human face and respond to smiles with smiles.

A significant proportion of the readers of this book are likely to adopt newborns, older infants, and toddlers. Until quite recently, little has been written for them about attachment. There has been a basic assumption that there is nothing special to discuss. It is indeed true that when well-prepared parents adopt healthy newborns and take them straight home from the hospital, the odds are very high that their attachment to one another will be relatively uncomplicated.

Families adopting internationally and the professionals working with them seemed to acknowledge the possibility of attachment challenges with infants and toddlers a bit earlier than have those working with domestic infant adoption. While relatively little has been written either for clinical professionals or for adoptive parents about the possibility of attachment problems in infant adoptions, an exception, now out of print and providing only a taste at best, was a Holly Van Gulden booklet for those preparing to adopt babies from India. Holly wrote eloquently about the unusual high-pitched cry common to internationally adopted infants, and about their enormous eyes—seen later to be reflections of the fear of looking up into unfamiliar white faces for the first time. *OURS* magazine (a precursor to *Adoptive Families*) through the years featured articles on the adjustment difficulties common to children arriving from India, Asia, and South America. The symptoms discussed were the symptoms of grieving, as these children dealt with the loss of the familiar—familiar caretakers, familiar food, familiar sounds, familiar smells, familiar voices and language, familiar culture—and were forced to make a transitional adaptation. Once again, it has been those adopters who were, by virtue of the obvious in their family, unable to deny difference and forced to acknowledge it, who led the way in dealing with an important adoption-related issue.

Very young babies can suffer from attachment difficulties which, if unacknowledged, can affect them over a life time. A variety of factors, mentioned earlier but repeated here, including the baby's health, the baby's inborn personality and predisposition to adaptability, the stability and quality of early caregiving, and the attention to detail by social service professionals in transferring between caregivers can be important in assuring the development of a relatively uninterrupted cycle of attachment.

What we must acknowledge is that human babies are not malleable lumps of Playdoh which can be moved about at will for some predictable length of time before exposure to the air results in hardening. And we must continue to keep in mind that, as the leaders of the dance of attachment, new adoptive parents not well-prepared and supported can themselves be at risk for attachment challenges that may be tied up in their unrealistic expectations for themselves and, perhaps, in their buried and now brought-to-the surface losses.

> My husband's and my youngest child, Lindsey, was born healthy
> and full term to a birthmother who had been sure of her adoption plan

for several months. But the agency had not found parents for her by the time she was born, so she came to us at ten weeks old from two prior foster placements. It was her third move after leaving the hospital where she was born. This confusing beginning and our baby's innately pessimistic personality combined to create a difficult situation for all of us: she had learned, in her first three months of life, that you just can't trust mother figures. Just when you trust them, they leave.

As experienced parents and well-read adopters, we recognized our daughter's symptoms as attachment problems and actively pursued the help we needed, which resulted in a regimen of exercises, routines and other "tricks" that helped her, over the course of several months, attach more comfortably to us. I'll be sharing more details that you will find helpful about this in Part Four, but this vignette is not about the baby.

One of the biggest surprises of this challenging attachment experience was the reaction of my husband's mother (who, you will remember, adopted her own children) to our experience. She and I had always had a great relationship, and over the nine years that we had been parenting first one and then two and now three children, she had often told me what a good mother she thought I was. One day during a several-day visit at our house we began talking about Lindsey's evolution over her first year with us. Mother was very interested in understanding the details of how we had known what the problem was and how we had gone about solving it. As we talked, she suddenly started to cry.

It soon became clear that her sadness was not just about Lindsey, but it was also an old one of her own. You see, Helen's own children had each been six months old when they arrived from traditional, well-regarded 1940s "children's homes." It was standard practice in those days for agencies to care for healthy babies in their own nurseries for several months before placement to make certain that the babies were indeed "adoptable" and to "match them with the right parents." These babies were cared for by shifts of registered nurses in starched whites. This was considered to be best practice by adoption agencies of the time, so no one offered adoptive parents any information about possible adjustment problems to come, because no one expected there to be any. These children's first few months at home were often very difficult. But no one mentioned attachment issues as a possibility in those days of "love them as if they're your own and they will be" advising.

Helen, like many other mothers of her era, had never talked about her feelings about those days with her husband, fearing that he would see her at fault. Like most adoptive parents of this period, she had never talked about these difficulties with her social worker—after all, they might take the baby away. Instead, for nearly forty years, Helen Johnston, a loving, gentle woman who was the classic image of a perfect

1950s mother, had silently believed that her babies' early unhappiness was because she herself was not a good enough mother.

Since I first shared this story twenty years ago, I've heard from so many adoptive parents of that era and/or their now-adult children that this reflects their own experiences. And, unfortunately, I've also heard from adoptive mothers of my own era and I continue to hear from adoptive parents of children recently adopted that they, too, have had similar experiences. I share it again in hopes that you will have some insight about what may be happening if the social worker who should be reading over your shoulder and changing his practice, and thus taking a lot of time to assess your present attachment skills and teaching you the proper steps to the dance or helping you to refine your own, does not prepare you for the possibility of an attachment challenge with your baby.

What about Preschoolers?

As children tend to "age up" between the time of their referral and the time that they actually come home to a family, more and more families internationally are bringing home toddlers and preschoolers—children between 18 months and 5 years of age. There are a handful of excellent books about adoption in toddlerhood listed in the resources section, but preschoolers deserve a nod here, too, and the most important message to take home with you about choosing to adopt a toddler is that you really must have realistic expectations.

I hear parents talking about this age group being an advantage (especially to single parents) because the child is at the right age to go straight to pre-school. Yes and no. There is no question that day-care or preschool will feel comfortable to a toddler coming home from an institution. Day-cares are institutional settings. This, however, will not promote your toddler's most basic need: attachment to a single care giver—you. If you are planning to adopt a toddler aged child, please plan for as extended a period of parenting leave as you can manage before taking him to pre-school. Your toddler needs to learn to trust and depend on you in order to develop a healthy attachment. Additionally, you must realize that children adopted in toddlerhood have cognitive abilities that may give them clear memories of their past (both positive and negative) but they do not have the cognitive skills to make "talk therapy" useful. Furthermore, they may have limited conversational skills for some time as they learn a new language.

Toddlerhood is a very difficult time emotionally for children to make transitions, and finding placement agencies willing to offer enough transition time is challenging. In her book *Nurturing Adoptions*, therapist Deborah Gray advocates a 16-day transition time for children in this age group. She advocates for these children like this . . .

"Comments like, 'He won't remember this,' or 'She doesn't really understand what's happening, so let's get it over with,' are excuses for short cuts. In fact, children provide compelling descriptions of the pain slack casework and abrupt moves have caused in their lives. And, the DSM IV-TR describes foster care moves as one of the causative factors for reactive attachment disorder. Young children, who cannot speak out for themselves, need special care from our society when they must move between families."[1]

Attaching with Older Children

If there is too little information about attachment risks in young children, everyone who has even a little knowledge about adoption seems to be able to acknowledge that when families adopt older children there is a significant risk for attachment difficulties. Indeed, this information has been exaggerated to the point where far too many would-be parents are scared away from adopting older children by their fears of full blown RAD—reactive attachment disorder—the most serious and difficult of attachment problems. RAD exists, yes, but certainly does not affect anything near a majority of older children needing adoption.

Children of school age in need of adoption have often been victims of multiple breaks in attachment, for example moving between multiple caregivers, such as from birthparent to extended family member to birthparent to foster care to foster care. They may have been attached to people who neglected them or who hurt them in some way. The more moves they have, of course, the more likely it is that they will eventually experience trauma or neglect. The result of such treatment is that children coming to adoption beyond infancy and toddlerhood are prone to have difficulty learning to trust subsequent parenting figures.

Under these circumstances, it stands to reason that the process of building transferred attachments with children who are not infants is complex. It is, however, doable. Rather than do the topic an injustice in this attachment primer, I will instead refer you to the work of a number of well respected authors, trainers, and clinicians who have provided valuable material about attachment issues and practical solutions for families adopting older children. If you have adopted or are considering adopting a child older than infancy, do not pass Go and collect your child without reading Vera Fahlberg's previously mentioned books, those of Deborah Gray, a therapist with a practice specializing in adoption and foster care who wrote *Attaching in Adoption* (Perspectives Press, 2002) and *Nurturing Adoptions: Creating Resilience after Neglect and Trauma* (Perspectives Press, 2007) and Greg Keck and Regina Kupecky's *Adopting the Hurt Child* and *Parenting the Hurt Child* (both from Piñón Press). Another name with which to be familiar as you work on attachment issues with older children is Daniel Hughes. Most of these folks treat children only in their own geographic areas, but their writing, in-service trainings, and institutes for professionals as well as for consumers, may indeed bring their writing and their ideas within driving distance of parents hungry for good information. Your knowledge about these folks and their expertise will prove irreplaceably valuable to you and the local professionals you work with as you parent your older-adopted child.

Here is our bottom line in this primer section on attachment: Successful attachment between any adoptive parent and child involves several steps, including these gathered from the writing of several of the experts mentioned above.

- Parents must be aware of how their own prior experiences with loss, if unresolved, may make them vulnerable to attachment challenges.
- Parents need full information about their child's prior health issues, attachment experiences or lack of them, and issues of abuse, neglect and loss.
- Parents must clearly understand that adoption is an add-on in both their own lives and their children's lives, rather than a replacement experience.
- Parent and child must be well prepared for a transfer.
- Children must be supportively disengaged from earlier attachments and allowed to grieve for them.
- Children must be encouraged to open themselves to new parents.
- New parents must then find ways to stimulate an arousal-relaxation cycle with these children that will encourage their coming to trust them.
- Parents must understand that they should not take the predictable rejections of their efforts personally.

I would encourage any parent who suspects an attachment challenge between themselves and their child to go first to their agency for help and/or a referral. Having been given the Good Housekeeping Seal of Approval as perfect prospective parents, many parents are afraid to go to their adoption workers to ask questions about what they are experiencing because they fear that in doing so they could risk losing their child by admitting to their caseworker—the most powerful person they had had contact with in their lives—that there are problems. Not so! If you make sound choices in selecting the professionals with whom you will work (Chapter 8) you will find them ready and willing to offer their guidance and support!

Understanding How Children Learn

Over time you will have many opportunities to help your child learn about and process the elements of his life, including adoption. Doing so with confidence demands an understanding of the very way that children's brains work to acquire and store information. Let's begin with a highly simplified introduction to a very complex process—cognitive development in children, or how children learn any and all of the things they learn. The remarkable Swiss psychiatrist Jean Piaget, who began observing children during the 1920s and continued to refine what he learned for well over fifty years, changed forever the idea that children are more or less miniature adults.

In his research, Piaget discovered that the minds of babies and children are different from those of adults. Since a child views the world from a limited perspective, it is only after he has had many and varied experiences with the things he sees, hears, feels, tastes, and experiences in his environment that he is able to think in the very logical way which adults take entirely for granted.

Piaget discovered that kids grow intellectually in five orderly and progressive stages. While children may move at differing rates because of individual and cultural variations, each child moves progressively forward in pyramidal form from one stage to another. More than that, Piaget noted that intellectual development is also tied to physical development. So that even the academically gifted child will need to wait for his physical development to catch up before his cognitive growth can move on.

In moving from stage to stage, children use three processes in their learning. First they *assimilate* (taking in information about something new), then they *accommodate* (putting out information or ideas to be tested) and finally they *equilibrate* (balancing what they've learned and absorbing it for later application). This is true of all learning, so that learning about math, about riding a bike, about sexuality, about family roles and relationships, about morality, about rights and obligations, about interpersonal motives, and about the functioning of societal institutions is all learned slowly and progressively through the process of assimilating, accommodating, and equilibrating.

Anna Freud is one of the psychiatrists who has added significantly to Piaget's work. Here's my simplification of her refinements to Piaget's stages of intellectual development. During the Sensory/Motor Stage of intellectual development (from birth to about two years of age) a child's major tasks are learning to use and control his body and learning to distinguish himself from others. You will remember that when we spoke about the development of attachment, it was pointed out that child and parent engage in a dance—the child expresses needs, the parent meets those needs, and the result of doing this over and over is the child comes to trust that a consistent caring someone other than himself, a person to whom he becomes firmly attached, will always be there to meet his needs. At about 18 months, a child, having "mastered" his body to an amazing extent in so short a period, begins to move seriously to mental activity. For example, he can begin to understand that hidden things still do exist and enjoy peek-a-boo games.

Since during this time children are exploring the world, learning to move away from parents, and experimenting with whether a parent will be there when child returns, this stage gives adoptive parents' a first test of their sense of entitlement. Each parent needs to be able to enjoy and adjust to the child's moving away from and moving back, giving the child his first sense of permission to separate and to trust both his competent self and his parents.

In the Preconceptual Stage (from about age 2 to 4) children think very egocentrically, assuming that they are somehow magically omnipotent—personally responsible for all that occurs in their world. All things are alive and feel because, after all, he is and he does. The child assumes that the world is as it appears to him, and he cannot conceive of another point of view.

This stage is followed between ages 4 and 7 by the Pre-logical/Intuitive Stage. Now begins some pre-logical thinking, but only with one concept at a time. For example, a child in this stage is still likely to feel that half a cup of milk which fills a small glass seems more than half a cup of milk which doesn't fill a large glass. He might have trouble labeling blocks as both blue blocks and plastic blocks at the same time.

During this time the child begins to relate differently to his parents. Prior to this time, parents were largely seen as need-fulfilling persons. Now, increasingly the roles of mom and dad are differentiated, with boys beginning to feel competitive with dad and girls competing with mom. Huge strides in cognitive development at this stage mean that the child becomes curious about the surrounding world and will begin to ask some very important questions—where babies come from, for example. He is more active socially. This is the stage in which he is first likely to have some beginning awareness about basic adoption issues.

Commonly called middle childhood, the Concrete Operations Stage (ages 7 to 11 or even older) begins in about first or second grade. Children this age can begin to think logically about things they have personally experienced and to make deductions about them. They remain limited, however, by their actual experiences, and they are unable to think abstractly. By this time children are able to think backwards and forwards in time (so now can understand that the half a cup is half a cup whether in a small or large glass). Because this stage is so long and children grow so rapidly during this time, many psychologists have pointed out that middle childhood sometimes seems to have two distinct halves, 6 or 7 to 9 or so, and 8 or 9 to 11. This is a stage rich in all kinds of fantasies. It is also a stage during which children test and test and test!

The fifth and final stage of cognitive development is called the Formal Operations Stage, and it occurs sometime after the age of twelve. Children who become logical thinkers understand the theoretic and are thinking abstractly. They are able to form hypotheses, to deduce and induce—even about things that they have not themselves experienced. Sometimes we assume that because a child of twelve or older is physically mature he or she must be cognitively mature as well. In reality, the movement from concrete thinking to abstract thinking is a difficult transition that can take many years or not happen at all.

> When I was a teacher of 9th grade English, one of the things I learned in the field rather than as a part of my teacher education trainings was that 9th graders asked to provide concrete information in essay form on a literature test can nearly always do very well, but that an often unpredictable proportion (if assumptions are based on physical maturity) will be able to abstractly analyze the material in a novel or an essay. In addition to teaching 8th and 9th grade English for several years in public schools, I once taught freshman English part time in a very academically-oriented and well-respected private prep school. These students were all talented, self-directed, and parent-supported. Peer pressure mandated academic success in this environment, and most kids were expecting to go to very selective and prestigious colleges. But many of these ninth graders were having a difficult time in their first year in high school, not because the material itself was too hard, but because the assumption of all of their teachers and of the curriculum itself was that all of these students were already abstract thinkers. They weren't! Some were still operating cognitively as concrete thinkers.

Understanding how it is that children learn and at what ages they are intellectually able to understand information given to them is an important asset when dealing with sensitive issues in parenting—issues like sex education, adoption, and morality. If parents, in their role as their children's long term teachers, can learn to consider just how relatively sophisticated or unsophisticated their children are before trying to answer questions or deciding how to share certain information, their children will learn with far less likelihood of misunderstanding.

While giving children information that is too sophisticated for their level of cognitive development surely can't hurt them, it doesn't help them either. In essence, they simply don't learn it. To use the familiar cliché, it goes in one ear and right out the other. The sad reality of this is that most of the time parents don't even realize that this has happened, and they go blithely along their ways, feeling self-congratulatory about having "done their job" in sharing what they know about whatever imposing subject they've just rambled on about—sex education, adoption, etc. It seems almost a cliché to share that old tired joke again, but it does ram home the point about what happens when we try to teach children about things which they are simply unable to process.

If you are one of those parents who would enjoy learning more about how children learn, I recommend that you seek out, through a good children's bookseller, a book which presents Piaget for parents. As the parent of young children, I personally found helpful Mary Ann Spencer Pulaski's *Your Baby's Mind and How It Grows: Piaget's Theory for Parents* (Harper, 1978). This one is, however, out of print. Newer writing from two authors coming from slightly different perspectives will also be useful. Dr. Daniel J. Siegel, a neuropsychiatrist, synthesizes in accessible form neurological and anatomical brain research and adds that to clinical information in ways that offer groundbreaking new thinking about how the human mind and human relationships develop. Central to Siegel's work is his concept of how humans develop *mindsight*, which he defines as the ability to perceive the mental state of another.[2] Mindsightedness lies at the core of a parenting book Siegel has written with pre-school teacher Mary Hartzel, *Parenting from the Inside Out: How a Deeper Self-Understanding Can Help You Raise Children Who Thrive* (New York: Tarcher, 2004). Family therapist Michael Gurian's work is dependent on this new brain research too, as well as the burgeoning knowledge we've gained from DNA research that helps us understand how very much genetics influence personality, learning styles, and even how children might react to trauma. After writing *The Minds of Boys: Saving Our Sons From Falling Behind in School and Life* (Jossey Bass, 2006) and *The Wonder of Girls: Understanding the Hidden Nature of Our Daughters* (Jossey Bass, 2003), his intriguing and helpful new parenting book is *Nurture the Nature: Understanding and Supporting Your Child's Unique Core Personality* (Jossey Bass, 2007).

Learning about Adoption

It frustrated, and in some ways angered, my husband Dave that his sister Mary Jane claimed that she did not know that they had been adopted until she was 10 or 11 years old. Dave, after all, felt that he had always known they were adopted, and in fact one of the things he appreciated most about his parents' style of parenting had been their complete openness about adoption issues. They had used library books, had dinner table conversations, and answered every question he had asked entirely to his satisfaction. He figured that his sister was not telling the truth, and he couldn't understand why she would lie about something like this, which he felt would hurt their parents' feelings. It was not until we began learning about what kids understand about adoption that it dawned on Dave and me what likely had happened with MJ.

Dave is older than his sister by slightly over two years. Additionally, she had a learning disability, which made learning more difficult for her than for Dave. Though they were chronologically just two years apart, her cognitive development was probably more than three behind his during their early and middle childhood years. As Dave's parents shared books appropriate for children his age and age-appropriately answered the questions of their curious older son, his sister, though sitting there too, was not paying a whole lot of attention. By the time she was old enough and intellectually mature enough to process this information, Dave had entered that very introspective time when kids are doing a lot of fantasizing but not much talking. Their parents assumed that both kids were doing just fine.

It was really true that Mary Jane hadn't known she was adopted until later. Despite the fact that adoption talk had been going on around her for several years, it ended by the time she was cognitively ready to listen to it. It wasn't until her own questions came up at age 10 or so that the conversation started again, and when it did, the fact of her adoption came as a big surprise.

In a landmark study of what children understand about adoption and when they learn it which was conducted at Rutgers University, Dr. David Brodzinsky and a research team that included his wife, Anne Braff Brodzinsky, discovered that both adopted and non-adopted children tend to be able to understand the concepts of adoption logically at exactly the same time, though children who were themselves adopted do learn the jargon of adoption faster than do their non-adopted peers.[3] Few six-year-olds in the Brodzinsky study, for example, could differentiate between birth and adoption. They thought that people were either born or adopted. These few six-year-olds were unable to understand the motives that underlie adoption. The children in this study progressed, though, until both non-adopted and adopted adolescents were able to define adoption with sophistication as "a sociological form of substitute care that is based on the principle of protecting the rights and welfare of children."

The stages this study defines closely parallel the stages of cognitive development identified by Piaget and Freud. By about ages 3 to 5, the Brodzinsky study showed children may know the words and can effectively parrot their own arrival story, but they don't understand the concepts involved. For example, many children ages 3 to 5 don't know the difference between birth and adoption and so equate the two ("Well, John was born, but I was adopted.") They need to be helped to understand that they were indeed born and then adopted (More on this in a later section on sex education.).

By about age 6, kids know that birth and adoption are different but have trouble with how adoption works and can't quite grasp its permanency. During this stage, which is colored by rich fantasies and a great deal of magical thinking for all children, adoptees are likely to have some fears about being abandoned by their adoptive parents. After all, they may reason poorly, I was bad enough that my birthparents, who supposedly loved me, let me go. This knowledge has some important ramifications for parents who are considering how best to impart their children's adoption stories. Many adoptive parents who are committed to transferring a clear message that their children's birthparents are good people, worthy of respect and affection, tell their children that their birthparents loved them very much and so chose adoption for them. To a child unable to reason and think abstractly, this story doesn't wash. Thinking concretely, children told this story are likely to make a progression which says that if their birthparents loved them and so chose to let them go when things were hard, then since their adoptive parents love them also, if things get hard they, too, will find new parents for them.

Educators have noted that when children of this age are given more information than they are comfortable with, they may actually feel that curiosity in general is potentially painful. So they try to suppress their curiosity, and this can lead to some school problems, as they become quite inhibited. A few adoption educators have actually suggested that the likelihood of conflicted thinking about such weighty issues as adoption in the very young is a good reason for not sharing the fact of adoption with a child until he is 7 or 8. Those who disagree with this position (including me) and continue to advocate early telling do so primarily because they fear that the presence of "secrets" in a family can be lethal to relationships and they have not been able to develop a compromise model that takes all of these factors into account.

Brodzinsky's work demonstrated that somewhere during that middle childhood span of ages 7 to 11 children begin to understand adoption's permanence, even though they are often still unable to understand the function of the intermediary. Since all children of this age do lots of fantasizing with friends, envisioning what it would be like to have idyllic, permissive parents, children who were adopted experience a conflict. For them, there really is another set of parents out there, so for adopted children—especially those in confidential adoptions—the typical fantasies of middle childhood are also possibilities.

We have noted earlier the six losses felt by adults in the infertility experience—loss of control, genetic continuity, a jointly conceived child, the physical and emotional satisfactions accompanying pregnancy or the ability to impregnate, and, if they do not adopt, the opportunity to parent. In his book *The Psychology of Adoption* (Oxford University Press, 1989), Dr. Brodzinsky includes an essay called "The Stress and Coping Model of Adoption Adjustment" in which he writes about the losses which children experience in adoption. He draws our attention to the work of many researchers—Nickman, Sants, Brinich, Kirk—who have noted various individual losses experienced by adoptees, and Dr. Brodzinsky gathers them here for us to consider: the loss of their biological parents, the loss of a genetic connection and genetic continuity, a loss of status associated with being different, a loss of confidence about who they are, and, as a result, to some extent the loss of a feeling of stability in their relationship with their adoptive family.[4]

These are enormous losses for one so young to handle, far beyond the kinds of progressively more difficult losses which normally teach us how to deal with loss. It is not at all atypical for adopted children to begin to exhibit signs of grieving and loss during these middle childhood years—the denial, the anger, the bargaining, and so forth. All too frequently these changes in behavior go unrecognized by the child, parents, and professionals as being related to the feelings of loss about adoption which these children are simply too cognitively immature to put words to without help.

Middle childhood aged children can either be very verbal or very quiet, and they can be more or less talkative than they were before. Because so much fantasizing is going on in the normal child now, adoption issues must be kept in the open during this time, and parents must take great care to send positive messages about adoption being a good thing to wonder about and inquire about. Claudia Jewett-Jarrett points out in her trainings that this is a time when a great deal of confused thinking goes on, despite parents' best efforts at adoption education.

> I went to a Claudia Jewett training one fall when my son, Joel, was eight or nine. Her book *Helping Children Cope with Separation and Loss*, which is now considered a classic, was new at the time, and it formed the basis for her training that day. I remember feeling smug and self-satisfied when she mentioned how common it was for middle graders—especially boys, who tended to begin to have negative feelings about themselves at this time—to begin to let their tendency toward magical thinking confuse what they had already been told about their adoptions.
>
> "No, not my son," I thought. "We've told him the story and he knows it. His birthparents were very young and weren't themselves finished growing up yet. They were not ready to be parents to any baby, so they planned adoption for him because they wanted him to have a mom and a dad who were ready to be parents."
>
> Still, one day the next week as we sat and folded socks and sorted laundry, he began to talk about a neighbor girl who was pregnant. I used the entree. "Joel, do you ever wonder why your birthmother chose Daddy and me to be your parents instead of being your mom herself?"
>
> "Oh, I know why she gave me away," he replied (the negative adoption language which he'd never heard from us sent chills up my spine) "It's because I was ugly."
>
> Ugly? My handsome son thought he was ugly? Reality check, Mom! Try that story one more time.

Somewhere beyond the age of nine, as they move toward adolescence, adoptees begin to understand the permanence of adoption as well the active role of the intermediary. They can begin to understand that a transfer of parental rights occurred and that this has had a legal impact. During these years children begin to have many questions, but they are often driven underground. During middle school or junior high years is the perfect time to introduce Susan Gabel's *Filling in the Blanks: A Guided Look at Growing Up Adopted* (Perspectives Press, 1988). This workbook is designed to be used by a child with the assistance of an adult—parent, counselor, social worker, therapist—and has been carefully crafted to take into account children of all backgrounds, colors and abilities being raised by families of all configurations formed by all styles of adoption. This is a particularly good book for parents to own and read before their children arrive, so that they can begin to understand how children of this age will be thinking several years down the road and begin to gather the data and information that will be needed to fill in the book at that time.

Since a major task during the adolescent years for all kids is separation, adoptees often struggle with identity issues. Conformity is an important part of being a teen, and adoptees often feel "different." Envy is a common emotion during adolescence, and adoptees often envy the genetic connections of their peers' families. Most teens and their parents spend a good deal of their time being angry at one another, but for teens who were adopted, the complication of that anger can include an unexpressed fear of being abandoned again. They may feel a need either to over-identify with their adoptive parents and reject their birthfamily or vice versa. For many adolescents whose birthparents were themselves young and still in school, the new ability to reason brings their birthparents' dilemma clearly into focus. Those adopted internationally and now learning about cultural differences and mores may begin to think differently about their having been abandoned at a police station, about government policies which forced their parents toward adoption, etc. They begin to empathize with their birthparents, even to the point where normal teen rebellion against "systems" becomes focused on an angry perception (true in some cases) that their birthparents were cheated by "the system."

The struggle to avoid losing control is powerful. Sometimes, this can frighten adoptive parents who have a shaky sense of entitlement. What if she's "just like her birthmother" and gets pregnant? What if he embarrasses us by defying our values? As our children begin the final stage of learning to be independent, the one we know will result in their really leaving us and our home to be independent young adults, families can find this testing overwhelming.

> Constance's younger daughter Lauralie rebelled thoroughly as a teen. Her older sister, also adopted but psychologically more "like" Constance, had seemed to be perfect. Lauralie refused to compete with her sister. Her choice of friends was from the group her mother considered "losers." She experimented with dangerous substances, activities, and relationships. Very bright, her grades suffered.

Constance found her infertility before her again. Not only did she resent being so completely out of control of her situation, but she also harbored a terrible, unspeakable belief. A child born to her wouldn't have been like this.

What Constance had forgotten—or perhaps never recognized at all—was that there are no guarantees in parenting. While Laurelie's behavior might have been adoption-related, many teens born to the parents who are raising them test in the same fashion. Constance, however, in her disappointment, needed a scapegoat. Adoption was it.

Finally, having reached the age of abstract thinking, kids can begin to understand the evaluative role of an adoption intermediary who functions to protect a child's best interests. Also, they can begin to understand the motivations of both birth and adoptive parents. During these years when all teens are most prone to be uncommunicative with their parents, adoptees are likely to be receiving an important message from their peers: what you are thinking may hurt your parents' feelings, so don't talk about this adoption stuff with them. Adoptive parents need to work hard to make it clear that this is not true. Keeping communication open is the key to it all. Kids need to feel that it is okay to talk about anything with their parents.

Even more importantly, in order to consistently reinforce the sense of trust that comes with firm attachment, from their earliest questions, children must be able to trust that their parents will tell them the absolute truth. Whether adopting an older child or an infant, parents must be committed to helping their children do what Kay Donley has called "making friends with the ghosts of the past"—fully accepting the importance of their placement history.

In an on-line discussion on the FRUA boards, MaryAlice Raabe offered this insight . . .

Kids don't hear what we hear, don't process info as we do, don't see the same "logic" in situations that we do (have been trained to see in some cases). Even the most logical, analytical little kid, can, if they are dysregulated, not be able to find their way out of a clear plastic bag. That "I don't know" answer that pushes my buttons is sometimes not defiance, it's that at that moment, with her overactive, congested brain, she honestly doesn't know!

Expecting a little kid, especially one whose emotional development has been irregular, (as that of children who have been in institutional care as babies and toddlers or in and out of foster care often is) to follow the same lines of logic adults do, is, well asMr. Spock would say, "Illogical, Jim." It's so easy to see and celebrate this child mind when it's about "cute" things, but it's important to give the same grace to child logic when it comes to less charming behaviors."

Seen in a certain light, even the things they say and do that aren't so charming, can be endearing too. It's just that applying adult logic to situations may not work with a child and thank goodness they are not little adults, that's how we all get to revisit our childhoods.

Opening the Lines of Communication

My six year old son and I had spent the summer afternoon at Rosi's. He had played in the backyard and fussed over Rosi's baby, John-David, while Rosi, Cindy, and I folded and stuffed newsletters for Resolve of Indiana. Cindy was still waiting for her first child, and I felt a little guilty as the conversation turned to the any-time-now excitement simmering at our house about the possibility of another adoption. But it was hard—and really unnecessary with these good friends who were all in the same place—to suppress the anticipatory nervousness. Despite the fact that for two years the nursery had been sitting completely ready—sheets on the bed, Pampers in the changing table, handmade quilt awaiting only the embroidered birthdate carefully folded over the rocker—I had more or less steeled myself for another possible disappointment. She might, after all, change her mind.

Several years later, when all of us had our children and got them together, we sometimes reminisced about that afternoon when we'd all been part of a real, for sure arrival. I had returned home to a ringing phone, and picked up to hear my friend Mary's voice, "Where were you all afternoon? Congratulations! You have a daughter!"

She had arrived. At long last Erica Brooke was here.

Families who adopt have arrival stories which they and their children love to hear in the same way that families formed by birth love to recite the tales of racing through rush hour traffic to get to the hospital on time. "The call" or "the email" become part of family lore, along with how Mom and Dad got engaged, Grandpa's brush with death on the ice at the village pond when he was seven, and the time Johnny got lost on vacation. Repeating these stories over and over and over is a part of the way that families claim one another as "us" as opposed to the "them" that is the rest of the world.

These stories are the first ways that we begin to talk about adoption with our children. For the youngest of children, adoption information is both offered and received as an experience of gain. But as children approach middle childhood, they are likely to become increasingly aware that in order for the gain to occur, they and their birthparents had to experience an enormous loss. (Remember the story in Chapter 4 about Erica's teacher who told her that if her parents ever wanted to give her away, she'd love to have her?) If children haven't felt that loss themselves, as they enter school they will soon be exposed to the negative societal reactions to adoption.

When children are very young they accept adoption so matter-of-factly that they are likely to bring up adoption quite frequently on their own. It will be several years before children become uncomfortable enough about adoption's differences to feel that it is not something to share freely.

> When Joel was in second grade he brought a friend home from school to spend the night. The boys were followed everywhere by Erica, then about 15 months old, who adored her big brother. She was not talking much, but engaging in long conversational sentences of babble and baby talk.
>
> At dinner she began an animated monologue directed at Joel's friend, Danny. She was so obviously trying to communicate something specific, that Danny turned to Joel at the end of the speech and asked, "What did she say?"
>
> Joel casually replied, "I dunno. I think her birthmother might have been Chinese."
>
> (Note also the concrete thinking about how language is acquired demonstrated in this anecdote.)

But through the years, talking about adoption becomes more complicated, because what children are worrying or wondering about and what we want them to know become more complex. As children enter the later stages of middle childhood and move into adolescence, they may be particularly unlikely to initiate discussion about adoption on their own. It becomes a challenge for parents to look for news stories and other ways to "casually" open the door to discussion for their children.

> As usual, the holiday season brought a spate of human interest stories in the news which included a reunion between adopted-away siblings. One television station was especially entranced by the story of the children of a dying birthmother who were attempting to find their older half sibling, who had been adopted at birth in a confidential placement. With so much visibility focused on the story, the adoptee was soon found, and the T.V. station filmed an emotional reunion (no mention at all of the adopting parents, of course) in a hospital room.
>
> Evan, who was 15, watched intently. He turned to his parents and said, "Why would she do that, after all her parents have done for her? That woman isn't her real mother."
>
> His mother, Kathleen, remained casual and calm. "I don't know about that, Evan. I think that if I'd been adopted I'd think sometimes about my birth family and be interested in meeting them. I think sometimes about your birthmother and your birthfather, who were pretty close to the age you are now when you were born. I wonder sometimes

about which one you look like and I wonder how they are doing now. Don't you?"

A long discussion ensued. (Just testing, Mom. What's okay to ask? What's okay to feel?)

For many families the car becomes the place where lots of significant talking takes place. Most parents quickly learn to play the cards they are dealt and to use every opportunity they can find for education.

> "Tell me again, Daddy, about when you, Chad and Mommy came to meet me at the airport when I came home from India."
>
> "My birthfather, Darryl, was mean to me sometimes, but not always. I remember once, when . . ."
>
> "Do you 'member that time, Aunt Cassandra, when we all went to the hospital to try to see Sam in the nursery before he came home?"
>
> "I remember when my foster mom, Mrs. B., made a big cake for my fifth birthday and invited my kindergarten class to walk to our house to see the new puppies and have some cake."

On the other hand, it's important for new parents to realize that children learn quickly which buttons when pushed get the most interesting reactions from their parents, and for many adoptive parents, adoption produces an interesting reaction. Middle childhood youngsters are particularly adept at "using" adoption. At bedtime, for example, many children who know that their conscientious parents who stand for no delays will drop everything to deal with an adoption-related issue, and will stall lights-out with an adoption-related question.

By the time their children reach adolescence few adopters have not been hit squarely between the eyes with an angry child's bullet, "You're not my *real* mom. My *real* mom wouldn't treat me like this!" Most of the time such comments are not really adoption related! They are diversionary tactics designed to throw parents off balance enough that the child can win the battle.

> "Hurry up, Dad, I'm gonna miss the opening tip-off if we don't leave now."
>
> "Brian, we can't leave until you finish the list of jobs I asked you to accomplish this weekend. I sure would hate to see you miss that basketball game," says Dad.
>
> "But I'll do it tomorrow, Dad. I have to leave now," is the reply.
>
> "Sorry, but that's not the way it works. I'll be happy to drive you to the fieldhouse as soon as the jobs are completed."
>
> "I hate you!" screams Brian. "You can't tell me what to do! You're not my real father!"

Dad remains cool. "Well, you know, Brian, I understand that you aren't very happy with me right now, and I can understand that you might have some concerns about your adoption that you'd like to talk about, too. I'll be happy to talk about those things with you as soon as that list of jobs is completed."

Using Books to Talk about Adoption

Many families find books a good way to open conversation. Books do provide a good start, but they can't become the only source for stimulating adoption discussions. Using books to open conversation must never become a crutch to dealing positively, specifically, and personally with your own and your child's personal issues. I offer here some brief guidelines for incorporating books into the way you teach your children about themselves and their family.

From the beginning, understand that even though a book does not describe a family just like your own it may provide some valuable discussion points for you and your children. Just because you adopted in-racially, for example, doesn't mean that a book about transracial adoption doesn't offer a good opportunity to think and talk about adoption. Just because you adopted transracially doesn't mean that a book with a main character who matches his parents racially wouldn't interest and help your child. Because your family was not built by both birth and adoption does not mean that your children wouldn't find value in a book about a family that was. Just because you are fertile rather than infertile doesn't make books which portray families built entirely by adoption inappropriate.

Every child's favorite book, of course, is his own. Most families purchase a traditional baby book for their children, but families built by adoption have in the past been reluctant to participate in this tradition. At issue has been that baby books are traditionally oriented to begin with pregnancy and birth, so that often adoptive parents felt awkward and uncomfortable about the missing blanks in their children's books. Some adoption educators of the past who were concerned that children would feel different without a baby book advocated that parents use a regular baby book anyway. Today's adoption-expanded families have more choices if only they will take the time to look. Although specific products may change as items go out of print and new titles come into print, I have not known a time over the last twenty-five years when two or more baby books designed specifically for adoptive families have not been marketed through the larger greeting card manufacturers, or through the many adoption-niche marketers easily located through the Internet or in advertising in adoption-related periodicals.

Adoptees placed beyond infancy should be accompanied by a lifebook (when their cases have been managed by really good caseworkers at highly professional agencies). Lifebooks are a combination baby book, photo album, scrap book, etc. which has been designed to pull together the significant paperwork, photographs, mementoes and anecdotes that record a child's life. In reality, every child, including those born to the families in which they live, but most especially including children adopted at any age from birth on up, should have a lifebook. As scrapbooking products are so readily available, making a lifebook becomes easier and easier for families to accomplish. If your older-adopted child does not yet have a lifebook, please contact your agency and ask for their help in pulling together the materials from his past caregivers that can help you to build one.

These and the family photo albums or photo boxes will provide the most consistent opportunity to talk about adoption. But other books—books about adoption, books about families, books about cultures, books about differences, books which carry subtle messages about permanence and continuity—can provide a comfortable way either to introduce information or to open the door to communication.

My background in both library and literature means that our house is filled to the top with books. When I was teaching school, the idea of using books to help children deal with difficult issues—a specialty called bibliotherapy—was a new and innovative idea that is mainstream now. Because my job is as an infertility and adoption educator, my office is overflowing with children's books—both good ones and bad ones—about adoption.

My kids did not have shelves full of adoption books, though. They each had a few adoption titles on their personal shelves—books which they asked me to read over and over. Beyond that, we used the library. Filling the family shelves with every adoption book on the market, it seemed to me, overemphasized the impact of adoption, creating a situation bordering on insistence of difference (ID behavior) discussed in Chapter 4.

Robert Munche's funny (yet so sentimental that it always makes me cry) story *Love You Forever* sends a wonderful message about permanence and continuity to children in adoption-expanded families, as does the classic by Margaret Wise Brown *The Runaway Bunny* and *Guess How Much I Love You?* by Sam McBratney and Anita Jeram. Many people would add Shel Silverstein's *The Giving Tree* to this list of classic non-adoption books for adoption-expanded families.

In choosing books you also need to be careful. For example, the Dr. Seuss book *Horton Hatches an Egg* carries positive messages about what makes a real parent, but it paints the birthparent, Maizie, in a terribly negative light. My collection of books not to use includes the P.D. Eastman title *Are You my Mother?* Even some adoption-specific books need to be avoided because of their negative adoption language (though creative parents have always known that there's a lot to be said for changing the script of a read aloud book when necessary).

Consider that information about "differences" of all kinds will help your adopted child feel less isolated and different herself. Embrace books from diverse cultures or featuring characters which don't necessarily "match" your child. Why not embrace the universe of diversity? Perhaps your child would enjoy collecting beautifully illustrated Cinderella tales (or some other universal theme retold in many countries) from around the world.

If you are a book lover and a book buyer, consider that it isn't just your own children who need to learn about adoption. Your child's friends, cousins, and schoolmates need this education too. Consider giving copies of some of your family's favorite adoption-positive titles as gifts at birthday parties. Most particularly make it a practice to donate copies of books on adoption to your school's and your place of worship's libraries.

More than the stories that are specifically about adoption, I find that adoption education works even better when the stories aren't about adoption at all. Every child personally touched by his own, a friend's, or a relative's adoption should own the most beautifully illustrated version of Margery Williams' *The Velveteen Rabbit* that his parents can find. Here we can begin the discussions of "realness" as a part of relationships.

> "What is real?" asked the rabbit. "Does it mean having things that buzz inside you and a stick-out handle?"
>
> Real isn't how you are made," said the skin horse. "It's a thing that happens to you. When a child loves you for a long, long, time, not just to play with, but REALLY loves you, then you become real."
>
> "Does it hurt?" asked the rabbit.
>
> "Sometimes," said the skin horse, for he was always truthful. "When you are real you don't mind being hurt."
>
> "Does it happen all at once, like being wound up," he asked, "or bit by bit?"
>
> "It doesn't happen all at once," said the skin horse. "You become. It takes a long time. That's why it doesn't often happen to people who break easily or have sharp edges or who have to be carefully kept. Generally, by the time you are real, most of your hair has been loved off, and your eyes drop out and you get loose in the joints and very shabby. But those things don't matter at all, because once you are REAL, you can't be ugly, except to people who don't understand."

Embracing Diversity

As adoptive families, we are—even those of us who are Caucasian and have adopted white children—minority families. And thus we have been given a rare opportunity to help our children become part of a less biased and bigoted future. Our challenge is to help our families celebrate diversity and multiculturalism without moving beyond A.D. (acceptance of difference) behavior to I.D. (insistence on difference) behavior. It is an exciting opportunity.

Once again, books are a good way to begin. In addition to the wonderfully inclusive books whose very purpose is to embrace diversity (for example *Free to be a Family* by Marlo Thomas and friends, and *People* by Peter Spier), some of the best books to use in trying to help your child learn to celebrate differences rather than to be intimidated by them are those that are general interest stories featuring ethnically-inclusive illustrations (anything illustrated by Jerry Pinckney, John Steptoe or Alan Say are good bets). Vera Williams' Caldecott Honor Book *More, More, More! Said the Baby* embraces a wide variety of cultures and combinations of cultures without mentioning that fact at all. Robert Munche's hilarious story *Something Good* features a pair of Caucasian parents with two daughters of color, doesn't mention adoption, and tells a wonderful tale of the relative value of children.

Families who have adopted transculturally or transracially will, most importantly, need to do the very hard work of making their lives as diverse as possible. Many transracial adoptive parents will need to move, will need to change some service providers and professional services, will want to build a wider circle of friends, may choose a different house of worship. We'll talk more about this later. When it comes to using books they need to find sources which will help their children learn about their cultures of origin in ways that help them to integrate that culture into a positive sense of self. It is, however, equally important that children who have been adopted have many books which embrace the cultures of the families into which they have been adopted. Families who celebrate their Irish, Italian, Jewish, Latvian, or whatever heritage (through the way they worship, the way they eat, the way they observe holidays, the mixture of languages they use) claim their children by bringing them into the fold. Your own family's culture is the one you will share sociologically with your child, and it may be quite different from the genetic heritage he shares with his birthparents.

Connecting with Other Adoptive Families

One of the things kids dislike most is being different from their peers. Finding himself the only one he knows who has been adopted can make a kid feel pretty weird, geeky, nerdy, and different. It's enough to make a person just hide, forget about it, and try not to call attention to oneself.

Just as every child deserves to be wanted for who he is, every kid deserves to know somebody something like himself—someone with whom he can identify, and hopefully, in whom he can confide. Since adoptees represent only about 2% of the population of children in the U.S., parents need to find ways to insure that their children know other adoptees. Parent groups are the easiest place to begin.

There are interesting patterns observed by the volunteer leaders of adoptive parent support groups across the world. Traditional (infertile couple) adopters of healthy, same race infants are the least likely of adopters to belong to a parent group from their child's earliest days (denial of difference at work), while it is this same group of parents who are most likely to make contact with a group looking for help with problems when their children reach adolescence. Also observed is the fact that intercountry adopters and the adopters of special needs children tend to belong to the group during their children's preschool years and move away from the group during middle childhood, often coming back again as their children reach pre-adolescence.

Middle childhood is a busy time in family life. It is during these years that families become caught up in an overwhelming schedule of school, lessons, teams, clubs, and so on. Often the adoptive parent support group is the easiest thing to let slide. Yet children who know other children who joined their families by adoption tend to feel less different, more entitled as members of adoption-built families. Additionally, adoptive parents groups are a family's best source for referral to an adoption-sensitized and adoption-informed professional should you at any time need help along the way.

But what if a formal support group is not for you? What if there isn't one near? What if the nearby one focuses on a particular style of adoption or a particular country or continent of origin and you don't feel a fit? What if you just aren't a joiner, much less one who would feel comfortable with the possibility that someone might expect you to do something as a volunteer for the group? Informal support can be almost as valuable. Making an effort to make and nurture social relationships with other adoption-expanded families you meet through your agency, through a parent group or infertility support group, through your house of worship, through your children's school, can be a comfortable way to accomplish this goal. BUT, if you choose this route, I encourage you to remain connected to the more formal world of adoption support and education by maintaining at least one subscription/membership to a national level periodical, never allowing the subscription to lapse—even during those years when adoption is the last thing on every family member's mind.

Continuing Education

Whether you choose to maintain your local adoption connections formally or informally, resolve from the beginning to continue your adoption education. In many communities half day or day-long conferences on adoption-related issues are an annual or biennial event. ACONE (Adoption Community of New England), Adoptive Parents Committee of New York/New Jersey, OURS of Northeastern Wisconsin, CAFFA (Chicago Area Families for Adoption), Concerned Persons for Adoption in New Jersey, and dozens more groups throughout the country sponsor significantly-sized regular conferences aimed at ongoing adoption education. Stay in touch with your agency or with NACAC (North American Council on Adoptable Children) and their affiliated groups in order to remain well-informed about these opportunities.

Just as you will want to include an up-to-date general parenting handbook (just as Dr. Spock was probably on your own parents' bookshelf), use your periodicals, Amazon.com., one of the several adoption-niche bookstores, your parent group, and your local library to help you select at least one of the several excellent handbooks for adoptive parents. New titles are being introduced every year, and staying in touch can help you to find just the right book for parenting adopted toddlers or adopted teens just when you need it.

Parenting Isn't Easy

I am a person who has worn several occupational hats—some of them at the same time. I have been a teacher, a librarian, an audio-visual specialist, a sales manager, a writer and editor and publisher, an infertility and adoption educator, and an advocate. Once I was even a professional popcorn popper! The hardest job I have ever had is also the one that has given me the most pleasure and the one that was the hardest for me to get—becoming a parent.

One of the things that made the job seem hard is that I expected it to come so easily—as a simple by-product of making love to a man I loved very much and found extremely attractive. Of course it didn't. I also expected it to come naturally—kind of by instinct. And of course after I became a parent I wondered along the way if it was harder for me because the "instinct" hadn't been triggered by that mystical experience of "bonding" that all the movies and magazines seem to imply comes magically with the pregnancy and birth experience, and creates a kind of super glue that holds families together.

The process of being a parent has been an incredible learning experience. I've done a lot of reading, a lot of questioning, a lot of listening, a lot of conferencing, a lot of thinking, and at this point a lot of parenting—to three kids who aren't kids anymore, but young adults. Are my kids gorgeous? Of course they are—because they're mine! And one of the great things about that is I feel no embarrassment about telling you that they are good-looking, smart, and savvy people. They look nothing like me and nothing like Dave. They don't have my weight problem or my couch-potato attitude toward athletics. They don't have my family's hereditary lazy eye or their dad's nearsightedness and lousy teeth. We can take credit for imparting our values, but none for imparting our genes.

Now, thirty years ago you'd never have convinced me that I'd ever feel that it was great to have kids who were unlike me. Nor could I have imagined that I could look at my two sisters' five children who do resemble me somewhat, and then at these three children genetically unrelated to their parents or to one another, and have felt so total a sense of claiming and overwhelming love of these three, and such a "they're nice kids, but I'm sure glad they're going home with their mother" attitude about those five who are biologically related to me. But I do.

The fact is that I know now that child rearing is a difficult task for all parents. All parents make mistakes, and you will too. All parents have issues that make them feel uncomfortable because they don't feel "expert" enough to teach their children about them. One of yours may be adoption. Parents in adoption have some different issues to deal with than do parents by birth (and it's also true that as adoptive parents there are some uncomfortable issues related to genetic connection that we are relieved of). How difficult the differences are to deal with depends on several factors, among which are how far the parents have come in the process of building that sense of entitlement to their children that we spoke about, and how far their children have come in building their own senses of entitlement to their parents.

Resources

Attachment

There will be additional attachment resources in Part Four.

Adoption Learning Partners (www.adoptionlearningpartners.org) offers on-line interactive courses for parents-to-be which some agencies require and/or accept for credit. These are introductory level classes, and most do not take the place of a more detailed book, but they can be an excellent alternative for those who are just not "readers." One helpful here is "The Journey of Attachment."

Fahlberg, Vera I. *A Child's Journey through Placement* (Indianapolis: Perspectives Press, Inc., 1991, 1994, 1998)

Gray, Deborah D. *Attaching in Adoption: Practical Tools for Today's Parents* (Indianapolis: Perspectives Press, Inc., 2005)

Hopkins-Best, Mary. *Toddler Adoption: The Weaver's Craft.* (Indianapolis: Perspectives Press, Inc., 1997)

Learning (Psychological and Social Issues)

Brodzinsky, David, Marshall D. Schecter, and Robin Marantz Henig. *Being Adopted: The Lifelong Search for Self.* (New York: Doubleday, 1992)

Brodzinsky, David, ed. *The Psychology of Adoption.* (New York: Oxford University Press, 1990)

Bernstein, Anne C. *Flight of the Stork: What Children Think (and When) about Sex and Family Building.* (Indianapolis: Perspectives Press, Inc.: 1994)

Gurian, Michael. *Nurture the Nature: Understanding and Supporting Your Child's Unique Core Personality*. (Boston: Jossey-Bass, 2007)

Kirk, H. David. *Shared Fate: A Theory and Method of Adoptive Relations*. (New York: Free Press, 1965)

Kirk, H. David. *Looking Back, Looking Forward: An Adoptive Father's Sociological Testament*. (Indianapolis: Perspectives Press, 1995)

Pavao, Joyce Maguire. *The Family of Adoption*. (Boston: Beacon Press, 2005)

Piaget, Jean and Barbel Inhelder. *The Psychology of the Child: The Definitive Summary of the Work of the World's Most Renowned Psychologist*. (New York: Basic Books, 2000)

Siegel, Daniel J. and Mary Hartzell. *Parenting from the Inside Out*. (Jeremy Tarcher, 2004)

Smith, Jerome. *You're Our Child: A Social/Psychological Approach to Adoption*. (Baltimore: University Press of America, 1981)

Communication in Adoptive Families

Adoption Learning Partners (www.adoptionlearningpartners.org) offers on-line interactive courses for parents-to-be which some agencies require and/or accept for credit. These are introductory level classes, and most do not take the place of a more detailed book, but they can be an excellent alternative for those who are just not "readers." Among the ones helpful here are "Let's Talk Adoption," "Finding the Missing Pieces," and "Lifebooks."

Elderidge, Sherrie, *Twenty Things Adopted Kids Wish Their Adoptive Parents Knew*. (Delta, 1999)

Keefer, Betsy and Jayne Schooler. *Telling the Truth to Your Adopted or Foster Child: Making Sense of the Past*. (Westport, CT: Bergin & Garvey, 2000)

O'Malley, Beth. *LifeBooks: Creating a Treasure for the Adopted Child*. (Adoption-Works Press, 2000)

Riley, Debbie. *Beneath the Mask: Understanding Adopted Teens*. (Baltimore, MD: Center for Adoption Support and Education [CASE], 2005)

Schoettle, Marilyn. *W.I.S.E. Up! Powerbook* (Baltimore: Center for Adoption Support and Education [CASE], 2000)

Van Gulden, Holly and Lisa Bartels-Raab. *Real Parents, Real Children: Parenting the Adopted Child*. (Minneapolis: Crossroad Classic, 1995)

Watkins, Mary and Susan Fisher. *Talking with Young Children about Adoption*. (New Haven, CT: Yale University Press, 1995)

Connecting and Continuing Education[5]

Adoptive Families magazine
"Everything you need to know about adoption, whether you want to adopt or you're a veteran adoptive parent."
New Hope Media

39 West 37th Street, 15th Floor
New York, NY 10018
Telephone: 646-366-0830 • Fax: 646-366-0842
Subscription Customer Service: 800-372-3300
www.adoptivefamilies.com

Adoption Today magazine
"Your guide to the issues and answers surrounding intercountry and domestic adoption."
Louis & Co.
541 E Garden Dr Unit N
Windsor, CO 80550
Telephone: 970-686-7412 • Fax: 970-686-7412
Toll Free: 888-924-6736
www.adoptinfo.net

Fostering Families Today magazine
A bi-monthly foster care and adoption resource for America."
Louis & Co.
541 E Garden Dr Unit N
Windsor, CO 80550
Telephone: 970-686-7412 • Fax: 970-686-7412
Toll Free: 888-924-6736
www.adoptinfo.net

North American Council on Adoptable Children (NACAC)
publishes *Adoptalk* newsletter, quarterly
"Founded in 1974 by adoptive parents, the North American Council on Adoptable Children is committed to meeting the needs of waiting children and the families who adopt them."
970 Raymond Avenue, Suite 106
St. Paul, MN 55114
Telephone: 651-644-3036 • Fax: 651-644-9848
www.nacac.org

Pact: An Adoption Alliance
"Pact specializes in the placement of children of color, but aside from their placement services, they are the premier organization and site for education and materials about transracial parenting. Their excellent newsletter (quarterly) is *Pact Press*. They also offer an annual family camp with education and activities for parents and children."
4179 Piedmont Avenue, Suite 330
Oakland, CA 94611
Telephone: 510-243-9460 • Fax: 510-243-9970
800-750-7590 (Birth Parent Line)
www.pactadopt.org

Families for Russian and Ukrainian Adoption Including Neighboring Countries (FRUA)
"FRUA exists to support adoptive families who are considering adoption, in the process of adopting, and those who have returned home with their precious children! Local chapters and strong Internet discussion presence."
P.O. Box 2944

Merrifield, VA 22115
Telephone: 703-560-684 • Fax: 413-480-8257
www.frua.org

Families with Children from China (FCC)
"Nondenominational network of families who have adopted children from China. Includes a listing of chapters around the world."
Find a chapter near you at www.fwcc.org/contacts.html
www.fwcc.org

Families with Children from Vietnam (FCVN)
"Families with Children from Vietnam is the national organization for families who have adopted from Vietnam and for prospective parents who wish to adopt a child from Vietnam"
Chapter information: www.fcvn.org/fcv_chapters.htm
www.fcvn.org

Guatemala Adoptive Families Network
"The Guatemala Adoptive Families Network was founded by families with children adopted from Guatemala to contribute to the well-being of all Guatemalan families and children. We initiate and support projects that help raise the standard of living for Guatemalan children and their families, that improve conditions in Guatemalan orphanages, and that promote ethical adoptions for Guatemalan children whose birth families voluntarily relinquish them, or who are otherwise legally placed for adoption. We offer opportunities for families with children adopted from Guatemala to participate in this work and to maintain lasting connections to Guatemala and its people. Online support lists are active and helpful"
P.O. Box 176
Watertown, MA 02471
www.guatefam.org

IChild
"ICHILD was founded in 1995, and is an Internet-based, world-wide support group and source of information & resources for those interested in adoption from India & the Subcontinent. Offers references, resources, and on-line support groups."
www.serve.com/ichild/

Korean Focus
"Korean Focus offers information, support, and friendship to families with an interest in Korean culture and the Korean American community."
1906 Sword Lane
Alexandria, VA 22308
Find a chapter: koreanfocus.org/koreanfocuschapters.html
www.koreanfocus.org

Choosing Children's Books

There are a number of excellent on-line resources for reading reviews and choosing books about adoption and about multi-culturalism. Check these out:

www.pactadopt.org
www.adoptivefamiliesmagazine.com/books.php
www.adoptshoppe.com
www.tapestrybooks.com
www.comeunity.com/adoption/books/index.html
www.adoptionbooks.com
adoptionshop.com/

Keeping in mind that the Internet changes rapidly, do a search every now and then on "adoption books for children" or "teaching children about race."

CHAPTER 6

Special Issues Along the Way

Educator Kay Donley has referred to adoption as an "add on" rather than a "replacement" experience for both children and adults. That means that growing up in an adoption-expanded family brings added challenges for children to acknowledge, accept, and master. Similarly, parenting in adoption presents different, but not necessarily worse, challenges for parents. Acknowledging these "add-ons" is crucial to success in families built by adoption. They represent a significant proportion of the challenges to consistently practicing AD behavior discussed earlier in talking about building a sense of entitlement within adoptive families. In this chapter we will explore a variety of issues which may (and in a few instances may not) arise as your adopted family matures.

Your Child at School

From at least the age of six (and often earlier) the center of family life tends to shift from home and house of worship to the controlling factors of school. Everything begins to revolve around the school day, the winter/spring/summer vacation schedules, homework, playmates who are classmates, etc. Music lessons, scouts, athletic teams, all seem to be influenced in some way by school. Even for children who have been in large daycare centers each day during their preschool years, the onset of school takes on special significance and colors family life in a new and unique way.

At school, for the first time, parents will forfeit an important measure of protective control over their child's environment. You will not necessarily know all of the parents of your child's classmates. You will not have an opportunity to assess your child's teachers' adoption sensitivity. To complicate things even more, soon after children enter the formal education system, they also make an important intellectual shift. Having reached a new cognitive level of development, they will be primed to view adoption in an entirely new way.

Early elementary-aged children are often more competitive with peers than they were before ("My dad is taller than your dad" . . . "Well my dad is smarter!") and have learned to look for the special chinks in the armor of their peers that will allow them to sling just the right insults ("Fatty Patty two by four, couldn't get through the kitchen door!" . . . "Who set your hair on fire?" . . . "I know why you look different than your brother. You're adopted. Nobody wanted you!")

It is nearly always at school that children, for the first time, suddenly and forever, will be made aware of the important fact that adoption isn't just gain ("Mommy and I were sooooo happy when the lady called and told us you were born, and so were Grandpa and Grandma and Auntie Tess and cousin Sadie . . .") but that it also means some rather profound losses ("Well, what was the matter with your real mother that she couldn't keep you?" . . . "Gosh, I wouldn't want to be adopted. Then I wouldn't have my daddy.")

Perhaps the most important thing for parents to become openly, solidly conscious of when it comes to the experience of their children at school is that you won't necessarily know what goes on there. Many hurtful things can be said out of earshot of protective or mediating adults on the playground, in the restroom, on the school bus, and in the hall. Ambiguous comments may come out of the mouths of caring but uninformed or downright insensitive teachers.

Some kids tell their parents everything. Most do not. Conscientious parents, then, spend significant time checking in with their kids—using quiet time before bed, the breakfast table, transportation time in the car—to carefully explore (while at the same time not prying into a newly found need for privacy) and—more than anything—sending the message that they are available, accessible, ready to talk about anything and everything.

Somewhere in second or third grade the family tree assignment will come home for the first time (it will come again in late grade school and again in high school). For many parents, this is a real tough one, and often it isn't because the child is uncomfortable, so much as it is a painful reminder to parents of their lack of genetic connection to a child they have by now come to see as so profoundly their own.

First, keep in mind that this first pass at the family tree is not a genogram. The point of this assignment is not to learn which of our relatives were brown eyed and which blue eyed and what recessive traits we are likely to carry. That one comes later—at about eighth or ninth grade—as a part of a science biology project. It's going to be a bummer. But let's deal with the first grade family tree first.

This first assignment of a family tree is part of a social studies project. The class is most likely to be discussing what countries everybody's ancestors immigrated from or for how long their family members have all been born in this country. For this kind of project it is important for both you and your child—as a claiming mechanism—to remember that socially, your child is your own. Your values and your cultural background are your child's too. The fact that your great-grandmother was a missionary in China or that your great-grandfather died in a concentration camp or that someone in your family experienced the internment of Japanese-Americans during World War II is a part of who your child is as well. This is not to suggest that one can ignore the fact that genetically your child has a different background. He does—and it may bring with it racial difference as well. Parents definitely need to keep these differences in mind. But this first family tree experience is a good time to explore family lore. When placing Great-Grandma Rohrer's name on the right line we can talk about the fact that it is her recipe for raisin-filled cookies that we make for Daddy every Christmas because it is a family tradition. It might be a good time to take Great-Great-Grandfather Selby's Civil War hat out of the closet and hang it on Kareem's wall (he is, after all, the oldest son in this generation).

As the years go by, there will be time nearly every year to add to this discussion of the nature and the nurture that is a part of who we are. And there are several ways to approach it.

> Adoption educator and therapist Joyce Maguire Pavao, who was herself adopted as a child, has suggested that we no longer really have family trees. With so many children growing up in families which include birthparents, stepparents, adoptive parents, and foster parents, more and more of us have something more akin to a family orchard. This concept provides an opportunity to do a uniquely personal art project which depicts the various trees (of many varieties) in your family's orchard.

> In a past issue of a Maryland APSG's newsletter, adoptive parent Pat Hall described her approach to the family tree project. Pat drew and cut out a pair of family trees and explained that sometimes trees get sick or for some reason can't be saved and that horticulturalists (she called them "tree doctors") will remove healthy branches from one tree and graft them onto another tree in order to keep the first tree's fruit available. Healthy trees that have room for more branches and a good space in which to grow and flourish are the family trees to which these baby branches are grafted. Pat's daughter had an interesting twist to her show-and-tell the next day. She wanted to take in her lifebook and explain the grafting process.

This brings us to another issue about school and adoption. Should the school know? When parents and children are visibly very different, the issue is moot. But this is one of the questions posed most frequently to me on the Internet chat boards that I moderate by parents raising racially matched children. The concern parents have about this is that in unnecessarily identifying one's child's difference publicly one unnecessarily exposes the child to the stereotypes of adoption-ignorant or adoption-insensitive or adoption-prejudiced people.

This is a legitimate concern. Quite frankly, I can understand why parents refuse to automatically check unnecessary boxes that ask about adoption on registration forms. I have myself approached a preschool or elementary school or two and asked them to tell me why they felt they needed this information. In most cases, the administrators don't know. If that is the case, there is no reason to supply the information, and in fact there is reason to request of the school system that the block be dropped from the form.

Teachers should not be expected to have any more accurate or in-depth knowledge of or sensitivity to adoption facts and issues than would any other member of the general public. Adoption is not part of the curriculum in universities offering degrees in education. It is rarely a topic of in-service training. Teachers are just as likely as are next-door neighbors, scout leaders, or old friends to be adoption-illiterate. This being the case, my own opinion about dealing with adoption as an informational piece at school is that this information does not belong on general forms in school records (and you can ask to have it removed), but that parents should plan to meet with their child's teachers at the beginning of every year from kindergarten through at least sixth grade. During this meeting you should personally share this information with those teachers in a manner which conveys that you want to help the teacher learn what he or she needs to know about adoption and adoptive families in general so that it is covered positively in the classroom and in the curriculum, and so that he or she can be on the lookout for inappropriate gossip among parents or taunting among schoolmates. There are some very good materials available which have been specifically designed to educate the educators. See the Resources section at the end of this chapter for a list.

There is another, perhaps more important, factor to consider in deciding whether the school and the teacher should be told that your child was adopted. Even if you don't tell, your children probably will—especially at a very young age when they still consider adoption an exciting source of their being special and thus feel pride about it, before peers have burst their bubbles. Certainly it is unhealthy to suggest that adoption be a family secret. This implies that there is something wrong with it. What you can do instead is help your children understand that there is a balance between secrecy and privacy. There are very personal pieces of information in their adoption stories which are theirs to share selectively with people who care about them and with whom they want to share, but that because some things are personal and private, they need to feel that they are themselves in control of sharing it.

By middle school, adoptees will have experienced multiple exposures to other people's positive and negative reactions to adoption. They may have taken it "inside" for a time and decided not to share it all if that can be avoided. On the other hand, adolescence, with its attendant body changes, often makes adopted children very curious about their genetic heritage. Girls may wonder whether their breasts are likely to be large or small, and without a very detailed history or in the absence of a communicative adoption, when a young woman will begin to menstruate is a guessing game. Boys who do not have a genetic parent present against which to gage themselves may wonder if they will ever be tall, if they will be muscular, if they will have athletic abilities in any sport. Encouraging and supporting these natural curiosities is an important part of allowing your child to begin to separate. Many middle school-aged children will enjoy the experience of working through adoption-related interests in a new light by using Susan Gabel's *Filling in the Blanks: A Guided Look at Growing Up Adopted* with their parents or another adult. Others may balk completely at this idea and consider it intrusive. As we discussed earlier, the most important adoption-related parenting task of middle school through high school aged children is to keep the doors of communication open.

Learning Problems and Mental Health Issues

Though several well done research studies make clear that the fact of adoption does not appear in any way to diminish the self esteem and general environmentally-fed mental health of children and adolescents who have been adopted (indeed more than one study has revealed that adolescent adoptees had better self esteem when compared to their non-adopted peers), statistically, children who were adopted tend to have a higher incidence of learning disabilities and attention deficit problems than do children raised in their families of birth. We cannot be certain why this is true, but there are some obvious risk factors common to some (though certainly not all) people who make adoption plans which are known to influence learning problems. First, children who are adopted are often born to very young mothers. As a group these young mothers not only have had poor or very limited prenatal care, but sometimes they have denied their pregnancies for a long time and have had poor nutrition. Their pregnancies are complicated by the fact that they are themselves still growing. Second, sometimes birthparents have used dangerous chemical substances (drugs, alcohol) which produce dangerous amniotic baths in which their children spend nine months (or less). Third, one of the primary causes of unplanned pregnancies is impulsivity and poor judgment, traits which are often related to ADHD and several learning disabilities, and to a handful of mental health disorders which have a strong genetic component. And then there are the children who have become adoptable after being removed from abusive or neglectful family situations, kids who have been moved multiple times from caregiver to caregiver, and those who have been institutionalized—all of these children are at high risk for post traumatic stress issues, though not all will manifest them.

It is nearly always impossible to predict, and thus to avoid, adopting a newborn with a learning disability, but this is probably not the issue for most would-be parents, anyway. What they want, what they need, is solid and thorough background information which will prepare them to look for and identify potential risk factors early enough so that their children get the best possible interventional opportunities. Indeed, some of us know someone, or have experienced ourselves, a biological pregnancy which throughout appeared normal and healthy, yet once the baby was born, a problem was detected. Sometimes, too, problems can arise as a child develops. The point is that just as with adoptive parents, no one ever really knows for sure about the health of their biological child until their baby is born and medically evaluated.

> P.W. was an apparently healthy baby when placed into Ann and George's eager arms. The agency had minimal information about his birthmother, who had arrived in their offices late in her pregnancy. His birthfather was listed as unknown. Always active and curious, it was when he entered preschool that more serious questions arose about P.W.'s distractibility and inability to follow directions. At age three, P.W. went through speech and hearing screening, psychological testing, observation, and more. Nothing specific was identified. Ann and George felt intensely guilty. Maybe they were just inconsistent in their discipline. Maybe they hadn't read to him enough. Were they just bad parents?

> It was when P.W. was in third grade that persistent Ann finally made the professional connection that led to her family's getting the help for P.W. that was needed. Despite requests from an adoption-sensitive and internationally respected psychiatrist, the agency which had arranged P.W.'s adoption refused to release delivery records or the data they held about this boy's birthfamily. They refused to attempt a follow-up contact with P.W.'s birthmother to obtain a family medical history. The doctor, determined to find this young man the help that he needed, was furious, but referred the family to extensive and expensive testing sources. It turned out that P.W. had a severe and complex form of dyslexia (more than likely hereditary), as well as an attention deficit, hyperactivity disorder (ADHD—also most likely hereditary). P.W. began to receive helpful medication. His family used private tutors and even special schooling for his dyslexia.

> Now that P.W. is a happy, fully-functioning adult, his parents say that it has never occurred to them that they wouldn't have accepted P.W.'s placement had they had full knowledge of his genetic background, but they are resentful of the many years of butting up again

brick walls, the significant amount of wasted money, the enormous family stress, and the wasted time that it took them in order to identify P.W.'s problems and to obtain the help they needed.

Mariah's daughter Robin came home as an infant in a domestic adoption. She was accompanied by detailed physical descriptions of birthparents, but sketchy social background. Throughout her child-hood Robin had social and educational problems. By age six she was relatively socially isolated. Mariah made numerous attempts to get her daughter's problems properly identified, but pediatricians looking at a "nice, normal, well-educated, upper middle class family" (even though they knew that Robin had been adopted) were disinclined to consider serious diagnoses.

Mariah believes that Robin's painful growing up years would have been less difficult for her (as well as for her parents), and that a mid-teen psychotic break might have been prevented by earlier medicating, had the agency released the information well before seventeen years after the placement, that this young woman's birthfather had been hospitalized shortly after her birth, diagnosed with bi-polar and schizo-affective disorders. Full birth siblings had mental health problems as well.

Mariah's daughter's being treated earlier was further prevented by the placing agency's refusal to do an outreach to her birthfamily for more information requested several times, beginning when this troubled adoptee was a young child. In a flagrant example of non-baby-centered practice excused by a promise of confidentiality, the agency which had been receiving updates and pleas for help from Mariah for years, waited until Robin's birthmother contacted them on her own when Robin was 24 to put these families in contact.

As for the prevention-of-a-self-fulfilling-prophecy notion some-times raised by social workers, Mariah feels confident that with full information from the beginning she would indeed have said yes to this placement. She wanted a baby and believed at that point that nurture was much more important than nature. And there's this to consider . . . with full information and proper support, Robin's parent, unencumbered herself by the genetic baggage of mental illness, would still surely have been an even more effective parent than Robin's birth-parents could have been.

Adoption professionals *must* responsibly provide disclosure of any-thing that may help families built by adoption parent their children effec-tively. The lesson for adopting families to learn from Ann and George's and Mariah's experiences is that there are no guarantees in adopting a child, just as there are no guarantees with giving birth biologically, and that they must be insistent with placement professionals that serious attempts be made before placement to gather as much medical and social history as possible. In addition, they must insist that these placement professionals set the stage for further contact between the birth and adoptive parents should it become important for the child. Adoptive parents should expect the best, but must also be alert to early symptoms of problems and be prepared to deal with them. In the absence of access to full clarifying information, parents must learn to be open-minded, clear-thinking, strong advocates on behalf of their children and their needs, present and future.

Sex Education and the Child Who Was Adopted

There's the old joke . . .

Billy ran in from playing to where his dad sat working on a complex report on his computer.

"Dad, Dad, where did I come from?" he asked breathlessly.

A jolt ran through his father. Here it was, the question for which he had rehearsed in his head for so long. He saved his document, pulled his son up into his lap and began to tell the story. "Man, woman, falling in love, feeling a special way . . ."

Billy squirmed every now and then, but was quiet as Dad droned on, "Penis, sperm, vagina, egg, uterus, nine months wait, birth. . . . Does that answer your question, Billy?"

"I guess so," said Billy. "Did you know that Ronnie comes from Moscow?"

It's universal. Sex education makes nearly all parents anxious. The anxiety felt by adoptive parents, then, is not necessarily related to the fact of adoption, though adoption does add a layer to how we present certain elements of sex education to our children. For example, our ethical or religious values about the rightness or wrongness of premarital or extramarital intercourse; our definition of responsible, safe sex; our attitude about various family planning options; and so forth may make our educating our children about sexuality more complicated. Sex education is another case of clear difference between families genetically related and those formed by adoption.

Dr. Anne Bernstein is a child and family psychologist, who, for her doctoral dissertation in psychology, worked on a study of what children understand about reproduction from their earliest ability to verbalize through their intellectual maturation as abstract thinkers. Her study formed the basis of a great guide for parents to use in sex education called *Flight of the Stork: What Children Think (and When) about Sex and Family Building.* This is not an adoption book. Indeed it was written for a general parenting audience. My husband and I found the original version of this book, to which we were referred when our first child was about 6 years old. When I discovered several years later that it had gone out of print, I contacted the author and asked her about updating her study and revising her book. She did, and a revised, expanded (to include full add-on chapters for special situations such as step-families, adoptive families, families formed by collaborative reproduction, etc.) and research-confirmed edition was published by Perspectives Press, Inc. in 1994. It remains one of my favorite and most often recommended books for parents of young children, because it is also a wonderful introduction to Piaget for parents.

What Bernstein's studies have demonstrated is that children's understanding of adoption follows their intellectual development in a pattern that parallels Piaget (Chapter 4) right from the beginning. Remembering that Brodzinsky (also in Chapter 4) had already discovered that kids don't even differentiate adoption from birth until ages 5 or 6 or so, and that they progress through the ages of understanding about adoption in a very predictable way, parents who have adopted can link what they've learned from Piaget and Brodzinsky to what Bernstein has to say about awareness about sexuality and reproduction in order to handle the difficult issue of sex education. Bernstein summarizes several levels of understanding and attaches colorful labels and entertaining anecdotes to each:

1. **The Geographer** (ages 3–7) At this level of understanding, kids think that babies have always existed and come from some*place* like a star or heaven and that all grownups are mommies and daddies.

2. **The Manufacturer** (ages 4–8) These children have come to believe that babies are built like houses or cars, but how? They can only imagine from their own experience and knowledge. Maybe babies were made outside the body and then swallowed, coming out like a bowel movement? If it comes from eggs, am I eating a baby for breakfast?

3. **In Between** (ages 5–10—Piaget's Pre-operational) Early reasoning has begun, but the child limits herself to what is technically possible from personal experience and has trouble letting go of old beliefs, so there's still quite a bit of magical thinking. Children this age still think very literally.

4. **Theoretician** (ages 10–13) These children still struggle to understand why the ova and sperm have to get together (couldn't there be a complete baby in just the sperm or in just the egg?), but are willing to speculate. Now is the time when children are able to understand that parenthood has both a social and a biological component. For some children, this is the last stage of intellectual growth—as sophisticated as they will become.

5. **Reasoner** (age 11+) Finally able to reason like an adult, children at this level can put it all together. The young person can now understand that two different entities—sperm and ovum—can combine to form another completely different entity. Children who have achieved this level of cognitive sophistication (and remember from Piaget, some people never do) can think morally and socially.

Just as it is with all other education, the challenge of sharing just enough to be helpful and satisfying but not too much to become boring, demands that parents try hard to be constantly aware of their children's developmental and cognitive maturity levels. Do remember that all sex educators suggest that in order to lay the foundation for good communication later, it is important to avoid euphemistic labels for body parts and body functions.

As adolescents separate, sexuality can become a central issue for those who were adopted. Can you remember when it first occurred to you that your parents actually had sex together and how ludicrous that seemed? Adopted children have two sets of parents about which to fantasize. One set—the birthparents—may be (for children in confidential adoptions, which remain a large segment of today's adoptions) perpetually young and vibrantly sexual. In fantasy they may be frozen in time at the ages when the adoptee's conception and birth occurred—an age which might be very close to the adoptee's current age. The other set of parents—his social and psychological parents—are, to an adolescent, *old*, not with it, behind in the times, and definitely more conservative than everybody else's parents. On top of this, some adopted children will know that their parents are infertile, and this may color fantasies about them. Do they make love at all? Are they sexual if they are not fertile?

Fears about sexuality are common among teens. Teen culture is often homophobic and kids may go out of their way to establish themselves as proudly and publicly heterosexual (even if they are not). Some may find a parent's infertility or homosexuality threatening. They may feel a need to distance themselves from this frightening specter by refusing to identify with their parents or even by finding ways to remind them of their status as "not real" parents.

At the same time, adoptive parents are often fantasizing too. Those same forever young birthparents in a confidential adoption linger for them as well. Will their children work so hard at detaching themselves from their social parents that they will need to identify so strongly with their genetic parents to recreate the situation of an early conception and birth? Will these separating teens ever talk to us again?

It wasn't until I had an adolescent that I realized that there are clear reasons for why God makes babies and teens as he does. He makes babies entrancing so that a healthy adult will be pulled almost automatically into the bonding and attachment cycle. He makes teens so difficult so that healthy parents can let go! Adolescence is not much fun for parents. But then, you may remember that it wasn't much fun being an adolescent kid either. It gets better.

Cultural Issues in Claiming Your Child

My Daughter's Dowry
by Arthur Dobrin[1]

This you inherit:
The gold of Africa's sun
Bathing a boma of straw;
Gospel singing to close the sores.
And your other part
Chosen to keep the Word
In two thousand years of wandering.
This is yours,
You who came to us
The color of fawn,
African girl,
Daughter of Jerusalem

Who is your child? What is his or her cultural heritage? In reality all of us are a blend of nature and nurture, heredity and environment. Some of us were born to and raised in families with a strong ethnic, religious, or national identification, and others come from what my own family has called a "Heinz 57 varieties" family. Some of us choose partners from cultural backgrounds similar to our own and others do not. Who our children are is a blend of all that we are and were, as well as what their birthfamilies are and were.

Genes you and I can do nothing about. We will not influence how tall, how fair or dark, or how intelligent or athletic our children brought to us through adoption become. Twins research seems to indicate that some personality factors, such as shyness, have a strong genetic component that environment can only influence to a small degree. But much of who our children become we will help them become.

One of the ways in which families claim their own is by sharing their cultural heritage with one another. We are the psychological and sociological children of the parents who raised us—whether those parents were our birthparents, our stepparents, our grandparents, our foster parents, or our adoptive parents. Your religious beliefs, your ethical values, your holiday customs, your family rituals are the ones which your children will live. In healthy families, adolescents tend to work very hard to reject much of that, but as adults, most people from functional families see themselves as culturally bound by and extended from the families in which they were raised.

You and your extended family will be your child's family. You must take ownership of this responsibility. Recently I realized that some families who are trying hard to follow David Kirk's advice about consistently acknowledging difference in adoption may have in fact been pushed over the edge toward an unhealthy insistence of difference because they have misunderstood what adoption educators are saying about cultural education.

> Maddy and Erv had adopted Anjulie from India when she was only three months old. Practicing Jews, they had taken Anjulie through a formal conversion, giving her the Hebrew name Elizabeth as her middle name and retaining her Indian name, Anjulie, as her first. The Cohens made a conscientious effort to make Anjulie aware and appreciative of her Indian heritage, including ethnic foods in their menus, reading colorful tales of Indian heritage, ordering wonderful costumes and toys from catalogs and Internet stores. Alongside that, they were raising Anjulie as a proud Jew, taking her to Tot Shabbat on Friday evenings and religious education on Sunday mornings. Their family was thrilled. Everyone was already planning for this 4-year-old's Bat Mitzvah to occur in nine years.
>
> Maddy and Erv thought they were doing a good job until they went to "The Conference" sponsored by their adoptive parents' group. At the adoption conference they attended a session on embracing your child's cultural heritage. A panel of parents went on and on about their successes with culture camp, their efforts to bring families of their child's culture into their circle of acquaintances, their dependence on the adoption group to provide playmates of similar cultural background for their children.
>
> Maddy was nodding in agreement right up to the point when the discussion turned to religion. The Korean adopters pointed out that in their very large city they had a Korean Methodist church, and that they had started worshipping there. Two once-Presbyterian adopters had immersed themselves and their three children—two biracial and one Caucasian—in a mostly African-American Baptist church in the inner city, and were "learning to be comfortable." Maddy knew that she couldn't go this far. Their Reform synagogue was as inclusive as any in their city. There were people of Ashkenazi and Sephardic origin. There was not, however, anyone of Ethiopian heritage as she knew there to be in a scattering of congregations in other cities. There were no Indians. There would be no Indians. Maddy and Erv were angry. They dropped out of the group.
>
> Had they missed the point, or had the parent group?

This is one of those tightrope issues. When a child who has been adopted "matches" his family racially—all of European extraction, all of African background, all Asian—families face this conflict relatively simply. Their children become the religion and absorb the cultural heritage of their parents with no questions. Had Anjulie been of European heritage, Maddy and Erv would have experienced no conflict.

But when a family adopts cross culturally—European Americans adopting a Latino son, Japanese-Americans adopting a Chinese daughter—their challenge becomes to help their child embrace the culture of their adoptive families—becoming Catholic, Jewish or Assemblies of God, learning to love Italian, Irish or Lithuanian food, celebrating holidays with special traditions—and to consider themselves and their children entitled to this family heritage, while at the same time helping their children become interested in, learn about, feel comfortable with, and be proud of their racially or ethnically different genetic background.

The purpose of this is not to emphasize one as more important or to preserve the heritage different from the one in which they will be raised. This would be impossible. The purpose is to prepare these children to move in a world which will automatically identify them, label them, make assumptions about them based on the way they look. Other people of Asian, African, Hispanic or another heritage will be attracted to your children as they grow, will expect them to identify with them, will be confused and perhaps judgmental and intolerant if these children are isolated from and ignorant about or rejecting of their Korean-ness, their African-ness, their Chicano-ness, their Pakistani-ness. The point is to instill a sense of pride in our child about all of who they are.

Yes, as a transcultural adopter, your family becomes a family of color. But you are not expected to reject your own heritage so much as you are expected to expand it and to help your child do the same. Ideally you have always been comfortable with and interested in cultures other than your own. If so, you will eagerly explore the diversity of your child's birth heritage and other diverse cultures as well—embracing difference.

I wrote the book which this replaces, *Adopting after Infertility*, when our youngest, and only transracially-adopted, child (Latina and African-American) was in early grade school. Though probably better-than-averagely prepared and connected as transracial adopters (already making good decisions about where we would live and how our world looked), in retrospect, as our daughter is now in her 20s, Dave and I see that we could have and should have done some things differently. That's why, when I am speaking to a group of would-be or new transracial adoptive parents, I often find myself unpopular when I tell them quite directly that probably the most important thing they must do in the best interests of their child, if they have already adopted transracially, is to **move**, and that if they have not adopted yet and are not willing to move, then they should not adopt transracially.

Why do I say this so strongly? The fact is that most people of all cultures tend to live in areas in which their socio-economic position, first, and their race or cultural ethnicity, second, are more than just predominant. There are exceptions, of course, but exceptions prove the rule. Statistically, the majority of transracial-adopters are white, and most are well educated and from the middle to upper socioeconomic classes. They tend to live in upscale middle-of-the-city areas (where their kids often go to private schools) and in small towns and in suburbs that are not very culturally diverse. It is simply not OK for a child of color to be raised as a token Asian or Latino or African child in a white culture. Sure there are likely to be well-to-do and upwardly mobile families of color living in these areas. So your child may know a few children of his ethnic appearance, but those children will be being raised by parents who know their culture from the inside out. They will maintain ties to their ethnic groups from throughout the city or in other cities in ways which white parents simply cannot do.

You may get away with this just fine while your child is in early grade school, and you are making the monthly trip to the ethnic restaurant, participating in the annual cultural festival in the nearby big city, making sure that the books in your home and the music on your child's CDs reflects his culture of origin. But by middle school your child (not you) may be experiencing racism that he doesn't understand as racism, and which he will not talk to you about. He will simply see himself as different and unwelcome for reasons that he cannot explain by anything other than there being "something wrong" with his whole being. High school is even harder for tokens. While the black daughter of the black attorney in your neighborhood may have a good black friend from her black church with whom to go to the prom, your son—oh so popular for so long—may not be a parent-welcomed date for the daughter of your white neighbor.

Racism is alive and real all over the world, not just in the U.S. Classism is alive and well too. To be raised to feel a sense of entitlement as a member of her race and culture, your child must have the opportunity to be immersed in that culture for a significant part of her growing up years. He must know people of his race from diverse educational and socio-economic backgrounds to "get" that his race and culture are not monolithic. He must have close friends who look like him and interact with their same-race families to feel a "fit" in those circles.

And still it won't be easy for our children.

> My daughter, Lindsey, grew up in an upper-middle class neighborhood in a public school district that is the most racially balanced in our part of the country. Poor, rich, and middle class white kids are educated in our district, as are poor, rich, and middle class African American kids. A smattering of Latino kids are represented—most from poor, immigrant families to this city that had not had a Latino population at all when I was growing up here. A smattering of Asian children are

schooled in this district too, but again, we live in the middle of the country and there aren't that many Asian families here—the closest Chinatown or Koreatown is 250 miles away.

In grade school, Lindsey had a mix of friends—many white, many black. By middle school she was rejected by many black girls because she "acted white" and "had white friends." In high school she worked her way into a group of black friends from educated, two-parent families (like hers) and they almost rejected her when she began to be asked out by the sons of poor, single mothers. She had a hard time figuring out how class worked for or against her in African American culture.

It was when she got to college at a historically black university (her choice, and we were thrilled) that she was able to be totally immersed in the multi-cultural-ness of her black heritage. Here she met young people who were the sons and daughters of African American professionals who themselves had been tokens in private schools in their hometowns, black kids from inner city schools who were the first in their families to go to college, the sons and daughters of diplomats from African nations, and men and women from the Caribbean Islands. She saw that these diverse groups didn't always "get" one another and that sometimes she "got" more groups than others did. She loved it.

And it was here that she was first asked whether she was bi-racial. Black folks saw her as "something else," while white people had not. She decided to do a summer school Spanish immersion program in a Spanish speaking country with a mostly black and mixed race population. She learned about black-on-white racism and found herself defending her white family. She found herself unique as an adopted person—not just transracially.

Her experience is not "typical" of transracial children, but she's convinced that we did it "relatively right."

What was hardest for our family? Martin Luther King once said that 11:00 AM on Sunday morning is the most segregated hour in America. He's still right. We never did get that part "right."

Still there is no formula that always works for every kid.

I have friends in the Twin Cities area who are raising Korean daughters following principles very much like ours. I can't imagine a better U.S. city to be doing that in. The Twin Cities are remarkably diverse, and they have a very visible multi-generational (immigrants, first and second generation American-born) Korean community that has embraced two generations of Korean adoptees and helped them learn about and claim their culture of origin.

These girls were never tokens, attended culture camps and took Korean language lessons, and each has visited Korea more than once.

The older daughter decided in middle school that she wanted to attend college in Vancouver, BC, which has a very large Asian community. For her, this didn't work. She didn't like "fitting in" as much as she thought she would and came home mid-way through the first semester.

And then there is the absolutely wonderful family I know who represent many families I frequently meet at conferences. They have chosen to raise their black (or Hispanic, or Latino or Asian) sons (or daughters) in upper middle class suburban enclaves (where parents are comfortable) with excellent schools and amazing opportunities. This family's boys, now in early teens, are among the less than 7% of children of color in their community and part of less than 2% of the community who are of African American heritage. Their mom says that these teens have never reported any incidents of racism. She only wonders whether there will be "what about the children" questions when they choose life partners.

But, you see, that kind of comment concerns me. Does it not assume that this mom's children will marry non-black women? I'm wondering if it might not be an example of unconscious incompetence (see the Jim Mahoney discussion in Chapter 4). I'm not surprised to hear that they've not reported racism. They've lived in this community all their lives and their exotic status is a positive. Their friends' parents can truthfully say that "Some of my kids' best friends are black." But they are not dating yet, and they have not had much opportunity to meet and know well many black families of their own or other socio-economic backgrounds. I would be willing to bet that a crash is coming. And their status as cultural tourists who listen to African America-inspired music, occasionally attend an African American church, and visit cultural events will not serve them well if or when they move out into a more racially normalized community as young adults. Could be wrong on that, of course, but I remain absolutely convinced that my advice is right, even though it rankles. If you are set on adopting transracially, you must be ready to move completely outside your own comfort zone—culture and class, neighborhood, city, or even state, if necessary—to see to it that your child has the best possible opportunities to become a "real" functioning member of his culture of ethnicity or origin, rather than just a cultural tourist. And the sooner you do this, the better it will be for your child. Adopting transracially is one of the clearest examples of how adoption is an add-on rather than replacement experience for all of those whom it touches.

About Those Other Parents

There remain some confidential adoptions in the U.S. today. Some of those are public adoptions involving children removed from parents and seen by social workers and the courts to be too dangerous to the children to allow for openness. Steadily diminishing percentages are through private agencies or in independent adoptions. The overwhelming majority of U.S. adoptions—both of babies and of older children—involve some degree of openness. The spectrum of interaction in adoptions defined as "open adoptions" is, however, a wide one. At one end are birth and adoptive families who may have met once or a few times during the pregnancy, at the hospital, or shortly after placement at an agency, but who have shared no identifying information with one another. Also at this end of the spectrum are those who did not meet at all, but who exchanged phone calls or letters mediated by their service providers before and right around the time of birth. These families have few or no expectations about having future contact with one another—at least until the child has reached adulthood. At the other end of the spectrum are birth and adoptive families which develop close connections akin to extended family, involving regular and mostly spontaneous visits, phone calls, and emails back and forth between members of both immediate families and extended families, adoptive and birth. Most adoptions defined as open fall somewhere in the middle of these two "extremes." Contact happens, but may be infrequent or even scheduled. In a smaller number of relationships the contacts are through the professional service provider, and in far more, the contacts are direct.

As in all important relationships, open adoption relationships tend to ebb and flow over time. Some are more formal, such as those with distant aunts and uncles and cousins, involving mostly written summaries and rafts of pictures a couple of times a year. Some are much closer and less formal, and include birthday parties and/or holidays spent together. Some involve just birthparents and adopting family, and occasionally birthparents themselves are not involved but grandparents or other extended family members are. Half siblings may or may not be part of the picture.

With very few exceptions, intercountry adoptions remain confidential, but this is changing with wide variations from country to country. It is not now common, but far from unusual, for families adopting from South America to have met members of their child's birthfamily around the time of placement. There are several Internet sources offering to assist those adopting from Russia with post-placement tracing of and contact with birth families. Ethiopia is encouraging open adoptions where adoptive families are able to travel to meet birth family while in country and are able to provide updates. Many adult adoptees from Korea—the country with which there is the longest history of intercountry adoption (nearing 60 years)—are now returning to Korea to look for answers. They advertise in newspapers, appear on television shows, and otherwise search and are often connected with members of their birthfamily. Readers may remember that a U.S. competitive skier raised in Colorado was connected with his Korean birthfather as a result of publicity about his status as an adoptee after the 2007 Olympics.

While it remains true that a significant proportion of those adopting internationally freely admit that one of their motivations for choosing inter-country adoption is to avoid contact with or involvement of birthfamilies, the fact is that intercountry adoption is unlikely to remain a way to maintain an anonymous confidential adoption like those of the 1930s through the 1970s. Most parents, advocates, and professionals with long experience in the field believe that by the time today's internationally adopted children are adults, there will be ways to make contact with birthparents in almost all countries. Bottom line? If confidentiality is your motivation for adopting internationally, don't bank on it to be successful. What you may instead need to do is open yourself to learning more about contact with birthfamilies or reconsider adopting.

Yet Another Shifting Paradigm

Adoption has been institutionalized—that is, regulated by law—for about 150 years now. Massachusetts passed the first modern adoption law in 1851, directing judges to insure that adoption decrees were "fit and proper." Before its institutionalization, for centuries all over the world most adoptions were between extended family members or family friends and so involved openness. Then, when adoption was formalized under the law beginning with the Orphan Train movement of the 1850s, it was soon decided that the stigmas associated with it—out of wedlock pregnancy, infertility, illegitimacy—demanded confidentiality. Beginning with Minne-sota in 1917, one by one each state passed laws sealing adoption records from public scrutiny and issuing "amended" birth certificates to adoptees. It was the adoption reform movement of the 1970s, led by adoptees and a smaller group of birthparents seeking access to one another, that brought about a slow but steady movement first toward opening sealed records and then toward the practice of open adoption.[2]

We've now had an entire generation of U.S. children grow up in various forms of open adoption, and what we know is that they are doing just fine. They aren't confused about who these two sets of mothers and fathers are to them. They know who their parents are. The longitudinal research that has been done with families across the open adoption spectrum (most of it by the University of Minnesota-University of Texas at Austin team run by Dr. Harold Grotevant and Dr. Ruth McRoy) confirms this. It also shows that, whatever the level of openness that has been negotiated between the families, most of them are satisfied with that level of communication, rather than wanting more or less. In other words, being given control of making a personal plan seems to create birth and adoptive families who are confident and content with their decisions.

Now, here's where the myth comes in. Though kids in open adoptions are doing just fine and their two sets of parents—birth and adoptive—are feeling that openness has worked for them, we have absolutely no research comparing today's families involved in open adoption with comparable families involved in confidential adoptions and therefore are unable to demonstrate in any way that open adoption is "better" for the children involved. There is still the assumption that it should be, but we have no proof one way or the other that either type of adoption in childhood results in healthier, more well-adjusted adults.

The trend, though, is going to continue to move in the direction of more and more openness, and communication between birth and adoptive families is likely to become an intercountry norm, as well as a domestic norm. It just seems to "make sense" to birthparents making an adoption plan, to adult adoptees who have grown up in confidential adoptions, to professionals who have worked in this field for a long time and are training new workers, to families now living in open adoptions, and to growing numbers of would-be adopting families.

Even now, in the early part of the 21st century when the majority of domestic adoptions are open to some extent, the sealed record controversy rages on in state legislatures. But frankly, more and more adoption professionals—even those who continue to feel that promises about confidentiality already made must be kept, even those who argue most vehemently against open adoptions through the childhood years—are coming to feel that in the future records and contact should be accessible to consenting adults. And they are thinking in more child-centered ways about how adoptions should begin.

Can you imagine, really, looking at your face in the mirror every day, watching your body develop, noticing the interests and tastes that seem so "foreign" to other members of your family and not even wondering? I didn't think so. It is normal and natural for children who were adopted to fantasize liberally about their birthfamilies and to wonder how like or unlike them they are. The late psychiatrist and adoption researcher Dr. Marshall Shecter often said that every adoptee searches in some way, though that search may not be a concrete one that results in information about or contact with a family of origin.

Many adoptive parents whose domestic or intercountry adoptions begin confidentially decide, over time and often while their children are still quite young, that access to birthfamilies and the information they hold makes sense. When you think about this carefully, it makes sense, too. It's an entitlement thing.

Having claimed their children, having built healthy attachments between them, having allowed their children to test the moving away from and coming back cycle throughout their childhoods, most adoptive parents do become confident in the realness and the permanence of their relationship with their children. They also become nearly as curious as their children. Where did that crooked smile come from? What kind of stomach can tolerate all that pepper sauce on scrambled eggs? What genes created the scrappy athlete who is this tiny girl? This intellectual dreamer planted in a family of active outdoors-people—who shares that philosophical bent?

Most professionals in the field of adoption, though not all, believe that while connecting with birthparents during early childhood can be a good idea, adolescence is not a good time to open an adoption that has been confidential to that point. Adolescence is a time of such overwhelming change with so many factors pulling at the need to detach from the security of family or to rush back to its shelter that most adolescents are not prepared for such a jolting new connection. While a full generation of open adoptions now has shown us that most adolescents cope quite well with an adoption that has been open from birth or at least since very early childhood, adolescence—despite the fact that this is the time when adoptees may begin to become insistent about it—is not a good time for making a first time connection with birthfamilies. A suggested alternative is that this is a time to reach out for more detailed information from the agency or the intermediary. With the visible and vocal support of their adoptive parents in this quest, young adoptees can be reassured that when they have reached adulthood, they may count on their parents to support their needs.

Statistically it remains true that the majority of adult adoptees do not make use of open records in places where they already exist, but the numbers are increasing. We don't know specifically why these changes are taking place. Is it because adoptees are feeling less guilty about their interest, less constrained? Is it because they are being pressured by society when they aren't really interested at all? Could it be that they search in order to take control—to protect themselves from a surprise contact from a birthparent? The why is not as important as is the fact. More and more adoptees raised in confidential adoptions are reaching a place in their lives when they search.

Not all comings together between birth relatives and the adults or nearly grown children for whom adoption plans were made years before are successful. Sometimes expectations are unrealistic. They are, after all, a large extent based on fantasy and conjecture. Birthparents for whom adoptees have remained frozen as infants may find that they don't like the adults their children have become. They may hope for a parental connection and find instead arms-length resistance. Adoptees who have felt "different" from their adoptive families may find that the birthparent with whom they first connect is not like them either. They may be surprised by the differences in values and interests that may well have come as a result of their taking on more of their adopters' cultural heritage than they realized. New relationships are always awkward. The genetic connection between social strangers often results in ambivalence.

Most connections, however, are successful to the extent that both families are comfortable with them. And we do know this: that in spite of the horror stories that circulate and feed fantasy, in the overwhelming majority of cases once a birthfamily and an adoptee have made contact the adoptee does not abandon his psychological and cultural family. Once curiosity has been satisfied, most adoptees find that indeed their closest connections are not with the people who look like them and share their genes, but with the people who raised them and provided the secure base from which they move out into the world—their parents. Eventually most "reunions" result in a pleasant, though not intense, ongoing relationship. For most adoptive parents who choose an entirely confidential adoption, then, there is nothing to fear in the search that may come. In fact, there is much to be said for supporting your children's possible interest in searching so openly that you will be automatically included in the process.

Social worker and adoption educator Sharon Kaplan Roszia (co-author with Lois Melina of *The Open Adoption Experience*) offers important advice. The decision to search from the base of a confidential adoption can and should only be the child's. It is tempting for parents who consider themselves liberated and progressive to consider doing a search on their own and presenting the information tied in a large bow as a gift to their children on some significant birthday or other special event. Don't, advises Roszia. Adoptees are the people least in control in an adoption plan. If adoptive parents thought they were out of control, if birthparents believed that they weren't given supported choices, adoptees had no say in the matter at all. It is important, then, that adoptees be given the opportunity to make their own decisions about whether or not to make a contact with birthfamily and when. Your role, Mom or Dad, is to be supportive of that decision.

Parenting is a challenging responsibility. Those of us who have chosen to adopt have more than likely reaffirmed our interest in assuming this responsibility many more times before reaching our goal than do most parents by birth. Perhaps that is why we as adoptive parents tend to feel so guilty when we experience those perfectly normal days that every parent has when we wonder why we ever got ourselves into this. Sometimes, in the very middle of parenting, it can look as if we'll never have privacy again, never have another night of full sleep, never have "extra" money.

But far more frequent and important are those days when you realize how fast time is flying and you wish for it all back—when that big guy who wouldn't be caught dead in your lap any longer snuggles up for a back rub when nobody else is around, when you go through some old things and pull out a baby dress that you can't even imagine she ever fit and she grabs you from behind smelling all summery and sunny, when you attend a concert at school and actually find beautiful the music of the sixth grade band. It is these moments, common to all parents, which reaffirm that being parents is more important than becoming parents, and cause the differences in adoptive parenting to recede to insignificance.

Resources

School

Adoptive Families' collection of articles on dealing with adoption at school www.
adoptivefamilies.com/school/index.php

Schoettle, Marilyn. *S.A.F.E. at School: Support for Adoptive Families by Educators, a Manual for Teachers and Counselors.* (Baltimore, MD: CASE, 2000)

Wood, Lansing and Nancy Ng. *Adoption and the Schools: Resources for Parents and Teachers.* (Palo Alto, CA: Families Adoption in Response [FAIR], 2000)

Evan B. Donaldson Institute and C.A.S.E. "Adoption in the Schools: A Lot to Learn (Promoting Fairness and Equality for All Children and Their Families). www.adoptioninstitute.org/publications/2006_09_Adoption_in_the_Schools _FullReport.pdf

Sex Education

Bernstein, Anne. *Flight of the Stork: What Children Think (and When) about Sex and Family Building.* (Indianapolis: Perspectives Press, Inc., 1994)

Race and Culture

Alperson, Myra. *Dim Sum, Bagels, and Grits: A Sourcebook for Multicultural Families.* (New York: Farrar, Strauss, Giroux, 2001)

Anwar, Muhammad. *Between Cultures: Continuity and Change in the Lives of Young Asians.* (UK: Routledge, 1998)

Coughlin, Amy and Caryn Abramowitz. *Cross Cultural Adoption: How To Answer Questions from Family, Friends & Community.* (Washington, DC: Lifeline Press, 2004)

Hopson, Darlene. *Different and Wonderful: Raising Black Children in a Race-Conscious Society.* (New York: Fireside, 1992)

John, Jaiya. *Black Baby, White Hands: A View from the Crib.* (Silver Spring, MD: Soul Water Rising, 2005)

Liu, Eric. *The Accidental Asian: Notes of a Native Speaker.* (New York: Vintage, 1999)

McIntosh, Peggy, Ph.D. "White Privilege: Unpacking the Invisible Knapsack." www.case.edu/president/aaction/unpackingThe Knapsack.pdf was excerpted from Winter 1990 issue of *Independent School* and from *Working Paper 189* (1989). Wellesley College Center for Research, Wellesley MA 02181.

Nakazawa, Donna Jackson. *Does Anybody Else Look Like Me?: A Parent's Guide to Raising Multiracial Children.* (Cambridge, MA: Da Capo Press, 2004)

Register, Cheri. *Are Those Kids Yours?: American Families With Children Adopted From Other Countries.* (New York: Free Press, 1990)

Register, Cheri. *Beyond Good Intentions: A Mother Reflects On Raising Internationally Adopted Children.* (St Paul, MN: Yeong & Yeong Book Company, 2005)

Roberts, Marsha. "White Privilege in Children." www.informedadoptions.com/ index.php?option=com_content& task=view&id=01+&Itemid=41. *PJ's note: I believe this author really is referring to "birth privilege," but it is an interesting adaptation of Peggy McIntosh's concept*

Steinberg, Gail and Beth Hall. *Inside Transracial Adoption: Strength-Based, Culture-Sensitizing Parenting Strategies for Inter-Country or Domestic Adoptive Families that Don't "Match".* (Indianapolis: Perspectives Press, Inc., 2000)

Wright, Marguerite. *I'm Chocolate, You're Vanilla: Raising Healthy Black and Biracial Children in a Race-Conscious World.* (Boston: Jossey-Bass, 2000)

Wu, Frank. *Yellow: Race in America Beyond Black and White* (New York: Basic Books, 2003)

Birthfamilies

Dischler, Patricia. *Because I Loved You: A Birthmother's View of Open Adoption* (Madison, WI: Goblin Fern Press, 2006)

Dorow, Sara, ed. *I Wish for You a Beautiful Life: Letters from the Korean Birth Mothers of Ae Ran Won to Their Children* (St Paul, MN: Yeong and Yeong Book Company, 1999)

Eldridge, Sherrie. *Twenty Things Adopted Kids Wish Their Adoptive Parents Knew.* (Delta, 1999)

Hern, Katie and Ellen McGarry Carlson. *Reunion: A Year in Letters Between a Birthmother and the Daughter She Couldn't Keep.* (Emeryville, CA: Seal Press, 1999)

Jones, Merri Bloch. *Birthmothers: Women Who Have Relinquished Babies for Adoption Tell Their Stories.* (Lincoln, NE: Backinprint.com, 2000)

Koenig, Mary Ann. *Sacred Connections: Stories of Adoption.* (Philadelphia, PA: Running Press, 2001)

CHAPTER 7

Ethics—Assuring a Firm Foundation

There's a single clear and compelling reason why you want to feel confident and conscience-clear about all of the choices you will need to make if you choose to adopt—choices about how to adopt and with what kind of assistance, choices about who to adopt and from where, choices about the statements you make and the agreements you negotiate and how you will follow through on them, and more. That reason is that someday you will more than likely need to explain how you made those decisions, why you followed that path, why you behaved in a certain way in order to answer questions from the most important person in all of this—your child.

Her questions will be simple ones early on, but as the years pass, and as she matures intellectually and emotionally, your child will have some sorting out to do. She may hear from her birthfamily or initiate contact with them. He may see a news story about the agency or other professionals who facilitated his placement. He may begin to read about the political and social climate in the area of the world where he was born. He or she will have questions. You will need to answer them truthfully. To do so, you will need to feel confident that your past decisions reflect the value system that you have tried to teach to and model for the child you have raised. After all, if you have not been truthful and honest in how your family came together, your child can only wonder just how trustworthy you are in general.

Most of us make decisions in our lives about which we later feel a little less confident—perhaps even a little guilty. Have I ever made an adoption-related decision I wish I could take back? Yes, I have, which is one of the reasons for the work I do. Hindsight and experience have taught me that the very integrity of our family relationships demands that we make decisions related to family building with utmost care, so that later they won't produce shame or self-doubt. This chapter is designed to look at some of the ethical issues that are put before those who seek to adopt.

Ethical issues in adoption all center around two main concepts:

- The best interests of the child must be paramount in all decisions made by would-be adopting parents, expectant parents considering an adoption plan, and all individuals who make their livings in businesses related to adoption.
- Birthparents and birth culture must be respected by adoptive parents.

Making a Paradigm Shift

The first thing to understand in considering the ethics of adoption is that in choosing to follow this path, your journey toward family building is not just another fork in a road. You will be making a paradigm shift. In transferring from the process and the culture of trying to build a family the "natural way" or with medical assistance to the process and culture of adoption, consumers are required to make a shift which may come as a real surprise to them. That shift? Medical treatment is centered on the needs and wishes of the client who pays the bills—the adult who wants a baby. Adoption's culture is centered on the needs and best interests of the one client who has no say in the process and who bears no financial responsibility—the child. Adoption's very existence is child-centered rather than adult-centered. While both sets of adults, birthparents and adoptive parents, are acknowledged to carry huge emotional burdens, as would-be adopters, you will carry *all* of the financial risk and burden.

Not fair, you say? I understand. Been there; felt that. I grew up in a closely connected family expanded exclusively by birth and then married a person who grew up in a family expanded in several directions by adoption. I am wife and sister-in-law and cousin-by-marriage to adoptees; I am daughter-in-law to parents by adoption. I have never given birth, but I have mothered three children who came to me as babies through adoption and have now grown to young adulthood. Some of this family's adoptions were confidential and some have been open. Some of these two generations of adoptions have been through agencies and some independent of agency assistance. Some of these adoptions were in-racial and some transracial. Adoption has been an important part of this family's life, already directly affecting four generations of people, with a fifth expected soon after this book is published.

I can identify, then, with adults in crisis who have a hard time seeing adoption as more than a way of meeting their own personal family planning and emotional needs—whether that means their needs not to parent at this time or their needs to find a child to parent. The crisis of an untimely pregnancy and the crisis of infertility have much more in common than most people would realize on casual observation, which is part of what troubles me so about the way some seem to frame adoption as a competition of sorts. I understand how people in crisis have a difficult time not being self-focused and demanding that their own needs take priority. I've been at this place myself.

But adoption is, and must remain, primarily about the needs of children. Because children have no power, no input into the process of what will happen to them, this book has been written to provide everybody who will exercise power over babies, who will make the decisions about how their lives will begin and how they will be launched toward adulthood in families different from the ones into which they were born, with some things to consider and some practical strategies for making a child's family life the best that it can be. I believe that if we talk about these issues out loud and look for strategies for avoiding problems or dealing with them once they occur, children really will become the center of every adoption. The result will be that the needs of children who have been adopted—the most important needs of all—will be properly met in ways about which both sets of parents can eventually feel confident and comfortable.

Parenting Changes Everything

Here's something you probably don't understand if you are not yet a parent (and most readers of this book are not yet parents). Parenting itself changes *everything*. No matter how you become a parent, from that moment forward, your child's needs *will* always come before your own and before anyone else's in your life. For those who conceive their children, that shift comes subtly, but automatically, as part of the pregnancy experience. Indeed, it's that enormous shift from thinking about *what I want* to *what my child needs* that makes it possible for birthparents to consider and choose adoption.

For those who adopt, however, making that shift is not automatic. Unless one makes a deliberate choice to shift thinking, to participate in an adoption expectancy period (Chapter 13), the shift won't likely happen until after the child arrives, which can make those early weeks and months difficult. By then, many of those who have turned to adoption after having their family planning challenged by other circumstances can have made some pretty poor choices already—choices rooted in their frustration, in their ticking clocks, and in their reactions to the many losses that infertility, or being a gay couple, or being without a partner has created. Far too many would-be parents become singly-focused on "*getting* a child" as if children were a commodity for which to shop. Far too often these parent wannabes have not begun to think beyond arrival—to a lifetime of responsibility and challenges that come with parenthood, let alone to specific challenges that come as a result of the particular route to adoption that they have chosen to pursue. Those who have not made that paradigm shift in thinking are at risk for making poor choices along the road to parenthood and beyond.

The Competition

We live in a fast-paced world and we have busy lives. Each generation from the middle of the 20th century forward has found it harder to slow down, harder to keep up, harder to accept delays, harder to face hurdles put before them. Too many of those involved in adoption right now seem to experience it as a competition. Agencies compete with other agencies and independent service providers to draw in limited numbers of pregnant clients whose healthy babies can be offered to an apparently unlimited supply of prospective adopters. Special needs agencies compete with one another for public and private grant money, and often trash one another and their differing approaches to counseling and preparation. Prospective adopters compete with other prospective adopters for the opportunity to adopt available babies. Intercountry adopters compete with native citizens of countries to adopt the "healthiest" children without parents. Adopters attempt to demonstrate to expectant parents that their adoptive family would offer a "better" life for the child about to be born than would the child's family of origin or any other prospective adopter.

Too many adopting parents look for too many shortcuts to "faster" placements by looking for providers who will not require "too much" education, extensive preparation, and screening, because it is too "invasive and unfair." On the other hand, many others look for ways to skirt regulations or avoid bureaucracies by "going independent" in countries where it's well known that that usually also means paying someone off, or working with a facilitator who is coercing birthparents, or ignoring the rights of citizens of that country. They're willing to pay more money to get faster, though often inferior, service.

When an expectant parent has a change of heart about adoption during the window of time a state or province grants for the change-of-mind process, many adopters and their professional advisors take the stance that possession-is-nine-tenths-of-the-law and go to court so that they might "keep" the baby, even though they are not yet the legal parents. (This fact—that the adopting couple was not yet the legal parents when the disagreement began within days of the birth of the child—has been at the core of every single one of the media-boosted horror stories involving birthparents wanting to reclaim children that has occurred in the last twenty years.)

Birthparents often spurn the idea that counseling could be beneficial to them in making such an enormous decision. Birthmothers and some professionals sometimes conspire to keep birthfathers and their families out of the picture entirely. None of this is reflects ethical decision making. None of it is child-centered.

As an adoptive parent, wife, extended family member, sister-in-open-adoption to my child's birthmother, and adoption educator, I hold those who elect to come together and work out an adoption to the highest of ethical standards. That's because this is what children deserve from their parents—in adoption that means both sets of parents.

Choosing a Child-Centered Adoption Practice

All four parts of this book are designed to provide practical strategies for grown ups who are preparing for the arrival and smoothing the first transitional year of a child who is to be adopted. That begins, in my opinion, when expectant parents considering adoption and would-be parents do the work they must do to select child-centered adoption practitioners. Chapter 11 focuses on the people who make their livings from adoption. This short section addresses not their qualifications, but rather their business practices.

Whether the practice is in the form of a public or a private agency or independent of an agency, whether the adoptions arranged are intercountry or domestic, the core of a child-centered adoption practice should include these services, at a minimum:

- The hands-on, day-to-day, the-buck-stops-here, accessible and compassionate leadership of an experienced, professionally trained and licensed (or otherwise accredited) specialist in adoption.

- A direct-services staff (those who will be counseling, educating, screening, and supporting pregnant parents, prospective adoptive parents and foster families) made up entirely of people with college degrees in practice-related fields (social work, sociology, psychology, medicine, law) who have been well-oriented to adoption issues and who are supported by the business in pursuing regular, ongoing continuing education in the field. This direct-services staff should reflect the racial and ethnic diversity of the organization's child clients and, whenever possible, should include people who have personally experienced adoption.

- A commitment to objectively serving the needs of each expectant parent who contacts the business to explore adoption through required counseling (by trained and licensed mental health or social service professionals) about the full range of options for dealing with an untimely pregnancy—from parenting to planning an adoption—and about the predictable emotional aftermath of any and all of those decisions.

- A commitment to the recruitment and acceptance for service of would-be-adopter clients not on the basis of their income or their formal education, but on the basis of how these people reflect the best interests of the children born to birthparent clients, and these clients' willingness to learn about and incorporate into their parenting adoption's core issues on behalf of their children. The preponderance of this learning needs to be done face-to-face through a thorough and realistic preparation course offered by, connected to, or carefully monitored by the adoption provider's leadership (more on this later in Chapter 11: The Homestudy).

- A commitment to providing post-adoption support and education services for adoptees, birthfamilies, and adopting families over their lifetimes.

For an adoption's launch to be optimal, everyone involved must be committed to being honest with everyone else in the adoption. Birthparents must be honest with one another, helping professionals, and prospective adopters. Adopters must be scrupulously honest with themselves, with one another, with professionals both here and abroad, and with birthparents. Intermediaries must be honest with birthparents and with prospective adoptive parents.

A well-prepared birthparent planning a baby-centered adoption would provide the professionals and prospective parents with full medical information. She would understand that there are prospective parents prepared to deal with nearly any "problem" that she might disclose. She would understand that, since what she wants most is the brightest possible future for her baby, she can best help to ensure that by providing full disclosure. In this way she can be certain that her child's parents do not need to play unnecessary and lengthy guessing games in attempting to identify the right resources for launching their child to the healthiest and most productive adulthood possible.

> Overwhelmed with guilt about the drinking she had done during the early stages of her pregnancy, Selena decided not to say anything about it to her social worker. In filling out a medical history form required by the state, she simply lied about her use of alcohol. Her caseworker accepted the forms at face value, never probing more deeply, not discussing the importance of the information contained there for her baby and his parents-to-be.
>
> Selena's baby, Brandon, presumed by all to be healthy and fit, went home with his new parents 48 hours after his birth. Brandon was a difficult baby and a difficult toddler. While his parents loved and were committed to him, they felt little emotional "giving back" from Brandon. In school Brandon had many problems learning and operating in the classroom. His parents did all that they could to be supportive, but they did not have a clue as to what to do. An early teacher alleged that Brandon's "adoption" explained a lot: "everybody knows" adopted kids have problems. As years went by, Brandon's parents blamed each other for Brandon's behavior problems and came to the brink of divorcing.

Meanwhile, Brandon's self esteem sank further and further. The adults around him expected him to be "able" to control himself, to be "able" to perform better at school. He did not feel that he was being deliberately uncooperative, but he just couldn't seem to do things "right."

Finally, a perceptive educator suggested that Brandon be screened at a children's hospital for the possibility of fetal alcohol spectrum disorders (FASD). Brandon's own family doctor had never mentioned this condition, and his parents had never heard of it. Doctors confirmed that fetal alcohol effect was indeed the major contributing factor to Brandon's learning and behavior problems.

Armed with this information, Brandon's parents and teachers could help him to get the special services he required. While FASD are not "curable," with knowledge about it his parents were able to get appropriate support and information which enabled them to manage it more effectively and—equally important to their family's overall health—to stop blaming themselves and one another for Brandon's problems.

Child-centered adoption practitioners will make education about the need for full disclosure an important part of their expectant parent counseling.

In child-centered adoptions, adoption professionals working with both domestic and intercountry adoptions are expected to be thoroughly educated about adoption in general—about its core, which includes both gain and loss for all whom it touches, and about prenatal exposure to harmful substances, sensory integration disorders, etc. Certainly all practitioners of intercountry adoptions should be trained about the effects of institutionalization, as well as many other increasingly common potential health and emotional problems, and they should be prepared to share these risks with would-be adopters.

At Marguerite's agency the budget had not allowed for good continuing education for years. She was sorry about that, but with 15 years of experience, Marguerite figured she knew pretty much what there was to know about adoption by now. Then the North American Council on Adoptable Children planned their annual training conference right in her own city. The fee was so affordable that she decided to go and was amazed at the "new" stuff she brought back.

She learned, for example, about the statistically higher incidence of attention deficit disorder (both with and without hyperactivity) among children who have been adopted. She listened with awe to speakers explain one of the more logical theories about why this is true: ADD, a hallmark of which is poor impulse control, is often genetically transmitted. Parents with impulse control problems are at significantly high risk for unplanned pregnancies. Marguerite thought back over 15 years to the number of birthparents she had interviewed who, despite high intelligence, were experiencing unexplainable school-related problems or who had dropped out of school altogether. Parents who hadn't set the right limits, she had supposed. Hmmm . . . ADD? She had routinely glossed over these kinds of problems in providing social histories to parents. No need to set up a self-fulfilling prophecy of problems, she had thought. Were some of those pre-adolescents she had placed as babies now experiencing ADD problems? Had their parents figured them out?

Marguerite listened to the internationally-respected attachment expert talk about toddler adoptions. He stated that toddlerhood might be a particularly difficult time for children to move. Toddlers were, he said, cognitively and verbally immature and so could not talk about their fears and impressions about what was going on in their lives. Toddlers were, he said, much more difficult to prepare for a move than were older children, and just as likely to have experienced trauma from the life circumstances that separated them from their birthfamilies. Their adopters were too often given what the speaker believed to be a mistaken impression that toddlers were even easier to parent than babies, since they were out of diapers, somewhat more independent and mobile, etc.

Marguerite's agency didn't have a formal intercountry program, but they had been doing more and more international homestudies, many of them adoptions of children older than infancy. Had they been preparing these families properly? Since the placement responsibilities were not her agency's and there was no active post-adoption program, she wasn't sure.

Child-centered adoption professionals see it as their absolute responsibility to educate prospective parents about these risks, and yet this is not happening now. Several of the professionals with whom I have talked about parent preparation expressed their dismay at the number of prospective parents with whom they had come in contact whose choice of intercountry adoption was based on myth and misinformation. Initially, pulled toward intercountry adoption because it might be faster, even though often more expensive than domestic adoptions, these adopters had ultimately rejected domestic adoption because they were frightened at the thought of a birthparent being able to reclaim a child. Additionally, these relatively large numbers of parents were so deeply immersed in denial about the realities of adoption that, despite agencies' attempts to make them aware of the risks of having absolutely no medical and health history on one or both birthparents—a situation that is more the rule than the exception in adoptions from some countries—these prospective parents thought that their internationally formed family-to-be would be somehow safer than they would be had they pursued a domestic infant adoption with fully available birthparent health information.

Today when agencies don't pass information on it is less often because they claim the restrictions of confidentiality, but more often because that agency has not obtained the information in the first place—either because they don't know that they should or because they haven't figured out how or because they are afraid that it would turn would-be parents away. This is far from child-centered practice.

Child-centered adoption professionals see it as their responsibility not just to know about risks as generalities, but to tenaciously gather detailed information from birthparents and subsequent caregivers of a particular child, and, because the child deserves to have fully informed and thus fully prepared parents, to pass every bit of what they know about a particular child, and every bit they know about possibilities, to adopters. Adopting parents don't need to be "protected" from difficult information, they need to be prepared for eventualities.

> Social workers, psychologists, and attorneys are not the only professionals with specialties in adoption anymore. For nearly a generation now, what began as a handful of pediatricians (led by Dr. Dana Johnson in Minnesota and Dr. Jeri Jenista in Michigan) interested in the unique medical issues of internationally-adopted youngsters has grown to a cadre of physician-led intercountry adoption clinics and practices throughout the country. Staff members often include specialists in pediatrics, infectious disease, neurophysiology, behavioral neurology, neuropsychiatry, educational testing, and more. These doctors have visited dozens of orphanages worldwide and examined children there. They have seen thousands of adopted children personally in their clinics and examined the medical records of thousands more. For years they have maintained that age at placement, poor nutrition, institutionalization, etc. should mandate that *all intercountry adoptions be considered special needs adoptions*, and that all adoptive parents must be taught this going in. Only the best agencies are doing so. The rest are falsely reassuring parents that they should expect smooth transitions and no difficult or uncorrectable problems from their children adopted from months or years in institutional care in impoverished nations. The results of this poor preparation are growth in abuse of internationally adopted children and alarmingly rising rates of disruption.

But wait! It's not always the adoption professional who is at fault for missing information. Too many prospective adopters don't ask . . . or maybe it's that they don't listen. Some adopters later claim that they were so trusting of professionals that they didn't think they needed to ask, that they had such confidence in their professionals that they expected they would be given everything they needed.

Sorry, but as one who has spent a quarter of a century first as a consumer of infertility and adoption services and then as a consumer advocate, this explanation doesn't wash with me. It's an excuse that might have worked generations ago, before the consumer advocacy era, when people routinely put their medical, legal, clergical, and other professionals on pedestals. But the world hasn't operated like this in a long time, and as consumers, infertility patients in particular have almost always left that ordeal having learned the lesson that it's not in their best interests to forfeit control over their family planning to others.

In the U.S it is rarely the case that parents are not able to get information. More often it's that parents-to-be were so tired from the battle to become parents that they just wanted to take their child and run. They didn't want to hear anything "negative." They didn't want to be educated. They didn't want to believe that nature carried any more weight than would nurture.

> At an Indianapolis conference, developmental neuropsychologist Dr. Ronald Federici, himself the adoptive parent of seven older-arrived children from Eastern Europe's orphanages and a frequent traveler offering care in orphanages around the world, shared anecdotes about some of the families treated in his "last stop" practice.
>
> There was the well-educated couple who brought their school-age adopted daughter for an evaluation. The girl had spent her first 5 years in an institution. Her problems had not "fixed themselves" and they were ready to disrupt if Dr. Federicci could not assure them of a treatment that would ensure that this child would be able to follow her mother to Georgetown Law School. There was no such treatment. (What agency had prepared a family with such unrealistic expectations?)
>
> There was the family who had adopted a toddler who was now four from one Asian country and an infant now under a year old from a second. The mother had never felt she had bonded with the first child, but was attaching well to the second. They were considering disrupting their adoption with the first and were searching the Internet for possible adopters. (Who had approved this couple for a second adoption under such circumstances?)

Yes, it's true that some agencies are guilty of malpractice (and that isn't too strong a word) in covering up information. Yes, it's true that other agencies are guilty of neglect by not making sure that their professionals' educations are up-to-date and being more forceful in offering parents the opportunity to learn. But it's also true that some of the formal complaints and adoption malpractice cases proliferating today are inappropriately filed by people who played ostrich until their heads were forcibly yanked from the sand. They now want to blame anyone but themselves for their disappointment that their child is not like them genetically and that, by nature, he has some problems they'd rather not have to face. This isn't child-centered adoption thinking either.

> Adoption, says social worker and adoptive parent Mary Anne Maiser, is like planting a seed in a garden. Someone else produces the seed and the adoptive parents as gardeners nurture it. They may till the soil, add fertilizer and water, weed the plot, and keep predators away. They may protect the seedling from hard freezes and from too much heat. Those who choose to garden do so because they enjoy the process—though it can be challenging—taking pride in the fruits of their labor.
>
> Gardeners who work hard most often grow fine plants, though whether that plant is a rose or a rutabaga has nothing to do with how well they gardened, but is instead a function of what kind of seed was planted. What's more, it isn't uncommon for gardeners to find that the plant they've nurtured is quite different from the one they expected. Those leaves that looked something like daisies might turn out to be carrots, the blooms on the mum may be pink instead of yellow. To the one who gardens for the love of it, these surprises are rarely disappointments—just interestingly unexpected outcomes.

Respecting a Nation's Customs, Rights and Rules

Many readers are considering intercountry adoptions, which represents about 20% of adoptions by U.S. citizens each year. There are a limited number of countries with formal intercountry adoption programs. We'll talk about them more specifically in Part Three, but for now, in thinking about ethics and international adoption, it's important that readers first understand that intercountry adoptions come primarily from countries which are underdeveloped, war-torn, or suffering economically after political turmoil. It is rare to be able to adopt internationally from an English-speaking nation or from most of the countries in Western Europe. Thriving intercountry adoption programs are not a good sign for a nation. And yet, the existence of a formal system for regulating orphanages and setting up an adoption system, making it possible for institutionalized children to find permanent homes in other countries, is actually a step up from the worst case scenario for children. Some countries are so poor and struggle so hard for stability that they have not even had the resources to develop formal adoption programs. In those instances, independent adoptions can and often do swiftly degenerate into baby-stealing/baby-selling enterprises.

The most basic ethical issue to understand about intercountry adoption, then, is that no country considers it a positive to "export" its children. Even when national ethnic or religious culture does not make domestic adoption of children without parents "acceptable," most nations find the fact that their children suffer socially and politically embarrassing. Korea provides an example of several common issues which should be understood by those who adopt from a country other than their own.

One of the first nations from which children were adopted internationally in large numbers was South Korea (after the Korean War of the 1950s). A war-torn country with a struggling, mostly agrarian economy at the time, this country's patriarchal Confucian heritage made domestic adoption of its many children orphaned by war nearly impossible. In addition to not having a cultural history of adoption and to being unaccepting of illegitimacy, many Asian cultures have also historically rejected people of mixed racial heritage. Many of the 1950s-era children in Korea's orphanages were not technically orphaned, but were the offspring of Korean women and U.S. soldiers, both black and white, who were abandoned by their mothers when they were ostracized by her neighbors and family.

The result of these problems, common among countries from which Westerners adopt, was that thousands of children of both mixed and full Korean heritage were adopted by U.S., Canadian, Australian, New Zealand, United Kingdom, and Western European families. It is estimated that the number of children adopted from Korea to other countries from the 1950s through the early 1980s was at least 150,000.

Meanwhile, South Korea's economy grew, and Korea became more and more modernized and "westernized." The political and cultural climate changed, too. When South Korea proudly hosted the summer Olympic games in 1988 in Seoul, the country was proud to showcase its progress, only to be embarrassed by several media stories which implied that children were the country's main "export."

Intercountry adoption screeched to a halt, while South Korea examined its child welfare system, began an overhaul, and rolled out an aggressive domestic adoption education campaign. Today, Korea encourages domestic adoption, which has resulted in far fewer intercountry adoptions.

The fact that as a developed nation South Korea can now care for most of its children domestically in loving adoptive homes and decreasingly needs the help of other countries with its child welfare problems is a positive when thinking is child-centered. And yet there are many people desperate for children who instead see a door closed to them. *Theirs is self-interested rather than child-centered thinking.*

Who Can Adopt

Similar political and cultural differences drive countries which are still sending their children to adoptive homes abroad to set their own rules about who can adopt these children. Some countries have age requirements; some have health requirements; some will not allow singles or same-sex couples to adopt. It's easy to see these as barriers to family building, and they are. But it is equally important to respect that every nation and every culture has a right to set standards it believes are in its children's best interests.

> A gay couple was interviewed by a national magazine shortly after bringing their newly adopted daughter home from an Asian country which does not allow same-sex couples to adopt. In the article they made clear that their agency had a "don't ask, don't tell" policy when it came to placing children with same-sex couples. Instead of bringing up the issue of homosexuality, the agency recommended single parent adoption. One partner had gone through the adoption homestudy and been approved to adopt. That partner's documents and information was all that was submitted to the government in the sending country. Both agency and family had deliberately chosen to lie by omission in order to facilitate the adoption. The interviewer asked about this and the couple's answer was that they disapproved of the rule and so felt no qualms about breaking it. They had not even considered other countries where their sexual preference would have been judged differently.
>
> The result of this national article was a political embarrassment for the sending country, which then invoked a several month slow down (with threats of full program closure) for other families already in the queue to adopt.

Bending the Truth

Think twice about any agency in this country which would encourage you to lie in any way in your process. You should never feel that it is acceptable to lie—by commission or by omission—on your paperwork. You should not believe that it is acceptable to answer direct questions in a foreign court with false information (for example being led to change the name of your agency or to lie about the total of fees paid and to whom, etc.) Doing so has two results: it taints your own adoption and it risks future adoptions for other would-be parents.

Payment or Payoff?

Families adopting from some countries are playing ostrich when it comes to the level of corruption that accompanies adoption practice in those countries. Under what circumstances, for example, can those who could never justify birthparents asking for money for college tuition in a domestic adoption justify greasing palms in other countries—taking "suggested" expensive gifts to orphanage directors and hiding U.S. cash in your luggage to be used to pay "certain fees" that will not appear on your adoption's documentation—and paying local agency staff fees that would be the equivalent of a year's salary or more for their country-men. Yet, such payments and gifts to officials are "customary' in some countries.

Post Placement

Sometimes, when they are safely home with their children, adop-tive parents are tempted to give in to their negative feeling about being "forced" to file post placement reports or to register their child's ongoing whereabouts with a foreign embassy. After all, they reason, the adoption is final. They can't take him from me now! There are two problems with this reasoning. The one you already feel—it's your conscience talking—that you made a commitment, and the right thing to do from an ethical per-spective is to follow through. The second may not occur to you, but has a far reaching impact. It is that countries count on every parent filing these reports to help them feel assured of two things—that children are doing well, and that adoptive parents are respecting, with their compliance, the country of origin's culture and its value in the child's life. Several times in the brief history of intercountry adoption, bubbles of noncompliance with PPRs have caused countries to consider ending their adoption program with the U.S. Your failure to comply with this requirement, then, puts at risks adoptions for future parents and for children who will remain without homes.

The Hague Treaty

Intercountry adoption has ebbed and flowed between many countries for years now. During the last quarter of the 20th century, however, a num-ber of intercountry adoption scandals arose. Some countries reported that babies were being stolen by attorneys and social workers interested in sell-ing them to Americans and Europeans. Governments saw that local officials were willing to be bribed to provide faster service or healthier children. Businesses arose completely outside of the regulated system, so that in some cases, false documentation was provided for "orphans."

The Hague Adoption Convention on Protection of Children and Co-operation in Respect of Intercountry Adoption was developed (beginning with a conference in 1993) specifically because it had become increas-ingly common for the interest in adopting by family-challenged people in "richer" nations to cause ethically questionable practices to pop up in struggling countries. This multilateral treaty to date involves 68 nations, including the U.S., which will have its full program in place sometime in late 2008. The Treaty seeks to set up minimal norms for entities in the adoption business worldwide, to have these entities regulated by the countries in which they reside, and to set standards for the services they provide to birthfamilies and adopting families. The goal is to ensure that birthparents' rights are respected, that children are safe in placements, and to prevent child-trafficking.

Child advocates are hopeful about the changes that Hague practices will produce, but nearly everyone involved believes that the standards it sets are not strong enough to fully prevent unethical practices in adoption. Remembering that you will one day be called upon to explain your child's adoption in detail, those adopting internationally should think carefully about the countries they choose, the services providers they select, and how each shows its respect for children and their birth heritage and ask themselves and their chosen providers many questions before moving forward. For example, we live in a country which sees bribes to officials as unethical (and illegal) and yet bribes in the form of expensive gifts are common practice in many parts of Eastern Europe and South and Central America. How do you comfortably resolve these disparities?

Working Ethically with Expectant Parents

Those exploring adoption hear these days about scams which allege that women claiming to be birthmothers victimize desperate would-be adopters. A number of media outlets have covered stories about these kinds of scams, both domestic and intercountry. The scenarios include

- Women who are not pregnant, but are claiming to be pregnant, who scam one (or more) set of prospective adopters for support money. (Often adopters are later told that there has been a miscarriage or neonatal death.)
- Women who really are pregnant, but who have no intention of making an adoption plan working (almost always long distance) with several agencies, facilitators, or attorneys and collecting support money from all.
- Scammers from foreign countries (frequently African or Asian or Eastern European nations) claiming to be needy birthparents interested in placing children in the U.S.
- Scammers from foreign countries claiming to be American expectant mothers and identified as foreign only by careful examination of the hidden headers which track their email.

This is unconscionable behavior, but it is real. These people, however, are not a norm. We'll talk more in Part Three about how to avoid such scams.

There is little discussion, though, about adoptive parents who misbehave. We're going to talk about that here.

When Is He Yours?

Making adoption permanent as quickly as possible is definitely child-centered thinking. What's less clear, however, is how to make that happen while still protecting the parental rights of genetic parents. Adoption does involve emotional risk for those who would become parents in this way. The bottom line is that adoptive parents do not and cannot become legal, permanent parents until both birthparents' legal rights have been cleanly terminated—voluntarily or by court revocation.

Recognizing that children are best served over a lifetime by having made as few caregiving and attachment figure transitions as possible, public agencies have been recruiting foster-to-adopt families for some time now. Since many of the children served by public agencies are toddlers and older, removed from situations of abuse and neglect, these hopeful parents take the substantial emotional risk of parenting these children while their birthparents are given the opportunity to rehabilitate themselves and re-claim their parental rights. More and more public agency foster parents are fostering in hopes of adopting.

Not wanting to accept the emotional risk inherent in such a situation is one of the reasons that many readers of this book look instead at either private agency or independent domestic adoption, or at intercountry adoption. These options are often less emotionally risky for parents-to-be, but they put children at substantial risk. Here's why.

Practitioners of genuinely child-centered rather than adult-centered adoption know that pregnant women considering adoption (and their partners, when available) need a minimum of several weeks of careful counseling by an adoption-experienced trained mental health or social service professional, and sign voluntary termination of the parental rights only after they are clear about their ultimate decision. Then follow-up with these mothers is needed to provide post-placement grief counseling for those who made placement plans. When birthparents approach their chosen adoption practitioner at least by the end of the seventh month of their pregnancy and take advantage of these counseling services, the period between birth and irrevocable termination of parental right can—and should be very, very brief—a matter of mere days, not weeks. These optimal situations result in direct placements and avoid the confusion of foster care (sometimes called cradle care) for the baby.

Sometimes, however, women experiencing an untimely pregnancy put off investigating adoption, making a first contact with a placement professional days before giving birth or even after delivery, often through a hospital's social service staff. Most often these last minute adoption decisions happen because these mothers have hoped against hope that they could avoid making this difficult choice. Perhaps the birthfather would step forward and propose marriage. Perhaps new grandparents will agree to support mother and baby. Perhaps she will find a way to support herself and her baby alone. In these situations, because birthparents have not had time to avail themselves of needed counseling about their options and the aftermath of any of the decisions they make, ethics should demand that this mother have professional counseling and support for a time after her baby's birth before terminating her parental rights.

But what happens to the baby? Sometimes the stressed birthmother and/or her family care for the child during this period. Sometimes, (mandated in the state of Wisconsin, but offered by few agencies in other states) the child goes to an experienced cradle/foster care home. Ideally, in a child-centered adoption, that trained foster care would be provided by agency clients hoping to adopt a newborn—this newborn—should her birthparents make an adoption plan.

Most often in these situations, however, the child is placed with an adoptive family and birthparents are given little to no counseling. The result can be an adoption at risk. When such adopters don't understand the value of—or even deny the reality term of that "change of heart" or "cooling off" period before termination of parental rights, they can be thrown completely off kilter by a change of heart. In crisis, they are prone to accepting the advice of less than ethical professionals to refuse to relinquish the child and take the battle to court. And even when adoptive parents do "understand" the concept—it can still be emotionally devastating to handle a change of heart.

This scenario has been repeated several times in the last two decades—always in situations where parental rights were improperly terminated and/or in which birthparents and adoptive parents received less than optimal professional services!

> In 2006 a single woman from a Midatlantic state decided that she had waited too long for a parenting partner and did an IVF with donor sperm. She then developed a medically and emotionally debilitating pregnancy-related condition called hyperemesis gravidarum which kept her in pain and bedridden throughout her pregnancy. After a difficult birth, and possibly in a state of post-natal depression, she signed a voluntary relinquishment of her parental rights in favor of an open adoption with a family introduced to her by a friend. Twelve hours later, she asserted that she had done the wrong thing.
>
> The adoption was done in a state different from the one in which the birth and adoptive parents live. Then the birthmother was charged with international kidnapping after taking the children—while on an allowed visit—to Canada. The kidnapping case has had the birthmother in jail without bond for over six months, and the adoption case has continued in dispute for over eighteen months as I write.

Despite their claims (and perhaps even despite their heart-felt beliefs) adoptive parents are not really acting in a baby's best interests when they fight such a case. No matter who wins a legal battle in such a situation, it is the child who is likely to suffer.

Though some advocates have been outspoken in their opinions about how hard a move from their known home with adopting parents back to their birthfamily will be on a child, little has been written about the possible long term impact of such a battle on a family when the adopting parents ultimately "win." These cases are never decided swiftly. They create many months or even years of emotional limbo. Adopting parents are under a great deal of stress and pain. They may feel anxious and even desperate. Such stress in the family is nearly impossible to hide from a young child, even when parents think the child is too young to understand what is going on. Might not children at the center of such Solomon-and-the-two-mothers scenarios be best off in objective foster care while the outcome is decided? Without access to the child, might both sets of feuding parents see things more clearly and from a more child-centered view? Most of all, should not judges in such cases behave more like the biblical Solomon, deciding the case quickly?

Birthfathers' Rights

A case from the media involving birthfather rights (among other legal issues) will be familiar to many readers.

> A couple from Michigan (where independent adoption is not legal) feeling that the agency process was too long, decided to go to Iowa—a state which not only allowed independent adoption, but also allowed non-residents to finalize their adoptions there—to adopt a newborn privately. They were matched with an uncounseled birthmother who had decided that she did not want the father of her child, with whom she had broken up, to know about the pregnancy and the adoption. She named another man as the father and signed her consent 40 hours (rather than Iowa's required 72 hours) after the baby was born. The adoption attorney (who was representing both clients) accepted these decisions without question.
>
> Within days, the birthmother had a change of heart. The adopting couple would not return the baby and fled to Michigan. The grieving birthmother contacted another attorney who recommended that she contact the baby's actual birthfather and have him file a fraud action, since he had not been notified of the pregnancy.
>
> A court battle ensued, during which time the adoption was never finalized, but custody of the little girl remained with the Michigan couple. Nearly three years later, after court decisions and appeals, the child was finally ordered returned to her birthfather, who had married the child's birthmother and had another child with her.
>
> Print and visual media coverage plastered pictures of the screaming child "ripped from her adoptive mother's arms" and taken away by her

> birthfamily. No matter whose "side" they were on, the general public
> could only agree that we were witnessing a genuine tragedy.
>   Both sets of parents eventually divorced. This child now lives with
> her birthfather and her sister. She appears to be doing well.

For years in many locations it was common advice from lawyers and social workers counseling birthmothers who were strongly against bringing their child's birthfather into the decision-making process to follow the letter, but not the spirit, of laws granting birthfathers rights in an adoption. By claiming not to know who the birthfather was or where he was, and by attempting to avoid letting him know about the pregnancy, birthmothers could enable adoption facilitators to use legal loopholes that allowed for all but anonymous and all but buried "advertising" for birthfathers to come forward if they wished to claim their parental rights. Some birthmothers, as in the case above, were allowed—or even encouraged—to go so far as to lie, naming a cooperative friend or duping another man into believing he was the birthfather so that he could sign off, leaving the birthmother to make the adoption decision without the actual birthfather's knowledge. This approach is neither ethical nor child-centered, but it has continued to occur, and it puts adoptions at risk.

Sure, birthmothers might feel at first that it would be "easier" if they could decide about adoption without involving the birthfather at all. This becomes especially true when a large part of what has led a birthmother to explore adoption has been that she feels betrayed or abandoned by her child's birthfather. But the child's needs for permanency now and his possible need for information later demand that each birthparent's parental rights be transferred in a straightforward and honest fashion. Not to deal directly with the issues of a father's parental rights creates shadows which may loom over the adoption for a long time to come.

To deal with these risks, and acknowledging the difficulty of contacting fathers who do not stay with their sexual partners or may have had an extramarital affair with a married woman who becomes pregnant, several states have established *putative father registries*, which outline a legal process by which men who may have impregnated a woman and want to protect their parental rights can insure that they are notified when a sexual partner has given birth and is considering an adoption plan. These laws vary from state to state, and it is wise for would-be adopters to be aware of how they work in any state touching their agency or independent adoption.

Adoption practitioners who are child-centered would never suggest an end run around either birthparent's parental rights, and yet there are adoption practitioners who do so routinely. One western state is known to have particularly relaxed attitudes about termination of parental rights. According to a 2004 column in the *Chicago Sun-Times* by Mary Mitchell,[1] every year hundreds of birthmothers are flown to this state at agency expense to terminate their parental rights in a state which does not require contact with the birthfather unless he has established a relationship with the mother and the child. Indeed some adoption attorneys and agencies in other states have been encouraged to "run adoptions" through an attorney in that state even in circumstances where nothing about the adoption—not the baby's place of birth, not the birthparents' or the adoptive parents' places of residence—are in this state. Birthfathers in at least five states have lawsuits going in this state. If any adoption provider suggests looking outside the states where you and a child's birthparents live to avoid "adoption unfriendly" laws, I hope that you will run, not walk, to another service provider!

Because most of these cases make news headlines, eventually the children at their centers will need and want more information about them. How does an adoptive parent explain to a young adult their rationale for having created an unnecessarily lengthy period of limbo in his life? For having felt such disrespect for the rights of his birthparents as to have held him hostage in hopes that a court would disregard the law to allow them to "keep" him?

Full Disclosure

Child-centered thinking demands that adoptive parents be completely honest with birthparents. A profile need not and should not contain lies or half truths. An agreement about confidentiality or openness should be heartfelt and honest.

> As the single parent of a toddler, my friend, Moira, made the courageous choice to plan an adoption for her second child. She did a lot of research first. Since she was already parenting a child, Moira knew what it would be like to parent again and she felt she couldn't handle two children as a single mom. She also realized that she could never choose a babysitter for her toddler sight-unseen, and so it became clear to her that she would not be able to live with an adoption plan for her coming baby unless she had a hand in selecting her baby's parents-to-be.
>
> At a time when open adoption was still very new and agencies in her area were not doing it, Moira chose an attorney who would help her to find a couple willing to maintain a confidential, but communicative (through the attorney), adoption. Neither Moira nor the adopters had counseling, but they met several times (sharing no last names) and Moira was convinced that they shared common goals.
>
> After her baby's birth and placement, things went well for a while, and, despite her predictable grief, Moira continued to feel that adoption had been the best choice for herself, her new baby, and her older child. But soon the adopting parents who had promised letters and pictures began to default, using as their excuse that they wanted to control what Moira did with any pictures and letters they sent (specifically, they wanted to tell Moira whether or not it was okay to share these with

the child she was parenting). Later they made it clear that they had not been sharing Moira's annual letters with their son, and—despite their preplacement agreement—did not intend to do so until he was 18.

When their son was about 6, Moira convinced his adoptive parents to go to a mediator with her to try to work these disagreements out. The mediation did facilitate some communication, all right . . . it enabled the adopting parents to share even worse news: they had known that they were pregnant when they adopted Moira's baby, but had chosen not to tell her because they had feared that she would change her mind about adoption. Subsequently they had given birth to other children, but, because their letters and pictures had been carefully edited to exclude these siblings, Moira had always believed (with some sadness) that her son was an only child.

Moira was shocked and dismayed, not by the fact that her son had siblings—she had hoped that he would have siblings someday—but that for several years the people to whom she had entrusted her baby had been carrying on an elaborate fiction with her. She felt betrayed.

In competing to get a baby at any cost these adopters had created a far worse problem than they realized. In the name of protecting their son and defending their parenthood they planted a land mine. The son they love and who loves them learned about their deception of his birthmother and her resulting shock and pain when he made contact with her in his 20s. He was furious. He, too, felt betrayed.

His adoptive parents had not been not well-prepared for what adoption itself means in the lives of all who are part of it. Their lack of good education and their fear led to one lie after another, and the accumulation of their own lies was responsible for a nearly irreparable rift in their family.

Moira's situation is far from unique . . .

Joanne's second child was born with a chromosomal abnormality. After much agonizing she and her husband decided that they were simply unable to meet his needs. They decided on adoption and soon met, interviewed and selected a couple who agreed to openness which included letters, phone calls, and visitations. Four years or so into the adoption, after many months of attempting to arrange a visit, Joanne was told that the adopting parents had no intention of having any further visits, and that in fact they did not intend to tell their children, including Joanne's son, that he had been adopted.

Joanne had absolutely no recourse. Agreements in open adoption are not, in most states, legally enforceable (though, thank goodness, most families consider them morally obligatory). Today Joanne's regrets involve her older child. She had expected that she could be honest with this child about the baby for whom adoption was planned.

Though we hear only one side of these stories, I have great difficulty understanding how adopting parents can betray the trust of birthparents and expect to remain unscathed. Though the explanations in most such cases claim that these parents are working in the baby's best interests, it's hard for most of us to understand how betraying the trust of a functional and cooperative birthparent is in anyone's best interest. Too many of the cases like this that I've heard about or observed involve no ongoing professional support for the two sets of parents and the child they have in common. Realistic preparation of birthparents and adoptive parents by well-educated, experienced adoption professionals and the commitment of such professionals to ongoing education, mediation, and support services is a vital part of child-centered adoption.

The Commitment²

What's wrong with this picture?

> Bob and Alice met through a popular dating service. Each had signed up—a bit reluctant at first—at the urging of friends. Each worked carefully on a "personal profile" to be posted for others to see. Each was "matched" a few times; sometimes those matches "clicked" and sometimes they didn't. When Alice emailed Bob in response to his profile, and he returned her email promptly, she considered this one a "clicker" and so did he. They emailed for several days, graduated to phone calls, and decided to meet. The meeting went well and led to several months of casual dating while each dated others as well. Then came a moment of truth: Bob and Alice decided that they loved one another and were meant to be together. They decided to marry and set a wedding date several months in advance. Each worked on the details of their coming wedding—there were bookings to be made, a caterer to choose, invitations to order, living arrangements to decide, and more. One day, however, Bob was shocked to discover that Alice was continuing to date others! When he confronted her, her surprised response was, "Bob, I'm so surprised at your lack of understanding about this! I'm 40-something and the clock is ticking for me. I've had one marriage fail already. Surely you don't expect me to put my partner-finding hopes on hold because we're engaged. What if you change your mind before the wedding or right after? I'd be back at ground zero. Besides, I'd be very happy to have both a husband and a lover. Why is this a problem for you? Our life will be wonderful." Bob broke the engagement. Alice was stunned.

Now make a minor adjustment or two and read the anecdote again.

> A pregnant woman and would-be adopters met through a popular matching service. Each had signed up—a bit reluctant at first—at the urging of friends. Each worked carefully on a "personal profile" to be posted for others to see. Each was "matched" a few times; sometimes those matches "clicked" and sometimes they didn't. When these particular would-be adopters emailed this pregnant woman in response to her profile, and she returned their email promptly, they considered this one a "clicker," and so did she. They emailed for several days, graduated to phone calls, and decided to meet. The meeting went well and led to several weeks of conversation while each talked to others as well. Then came a moment of truth: this pregnant woman and these would-be adopters decided that theirs was the right match for the coming baby. They decided to plan an adoption. Each worked on the details of the pending birth—there were doctors' appointments to go to, baby-arrival arrangements to be made, classes to take, post-adoption planning, and more. One day, however, the expectant mother was shocked to discover that the adopting parents were continuing to circulate their profile online and were continuing infertility treatment as well! When she confronted them, their surprised response was, "We're so surprised at your lack of understanding about this! We're 40-something and the clock is ticking for us. We've had multiple miscarriages and a failed adoption. Surely you didn't expect us to put our baby-finding hopes on hold until after you give birth. What if you change your mind before the birth or right after? That would put us back at ground zero. Besides, we'd be very happy to have two children. No problem for us. Why is this a problem for you? We'll have a wonderful life." The birthmother broke the adoption plan. The would-be adopters were stunned.

Interestingly, though readers would almost universally criticize Alice, and understand Bob's position and decision in the first anecdote, many would-be adopters—and even a very few adoption service providers—would have a hard time seeing the parallel in the adoption anecdote. Yet the problem with each picture is the same—two vulnerable people in crisis think that they've made a permanent commitment to one another, and the failure on the part of one party to fully commit to the other has led one party to feel irreparably betrayed.

I've been putting myself on the line for years with my child-centered position. It is important for would-be adopters to do their basic adoption decision-making as early as possible in the infertility treatment or family-planning process and to put adoption itself and then various styles and approaches to adoption in or out of the mix while still in treatment. Then, no matter how large they hope that their family will actually grow, to actively pursue (the key word is "actively" here) only one family-planning option at a time. Engage in treatments. Plan a private adoption. Accept an intercountry referral. But do so one at a time.

The core of my beliefs on this topic is this: Every child deserves to be wanted, to be dreamed about, to be prepared for, for who he is and will become, not as a substitute for a child one might have had, not as a prize in a race to see how quickly one can become a parent against great odds. The biggest difference between the two anecdotes shared above is not with the adults involved at all; the adoption story would be just as applicable to single adopters as to coupled-adopters. Instead the most important difference between these anecdotes is that the various possible outcomes of the adoption story each put an innocent child at substantial, and completely avoidable, risk. At risk how?

- At risk physically because of the hormonal effects (increased cortisol and other stress-produced hormones) on his prenatal environment of this confusion and betrayal to his already-stressed expectant mother.

- At risk because his adoptive parents didn't "believe" enough in his coming to fully prepare themselves (through a psychological pregnancy), their home, lives, and their family and friends for him and him alone, and so they may be slow in developing a comfortable sense of entitlement and/or attachment.

- At risk for the negative effects of being "artificially twinned" (see section which follows)—parental stress and divided attention for the first few months after birth are obvious, but artificial twinning carries potential long-term problems, too.

- At risk because his birthmother may or may not be able to resolve this crisis in his best interests over either the short or the long term. What if her sense of betrayal leads her to decide that the falling apart of a carefully made adoption plan means that adoption itself was the wrong choice; will she be prepared to parent effectively when she didn't think she was before? Even more, might she feel powerless, in the face of crisis, to change her mind and feel "forced" to place her baby with people she no longer trusts? What if she does say no to the first couple and follows through with a plan for adoption; will she have enough time and support to find another couple without feeling "pushed into it"? Will the second-chosen adopters have enough time to prepare adequately? Will the birthmother regain her ability to trust?

Many of the most important developments in the lives of adults require sacrificial commitment, but none more so than parenting. Parenting requires putting the short and long term needs and best interests of a child far above the short-term wants and conveniences of the adults in his life.

Birthparents who choose adoption certainly recognize that, and in doing so set aside short-term emotional and physical comfort during pregnancy and their long-term emotional desires to parent for the long-term best interests of a baby born when they simply were not prepared to parent that child effectively immediately. Because they are thinking in a child-centered way, birthparents choose a permanent solution to what, for them (but not for Baby) may well be a short-term problem.

Adopting parents must be prepared to make similarly difficult choices. They must risk experiencing devastating emotional disappointment by preparing for a single child's arrival in their lives. Once matched with a particular pregnant woman or having accepted the referral of a child waiting for them in another country, unless they are able to set aside treatment (at least until they and their child are both ready to add a sibling to their families), and set aside other adoption possibilities to focus on this single opportunity, they are not committed to adoption. Adoption is not about the wants of adults. It's about the needs of children. When those wants and needs come together unselfishly, we have commitment.

A Case Against Artificial Twinning[3]

While we're talking about what ways parents-to-be use to increase their odds of adopting children faster, I'm going to open an unpopular subject among family-challenged people trying to build a family. This is a subject often met with angry defensiveness by people who have already built their families in exactly the manner I argue against here. Given that for a long time now I've been seen by most advocates of the infertile and many couples themselves as a hero of sorts—one of those outspoken and visible few who can be counted upon to defend and argue the position of infertile people facing a world which doesn't "get it"—it was not easy for me to decide to become so public on an issue of such controversy. While I'm used to having professionals in the fields of infertility and adoption occasionally mad at me when I take them to task in their treatment of their clients, to have family-challenged people—no matter how few—react angrily is more difficult to accept.

But the topic at hand is an important one. And the reality is that, having struggled through the thicket that is challenged family building, I'm far enough into the completely different journey that is parenting that I've come to believe that the best thing I can do as an advocate for you is to be, first and foremost, an advocate for the children you will someday parent.

So, dear reader, be prepared as you read what follows to experience an intellectual "itch" about the subject of artificial twinning that will demand that you "scratch it" by thinking carefully about why it upsets you so much. That kind of deep thinking is what helps us really to understand ourselves and to build our personal convictions. While you read what follows, I urge you to try to do so not with attempted objectivity . . . objectivity is the op-posite of my point here . . . but instead to listen with subjective compassion for the children you so very much want to parent.

The Issue

Artificial twinning, false twinning, virtual twinning, and pseudo-twinning are synonymous terms coined to describe the increasingly frequent situa-tion of genetically unrelated children born very close in age (less than eight months apart) to different birthparents being raised as siblings by the same social/legal parent(s). Though this definition can include children of any age, I'm writing about unrelated healthy infants who are raised as siblings from their very first year of life.

Let me be absolutely clear: This section of Adopting: Sound Choices, Strong Families is directed specifically at prospective parents; I've no inten-tion of scolding families who have already made the choice to adopt two newborns during the same year (and indeed I have some positive advice for them later in this section). Moreover, I am not talking here about families who propose to adopt a toddler or older child whose age happens to match a child already born to or adopted by the family many months before. I'm not speaking to families whose children are close, but are more than nine months apart in chronological age. Nor will we talk about prospective fami-lies who want to adopt a close-in-age birth-sibling group, or about interim care givers of special needs babies who decide to adopt their charges. Nei-ther is this section directed at those families who travel abroad to adopt and bring home two close-in-age toddlers or older children at the same time (though I do direct it at families traveling abroad to adopt two unrelated children under the age of nine months).

Not that families like the above don't have issues. They do. But my position against pseudo-twinning focuses narrowly on the unique issues of genetically unrelated healthy infants—babies less than nine months apart in age, who, during the cognitively, physically, and emotionally crucial first year of their lives, become "twins." My goal is to help parents-to-be see that creating families in this way is not in either baby's best interest.

How it Happens

The goal of parents who artificially twin babies is almost always the same, no matter how these babies arrive: instant family. It is a logical, un-derstandable goal, born out of great frustration, long-term disappointment, and pain. But pseudo-twinning is usually not a carefully thought through or researched goal and it comes from self-centered thinking rather than baby-centered thinking. Most of the time it reflects parents' nearly desper-ate need to regain control over their family planning and to "get" a child. Would-be parents who have "failed" in so many ways during infertility treatment, for example, are often unable to believe in their potential for success in becoming parents to an extent that allows them to think in the baby-centered way that is the heart of effective parenting. They simply don't know about or understand the need for emotional and practical preparation through a psychological pregnancy with each of their children unless adoption professionals take extra, careful time to explain the concept and its benefits to them.

Actually, most people enmeshed for a long time in a quest to become parents have great difficulty projecting beyond having a baby placed in their aching, empty arms. Partially because medical providers often have not insisted that patients think about and communicate about anything beyond today's test and next month's treatment regimen, infertile couples who get to the point of exploring adoption and find the waits long, the qualifications and costs creating barriers, and that adoption professionals want them to end treatment and take up more precious time thinking, talking, and questioning rather than just to follow a series of steps and "get the baby," find it just too much.

The result is that many would-be adopters are inclined to look for ways to avoid "the system" of institutionalized, licensed agency adoption and to hedge their bets when looking for a child to parent. Sometimes they avoid agencies altogether, other times they work with two adoption agencies or facilitators but tell neither about the other's existence. Caught up in the kind of uninformed, surface thinking that produced treatment-related questions like, "Well, why not put in all eight embryos? We'd be real happy to have triplets!" These couples may also think that it's a good idea to do their "last couple" of ART attempts while actively working the phone lines with expectant parents responding to their ads, or to make plans and commitments with two different pregnant women simultaneously. They often make such comments as, "Well, so what if we do get a couple of kids close together? That will be great! Instant family."

Rarely do already-experienced parents (people dealing with secondary infertility, or couples who have already adopted once) artificially twin two babies under nine months of age. This is because most people who have already had the opportunity to parent a newborn understand from experience the unique intensity of the first year of life: the vulnerability and the rapid cognitive, physical, and emotional changes that make a 6-month-old extraordinarily less similar to a 4-month-old than the same children will be at 30 and 28 months of age.

Pseudo-twinning of babies most often does not reflect an understanding of the needs of newborns and under-one-year-olds or the realities of parenting and family life with an infant. Indeed among the most common reactions to earlier versions of this material have been those from parents who had themselves artificially twinned newborns and who felt angrily defensive about what I had to say on the one hand, but on the other hand said that they would never recommend that others do what they had already done.

Most often artificial twins are the children of different birthmothers adopted by one family using two separate adoption facilitators. After all, think couples pursuing two adoptions at once, birthparents have changes of heart so often that this way maybe at least we'll end of up with one child. People still in treatment often think similarly—well treatment hasn't worked so far, but adoption is risky too. Why not save time and pursue both routes to parenthood, hoping one or the other works? Such couples stay in treatment and become pregnant while at the same time working with an already pregnant birthmother to adopt her child. A third route to artificial twinning involves parents adopting a newborn knowing that they are already pregnant, but having little faith that the pregnancy will result in a successful live birth. Finally, there are the small but growing numbers of never-before-parents seeking to adopt healthy newborns who travel overseas to countries where the media tells them that otherwise healthy babies who just need a little love and attention currently languish in orphanages. They travel not to adopt a baby that an agency and a foreign government have already identified as their child-to-be and prepared them to adopt, but intending to shop from orphanage to orphanage for the healthiest infants, hoping to bring back two. Their explanation to both self and others is that they want to "save" these babies but can afford to make such an expensive trip only once.

Parents of exceptionally close-in-age babies who protest that they didn't do this on purpose (and many do take this position) are kidding themselves. Adoption doesn't happen accidentally in the way that birth control fails. Getting the word out that you want to adopt and/or applying with agencies and contracting with facilitators is a very deliberate act. So is treatment for infertility or continuing to have unprotected intercourse.

When you know that you are pregnant or when you are offered the opportunity to adopt two close-in-age infants from separate sources, you *can* say no. We are, after all, talking about healthy babies here, and healthy babies have long lines of as many as one hundred prospective adopters waiting to learn about them. If you say no to the opportunity to adopt a healthy baby, he will not go unparented. Artificial twinning is deliberate, and the fact is that it reflects the needs of parents more than the needs of children.

The Ethical Questions in Virtual/Artificial Twinning

Today, as would-be parents—especially well-educated, two-income professional couples of advancing age—delay longer and longer the decision to become parents and then spend extended periods of time pursuing a lengthening menu of treatments which includes a variety of quasi-adoption, medically assisted alternatives like donor eggs, gestational care, and surrogacy, artificial twinning is becoming every bit as much of an ethical "problem" for medical treatment providers to address as it has been for adoption providers for quite a while now.

Artificial twinning has long been of concern to adoption professionals, who argue that it is not in babies' best interests. Avoiding artificial twinning and promoting the need for a psychological pregnancy are the main reasons that many agencies require that couples end treatment before beginning a parent preparation process. It's understandable why patients not provided with careful and thorough counseling and guidance around these issues would have a difficult time understanding a requirement like this, and it behooves professionals to do a better job of explaining the need for such a mandate.

The ethical problems already of concern to adoption professionals closely parallel some of the ethical concerns about the 63-year-old mother-through-egg-donation whose deception of her doctors (and, indirectly, her child's donor mother) by lying to her ART clinic about her age was splashed throughout the world media several years ago. Couples who adopt an infant while still in treatment or couples who adopt two babies a few weeks or months apart almost never do so through agencies that are aware of what they are doing, or from countries which have long-standing intercountry adoption programs, and rarely do they adopt through the same independent intermediary for both placements.

Perhaps even more troubling, rarely do these "artificial twinnings" happen with the knowledge and approval of the adopted babies' birthparents. Adoptive parents who artificially twin often do so by behaving less than truthfully and honorably with their children's birthfamilies in fully confidential adoptions or in adoptions expected to be communicative only until the child is placed. These would-be parents assume that deceptions by omission can have no future impact on themselves or their families. But they are wrong.

Birthparents deserve more respect than they get from adopters who are not honest with them about their intention to artificially twin newborns. After experiencing the trauma of an untimely pregnancy and courageously pursuing adoption, birthparents are likely to receive little support from the world at large. In making an adoption plan they present an adopting couple with a priceless gift. Birthparents given the power to do so select their baby's adopters with great care, looking for the parents they believe to be the most likely to appreciate this gift and treat it with utmost love and respect. While they do often wish that their children will be placed with a family who will offer them the possibility of a sibling, the majority of birthparents are put off by the perceived baby greed of families intent on adopting two babies at once. And they have every right to feel this way.

Though a few birthparents will agree to artificial twinning—especially those who have not been well-counseled to feel confident about their own "worthiness" to make careful, best-option decisions on behalf of their newborns—most birthparents who know that the possibility of artificial twinning exists with a prospective family will not agree to such a placement. Even if thinking only of themselves, birthparents legitimately worry about whether would-be parents working on two separate babies-to-be at a time could be expected to be fully committed on an emotional level to both options. So, could birthparents seeking a solution to an overwhelming crisis fully depend upon such a couple to remain committed to them no matter what the outcome of their own treatment or pregnancy or the adoption of an earlier-born baby? Additionally, given the fact that there are so many couples waiting to adopt, it's important that infertile couples ask themselves the question why would any expectant parent—or an egg or embryo donor, for that matter—deliberately choose a couple already pregnant or hoping to be any day, a couple who would be distracted by a second needy infant genetically unrelated to the first and at a slightly different developmental stage?

Try thinking about it in a framework similar to the anecdote about Bob and Alice shared earlier . . . suppose you fell in love with two suitors. Each asked you to marry, but you weren't quite sure which one would work out in the long run. How logical, how ethical, or how loving does it seem that you "solve" the dilemma by hedging your bets, accepting both proposals, setting wedding dates, and beginning the financial and emotional preparations for marriage with both suitors? Is it reasonable to expect that either one would accept this situation if the truth were known about the existence of the other suitor and parallel wedding plans? Probably not! In order to follow such a plan, then, one would have to lie to both suitors right up until making a final decision.

Twinning "on the sly" often creates worries for adopters (and it should) that the birthparents will "find out" and attempt to disrupt the adoption. They also worry (and they should) that they will eventually have to explain and justify a deception to their teen or adult children who hear of it from birthparents who search for them (and they likely will). Such situations add that much more pressure to adoptive parents' ability to feel confident, authentic, and fully entitled to their parenthood.

The Professional View

Though most adoption professionals want to offer appropriate support and education to families already created, I have found no responsible adoption providers who encourage pseudo-twinning of newborns or argue on its behalf. Few willingly engage in it. Still, there has been no professional call to have artificial twinning banned by law, and there is unlikely to be one. Rutgers researcher and clinical professional Dr. David Brodzinsky cautions that if children are raised as if they are twins there can be drastic consequences, and he advises against artificial twinning in general. But he points out something very important for us to hear: that when parents of back-to-back children are realistic in their expectations and are well supported, most families appear to function quite well.

Child therapist Michael Trout, an expert on infant attachment issues and director of the Infant-Parent Institute in Champaign, Illinois, believes that healthy preparation for parenting in adoption can't happen when adopters' don't give themselves the unencumbered opportunity to experience a psychological pregnancy, but instead the adopters' focus is on "getting the baby out of there (away from the birth family)."

> "This is unnatural," writes Trout in an issue of *Pact Press*, "and it makes people manipulative, dishonest with themselves and incomplete," reminding us, "A pregnant woman does not begin pregnancy thinking only of how to get the baby out of there (away from her uterus). She and the baby's father get to linger over the separateness and reality of the baby in this place they cannot touch. They get to ponder all the ways their lives will be changed and they get a chance to fantasize running away, as well as to fantasize the wonder of opening their space and their hearts to this new, separate and mysterious new person." Trout joins me in advocating for a psychological pregnancy for adopters—an almost impossible task for would-be parents hedging their bets by "working all the options."

According to Joyce Maguire Pavao, a well-known family therapist specializing in adoption and who was herself adopted, artificial twinning should be avoided. "It's difficult, if not impossible, to fulfill both children's needs," she states in an interview with the *New York Times* (December 26, 1991), noting also that adolescence may be a particularly difficult time for artificially twinned adoptees.

The consensus of professional opinion seems to be that adopting two children at once, adopting while in treatment, or pursuing treatment while actively working on an adoption are bad ideas for everybody: for would-be parents, for birthparents and gamete donors, for the professionals who care about each of these clients, and, most of all, for the children.

A Kids-Eye View . . .

It's hard enough to be one of a set of twins or triplets genetically related and born together. Though most gestational multiples are very much wanted and ultimately they and their families do very well, from the beginning of their lives their families are under unusual stress and scrutiny. Gestational multiples compete for their parents' arms, time and attention, as well as for all other family resources. Their early months are often marked by overworked and overtired parents or—perhaps even worse for children—by inconsistent, and therefore unpredictable, care from a variety of well-meaning "helpers." Multiples are at risk for an early awareness that they are not the center of the universe during a time in their emotional lives when they should be. Families of gestational multiples fight for privacy amidst a public fascinated by multiples. But at least genetic twins are matching age-mates and so are likely to have the same developmental needs, not to mention often having similar natural paces, rhythms, and personalities. They share one set of parents whose attention is focused upon them.

Pseudo-twins, on the other hand, are likely to be strikingly different from one another both temperamentally and physically. The fact that they are almost never born in the same month—let alone on the same day— means that throughout their first two years of crucial and dramatic growth and change they will be at vastly different developmental stages every single day of their lives. At no other period of human development beyond the vulnerable and dependent first year of life are cognitive, emotional, physical, and motor changes as rapid as they are in the first twelve months after birth, when changes are so dramatic as to be observable and measurable on a daily basis. The rapidity of these changes is one of the things that makes this first year so stressful on parents, as well, as they struggle to stay alert to new needs and new dangers produced by new skills and awarenesses. The differences between children who are two and five months apart in age or who are nine and eleven months apart in age are obvious, whereas the same two children will seem much more similar by the ages of 24 and 27 months. The result is that, unlike genetic twins, pseudo twins will be on different eating, sleeping, waking, and playing schedules, making it impossible for their often sleep-deprived parents to take advantage of synchronized schedules most common with genetic multiples to relax and refresh themselves.

Because at least one or both of them will have joined the family by some form of adoption, quasi-twins' parents' attention will be diverted either by a combination of their own recovery from pregnancy and birth and the psychological, social, and legal details of the adoption or by two sets of differing adoption-related details and concerns. Pseudo-twins will share social and legal parents but not genetic parents, and, in these days of increasing openness in adoption, the non-parenting genetic parent of at least one of these age-mates is increasingly likely to be part of the lives of their shared parents.

To a greater extent than is the case with differing aged children adopted into the same family, pseudo-twinning puts children's adoption status front and center. Being of differing genetic backgrounds and not quite the same age will make these children's unusual situation something they can never escape, placing them in the social position of being compared and questioned by teachers, peers and perfect strangers throughout their childhoods, despite the unlikelihood that they are athletically, socially, psychologically, or academically—and sometimes racially—similar.

None of these down sides for children who are pseudo-twinned can be made up for by the sole argued benefit for these children: having close-in-age playmates.

The truth is that artificial twinning happens in order to meet the needs/desires of parents, not children. As advocates for children, we should work to insure that parents-to-be understand that every child is a unique gift deserving to be wanted and cherished for who he is, not as a second-best substitute for the child one "really" wants, not as a stop gap, not as insurance against "failure." Families who do understand this also understand the importance to every baby of having the opportunity to be the center of her parents' universe for at least the amount of time nature would take to bring a pregnancy to a live birth. Professionals and advocates should help adopters-to-be understand the value of experiencing a psychological, if not a physical, pregnancy for each of their children, and the value to each child of finding and having his own place in the family's life.

So You've Already Got Pseudo-Twins. Now What?

A word of caution: Families of separately arrived, close-in-age children who arrived *beyond* the infant stage may find some, but not all, of the advice here of value. If your similarly-aged children have arrived in the family several years apart (for example one as a newborn and the other as a toddler), your own and outsiders' inclination to twin these children may be significantly less pronounced. The advice offered here has been designed specifically for those parenting two children six to seven months or less apart in age, both of whom arrived in infancy.

OK, so maybe upon reflection you agree with this article that artificial twinning is not the best idea, but it's too late . . . you're already parenting two children less than nine months apart in age who each arrived as an under-one-year-old. What should you do . . . give one back?

Of course not. No one would advocate that. In fact, as pointed out earlier, even those professionals with the strongest feelings against pseudo-twinning agree that families who acknowledge its difficulties and address them head-on are likely to raise healthy, happy children.

If you make your babies' individual needs paramount, without a doubt, your family's life will be more complex than most, and your work as a parent will be significantly more complicated than that of parents of children nine months or more apart or that of parents of gestational multiples, but you can do this.

You are simply going to need to be even more adept than most parents by adoption must be at walking a tight rope of issues peculiar to your family's situation. The fact is that you don't want to lump your children together as an inseparable pair (neither do the parents of genetic twins), but you don't want to drive a wedge between them either.

Here are nine practical strategies for parents of very close-in-age siblings who arrived as babies.

- People are fascinated by multiple births and will expect your family to want to do "twin things" because they think twinning is neat and desirable and because they presume that lumping twins together is "easier" on parents. You will need to go to extra lengths to refuse to allow yourself or anyone else in your children's lives—daycare providers, teachers, grandparents, etc.—to "treat" your children as twins. Dress them differently, give them individual toys (and rooms, if possible), acknowledge birthdays separately, etc. No matter how close they are in age, treat them not as a twinned pair but as you would treat children born at least a year apart.

- Become acutely tuned in to your babies' age-related developmental differences, particularly during their first two years of life when change and growth is rapid, and be individually responsive to these differences. As they grow older, be especially observant supportive of your children's individual interests and talents while at the same time fostering their sibling interactions.

- Remain aware that in all families parents and others have a natural tendency to "lump" close-in-age children together even when they are not twins. This is more often about accomplishing the tasks of family life as efficiently as possible than about not wanting to see children as individuals. In your family this issue becomes more important than in families whose close-in-age children are genetically related.

- The common fascination with multiples also means that you will need to be particularly aware when your children are babies of the need to establish family privacy boundaries concerning who really "needs" detailed information about the unusual beginnings of your family. As your children become older, help them to develop their own scripts about how to respond to the curious.

- Being artificially twinned is likely to be harder on same-sex siblings than on opposite sex pairs. If your children are the same sex, you'll need to work even harder not to twin them.

- If your children are of the same race, the assumption that they are fraternal twins will be even greater than it will be if they are of opposite sexes or racially/ethnically different. On the other hand, close siblings of differing races may draw even more questions from the curious, causing the children to feel awkward and uncomfortably "different."

- As your children grow, support their close friendship but discourage what could be their inclination to become "twin entwined" as exclusive friends who are frightened of separation from one another.

- Give serious consideration to planning from preschool forward to separate your children in school by more than just different rooms and teachers for the same grade. There are two ways to do this: you may decide to hold one back from the beginning (boys in particular often benefit from starting formal kindergarten at 6 rather than 5) or, if the cognitive development of both children makes it in their individual best interests to start school at the same time, you might consider sending them to separate schools.

• If there was a birthparent deception involved in one or both of your babies' arrivals, honor your child and his genetic parents by fixing the lie as soon as possible. Allowing this potential problem to exist unaddressed can and will begin to feel like a sword hanging over parents' heads. Furthermore, the longer you wait, the more likely your child's birthparent—and eventually your child himself—will feel betrayed. Consider engaging the help of a professional social worker or other mental health professional with mediation training to assist you in sharing this information with your child's birthparent and establishing a more honest relationship.

Above all, give yourself credit for having had the best of intentions in being so eager to build a family that your children arrived close together. Be the best parent you can be to your individual children. If you acknowledge and address your family's unique issues, allowing yourselves to reach out for support or help when you need it, your family will do very well!

The Ethics of Disruption or Dissolution[4]

Sometimes—but it should be hardly ever—an adoption doesn't work out. A child's needs may be simply more than a family can handle. The disparate psychological natures of a parent and an older-adopted child will put them at permanent loggerheads. But disruptions rarely if ever happen without clear indications that specific things went wrong in the placement to begin with, and almost all of those things can, and should, be avoided. A 2004 Child Information Gateway article summarizes these causes like this.

> Although specific causes of disruption may vary with each situation, the primary factors (correlates) in disruptions are well-documented. Several studies have shown that the rate of disruption increases with the age of the child. Other correlates include the number of placements the child experienced while in foster care, the behavioral and emotional needs of the child, and agency staff turnover (Barth & Miller, 2000; Berry, 1997; Groza & Rosenberg, 2001; Festinger, 2001; Smith & Howard, 1999). Research suggests that disruption is probably less likely when services have been provided (Goerge et al., 1997), although no direct links have been shown between particular services and disruption rates. However, various service characteristics, such as staff discontinui-

ties (different workers responsible for preparing child and family), have been linked to disruption (Festinger, 1990).[5]

Are you hearing this accurately? Disruptions and dissolutions happen when parents have not been realistic about the history of the referred child, when the child's needs have not been adequately assessed and shared ahead of time, and when adequate services have not been provided to the family. As an adoptive parent-to-be, what you can, and indeed *must* do to help to insure that there is no disruption or dissolution of your adoptive family are these things:

- Know your emotional, physical, and financial limits going in to any placement.
- Educate yourself thoroughly about overall options and about specific providers and programs, and then about specific adoption opportunities-and choose agencies which will expect and provide even more education.
- Make sure that any children already in your home are appropriately prepared for this placement and that services are available to them later should they be needed.
- Be sure that you have access to support—from family and from parent peers.
- Educate yourself ahead of time about local programs available to you for the type and age child you propose to adopt.
- Be your family's best advocate in assuring yourself that you have received all of the information that can be obtained about your referral before accepting it.
- Ask for advice from medical and psychological experts outside your family in looking over this information.
- Make absolutely certain that you are "hearing" everything that you have been told. If you suspect that you might not be, have someone more objective with you.
- Follow your instincts about whether this referral "feels" right. Don't be pressured to say yes if it does not.
- If problems beyond "normal" adjustment persist several months after placement, demand that your agency provide services and help you to find services beyond their capabilities.
- Give this placement your very best shot—do everything you can humanly do and obtain all of the services you possibly can obtain to avoid disruption. If the placement must end, respect this child's need for an explanation, for a smooth transition, and for a formal goodbye to those he has come to know and perhaps love in your home, extended family and neighborhood.
- This is child-centered thinking about even worst case scenarios.

Summing Up Parts I and II

These first two sections, the first half of *Adopting: Sound Choices, Strong Families*, have provided the material I think is essential for those who are considering adoption to digest before they decide whether or not to pursue adoption. I realize that it has not provided an easy read. Topics like loss, making a leap to an entirely new culture, and ethics-based decision-making raise some difficult issues to ponder.

If you find yourself needing a break, or feeling that this has been entirely too intimidating, this is a good place to stop and reconsider what has been shared about family building in the previous seven chapters, perhaps going back to the decision-making model in Chapter 3 to look at other options.

Some readers will have found these chapters stimulating, thought and discussion provoking, but, ultimately, affirming. Those families will be ready for Parts Three and Four, which will walk parents-to-be through making decisions about who to adopt, where to adopt, who to use for assistance, and then how to launch your newly adoption-expanded family in the most optimal way.

Resources

Ethics in Adoption

Babb, L. Anne. *Ethics in American Adoption*. (Westport, CT: Bergin & Garvey, 1999)

Erichsen, Jean Nelson. *Inside the Adoption Agency: Understanding Intercountry Adoption in the Era of the Hague Convention*. (New York: i-Universe, 2007)

Fogg-Davis, Hawley. *The Ethics of Transracial Adoption*. (Ithaca, NY: Cornell University Press, 2002)

Freundlich, Madelyn. *Adoption and Ethics: The Role of Race, Culture, and National Origin in Adoption*. (Washington, DC: CWLA Press, 2000)

Freundlich, Madelyn. *Adoption and Ethics: The Market Forces in Adoption*. (Washington, DC: CWLA Press, 2000)

Freundlich, Madelyn. *Adoption and Ethics: The Impact of Adoption on Members of the Triad*. (Washington, DC: CWLA Press, 2000)

Freundlich, Madelyn. *Adoption and Ethics: Adoption and Assisted Reproduction*. (Washington, DC: CWLA Press, 2001)

Hague Treaty

Information about the Hague Treaty can be found in many places on the Internet. I recommend this discussion on the U.S. State Department website travel.state.gov/family/adoption/convention/convention2290.html and this one on the website of Holt International Children's Services www. holtintl.org/hague.shtml as good places to begin.

Barth, R. P., & Miller, J. M. (2000). Building effective post-adoption services: What is the empirical foundation? *Family Relations, 49*(4), 447–455

Berry, M. (1997). Adoption disruption. In R.J. Avery (Ed.), *Adoption policy and special needs children* (pp. 77–106). Westport, CT: Auburn House Press

Festinger, T. (2001). *After adoption: A study of placement stability and parents' service needs*. New York: New York University, Ehrenkranz School of Social Work

Goerge, R. M., Howard, E. C., Yu, D., & Radomsky, S. (1997). *Adoption, disruption, and displacement in the child welfare system, 1976–94*. Chicago: University of Chicago, Chapin Hall Center for Children

Groza, V., & Rosenberg, K. F. (2001). *Clinical and practice issues in adoption: Bridging the gap between adoptees placed as infants and as older children*. Westport, CT: Bergin and Garvey.

Smith, S. L., & Howard, J. A. (1999). *Promoting successful adoptions: Practice with troubled families*.

PART THREE

Embracing Adoption and Making Sound Choices

So you've decided that adoption is a good option for you. I'm so happy that you've been able to make that leap. You may still be wondering whether you will be eligible for adoption. You can skip ahead to Chapter 12 for more detail, but, basically, the answer is that unless you have a criminal history, uncontrolled substance abuse in your background, or a potentially fatal health condition that is not convincingly explained as under control, there is very likely a route to adoption for you. Yes, would-be parents who are beyond "normal" childbearing age have narrowed choices. It is a fact of life—fair or not—that our personal circumstances and our past life choices *do* impact our family building options. Yes, singles and unmarried couples do adopt, but they have fewer options than do married couples of child-bearing age. Current (2007) Department of Health and Human Services statistics show that 68% of adoptive families are headed by married couples, 27% by single women, 2% by single men and 2% by unmarried couples.

Now comes the complicated part: You have some complex decisions to make about how to adopt. Sixty years ago there would have been many children available, but few choices to make. Adoption agencies made nearly all placements then, and they made all of the decisions for both birthparents and adoptive parents. Agencies matched adopters and birthparents with minimal input from either. After all, children considered adoptable were healthy (often spending several weeks or months in a foster home or a foundling hospital to assure this), and children with serious disabilities were routinely institutionalized. Confidentiality (a lack of contact between birth and adoptive families) was the norm. Professional practice standards dictated that most adopters be under 40, well employed, married once, and practice the same religion. Most adoptions were of children under a year of age who "matched" their new parents as closely as possible—in ethnicity, physical type and appearance, "background," religion, etc. There was relatively little intercountry adoption. There was a brief window after World War II of European orphans arriving in the U.S., but it was not until the Korean War that an actual system was put into place to help American families adopt children in need overseas. That first system emerged from Bertha and Henry Holt's mission work in Korea and produced Holt International Children's Services.

Things could not be more different now. Today, clients of agencies which practice domestic adoptions are empowered to make many more decisions. As we'll discuss in Chapter 10, today's adoptions may occur either through an agency (publicly or privately supported) or independently, either directly between birth and adoptive parents or with the assistance of an intermediary. In domestic infant adoptions there has been an almost complete reversal in standard practice regarding birthparent empowerment over the last 25 years. With few exceptions today, birthparents ask for and are encouraged to look at detailed profiles of people interested in adopting and to select adopting parents. Prospective parents are asked to consider carefully what health and developmental challenges they feel they might be able to handle effectively, and no child is considered unadoptable today. While many private agencies and/or foreign countries continue to have guidelines regarding age of parents, marital status, religion, health, sexual orientation, etc., families who do not meet the guidelines at one agency will find that there are other options for adopting open to them. While most adoption professionals still believe that race- or ethnicity-matching is the optimal situation for a child who is to be adopted, federal law mandates that race not be a barrier to the goal of permanency for every child. Both domestically and internationally, it is now common for children who are adopted to be racially different from their new parents.

The approach for this section is to begin by looking again at The Plan (Chapter 3), especially as it pertains to how to assess priorities and allocate resources as you go along. With your resources in mind, you must then make a series of decisions.

- You must first decide what kind of child you are prepared to parent (baby/older, relative health/ability, inracial/transracial) and what kind of children will be available to you, depending on your circumstances. This is the focus of Chapter 9.

- Then, with the help of Chapter 10, you must decide about the adoption process (domestic or intercountry, agency vs. independent) and style (confidential vs. open) which will work best for your circumstances. This chapter will also introduce you to an array of paid-for services offered to those who adopt, the qualifications of the people who offer those services, and will help you to decide just which of those services will work best for you.

Each option explored here has its own set of risks and benefits unique to the particular family making the decision. All of Part Three is designed to walk you through those decisions, offering you information and raising issues that will help you to make sound choices that will help you build a strong family.

Chapter 12 wraps up Part Three, talking you through some of the emotional challenges of the process known as a homestudy—but more appropriately thought of as a preparation process for the unique approach to family building that is adoption.

And a reminder . . . rather than being a "how-to" book which tells you *how* to find the particular child or the particular service provider that these questions lead you to decide to pursue, I will provide some suggestions for finding the best and most current how-to information as we go along and in the Resources sections.

CHAPTER 8

The Plan, Revisited

In Chapter 3, I outlined a series of steps for making any good plan. Those steps were

1. Personal reflection.
2. Sharing your discoveries about yourself with your partner, if you have one.
3. Discussing ways to blend your separate needs and wishes in order to select a consensus or compromise course of action.
4. Inventorying personal resources—time, money, emotional energy, and physical capacity.
5. Gathering information about the options you find of interest.
6. Building a detailed plan for pursuing that course of action—developing strategies, assigning tasks, allocating resources, and setting a time for evaluation.
7. Pursuing the course of action.
8. Evaluating and adjusting the plan as needed.

As part of reflecting, sharing, and discussing, you've come a long way in working through some very important issues in order to decide that parenting through adoption is a choice you wish to make. You aren't finished making decisions, though. The series of chapters in Part Three will help you to make the decisions about who and where and how to adopt. In this chapter, I'd like to raise some status and resource-related issues which could become challenges for some readers and then talk you through some potential opportunities and solutions, introducing some alternatives for challenges that simply cannot be changed.

Your Status—Who You Are

Whether you adopt, who you adopt, where you adopt, and how you adopt are going to be greatly affected by the reality of who you are. This section will attempt to help you understand how various aspects of who you are can become challenges in your attempts to build a family, and offer some potential solutions or alternatives for you to consider.

Your Marital History and Status

The facts have already been shared: the overwhelming majority of people who adopt both domestically and internationally are married, heterosexual couples. If yours is a first-time marriage of at least two years duration, your marital status itself is unlikely to be a challenge at all. Agencies supported by a religious denomination may have restrictions or at least extra questions concerning those who have divorced, but public and non-denominational agencies and those providing services in independent domestic adoptions will not. Whether pursuing domestic or intercountry adoption, couples with a history of more than two marriages will face closer scrutiny but are likely to make the cut as well. The agency, or perhaps a pregnant woman, is simply going to want to talk about what went wrong that first time and how you have worked on your relationship skills to support your current relationship.

Unmarried heterosexual couples can and do adopt in some jurisdictions, but at significantly lower rates than do married couples. Many states and local jurists continue to prefer the institution of marriage, as do many expectant parents making adoption plans. While the issue is being debated in some locales, not being married could present a challenge. Some couples in this situation deal with this challenge by having one of them adopt as a single. (Sometimes the other partner subsequently adopts as a co-parent or second-parent.) This is a reasonable alternative as long as you are being honest with your agency and/or your child's birthmother about the fact that you do live as a committed but unmarried couple and/or you are making no attempt to sidestep the adoption regulations of a foreign country. If your agency or intermediary will be circulating a profile, your marital status and your living arrangements should be clear and honest. Expect to face questions about why you have chosen not to marry and whether you would consider marrying to give your child the legal protection of a two-parent adoption.

Singles face some hurdles, but most find those hurdles manageable. An important task for singles wanting to adopt is being able to demonstrate to agencies or to expectant parents that they have in place a strong support system of family and friends who will commit to involving themselves with the family, providing opposite gender role models and assisting in times of crisis. Additionally, singles will be asked to produce a solid plan for guardianship and ongoing care for their children should the parent die.

In domestic adoption singles frequently adopt waiting children through both public and private agencies. Adoptions of healthy newborn children (and especially white and Asian children) are significantly more challenging for singles, so that most who stick to this preference and are successful have worked every angle they can think of and have most likely waited a much longer time than would a married couple or a single more open to toddler, sibling group, or transracial adoption. Statistically, however, the Adoption and Foster Care Analysis and Reporting System (AFCARS) reports demonstrate that single women (and especially African American and Latina women) adopt children of color and older children from the U.S. child welfare system (often serving first as foster parents) at higher rates than do married couples. Intercountry adoptions by singles is shrinking somewhat. Again, children with age, race, or abilities "issues" are more readily available, but some countries have closed their doors to single adopters so that as I write, only Russia, Kazakhstan, Vietnam, Guatemala, and Nepal are open to adoptions by singles. Just as all of adoption is constantly changing, this list is likely to change, with some countries opening to singles while others close.

Your Gender

AFCARS data shows that about 3% of adoptions from U.S. foster care are by single men, while ten times as many single women (30% of adoptions from foster care) adopt![1] Most of the barriers are not legal, but social. That is not necessarily because men are being turned down for domestic adoption. Actually, far fewer single men than women even present themselves as candidates for adoption.

Many men are put off by intense scrutiny of their motivations, their social life, etc. by caseworkers and birthparents who seem to suspect them of being potential child-abusers. It takes courage, stamina and a strong sense of self-confidence to leap hurdles like that, but it can work for the single man who is motivated to become a parent.

The truth is that while very few countries where intercountry adoption is common encourage adoption by single men, when it comes to domestic adoption, there is nothing in any state's law which specifically prevents single men from adopting.

Your Race

Though the Multi-Ethnic Placement Act prevents the fact of race from being the sole barrier to a U.S.-born child's placement with a family of a race different from his own, all agencies everywhere prefer that children be fostered and/or adopted by families of their own race and ethnicity where possible. A few domestic adoption agencies do a very good job of recruiting from among non-white populations so that they routinely place black children with black parents, Hispanic children with Hispanic parents, Asian children with Asian parents, and so on. Most domestic agencies, however, are not so good at these recruitment issues, so that many children of color are placed with white parents. Similarly, intercountry adoption results in far more trans-racial than in-racial placements, with the preponderance of adopters being Caucasian. Asian Americans wanting to adopt are often adopting internationally from both Asian and non-Asian countries. Most agencies specializing in adoptions from African nations have mostly white clients, with a smattering of African American clients.

Being a person of color or an interracial couple can actually be a plus for those wanting to adopt within the U.S. There are adoptable European American, African American, and Latino children from newborns to teenagers available through the public and private agency systems, as well as independently right here in the United States. Indeed, African Americans should know that there are U.S. adoption attorneys with large practices who are placing U.S.-born children of color with white families in Canada and in Europe because they have not recruited enough families of color with whom to place these children. Families of these ethnicities are also recruited and welcomed by public agencies responsible for finding homes for older children of these ethnicities. Here's one place where being a person or a couple of color can serve as a distinct advantage, so stand up and identify yourselves.

The same is less true for people from Asian American backgrounds. Fewer children of Asian heritage than other ethnicities, including white, become available to be adopted in the U.S. This is in part because statistically fewer U.S. Asian families live in poverty, which often draws children into the public welfare system. Additionally, American Asians are statistically better educated and so may have better access to birth control. When healthy babies of Asian extraction present as adoptable, they are often bi-racial. This is one reason why ethnically Asian adopters often turn to intercountry adoption, where children of many, but certainly not all, Asian ethnicities are readily adoptable. Still, fully Asian and interracial families considering adoption would do well to carefully explore agencies and attorneys based in cities with large Asian communities in their quest to adopt.

As is recommend in every instance, adopters are wise to begin by talking to local agencies and private adoption practitioners, but if what you hear from them is discouraging, begin to contact agencies and independent adoption practitioners in cities and states with larger populations of your race. For all practical purposes, race need not be a barrier to successful and fairly quick family building.

Your Sexual Orientation

People who are gay or lesbian have adopted as singles for years in a don't-ask-don't-tell climate. Florida is the only state which currently (2007) has a complete ban on gays/lesbians adopting. All other states allow—at least in practice, if not clearly written in statute—non-cohabiting singles who are gay or lesbian to adopt, but are less clear about whether or not gay or lesbian domestic partners can do second-parent adoptions. Many states are currently debating whether to ban adoptions by gay/lesbian couples. There are several excellent websites listed in the Resources section following this chapter which stay up-to-date on current legal status for homosexual parents-to-be.

It is important to realize, however, that lying about sexual orientation is not in any would-be parent's best interests. It is not considered lying to omit information, but when directly asked about sexual orientation, you must be honest or risk being accused of fraud and having an adoption disrupted.

The bottom line is that openly gay and lesbian people—both singles and couples—may find it more challenging to adopt than do heterosexual couples and singles, but they *do* adopt. These would-be parents work with agencies and intermediaries friendly to their sexual orientation to adopt same-race babies (after longish waits) and babies of other races, and to adopt older children and sibling groups through the public agency systems of many states, often starting out their journey to parenthood through fostering. They adopt internationally, too, but in a limited number of countries.

Your Religion

Only when an agency accepts no public assistance (from, for example, United Way or state or federal government) can it refuse to work with people of other religions. Still, religiously oriented agencies tend to recruit more birthparents (who may make ultimate parental choices) and adoptive families of their denominations. Christians adopt readily and easily both domestically and internationally in the United States. Many denominations—Catholic, Lutheran, Baptist, Methodist, LDS, etc.—sponsor their own adoption agencies. There are, additionally, numerous Christian agencies not identified with a specific church, some of them quite large—the network of Bethany Christian Services agencies, for example. Jewish Social Services agencies exist in virtually every city with a sizable Jewish population, though many of these agencies either no longer provide adoption services at all, place only disabled children of Jewish heritage, or are primarily offering intercountry adoptions to Jewish couples. Many Jewish families, as well as agnostic or atheist families, find independent adoption and intercountry adoption faster routes to family building.

In Islam, children are cared for under the rules of kafala, which mandates not an adoption which terminates birth family connections, but rather a guardianship under which a child's surname not be changed, relationships with blood kin remain open, and any inherited money from birthfamily not be intermingled with the funds of the guardianship. Assuring that the child is raised in Islam is imperative. For these reasons, formal institutional adoption is unusual within American Muslim families, and trans-religious adoptions are not permitted. Intercountry adoptions from countries with Islamic governments do happen occasionally, but are extremely rare—even for American Muslim families operating under the rules of kafala.[2]

Your Age

Private agencies often set age restrictions for those they will accept as clients. Sometimes these rules relate to their not wanting to put the children they represent at risk for early loss of yet another parent. Just as frequently, however, such restrictions are imposed simply as one way to keep the size of an agency's list of applicants manageable. After all, the rules of supply and demand come into play when agencies are working with a limited supply of healthy newborns versus enormous numbers of adults interested in adopting those newborns.

For either of these reasons, single and coupled applicants who are much beyond 40 may begin to find that both domestic agencies and many foreign countries will consider them to have "aged out" of adoption. And yet older parents do adopt. A few countries in the world have great respect for older parents and actually bar younger would-be parents from adopting rather than older applicants. In the U.S. often older parents adopt independently. They adopt children considered harder to place because of their physical, emotional or cognitive challenges, their age or race, or the fact that they come as a group of siblings.

"May-December" partnerships, where one parent-to-be is 30-something and the other is over 50, usually find fewer barriers than do older singles. Many (but not all) agencies and many (but not all) countries pay closer attention to the age of the younger parent than the older. They will, of course, expect such couples to make practical and financial plans for the possibility of a widowed younger spouse.

Your Health

Every route to adoption will require that the applicants have a full physical exam and share medical history and status as part of the home-study documentation. If chronic health or abilities issues are part of your profile, you will want your doctors and other health and disability support professionals on your team when it comes to endorsing your ability to parent effectively despite any challenges you bring to the process of adoption.

People with disabilities (physical or mental disabilities which substantially inhibit or impair one or more major life activities) are protected under the Americans with Disabilities Act (ADA) when it comes to access in employment and many other aspects of their lives. The ADA applies to both public and private agencies (the second because they are seen as "public accommodations"). Court cases, however, have so far determined that agencies can use clear and narrow "safety" and "public threat" issues to bar some people with disabilities from adopting.[3]

The ADA does not apply to intercountry adoptions, however. Each country takes its own stand about the relative health of parents it approves to adopt its children. Some countries have stricter guidelines about the health of prospective adopters than others. China, for example, announced in 2007 that it would no longer allow adoptions by people who had been on anti-depressant or anti-anxiety medications for two or more years, people above a body mass index of 40 or people who are blind, facially deformed, or have paralyzed limbs. Already in a few parts of the U.K, domestic placement agencies are refusing to place children under age 5 with smokers. This could be expected to become an issue in other parts of the world as well.

While such limitation issues may make many Americans fume with indignation, it is important to keep in mind what has been mentioned before: that a country with enough children in need of permanency that it is forced to "export" them for adoption has both the right—and many would say the cultural responsibility—to set standards that respect its own people's culture.

Those with health concerns, whether those concerns are "just" disabling or they are life-threatening, should understand that the key to adopting successfully is in the ability to convince social workers and/or expectant parents that they have carefully thought through the impact of their health on the child they want to adopt and have made careful, specific plans and accommodations for parenting that child successfully and safely. Such prospective adopters will want to demonstrate how their home and their lifestyle accommodate these issues, that they have made arrangements for assistance with care as needed, that partners have carefully thought through and planned for how a surviving partner might manage parenting issues should the other partner die, etc.

All of this requires carefully child-centered thinking. For example, it is important to understand why most adoption professionals will require that those who have had treatment for life-threatening diseases such as cancer wait to begin a matching process after they have been in remission past what medical professionals consider to be "cure" status—often three to five years. Child-centered thinking also requires those who are at high risk for recurrence of a chronic illness and/or early death to carefully consider how the impact of their immersion in treatment, as well as their possible death, could affect the children they wish to parent. Children in need of adoption have already experienced the loss of a parent. Is it reasonable, therefore, for a person at substantial risk of a long debilitating illness to deliberately ask that such a child be subjected to substantial risk of another loss of this magnitude?

Mental Health

When adopting domestically, most people with managed and controlled mental health issues, such as chronic depression, anxiety, obsessive compulsive disorders, and bi-polar disorders, will find that most agencies are open to working with them and to helping their expectant parent clients move beyond myth and stereotypes. But even professionals such as social workers and attorneys, like the general public, are sometimes constricted by their own prejudices fed by myth. The support and endorsement of your physician and therapist can be critical to making productive connections with adoption professionals.

When it comes to intercountry adoption, let me remind you that every country makes its own rules, and that these change frequently. Doing necessary research will prevent your being shocked by a situation such as China's 2007 decision not to place its children with parents with a history of more than two years on mental health-related medications.

Substance Abuse

Would-be parents with a history of *past* drug abuse or alcoholism can and do adopt, but with added layers of questions and conversations to be expected. Once again, a key to success is finding treatment professionals willing to vouch for your progress in the life-long process of recovery.

You and the Law

A criminal background check is a routine part of the homestudy documentation in most states and in all intercountry adoption. The primary purpose of this check is to assure that would-be adopters have no history of sexual predation with children. Convictions for other crimes will, of course, be examined and discussed at length, but will not necessarily prevent a person from adopting. Factors, such as whether a criminal conviction was a part of a pattern or a result of a single act, age at conviction, and rehabilitation status, will often be considered. Indeed, if your criminal background check would reveal a single conviction of relatively minor nature or problems only before you reached age 21, it makes sense to contact an attorney about the possibility of having these convictions expunged, wiping the slate clean. Many now-successful people with difficult histories in their youth have much to bring to the table in parenting children in danger of making wrong turns in their journey to adulthood.

We will talk more about all of these issues that are a part of who you are as a candidate for adoption in the next chapter, in thinking about what child you might wish to adopt versus children who are likely to be available for adoption.

Money Matters

Perhaps no issue incites more debate than the issue of fees in adoption, and the rhetoric involved in such a debate is schizophrenic at best. People working in adoptions are highly offended at the mention of the word purchase when applied to the placement of a baby, yet it is a fact that healthy, white infants command the highest fees. Minority children, older children, and children with disabilities wait to be adopted, and in order to promote their adoptions, agencies are forced to recruit parents from outside of their approved-and-waiting lists, to waive fees entirely, and to ensure that children with problems which will require professional intervention and assistance are accompanied by federal adoption subsidies.

In the real world of adoption the healthy white babies most traditional adopters seek are a valuable commodity. Because the pool of waiting parents for healthy Caucasian babies is large and the supply small, there is competition among prospective adopters. Agencies and intermediaries placing babies can be picky about qualifications and unyielding about fees, which can be, and are, high enough to cover the costs of these adoptions as well as to subsidize other less lucrative services.

Public agencies usually handle both infant adoptions and the adoption of older children, yet because public agencies are able to offer birthparent clients only clinic-based and publicly-assisted medical care, far more birthparents seek the help of private agencies or of non-agency intermediaries (adoption consultants, physicians, attorneys), who, when local law allows, are often able to offer private medical care, support, and living assistance.

Private agencies and non-agency intermediaries, on the other hand, are far less often involved in the placement of older children or sibling groups, and they often refer babies born with disabilities to the public sector agencies. This, coupled with the fact that most older adoptable children become available because their families have become, in some way, embroiled in the public "system," means that public agencies are saddled with enormous expenses that private agencies rarely experience. Who pays for these expenses?

Many public agencies do not charge fees at all and are instead supported by public funds—your tax dollars. Nearly all private agencies do charge fees, but the size of the fee and the method by which it is determined vary considerably. Private agency fees may be based on a flat across-the-board sum for all applicants, on direct costs of services, or on a percentage of income with or without a ceiling. At some agencies fees include everything from the homestudy through the legal costs of finalization, which will be processed by the agency's law firm. At other agencies each service is paid for separately, beginning with an application fee and following up with a specific fee for each counseling session or group workshop.

The allocation of funds collected from placement fees varies considerably from agency to agency, too. At some agencies, fees become part of a general fund which supports the expenses of a wide range of community and social services. At other agencies, adoption fees remain exclusively within the adoption program. Some agencies further divide their adoption program so that funds collected from adoption fees are not applied to expenses incurred in providing services to birthparents who do not make adoption plans. However, it is more common that the services supplied to the over 95% of birthparents who do not make adoption plans are paid for from the fees collected from those who adopt the children of the 5% of birthparents who do choose adoption.

Agencies usually try to explain that there are expenses in adoption services and, since somebody must pay for them, why not adopters, who benefit most from their services? On the surface this is logical, but adopters ask themselves, how do we benefit from services supplied to non-placing parents? Of course there are expenses in adoption, but no one involved in special needs adoption suggests that adopting families should reimburse custodial agencies for several years of counseling and foster care in making these placements, so at what age or in what condition do children cease to become worth paying for? How is it logical that a percentage of income is a "fair" assessment as a placement fee when parents by birth do not pay for the professional assistance they use in their children's arrival in this manner?

Few adopters would argue that someone has to pay for services. Few would argue that direct service provided to them and to their family should be paid for by them. There is seldom an argument about whether or not adopters should pay for their own counseling time, their own psychological testing, and most would extend this same logic to include their assuming their own child's birthparents' counseling fees, medical expenses, and legal fees. But many adopters come to the personal limits of their dignity when asked to carry the financial burden for children not placed for adoption or for placements other than their own. They experience this as one more punishment for their infertility and it becomes yet one more source of unvalidated anger.

Indeed, it is this very issue which drives increasing numbers of prospective adopters of infants out of the system of licensed public and private agencies and into the unchecked world of independent adoption, where flat fees or percentage of income fees are atypical, and are, in fact, often indicative of an unethical practice. In general, most professionals feel that only direct reimbursement-for-service charges are ethical in independent adoptions, and these fees may be paid to several service suppliers, from physicians and hospitals to social workers/counselors/educators (birthparents' and adopting couple's), to attorneys (birthparents' and adopters').

Perhaps no aspect of the relationship between prospective adopters and the intermediaries with whom they work is more uniformly uncomfortable for everyone involved than is the issue of finances. Caseworkers don't like to talk about it, often to the extent that they gloss over this topic in their presentations to families, resulting in misunderstandings. Families don't like to think about it, as it points out another way in which they are singled out as very different from families formed by birth. Agency directors are almost always people firmly committed to human services, so that they care very much about the negative impact of fees on their clients, but then again, fees are their programs' life blood.

Because the issue of fees is so complex and difficult, this is one more area which should be clearly discussed and well-presented in written form by an adoption agency or service provider. Financial information should be shared with prospective adopters at the very beginning of a potential working relationship with an agency or intermediary.

The issue of fees does not end at placement. Feelings about the process of adoption color our lives into the future. Children eventually ask questions. Consider several examples.

> Pam and Dan adopted a healthy white baby from a highly respected religiously based adoption agency. Their fee was a percentage of their combined income for one year, and amounted to a five digit sum. Two years later they began the adoption process again. Feeling much more self-assured about their parenting abilities, they broadened their thinking and began to ask about minority children and children with disabilities, and decided that they could handle this. The social worker profiled a baby—a beautiful Hispanic daughter with a minor correctable medical problem—and they were thrilled. But then she added, "And because this baby would be more difficult to place, we are prepared to adjust the fee to $7500." Their answer was yes!
>
> It was months later that they began to feel uncomfortable and indignant. Their much-loved daughter was a bargain basement baby? On sale because of her color and a slight imperfection? What message did this send to her and to her older brother? If asked, how would they explain it? They sent a donation check to the agency for the other $7500.
>
> Tom and Caroline, an African-American couple, had dealt with infertility for a long time. They wanted to parent, and, in the community in which they were raised, informal adoptions of kids in need of parenting by extended family members or friends is a warmly embraced tradition. But Caroline and Tom, upwardly mobile and middle class, thought that they wanted to do it "right." They would go through a homestudy. They would adopt confidentially. They would have assurances about the birthmother's prenatal care.
>
> They approached a large local agency about adopting through the process. They were shocked to hear about fees at all. For both Tom and Caroline this idea stirred up deeply rooted feelings about people as commodities. They couldn't do it—buy a baby. Several months later, they adopted privately after making a less formal connection through their pastor.

These are the uncomfortable, uncompromising facts. There are few clear answers to the harsh realities of adoption's financial complexities for agencies or for clients. Adoption is a big money business, and prospective adopters need to find a way to deal with this set of realities.

I struggled to decide where the material which follows belonged in *Adopting: Sound Choices, Strong Families*, and ultimately decided that, while it could have fit in the chapter on ethics, it fit best where you would be thinking about financial issues in adoption.

Money questions produce all kinds of concerns, misunderstandings and even long term "issues" for adoptive families, and those issues are not all about how to find the cash to pay for an adoption. The very fact that adoption costs money at all is a political hot potato. On the one hand, society and its laws claim that adoption is about serving the best interests of children in need of replacement parents, but at the same time society at large (in the form of the government) is unwilling to fund adoption fully by making adoption available only through tax-supported public agencies. If it did, the playing field for would-be adoptive parents would be better leveled, and children could never be seen by themselves or by the world outside to be commoditized because of their age, race, or health and abilities.

Money is an issue in adoption, and the result is that within the culture of adoption it can almost be said that there are two or even more "classes" of adoptive families and their children who have been adopted.

On the one hand there are those families who adopt through the public child welfare system. Because the government pays for these services to families and waiting children, their adoptions cost little to nothing. In fact, many of these families receive subsidies for the long-term care of their children. That's because the children adopted are rarely healthy newborns, and instead are considered to have "special needs" because of their race, age, health/abilities status, the fact that they are part of a sibling group, or because they have been abused and neglected—or some combination of this long list. Within this group of families there are subgroups, which include people who choose this route because it is what they can afford, people who choose this route because they believe that they should try to make a difference in the lives of waiting children within their own country, people who foster in order to adopt, people who foster as a career or life mission and sometimes adopt, etc. Sometimes these motivations for adoption collide.

> The week before I wrote this chapter, I had a conversation with a father who fostered to adopt. He and his wife chose this route not because they couldn't afford private agency or independent adoption, rather because they liked the idea that they would be adopting kids who really needed them. They fostered a sibling pair, and the public agency had thoughtfully connected them to the agency's support group for fostering and adoptive parents. They eagerly attended.
>
> But they came away from that meeting feeling that, while they wanted and needed support, they didn't "belong" there. Most of those in attendance that particular night were "professional foster parents."

Their role—an important and really needed one—is not to adopt children who need parenting, but to nurture children and keep them safe while the system decides whether they will go back to their birth family or be adopted. Most of these parents expect that these relationships won't be permanent, though sometimes they do adopt when a child they fostered becomes available for adoption.

The world of these parents seemed so different to this previously childless couple. Most had rather large families that included children by birth and children by adoption. Much of the conversation had been about subsidy payment shortages, kids that simply "had to be moved," and more about the "business" side of special needs adoption. Theirs is, to this foster-to-adopt father, another whole world with which he has little in common. Where does he "belong" to get the support he and his wife want and need?

On the other hand, there are those families who adopt through private agencies or through independent adoptions. Some of these families adopt domestically, often motivated by wanting to adopt a newborn, wanting that baby to match them racially, and sometimes because they feel pulled to know and form some sort of relationship with their child's birthfamily. Others using private agencies are adopting internationally and, in addition to wanting to make a difference in the life of a child suffering circumstances likely to be far worse than the circumstances of kids in U.S. foster care, they may be pulled to a particular country's culture and feel that this will be a faster route than U.S. adoption. Still others adopt internationally, in part, to avoid the issue of openness in adoption. All of these families—including those who will be adopting children known to have significant special needs—will be spending tens of thousands of dollars to adopt.

This wide variation in motivations and in investment of time, money, and emotional energy makes clear that adoption is not just its own world, but perhaps its own universe and much of the division has something to do with money.

As a member of a multi-generational adoption-grown family, I find the issue of money and adoption particularly distasteful. I've witnessed money issues as they have affected members of my own family, and in every case what I observed caused me to feel some element of embarrassment, and ultimately, as you will read, shame. The following progression of four anecdotes may help you understand my conflict, which is representative, I think, of how many adopting parents feel.

When Dave and I first actively pursued adoption we were in our 20s and married six or seven years. The first appointment we were able to get was with a venerable old agency (and the equally venerable and old social worker who ran the place) in the city where we then lived. We spent about an hour in her office while she talked about how the process of adopting a baby worked. She asked us a series of questions, handed us an application, and we left.

As we walked to the car, I was as excited as I could be, thinking about how quickly I could get that paperwork filled out and returned. Imagine my shock when Dave slammed the car door, turned to me and angrily blurted, "No way am I adopting through that agency!"

In shock, I listened to his tirade. What he had heard and what I had heard in the same meeting with the same person had been received totally differently. He remembered that the questions all concerned our finances—what we earned, what we owned, what we had saved, how much we were prepared to pay. I had heard those questions, yet I thought I remembered more.

But here was the difference . . . Dave had been adopted himself as an infant, and the issue of paying money to adopt a child had felt quite personal. Raised in a family where adoption was an open subject, he thought he "got it," but none of those conversations had ever involved how much it had cost his parents to adopt him, an older brother who had died before Dave was even born, and his younger sister. He was shocked and offended by what felt like his commodification—something adoption-related that he had never faced before.

He needed to process this issue, and he did, successfully (much to my relief), but when we adopted some three years later, it was not through this agency.

My son Joel has always been something of a news junky. He was about 9 the Christmas when Cabbage Patch dolls became all the rage, and he listened intently to a news story on one of the networks which spotlighted a perceived "shortage" in Cabbage Patch dolls which had created a kind of black market for them. Classified ads offered thousands of dollars for a doll for a beloved child or grandchild—while cameras panned over black Cabbage Patch dolls languishing on department store shelves. I could see the wheels turning. First, he turned and examined his baby sister—African American/Latina. But he didn't ask about her "value." Instead, after a few minutes went by, his question focused on the bidding war. "Is that the way adoption works, Mommy? Do they give the babies to the people with the most money?"

Oh my gosh! This is the hardest adoption question I have ever been asked by one of my kids. And what is the answer, really? Isn't the honest answer, "Yes, sometimes?" That wasn't what I told my son.

Erica's 1981 arrival coincided with our selling Dave's beloved 1973 Porsche 911 Targa. We had bought this far too expensive car to replace a car that had been totaled when I was in a serious automobile accident. A few months before the accident I had had an unsuccessful infertility surgery and we knew for sure that we would never conceive. We were exploring adoption with enthusiasm, but it seemed so far away. We were both so sad. When we had to replace the totaled car, Dave convinced me to spend our "baby money" on the Porsche of his dreams—a gift to ourselves to make "us" (read *Dave*—I needed medication) feel better.

That car is legendary in our family—immediate and extended. We loved it and enjoyed every minute of owning it. A picture of it is framed on Dave's office wall and a small stained glass replica sits on a shelf. He kept the plaque with his name on it that came with it from the factory. In 1975, precious Joel came home in style from the hospital in a car seat that didn't really fit in the jump seat in the Targa's back. We kept it far longer than we should have, considering that Dave had a company car, and since the family of three couldn't really ride in it, I drove a larger car.

In June, we sold the nearly pristine Porsche to a buyer who loved it as much as we did and paid us $500 more than the original purchase price. We were waiting for an adoption through an agency, but the next month Erica's adoption "fell out of the sky" and we used the money to fund the private adoption of our newborn daughter. She knows the story, and even as an adult she sometimes tells it—even to people she doesn't know that well—when the subject of her adoption or even of sports cars, comes up.

But then there's my reaction over 25 years later to that same story. Hearing it reminds me of the only adoption-related thing I've ever done of which I am ashamed. I'm sharing this anecdote here for the first time ever.

Erica's private adoption was one of those friend-of-a-friend connections, and it was completed by an attorney who was not really that adoption-experienced. We look back now and we aren't so sure that he did things as we expected or asked. For example, we asked him to offer an open adoption. He was shocked—couldn't imagine it! He reported back that Erica's birthparents did not want openness. I sometimes wonder now—did he really even offer it?

Because we were waiting, approved for an agency placement, and because I was already volunteering a lot in the field of adoption, I felt that we were pretty adoption-literate (we were considering open adoption at a time when it was really, really revolutionary). But in retrospect, I see now that resentments lingered. I really hated being so out of control of our family building.

The attorney called when Erica had been home for quite a while to say that the physician who had delivered her had told her birth grandparents that they shouldn't bother to file for the insurance coverage on their daughter's pregnancy and birth, and he was calling to ask us for yet another check. The doctor felt it was "only right" that we pay those bills, and he refused to submit claims. I was furious. I wrote the doctor a long and scathing letter (I'm famous for my letters) about his profound insensitivity, and I copied it to the attorney. If insurance coverage was available, I wrote, it should be used. We (poor us with the beautiful brand new baby while they and their daughter grieved her loss) had spent thousands of dollars over many years on infertility treatments not fully covered by our insurance, and this adoption was not going to be covered by our insurance's maternity benefits. We didn't deserve further "punishment."

We did not hear from the doctor again, but a year or so later I began to think of that crisis time and my letter with deep shame, and I still do. That letter was incredibly insensitive, and an experienced adoption professional would have told me so. The truth is that I'm not sure how those medical bills were covered. Did the family file for the insurance or did they pay the costs out of pocket? I didn't even consider at the time their own possible discomfort about claiming insurance coverage for a pregnancy and birth that had resulted in an adoption. I didn't consider that the physician—or the attorney—might have shared that ugly letter with them.

What Does it Really Cost to Adopt?

We've mentioned before that the range in the cost of adding a child to your family by adoption can run from $0 to over $40,000 before adding in any of the costs of being a parent at all. Figuring out where your adoption will fall on that broad range will depend on who, how, and where you adopt.

When adopting through a public agency, the chances are that your fees will be very low to nothing at all. That's because these adoptions are supported by state and federal tax dollars. Most often the homestudy/parent preparation process involves a significant investment of time, but probably no investment of money. In some states even the legal costs of finalizing a public agency adoption are covered by the state. That's how an adoption can cost absolutely nothing. In some states small fees are charged for a homestudy primarily to establish a "commitment" on the part of the person asking to adopt. In other states, families are required to hire their own attorney to finalize a public agency adoption, though the legal paperwork involved is so routine that the costs of such a finalization usually involve less than four billable professional hours.

Adopting through a private agency works far differently. When the agency is working under a contract with the state to find and prepare homes for wards of the state system, the adoption is usually a virtual public agency adoption, at low to no cost. An adoption worked entirely through a private agency may be billed in several different ways, but before we discuss those, let's think about what services go into the overhead of a private agency and therefore must be figured into the fees charged clients. Some agencies set their fees proportionate to clients' incomes rather than as flat fees or actual costs of services. A growing number of employers now offer adoption reimbursement benefits of a few thousand dollars, and currently the federal government allows a several thousand dollar tax credit for non-recurring adoption expenses. There are also a very small number of grants available from houses of worship and from foundations.

Evaluating Your Own Financial Situation

Before you even consider how you are going to adopt, you must determine that you can afford to parent a child. The first year alone can make an enormous difference. The U.S. Department of Agriculture does an annual report on the costs of parenting. The most recent year available while I was writing reported 2005 figures in 2006 and reported that the average *annual* cost of raising a 0–2-year-old, depending on the income and dual or single parent status of the child, ranged from $7580 to $15,760. The average annual costs for raising 6–8-year-olds, using the same parental variables, ranged from $7780 to $15,790. Parents of 15–17-year-olds were spending, on average, $8540 to 15,970 annually. If child care will be a necessity, you should know that the states' rules about the caregiver to child ratio, and about health and sanitation issues, make daycare over twice as expensive for a child under 12–18 months of age than for a toddler-aged child. There are families whose decision to adopt a toddler-aged child rather than a newborn is ultimately determined by this financial reality.[4] Financial figures such as this help to explain why it is so important to get rid of as much debt as you possibly can and to begin to adjust your lifestyle budgeting before a child arrives.

You will be sharing rather intimate financial information as part of a homestudy. A credit check will be run; your employment will be verified; tax records for recent years may be requested. In looking at this information, agencies are not looking for wealth, but for reasonable and responsible financial management. Low debt ratio speaks more highly of those who want to be parents than do assets secured by large mortgages, loans, and credit card debt.

Parenting is an expensive proposition. Agencies and birthparents want to be assured that you understand this and have planned for it. They will ask questions about the number of hours you work and about your plans for daycare. They will ask you to explore your health insurance benefits and, depending on whether you are a couple or a single, they may ask you to produce future guardianship plans.

Some agencies still require that one parent be able to stay home for at least half a year, and most of a year if your child is not going to be arriving as a newborn. This is a reasonable and fully child-centered requirement. You will need to explore your eligibility for parenting leave.

The bottom line is that anyone planning to become a parent through a process as expensive as the process of adoption will need to have taken a careful look at their budget, and adjusted it and their life accordingly.

Exploring Financial Options and Assistance

The National Endowment for Financial Education worked with several organizations within the adoption community to develop a resource on financing an adoption. The title is *How to Make Adoption an Affordable Option*, and it is available in its entirety online through the Federal Citizen Information Center at www.pueblo.gsa.gov/cic_text/family/adoption/. This is a wonderful place to start.

Additionally, no matter what approach to adoption you are initially leaning toward, you should learn about adoption subsidies available to those adopting waiting children, about federal tax credits and deductions of adoption expenses (capped on a sliding scale based upon family income, but open to those adopting through any route), and about corporate adoption benefits offered by increasing numbers of employers. Online places for exploring these resources include

- The Child Welfare Information Gateway (www.childwelfare.gov/)
- Courses on Adoption Subsidies and Financial Assistance from the National Adoption Center (www.adoptnet.org)
- The Casey National Center for Family Support (CNC) (www.casey.org) makes available a federal tax benefits booklet that highlights deductions, exemptions, and tax credits of particular interest to foster and adoptive families and kinship caregivers. Copies can be reproduced from their website
- The Dave Thomas Foundation for Adoption (www.davethomas foundationforadoption.org) and the Child Welfare Information Gateway both offer information you can share with your employer to encourage the company to offer employee adoption benefits if they do not already do so. (This is becoming increasingly common, so you may be surprised to find that your employer already offers such a benefit.)

Many would-be adopters are unaware of some readily available financial aid and incentives available to most families.

- **Dependency Exemptions.** It may be obvious to many, but it is surprising how many non-parents forget to consider that adoptive parents are eligible for federal and state dependency tax exemption for their adopted children just like parents by birth. The amount of exemption is adjusted annually and helps by reducing your taxable income.

- **Tax Credits** are available at the federal level to adopters of infants and older children in both intercountry and domestic adoptions. Because specific limits on the credit and eligible income limits may change from year to year, consult a tax advisor before filing Federal Form 8839 or a comparable state form.
- **Federal.** The federal adoption tax credit is more beneficial than a simple tax deduction. Under the Hope for Children Act (Public Law 107-16) "qualifying adoption expenses" up to almost $11,000 (for families with gross incomes under $170,820[5]) may be deducted from overall federal tax liability. For example, if your federal tax obligation is $6,000 and you have $4,000 in adoption expenses, your tax liability would be reduced to $2,000. If your tax bill is smaller than the amount of your expenses, you can carry forward the unused portion of your adoption tax credit for the next several years. Qualified adoption expenses must be legal, and may include adoption fees, attorney fees, birth parent expenses and travel costs, including necessary transportation, meals and lodging.
- **State.** Some states offer a tax credit or deduction in addition to the federal tax credit. Ask your tax advisor about possible state credits.
- **Employee Benefits.** At least 25% of corporations in the United States offer some form of adoption benefits to their employees. Typical benefits may include reimbursements of adoption expenses (typically $1,000 to $10,000); paid leave in addition to vacation time, sick leave, or personal days; and unpaid leave. The human resources office where you work can tell you what benefits your employer may offer. To encourage your employer to consider adding adoption benefits (which costs them little but earns them high marks in internal PR) see the Resources section for several articles and booklets already prepared to offer them facts, statistics, and lists of other corporations who offer these.
- **Subsidies.** Families who domestically adopt children with special medical, emotional, and/or developmental needs; older children; or members of a sibling group may find that their children are eligible for an adoption subsidy from federal and state governments. Subsidies are used to cover special educational, health, and therapeutic needs of children adopted with special needs. Unless an intercountry adoption disrupts, throwing the child into the U.S. child welfare system, internationally adopted children are not eligible for these subsidies. Check with your state government or social worker for details, and don't accept a first "no" answer. Subsidies are for the benefit of children, and they are not based on family financial need,

but on the needs of the child, so it can be important to make yourself a strong advocate for your child.

- **Military Subsidies.** After an adoption has been finalized, active-duty military personnel can receive up to $2,000 reimbursement per child for many adoption-related expenses up to a maximum of $5,000 in one year. Reimbursement does not include travel costs, but does include medical costs for a birthmother and the child.

- **Credit Cards.** Some adoption service providers accept major credit cards as payment. Not only does this provide a way for financing large expenses over time, but when tied to any kind of "rewards" program (airline miles, store discounts, etc.) it can also provide the family with an offsetting "benefit" to charge card fees.

- **Loans** are a frequent form of adoption financing. Some financial institutions have specific loan programs for adoption, and virtually all provide home equity loans for those who own their homes. Think about whether you have a close friend or family member who might be willing to extend a loan for this purpose (be sure to make it formal, writing up an agreement and formalizing a schedule of payments you can stick to). Additionally, you might explore loans against life insurance policies and 401Ks (being careful not to deplete these resources, which can become very important later).

- **Health Insurance.** Will your plan cover any pre-adoption expenses such as childbirth? Most do not, but some plans do in some states. All private and group insurance plans are required, by federal law, to cover even pre-existing conditions from the time a child becomes your legal responsibility.

- **Fundraising.** Internet discussion groups frequently include threads about adoption financing. From these discussions I've seen numerous creative ideas, including
  — Selling fundraising items such as candy, popcorn, magazine subscriptions, etc. through companies established to offer these kinds of products to schools and houses of worship.
  — Holding garage and yard sales, and online auctions like eBay. Ask friends and family to donate items too.
  — Participating in runs, walks, bikathons, etc. to which family, friends, and co-workers pledge or in which they participate, bringing their own friends' pledges.
  — Asking for a money shower in lieu of the more traditional type.
  — Earning a little extra money through participating in survey groups or clinical research trials.
  — Seeking financial help from the members of your religious congregation.

- **Shrinking Your Lifestyle.** Live below your means rather than above them. Downsize your house and your car to save payment money, use public transportation, practice energy conservation to save on utility bills, prune your cable, telephone and cell phone subscription to more basic options, eat out less often and pack your lunch, eliminate the $5 coffee splurges, put each day's change into a savings jar, shop at thrift stores, etc. Subscribe to or participate in frugal living periodicals and websites such as *Frugal Families*, *Living on a Dime*, and *Frugal Mom*.

Gathering this information will give you a starting point for asking yourselves some hard financial questions about your financial budget for adoption, as well as for parenting.

What you learn about these financial resources can influence a number of your decisions about adoption—from the style of adoption to the age of the child (a school-aged child will not require the additional expense of daycare), to the health of the child (the possibility of a subsidy may make it possible for you to take on the expenses of a disability with which you are already comfortable and familiar), to whether you can adopt at all (the existence of an employee benefit plan and the federal tax deduction may make adoption far more affordable than you thought it would be).

Adoption Insurance

Since I wrote *Adopting after Infertility* in 1992, an experiment by several large insurance companies in offering adoption insurance, which would reimburse would-be parents the expenses they had paid should an adoption fall through, seems to have failed for the most part. Few insurers offer adoption insurance these days, and when they do, it is offered only to clients of specific service providers.

The problem with this is that it would indicate that such a provider experiences a particularly low proportion of changes of heart during the pregnancy, yet the proportion greatly increases before a placement is actually made. This would make most advocates very nervous. The average ethical adoption provider who provides good options counseling for expectant parent clients finds that well over 75% of them, and often as high a proportion of 95% of them, decide at some point during the pregnancy (often very early) not to make an adoption plan. This is why so many of those services providers don't match expectant parents with would-be adoptive parents until at least the third trimester of a pregnancy. A select few agencies continue to prefer to make matches only after the child is born, so that would-be adopters are not exposed to repeated disappointments, which can impair their ability to lead the dance of attachment.

In the next chapter on choosing what kind of child to adopt and again in the anticipation chapter in Part Four, we will discuss investigating the educational, medical, and counseling support services that may be important for the individual child you adopt. For example, it makes no sense, if thinking in a child-centered way, to move a child of color into a totally white neighborhood or small town, and it is important that those who will be adopting older post-institutionalized children know whether the specialized medical and counseling services for these children are readily available to the family without having to travel unmanageable distances. These issues, and others, will become part of your evolving plan of action when it comes to adopting and effectively parenting your child.

Resources

Marital Status

National Council for Single Adoptive Parents. www.ncsap.org/

Child Welfare Information Gateway. "Single Parent Adoption: What You Need to Know" www.childwelfare.gov/pubs/f_single/index.cfm

Coleman, Thomas F. "Debates over unmarried adoptions heating up." Umarriedamerica.com www.unmarriedamerica.org/column-one/05-13-07-unmarried-adoptions.htm

Engber, Andrea and Leah Kungless. *The Complete Single Mother: Reassuring Answers to Your Most Challenging Concerns.* (Cincinnati, OH: Adams Media Corp., 2005)

Hertz, Rosanna. *Single by Chance, Mothers by Choice: How Women are Choosing Parenthood without Marriage and Creating the New American Family.* (New York: Oxford University Press USA, 2006)

Osborn, Martha "Single Parent Adoption and Women" Adoption at About.com adoption.about.com/od/nontraditional/a/singleapar.htm

Mattes, Jane. *Single Mothers by Choice: Guidebook for Single Women Who Are Considering or Have Chosen Motherhood.* (New York: Three Rivers Press, 1994)

Nolo: Your Legal Companion's "Parenting Issues for Unmarried Couples FAQ" www.nolo.com/article.cfm/objectID/893B37A0-D0E8-4B7D-9FD90CE5DCB C3BE7/118/304/145/FAQ/

Varon, Lee. *Adopting On Your Own: The Complete Guide to Adoption for Single Parents.* (New York: Farrar, Strauss and Giroux, 2000)

"Why Is Single Parent Adoption Becoming More Prevalent?" family.findlaw.com/ adoption/adoption-types/single-parent-adoption(1).html

Sexual Orientation

ACLU Position Statement "Adoption and Co-parenting of Children by Same-sex Couples" www.aclu.org/getequal/ffm/section1/1c7apa.pdf

Belge, Kathy. "Gay and Lesbian Adoption Rights: Both Sides of the Issue" About. com:Lesbian Life. lesbianlife.about.com/cs/families/a/adoption.htm

Families Joined by Love: Books and Resources for LGBT Families is a site (with bookstore) devoted to this niche. www.familiesjoinedbylove.com/

Family Pride's Blog. "New Numbers Released on Gay/Lesbian Adoption and Foster Care" www.familypride.org/blog/2007/04/new-numbers-released-on-gay-and-lesbian-adoptionfoster-care.html

Hicks, Stephen and Janet McDermott. *Lesbian and Gay Fostering and Adoption: Extraordinary yet Ordinary.* (London and Philadelphia: Jessica Kingsley Publishers, 1998)

McGarry, Kevin. *Fatherhood for Gay Men: An Emotional and Practical Guide to Becoming a Gay Dad.* (Binghampton, NY: Harrington Park Press, 2003)

Mallon, Gerald P. *Lesbian and Gay Foster and Adoptive Parents: Recruiting, Assessing, And Supporting an Untapped Resource for Children And Youth.* (Washington DC: CWLA Press, 2006)

Sember, Brette McWhorter. *Gay & Lesbian Parenting Choices: From Adopting or Using a Surrogate to Choosing the Perfect Father.* (Franklin Lakes, NJ: Career Press, 2006)

Religion

"Adoption of Children from Countries in which Islamic Shari'a law is observed" U.S. Department of State Travel Section. www.travel.state.gov/family/adoption/intercountry/intercountry_3132.html

Huda. "Adopting a Child in Islam" About.com.islam islam.about.com/cs/parenting/a/adoption.htm

Health

"ADA Home Page" www.usdoj.gov/crt/ada/adahom1.htm U.S. Department of Justice

Adopting after Cancer online support group: groups.yahoo.com/group/adoption-after-cancer/

Evan B Donaldson Adoption Institute "FAQs on the ADA" www.adoptioninstitute.org/policy/adafaq.html

Freundlich, Madelyn, MSW, MPH, JD, LLM. "The Americans with Disabilities Act: What Adoption Agencies Need to Know" www.adoptioninstitute.org/policy/ada.html

Peterson, Lisa, Esq. "Legal Update: Decision under the Americans with Disabilities Act" www.adoptioninstitute.org/policy/polada.html

Finances

Christianson, Laura. "The Price of Parenthood: Financing Adoption." Preconception.com www.preconception.com/resources/articles/priceofadoption.htm

Dave Thomas Foundation's "Adoption Friendly Workplace" page www.adoptionfriendlyworkplace.org/afw/afw_index.asp

IRS FORM 8839 Qualified Adoption Expenses (and related instructions) www.irs.gov/taxpros/providers/article/0,,id=167290,00.html

Marchetti, Michelle. "Ten Things Your Adoption Agency Won't Tell You" Smart Money.com. www.smartmoney.com/10things/index.cfm?story=april2004

NACAC's Adoption Subsidy Information, State-by-State Profiles www.nacac.org/subsidy_stateprofiles.html

Saenz, George. "Adoption expenses provide tax credit" Detroit News Online, April 2007. www.detnews.com/apps/pbcs.dll/article?AID=/20070402/BIZ01/704020317/1010&template=printart

Subsidy info. from the National Adoption Assistance Training Resource and Information Network Helpline at 1-800-470-6665

Grant Sources and fundraising options are detailed on the following agency and APSG websites:

- Bethany Christian Services www.bethany.org/A55798/bethanyWWW.nsf/0/5BC861840817259285256D9E0066DE24

- Families with Children from China fwcc.org/financing.htm

CHAPTER 9

Which Child?

Now that you've decided to adopt, and you have a realistic grip on your resources and what challenges may lie before you, what kind of child will best fit into your family?

For many years—until the mid 1960s to the early '70s—it was realistic to expect that you could fairly quickly adopt a healthy infant who matched you racially. The number of infants available for adoption and the number of families wishing to adopt were relatively close. During the '30s, '40s and '50s there were actually more babies in need of parents than families interested in adopting. In fact, in those years couples were often allowed to view and select from two or more healthy babies. Though treatments for infertility were less successful a generation or more ago, a solution to childlessness was easier. Couples who lost control of their fertility regained control of the family planning aspect of their lives by actually "choosing" their child. At this same time, however, singles and same-sex couples were left completely out of the adoptive parenting picture and so had no expectations at all about adopting.

Today there are still more children to adopt than there are potential parents asking for them. But those children aren't necessarily babies and aren't necessarily perfectly healthy. For couples of African American, Native American, or Hispanic origin, there remains a surplus of babies for adoption. For certain Asian ethnic groups, intercountry adoption can provide an opportunity to adopt a same-ethnicity infant. But statistics have changed dramatically for European-American couples, which is one of the things that has driven intercountry adoption to all-time highs. Whether adopting domestically or internationally, for all parents-to-be the risks that a baby born apparently healthy may later develop problems brought about by poor prenatal care, in utero exposure to drugs and alcohol, or that he may develop AIDS or suffer the most sobering deprivational effects of institutionalization are higher today than they were in the past.

Various sources claim that there may be 40 to as many as 100 would-be parents hoping to adopt every available healthy, Caucasian infant. This statistical swing has produced the need for adopters to realistically examine their limitations, as well as their wishes about parenting and to consider whether horizons could be expanded. But that is a hard thing to do, and it isn't the right choice for many people.

In fact, just in case no one else around you tells you this, let me make absolutely clear what I think about pushing never-before-parents—singles, infertile couples, same-sex couples—to consider special needs adoption when they haven't volunteered to do so. Despite the changes in adoption that make inracial adoption of a healthy baby more difficult than it was twenty years ago, it is still perfectly normal, perfectly healthy, perfectly acceptable to make the decision that the right way for you to begin parenting is with a healthy newborn baby matched racially to you. Still . . . it doesn't hurt to think about those other options, so that, if you do decide to reject them (for now at least) you will have done so not out of panicky fear and ignorance, but after reasoned exploration, discussion, and decision making.

Boy or Girl?

Now here's a place where adopting parents can still exert some of that lost control—gender selection! You can indeed choose your baby's gender if this is important to you, though it is rarely available in newborn domestic adoption and less and less the case in international adoption. This can be a real advantage to those for whom lost control is a big deal—and to some parents it can be absolutely unimportant.

Deciding to specify boy or girl will have only a small impact on your chances of adopting, but it can impact the timing and it can influence both age and location of the boy or girl who is to be yours. In general, in North America, slightly more boys are available for adoption than girls. In many parts of the world, however—in Asia and South America, Africa and the Indian subcontinent, and in other cultures where girls are much less valued than are boys—there are many more adoptable girls than boys.

It's not at all unusual for people to have a preference about the gender of their children. Actually, research shows that most parents expecting by birth do have a preference about whether their child will be a boy or a girl. But for several generations now, attitudes about sex selection of first children has been opposite between parents who give birth and parents who adopt. When pregnant couples expecting a first baby are asked in opinion polls whether they prefer a boy or a girl, even in Western cultures, boy children tend to be more desired than girls by those who have a preference at all. But the reverse has been and continues to be true in adoption. More adoptive parents-to-be express a preference for girls than for boys. This is not true just in intercountry adoption, where it has long been openly discussed, but also in domestic infant adoption.

Why would it be that adopting parents might prefer a girl to a boy, when birthing couples seem to prefer a boy to a girl first child? It has been speculated that for some couples this is a reaction to their loss of genetic continuity. Boy children are still perceived as the continuers of family—carrying a family name from generation to generation. Girl children, whose names are still frequently changed at marriage, do not carry the same responsibility for family continuity. Is it easier for a man feeling the blow of the ending of his family blood line to adopt a girl than a boy? Is it easier for extended families to accept the adoption of girls than boys?

While those adopting a first child less frequently specify gender, seeming to prefer instead to be surprised, those adopting a second child (either after a first adoption or in the case of those adopting after secondary infertility) very often find it empowering to make a choice about the gender of their child-to-be. It is not uncommon for parents who have children to specify a particular sex as their preference.

It is probably a good idea for you to examine your motivations for wanting a child of a particular sex—not because having a preference is wrong, but because it is always valuable to understand why we feel as we do. In adoption, understanding our motivations contributes greatly to our ability to build a sense of entitlement.

> Karen had always seen herself as the mother of a daughter. Through all those long years of infertility she mourned what she feared would be the loss of the little girl with long hair to braid, a shared interest in flowers—all those things she'd dreamed about as a little girl playing with dolls.
>
> On their third cycle of GIFT, Karen conceived twin sons born healthy. She and Roger were thrilled, but Karen didn't feel "finished." When the boys were five, Roger suggested GIFT again, but Karen knew what she needed, and Roger agreed. They adopted a two-year-old girl, Angelina, from South America.

Actually, beyond just having the power to decide, there are some very practical reasons why many adoptive parents think about the sex of their children in relationship to one another.

> Barry remembered vividly how he was compared to his two-years-older brother, Brian, in grade school. Brian was smart, athletic, and gregarious. Barry was quiet, awkward, and painfully shy. It seemed that almost every teacher remembered Brian, and Barry remembered their reactions as being "You're Brian's brother? Wow! I'd never have guessed!" He had always felt that he was being negatively compared.
>
> Barry didn't want to see that happen to his own children, and he figured two same sex kids were more likely to be compared than siblings of different genders. Furthermore, it seemed to Barry that if his children were genetically unrelated, the likelihood of their being very different from one another was even greater than it had been for himself and Brian.

Yes, Barry wanted this second child to be a son—not necessarily because he had always wanted a son, but because he didn't want his much-loved daughter, adopted at birth, or her younger sibling to feel the pain that he had felt as a child.

Make no mistake, though. If you do have a preference for gender, your choices about routes to adoption are changed. A generation ago this would not have been the case, but in today's domestic newborn adoptions, the odds are very good that service providers will want to match you not with a child already born, but with his pregnant mother. Depending on circumstances, she may or may not know the gender of the child she is carrying. Furthermore, when expectant parents (rather than more objective social workers) are choosing prospective adopters (as more and more do in today's domestic adoptions) things feel far more "personal," and being seen as "picky" about anything at all, including gender, can be a cause to put a profile down and pick up the next one. It's important to understand that this may not be seen as child-centered adoption thinking. What happens to the child who once born is not the correct gender? What happens to the mother who thought she had found a family for her child and now her plan for her child's future has now collapsed? It is an issue of ethics and most ethical agencies will not allow prospective adoptive parents to sex select when planning a newborn adoption. Gender selection is most often an easy thing in intercountry adoption, where matches are made by professionals and referrals come after the child has been born.

Gender selection can be important and, as shown in the vignettes above, reasonably so. If gender selection is one of your priorities in becoming a parent, you may want to look more closely at intercountry adoption, fostering-to-adopt a U.S.-born baby, and/or adopting an older child.

Health and Abilities Issues

Sure, healthy is easiest, but health is a relative thing. What represents compromise to you? Where is the line over which you just can't go?

First, be realistic. It is utterly, completely, totally impossible for an agency, intermediary, or birthparent to guarantee you a completely healthy child. Children who are born apparently healthy and whose gene pools do not indicate the likelihood of impairments regularly develop illnesses and conditions that could not be predicted. This happens in families of the sturdiest stock and to mothers with the best of prenatal care, and it could just as likely have happened to you, had you given birth. There are no guarantees in parenting. Your ability to be as flexible as possible in this area will significantly increase your odds of becoming a parent sooner and to a younger child.

Agencies will definitely ask you to carefully consider your limitations regarding the predictable health and abilities of a child. Most are likely to

provide you with a checklist filled with the names of illnesses and disabilities, and ask you to check off yes, no, or maybe. What they will not likely
do is offer you any specific information about the problems on those lists.
Here's more homework for you.

Of course you can Google a lot of this, and that will give you helpful
definitions and explanations, but it won't give you firsthand experience
from parents who have been there and done that. Once again consider
NACAC and a referral to local adoptive parent groups as your first line
resource. In addition to grassroots adoptive parent support groups (APSGs)
every state has an organization of foster and adoptive parents supported
by federal funds. It may have a name like Indiana's, which is IFCAA—the
Indiana Foster Care and Adoption Association, or like Connecticut's, which
is CAFAP—Connecticut Association of Foster and Adoptive Parents. These
groups have small paid staffs and multiple goals. They are part of the recruitment and support system for those who foster children for the state,
offering them respite care, providing continuing education opportunities
for the maintenance of their licensure as foster parents, and providing peer
support. They also serve the foster parents who eventually adopt the children in their care and those who adopt outright from the public welfare
system. This group in your state is an invaluable source of information
and referral.

Also contact your local United Way or other community clearinghouse
and ask for referrals to agencies and support groups dealing with the health
problems which you would like to learn more about. Talk directly to parents dealing with these problems. In doing so you will discover that the
vast majority of things on those lists are problems that can range in severity from quite minor to overwhelmingly disabling. And, some things that
could appear on the surface to be fully correctable or purely cosmetic can
be symptomatic of far more serious conditions.

> Jesse and Vic were pretty clear—perfectly healthy babies were
> what they wanted. Three of them—as closely matched to them as pos-
> sible. To assure that, they were pretty certain about their expectations
> about a birthparent, too: She wasn't to have drank, smoked, or taken
> drugs during pregnancy. They wanted a full family social and medical
> history on each birthparent.
>
> Because of their clearly defined limits, they had ruled out inter-
> country adoption (too many of those babies were abandoned, so health
> and prenatal history weren't available). They had ruled out parent-
> initiated private adoption because they were unwilling to commit to an
> expectant parent during her pregnancy—they wanted to be sure the
> baby was healthy. So Jesse and Vic were waiting in line at a traditional
> private agency practicing confidential adoption.
>
> Their group homestudy included four other couples, all of whom
> were told to expect that they would likely receive a baby within a year

of approval. The first couple to adopt got a gorgeous little boy. The second couple's little girl had bright red hair. The third couple received tiny twins born four weeks prematurely. The fourth couple adopted a biracial boy.

Sixteen months after the end of their homestudy, Jesse and Vic still waited. They had discovered that couples who had been in the group following theirs had already received placements. They went to see their caseworker. "Well, we wouldn't have been able to deal with the biracial baby," Jesse said, "but those other kids would have been perfect. When will it be our turn?"

"To be honest," came the reply, "we didn't think of you for any of these children. The backgrounds of all of them included something on your listed limitations. The first boy's birthfather's family had a strong history of strabismus (crossed eye), but the baby didn't appear to have the problem, and this couple figured that was correctable if it showed up later. The little girl with red hair sure wouldn't have looked like you at all, and would have drawn comments from others. Besides, we couldn't make contact with the alleged birthfather and so we had no medical history on him. The twins were so small and so early that there was a significant risk of problems. They spent some time in the preemie nursery, where their adopting parents were able to visit daily to feed and hold them."

Vic and Jesse reevaluated their list, and one month later they were the parents of a little girl. When the call came, they were hesitant. Hers had been a difficult birth and she had a dislocated hip. But they called the pediatrician they had pre-selected and asked him to look at the records and the family history. He was encouraging. APGAR scores were good. Baby would be in a cast for a while, but she would be a fully functioning, rambunctious toddler in no time.

My advice is this: the more maybes you can check, the better. If your answers are mostly no's you're going to be called only when pure perfection is available. If your answers are yes or maybe, you'll probably be on the short list for a lot of possibilities. Remember, you can always say no to a specific situation that just feels wrong. This is something over which you do have absolute control. (No, it won't necessarily be easy to allow yourself to do this.) You can always take the time to fully investigate the health issues presented to you before saying yes or no to the adoption. On the other hand, you can't say yes to something you don't even know about.

If possible, establish rapport with the physician who will be your child's pediatrician before your child arrives. Choosing a pediatrician who is knowledgeable about adoption issues can be important for any family. It may become even more important if you are adopting a child with emotional problems or a child from another country who may be at risk for infectious diseases less commonly seen in this country. Speak with other adoptive parents about their pediatricians. Look for the possibility in your community of an adoption medicine clinic (often a part of a teaching hospital, but sometimes a private practice choice for a pediatrician—especially one who is herself an adoptive or foster parent). Ask whether this doctor would be willing to review health and birth records and offer a medical opinion before you accept a referral either internationally or domestically. If you are adopting a newborn, sometimes your doctor will be willing and able to check the baby out in the hospital. If your adoption comes so suddenly that you have not able to engage a pediatrician before your child's arrival, ask your own primary care physician if he or she would be willing either to examine these records or to refer you to specialized help if needed.

Race and Ethnicity

The overwhelming majority of those who adopt do so within their own race. European Americans primarily adopt white children. African Americans most often adopt black children. Asians adopt Asians of their ethnic heritage. Latinos seek to adopt children from within their own segment of Latin culture. Interracial couples look for children of the same bi-racial mixture as their family. This makes perfect sense. These decisions would have been the ethnicity of children born to you, and in choosing to race-match, your family will not "stand out" in a crowd. That in itself rules out one layer of complication and difference in becoming an adoptive family.

But for over 50 years there have been adoptive families made up of parents and children who do not "match": European American parents with Asian children, African American parents with biracial children, and just about any other combination. The truth is that these families, when they practice what David Kirk would call AD (acknowledgment of difference) behavior (Chapter 4), when they are well educated and prepared going into adoption, and when they are well supported afterwards do very well.

But the issue of race matching vs. transracial placement in adoption incites both political and

> **Myth:** Adopting a child of a different race or ethnicity is bound to cause problems for both parents and children.
>
> **Fact:** It is true that the decision to adopt transracially should not be taken lightly and should be done only by parents willing to face racism proactively. Many of these families will need to commit to making major changes in their lives and lifestyles. However the first transracial adoptions (of Korean war orphans) have provided over half a century of opportunity for research, which has demonstrated that, when parented by realistic, racially-conscious parents willing to connect their children with their ethnic and racial heritage, most transracial adoptees have strong racial identity as well as strong attachments to their families.

moral debates. The facts are clear. While European-American babies are at a premium and Caucasian adopters are lined up 40–100 deep to adopt them, there are significant numbers of minority children—particularly African American, Hispanic, and Native American—waiting for adoption in the United States. Their numbers outnumber the minority families waiting to adopt. Throughout the world in third world nations and now in the European countries struggling from behind what was once the Iron Curtain, millions of babies and children cry out for parents.

Why children wait in the U.S. is an issue of debate. Certainly some minority cultures, which experience poverty and lack of education in much higher proportionate numbers than do white families, are more at risk for the problems that lead to separation of parents and children. And then there's the fact that minority families have been reluctant to adopt through the system (partially because recruitment among minority families has been poorly done at best), even though minority communities have, historically, practiced informal adoption—"taking care of our own"—at very high rates.

Is transracial adoption in the best interests of a child? Keeping in mind the child-centered thinking that adoption is primarily a service for children, not a service for adults, the solutions to the problem of waiting children are controversial. While many European-American couples express interest in adopting minority children, professionals in the minority community are rightfully resistant to such actions. Most certainly, agencies working with birthparents who will deliver children of color need to do a far better job of recruiting parents among people of color, and there are some agencies out there which are doing a wonderful job of that.

Native Americans concerned about the large numbers of children being adopted by whites and removed from their cultural heritage successfully lobbied for the 1978 passage of the Indian Child Welfare Act (ICWA), a special law which, recognizing the sovereignty of Indian nations, gives tribes the absolute power to make foster and adoptive placement decisions about their children and discourages the placement of Native American children with families who are not themselves Native American.

The National Association of Black Social Workers has called transracial adoption a form of cultural genocide and has fought unsuccessfully for protection similar to the ICWA. While child advocates in some states, such as Michigan, have successfully defeated official policies which require the placement of minority children in minority homes, some states, notably Minnesota, have passed cultural heritage acts which mandate that agencies must go to tremendous lengths to place children in families of like ethnic backgrounds.

Elizabeth Bartholet, an adoptive parent who is a professor of law at Harvard University, met the issues head on in an article she wrote for the University of Pennsylvania Law Review (Volume 139, Number 5: May,

1991). In her article "Where Do Black Children Belong? The Politics of Race Matching in Adoption," Ms. Bartholet wrote,

> My thesis is that thinking that promotes racial matching to the exclusion of permanency comes from powerful and related ideologies— old fashioned white racism, modern-day black racism and nationalism, and what I will call "biologism"—the idea that what is "natural" in the context of the biological family is what is most desirable in the context of adoption. Biological families have same-race parents and children. The law and policies surrounding adoption in this country have generally structured adoption in imitation of biology, giving the adopted child a new birth certificate as if the child had been born to the adoptive parents, sealing off the birthparents as if they had never existed, and attempting to match adoptive parents and children with respect to looks, intellect and religion. The implicit goal has been to create an adoptive family which will resemble as much as possible "the real thing"—the "natural" or biological family—which it is not. These laws and policies reflect, I believe, widespread and powerful feelings that parent-child relationships can only work, or at least will work best, between those who are biologically related. They also reflect widespread and powerful fears that parents will not be able to truly love and nurture children not biologically related to them. These feelings and fears have much in common with the feelings and fears among both blacks and whites in our society about the danger of crossing racial boundaries. It is thus understandable that there would be much support for racial matching in the context of adoption.[1]

Her article was later incorporated in her 1999 book called *Family Bonds: Adoption, Infertility, and the New World of Child Production*. It continues to inspire much needed discussion.

In 1994 President Clinton signed the Multiethnic Placement Act (MEPA) into law. This law's main provisions included barring racial discrimination practice in delaying or denying children placement, preventing agencies from using race alone as a barrier to becoming a foster or adoptive parent, and requiring that agencies would diligently recruit foster and adoptive families reflective of the racial diversity of the children in each state's care. Unfortunately, the original MEPA was weakened in 1996 when, without any hearings or recorded statements, the Interethnic Placement Act (IEPA) which became MEPA's Interethnic Provisions (IEP) quietly sailed through Congress. These provisions prohibit all consideration of race in placement.[2] NACAC and other advocates for children are currently (2007) lobbying for changes which would once again bring MEPA into a child-centered focus.

Beyond Politics

But all of this discussion has been politics. Most family-challenged people aren't adopting out of political motivation. They are adopting in order to become parents! That's great, yet it is easy for people desperate to adopt a child to make an idealistic leap of faith in an information vacuum.

"A child is a child," they say. "Kids grow better in families, and these are kids without families. Give me this child to love." The reality of transracial or transethnic adoption and parenting is more complex than that. Love does not conquer all. The problems inherent in interracial dating or interracial marriage are also a part of interracial adoption. In either case, the result is a multiracial or interracial family. There's no room for naiveté or surface idealism in such families if the children raised there are to become healthy, competent, self-confident adults.

Most North Americans of European heritage are completely unaware of the extent of racism in this culture. In Chapter 4, I mentioned Jim Mahoney's discussion of the adult learning model (moving from unconscious incompetence to conscious incompetence to conscious competence to unconscious competence). Understanding this learning model is helpful in comprehending the process of acquiring any new life skill or situation. Race is one of the places where awareness of that learning model can be useful.

Many would-be parents who would not even consider adopting an American black child adopt internationally from Asia, India, South America, etc. without considering it a transracial or transethnic placement. Often these decisions are made in a state of unconscious incompetence about racism in North America. Since much of American racism is based upon an often unacknowledged hierarchy of skin shade, these adopters believe that because these children are not of African Negro heritage (not true of most adoptable South American children), and because these children will be lighter of skin than American people of African heritage (also frequently untrue), their children adopted from overseas and their families will experience little if any prejudice. It is not until their growing children run smack into racism that such naive adopters are brought up short.

> Dave and I adopted Lindsey, of African-American and Hispanic heritage, feeling comfortable that we knew what we were doing. We knew other transracial adopters, we knew people of color, and we lived in an integrated community and were committed to continuing to do so.
>
> Thinking that we were consciously competent, I realize now that we were probably somewhere between unconscious incompetence and conscious incompetence in our understanding of racial issues. Truth be told, in making the decision, early on we focused a lot on the fact that her birthmother, with whom we would have an open adoption, was after all, Latina. Lindsey, we reasoned then, was as much Latina as African American.

The fact is that Lindsey looks exactly like her handsome African-American birthfather. While her Latina heritage is an important, wonderful, and positive part of who she is (something she has embraced by becoming fluent in Spanish and choosing to do her college studying abroad in the Dominican Republic), to the world at large—most especially the white world—she will always be recognized and reacted to as an African-American person. So, it was really important that she come to identify herself positively in this way.

We were quite unprepared for the silent blatancy of racism until we became a family of color. Early on we were not surprised to find that when we went out as a family—white Mom, white Dad, two white children and black baby—there was a great deal of positive attention of the aren't-you-people-wonderful, isn't-she-cute variety. On the other hand, we were shocked to find that when one parent went out with baby Lindsey, reactions from both black and white people were cold and standoffish. There was a definite unspoken criticism, which we finally came to understand came from the assumption that they were observing an adult involved in a transracial sexual relationship.

It is one thing to share, as I still do, the family-of-man ideals of many transracial adopters, who loudly—and accurately—point out that biracial children are genetically no more black, brown, yellow, or red than they are white and argue for an acceptance of biracial people as a group separate and equal to either of the races of which they are blended. It is quite another to deal yourself with, and to help your children learn to deal with, day-to-day racism based on their perceived minority heritage.

In her article mentioned above, Elizabeth Bartholet refers to a number of studies which have attempted to measure the success of transracial adoptions. These same studies are also cited in Cheri Register's excellent book on intercountry transethnic adoption, *Are Those Kids Yours: American Families with Children Adopted from Other Countries* (The Free Press, 1991). Most of these studies produce similar results: transracial adoptions are successful (when measured by children's self esteem and cultural pride) to the degree to which adopting parents are willing to make themselves culturally competent—willing to learn about, live within, and embrace the culture and the people of a child's minority background.

If you are considering a transethnic domestic or intercountry adoption, you should read the studies that Register and Bartholet digest for you, you should speak directly to local families who have adopted transracially, and you should attend a NACAC conference or listen to the appropriate audiotapes from recent conferences on these issues.

Interestingly—and importantly—many of us who have adopted transracially have a lot to say retrospectively about our own unconscious incompetence. In addition to my own thoughts shared throughout this book, Gail Steinberg and Beth Hall talk about their personal evolutions as parents of interracial families in *Inside Transracial Adoption* (Perspectives Press,

Inc., 2000). And in addition to her first book, mentioned above, Cheri Register's *Beyond Good Intentions: A Mother Reflects on Raising Internationally Adopted Children* (Yeong and Yeong Book Co., 2005) looks back after 14 years and offers some important modifications to her original thinking. Please listen to us—as our kids have reached adulthood, we really do know more than do the less experienced white parents of toddlers and elementary school-aged children of color who populate most Internet chat groups.

As discussed in the ethics section of Chapter 7, developing cultural competence first means becoming conscious of our own subconscious feelings about race. A valuable place to start is by taking the Implicit Association Test, a research-based ten minute online survey which will likely reveal some degree of bias of which you may not be aware. The IAT has been given over a million times. Its introduction says this,

> "When it comes to gender and racial equality, most people know what their opinions are. But what about unconscious attitudes and associations? Would you be surprised to learn, for example, that you unconsciously favor one gender or racial group over another?
>
> "The 'Implicit Association Test' offers one way to probe unconscious biases. In this 10-minute test, you will be presented with words or images and asked to respond as quickly as possible. At the end, your responses will be tallied so that you can see how your score compares to others and to your expectations (these responses will also be saved and tabulated as part of an investigation of implicit associations)."

If you are considering adopting transracially, I would encourage you to stop here and take the IAT as a way to begin to think more objectively about where you are on the adult learning model scale and how far you may need to go to become culturally competent. Be prepared to add some confusion and surprise to your discussion about adopting a child who is racially different from you and/or your partner.

Put this book down and go to www.understandingprejudice.org/iat/ to take the test. We'll resume in ten minutes.

Welcome back. Were you surprised by your own results? Even after living in an interracial family for almost a quarter of a century, I was. You may have a lot of work to do. Becoming competent culturally also means being sensitive to the issues surrounding moving an Asian child to a rural American community. It means understanding the problems inherent in sending an African-American child to a mostly white school. It means developing an excited interest in living in an integrated community, eating ethnic foods, extending one's circle of support and friendship to include people of color, and more. For most middle and upper middle class people of European heritage, developing cultural competence will not be easy, because the fact is that most of us are much more racist than we care to believe.

No matter how hard we, her white parents, worked to develop cultural competence, to some extent Lindsey had to grow up precisely what the derogatory term "Oreo" refers to—black on the outside, white within. I've heard similar terms, "Twinkie" and "banana," used to describe Asian children who are immersed in white culture.

I like the approach of adoptive parent (of Korean-born children) Gregory Gross on this issue. Writing in the March/April 1992 issue of *Interrace* magazine, Gross said that he sees his task as teaching his children to value their outside coating so that they can value their inside core. The banana skin (or the Oreo outside) will be tough, the filling soft and sweet.[3]

Dave and I love our now-grown child unconditionally. She is ours in the same gut-wrenching, I'd-die-for-her way as are our other two children, who are white. We feel that we were good parents, and you would never get us to go so far as to say that we were not the best parents Lindsey could have had. On the other hand, we are ready to admit that we were typical educated white liberals—very idealistic, but also naïve in some important ways. We worked as hard as we could, and the best answer to whether it worked out comes from our African-American/Latina daughter, a proud alumna (as you read this) of Howard University (a historically black college), who says we did just fine. We still wonder about some things we should have done differently. But all parents feel that way about something.

Adopting transracially can be a beautiful way to form a family. It has been a successful way to form families for thousands of parents and thousands of children. What's more, if you can be flexible about the color of your children-to-be, you can adopt much more quickly and possibly less expensively (though this offends my thinking, as you will read elsewhere). However, for exactly the same reasons that interracial marriage is not for everyone, transracial adoption is not the right choice for every adopter and, as mentioned in Chapter 7, it demands huge changes and constant awareness, as well as the ability to be kind to yourself when you blow it—because you will.

It is perfectly reasonable for you to decide that you wish to pursue an inracial adoption.

A Baby? Maybe Not!

Of course you first thought about a baby—it was logical. But what about an older child? Have you considered the older children who wait? Age of child should not become the most important element in deciding to adopt. Babies grow to toddlers who grow to school age who grow to teens. Each age has its positives and negatives, and parents who deliberate carefully may find that they actually enjoy children of a certain age more than others.

The truth is that not everyone wants to adopt a baby. Many would-be adopters have done most of their fantasizing about parenting not about babies, but about toddlers, or about reading stories with a pre-reader, or about coaching a grade school sports team. Consider your fantasies when deciding what age child is for you.

Consider your own age and your health with great care as well. When we are bombarded today with news about people and celebrities who are well past traditional child bearing years beginning new families or second families by adopting or by giving birth using advanced technologies, it can be tempting to think that it really is possible to have it all—long and important career first, parenthood to an infant or two in later life. Indeed, many people do manage this successfully—often with substantial help from others. Baby boomers who have reached their 40s and 50s vigorous and in good health have been especially prone to this kind of thinking. But there are the less cheery stories we don't read about parents. In parenting, age does matter.

> **Myth:** Newborns are the "easiest" to parent.
>
> **Fact:** Certainly newborns aren't the easiest from a practical perspective. They are totally dependent, require constant care, create havoc with parental sleep schedules, often require expensive daycare, and so on. There are many practical reasons that make adopting older children "easier"—no diapers, longer nights, ability to interact through play with adults, and they often recognizing the value of having a family. On the other hand, from a psychological perspective, infants probably are "easier." Certainly experiences of early life—being in a neglectful birth home, experiencing moves in foster care, or growing up in orphanages—do matter, but well prepared and educated parents can lower their risks and can handle those that appear unpredictably with proper support and personal commitment.

When I raise this issue, I'm frequently met by such replies as, "Oh, but a 25-year-old mother could be hit by a truck tomorrow. Why should a worse case scenario prevent me from doing something I've always wanted to do—parent a baby?" And, "Why, 40 is the new 30!" In reality, the odds of that very young mother being seriously disabled or dying are very low. Equally as true is that not every 40-something is in as good of shape as they could be. But actuarial statistics are very different for the nameless average 25-year-old than they are for the anonymous average 50-year-old. February 2007 tables from the Centers for Disease Control[4] predict average life expectancies for people of both sexes and all races born at the beginning of the decades from 1960 to look much like Table 9-1.

Table 9-1

Decade of Birth	Life Expectancy in Years
1960	69.7
1970	70.8
1980	73.7
1990	75.4

Now of course these are averages, and it should be noted that European-American men, on average, live 5–7 years longer than do African-American men and that all women are expected, on average, to live 5–9 years longer than men. Healthy eating and exercising, maintaining a good weight ratio, not smoking or engaging in other life-altering substance abuse all contribute to higher life expectancies. Genes contribute, too. In fact, in light of the revelations which have come from the Human Genome Project and have been influenced by studies of twins reared together and apart, scientists estimate that longevity due to genetic inheritance is between 25–30 percent; individual interaction with the environment accounts for the rest.[5]

This means that the healthy lifestyle you've adopted is important. But it also means that when predicting your health and abilities status during prime-impact parenting years when your child will be between 5 and 20 years of age, you need to take a close, hard, objective look at your family health history. If you are a male adopting at 50, you need to consider just how healthy your grandfathers and their brothers, your father, your uncles, and your older brothers were or are at 60 and at 70. If you are a woman adopting at 45, you need to consider the health history and status of your grandmothers and their sisters, your mother, your aunts, and your older sisters at 55 and at 65 and older. If, for example, Alzheimer's runs in your family, or early death due to blood pressure problems, heart disease, or a particular form of cancer is common despite medical interventions, you should screen for these problems and apply preventative procedures, but you should also be realistic about your would-be child's risk for being placed in a precarious position at an early age.

Consider your child-to-be's extended adoptive family—are there to be cousins? If so, what are their ages? What about the ages of kids in the families of close friends?

Of course you will plan for negative eventualities with life insurance, long-term care insurance, guardianship agreements, etc. But beyond that, should a 25-year-old new to his adulthood and independent be expected to provide care for an aging parent? Will a 16-year-old really do "just fine" with the loss of yet another father?

> Becky and Joe built a large family by birth and adoption. Their adoptions began with children of color and later included children with very special medical needs. When Becky developed cancer while still

parenting 10 kids at home, her friends worried. They grew even more concerned when, in the midst of treatment, two different agencies placed two more medically fragile children in her care. Becky died with 12 children still in need of daily care. Her husband, Joe, died of a heart attack just three years later, with 8 children still in the home. Their older children were simply too young and emotionally unprepared for parenting these children. The family dissolved.

Consider your lifestyle and the expectations it creates for your children.

Two busy big city bankers adopted 3-year-old Natasha from Ukraine. They delighted in her blue-eyed blond good looks. She was a perfect "match." They hired an au pair from Ukraine to be her caregiver for the first year, followed that with other live-in nannies, and felt positive that Natasha was doing fine. She loved her nannies—why it sometimes seemed that she preferred them to her parents, who worked long hours. It was great that Natasha and nanny could often be carted right along on Mom's or Dad's business trips. The parents were only frustrated by the annual turnover in these care providers. They had expected a longer term commitment.

When Natasha was 7, her first grade teacher became a pain in the rear, with frequent calls and notes home. When Natasha's parents finally found time to meet with him, they were shocked to find that Natasha's behavior in class was problematic, and her learning was slow and not even methodical. Suddenly, seven years into the adoption of their daughter, Natasha's parents were faced with the need to find expert diagnosis and care for a child in trouble. Their less than full-time interaction with this lovely child from a neglectful background who had continued to be cared for by a series of parent substitutes long after she left the orphanage had indeed worsened the trauma she brought with her. Getting Natasha the help that she needed called for major disruption in the family "routine." It happened, and Natasha improved greatly, but not without major upheaval that was far more difficult than a smoother transition and care plan might have been.

Families with a twist—single parents, gay and lesbian couples, couples who are older than their mid-40s—should understand that their options for adopting a newborn are diminished by the fact that there are many two-parent heterosexual couples younger than 40 eager to adopt. While it may seem unfair that this stereotypical "ideal family" will have a better shot at the stereotypical "ideal child," those are the facts. It won't be impossible for families with a twist to adopt a newborn; it will, however, be significantly slower for them to adopt a newborn. Many just don't want to wait, and so they will need to become more open to adopting a child who is not a newborn. Additionally, many agencies will automatically steer them in that direction.

So, what is "older" anyway? Most advocates believe that any child who is not a newborn should be considered an "older" child. Why? Because if he has not been adopted at birth, he will have had prior experiences in care before coming to your home. The older he gets, the more experiences—both good and bad—he will have had, and the more risks he has been exposed to. Agencies, however, define older differently. Both in the U.S. and abroad, a child is considered "older" if he or she is beyond the toddler years and into what is defined as school-aged—generally 5 years old and up. Indeed, age alone is enough to define these children as harder to place or as having special needs, terms which themselves may frighten off those beginning to explore adoption.

Rumors abound, and the stories one hears about older kids—both those who wait in the U.S. and those who wait in other countries—are awful. Some are true. Some of these kids have indeed had horrible beginnings. Abandoned or willingly placed by birthparents simply unable to make it, or removed from their parents due to abuse or neglect, some waiting children have been moved from family member to family member or from foster home to foster home for years. Children from the many countries who continue to use institutional care settings rather than foster homes for their parentless children have all suffered some degree of neglect, if not abuse, in that setting—let alone what they were exposed to either in utero or in early family care settings. But myth exaggerates fact. In the media business there is an adage: if it bleeds, it leads. That means that when adoption is covered at all in the media, the coverage is not likely to be about the many families parenting children from an orphanage on the other side of the world or from a U.S. foster family who is doing very well. Instead the coverage is likely to be about the far less common cases of incorrigible, rage-filled, and attachment disordered children who are murdered by their adoptive parents or who murder their parents. It's enough to seem to "prove" the old bad seed myths that used to surround adoption. Do any of these news stories offer us any proof that adoption itself was the responsible factor in these horror stories? When was the last time, that you saw a news story that made clear to you that a caesarean-section-born or birth-control-failure child murdered his mother?

Some of these "older" kids have had pretty good starts and relatively stable relationships with long-term caregivers. Perhaps they started out in a stable birth family relationship which has now dissolved due to illness, death, divorce, unemployment, or any one of dozens of other factors. Perhaps they've lived nearly all their lives in one foster home with a set of well-trained interim caregivers while the agency tried unsuccessfully to help the birthfamily get itself together. Perhaps their care in their home country was in an orphanage modeling the best possible institutional care. Perhaps (and this is something we just don't talk about often) these kids have simply been born more resilient than the children in the cribs around them.

Love absolutely does not conquer all, yet the truth is that with a combination of realistic expectations, appropriate pre-adoption education, and post adoption services from a really good agency which will respect the need parents have for full disclosure and honesty; with the support of a good adoptive parents' group; with a commitment on your part to advocate for yourself and your child, adopting an older child can be, and most often is, completely successful.

Do You Have a Particular Age in Mind?

It has become increasingly common for those adopting today (who are older, on average, than prior generations of would-be adopters) to think seriously, and first, about adopting a toddler. As a result, a question I see posted more and more often on the adoption support boards I moderate for INCIID.org concerns the adoption of toddlers. "We're fine without a newborn, but where are the toddlers?" ask these would-be parents at the initial stages of exploring adoption.

Lots of toddlers (1- to 4-year-olds) are waiting in other countries. These children are readily adoptable. The most important thing you must keep in mind (because it often just doesn't come up in the preparation process) when thinking about adopting a toddler from another country is that toddlerhood can be, developmentally, a difficult age for a child to move. One particularly challenging issue is that these children have had many experiences—some of them creating various levels of trauma and loss—but they do not have the cognitive and verbal skills to talk about these things, which makes remedial therapy challenging. Additionally, children adopted internationally will take some time to understand and use a new language. Understanding these challenges and putting into place (well ahead of placement) a support team for an internationally adopted toddler that includes an intercountry medicine clinic (with adoption-literate and -experienced developmental pediatricians, neuropsychiatrists or neuropsychologists, occupational therapists, speech and language specialists, attachment specialists, etc.), a translator, and more can result in a highly successful adoption. Going in with eyes closed to realities other than how cute that little person is can result in disaster.

Shaqia wasn't interested in reading ahead of time—too scary. Just get her that little racially matched Haitian toddler like the boy she had seen in a church bulletin and she'd know what to do. After all, she had lots of nieces and nephews, so plenty of experience with toddlers.

René (whose name was immediately changed to Montel) arrived at age 3, AIDS-positive but on medication, and developmentally delayed partially due to serious malnourishment. (Shaqia would fatten him up!) He wasn't talking, though he understood spoken Haitian French. (Shaqia and her supportive family spoke no French).

Surrounded and passed around by noisy aunts, uncles, and cousins speaking a language he didn't know, Montel withdrew to a dissociative shell. Shaqia tried her best to love him out of it, but he wouldn't respond. He shrank from her touch, woke with terrors in the night, and cried when picked up from daycare.

Shaqia reached out for help from her agency—which was half way across the country from her home—and got little response other than to "relax," so she turned to the Internet. There, after weeks on a message board for others who had adopted troubled toddlers, she found her answer—not support, not education, not services, but another parent willing to "take him." An independent adoption was arranged, and Montel, to be renamed René, moved across the country to a new home, a new family—and new challenges.

Shaqia had no support for her decision—not even in her family, members of which were quite vocal about her having "given up." Where were they when she needed help and respite? Her parenting dream was shattered.

Angel's story could not have been more different. A career military officer, he had never married, but with his 20 years in and now retired from the service, he was ready to become a full-time dad. He moved back to the city where most of his family lived and began the process of adopting from Guatemala, the country from which his family had emigrated a generation before his own birth in the U.S. His sisters and his brothers were on board and supportive.

His agency, a state away, put him in touch with an independent social worker in his own city who was herself a single adoptive parent—domestically. Sylvia helped him find books to read (Mary Hopkins-Best's *Toddler Adoption* from Perspectives Press was on the list), linked him to two different local parent groups—one serving families who had adopted from Guatemala, the other who had adopted older children, mostly from the foster care system—and to an intercountry medicine clinic at the university medical school just 75 miles away. He found ready ears and great ideas in both places.

When Angel brought Guillermo home after their several week stay together in Guatemala, they had already forged the beginning of a good attachment. Angel spoke Spanish, an advantage in communicating with his new son. Together with Guillermo's new Abuela, who had accompanied her son on the journey, father and son had lived for several weeks on Guillermo's familiar "turf" of sights, sounds, smells and foods, making for a smoother transition for Guillermo. Abuela's experienced hands guided her son into new parenthood, and she was careful to take the advice of the books she had read—mostly advising, allowing Angel to do the hands-on parenting.

After arriving home, Guillermo took the advice not of his eager family—who had never experienced adoption—but of those parent group experts. He and Guillermo cocooned for several weeks before entering the big new world. During this time family members came to visit one or two at a time and for short periods (Angel and Abuela had prepared them ahead of time). Guillermo was fed familiar foods, listened to tapes of music from his home country play in the background, and slept for a while on a mat near Papí's bed so that when he woke at night his daddy was near to help soothe him back to sleep. His visit to the intercountry medicine clinic discovered some parasite in need of treatment, but beyond that, Guillermo appeared to be in pretty good health. He would need more testing later, of course, but he would get that at the clinic, which would consult as needed with his local pediatrician.

Three years later Guillermo and Papí are doing well. Dad and son, and extended family have merged seamlessly. Papí coaches Guillermo's Little League team—his dream for fatherhood satisfied.

In the U.S., there a great many toddlers in foster care, but many of them are not yet free for adoption. Most toddlers in the foster care system who are already available for adoption and waiting for a permanent family are the youngest of sibling groups or have more complicated medical, physical, or emotional challenges.

Where are the healthier or only-child toddlers? Well, let's look at how the public child welfare system works. The primary goal of the American child welfare system is not to remove children and get them to new homes. The primary goal of child welfare is to keep children safe while at the same time trying to keep families together. So when a baby (or toddler) is removed from an abusive or neglectful situation and placed in safe foster care, the first order of business is to try to offer supportive and rehabilitative services to the birthparent(s) with the goal of reunification. This process can take up to a year—sometimes more. According to the Adoption and Foster Care Analysis and Reporting System (AFCARS), about 54% of the time rehabilitation and reunification works. Sometimes it works for a while, but then the child is back in foster care.

When reunification is not an option, the "second best" option, according to the system, is to find extended family members to adopt the child. When that doesn't work, the child is deemed generally adoptable. By this time, the baby removed from his birth home has become a toddler, and the toddler removed from his home has reached pre-K age.

We will talk in Chapter 10 about the option of fostering-to-adopt, which brings together children of younger ages with would-be permanent parents willing to take the emotional risk of caring for a child while birthparent rehabilitation and reunification is attempted, knowing that they have at least a 46% (or better, because of how these placements are made) chance of becoming this child's adoptive parents.

Finding that Older Child Meant for You

Statistically, according to AFCARS reports, the mean age of children free for adoption in the U.S. foster care system in FY2005 (the most recent statistic available in summer 2007) was about 8.5 years, with the range of ages being from newborn to 17 years.[6] The average age of children adopted internationally from all countries is under 5 years but older than 10 months.

Before beginning to inquire about the photo listing books that catalog specific waiting U.S. children, begin the decision-making process by clarifying your goals in parenting, taking into account your personal fears, your personal needs, your specific situation regarding age and health, where you live, careers, etc. You should try to list any and all benefits you can think of in adopting a baby (e.g. having the opportunity to be the child's only psychological parent, babies are so easy for everyone to relate to, etc.). Then list the disadvantages that each of you sees in beginning with a baby (e.g. we'll be older than our child's peers' parents, we'd have to deal with daycare problems, etc.).

Next list any and all benefits you can think of in adopting an older child or a child of a particular age (e.g. we get out of the dirty diaper and two o'clock feeding stage and go straight to the good stuff like Cub Scouts and gourmet cooking lessons, we won't have to interrupt careers with significantly long parenting leaves, etc.) and any and all disadvantages you can see to starting with an older child (e.g. we won't have control over what's happened in his past, our parents may not relate well to her, etc.).

Then, whether you may be adopting domestically or internationally, *really* investigate both family resources in your own community and the agencies which specialize in special needs placements because most older children will have specialized needs, whether your agency categorizes them this way or not. Is there a strong post-adoption program? You can expect to need post adoption services, and many agencies don't have them—so choose another. Are mental health providers in your town adoption-educated and adoption- and attachment-sensitive? If you are considering a child with physical or learning disabilities, how are the educational and social services? What kinds of specially focused programs exist for kids with problems, and *how do parents already using them feel about them*?

Look for, and check in on, foster and adoptive family support groups both domestic and intercountry in your area. Talk to these parents, many of whom will have already had experience with kids adopted at the ages you are considering and so may have become real experts at locating local resources. Strongly consider attending one of NACAC's annual North American Conferences on Adoptable Children, held every year in late July or early August at rotating sites throughout North America. This is the largest adoption conference in the world. It is here that you will come in contact with the world's most well-respected experts in the field, all of whom provide wonderful training, but some of whom have not written books or articles easily accessible to consumers. NACAC sessions are taped, and the tape catalog for several years' worth of conferences is available from them on request.

Don't limit your contact with parents of children with special needs just to adoptive and foster families. Look as well at the support groups in your area which focus narrowly on specific educational and disabilities needs, and which include families formed just by birth.

Both domestic agencies which have expertise in special needs adoption and intercountry programs which are really good at placing older children have strong local post-adoption programs. If a local agency does not offer such a program, this is not the agency for you. Those agencies working with U.S.-born older children should be mentioning the possibility of subsidies (as mentioned in the finance section in Chapter 8) to help with any medical or education problems, or with ongoing counseling. Subsidies are most often not available to intercountry adopters.

Whether adopting domestically or internationally, expect to hear terms like life book, disengagement therapy, attachment challenges, attachment therapy, and more. Expect to be referred to the books and tapes of some of the experts mentioned in the resources section. If you don't hear these things from your agency, bring them up. If you feel that your agency does not immediately understand what you are talking about and does not actively engage in discussion about these things, *consider this a red flag!*

Leah and Ned lived in a small town served mainly by the public agency. There weren't many babies, but their caseworker was more than delighted to share the state's photo listing book of waiting children. Leah and Ned were swept into the adoption of Mia, a 3-year-old described as bright, mischievous and affectionate, after waiting for several years and losing hope that there would ever be a newborn.

"Mia just needs undivided attention and a lot of love," the caseworker assured them. "You'll do fine."

Mia was affectionate, all right—indiscriminately so, and especially with men, even strangers. She masturbated in public—even at church. She was cuddly with her new daddy, but she was aloof from Leah. She was sneaky—hoarding food and seeming to deliberately look for ways to be naughty, which brought her attention—the negative kind.

Leah approached the agency, but no one there had any ideas. "Just be consistent and give her lots of love," they said.

Leah and Ned were dealing with a child who had been sexually abused, but they didn't know that. They needed special therapy—but none was available. Their child was unattached, though not unattach-able—but no one was supporting them in getting the help they needed. Love could not be enough to meet this family's needs. The adoption disrupted and Leah and Ned felt like complete failures—afraid to try parenting again.

Leah and Ned had not *decided* on a special needs adoption. They had *settled* for one. Furthermore, their agency had prepared them badly, with-held important information from them, and failed to provide the support and post-adoption services this family needed and deserved. The disrup-tion of Leah, Ned, and Mia's adoption wasn't their fault. It was a failure of the system. But the system can and does work.

At 55 and 36, Rich and Maryanne were in a second marriage. Neither had children and both wanted to parent, but Rich's age had been a factor which blocked them from applying for a baby at several agencies. They had optimistically pursued private adoption, but had given up when three birthparents expressed hesitance because Rich was older than their own fathers, whom they sure didn't want to parent their babies. On investigating intercountry adoption, they discovered that Rich's age was a factor with nearly all of the countries local agencies could help them with.

They were about to give up when they ran into an adoption worker they knew socially at a party and she laughed, "Have I got a 10-year-old for you!" She was kidding, of course, but it got them thinking.

At 55, college-athlete Rich still harbored a desire to be a PeeWee football coach for his son's team. He wondered if he'd be as physically fit at 65 or 70. Maryanne had spent a lot of time getting her small business off the ground. She was its key employee; it was going to be difficult for her to arrange to be home full-time with an infant for a while and then juggle daycare for six years.

Looking through the photo listing books, they found Morrie, an 8-year-old boy from a state half way across the country. He was healthy and handsome, but hyperactive and dyslexic. The foster mother with whom he had lived since the age of 4 months was elderly and ailing. Morrie had to move.

It sounded challenging, but Rich and Maryanne decided to check it out. They read books on both ADD and dyslexia and felt confident that these were challenges they were prepared to handle. Rich was especially pleased to read how important channeling extra energy through sports can be to many hyperactive boys. Their local research produced some encouraging news. Their city had a well-respected private school that specialized in dyslexia. A significant proportion of its graduates went on to college. A subsidy which was a part of Morrie's adoption planning would help to offset the tuition.

The local agency put Rich and Maryanne in touch with an active adoptive parents' group, and they discovered that there was a smaller support group within the group for families of children adopted at an older age. Their pediatrician spoke with Morrie's current doctor and was reassured that drug therapy effectively managed his attention deficit/hyperactivity disorder.

Morrie, Rich, and Maryanne became a family—a successful one.

You do yourself a serious disservice if you don't realistically look at the option of adopting an older child. But do so in light of what you know about your personal resources—time, money, emotional reserves, physical capacities—and about your community's resources as identified from your research. It is perfectly reasonable that the result of this soul searching might be to decide that you still want to parent a baby.

Muddied Thinking about the Choice of a "Waiting" Child

One of the most important reasons for the inability of many family-challenged never-before-parents to consider special needs adoption is that they are normal. Like everyone else, they have fears, doubts, and prejudices. As a group they have the same needs, dreams, and values as do people who give birth to their children. Proportionately, then, they are no more likely to see special needs adoption as a first choice for family building than are their fertile counterparts.

Since friends, neighbors, and family members look at adoption as second best and for the most part reject it as a family building alternative for themselves, singles, same-sex couples and infertile people are frequently unable to see themselves as potential adopters of waiting children either. They often hold a buried feeling that they are being treated as "second class citizens" offered what society sees as "second rate goods" rejected by everyone else, but seen as "all they can get" or "all they deserve." This too-negative-to-voice feeling is a part of the traditional adopter's feeling of powerlessness, but it is fed by the approach to special needs adoption taken by too many agencies.

Though substantial training is required to adopt a child with special needs, other qualifications may seem "easier." There are fewer restrictions about age, religion, marital status, etc. Agency fees are often lower or non-existent; when adopting domestically, subsidies often exist which appear to "pay" people to accept such children. To a would-be parent looking from the outside, not able to get close enough to the realities of special needs adoption to be properly educated, and thus primed to misinterpret

Myth: Kids with "special needs" are irreparably damaged. It's safer to adopt a child from abroad than a child from foster care.

Fact: The idea of "special needs" is misunderstood, first because children in the U.S. system may be labeled as having special needs just because of their age, their race, or the fact that they come as part of a sibling group, rather than because they have any significant educational, emotional or physical problems. Additionally, adoption medical experts steadfastly maintain that adoptive parents must enter intercountry adoption only if willing to accept that virtually all internationally-adopted children should be considered to have special needs of an emotional or physical nature (more on this later). Though not without challenges, both those adopted internationally and those adopted domestically thrive when placed in loving, committed, and appropriately prepared and supported permanent homes. Even those children who need years of physical, emotional, or educational therapy most often grow into happy, productive adults.

what little they do know, such facts and fantasies are frightening and even demeaning.

Parenting is never easy, but it becomes more difficult when the baggage of several years spent with other families, racial differences, or profound disabilities is added to it. This is the primary reason that the vast majority of parents considering family expansion prefer to do so by giving birth over and over again rather than by adopting children already born and in need of permanent, loving families. All of society accepts this reasoning on the part of fertile couples and do not think poorly of them when they choose not to adopt.

The common value system declares that birth is superior to adoption as a method of family planning. Most people, then, are delighted but somewhat surprised by the fertile couple who chooses to adopt rather than to give birth to some of their children. They tend to heap praise and admiration on such adopters ("Aren't you people wonderful to take that child! I don't know how you do it. I don't think I could, but I'm sure glad that there are people out there like you!"), while at the same time viewing their motivations as somewhat suspect ("Why would you want to take someone else's reject when you could have a baby? You're asking for trouble.").

Because most of the challenges to family building experienced by readers of this book—sexual orientation, infertility, single status—often damage self esteem, these hopeful parents, who have not had the opportunity to parent by the traditional method, often harbor the unexpressed fear that they will be unable to do a good job. Some even feel, as I did briefly about my infertility, that their status was a signal from God that they wouldn't make good parents. They desperately want to get as close to the "real thing" as they can in order to test their fitness for parenting. Children with special problems, such couples feel, need special parenting skills, and they question whether they have the ability to acquire such skills. Some professionals question this as well.

Finally, adoption is often difficult for extended families to accept in principle. Couples sometimes feel that they have let their families down with their infertility and thus fear being rejected by them. They feel that a baby—one of their own ethnicity—might be more easily accepted by their families, allowing both themselves and their children to experience the "realness" of multigenerational family dynamics that they might miss out on if their family did not accept a special needs adoptee. While this is a solvable problem, and indeed we will spend some time talking specifically about bringing families along in the adoption experience, the fact that this fear is rooted not in myth but in reality makes it a difficult fear to erase.

The facts are clear. Waiting children, who were once seen as unadoptable and shuffled off to institutions with little attempt to find adoptive homes for them, exist in large numbers here and in the rest of the world. Child welfare advocates have done an admirable job of changing professional attitudes about such children. Now, permanency is the goal for every child and caseworkers are pressured to find homes for these children.

Many prospective adopters comment that they have felt uncomfortably pressured by their agencies to consider special needs adoption. Rarely is such pressure intended or consequential. In most cases the sense of pressure comes as a result of adopters feeling their own sense of guilt in response to the reasonable suggestion from agency workers that they give at least careful thought to all of the options open to them in building a family by adoption. Sometimes, however, the pressure is real. Social workers are real normal people. They share the same value system held by the majority of the society in which they live, and thus some of them send the same set of mixed messages to the family challenged that they are receiving from family and friends. Frustrated by the need to find homes for children in need, as well as increasing numbers of potential adopters inquiring about the increasingly harder to find "Gerber baby," adoption workers wish that the ideal could be met: that children in need of homes and families who want children could meet each other's needs. Faced with this practical crisis, adoption workers sometimes subconsciously buy into the old adage "beggars can't be choosers" as they consider would-

> **Myth:** Adopted kids aren't as mentally healthy as kids raised in their birth homes.
>
> **Fact:** There are many recent longitudinal studies that demonstrate that adoptees fare very well in adolescence and adulthood psychologically, socially, and emotionally—most often just as well as children living with their families of origin. Older studies which claim that adopted children are overrepresented in mental health systems rarely account for complicating factors such as age and situation of child at placement, the fact that adoptive parents may indeed be more likely to look for help for their children, etc.

be parents in the adoption approval process. The message goes out, this time not just from the uninformed neighbor, but from the most powerful person in family-challenged lives, "If you really wanted a child, you'd take one of those homeless kids they advertise in the papers."

So the double standard which has always been at work in society at large has filtered down to some social work professionals. An adoption worker who would not judge negatively a fertile couple's decision to give birth rather than to adopt an older child reacts impatiently toward, and even questions the motivation for parenthood of, the singles, gay couples and infertile heterosexuals seeking a healthy infant, and the credibility gap widens.

Just as you carefully explored all of your choices in medical treatment, it makes sense that you would do yourself the service of fully exploring the entire range of adoptions. Understand, however, that ultimately only you can decide whether to adopt a baby or a waiting child.

Adoption itself is an enormous leap! Few fertile people have the courage to make that leap. Leaping even farther—to create a multiracial family, to accept the challenges of parenting a child who comes to you with several years' worth of less than optimal parenting experiences—takes superior courage. Since readers of this book are perfectly normal people, there is no reason to presume that you will be prepared to make this leap in numbers proportionately higher than the fertile population.

Obviously, the decisions to be made are enormous, and they are made more difficult by the complexities of your challenges to family building and the process of adopting itself. In order to make these decisions, you will find it helpful to work on the decision-making process of developing goals and objectives, examining alternatives and strategies, and allocating resources again. In addition to the material I share here, at the end of Part Three you will find a selected list of recommended resources which will help you in the data collection process that is part of your decision-making routine. These materials will help you to examine in more detail the various adoption options which you find yourselves willing to explore, and they will offer quite practical advice for pursuing your objectives.

Adopting a Newborn— Back to that First Thought

> **Myth:** There are no healthy newborns to adopt anymore.
>
> **Fact:** There continue to be many thousands of healthy newborns adopted every year.

Though there are very few newborn babies adopted internationally, there are babies to adopt. At least 100,000 of them are adopted in the U.S. every year. What many would-be parents don't realize is that more newborns are adopted independently than are adopted through licensed adoption agencies. The next chapter will describe in more detail the issues to consider when thinking about choosing independent adoption.

Adopting a Second Child

For first-time parents, decisions about sex, age, able-ness, and ethnicity of their children are probably more complex and difficult to make than are those same decisions for parents who are adopting for the second, third, or fourth time. Oftentimes, though certainly not universally, second-time adopters find that they are feeling much more flexible about many of these issues.

There are a number of reasons for this common change in flexibility, but the big one is clear—experience. The lack of experience with parenting that made non-parents so needy of getting as close to the "real" thing disappears when one has successfully parented for a while. Babies grow quickly and, usually, so does love. It becomes easier, with experience, to imagine being successful with a slightly older child, to understand falling in love with a child of a different skin tone. It is clear, for most, that adoption is a real and solid way for families to be formed.

This is often less true for secondarily infertile people adopting after having given birth to a first child. For these couples, adoption itself remains the great and frightening unknown. While they are often more confident in their competence with parenting skills, they are often every bit as frightened as are the childless who become parents for the first time through adoption about those nearly unspeakable fears—Can I love a child not genetically related to me? Can the rest of my family? Will I be a "real" parent to this child? For couples dealing with secondary infertility, perhaps the best resources for exploring concerns and finding support are not infertile couples who have already adopted (but have never given birth), but instead preferential adopters—fertile couples who have chosen to expand their families by adoption despite their continued ability to expand it by birth.

Final decisions about the sex, age, challenges, and race of your child are yours. Beyond the unforeseen circumstances that become a part of any parenting experience, you have enormous control and power here. In order to exercise that power and control, you must be well-informed and willing to demand your right and the right of your child to full disclosure of any and all pertinent facts from the intermediaries involved in your adoption. And remember . . . you are not a beggar; you are a chooser in this case. Be sure that you make careful and clear decisions that you will be able and willing to claim as your own, whatever they may be.

And a final word . . . I have a strong bias as an adoption advocate and a parent educator. I am offended by what I see as a growing phenomenon among some prospective adopters who seem to be embarked on what I've come to call The Search for the Good Enough Baby. In my books, and in the speaking that I do, I offer advice about "problems" that may arise during the parenting experience because I believe that well-informed parents can do the best job for their children. But if a perfect match to what you believe your birth child would likely have been or guaranteeable assurance that an agency has found for you a baby who carries something akin to a Good Housekeeping Seal of Approval is what you are expecting before saying yes or no to adoption in general or to a specific child offered to you, please don't adopt at all. Parenting doesn't come with guarantees, and if you expect one, you are bound to be disappointed. Any child deserves more than that. Every child deserves to be wanted for who he is rather than as a substitute for what might have been.

Resources

Kids with Special Needs

See also the Resources at the end of Chapter 11.

Adoption Learning Partners (www.adoptionlearningpartners.org) offers online interactive courses for parents-to-be which some agencies require and/or accept for credit. These are introductory level classes, and most do not take the place of a more detailed book, but they can be an excellent alternative for those who are just not "readers." Among the ones helpful here are "With Eyes Wide Open" (see book on which it is based, below), "Adopting the Older Child," and "Becoming Your Child's Best Advocate."

Children's Home Society of Minnesota. *With Eyes Wide Open: A Workbook for Parents Adopting International Children*, a workbook (St Paul, MN: 2000) and the related eponymous online preparation course from Adoption Learning Partners which can be taken for credit to satisfy preparation hours with many agencies. www.adoptionlearningpartners.org/courses/wewo.cfm

Cline, Foster, MD and Lisa Greene. *Parenting Children with Health Issues.* (Golden, CO: Love and Logic Press, 2007) and the related web site www.parentingchildrenwithhealthissues.com/index.html

Erichsen, Jean, MA, LBSW. *Inside the Adoption Agency: Understanding Intercountry Adoption in the Era of the Hague Convention.* (Lincoln, NE: iUniverse, 2007)

Hoppenhauer, Denise Harris. *Adopting a Toddler: What Size Shoe Does She Wear?* (iUniverse Star, 2004)

Hopkins-Best, Mary. *Toddler Adoption: The Weaver's Craft* (Indianapolis: Perspectives Press, Inc., 1997)

Keck, Gregory, PhD. and Regina Kupecky. *Adopting the Hurt Child.* (Colorado Springs: Piñon Press, 1998)

Keck, Gregory, PhD and Regina Kupecky. *Parenting the Hurt Child.* (Colorado Springs: Piñon Press, 2002)

Maskew, Trish. *Our Own: Adopting and Parenting the Older Child.* (Longmont, CO: Snowcap Press, 1999)

North American Council on Adoptable Children: (www.nacac.org) North America's premier advocacy network for waiting children, NACAC lobbies for legislative action; educates through its annual conference, its training programs, its website, and its newsletter (Adoptalk); offers a supportive training and networking system for parent groups throughout the country; and much, much more.

McReight, Brenda, PhD. *Parenting Your Adopted Older Child*. (Oakland, CA: New Harbinger Publications, Inc., 2002)

Financial Assistance and Subsidies

See also the Finance section in the Resources for Chapter 8.

Adoption.com's guide to financial assistance and subsidy. www.adopting.org/adoptions/special-needs-adoption-subsidies-assistance-payments.html

Adoption Policy Resource Center (www.fpsol.com/adoption/), run by advocate and assistance expert Tim O'Hanlon, can help you to understand what assistance resources your child may eligible for and how to advocate effectively for what your child is entitled to. Available as downloadable ebooks by O'Hanlon and by Rita Laws are several excellent resources which, because they are in electronic format, can be kept constantly up-to-date. Well worth the investment!

Laws, Rita and Tim O'Hanlon. *Adoption and Financial Assistance: Tools for Navigating the Bureaucracy*. (Westport, CT: Bergin & Garvey, 1999)

Race and Ethnicity Issues

AdoptKorea (www.adoptkorea.com), adoptive parent Roberta Rosenberg's comprehensive site, focuses on all things Korean-adoption-related.

Adoption Learning Partners (www.adoptionlearningpartners.org) offers online interactive courses for parents-to-be which some agencies require and/or accept for credit. These are introductory level classes, and most do not take the place of a more detailed book, but they can be an excellent alternative for those who are just not "readers." Among the ones helpful here is "Conspicuous Families."

Alperson, Myra. *Dim Sum, Bagels, and Grits: A Sourcebook for Multicultural Families*. (New York: Farrar, Strauss & Giroux, 2001)

Bridge Communications www.bridgecommunications.org

Families with Children from China (www.fwcc.org) is the website for a national network of local groups of adoptive parents who have adopted daughters from China. FCC chapters provide support, education, networking, online discussion groups, cultural links, and more.

Pact, An Adoption Alliance (www.pactadopt.org) "provides the highest quality adoption services to children of color. Our primary client is the child. In order to serve the child, we address the needs of all the child's parents, by advising families facing a crisis pregnancy and by offering lifelong education to adoptive families and birth families on matters of race and adoption. Our goal is for every child to feel wanted, honored and loved, a cherished member of a strong family with proud connections to the rich cultural heritage that is his or her birthright. Pact was incorporated in 1991 as a non-profit 501(c)(3) charitable organization."

Klatzkin, Amy, ed. *A Passage to the Heart: Writings from Families with Children from China.* (St Paul, MN: Yeong and Yeong Book Co., 1999)

Register, Cheri. *Are Those Kids Yours?: American Families With Children Adopted From Other Countries.* (New York: Free Press, 1990)

Register, Cheri. *Beyond Good Intentions: A Mother Reflects On Raising Internationally Adopted Children.* (St. Paul, MN: Yeong and Yeong Book Co., 2005)

Steinberg, Gail and Beth Hall. *Inside Transracial Adoption.* (Indianapolis: Perspectives Press, Inc., 2000)

Intercountry Adoption

See also the Resources at the end of Chapter 11.

Adoption Learning Partners (www.adoptionlearningpartners.org) offers online interactive courses for parents-to-be which some agencies require and/or accept for credit. These are introductory level classes, and most do not take the place of a more detailed book, but they can be an excellent alternative for those who are just not "readers." Among the ones helpful here are "With Eyes Wide Open" (see book on which it is based, below), "Adopting the Older Child," "Becoming Your Child's Best Advocate," and "Medical Issues in International Adoption."

Davenport, Dawn. *The Complete Book of International Adoption: A Step by Step Guide for Finding Your Child* (New York: Broadway Books, 2007) and the author's info-packed related website www.findingyourchild.com/

Uekert, Brenda K. PhD. *10 Steps to Successful International Adoption: a Guided Workbook for Prospective Parents.* (Williamsburg, VA: Third Avenue Press, 2007) and the author's related website www.10steps2adoption.com/

U.S. State Department's International Adoption booklet travel.state.gov/family/adoption/intercountry/intercountry_473.html

U.S. State Department Country-Specific Inter-Country Adoption Information www.travel.state.gov/family/adoption/country/country_369.html

CHAPTER 10

Openness

Stop! Don't flip ahead to the next chapter because you've already decided that open adoption is not for you and you've chosen intercountry adoption for that very reason.

I've got news for you. That "out" is no guarantee that you aren't going to hear from, or about, a birthfamily. It isn't going to stop "searching" on your child's part either. More and more families are indeed meeting their children's birthfamily members in their countries of origin; more and more young adult adoptees are returning to their countries of origin (often with their adopting parents' support) to try to make contact with birth relatives; and more and more adoptive parents are finding, after their children have been home with them for a while and they are all feeling "entitled," that they wish they knew more, so they are initiating intercountry searches. Funny, how time and experience can change a person's point of view.

You'd better stop now and learn more about openness in adoption, because it may very well be a part of your family's future.

After living with adoption for so long, when I use the word *openness* in the context of adoption, I may actually be talking about two different things. That's true of many of us who have been working and/or living in adoption for a long time, and that could confuse many readers of this book—"newbies" to the adoption world.

The first way I use *openness* is to describe the concept of families' abilities to communicate without barriers, to their having developed family cultures where children feel that they can ask their parents anything without fear of hurting their feelings, or having them dismiss their fears or their discomfort as unimportant. The extent to which families are able to do this is tied into the development of each individual's sense of entitlement (which may be a fluctuating thing) as well as to how successful the parents have been in consistently acknowledging that adoptive relationships and adoptive families are different from families whose connections are by birth (Chapter 4).

The other way that the term *openness* is used in the context of adoptive family life is to describe the degree to which adoptive families and birthfamilies are in communication with one another—or at the very least have some knowledge of one another.

I suspect that this second use is what most readers are thinking about right now. Because issues around contact between birth and adoptive families remain one of the things that most worry those who are considering adoption (not quite as much as attachment, but close), I decided that the topic really needs its own chapter.

A Little Background

Let's begin with a discussion of the history of adoption and some philosophical debates going on today in order to be prepared to discuss the question of whether you are prepared for an open adoption.

You may be surprised to know that confidential adoption—the kind of adoptions where birthparents and adoptive parents have virtually no identifying information about one another and are expected never to contact one another—is actually much newer than is open adoption.

For centuries, in nearly every culture around the world, children in need of parents were cared for by extended family members or someone else known to them in close-knit communities. There was no secrecy about the issue of being fostered or adopted then, primarily because "everyone knew" who the birthparents of these children in need were and there was no attempt to try to hide the fact that these children were not the genetic children of the family raising them. Social custom was what linked these families, not law. Adoption still works this way in most tribal cultures around the world, and indeed much about this traditional approach to adoption in western culture is like the practice of *kafala* in Islamic culture, in which children in need are taken into guardianship by caregivers. Huda, about.com's guide to Islam, describes the relationship like this.

> The guardian/child relationship has specific rules under Islamic law, which render the relationship a bit different than what is common adoption practice today. The Islamic term for what is commonly called adoption is kafala, which comes from a word that means "to feed." In essence, it describes more of a foster-parent relationship. Some of the rules in Islam surrounding this relationship:
>
> An adopted child retains his or her own biological family name (surname) and does not change his or her name to match that of the adoptive family.
>
> An adopted child inherits from his or her biological parents, not automatically from the adoptive parents.

When the child is grown, members of the adoptive family are not considered blood relatives, and are therefore not muhrim to him or her. "Muhrim" refers to a specific legal relationship that regulates marriage and other aspects of life. Essentially, members of the adoptive family would be permissible as possible marriage partners, and rules of modesty exist between the grown child and adoptive family members of the opposite sex.

If the child is provided with property/wealth from the biological family, adoptive parents are commanded to take care and not intermingle that property/wealth with their own. They serve merely as trustees.

These Islamic rules emphasize to the adoptive family that they are not taking the place of the biological family—they are trustees and caretakers of *someone else's* child. Their role is very clearly defined, but nevertheless very valued and important.[1]

Customs about caring for orphans began to change in western culture with the advent of the Industrial Revolution. As families moved from an agrarian existence to an industrial one, they also moved away from their extended family—leaving rural areas to find work in rapidly growing cities. It became increasingly common for immediate family groups to be isolated from the support common among extended families. Living in close quarters, in filthy conditions, with contaminated water and food supplies, disease rapidly moved through the quarters of industrial workers. People worked in unsafe conditions, so that both parents and children were at substantial risk for being killed on the job. For the first time, western society saw a need to "do something" about growing numbers of orphaned children.

Orphanages and work houses were the first tries, but conditions in orphanages and workhouses were so bad that "do-gooders" soon intervened, looking for ways to move these children into families. The result, during the first years of the 20th century, was the birth of charities which became child welfare agencies. This was the time of the orphan trains in America. Orphaned children from eastern cities were sent west on the new railroads, stopping at cities and towns along the way, to be "put up" on the platform in hopes that families who had been notified by telegrams to their pastors might adopt them. Some of the subsequent adoptions produced wonderful relationships. Others were little more than indentured servant/owner relationships.

But this trial seemed successful enough that, over the course of about twenty years, adoption became a structured social service with laws in each state which governed how it worked. Parents were matched with children previously unknown to one another, and thinking began to change. The new way of looking at things first suggested that children be transplanted from one family to another and not even know that they had not been born to the parents who raised them. This approach seemed to "solve" two social problems: the stigmas of illegitimacy and infertility.

After twenty or so more years, it was decided that children did need to be told of the adoption, but that, in order to protect both adoptees and birthparents from the shame of illegitimacy and to protect the wounded egos of infertile adopters, birth certificates would be amended to pretend that adopters had given birth to these children. Under this system, in order to prevent competition between parents and confusion in children, adoptive families and the birthfamilies would never meet one another, nor would they have identifying information about one another.

This was the way adoption grew for about half a century. Even as societal changes made the stigma surrounding both infertility and illegitimacy all but disappear, the majority of adoption agencies continued for decades to support the idea that birth and adoptive families should not be in communication with one another throughout the child's growing up years.

At the same time there was a slowly shifting attitude about whether or not adult adoptees should have access to identifying information about their birthparents. Beginning in the 1950s with adoptee Betty Jean Lifton and her organization Orphan Voyage, an increasing number of people— adult adoptees, adoptive parents, birthparents, and professionals—began challenging the wisdom of maintaining secrecy and anonymity in adoption across the life span. They pointed out that many adoptees experienced significant confusion during their adolescence, and later as they struggled to understand who they were and why adoption was planned for them. By the 1970s, this led to ongoing discussions about whether there was a need for more openness in adoption. Although the debate often got muddled, in reality there were several separate issues involved here.

One issue came out of the research revealing confusion among adopted children and related to David Kirk's Shared Fate theory (Chapter 4). Families forge stronger, more empathic relationships when they acknowledge differences in adoption with relative consistency. This calls for establishing an open communication style—a family climate where asking questions and talking about feelings and fears is encouraged and supported. This element of the openness debate has certainly reached maturity. Open communication is universally accepted by experts and taught to adoptive families.

A second issue related to openness in adoption was (and remains) the debate over access to records for adult adoptees and/or to birthparents of adult adoptees. This debate has been raised in legislatures throughout the U.S. for 50 years now, with very slow progress. In most states "progress" on this issue is represented by the establishment of rather restrictive, difficult to use, and poorly advertised mutual consent registries, which require that all parties to an adoption register their consent to and interest in contact before records can be opened. Even 25 years after open adoption began to grow slowly more common, no legislatures have even been willing to declare that records will be open to future adoptees and birthparents after X year.

A third issue pertained to just how much information families should be given about birthfamilies and the earlier life experiences of older children who are being adopted. Law has now established that agencies are bound to share all information to which they have access (short of identifying information) with adoptive parents of waiting children. Failure to disclose important information has been the basis for several successful wrongful adoption lawsuits.

The fourth issue is the debate over whether birthfamilies and adoptive families should be in communication from the beginning of an adoption and perhaps throughout a child's growing up years. In order to deal with the last issue, which is really emerging as the predominant style of adoption, we need to give careful thought to the other issues. While extremist proponents of one view or the other often see these issues as one and the same, many adoption educators—and I am one of them—feel that, while they are interconnected, they are indeed separate, and that it is possible to feel quite differently about each matter.

Opening adoption records to adults continues to feel uncomfortable to many people, including adoptees and birth parents. The central concern is no longer the fear that there is something intrinsically harmful to anyone in the adoption triad when they have contact with one another as adults. Contacts have been made outside of the system and records have been opened in some official way in several countries and in some U.S. states for a long enough period of time now that there are some things we know. We know that the majority of adoptees and birthparents living in places where records are accessible to them if they wish do not choose to make use of this access. But we also know that for the adoptees who do wish this access and are denied it, the ramifications of this lack of control over an issue as basic as the facts about their genetic identity can sometimes be overwhelming and almost disabling. We know that in the overwhelming majority of meetings between adult members of birth and adoptive families not only has there been the relatively successful formation of new relationships, but also that the relationship between adoptee and adoptive parent has been more often strengthened than impaired. On the other hand, we also know that there are birthparents who do not wish to have contact with their adopted-away children, who have been promised privacy and wish to keep it, and who may not even have told anyone else (parents, husbands, subsequent children) about the adoption.

All of which leads us to the question most debated of all.

Should Adoptions Be Open?

There are so many myths about open adoption. Let's look at some.

Myth: Open adoption is co-parenting. I don't want anyone else to interfere with my family.

Fact: Open adoption is not offered as an opportunity for birth-parents to continue to parent their children. Once an adoption is finalized, the adoptive parents are legally that child's only parents, able to make all decisions on behalf of their children without interference. In this regard, open adoption has nothing at all socially or legally in common with co-parenting agreements when parents divorce. Instead, open adoption is based on the goodwill belief of two families that the best interests of a child are served when he has access to information. Healthy, well-planned, and open adoption has clear boundaries which have been discussed and agreed upon by birth and adoptive parents with the support of experienced professionals.

Myth: Open adoption solves all children's adoption-related problems and ends the birthparent's feelings of grief and loss.

Fact: Open adoption is not a panacea. Nothing can "stop" feelings of loss other than healing support. Adoption is a unique family structure with its own challenges. Open adoption may help children answer some of their questions about their identity, but, as in all family relationships, access to birth families doesn't mean that relationships with them are always easy. Relationships take work.

Myth: Open adoption confuses children about who their "real" parents are.

Fact: All adopted children must at some point grapple with the fact that they have two sets of parents and two families—one by birth and one through adoption. Research over a full generation of open adoptions demonstrates that children rarely are confused by having relationships with members of their birthfamily and that adoptive parents, too, have fewer fears about birthparents when they are known to them.

Myth: Seeing her child, and knowing where we live, will just deepen a birthmother's grief and make her likely to want her child back.

Fact: Birthparents make adoption plans because they want what is best for their child. Having information, pictures, and contact, as opposed to fantasy, can only reduce curiosity and deepen a sense of reassurance that the plan was a good one and the child is doing well.

How Does Open Adoption Differ from "Closed" Adoption?

For nearly 30 years now—a generation and a half—a handful of pioneering agencies scattered from Michigan to Texas to California have been offering varying degrees of communication between birth and adoptive families in what has come to be called open adoption. As their system proved popular and successful with birthparents, who had begun to abandon adoption planning under the closed system, other agencies followed the trend. Even now, however, the spectrum of openness ranges from a one time exchange of letters without identifying information to what the experts in the field define as *continuing open adoption*: the ongoing back and forth sharing of information between an adoptee and his families of birth and adoption, designed to foster communication and cooperation for the adoptee's benefit throughout the lifespan.

As openness has matured over time, researchers have been watching to see how relationships work, and most are doing fairly well. In domestic infant adoptions today, it is almost a minimum standard that most birthparents examine profiles of prospective adopters and then have an opportunity either to meet them face to face or to speak with them over the telephone. Once that connection is made, it almost always continues for the remainder of the pregnancy. That's where things might begin to follow several different paths.

- Some birthparents believe, in their grief, that ongoing face-to-face contact with their child would be too hard on them. Most of these don't just disappear, though. Instead, they elect to ask that periodic updates and pictures be sent to them via the intermediary. Sometimes the adoption continues like this for the child's entire growing up years, or at least until the child begins to ask for more information. Sometimes, after having time to heal, the birthparent(s) may come back to the intermediary and suggest that they'd like to reconnect with the family.

- Some participants in open adoptions feel confident about continuing the relationship on their own and commit to staying in touch—mostly by letters and emails or telephone—for years. They do so in a casual, not particularly close, way. Many ebb and flow. Since contact doesn't feel intimate, these kinds of relationships tend to offer any participant not feeling fully satisfied by or valuable to the relationship "easy outs." "Well, she never answers my notes or responds to the pictures, so why should I keep sending them? She must have moved on." Or "The family just seems so busy! He doesn't have much to say to me when I call, so maybe, since he's doing fine, I should just let him decide when he wants to talk to me." Based on purely anecdotal evidence from the many agencies I have worked with and the many families I know, I suspect that most open adoptions right now are pretty much like this.

Advocates of open adoption would say of the two styles above that it's great to see adoptive parents and birthparents in contact with one another, but that no adoption is genuinely open unless the children themselves are actively involved. That usually works like this.

> Extended family relationships are those that most advocates for open adoption would say are the ideal. In these open relationships, families really do merge, at least to a noticeable extent. Birthfamily is invited to birthdays, adoptive family is invited to graduations and weddings, and even extended family members know one another well enough to chat comfortably at gatherings they both attend. Most of the time, these relationships wind up with birthparents being a lot like favorite aunts and uncles in genetic families, and while half siblings sharing a birthmother but not an immediate family rarely see themselves as "brothers and sisters" in the classic sense, they are at least as close as first cousins. As in all families, there can be disagreements. Teen years can be especially challenging, since teens don't even want to be with their moms and dads on weekends when visits typically get planned; they'd prefer to hang out with their friends.

What's most interesting to know about this generation and a half of open adoption is what the researchers who have been following families over time have found. Drs. Ruth McRoy of the University of Texas and Harold Grotevant of the University of Minnesota and their grad students have been following a sample of families in diverse geographic areas and serviced by more than one preparatory placing agency since their children were placed. They've interviewed and surveyed birthparents and adoptive parents several times, several years apart. What they've found is that most everyone feels the kids are doing fine and, beyond that, almost all birthparents and adoptive parents are satisfied with whatever level of openness they personally chose and agreed to—whether really open, or not so much so.[2] Being well-counseled and feeling empowered seems to have worked for these families.

But Does It Always Work?

Though you have probably heard them referred to as *closed adoptions* more frequently, adoptions which involve no sharing of identifying information between birth and adoptive families are called *confidential adoption* by its supporters.[3]

Proponents of confidential adoption[4] argue that not all birthparents and adoptive parents would be able to form successful relationships, and that is certainly true. Unless both families have been well-counseled, both families have respect for boundaries, and unless birthparents are emotionally healthy and are not abusing substances, there can be serious problems with openness. Mediators cannot be accessible to help deal with emotionally needy or mentally unbalanced people 24 hours a day. This is another reason to use well-trained professionals when planning adoptions. Experienced professionals are in the best position to determine whether openness can work with a particular situation.

Some children come to adoption from dangerous, abusive, or neglectful situations. Certainly unless those problems have been solved, it could be unsafe for these children to have their birthparents involved in their lives. On the other hand, it is often possible for the adoptive families of these children to forge important supportive and productive relationships with extended birth family members of the child, much to his or her benefit.

As mentioned in the ethics chapter, after a full generation of practicing openness in adoption, we do know that it is working for most families who have been well-prepared and supported. Careful objective analysis may at some point in the future give us clearer answers about the long-term effects of openness on children, birthfamilies, and adopting families. As previously mentioned, the work of professors Ruth McRoy (University of Texas) and Hal Grotevant (University of Minnesota) is ongoing. Preliminary findings seem to indicate that families operating in the mid-range of openness tend to be more satisfied with their arrangements than are the families on either end of the spectrum. On the other hand, Marianne Berry's study suggests that, while adoptive parents are often uneasy about open adoption, those who practice it feel more settled over time and, in fact, the more direct and the more frequent the contact, the less worried the adoptive parents are about being entitled to the child.

What is important for each parent to keep in mind while sorting through whether openness or confidentiality are appropriate for your family, is that what is best for the child who will be adopted needs to be central to the decision. Frankly, it matters little whether birthparents would like an open adoption if it is not in the child's best interests. It matters little if prospective adopters want to put the birthfamily behind them and pretend that they don't exist if it is not in the child's best interest. Children are the most important clients in adoption.

The Need for Education and Ongoing Support

Most openness arrangements work quite well. Of course there are awkward moments, and Berry's research indicates a clear need for the continued involvement of professionals serving in a mediating role. In agreeing to an ongoing relationship, adoptive families and birthparents are creating a new kind of extended family relationship. In some ways, a fully open adoption is like a marriage. It demands respect for one another and a commitment to maintaining a positive relationship. But marriages are hard work and usually they involve two people of similar ages, backgrounds, and value systems.

In fact, adoption often matches people who would not have much in common if it were not for the adoption. The two sets of parents are almost always of significantly different ages. This can be particularly difficult when the expectant mother begins to see the adopting couple as surrogate parents for herself. Sometimes this goes unnoticed when the adopting couple, so focused on the excitement of the coming baby, fails to understand the tenor of the relationship as viewed by the expectant parent.

> Pete and Nancy went through several months of Sandy's pregnancy with her, driving her to doctor's appointments and offering her a lot of emotional support. Sandy was far away from home, and she became dependent on the warmth and caring of Pete and Nancy's friendship. Nancy was her Lamaze coach and was with her when Aaron was born.
>
> But then they were gone, caught up in parenting Aaron and, while grateful to Sandy, much less inclined to spend long hours on the phone with her, have her over for dinner, or listen to her problems at work.
>
> Their caseworker, Camille, played an important role in helping Sandy deal with what really had become two losses—the loss of her baby and the loss of an intimate relationship with Pete and Nancy—and to help all of them negotiate a comfortable relationship for the future.
>
> Question to ponder: If Camille had not been available, how would this set of unmatched expectations have been successfully negotiated?

Sometimes the birth and adoptive families are of different educational and/or ethnicities or socioeconomic backgrounds—backgrounds that would not lend themselves to naturally occurring ongoing friendships. Skilled mediators can be helpful in mediating misunderstandings and helping both families develop the tools for building a successful long-term relationship.

At Issue

Because more and more birthparents are requesting openness as a condition of making an adoption plan, some prospective adopting couples are finding themselves feeling that they are being pushed into what feels like an uncomfortable corner, forced to agree to openness or be denied the opportunity to parent. Perhaps nothing about open adoption frightens me more than this. I am meeting more and more parties to adoptions who have in some way failed to live up to the bargains they made in negotiating with the other family in open adoptions, both agency arranged and privately parent-initiated. The great majority of these situations have involved adopting couples who agreed to some form of openness before placement and then decided at some point after the finalization of the adoption that they didn't want to continue with the communication. Some of these situations have involved semi-openness, where families maintain anonymity and communicate only through an intermediary. Others have involved fully open adoptions, where birthparents and adoptive parents have been in frequent direct contact with one another. In either case, the pain of betrayal felt by birthmothers in such situations is intense.

> Max and Cathy adopted through an agency in the Southwest which arranged only open adoptions and would not work with couples who wished confidentiality. They met Marcy during her sixth month of pregnancy, and were thrilled when she decided that the match was perfect. They communicated closely, and were able to be in the delivery room when Jillian (a name the three had chosen together) was born.
>
> After the birth, Cathy and Max were less eager to have Marcy remain a part of their day-to-day lives, but, as the social worker explained to Marcy, this was typical. They were very much involved in claiming this child as their own and building attachments within their newly expanded family. Marcy tried to be patient.
>
> Shortly after the adoption was finalized, both Marcy and the agency were shocked to find that Max and Cathy had moved. There was no forwarding address for their mail, no forwarding phone number. Max's employer refused to give out information about where they had gone. In fact they had moved to Chicago—a plan they had had in mind, and which the large national corporation for which Max worked had agreed to, since just before Jillian's birth. Marcy and the agency had both been betrayed. Max and Cathy had played a game with them and changed the rules after they had possession of the most valuable piece.

There are birthparents for whom confidential adoption remains the best option and birthparents who should have openness. Similarly, open adoption is right for some adopters and confidentiality better for others. Some children will do better with openness and others with confidentiality. The menu of options must remain open to the clients who are empowered to make the choices right for themselves. And key to the success of adoptions is the matching of birth and adopting parents who agree on and choose the same level of confidentiality/openness.

If you decide on an open adoption, do so only if you are absolutely certain that you are able to commit for your lifetime to living up to your promises and working on ways to negotiate through problems. This isn't just a matter of ethical responsibility to your child's birthfamily. It goes much farther than that. What is Dean going to think when Liz contacts him at age eighteen and learns as their relationship progresses that the parents whom he loves and who love him lied to her? What if an adult Jillian searches for and finds her birthmother, only to learn how Max and Cathy betrayed her? No matter how strong the attachments, no matter how fully entitled parents and children feel toward one another, how will these parent-child relationships be affected by such news?

In choosing an open adoption, be prepared for the ongoing changes that must be negotiated in any working relationship. Rather than look upon these negotiations as promises carved in stone, so that you risk being disappointed when either of you are unable to live up to those promises, look at the agreement less as a contract and more as the beginning of a flexible relationship based on trust that is similar to a marriage. Adoption educator and birthparent advocate Brenda Romanchik calls it a covenant. What you and your child's birthparent want and need now may not be what either of you feels you want or need later. Open adoption pioneer Kathleen Silber wrote in an article in *Adoptnet* (March/April, 1992) that birthparents nearly always decide later that they want more rather than less contact with the adopting family than they thought they would during their pregnancies. Therefore, she suggests that it is nearly always better to agree to an arrangement which is more conservative than you feel you could live with (for example, a birthparent seems to think she only needs one picture a year when you know in your heart that you would be comfortable with more frequent communication than that) rather than one which stretches you to what you believe are your furthest limits.

A Perspective after Living It Both Ways

If any one thing has made me open to the idea that confidentiality may not be the best way to practice adoption, it has been coming to understand that there was a great deal of deception practiced in many old-style confidential adoptions. Birthparents were often given assurances about the adopting family that were not kept. Adopting parents were too often given inaccurate or incomplete profiles on the birthfamilies.

Our first adoption was a traditionally confidential one, as were Dave's adoption and that of his sister. Maybe my husband's birthmother had no other choice and lived her life filled with regrets. We'll never know. She died before Dave tried to make contact with her. Maybe my son's birthmother, now in her fifties, has been unable to manage her grief and move on productively with her life. Or maybe both of these women were confident in the decisions they made. How do I know? Is it important that I know?

On the other hand, I remember the years when I felt a sense of disappointment when we didn't hear from our youngest daughter's birthmother for a while. She was moving on with her life. Did we expect too much from her and of ourselves in trying to maintain contact as our lives diverged and we were all so busy parenting young children?

What I do know is that all three of my children did well in three quite different forms of adoption. We had very little information for our oldest, but we made it clear that we stood ready to help him obtain whatever he wanted to have. So far, he remains relatively uninterested—not an atypical reaction from male adoptees. We have full identifying information about our middle child, though we have never had direct contact with her birth-family. We answered her questions and shared what we knew—including a picture. To this day—as she waits for the birth of her own first child—this has satisfied her needs. The adoption of our youngest has been continuously open. We are in at-will direct contact. Our daughter knows her maternal half siblings and grandparents and some cousins. She has a more distant relationship with her birthfather, who has not introduced her to his extended family.

All of our adopted children, despite the diverse kinds and amounts of information we had for them, did well. I am convinced that this had less to do with the confidentiality or the openness of their adoptions, than with the commitment we made as their parents to believing in them and in our relationship with them—the degree of our mutual senses of entitlement to one another. We clearly sent the message to our children that without question we consider ourselves a family, that we respect each of them as unique individuals, and that we respect their birthparents and their decisions. Of course they have questions! And we answer them honestly and straightforwardly without defensiveness and with no reservations.

Resources

Child Welfare Information Gateway. "Openness in Adoption: Bulletin for Professionals." www.childwelfare.gov/pubs/openadoptbulletin.cfm

Dorner, Patricia Martinez. *How to Open an Adoption: A guide for parents and birthparents of minors.* (Michigan: R-Squared Press, 1997)

Gritter, James L. *The Spirit of Open Adoption.* (Washington, DC: CWLA Press, 1997)

Gritter, James L. *Adoption Without Fear.* (San Antonio, TX: Corona Publishing, 1989)

Grotevant, Harold D. "What Works in Open Adoption" in *What Works in Child Welfare,* Edited by Miriam P. Kluger, G. Alexander and P. Curtis (Washington, DC: CWLA Press, 2000)

Grotevant, Harold D. and Ruth G, McRoy. *Open Adoption: Exploring Family Connections.* (Thousand Oaks, CA: Sage Publications, 2000)

Melina, Lois Ruskai and Sharon Kaplan Roszia. *Open Adoption Experience: Complete Guide for Adoptive and Birth Families—From Making the Decision Through the Child's Growing Up Years.* (New York: Harper-Collins, 1993)

Pavao, Joyce Maguire. *The Family of Adoption,* revised. (Boston: Beacon Press, 2005)

Romanchek, Brenda. *What is Open Adoption?* (Michigan: R-Squared Press, 1999)

Silber, Kathleen and Patricia Martinez Dorner. *The Children of Open Adoption.* (San Antonio, TX: Corona Publishing, 1990)

Silber, Kathleen and Phylis Speedlin, *Dear Birthmother*, 3rd Edition. (San Antonio, TX: Corona Publishing, 1991)

Waters, Jane. *Arms Wide Open: An Insight into Open Adoption.* (Bloomington, IN: AuthorHouse, 2005)

Wolff, Jana. *Secret Thoughts of an Adoptive Mother*, 2nd Edition. (Kansas City, MO: Vista Communications, 1999)

CHAPTER 11

Finding Your Path and a Guide

Sometimes, but hardly ever, adoptions happen without any or with only minimal outside assistance. A step-parent adoption, for example, rarely involves any counseling or even much of an assessment of the home and would-be parent. Step-parent adoptions are relatively routine legal processes that in some states may require only an attorney to file papers. Most non-relative adoptions, however, are much more complicated than this. Before you can be completely certain about adopting or not, and if so who, how, and from where, we need to spend some time focusing on how you might go about choosing service providers. After all, hiring the right people to help you in your quest for family is going to involve your investing a significant chunk of all of your resources—money, time, emotions, and physical energy. These are life-changing decisions.

So, what services are essential to an adoption? What can you just not do without?

Well, somebody needs to bring children in need of adoption and would-be adoptive parents together. Domestic and intercountry agencies can do that for a fee, but so can some attorneys, some facilitators, and some Internet advertising services. At the same time, a significant number of adoptions come together through friend-of-a-friend connections and through referrals from professionals outside the adoption field (e.g. doctors, clergy) involving no fees at all for the "matching."

> Phil and Cassie sent their "Hoping to Adopt" letter to their entire holiday card list and all of the professionals they personally knew who had contact with people who might be dealing with an untimely pregnancy—school counselors and coaches, doctors and nurses, friends who used teen babysitters, etc. At the same time they posted their profile on an Internet site.
>
> Within a month they heard from friends whose teen babysitter was indeed pregnant. They met at their friends' home with her, the baby's

271

father, and with the couple's parents. Things felt "right" for everyone, so they retained an adoption attorney. The attorney referred them to a local agency who agreed to counsel the birthfamily and do the adopting couple's homestudy/parent-prep.

Because this was a "directed adoption," both sets of professionals offered adjusted fees that excluded portions usually added to cover the recruitment and matching elements of their broader services.

For these families, there was added comfort in knowing that they had been brought together by people they all knew and trusted, and with whom they shared common values. This dispelled for them some of the fear that they had about adoption being "working with strangers."

Several years later, this open adoption is healthy and strong. The intermediary couple is the child's godparents.

The adoption needs to follow the laws of the states and the countries involved. Some courts and some states accept the paperwork of in-state licensed agencies and do not require that an attorney represent the agency's adoptive parent and birthparent clients at finalization. Other states require attorneys for everyone. In an independent adoption, there is the question that having a single attorney try to serve the best interests of two clients with conflicting interests—such as birthparents and adoptive parents each have—presents an ethical conundrum. Though some attorneys do this, arguing that it saves adoptive parents legal fees, many absolutely will not do so. Similarly, legal ethicists would also say that an attorney representing an agency has a conflict of interest in trying to represent the agency's birthparent and adoptive parent clients. Too often these decisions are made primarily thinking about finances rather than thinking about long term legal consequences. Adoption attorney (and former president of the American Academy of Adoption Attorneys) Mark McDermott points out that since adoption is the most important legal case adoptive parents will ever do, they need independent legal advice no matter how they adopt—independently or through an agency.

Everyone needs a homestudy. In most locations this must be done before a placement can be made, though in some states courts have the option of waiving the pre-placement homestudy requirement in favor of one done after the child is placed and before the adoption is finalized. Homestudies are traditionally done by licensed child placing agencies, but in several states licensed independent social workers or court-appointed and -supervised caseworkers may perform a homestudy. Unless your adoption is through the local public agency, and that agency has no fees for adoption, a homestudy is indeed a service you must pay for; but, depending on whether yours is an agency or independent adoption, a domestic or intercountry adoption, an adoption where all of the principals are located in one state, the homestudy fee may or may not be an "add on" to other fees that you must pay.

The least "layered" route to adoption (though it isn't always the cheapest and there is no guarantee that it won't be emotionally complex) is to use a full-service licensed agency in your own state which will match you with an expectant parent who is also using the agency's counseling services. In such an adoption you would pay just one fee—to the agency. There would be no advertising fees, no added homestudy fee, in many cases no added attorney fees, and no foster care for the child.

The most complicated adoptions are those which are fully independent, involving would-be parents who hire coaches to help them "sort out" whether to adopt internationally or domestically, publicly or privately, and what other services to use. These adoptions will involve paying for advertising services and/or facilitators to help locate an expectant parent with whom to make a "match." If these matches are made across state lines, they will involve two states' Interstate Compact Officers, legal advice in two states, and will require the hiring of an agency or an independent social worker to do a homestudy. Additionally, mental health or social work professionals should be available in the expectant parents' location to counsel and support them. Move this same adoption scenario to another country, and you have an additional several layers of services to pay for—including travel, facilitators, agencies or attorneys in the second country, the possibility of bribes or pay-offs, and U.S. Citizenship and Immigration Services paperwork and permissions.

Most adoptions (domestic or intercountry) fall somewhere in the middle of these examples in their complexity, as well as in emotional and financial risk. Most adopters find themselves selecting more than one professional and paying for more than one provider—which may include, for example, a homestudy-only agency or social worker in their home town, a placement agency in another state, and perhaps an adoption doctor in an intercountry adoption or an attorney in a domestic placement.

Sorting out just which approach to take can include factors ranging from personal budget to whether your heart is simply pulled in the direction of a certain kind of child or a certain country's culture.

Adoption as an approach to family building has substantial financial and emotional risks. There are, though, some things you can do to lessen your chances of being hurt:

1. Assess just how much risk—especially the financial and emotional risks—you are willing to take. For example, some adopters choose to use more traditional private agencies because they do not want to "shop" from among uncounseled expectant parents with whom to match, preferring instead to work with clients with whom the agency is already offering counseling, education, and support. This can lessen the emotional risks.

2. Recognize the risks of each of your choices going in. Identify for yourself what you see as the positives and negatives of each style of adoption we will discuss here.

3. Know going in what to expect. Ask for as much information as possible—in writing—about the services which will be offered, the projected timeline of the process, and the financial commitment.

4. Screen the practitioners with whom you will be working carefully. Contact local (in the practitioner's city) parent groups or infertility support groups and ask what experiences their members and clients have had with the provider. Ask the provider to put you in contact with half a dozen or so other adoptive parents who have had a placement within the last year. Contact the Better Business Bureau, the practitioner's home state's licensing and/or accreditation entities and the state attorney general's consumer protection office. When working with an unlicensed business, exercise even more due diligence in investigating.

5. Assess the availability and quality of education and support services the professional provides or refers to—both for expectant parent clients and prospective adoptive families. Just as you would have evaluated an IVF clinic's success rates before signing on for treatment, ask for the adoption provider's statistics concerning number of birthfamilies worked with in the last year, number of successful placements, number of changes of heart, etc. Understand that it is normal and reasonable that a substantial percentage of expectant parents who seriously explore adoption decide at some point in the pregnancy or at the hospital that they wish to parent. A very high proportion of expectant parent clients choosing adoption may signal coercive practices rather than "success."

6. Many practitioners do not require a contract at all. Those which do often write contracts that are less than consumer-friendly. If you are asked to sign a contract, have it legally vetted by someone experienced in adoption. It is unlikely that an entity requiring a contract will allow you to modify their contract, but discomfort with elements of the contract can be a good reason to choose another service provider.

7. Bottom line: agree to work only with professionals proven to be ethical and with whom you feel you can establish a relationship of mutual trust and cooperation.

Guides: Credentials and Qualifications

In the 21st century there are a lot of people who earn their livings by providing services paid for by families who want to adopt, many in positions that didn't even exist a generation ago. As an example, while the number of children placed overall both domestically and internationally has not changed much in 25 years, where they come from and how they are placed has. Over 300 state-licensed adoption agencies in the U.S. offer to help families adopt internationally today, whereas 25 years ago there were fewer than 50. This same period of time has seen the founding (1990) and rapid growth of a professional organization called the American Academy of Adoption Attorneys (AAAA or Quad A). Agencies licensed by one state to provide domestic or intercountry adoption services cannot operate as "agencies" in states where they are not licensed, so they become "facilitators" if operating outside their own home state, which means that rules—and consumer protections—change. Coaches, facilitators, consultants, and advertising services are all businesses which require no educational qualifications, professional licensure or government oversight, yet they charge from hundreds to thousands of dollars for services that those interested in adopting may or may not need. These services did not even exist a generation ago.

We need to start this chapter, then, with some definitions and descriptions of qualifications which the guides you choose to help you facilitate your adoption plan should have.

Individual Guides' Qualifications

Not everyone who earns money from adoption can legitimately be called a "professional" in the field. The noun *professional* is often used rather casually—and inaccurately—when it comes to adoption services. Let's reexamine its definition:

> Professional, *Noun*: 1. a person following a profession, especially a learned profession (*doctor, lawyer, pharmacist, teacher*, etc). 2. One who earns a living in a given or implied occupation: *hired a professional to decorate the house.* 3. A skilled practitioner; an expert.[1]

For the purposes of this book, I believe that we need to define *adoption professionals* more narrowly than "those who earn a living within the adoption world." I think it important for our understanding of how the world of adoption works on behalf of children and their birth and adoptive families to define a *genuine* adoption professional in the following way.

> Adoption Professional, *Noun*: One who works in a specialized adoption-focused, child-centered practice within the fields of social work, psychology, law, medicine, etc., who holds college degrees and required licensure in his or her field and/or accreditation qualifying for that work, and pursues a commitment to ongoing continuing education in the rapidly changing area of adoption.

In today's adoption world, such a refined definition of *adoption professional* would be limited to licensed social workers, credentialed mental health therapists, attorneys, and physicians for whom the majority of professional practice is devoted to people touched by adoption. The last part of that distinction—"for whom the majority of professional practice is devoted to people touched by adoption"—is just as important as the credentials.

Social work, mental health, law, and medicine are complex fields. Just as you would not choose a general practitioner or a podiatrist to perform reconstructive surgery on damaged fallopian tubes, you should not consider that a general practice pediatrician necessarily "gets" adoption, assume that a family therapist is attachment and adoption literate, or ask the attorney who wrote your will to finalize your adoption. Look for genuine specialty practices whenever possible, and expect services and credentials like the following.

Adoption Counselors

Counselors help those who are considering adoption sort through the many ramifications of this family planning alternative—pointing out options, providing information and education, and helping both birthparents and adopters make careful, objective choices. In principle, these individuals should be licensed counseling professionals such as social workers working at a licensed agency, degreed and credentialed independent social workers, licensed family therapists and psychologists, professional mediators, or other trained and licensed professionals in a related counseling field. In practice, however, many people who call themselves adoption counselors are not necessarily trained in mental health or social service fields, nor are they licensed.

Facilitators, as we will see below, are not regulated businesses, and for the most part they are not owned or staffed by people with mental health or social service educations and licenses. That means that any "counseling" these services provide to expectant parents considering adoption and would-be adoptive parents is not based in professional education and training. Similarly, one of the major criticisms about attorneys who serve not just as legal advisors in adoption but who also act as adoption intermediaries or facilitators has been that they are not trained in counseling or mental health fields. Yet, they often seem to be practicing in these fields, trying to provide counseling for birthparents and preparation for adoptive parents. For years, licensed adoption agencies have felt that the danger of exploitation rooted in inadequate preparation is exceedingly high in independent adoption.

In fairness, it must also be pointed out that as adoption in America becomes increasingly entrepreneurial, a significant number of formally licensed agencies have begun to provide services which are less than optimal too. For example, agencies which advertise nationwide find it difficult to mandate birthparent counseling for clients who do not live in the state where their office is located, and so, increasingly, some agencies don't insist that the birthparents who plan adoptions through them receive options counseling. Similarly, when clients pursuing intercountry adoption choose a placing agency in another state, they will need to have a homestudy done in their own state. Not all placing agencies do an adequate job of setting standards for the assessment and educational components of those homestudies.

Social Workers

Most adoption counseling and much intermediary work is done by social workers. In the United States, most general caseworkers working in licensed agencies have earned, at a minimum, a bachelor's degree, preferably in social work (BSW), but often in a related field—for example, sociology, psychology, or education. These caseworkers are trained and supervised by a person with a master's in social work (MSW). The MSW is a professional degree that prepares a candidate to practice social work supervision and do administrative work in the social service field. Licensed agencies in almost every state include a director of social work (often the executive director) who has that MSW. This person is responsible for the social work provided by those working beneath him or her. He or she provides training and supervision, and it is the flourish of the MSW's signature which completes a homestudy. There is no doctorate in social work approved by the Council on Social Work Education, though a few colleges now offer DSWs. DSW and PhD degrees prepare individuals to do research or policy analysis in either academic or non-academic research centers. College professors teaching social work often hold PhDs in related areas.

It may surprise you to learn that there are very few courses in schools of social work which focus solely on adoption issues, and none which focus only on infertility. Infertility and adoption issues are normally covered as segments of larger general courses on topics such as Child Welfare Issues or Marriage and Family. Almost any experienced social worker will tell you that most of what he or she has learned about adoption or infertility issues has been learned on the job; as a part of continuing education training through seminars offered by their employers or by their state's human services system; by attending conferences such as those of the Child Welfare League of America, the North American Conference on Adoptable Children, or the American Society for Reproductive Medicine; and by reading the journals of professionally-related organizations and consumer advocacy groups. But seminars and journal subscriptions are both expensive and time consuming, so that many social workers whose employers do not reimburse for such continuing education are able to pursue it only on a small scale. It is not unusual, then, for well-prepared consumers to be better informed about some adoption or infertility issues than an inexperienced recent graduate of a school of social work or a social worker not working in an adoption-related position.

Some states, but far from all, require that social workers practicing adoption be licensed or certified after receiving appropriate training and being mentored in a practicum. This results in a designation such as LSW (Licensed Social Workers) or CSW (Certified Social Worker). Beyond this, some states make available an examination which offers those who pass the designation LCSW (Licensed Clinical Social Worker)—a step above CSW. Some social workers acquire even more specialized professional status by working to achieve the nationally recognized designation ACSW—as fellows of the Academy of Certified Social Workers—conferred by the National Association of Social Workers.

To former infertility patients, this may not seem too unfamiliar a series of stepped qualifications. While in treatment, infertility patients usually became quite familiar with the training and certification steps physicians take from MD to graduate, Ob-Gyn to board-certified Ob-Gyn, to Sub-specialist in Infertility/Reproductive Endocrinology to Board-eligible in Infertility, and finally Board-certified Reproductive Endocrinologist/Infertility Specialist. What you will likely remember from those days with the doctors, though, is that unless you were a careful consumer and asked, most doctors would allow you to presume that they had the highest rank of training and credentialing. The same is true in the field of social work. To know what your social worker's qualifications, experience, and training are, you are going to have to specifically ask, and it is entirely appropriate that you do so. Social workers are required to post their credentials in their office and on their professional business cards.

The proper role of the social worker or other mental health professional is to build on a client's strengths. Not all counseling professionals are able to understand this concept and follow it, however. Finding the right independent social worker (in the few states which allow independent social workers to do homestudies) or individual caseworker at a licensed agency will make an enormous difference in your ability to make the parent preparation process a positive experience and a productive one for your future family.

Adoption Attorneys

Since adoption involves a permanent legal transfer of parental rights from one set of parents to another, it is impossible (or at the very least, unwise) to complete an adoption without the assistance of at least one attorney. Sometimes that attorney leads the adoption and may even be the facilitator, as is the case in many independent adoptions.

General practice attorneys are as unprepared for adoption's intricacies when armed only with their law school training as are freshly minted social workers. Law school students learn about the basics of the law and adoption in courses on family law, but most adoption practice is learned on the job, often under an experienced mentor, as well as through participation in continuing education. While adoptions which are arranged by well-regarded agencies usually involve fairly straightforward and simple legal work (often prepared by agency-retained attorneys), independent adoptions are much more complicated and require specialized expertise.

Attorneys who choose to specialize in this field must truly become legal experts. In essence, adoption law is as much a complicated specialty as is reproductive medicine. Of course you would not have had your brother-in-law the podiatrist perform tubal reconstruction surgery. Similarly, the person who closed your real estate deal or defended your neighbor falsely accused of theft is probably not the person to finalize your adoption. You will want to choose an attorney who has experience and expertise in adoption law to handle your independent adoption.

In all western countries, the termination of parental rights (TPR) is a carefully regulated legal procedure. In the United States, attorneys must assure the courts that both birthparents have agreed without coercion to this termination or that there is just cause for terminating those rights involuntarily. In instances where a birthfather is unknown, out of range of contact or unwilling to terminate rights, attorneys must follow a specific legal process for termination. A growing number of states have followed Indiana's lead and now make this process somewhat easier with their establishment of what is called a Putative Father Registry. This requires that men who are interested in retaining their parental rights to potential children pay close attention to the pregnancy status of women with whom they have had sex, and register themselves as putative fathers before the child is born or closely following the time of birth. Not doing so demonstrates to a court a legal lack of commitment to the children a man produces, and results in the start of an automatic process for termination of parental rights.

Increasingly, attorneys concerned about developing a high standard of ethics in the field of adoption law are speaking out as advocates on controversial issues such as birthfather rights, the need to refer clients to counseling services, the need for birthparents and adoptive parents to have separate attorneys each advocating for their particular rights, the need to bill for services on an hourly basis rather than as a flat fee, and more.

The American Academy of Adoption Attorneys is a professional association which holds as one of its goals the establishment of guidelines and ethical standards for attorneys practicing in this field. These are similar to the guidelines and standards established by professional organizations in the medical field such as the American College of Obstetrics and Gynecologists or the America Society of Reproductive Medicine. Membership in Quad A is one of the criteria adopters and birthparents can look for in selecting an adoption attorney.

Adoption Doctors—the Adoption-Focused Medical Practice

Yet another change in adoption in the last generation has been the appearance of medical practices specializing in adoption and foster care. These practices come in two forms: clinics which are often attached to teaching hospitals, and private practices, often run by a single general pediatrician with a strong interest and expertise in adoption issues (and sometimes a personal connection as a member of the adoption circle) to devote a significant portion of his or her practice to seeing these families.

Once again we are talking about fully credentialed medical professionals who have added adoption to their bag of skills not through courses in medical school, but as a separate layer of personal continuing education. Today, some pediatric fellows have chosen to build this training into their primary education by taking their residencies in hospitals which have adoption clinics with which they can be involved, often under the mentorship of someone who has learned "on the job" for years.

Twenty years ago there were less than a handful of adoption doctors. In my early trips to annual conferences of the North American Council on Adoptable Children I met two, both of whom are now looked up to by younger doctors as the founders of this subspecialty. Dana Johnson is a neonatologist at the University of Minnesota Hospitals and School of Medicine. Being an adoptive parent himself, Dana's personal interest in adoption and in orphanage experiences led him to pull together other university volunteers in fields such as psychiatry, psychology, educational testing, developmental pediatrics, neurology, infectious disease, and more. First these folks were all volunteers at this "second job" within the hospital, and in 1986 the University of Minnesota established the first Adoption Medicine Clinic. At about the same time, single adoptive mom and pediatrician Jeri Ann Jenista was beginning to focus exclusively on issues in adoption medicine in Michigan.

The work of these two remarkable physicians served as models for other pediatricians. The result was that the American Academy of Pediatrics Section on Adoption and Foster Care (SOAFC) was established in June 2000. It now has over 200 members. Who knows, in another generation adoption medicine may be a full fledged medical subspecialty! AAPSOAFC membership is an important indication of a physician's interest in and commitment to adoption research, intercountry orphanage voluntarism, and continuing education.

So what does an adoption medical practice do? Private practitioners and clinics are prepared to examine referral information about children available to be adopted, offer opinions about the relative health of the child, suggest future tests that should be done, and refer to specialists for more detailed information—even before a family accepts a referral. Most families make an initial connection with an adoption doctor before traveling—even when they are traveling "blind" (without a referral in hand). Then, when they have met the child in his home country they may send pictures and additional medical data via fax or email with questions that may concern them. After a child arrives home, teams of clinic members can be pulled together to perform comprehensive diagnostic tests—medical, developmental, psychological, educational, etc.—to help families determine what services they need to access on their child's behalf. Often these specialists are quite willing to serve as consultants to hometown pediatricians with less experience in adoption and/or international medicine.

While in their early days adoption medical clinics serviced families adopting internationally almost exclusively, more and more adoption medical clinics are being contacted by state agencies and parents adopting through the foster care system for help in diagnosing domestically born children's needs in an adoption-friendly way.

Nonprofessional Adoption Service Providers

People making a living in the field of adoption who do *not* have accreditations, licensures, and/or specific adoption-related educational backgrounds and credentials include people with titles like

- facilitators
- coaches
- marketers and advertising specialists
- consultants
- educators
- journalists and writers

These people may be (and often are) professionals in some field, but they are *not*, under this book's narrow definition, *adoption professionals*. As an adoption educator, I am an example of one of these. My master's degree is in education, not in social work, counseling, law, or medicine. I'm licensed to teach in public schools, but there is no adoption-related licensure for someone who does what I do (which is training professionals and consumers about infertility- and adoption-related issues, and about one another). Many of these non-professional service providers are very good at what they do and worth their fees. Others are not. Of course, it is also true that some accredited and licensed adoption professionals are very good at what they do, while others are not.

The biggest difference between adoption professionals as narrowly defined above, and that second tier of people and businesses offering services for a fee in the field of adoption without accreditation of any sort, is that the second tier are, basically, entrepreneurs. They do not report to, and so are not held accountable by, any standard-setting and monitoring organization or regulating body—private or governmental—which can, for cause, discipline them or remove them from the field. Without those professional standards and related monitoring in place, consumers who have bad experiences with an entrepreneur working in the field of adoption have no recourse other than to file an expensive and difficult-to-win civil lawsuit.

Qualifications of Business Guides

What Is an Adoption Agency?

An *adoption agency* is a business entity which is licensed, regulated and monitored by a state to provide adoption services, including options counseling for pregnant people considering adoption, and homestudies and parent preparation for those who want to adopt. Adoption agencies bring together these two types of clients and offer post-adoption services for all. States set minimum standards for how agencies are to be staffed and how they are to operate, and rules vary from widely state to state. Almost always those standards require that a person with a master's degree in social work supervise the work done by all other casework employees of the agency.

States monitor adoption agencies at regular intervals to be certain that they are following the financial standards, employee credentialing and training standards, and homestudy standards that the particular state requires. Because they are licensed, agencies are regulated, and that means that when something goes wrong because of suspected misbehavior, consumers can file a complaint with the state's licensing body and expect that that complaint will be thoroughly investigated.

There are both *public agencies* and *private agencies*. *Public agencies* are supported by the tax dollars of a state, province, county, or municipality and may also receive federal funds. Often these agencies carry names such as Whatever County Department of Family and Children's Services, This State Children's Services, Anywhere Department of Human Services, or Someplace Children's Aid Society. Public agencies serve the public at large, but this does not mean that they do not have requirements and prerequisites for adopters. Those prerequisites, though, are generally more flexible than those of many private agencies. Though public agencies rarely directly accept applications to adopt from people who are not legal residents of their tax-based service area, they do work cooperatively with agencies in other geographic locations to arrange placements of children with special needs outside of their service areas when necessary or appropriate.

Private agencies are supported by funds other than tax dollars, obtaining their financial support from sources such as adoption fees, private donations, United Way or a religious, fraternal, or family foundation benefactor (for example—Jewish Social Services, Latter Day Saints Social Services, Lutheran Family Services, Salvation Army Adoption Services, Spence Chapin Agency, The Cradle). Sectarian private agencies are religiously connected and may or may not serve only clients of a particular faith. Nonsectarian agencies have no connection with a specific religion. Many private agencies are supported by a combination of the above types of funding. Private agencies do not have to serve the public at large, but most often do serve a rather large pool of people who meet requirements set by their boards of directors. These agencies, like public agencies, are licensed by the states in which they operate, and must follow the same kind of minimal rules and regulations about how they operate. Their licenses to operate as agencies do not extend beyond the borders of any single state. A few agencies choose to be licensed in more than one state.

A license granted by a state assures that an adoption agency is qualified to provide full services. This means that an ethical full-service agency can

- advertise their services widely and in as many ways as they possibly can—yellow pages, display ads in newspapers and magazines, TV and radio commercials.
- provide counseling to families experiencing an untimely pregnancy—and they do so face-to-face, not over the phone—or, if the client is geographically distant, make sure that this service is provided to the client face-to-face in their location. This service may include counseling and even mediation services with the pregnant mother, the baby's father, and even the baby's grandparents. When agencies are doing their job ethically, such counseling is objective—offering these families information about all of their options, including both adoption, in all its detail, and parenting, as well as ways to find support for doing that.
- conduct the legally required investigational process which is called a "homestudy," and in addition provide many hours of parent preparation education—often accompanied by a variety of reading material such as books and photocopied articles. Their social workers visit client homes and offer workshops for groups of clients.
- offer ongoing supportive counseling, mediation, and education for their birthparent clients, their adopting parent clients, and their adoptee clients throughout their lifetimes—much of this at no additional fee.

Sometimes (though far less often than they did a generation or more ago) agencies provide housing for expectant parents. They may help them with other costs and expenses. Most of these family clients cannot afford to pay for these services, so the agency does not charge them—whether they choose to plan an adoption or not. Indeed, it is not unusual for an ethical full-service agency to provide some level of counseling services to 100 families and have 5 or fewer actually follow through with an adoption plan. The financial investment in the services to those 95 families comes from somewhere—much of it from the fees charged to families who adopt those five children.

Agencies, public or private, set their own policies about openness, and there is a wide variation among these policies, some of which are influenced by the laws of individual states. Some agencies facilitate open adoptions and some agencies continue to provide for full confidentiality—though these numbers are shrinking rapidly.

At one time all licensed agencies offered all of the services listed above. Recently, however, some agencies have chosen to devote almost all of their time to doing assessments and preparation—homestudies. These agencies do most or all of their business working with attorneys doing independent adoption, or with agencies in others states who have clients in need of a domestic or intercountry homestudy.

These agencies do not have their own programs in other countries, rarely if ever are contacted directly by an expectant parent exploring adoption, and less often actually make matches. These agencies, while licensed as full-service agencies, bill for the services they actually perform for clients—the homestudy and parent preparation process, counseling to a birthparent brought to them by the would-be adopter or an attorney. Perhaps (but not always) they provide post-adoption education and support. Most of these agencies have a menu of flat fees for services, and while they sometimes are able to make exceptions and lower fees in exceptional situations, their profit margin is very close to the wire.

Facilitation Services

If you are thinking about using an adoption facilitator as your intermediary, know that it is not currently considered a quantifiable professional field and that in some states these businesses are illegal—whether they are located in the state, or advertising and accepting clients from a home base outside that state. Instead, people from all sorts of educational and vocational backgrounds who have a strong interest in adoption issues simply set themselves up as adoption consultants. Consultants are often people who have adopted themselves and who wish to pass on their knowledge and experience about networking to find a baby, about how to write a resume, and about what books and articles will provide useful information to prospective parents. They do not make matches.

These can be very useful services. However, it is important for consumers to understand and be cautious concerning the entrepreneurial nature of such a profession. One cannot take courses to qualify for such a position. There is no degree. There is no licensing. There is no specific form of continuing education. The result of this is that there is even more variation among consultants than there is among social workers and attorneys. Consultants, however, do not run agencies and therefore don't have lists of qualifying factors for their clients, so the choice to use or not to use a specific consultant is perhaps much clearer and more easily made than the choice to use a particular agency.

Additionally, while shopping for service providers, it is very easy to make the mistaken assumption that a facilitation service or consultation service is a licensed agency. No law says that only licensed agencies can use the word *agency* in their names or in describing their services in brochures or on websites, and few consultants and facilitators go so far as to state up front that they are not an agency and are working without any licensure. Many licensed agencies forget to include the fact of their own licensure (and in what state or states) in their marketing materials.

Many people make the deliberate choice to use facilitators and consultants in planning fully independent adoptions, but others do so out of ignorance. Be sure that you know, when choosing any adoption service provider, just what licenses and credentials your chosen business has or does not have, as well as whether or not you even need the service being advertised or offered.

How Businesses Are Organized: For-Profit vs. Not-For-Profit

Until quite recently all licensed adoption agencies were also registered with the U.S. Internal Revenue Service as not-for-profit (501c3) organizations, though now in the U.S. a few states do provide for the licensing of for-profit organizations as adoption agencies. On the surface, the difference between for-profit and nonprofit agencies may seem to be that donations of money and in-kind services to for-profit organizations are not deductible. But the differences between for-profit and not-for-profit businesses are much more complicated than that, and the differences change perspective. These two types of businesses are simply by nature (and by regulation) operating under differing goals.

- A nonprofit is driven by its service mission philosophy rather than by the profit motive.
- A nonprofit serves those who cannot afford to pay full costs.
- In nonprofit, excess revenue over expenses is used to further the organization's exempt purpose.
- A nonprofit likely will remain in the community even if it suffers financial losses.
- A nonprofit is more accountable to its board and the public than are for-profit organizations.
- A nonprofit looks for ways to respond to community needs without regard to profit.
- A nonprofit may not compensate its employees higher than "reasonable" rates.

Comparing Not-For-Profit Corporations with For-Profit Business Corporations

	For Profit	Not-for-Profit
Advantage of corporate business model	Limited Liability, control over the business by the CEO.	Limited Liability, tax exempted, lower costs (for example postage exemptions)
Over-arching goal	Generate profits for owners	Change lives for the better
"Moral owners"	Shareholders	Varies: public, donors, a church, etc.
Primary beneficiaries	Owners, through profits	Varies: children, would-be families, etc.
Board of directors	Not required to have one unless stock is sold publicly. Often run by an entrepreneurial small number of stockholders	Board is community-based, hires and fires the executive director, and is bound to practice due diligence in seeing that the goals are met and clients served
Staff	Almost always paid, and often according to profit-building performance	Paid and nonpaid; relatively few compensated by performance, are required not to pay "above community norms."
Public accountability	Very private, disclosing only what law requires	Often anxious to provide reports and have activities known to as many as possible
How fees are set	High enough to generate profitability for owners and/or shareholders beyond overhead, business expenses, and salaries.	Low enough to be accessible to clients while still keeping the corporation viable.
Can apply for grants	No	Yes
Can accept tax deductible donations	No	Yes

- A nonprofit's board of directors is typically made up of unpaid community leaders motivated by public service.
- A charity attracts thousands of hours of volunteer time and philanthropic contributions.[2]

Here's another view. I was inspired by and so adapted the table on page 286, a board training handout developed by Dr. Robert Andringa for the Council for Christian Colleges and Universities. It compares the roles and goals of boards of for-profit and not-for profit organizations.[3]

Are We Confused Yet?

Sometimes it's hard to tell, on the surface, whether a business is a licensed agency or an unlicensed entrepreneur, whether an agency is public or private, whether an organization is for-profit or nonprofit. Public agencies and private agencies both facilitate the domestic adoptions of babies, older children, and children with special needs; although some private agencies do specialize in one of these types of adoption placements (for example the private, nonprofit Aid to Adoption of Special Kids focuses on special needs placements and the private nonprofit Homes for Black Children recruits minority adopters for minority children). Increasingly, the majority of agency-arranged infant placements are occurring through private agencies (which are often able to offer an expectant mother more financial support and/or private medical care as opposed to clinic care) and fewer infant adoptions are handled through public agencies. Facilitators, consultants, coaches, and law firms are almost always set up as for-profit businesses.

To further complicate issues, as some states privatize their social services, many private agencies have taken on contracts with individual states to provide recruitment, fostering, homestudy, parent preparation, post-adoption support, and other services for the families of waiting children who are wards of the state.

Most intercountry adoptions are done through private agencies. While a public agency could do a homestudy for an intercountry adoption, few do, as they are kept busy by their mandate to deal with children born locally who are in need of services. But U.S. licensed private agencies working in intercountry adoptions are not necessarily working with similarly well-trained and accredited business people in the countries from which they place children. Those countries themselves determine whether or not people who make money (often at fees substantially above the norms within their culture) need any training, licensure, or government oversight. Those sending countries alone police local service providers to ensure that they are operating legally and ethically. Each U.S. agency determines whether to hire and train its own in-country staff to work with government agencies, courts and orphanages or foster parents, or whether to use local "freelancers."

Although all agencies are licensed to offer a full range of services, not all do. There is a small but growing number of private agencies whose primary work is to assess and prepare adoptive parents whose adoptions are arranged independently or internationally. Most of their domestic adoption clients are being matched through a facilitator or a large adoption law practice. Those same services are doing most of the marketing that recruits expectant parents, so the agency does little to no recruitment of birthparent clients. They do, however, provide counseling for the expectant parents recruited by the facilitator or attorney. These homestudy-only agencies also forge relationships with out-of-state agencies which have programs in several foreign countries. The "placing agency" handles everything for the would-be adopter except local preparation and assessment, and post placement follow-up provided by the homestudy-only agency. Depending on the agencies and the relationship, there may or may not be available long term post-placement education and support available.

Paths to Adopting Domestically

First, you must understand that adoption is governed not by the federal government, but by each individual state. While the states often do work together to facilitate adoptions across state lines, each state makes its own laws and rules about how agencies are licensed, whether adoptions without agencies are legal, how parental rights are terminated and when, whether unlicensed facilitators can legally operate in the state, what kinds of expenses adoptive parents can legitimately assist an expectant parent with, whether some of the state's services to waiting children are outsourced to private agencies, etc. It's important for the safety and security of the family you hope to build by adoption that you have a handle on your own state's adoption laws, and two good places to find that information are on your own state government's website or on the website of the federal government's Child Welfare Information Gateway.

Public Agency Adoption

Sometimes it comes down to a question of budget. Adoption through the state-funded public agency in your county will involve very low to no fees at all. The children almost always come out of the foster care system. This means, of course, that in most cases there will be a delay between the time they are removed from their birth homes and the time that they are made available for adoption. Why the delay? Since, as we mentioned earlier, the goal of the child welfare system is reunification—ultimately, to try to keep families intact—that means that birthparents are given some time (usually a year or so) in which to rehabilitate the situation that created the need for the child or children to be removed. When children cannot be safely reunited with birthparents or adopted by members of their extended birth family, the next best choice is to maintain as much stability as possible. For this reason, foster parents are next in line should they wish to adopt. Those whose primary goal is to adopt through the foster care system and to adopt as young a child as possible, usually do so by becoming licensed foster parents and asking to care for young children seen as likely to be eventually adoptable. Many foster parents care for newborns whom they eventually adopt as toddlers through this process. Of course, there are many older children and sibling groups who are adopted through the public child welfare system too. Many adoptive parents, however, go through the child welfare system preferentially because they want to make a difference in the life of a waiting child, not because it is cheaper to adopt in this way.

> **Myth:** It's just too hard to adopt from the U.S. public system.
>
> **Fact:** No road to adoption is without "bumps." The Adoption and Safe Families Act of 1997 was the Congress's attempt to streamline the foster care process so that children do not linger there unnecessarily. It is working—in some places better than in others. There are resources available to help would-be parents adopt out of the bureaucracy of foster care, beginning with www.adoptUSkids.org and www.davethomasfoundation.org, which can refer you to advocacy resources within your own state.

Unless they live in particularly restrictive states, virtually all of the family-challenged people reading this book—infertile or genetically challenged couples, same-sex couples, singles, older parents, people of all races—can be approved to adopt through the public agency system. Bureaucracies can be frustrating, and public agencies are government-designed and -led bureaucracies, yet the person or couple willing to invest both energy and perseverance can and will succeed.

When budget is not a primary barrier, there are more choices. Most adoptions of newborns in the U.S. come into their adoptive families through private agencies and independent placements. If they can afford to do so, those wishing to adopt a newborn most often choose one of these two routes. Similarly, more expectant parents considering making a voluntary adoption plan seek out a private agency or an independent adoption service provider rather than going to "the state" or "the county."

Private Agencies

Adopting through private agencies appeals to would-be parents for a variety of reasons. Some are comforted working with agencies supported by their faith community. Others choose to adopt through private full-service agencies (i.e. agencies whose clients include both prospective adopters as well parents-to-be dealing with an untimely pregnancy, and which are able to provide both homestudies and matching services) because they feel less willing to expose themselves to the emotional risks of searching for a match with an expectant parent on their own and/or they understand that to do so is inherently riskier, both financially and emotionally.

Once again I remind you to be certain that the business you are working with and relying on for agency services really is licensed as an adoption agency in the state in which they, and your adoption, are working. Additionally, you need to feel confident that birthparent clients and adoptive parents are given quality, up-to-date educational and counseling services, and those life-long post-placement services (in some cases at an additional fee) are a part of the agency's ongoing commitment and mission.

Independent Adoption

An *independent adoption* is one which occurs outside of the licensed agency process. (In the U.S., this process is also sometimes called a *private adoption*.) In a non-agency or independent adoption it may be that expectant parents and prospective adoptive parents have found one another directly, or they may have been put in touch by an intermediary who does not work for a licensed child placing agency. Sometimes independent adoptions are the result of serendipitous connections between friends of friends. *Intermediaries* may be friends and neighbors, members of the clergy, physicians. In such situations there are no fees charged by the people who make these connections. Yet independent adoption is a business as well. Attorneys (primarily) but also independent social workers and, increasingly, businesses which call themselves *adoption consultants* or *adoption facilitators* earn their livings through making the connections which result in independent adoptions.

There are no federal adoption laws in the U.S., so those who arrange independent adoptions which involve the residents of two different states must be familiar with adoption law in both states, or network with attorneys in two states. The Interstate Compact on the Placement of Children is an agreement signed by all of the U.S. states which regulates the placement of children in foster care or adoption across state lines. Each participating state has a compact officer who assures that that state's regulations are being complied with, and assists attorneys or agency representatives with necessary paperwork needed by both states. Similarly, in Canada, the federal Ministry of Health and Welfare staffs an Adoption Desk which coordinates all inter-provincial (and intercountry) adoptions.

Domestic adoptions without the direct assistance of an agency are prohibited in a few U.S. states (at this writing Connecticut, Delaware, and Massachusetts) and Canadian provinces. Sometimes this means that residents of states where private adoption is not sanctioned cannot adopt privately in other states either. In the states which prohibit non-agency adoptions, however, it is possible to achieve what amounts to an independent adoption when would-be adoptive parents and birthparents identify each other without intervention by an agency and then arrange for parental rights to be relinquished through a specific agency. This is often called a *directed agency adoption* or a *designated adoption*.

Most state laws prohibit non-regulated intermediaries and birthparents from "profiting" in adoptions. Attorneys can charge their normal hourly rates for legal services, counselors for mental health services, physicians for the medical care they provide, consultants for training they may offer, but no one can charge something in the nature of a "finder's fee" for the service of bringing adopters and birthparents together, and this is where independent adoption can get "sticky."

Though independent adoptions can occur as the result of adoptive parents themselves spreading the word about their interest in adoption by handing out business cards, placing advertisements in newspapers and on community bulletin boards, etc. until they are contacted directly by a birthparent, increasingly these services are offered by private businesses which are completely unregulated and unlicensed. These business offer advertising options, where profiles can be posted on the Internet; maintain "matching services" where profiles of expectant parents and would-be adopters are filtered by the business (somewhat akin to online dating services); will place advertisements in newspapers throughout the country; and will help to create or refine profiles to be seen by women and couples exploring adoption. These contacts may be arranged in a way that maintains anonymity and confidentiality, or the adopters may choose an open adoption arrangement involving varying degrees of communication between birth and adoptive families.

Most of those working in adoption believe that independent adoptions should always involve payment only for direct services and that suggested flat fees ("I can get a baby for you for $40,000) are morally and ethically wrong. Flat fees may even violate many states' laws. Furthermore, most states have specific regulations about just what expenses of birthparents may be reimbursed. Nearly all approve the reimbursement of counseling and medical expenses. But some will allow for the payment of living expenses or clothing allowances and others will not. Birthparents are prohibited in every state from exchanging their parental rights for money, cars, tuition, etc. Before agreeing to anything, be absolutely certain of your own state or province's laws about reimbursements. Make sure you are operating from a point of education, rather than desperation.

Another term you may hear within the adoption community is *parent-initiated adoption*. This is not a separate type of adoption, but a style. It refers to the situation wherein prospective adopters or birthparents seeking adoptive parents for their baby, actively seek out a match in adoption without using intermediaries. Parents may advertise, send letters, circulate resumes, or use Internet advertising services. However they choose to go about their search, the point is that these would-be adopters do not rely exclusively upon an intermediary or an agency to locate the other set of parents for them. Birth or adoptive parents can take an active role in creating an adoption plan. Key to this process, and what can make it vary widely from that of a traditional confidential agency adoption, is the active pre-birth commitment of one particular set of adopting parents to one particular birthmother. From an ethical, moral perspective, this has to mean a willingness on the part of an adopting couple to parent the baby born to this birthmother no matter what the sex or health of the child she bears.

Mythology has it that independent adoptions are always parent-initiated. This is not true. The business of adoption intermediaries or consultants arose specifically to do pregnant parent recruitment and bush-beating for non-agency adoptions. The same mythology says that agencies don't like parent-initiated adoptions. This is also untrue as a blanket statement. Increasingly, agencies are becoming involved in parent-initiated adoptions—whether through the process called direct/designated adoption, or as a response to their clients' interest in asserting more control.

In a few states independent adoptions are not legal. (Check your state's current laws through its web site or that of the federal government's Child Welfare Information Gateway). It's legally, emotionally, and financially risky for residents of states not allowing independent adoption to try to do an independent adoption in another state, since they lose the blanket of consumer protection offered by a state to its own citizens. Almost all of the high profile adoption disasters of the last several years have involved adopters leaving non-independent states to adopt independently in another state, and not understanding or being given poor advice about the law there.

Where independent adoptions are allowed, they can be a valuable and viable resource for would-be adopters who feel that they face religious, age, marriage status, or sexual preference barriers. Some facilitators and consultants (unlicensed) and adoption attorneys actually specialize in helping certain of these family-challenged people adopt. They offer creative and non-traditional options for making matches. Some people choose independent adoption because they believe that they can speed up the process by aggressively marketing and advertising themselves in print and on the Internet, and are willing to accept the substantial emotional risks (and financial risks as well) of handling this kind of outreach and response with expectant parents on their own.

When considering adopting independently, check the reputation of your service providers carefully. Membership in the American Academy of Adoption Attorneys, while not an absolute guarantee, can be one good screening tool when choosing an attorney. Check facilitators, consultants, and advertising services (all of which will be established as for-profit ventures) with references, local parent groups and online discussion groups, and with consumer protection sources.

Also seriously consider the quality of support and education provided to expectant parent clients. Attorneys, facilitators, and consultants are not social workers; they are not trained to provide social service or mental health counseling, options counseling, or grief preparation work. Think carefully before committing to a legal practice or a facilitator who tells you that "our birthparents don't want counseling and we don't force it." Women and couples dealing with an untimely pregnancy are in the middle of a crisis. Few can make an informed decision without good counseling by a qualified professional. From an ethical perspective this is a service you should insist on for your child's birthparents—and expect to pay for.

If you adopt independently you will still need a homestudy. Depending on the state and even the county, your independent adoption may require that you complete a homestudy before a placement, provide for cradle care between birth and the completion of a post-placement adoption, or allow for the placement of a child with you while you complete a homestudy. It is a worthwhile investment in your future family not to simply choose the cheapest or fastest among homestudy service providers, rather to carefully evaluate those you are considering on the basis of the quality of the education component of the process.

Understand that in almost all independent adoptions, services end when the adoption is completed. With the fewest exceptions attorneys and facilitators are not set up to provide post-placement education and support to birthparent and adoptive parent clients. Chances are that if someone needs grief counseling, there is a need for mediation in a relationship, or you have other post-placement related concerns, you will need to look elsewhere for these services. Sometimes the social service professionals who completed your homestudy will be your first line of contact for locating and purchasing post-adoption services.

Adoptions without agencies are an issue of such concern to many people that bills to prohibit independent/private adoptions are introduced every year in dozens of state legislatures. Once again, be certain to check your state's *current* law before investing yourself too heavily in an independent adoption.

At Issue: Agency vs. Independent

The controversy over agency vs. independent adoption centers around the perceived possibility for exploitation of both birthparents and prospective adoptive parents, which of course can certainly determine whether an arrangement is being made in a child's best interests. Vocal opponents of independent adoption are most often those who believe that only social workers, practicing not independently but in an agency setting where they can be properly trained and supervised, can offer the education and counseling needed by birthparents and prospective adopters in considering and following through on an adoption. Critics also point out that without a licensing entity to monitor what goes on, there is the possibility for exploitation. Critics claim that birthparents can be poorly advised of their options and promised more than can be delivered. In effect, the critics say, babies can be snatched away from birthparents. Adopters, too, desperate for a baby, are at risk for exploitation. Opponents of independent adoption fear that when independent adoption is allowed to exist unregulated there is a genuine risk of black market baby selling, auctioning infants to the highest bidder, or even of creating babies as commodities.

Those who support non-agency adoption reply that the courts are responsible for monitoring both the expenses in an adoption and the proper termination of parental rights by birthparents, and thus can and should prevent the inappropriate termination of parental rights or the sale of babies. Advocates for independent adoption point out that one of the reasons that independent adoption has existed and has come to flourish is that not all birthparents and not all adopters want the education and counseling services of social workers, and that they should not be required by law to submit to this control.

Dave and I felt this way as we began to build our family by adoption. We resented the homestudy we had been required to participate in and had "passed" with the agency at which we applied, so that when our son arrived by private placement we were thrilled to be out from under the agency's thumb. We were full and unqualified supporters of independent adoption. We even testified at several Indiana legislative hearings when bills were introduced that might have outlawed independent placement. We used independent adoption twice (though in both instances we had been approved and were waiting for a placement at an agency) before adopting our third child entirely through the agency process.

Today, based not just on our own experiences but on the experiences of hundreds and hundreds of birth and adoptive parents I've met throughout the country in the last ten years, I have far more reservations about independent adoption than I had at one time. They are not strong enough reservations that I feel that independent placement is a bad idea. I continue to vigorously support the maintenance of independent adoption as an option for both birthparents and adopting parents. In fact, I believe that there are some terrible agencies licensed to do adoptions in this country and that there are a great many poorly trained social workers employed by relatively good agencies!

That translates to one clear belief on my part: licensing by a state does not a good professional or a good agency make! No matter how you adopt, you must choose your helping professionals carefully and wisely!

My reservations about independent adoption are rather specific. Though increasingly the professional intermediaries (attorneys, physicians, and adoption consultants) who facilitate large numbers of independent adoptions are ensuring that their clients get good preparation services—either by referring them to professional services, or in many instances by hiring professionals in the mental health or social service fields to work with them—there remain far too many attorneys and adoption consultants attempting to practice social work, and either doing it badly or ignoring the need for it at all.

I believe that a well-done parent preparation process (as opposed to an old-style homestudy) can be one of the most valuable steps parents can take in getting ready to parent in adoption. Attempting to avoid this process is far too often a rejection-of-difference behavior (remember Kirk?), too often a knee-jerk attempt to snatch back lost control (remember infertility's losses?), too often a reflection of an obsessive need to get a baby—any baby—and get on with life after infertility. Adoption is different. You need help to learn about this clearly in order to become a really good parent in adoption. And all of us who wish to be parents at all want to be really good parents.

But beyond and perhaps even above the preparation needs of adoptive parents, I've come to understand much more clearly over the years how vital it is to our children's birthparents that they get proper education and counseling services before making an adoption plan. Adoption is a forever decision, and it cannot help but represent an enormous loss to birthparents who choose this option. Adoption is not necessarily the correct choice for all people dealing with an untimely pregnancy.

Historically, far too few birthparents actually *made an adoption plan*. The old language that we optimistic (and defensive) adoptive parents and adoption professionals want to eliminate (as part of our drive to promote the use of respectful or positive adoption language) really did fit many birthparents of a generation ago, and continues to apply to too many poorly counseled and supported birthparents today. Their children were and are indeed often *given up for adoption*. Too many of these birthparents were not shown clear choices. Nobody actively supported the possibility of their parenting their children themselves. Far too many of these anonymous, faceless birthmothers (unknown to their children's adopting parents because confidentiality was mandated and there were no other choices) really did *relinquish* their children to adoption. They really did *surrender* to a paternalistic system. The odds are significantly higher that those birthparents whose adoptions were arranged outside of an agency had no counseling or mental health services and thus may not have actually *made an adoption plan* in years past.

This does not have to happen in an independent adoption, though. Whether the adoption is to be confidential or open, objective counseling is a necessity. Neither you, nor an intermediary who is not a trained mental health or social work professional, is in a position to assess how fully informed your child's birthmother is about her options. If the adoption is to be confidential, you should advocate even harder for this preparation and counseling. In a confidential adoption, over the years you will think often about your child's birthparents and wonder how they are doing. Having the knowledge that you did all that you could to ensure that they were supported in making the best possible decision for themselves, as well as for the child you share, will be valuable to you and to your relationship with your child.

Whether you are adopting through an agency or without one, you can, and indeed you must if you care about your child's birthfamily, willingly and actively offer to provide objective outside counseling services for a prospective birthmother who is considering placing her child with you. If the agency or the independent adoption intermediary whom you have contacted reacts negatively to this idea, consider this reaction a bright red flag and look elsewhere for the services you need.

Because of the wide spectrum of options within both independent adoptions and agency adoptions, deciding whether to adopt through an agency or without one requires careful soul searching and more specific information gathering. For example, the decisions you make about domestic or intercountry adoption, about confidentiality vs. openness, about your interest in being directly involved in the process vs. having someone else do the negotiating and the matching, can influence the decision to use an agency or not. The requirements and the style of the agencies at which you qualify may influence this decision. How strongly you feel about being able to control the relative health of your child may mean that a parent-initiated independent adoption which involves a direct commitment to one pregnant birthmother is not for you. Your limited resources of time and money may influence this decision. Here is another place to gather as much detailed information as you possibly can and then to use the process outlined before to set goals and objectives, develop strategies, and allocate resources.

> As Ron and Julie faced their infertility they came to realize that, if they had to make some choices, parenting a child from infancy was what they wanted more than a pregnancy. They evaluated their options and decided to invest their energies and financial resources into pursuing adoption. With the help of their RESOLVE support group they were guided to books to read, adoption forums to attend, and people to consult.
>
> After having initial meetings with two adoption agencies, Ron and Julie decided that they were not comfortable giving so much control of their lives to the agency social workers, so they began pursuing independent adoption while they waited for their names to move up on the agency waiting lists.
>
> They assessed their skills and talents and decided to write letters in search of a child. They began the process by reading more books, selecting an attorney and composing letters to doctors, attorneys, college fraternities and sororities, school counselors, and anyone else they thought might come in contact with birthparents who wanted to make an adoption plan. They felt they regained lots of lost control as they spread the word of their search to family, friends, and acquaintances.

Within a year, their efforts led them to an independent adoption that worked out beautifully. They brought home their healthy, same-race infant directly from the hospital in an adoption which happened to cost several thousand dollars less than what would have been their agency percentage-of-income fee. They were able to develop some openness with the paternal birth family which brought them lots of satisfaction in the years to come.

Two and a half years later, they were able to adopt a second child delivered by the same doctor in the same hospital with the same attorney at about the same cost as the first adoption. Their family building complete, they proceeded to preschool, soccer, and swing sets.

The Path to Adopting Internationally

Deciding whether to adopt a child born in your own country or one from another country is a complicated and very personal decision. Certainly intercountry adoption is more complex than most domestic adoptions, and, on average, international adoption is more expensive than is adopting domestically. But people have many motivations for choosing to pursue intercountry adoption.

If you are considering adopting from outside the U.S., first carefully consider all of the issues raised in Chapters 6 and 7 about transracial/trans-ethnic adoption. Some children adopted from Eastern Europe appear to be Caucasian, but many others do not. Certainly children adopted from Asia, India, the South Pacific, Africa, or Central or South America will be seen as children of color and will be exposed to the prejudices of many people. Your child should feel proud of his cultural and racial heritage, and you will need as a family to embrace that culture, to work hard to introduce and inform your child about that heritage and to bring it alive for him. Read the books, listen to tapes, speak to experienced parents, and explore as carefully as possible the culture of the country from which you are considering adopting before making a decision.

Be prepared as well to deal with two further concerns that will be pushed into your face. The first may come from people here at home: Why are you adopting a child from overseas when there are so many waiting children here? The second comes from those who see citizens of developed and prosperous Western countries as exploiters of the world's poverty, war, famine, and unhappiness. More and more the governments of countries who once allowed many babies to be adopted to North America are finding the exportation of children to be an embarrassment and are making adoption more difficult, demanding instead to know why the U.S. and Canadian governments, if they truly care about children, do not offer them humanitarian aid to care for their own children.

Some would-be parents have their hearts pulled by the people, culture, issues or problems of specific area of the world. Adopting internationally simply feels like the right thing to do. Since each country sets its own rules and requirements about who can adopt its children, your personal characteristics can either help or hinder you. Religion rarely gets in the way of adopting internationally. But it is possible to be too old or too young. Singles are welcomed or barred. It is often difficult or impossible for openly gay or lesbian people to adopt internationally. Investigating the rules and regulations, the current political climate, and the costs of adoption in a handful of countries whose children appeal to you will usually help adopters to make the decision to pursue intercountry adoption—or not.

Common motivations people report for choosing intercountry adoption include these:

1. We can adopt more quickly internationally.
2. We can select the sex of our child.
3. We think that orphanages are much worse places for children to be raised than is U.S. foster care.
4. We don't want to take the chance of a birthparent's involvement in our lives.

Let's talk about these motivations. If you are thinking that intercountry adoption may be a fast, cheap way to adopt a healthy white infant, you are completely misinformed. Throughout Canada, Western Europe, Israel, Australia, New Zealand, etc., prospective adopters of European heritage find a shortage of healthy same-race babies to adopt. American couples who travel to adopt from other countries anywhere in the world are often shocked to run into large numbers of non-American people of European heritage there to adopt too. On the other hand, if you are open to adopting transracially, intercountry adoption does often move more quickly that some domestic sources. The break up of the former Soviet Union did indeed result in a new "source" for children of European heritage, at least temporarily.[4] Most intercountry adoptions twenty years ago involved the adoption of children of color from East Indian, Asian, South and Latin American indigenous decent or mixed race children (Filipino, Caribbean Black, African Black, and other racial mixtures). In the last fifteen years, adoptions from the countries of the former Soviet Union have changed the racial picture of intercountry adoption.

As for speed, well, it can depend. In this, the summer of 2007, I am aware of enormous backups in the administrative process of adopting from all three of the current top sending countries. Accreditation of foreign agencies doing adoptions in Russia has been stalled for nearly six months, producing a backlog of waiting families that will be difficult under the best of circumstances to "clear out" within the next 18 months. Similarly, so many dossiers are in process in China that families already waiting for referrals from that country are waiting twice as long as ever before. And then there is Guatemala's reluctance to change its process to become Hague compliant. It is very possible that small agencies with programs in only one or two countries will drown financially in the backlog, unable to transfer clients from slower programs to faster ones. Some agencies which have, in the past, formed partnerships with larger agencies with programs in multiple countries may find that they are no longer able to do so when some of those countries decide that they want more control over each step of the preparation and follow-up process of families parenting their internationally adopted children. The bottom line is that in order to adopt internationally, families must keep themselves very up-to-date about international politics.

It is correct that, because the children have already been born when they are referred, it is possible to specify whether you wish to adopt a boy or a girl when adopting internationally. This is also true when adopting older children from the U.S. foster care system.

It's been my experience that a significant proportion of those adopting internationally say that one of their main motivations is that they can avoid contact with birthparents as in an open adoption, and that they will avoid the possibility of a change of heart. Neither of these beliefs is completely accurate.

First, while it is certainly far from common, more and more intercountry adoptions involve some contact between birth and adoptive families at the beginning. Second, more and more adoptive parents of internationally adopted children are following the predictable psychological path of becoming more open to the idea of contact with members of their children's birth families once they have settled comfortably into a sense of entitlement to their children. Finally, well over a generation of experience with internationally adopted children has demonstrated that at least as many, if not more, internationally adopted adults are interested in making a connection with their birth culture and their birthfamilies, and that they will do what it takes to make these contacts. So beginning an adoption primarily for the purpose of being able to avoid birthfamilies is not only not particularly healthy or child-centered, but it is also in all likelihood an unrealistic expectation. If this describes your motivation for adopting internationally, please revisit Chapter 10.

As for avoiding the possibility of being disappointed after making any kind of emotional connection to a referred child, this too is impossible to guarantee. You should know that changes of heart in domestic adoptions very rarely happen after a placement. They almost always occur during the pregnancy or right at the time of birth. When adopting internationally there are protections against changes of heart in those countries where children are anonymously abandoned, but in many countries (Russia, for example) birthparents have the right to reclaim their children right up until an adoptive family leaves the country. Beyond that, in Russia and many other countries, citizens of that country have first choice and can yank an adoption out from under a referred parent from another country even while those hopeful parents are in country and preparing to go to court. In those situations, the idea that intercountry adoption is somehow "safer" than is domestic adoption is a myth.

Similarly, many people are falsely convinced that children in orphanages in other countries are likely to be emotionally and physically healthier than children in U.S. foster care. There is no reason to believe that children raised in institutional settings—which are by nature emotionally neglectful at best—are healthier than children raised in one-on-one family care in a well-prepared foster home. Children the world around are at risk of neglect and abuse when their parents are impoverished or users of dangerous substances, or in any other way impaired.

Common motivations for selecting a particular country from which to adopt include these:

1. The country embraces singles, gays, older parents, younger parents, or people of our religion.
2. The adoptable children are younger here and come home more quickly.
3. The children will match us racially; our families wouldn't accept a transracial adoption.
4. We believe that the ethics of adoption in this country are higher than those in other countries.
5. It is cheaper to adopt from this country than others.
6. The culture supports "greasing the wheels" to move the process along, and we can afford to do that.
7. Our family shares this ethnic heritage.
8. We've traveled to that country and admire it.
9. We admire this country's culture and feel able to celebrate it with our child.
10. We speak the language of this country.
11. My health (weight, medications, etc.) is not an issue.

These are relatively reasonable and free of myth. Those adopting internationally for one of these reasons are likely to find satisfaction in their decision if they do all that they can to keep themselves up-to-date and well-informed of other risks and potential problems.

When I wrote this book's predecessor, *Adopting after Infertility*, statistics showed that between October 1990 and September 1991, Americans adopted a total of 7,801 children from 79 different countries outside the U.S. The largest number—2,287—came from Romania, whose current government has now banned intercountry adoptions. The second largest number came from South Korea. Where once over 4,000 children a year came to the U.S. from Korea, changes in government policy and social attitudes resulted in only 1,534 Korean adoptions to the U.S. in FY1991. India sent 397 children during that period and the Philippines 341. All together, the South and Central American countries of Peru, Colombia, Guatemala, Chile, and Honduras accounted for 1,753 adoptions.

As I write this book, today's statistics couldn't look more different. The overall numbers have more than doubled, with 20,679 children coming to the U.S. to be adopted in fiscal year 2006 (October 2005 through September 2006). On the other hand, the FY2006 statistics showed a drop from FY 2005 of more than 10% in the number of children internationally adopted. The sending countries are very different when comparing FY 1991 to FY 2006 too. In FY2006, the top ten countries from which children were adopted were China (6493), Guatemala (4135), Russia (3706, down from 4639 in FY2005), South Korea (1376), Ethiopia (732), Kazakhstan (587), Ukraine (460), Liberia (353), Colombia (344), and India (320).

These numbers and these countries are going to change even more. Why should we expect vast changes? First, the Hague Treaty will be coming into effect. The result in the U.S. will be that the government will strongly discourage adoptions from non-Hague-compliant countries. Under current political circumstances this would virtually eliminate adoptions from Guatemala, for example. Second, the political and economic climates in every country will influence whether or not children continue to be or begin to be adopted internationally. As war, famine, and political upheavals traverse the world, new countries will need help for their orphaned children. Similarly, as economies grow, governments stabilize, and countries become more able to promote domestic adoption, intercountry adoption will diminish. Other influences will be purely colored by international politics as countries work to assure that their native children are well cared for wherever they live and that their countries' own cultures are respected abroad.

Intercountry adoption can be both complex and expensive. Among the complexities is that very often families in smaller states or rural locations find that they are unable to adopt internationally without working with multiple service providers. One agency may maintain the program and political connections with the placing country and pass along the referrals, while still another agency or independent social worker may do the homestudy. Yet another service may help with dossier preparation of numerous documents that must be translated into the language of the sending country. The U.S. Citizenship and Immigration Services is yet another level of bureaucracy that must be satisfied. Some countries require that adopters travel to that country and live there for a few weeks before they will grant an adoption. Other countries allow children to be escorted by agency workers, airline personnel, etc. to meet their new parents in their new home country. Current how-to information is available to you from a variety of sources—The Adoptive Families magazine website, Adoption Council of Canada, and local and regional parent groups (such as Families Adopting Children from Everywhere in Maryland, Latin American Parents Association based in New York, the Adoption Community of New England,

and Adoptive Parents Committee of New York). Gather this information and then apply the decision-making process for yourself.

Are there right or wrong answers to questions like these? Not necessarily. Perhaps they are not even appropriately asked. But once again, understanding your own private motivations will help you in building a healthy sense of entitlement to your child.

Intercountry Agency Adoption

Choosing service providers for intercountry adoption is becoming increasingly difficult. That's because there are so many agencies working in intercountry adoption today and most of them work in just a handful of countries while advertising their services nationwide. There is a mixture of for-profit entities and not-for-profit businesses marketing intercountry adoption services, and many agencies are not completely open about how their placements and referrals come to them.

> In the year before this book was published, several other adoption activists and I spent thousands of hours trying to help the victims of an intercountry adoption quagmire. About 40 individual licensed adoption agencies from coast to coast, only two of which were accredited to make placements from Russia, had banded together under the "umbrella" of those two accredited agencies. Together they used the services of a for-profit facilitator which had hired and was supervising a staff in Russia, all of whom carried business cards falsely identifying themselves as employees of the accredited U.S. agencies. The owners of the facilitation company pulled large amounts of money out of the company in the form of loans, drove expensive cars, and owned lavish homes and business properties paid for with these loans. When they declared bankruptcy, these unethical facilitators took with them millions of dollars, and the adoption dreams of over 400 clients, not to mention the reputations of several agencies! The result was an FBI investigation and huge complaint lodged against member agencies with Joint Council on International Children's Services (JCICS), both still ongoing as I write.

I have some strong recommendations about choosing intercountry placement agencies. After very careful research has helped you to weed out all agencies that do not have squeaky clean reputations among parents who have used them, with the professional organizations with whom they may network (such as JCICS) and with consumer groups such as the Better Business Bureau and their home state's agency licensing and attorney general's offices, consider that the fewer processes and bureaucracies between you and your child, the less financially and emotionally risky your adoption. With this idea in mind, the following is recommended.

- Whenever possible, avoid using businesses which piggyback on, partner with, or umbrella under another agency. Using reputable placement agencies that have established their own programs on the ground—using local employees that they hire, train, pay (fairly), and supervise and/or agencies which build careful ethical relationships directly with local agencies or orphanages in the countries in which they work will eliminate several layers of emotional and financial risk.

- The fewer layers that must be gone through between you and your child, the less risky your process. When possible use the same agency for both homestudy and placement.

- Never use an agency which suggests that you lie by omission or commission on an application or to a foreign court. Run, don't walk, from a program which suggests that you identify yourself as a client of an agency other than theirs.

- The cultures and layers of some countries take for granted and encourage bribes and payoffs. Consider carefully whether you are willing to participate in a system which violates your own personal principles. Someday you may be called upon to explain this to your child.

Successful adoption is to a large extent dependent on finding the right resources to support a growing family. Your experience with other professionals in other fields has no doubt demonstrated for you that not all professionals are good at what they do—despite education and training, despite fulfilling licensing or specialization requirements. It is important that you, as prospective adoptive parents, understand and take hold of your power and responsibility if you choose this path to parenthood.

Avoiding Adoption Frauds and Scams

For the century since adoption has been part of a legal system, there have been people willing to try to take advantage of birthparents and adoptive parents for their own gain. The rise of the Internet has, however, created opportunities for the rapid escalation of scamming throughout the world.

Fraud takes place when an individual or a business intentionally misrepresents itself or a situation to another for personal gain. Most adoption frauds take the form of exorbitant fees charged by service providers, fees charged for services that are never rendered, coercing birthparents to sign away parental rights, vital information being withheld from adoptive parents by intermediaries about a potential adoption or a particular child, etc.

A facilitator advertising prolifically on the Internet posted pictures of "available children" and their descriptions. Prospective adopters responded in droves. Upon response, each would-be parent was asked for a several thousand dollar deposit to "hold" the child while the family gathered paperwork and submitted it to the facilitator to begin proceedings.

By chance, two hopeful parents participating in the same chat group suspected that they were expecting to mother the same child! After talking at length on the telephone with one another, they confirmed that this was indeed the case. They began spreading the word and found four other hopeful adoptive parents holding the same paperwork about the same dream child.

They went to local police, who, upon confronting the facilitator, advised these clients and many others that there were no children at all. She had been posting pictures cut and pasted from other sources. Most of their deposited funds were already gone.

Your best protections against fraud are

- reading books, magazines, journals and Internet sites, participating in Internet chat groups of experienced adoptive parents, and attending information meetings to meet other would-be adopters and ask about their experiences
- knowing what the law in your state (or any state in which you intend to adopt) says about what expenses you can pay, how fees can be determined, and from and by whom consents must be taken
- understanding that if it sounds amazingly fast, simple, or cheap, something is wrong
- if adopting intercountry, paying close attention to the U.S. State Department's frequently updated web pages about current issues in adoption in that country
- working with professionals who are local to you (Many readers will completely ignore this advice, wanting to "increase their odds" or "work with a bigger source," and that's fine. Just know that it is harder to protect yourself when working outside your own state.)
- using service providers who are directly associated with the source—the orphanage in the sending country, the expectant parent, the foster care agency—rather than service providers who "partner" with others or who are not licensed or accredited themselves, but subcontract with those who are
- carefully checking the reputation and credentials of any service provider you hire (Check with the Better Business Bureau in their location and in your location. Check with their state's Attorney General's Office—have they been sued? If so, what was the out-

come? Check with the appropriate licensing entities about com-plaints and resolutions—the agency licensing bodies in each state in which an agency claims to be licensed, the bar association for attorneys.)

- if working with an expectant parent not in your location and an agency, attorney, or facilitator not located in the same city as the expectant parent, insisting on proof of pregnancy from a physician with whom you and the professionals can speak by telephone

- listening critically to everything you are told by an expectant parent, a social worker at an agency, or an attorney and asking careful ques-tions about anything which seems odd, vague, or contradictory

- comparing the adoption laws and regulations between several states (or between several countries if you are doing incountry adop-tion) will give you a clearer sense of how the most child-centered processes are run

- understanding the "rules" of any sending country you may use and using service providers who follow those rules carefully (For ex-ample, some countries do not allow the Internet posting of photo-graphs of available children. When a service provider posts pictures of children it claims are available for adoption from that country, something is probably wrong. You are in danger of experiencing a "bait and switch" situation.)

- never agreeing to lie or to misrepresent in any way to a court or to a government official anything about yourself, who you are working with, or what you have paid and to whom

Scams are a bit different from frauds, and they seem to fall into two categories: emotional and financial. In some cases the two are combined.

Emotional scams are run primarily by people who are emotionally un-balanced. Most often they pose as expectant parents considering an adop-tion plan. They are seeking attention and sympathy, and look for it among the most vulnerable. They visit the websites on which hopeful adopters post their profiles, and then make contact, inventing a story about an un-timely pregnancy and a difficult life. Would-be parents are especially at risk for being taken advantage of by an emotional scammer because they have often waited so long to become parents that they are feeling desper-ate—willing to do anything to adopt. Hopeful adopters spend hours taking collect telephone calls and offer almost unlimited emotional support to these needy people. An adopter-to-be can be strung along for many weeks or even months because she doesn't want to believe that anyone would be so cruel as to pull off a con like this.

Many of these emotional scammers have several families on the string at the same time, allowing their scenarios to play out with each until their "pregnancy" should have come to birth. At this time many of these women can successfully convince would-be adopters that the baby has died, causing yet another devastating loss to a family who wants nothing more than to parent a baby.

> You may have viewed a *Dr. Phil Show* segment on adoption scamming in which a Wisconsin woman took advantage both emotionally and financially of at least three would-be adopters who stumbled on one another. They suspected that there were perhaps dozens more.
>
> She had used several names for herself, but virtually the same story about being pregnant and unable to raise a child. She spent hours on the telephone getting sympathy and support for her sad story. Eventually she agreed to meet one mother-to-be in Chicago, but failed to show up. At about the same time she told another would-be parent that she was in labor and on the way to the hospital. The parent bought a plane ticket, only to be called while waiting for a connection in an airport to be told that the baby had died.

Emotional scammers also seek attention from churches and charities working to prevent abortions. Volunteers may spend hours on the telephone with them, "convincing" them not to end the pregnancy, but to parent. The charity offers baby items, short-term financial assistance and more to mentally unbalanced people who have refined a highly successful emotional game.

Financial scammers have grown more and more bold. They include "facilitators" who collect deposits and "birthparent expenses" that go straight to their own pockets, as well as Internet offers to place children through independent adoptions from fake orphanages and charities in Africa, Asia, and Eastern Europe. People adept at reading headers and other Internet codes can tell whether these emails originate in the country they claim to represent, and most do not. Still, the proliferating numbers of offers such as these which are being made to families running profiles on the Internet only proves how successful they can be to the scammers.

> Foreign financial scammers are incredibly bold. They troll the Internet picking up email addresses which are adoption related. I get emails several times a week from people claiming to be missionaries, most often in African nations, who are working in villages ruined by war or famine. They seek my help "as a good Christian" in finding homes for dozens of babies and toddlers needing to be rescued from fighting, poverty, or malnourishment.
>
> When followed up, these scammers direct that money orders or bank transfers be wired (often to a third country) in care of a fictitious church or orphanage. When the money arrives, the email contact stops, cell phone contact (usually to temporary disposable numbers) ends.

Now, careful, logical thinking would tell most people to think twice about all of these kinds of contacts. But people seeking children are in crisis, and they want—even need—to believe that their quest is possible and probable. They are vulnerable to being defrauded or scammed when logic fails them and they follow their hearts.

The best protection against scam artists is to work only through *reputable* adoption professionals, who have been trained to recognize potential fraud and can, because they have less emotion invested than you, be more objective and critical of suspicious contacts. However, know as well that even agencies and attorneys can be and have been scammed by unscrupulous people! If you decide to distribute your profiles to be posted in public places, to buy newspaper advertising, or to post an online profile on one of the dozen or so sites that would be happy to sell you space, your risk of being taken advantage of will be cut if your contact information is directed to the office of your chosen adoption professional. If you can't bring yourself to take this simple step, preferring to direct contacts to yourself, keep these things in mind.

- Expect that a woman who is really pregnant and is seriously considering adoption should be willing to provide you, your agency, or your attorney with medical proof of a pregnancy and contact information for a confirming physician.
- Be wary of anyone who is unwilling to meet you face to face.
- Be concerned about an expectant parent who refuses to accept medical attention or counseling you are prepared to pay for.
- Ask careful questions of an expectant mother working with a professional service provider far from her own home turf. Scammers frequently do this to avoid having to "meet" anyone.
- Beware of people who are contacting you on behalf of someone else who is pregnant. If after one or two phone conversations you still are not put in contact with the "friend," suspect that this person may not exist.
- Never send money!

Filling in the Gaps— Notes for Consumers

Of course what adopters want is to be the best possible parent to their child no matter how that child arrives. The intermediaries who assist in adoption will provide valuable assistance in preparation for parenting, but parents, don't stop there. While you wait, read and listen to CDs—everything you can lay your hands on—beginning with the materials listed in the resource section. Attend adoption seminars and workshops sponsored by agencies, hospitals, infertility, or adoptive parent groups. Join a parent group, at least to get their newsletter, but hopefully to spur your active participation (many of them have parents-in-waiting sub-groups or support groups).

Allow yourself to begin to experience that psychological pregnancy we will talk about at length in Part 4. There's an almost tangible difference in the air around family-challenged people who have finally committed to adoption.

> An adoption attorney and I found ourselves on the faculties of two separate symposia in the same city about six months apart. It was the first time I'd spoken to two different groups in the same city so closely in time. At lunch at the second program I ran into the attorney and we ate together. She had presented well-received sessions on considering and pursuing private adoptions at both symposia. But today something felt different. We were each fascinated by our reactions to the crowds and were each surprised to have them confirmed by the other.
>
> The first symposium, held in dreary November, had been an all-day program on infertility issues—treatments, options, emotional issues—sponsored by the local RESOLVE chapter. It was attended by nearly 300 people who packed the rooms to listen to high-powered, well-qualified faculty of medical and mental health and adoption experts. I did a keynote address called "Life at the Crossroad" where I presented a cheerleading-style effort to help couples re-empower themselves. I also did workshops on decision making, dealing with family and friends, and considering adoption. The evaluations for the symposium were excellent. Nearly everybody there felt they got just what they needed from the day.
>
> Several months later, on a cold, grey February morning the conference at which we were speaking was offered by an adoptive parent group. Once again the list of offered sessions and speakers was impressive. Over 300 prospective adopters and adoptive parents attended. I was surprised at how many of the faces looked familiar from the RESOLVE seminar the previous fall. I spoke on promoting understanding of adoption issues, building a sense of entitlement, and talking to kids about adoption.
>
> Despite the fact that we were dealing with quite a few of the same people, the atmosphere was totally different on those two days. At the infertility conference attendees had been quiet and reserved; they hesitated to share with one another or to ask questions out loud. Interaction at lunch and at breaks was limited and somewhat muffled. The attorney and I had each felt what amounted to almost a pall over the day, despite the fact that it had been completely successful.

> Today registrants had milled excitedly over coffee and donuts
> waiting for the introductions to begin. The lunchroom buzzed and
> laughter pealed. Questions had been enthusiastic. The difference could
> be physically felt, and the difference here was hope!

Reach for that hope! Look for a preparation for parenting in adoption class in your community. These are the equivalent of Lamaze courses for adopters and they are wonderful. Often offered by infertility or adoptive parenting groups but sometimes by the parent educators at area hospitals, the Red Cross or at a YWCA/YMCA, these several week courses deal with the practicalities of getting ready to parent: bathing and diapering and other basic infant care skills, choosing a pediatrician, selecting nursery and clothing items, child-proofing your home, and deciding whether to try to do adoptive nursing or to bottle feed. They also provide a completely nonjudgmental atmosphere away from the perceived judgmental process of the homestudy to share nagging fears with other prospective adopters, to explore concerns about reactions from family and friends, to talk about choosing arrival announcements and baby books. Most of all, such classes make the coming child and your becoming a parent begin to seem real and exciting!

Resources

General—How to Adopt

"The (annual) Adoption Guide." (New York: *Adoptive Families* magazine annual) www.theadoptionguide.com/

Beauvais-Godwin, Laura. *The Complete Adoption Book: Everything You Need to Know to Adopt a Child*, 3rd edition. (Avon, MA: Adams Media, 2005)

Falker, Elizabeth Swire. *The Ultimate Insider's Guide to Adoption: Everything You Need to Know About Domestic and International Adoption*. (New York: Wellness Central, 2006)

Gilman, Lois. *The Adoption Resource Book*, 4th edition. (New York: Harper Collins, 1998)

Domestic Adoption

Independent Adoption

Caldwell, Mardie. *Adoption: Your Step-by-step Guide: Using Technology & Time-tested Techniques To Expedite A Safe, Successful Adoption*. (Nevada City, CA: American Carriage House Publishing, 2005)

Hicks, Randall B. *Adopting in America: How to Adopt Within One Year*. (San Diego: Wordslinger Press, 2004)

Waiting Children/ Public Agency Adoption

"The Children's Bureau presents: AdoptUSKids" U.S. Department of Health and Human Services www.adoptuskids.org/

"How to Adopt." National Adoption Center adopt.org/servlet/page?_pageid=67&_dad=portal30&_schema=PORTAL30

"How to Adopt." North American Council on Adoptable Children www.nacac.org/howtoadopt.html

Working with Birthparents

Burns, Susan. *Fast Track Adoption: The Faster, Safer Way to Privately Adopt a Baby.* (New York: St. Martin's Griffin, 2003)

Handel, Nelson. *Reaching Out: The Guide to Writing a Terrific Dear Birthmother Letter.* (Los Angeles: EasternEdge Press, 2002) also available as CD.

Intercountry Adoption

Davenport, Dawn. *The Complete Book of International Adoption: A Step by Step Guide to Finding Your Child.* (New York: Broadway, 2006)

Nelson-Erichsen, Jean and Heino Erichsen. *How to Adopt Internationally: A Guide for Agency-Directed and Independent Adoptions*, 2nd Edition. (Fort Worth: Mesa House Publishing, 2003)

Uekert, Brenda K, PhD. *10 Steps to Successful International Adoption: A Guided Workbook for Prospective Parents.* (Williamsburg, VA: Third Avenue Press, 2007)

Adoption Medicine

"Find an Adoption Doctor." *Adoptive Families.* www.theadoptionguide.com/tools/adoption-doctor-search

Miller, Laurie C. MD. *The Handbook of International Adoption Medicine: A Guide for Physicians, Parents, and Providers.* (New York: Oxford University Press, 2004)

Avoiding Adoption Scams

"International Adoption" U.S. Department of State. travel.state.gov/family/adoption/notices/notices_473.html

Adoption Agency Checklist web site. www.adoptionagencychecklist.com

Adoption Agency Research chat list groups.yahoo.com/group/Adoption_Agency_Research/

Advocates: Lynn Banks and Kelly Kiser-Mostrum, author of the book *The Cruel-est Con* (i-Universe, 2005) run Adoption Scams www.adoptionscams.net/ and its highly valuable related listserv Adoption Scams and Un-ethical Treatment groups.yahoo.com/group/adoptionscams/ and less active message boards.

Kiser-Mostrum, Kelly. *The Cruelest Con: The Guide for a S.A.F.E. Adoption Journey.* (i-Universe: 2005)

Smolin, David and Desiree. This couple, who adopted two children from India whom they later learned had been stolen from their family, maintain a blog (fleasbiting.blogspot.com/) and a website (www.adoptinginternationally. com/) devoted to current information about child trafficking for adoption and other illegal activities related to international adoption. www.adoptingin-ternationally.com/

CHAPTER 12

Approval (and Preparation!)

You've decided to adopt. You've made decisions about the age, gender, relative health, and ethnicity of the child you are hoping to parent. You've thought through the various approaches to adoption and decided on whether to pursue an agency or non-agency adoption, whether to commit to openness or confidentiality. What you need now is the piece that grates and frustrates—official permission to become a parent, societal approval to add a child to your family. This chapter will help you to understand—and hopefully to embrace—the elements of this process. The chapter's goals are

- to explain the purpose and the relative value of required special preparation for parenting for adopters
- to explore some of the common factors about traditional assessments that have been most disheartening and corroding for prospective adopters
- to help those who will experience this process prepare themselves to accomplish required steps in the process
- to consider some ways in which prospective adopters can become appropriately prepared for adoption if circumstances do not bring them in contact with sensitive and well-informed professionals.
- to offer suggestions for positive and productive change.

Muddied Thinking about the Homestudy

Just making it to the homestudy in this adoption process alone feels challenging. Having to "qualify" as a parent by meeting an agency's standards and requirements—especially when there is such a variation from agency to agency in those standards and requirements—is the first hurdle.

While we may be able to understand rather easily some requirements—being a member of a certain religion if the agency is sponsored by that religion, for example—other requirements really hurt. Why would a previous divorce, for example, in this era when well over 50% of marriages end in divorce, preclude parenting? As couples are marrying later and later, setting arbitrary numbers of years for length of marriage can mean that couples who made careful decisions later in life may fail to qualify by virtue of their age after being married long enough. And, speaking of age, how old is too old? In this era when it is more and more the rule, rather than the exception, for couples to delay childbearing into their 30s and where couples are succeeding at infertility treatment into their 40s, how realistic is it for an agency to say that they will not place babies with couples where one parent is over 40? At a nonsectarian agency, how can one require that applicants "practice a religion" when many people have an active and fulfilling spiritual life outside of organized religious denominations?

It's enough to drive a couple away from agency adoption. And it often does. The fact is, though, that that is expected. The truth, were it told, is that for some agencies, strict requirements such as these serve one purpose and one purpose only—they are effective gates which serve to slow the flow and make the work manageable. It isn't anything personal. It is simply an issue of supply and demand. If there are 40 to 100 couples waiting for each available newborn there has to be a way to weed the lists of applicants down to a manageable size. It just seems more acceptable in a society, which claims—on the surface at least—to be embracing of socioeconomic, cultural, racial, and educational diversity, to set qualifications about length of marriage, age, and so on than to require a certain level of education or of income, or to exclude people because of race.

From the perspective of those who promote agency adoption and are critical of independent adoption, however, such gatekeeping regulations and qualifications become counterproductive to their goals of ensuring that all prospective adopters are properly prepared for parenting in adoption. When people are turned away at the intake door, they don't necessarily stop their efforts to adopt. They keep looking. And in this age of rapidly increasing entrepreneurialism in adoption,

> **Myth:** Homestudies are invasive and judgmental. I'd never pass.
>
> **Fact:** There are no white glove tests. Social workers are looking for clean and safe homes that are appropriate for a child, with well-prepared parents who will be realistic, flexible, safe, and loving. The law requires an element of screening for criminal background. Some element of psychological screening will help to determine your potential strengths and weaknesses as a parent, mostly so that you can be better prepared to have realistic expectations. The process should include far more supportive preparation and education than it does screening per se and, if it does not, you are with the wrong service provider.

they are highly likely to find some intermediary somewhere who will help them adopt—with or without an "appropriate" assessment and preparation process!

"I know; we'll adopt independently. No agency, no homestudy!" It doesn't work quite that way.

In some jurisdictions non-agency placement is completely illegal. In other jurisdictions it is available in a hybrid form called direct adoption, where birthparents and adopters make their own match and then go to an agency for counseling and education which will win them court approval. In many places non-agency adoptions flourish, and indeed in some locales they are more common than agency adoptions. However, in the U.S., at the very least all courts require an approval process of some kind.

Yes, it is true that quite regularly the homestudies done in independent placements are done by court order after the placement and often seem to be just a formality with a few scary teeth. On the other hand, in quite a few cities and states, courts have decided to establish local policy—even when the law does not require it—that requires that a parent preparation process be completed before a court will grant even temporary custody of a child to be adopted.

An important question to ask yourself is why do you want to avoid this? If it is because you resent having to pass muster and prove yourself a fit parent, that's logical, but it probably isn't fair to the family you dream of building. For many people, the avoidance of conventional process is really a way to deny difference—a way to pretend that adoption is just like parenting by birth.

You read in Part 2 what I had to say about the importance of building a sense of entitlement—including acknowledging difference. Here's a place where you may very well need to sublimate your current need for control in the interests of doing what is best for your family over the long haul.

There is much to be said for the benefits of a true parent preparation process (as opposed to an old-style homestudy). In parent preparation you will meet other couples and share concerns. You will probably meet some birthparents (even if you are going to adopt confidentially) and have a more realistic picture of what birthparents are like. You will be introduced to parent groups, literature, and other educational and support opportunities which you are otherwise quite likely to miss. You will be offered parenting tips, practice in dealing with societal reaction to adoption, and suggestions for answering your child's questions. You will have an opportunity to polish the rough edges left on your feelings about infertility with a trained facilitator and to try on some adoption options that you may not know how to explore without committing to them. You will explore ways to bring your family aboard in embracing adoption. You will be encouraged to make an important first step in role transition—from non-parent to parent—with the support of some folks who can really make it happen.

Dave and I adopted twice independently—though in each case we had completed a homestudy process and were waiting with an agency. We adopted once entirely through an agency. There were pluses and minuses to both ways to adopt. I resented entirely having to go through the first homestudy, was somewhat indignant that we needed to do it again the second and third times, yet, retrospectively, I am absolutely certain that we are a healthier family for having had the experiences of going through both homestudies and parent preparations. We learned a lot more than we expected from these processes—about ourselves, about our children, about their birthparents, about adoption, about life.

Why Do We Have to Do This?

I know that most readers resent the idea that they are required be "approved" to wait on a list or have their independent adoption finalized. I did too, 30 years ago. Over that 30-plus years, though, I've never met an experienced adoptive parent (I'd define *experienced* as being at least 10 years into adoption) who claimed that the adoption professionals they had used had required *too much* pre-adoption education, either through face-to-face instruction or through required reading and discussion. Instead, virtually all of the adoptive parents I have come in contact with (literally thousands) have had at least one "I only wish that I had known (or that they had told me or that I had asked) . . ." this or that or another thing. I'd like to see you reach this point in your thinking before you even start the process of getting that "stamp of approval."

All who adopt will go through an assessment/preparation process of some sort. This is a legal requirement in developed countries where adoption is a part of the legal system. That's because a formal system of adoption exists as a service for children, not a service for adults. That being the official stand, gate keeping is indeed a part of society's responsibility to children in need of new caregivers. It is the judicial system's role in adoption to make decisions which are in the best interests of the child when deciding about terminating or assigning parental rights. This is the legal principle which gave rise to the concept of studying the home, the environment, the character, and the relationship of prospective adopters in order to determine which, of multiple potential parents, would best suit a particular child. The role of the social worker in preparing a homestudy or assessment, then, is to make a recommendation to the courts about the assignment of those parental rights—a recommendation based on professional evaluation.

Homestudy. Assessment. Evaluation. Approval process. There is traditional, *old fashioned* thinking reflected in these commonly used terms which describe the way in which government-licensed professionals learn about prospective adoptive families, educate them about adoption, and make recommendations to the courts regarding their suitability and readiness for parenting in adoption. These terms feel judgmental and seem to imply a gate-keeping responsibility on the part of paternalistic professionals. And certainly in a child-centered system for providing alternative families to children who have lost or been removed from their original ones, there needs to be some gate keeping to insure safety and stability for children who have already experienced loss.

The assessment process remains the core of the traditional homestudy, and it is in this part of the pre-adoption process that you will be asked to submit medical and perhaps psychological evaluations, have your criminal background and your fingerprints checked, be interviewed separately and together, provide references to be checked, and produce your financial data—complete with tax records and pay stubs—for examination. For many people considering adoption the process these older terms describe is the single most intimidating factor in deciding whether or not to adopt—can I submit myself to the white-gloved inspection of a homestudy by an authoritarian social worker who will pass final judgment on whether or not I can be a parent?

When I wrote my first book on adoption (*An Adoptor's Advocate*) in 1984 just as our third child arrived, part of my purpose was to help adoption professionals see why this kind of terminology and this outlook was met with such resistance by their clients. When a process is seen as judgmental, I reasoned, it's almost impossible for a client to feel supported by professionals. Instead they feel defensive and on guard. I suggested that the process needed change—adding strong education and support elements to the minimal requirements of a legal assessment and renaming the process *parent preparation*. Other advocates and the growing number of adoption professionals who have personally been touched by adoption agreed. Many agencies have remodeled and expanded their programs in just that way, and these agencies take great pride in their parent preparation process, which most often includes suggested reading, perhaps an online course or two, and attending several hours of face-to-face education—often with other hopeful adopters whom they might not have met under the old system, thus fostering another element to the process of becoming an adoptive parent: peer and agency support.

While the provisions of the Hague Treaty have legally established higher expectations about the amount and the quality of this education than the average agency provided before, the trend toward better education began among the most forward-thinking agencies doing both domestic and intercountry adoptions in the mid-80s—well before the U.S. began to implement the treaty. Domestic adoptions have less state-mandated education in their process. The new Hague parent preparation rules mandated by the federal government will, however, provide an impetus for state governments to consider beefing up their minimal adoptive parent preparation process for domestic adoptions. The results are likely to be that within the next handful of years nearly all adoptions will involve parent preparation rather than just "assessment." The days of the over-the-phone or fast visit "one hour homestudy" are numbered—and with good riddance! Families today deserve the tools that can be provided by well-informed, well-trained, and ethical agency staff members providing genuine parent preparation.

I guess this means that if you still don't "get" the extended process, you can blame me, in part, for the process. The truth is that in my (well-read-and-informed, many-years-retrospective and therefore not in the least humble) opinion, cooperative and open-minded participation in well-designed pre-adoption (and post-adoption) education is absolutely key to both short and long term success in adoption-expanded families.

Today, if you have chosen an ethical, experienced, child-centered agency, you should expect to be involved in two overlapping processes. The first is an assessment, the second is education. If your agency is not providing a multi-part education and support element, the truth is that you and your growing family are being short-changed, both emotionally and financially.

Building a Relationship between Agency and Client

First, you have to trust the agency itself. Having done your homework in selecting it is the best start. But then you must come to feel confident about a personal relationship—the one that must be forged between prospective adopters and social worker. Successful parent preparation results from trust built between client and professional, and building that trust is itself a challenge. Adoption workers are threatening. It goes with the territory. No matter how understanding, how knowledgeable, and how compassionate he or she is, the caseworker is still perceived as a threat by nearly every client—fertile or infertile, gay or straight, single or coupled prospective adopter, man or woman dealing with an untimely pregnancy—who walks through the office door.

Control is one of the issues that makes this so. In modern society a feeling of being in control of one's destiny is vital to a sense of well being. Losing control through illness, accident, or uncontrollable circumstances is difficult. Even people who consider themselves to be devoutly religious often have difficulty turning over control of their destiny to a supreme being. Yet this is what the concept of religious faith demands. To be asked to turn over to another human being complete control of an area of their lives which most people take very much for granted—family planning—is particularly hard for pre-adoptive parents of the birth control generations. Yet this is what adoption often appears to demand—of both adopters and birthfamilies.

There is no local, state, or federal license to parent. There are, however, controls on marriage and divorce which require societal intervention to do or to undo. We must meet certain requirements to complete education, to drive a car, to obtain a job, to qualify to vote, to buy property, but if one is biologically able to reproduce one is not required to qualify to become a parent. Our laws and social customs assume that the biological relationship between progenitor and offspring is inherently inviolable except under the direst of circumstances, that society generally has no business interfering in the parent/child relationship.

When adoption is looked at from the point of view of the would-be parent, who is asked to defend personal values, plans, goals, motivations, relationships, and finances under examination by one who has the absolute power to grant parenthood (whether of a first child or of a fifteenth), perhaps it isn't too difficult to understand why pre-adoptive parents find it hard to relinquish this control. After all, who is this person more powerful even than the physician who tried to help, but had no absolute power to ensure that we would become parents? What specific qualifications, educational or personal, equip him or her to hold this God-like power?

Since parents by birth aren't evaluated and licensed, how will the suitability of would-be adoptive parents be determined? Where are the written criteria for what constitutes parental fitness, and if such criteria are not written, what qualifies this person (perhaps young and/or unmarried and/or not a parent or at least rarely an adoptive parent) to decide whether or not we are parent material? If we are approved, what qualifies this person to decide which child, how young or how old, what sex or what color, how healthy or unhealthy, we are qualified to parent?

All pre-adoptive parents ask these questions silently—and it's important to note that birthparents considering adoption have a similar list and a similarly suspicious view of adoption social workers. Few of these clients, however, openly question the social worker. To other clients, such questions seem perfectly logical. To some adoption workers such questions seem insulting and even threatening. I am a professional, such workers say, qualified by training and study to do such work. Would you, they ask, seek only a diabetic doctor to treat you for diabetes? No. You would choose your doctor on the basis of his educational qualifications and trust his knowledge. If you didn't trust him you would change doctors. The same, then, should be true of your relationship with me.

In the crux of this argument—that one places trust in a professional by virtue of his education and thus his expertise, and that in the absence of this trust one finds a new professional—lies the heart of the problem. Adoption is a difficult and slow process. Potential adopters don't feel that they have the power to pick and choose their agencies as they would a doctor because there may not be a large number of agencies in the area and because due to restrictions on age, religion, length of marriage, etc. they do not qualify at all agencies. They may not feel that they have the power to pick and choose social workers within an agency because many agencies don't have a large number of adoption workers. As well, unlike the situation of a patient electing to see a doctor who practices in a group, where the patient is allowed to decide with which physician he wishes to make an appointment (and I might point out as a valuable aside that infertility patients are notorious for doctor hopping), at an adoption agency couples are usually randomly assigned to a worker and then may fear that a request for a change in worker may be negatively received and thus cause them to risk general disapproval by the agency.

What's more—and this is important—the adoption profession is learned primarily on-the-job. Even the largest and most notable schools of social work do not have courses devoted exclusively to adoption or to fostering. These topics are buried in other broader family-focused or child welfare courses. That means that there is some element of logic in the concerns that newly minted social workers who have not gone through the adoption process themselves may not "get it." Furthermore, a growing number of caseworkers at some of the newer agencies (most especially those that have been forced to find a way to "legitimize" themselves when facilitation services have been made illegal in a state) do not have a college background in a social services or mental health related field, and received less than appropriate on-the-job training and supervision by those at the agency who do.

Would-be parents feel powerless whether they actually are powerless or not. The degree of powerlessness they feel is in many cases directly proportional to their perceived need to adopt. The infertile couple or single person with no children at all and a deep desire to parent may feel most powerless. The couple with four biological children who have also adopted six times and are being asked to consider a sibling group may feel least powerless. Yet all of them probably do feel or have in the past felt the frustration of losing control to a social worker.

> Ashley and Del felt that they were lucky. Unlike many of their friends, they had forged a friendship with the social worker who had facilitated their first adoption, and, as a result of these warm, trusting feelings, they expected the second adoption to flow more smoothly for them emotionally. And it did, until the disaster.
>
> Ashley and Del's second placement was disrupted after several weeks when their child's birthmother had a change of heart. They and their older child grieved for months, and were comforted by the fact that many people, including their social worker, were able to offer them empathic support.
>
> Throughout the grieving, Ashley and Del, who had earlier worked very hard to understand the losses which accompanied their infertility, experienced real clarity about what was going on for them. They grieved the terrible loss of the actual child, of course, but beyond that, this loss had reopened the old wounds about lost control. They had rediscovered just how out-of-control their family planning was.

After grieving for her lost child, Ashley grieved her empty arms and her inability to do anything about filling them. Five months had passed and she was eager to adopt again, but she was dependent upon the caseworker's assessment of her readiness.

It did not even occur to Ashley that the caseworker would misinterpret her feelings, and so she made no attempt to hide her loneliness and longing for a child to fill the waiting nursery. However, the caseworker was concerned. "You sound far sadder than you were the last time we spoke," she said. "We must make sure that your grieving has progressed sufficiently; we don't want to place an unfair burden on the new baby. Let's work together on this to help you get ready."

Ready?! What would "ready" mean? Ashley and Del were frightened, and for the first time in their relationship with their caseworker, wondered if they had come to an impasse with her. Perhaps they shouldn't have been so open with their feelings after all. Perhaps that old-style thinking—the one that labels all loss in infertility the loss of a dream child, the one that expects there to be a finite point at which one's losses are "resolved"—would enchain them indefinitely.

There is no way for adoption workers to completely erase the adversarial relationship that traditional adopters may experience. This perception is part of the situation, and much of that can't be changed. There are ways, though, for caseworkers to ease the tension, and many workers and agencies today are in the process of doing this. And there are ways for would-be parents (and expectant parents too) to assure themselves ahead of time that they will be working with the most qualified of available adoption professionals. Agencies need to make clear to clients that such changes are possible. Clients should always feel assured that the option to ask for a change in social workers, if they are feeling discomfort about forging a good working relationship with the person assigned to their case, will not negatively impact their adoption process through that agency.

Today's professionals are getting better at accepting that they may be expecting too much from themselves in thinking that they alone can adequately prepare an adopter for parenting. In seeing oneself not as the grantor of children, rather as the preparer of parents, a professional becomes himself an adopter's advocate. If professionals truly see themselves in this role, they are eager for continuing education for themselves, and they work toward flexibility and humanness in the system, more responsiveness in and justification for policy, better training of social workers and foster parents, less theory and more practicality in parent preparation, and better communication with and referral to other helping professionals and adoption-related services. Adoption professionals have always seen their primary client as the child in need of parents. Yet only in forming a positive relationship with those new parents can social workers protect the child's best interests. Learning to educate, to empower, to support, and then to trust those clients is a key to forging that relationship.

In selecting the professionals who will work with you in your quest for expanding your family, would-be adopters need to reassert some of the important control that they do retain. Your most powerful and important asset is to feel free to ask probing questions about the agencies you are considering—questions about their philosophy; the adoption-related qualifications and experience of the management, board of directors, and staff members; the agency's view about and commitment to continuing education for the staffers; their experience networking within the world of adoption; their commitment to ethical standards, etc.

In order to work toward forging those solid relationships, professionals need to understand how adopters perceive certain aspects of traditional assessment. Adoption professionals, please read over our shoulders—your clients' and mine—as we examine some elements of traditional assessment and make suggestions for thinking differently about them.

Approval Part One: The Elements of Assessment

If other people live with you—perhaps a grandparent, an aunt or uncle, children over 18, a roommate—they too will be part of the assessment. They will be interviewed, and they will need to go through the background check process. How their presence there affects your finances will be discussed as well. They will need to assure the agency that their own health does not produce a threat to the child's health, and that a child who may come to the home with a communicable illness will not compromise this person's health. The extent to which this person will be involved in the care of the child you propose to adopt may call for his or her more active participation in the elements of assessment and preparation.

Currently, each state sets minimal standards for what the assessment must include, and agencies then decide what to add onto these minimums, if anything. What you would like most to have, I know, is a rulebook that explains exactly what a homestudy is, and how to play the game successfully enough to pass Go and collect your child. But the fact is that if this is to be likened to a game, it is a game with changing standards and rules. I doubt that you would be able to find any two unconnected agencies anywhere in the world whose assessment processes are the exactly the same. Some assessments are also more intensive than others.

For the most part, adopters don't often feel confident enough in their "approvability" to openly question the process, and this needs to change. It is the existence of these confusing, unexplained, and therefore misunderstood common elements juxtaposed against the absence of standardization (which would indicate professional agreement) which makes it so difficult for adopters to feel that the assessment/preparation process makes sense or has any real value for them. If a step is important at one agency, why is it left out at another? If one agency feels it unnecessary to require a certain procedure, why is the other so adamant about requiring it?

While there is still room for more standardization in the process, individual advocates, and consumer advocacy and support groups have raised enough questions over the years that there are certainly common elements to every agency's process. Of the two portions of a good parent-preparation process—assessment and education/support—assessments are most likely to be quite similar from agency to agency.

Personal History

Paperwork

Birth certificates, marriage license, divorce papers (if there has been one), and educational diplomas and professional certifications are the kinds of paperwork you should expect that you may need to produce as part of the personal history portion of the assessment process. These simply help you to verify your identity for the agency. After all, identity theft is a part of the modern world.

Autobiography

Most agencies begin to learn about their would-be-parent clients by asking that they write an autobiography, usually providing some guidelines for length and perhaps a list of suggested questions that should be answered in the process. This history will be an opportunity for the client to describe the family culture in which he or she was raised, the family in which the proposed adopted child will be raised and nurtured, and motivations for adoption. Most of the time, the autobiography only serves as a point of reference which the caseworker uses during her interview with you, as opposed to a document shared with birthparents.

Interviews—Sharing Intimacies

Most agencies set up a short series of interviews with clients. Usually when the prospective adopters are a couple, there will be interviews with each parent-to-be separately and then together. Good social workers expect that clients will be nervous about these chats, and they will do their best to help the client to relax, often suggesting that the interviews occur in their homes, as opposed to at the agency office, and as part of state-required home visits. The assumption is that the client is likely to feel more comfortable and open on home turf. But first visits are rarely easy.

> An amusing commercial for a popular laxative pops up now and then on television. Maureen and Roger sit on their front porch, Roger absorbed in his newspaper while Maureen carries on a conversation

with the camera. She proceeds to tell us that when Roger is feeling "you know, irregular" she offers him this product. Roger, amazed at what he is hearing, appears from behind the newspaper to express his indignation. "Maureen!" he cries.

"Well, it's true," she replies.

"But you don't even know these people!" cries Roger as he hides his face again behind the paper.

We are not a culture in which we are raised to feel comfortable sharing the facts of our most intimate lives. In many marriages, couples married many years consider their bathroom functions every bit as private—if not more so—as does Roger.

Imagine yourselves, then, being asked by a perfect stranger about the frequency and the satisfaction of your sex lives. Beyond imagining, expect that this may happen. A part of the assessment process for many agencies includes private discussions between each of you and your social worker and then the three of you together about many very intimate issues: your relationship with your parents and your siblings, your relationship with your partner, your feelings about religion or spirituality, your private value system, your goals for yourself, and even your sex lives.

Anna and Joe were frightened. Had they blown it? Totally unprepared for the fact that their caseworker might ask them about sex, each had answered his questions differently when they went in for private interviews. Joe had figured that it probably wasn't a good idea to admit to a social worker who was a priest that they had been intimate before they were married. Anna, on the other hand, had been unable to lie to a priest. Now they were worried. What would it mean that their answers were different? Did it matter anyway? What was the reason for asking these questions?

I've always wondered, and as a result I've asked many caseworkers I've met, what they do with the information they ask about sexuality and relationships. I've asked by what standards they evaluate this data. I've asked who trains them for this work. With the rarest of exceptions, the answers are strangely noncommittal. As it turns out, few adoption workers have received training on how to evaluate the answers to intimacy surveys, and few agencies have standards. Perhaps even more shocking, far too many adoption workers are so uninformed about the practical realities of infertility, for example, that they are unaware of how common temporary sexual dysfunction is for couples who have ended treatment and are simply too exhausted after years of scheduled intercourse to care about having intercourse for pleasure for a time. Since most couples are unaware of this common reaction also, the result of this mutual lack of knowledge is that the very people (mental health professionals) who might be able to assist a couple feeling frightened of this element of their reaction to infertility is in essence unavailable to offer help in working it through. I'm pleased to say that conversations about sexuality are less and less frequent in the assessment processes of today.

Beyond sexual intimacy issues, in this enlightened age of getting in touch with our feelings, most prospective adopters have at least a passing familiarity with such terms as *dysfunctional family*, *inner child*, *co-dependency*, and many more frightening and controversially defined issues such as *what constitutes child abuse* (though we all seem to know that the tendency toward it is passed on from generation to generation). So how does one answer questions about corporal punishment, for example? You may have been raised in a family where children were spanked. Do you intend to spank your children? These are issues which may or may not be important to share with an adoption worker.

The deciding factor in whether or not these intimate issues will prove valuable if shared is simple and straightforward. If the professional

- knows *why* he or she is asking the question
- understands and can convey to the client on what basis the answers will be interpreted
- is qualified to assess the information
- is trained to provide assistance if merited
- can help the client understand how it will be a valuable part of preparation for parenting

then it can be important to share this information. It is perfectly reasonable for prospective adopters to ask about these things before answering uncomfortably intimate questions. Of course you will want to do so in a pleasant, cooperative, and positive way, rather than to challenge the professional in a manner which serves to put him or her on the defensive.

References

The need to provide personal references, while perhaps the most easily justified and understood requirement of the approval process, is often uncomfortable and can even be agonizing. Numbers and types of references required vary considerably among agencies, as does the form in which they are to be submitted. References from some or all of the following may be requested: the prospective adopter's parents and siblings, employers, friends and neighbors, clergypersons, and the school of other children in the family.

Agencies need to understand why providing references is difficult for prospective adopters. Of course it begins with the frustration of having to get permission to parent at all. But that's not all. The need to supply references destroys completely and forever any remaining privacy the prospective parents may have had concerning their family expansion plans.

While people contemplating becoming pregnant may never need to make this known to others until they are successful in their efforts, the reference gathering aspect of the adoption process requires that adopters ask for the cooperation of others in gaining agency approval. It can be humiliating to ask for references for such a purpose, as it may seem as if one is requesting permission to do what for others is a totally natural and independent action—building a family. This enhances the adopter's feelings of being out of control. After all, what prospective parent by birth must depend on the positive reactions to themselves and their family plans from parents, neighbors, employers, etc. in order to add a child to their family? Of course, buried deep within the discomfort of asking for such a reference is the adopter's nagging fear that—no matter how squeakily clean and ready one knows oneself to be—one of those references may say "something" that may cause rejection by the agency. How would one ever explain being rejected to others who have supplied references?

> When Rashid and Esther applied to adopt, Rashid still felt a little reluctant. Concerned about what others would think and say about their inability to conceive, he resented having to get a social worker's approval. Things got worse when he was asked to send out reference forms.
> "From that point on," said Rashid, "it felt kinda like someone was watching us in bed. Everybody knew we were trying to start a family, and they might as well have been asking us about how the sex was going when asking us how the homestudy was going."

The format in which references are to be supplied can also be a cause for concern. Some agencies request general letters of reference with few if any specific guidelines, while others supply a highly detailed questionnaire to be completed. Most often there has been no attempt to design individual reference models for each type of reference supplier, so that the adopter is placed in the awkward position of asking people to supply information about which the referrer may not have knowledge.

Many of those asked to supply references are uncomfortable doing so. Aware that they themselves have not needed such public permission to parent, they feel awkward. When information is requested on a "general questionnaire" to which they feel that they cannot or should not appropriately respond, they feel the weight of responsibility given over to them by the person needing the reference and, to a certain extent intimidated by the authority of the system, they would be hesitant to question the agency's procedure and thereby risk jeopardizing the adopter's chances.

> Brenda and Stan were adopting for the first time. Their agency asked them to forward copies of a single standard reference form to

each of their parents, two friends, each of their employers, and their pastor. They complied and waited.

Brenda, a teacher, was called to her principal's office one afternoon during her prep period, where she faced an embarrassed man. "Ah, uh, Brenda, I, uh, got this form, and I sure do want to help you out here. Adoption is a great thing and all that. I guess I just don't quite know what you want me to say on a couple of questions, though . . . like 'How would you describe the stability of the marital relationship of this couple?' What would you think I'm supposed to say there? I don't know your husband."

He didn't mention specifically the other question that had stood out to Brenda as a tough one, "Would you feel comfortable placing your own children in this couple's care?"

After an awkward silence, they agreed on some "right" answers. A day or two later, Stan's boss placed a photocopy of his response to the agency in the interoffice mail. Some questions had been left blank.

The development of a specific written policy about references would have helped both agency and client here. What does the agency hope to learn from each type of reference requested? Have they made that clear by designing tools which take into account the differences in viewpoint of each referrer? What will be the agency's reaction to a questionable reference or an entirely negative one? Is a system of checks and balances in place that will guarantee the adopter the opportunity to defend himself while at the same time protecting the confidentiality of the referrer? When references are well-justified and carefully developed tools are used, agencies will receive more helpful information and couples will be feel less awkward about asking for references from others and less resentful of the need to supply them.

If, as a client, you are presented with a reference format or tool that seems awkward to you, and you have a good relationship with your social worker, please speak up. The fact is that some of these awkward elements of the assessment part of the approval process are things that nobody at the agency has taken a good look at for a while. A compassionate agency will always be open to suggestions offered in a spirit of constructive criticism.

Home Visits

You do not have to own your home in order to adopt. Adoptive parents live in rented and owned houses, apartments and condominiums, and in manufactured housing. Agencies usually require that children of opposite gender stop sharing rooms at school age, but, unless there is an issue of safety of one child against the other, same-sex children of not too disparate ages may share rooms.

Your social worker will visit your home at least once. She will not be wearing white gloves and swiping them across the top of your refrigerator. The purpose of this visit is to insure that the child coming into your home has a clean and safe environment in which to grow up. She will be looking for potential safety hazards and will be suggesting how those might be taken care of. For example, he or she may speak with you about the need for safety gates, electrical outlet covers, safety latches on cabinets, or repairing a broken stair. She may look at your yard and ask about plans to keep unsupervised children away from a pool or a hot tub, or from pets not yet used to children. If your pets are very large or breeds that have reputations for unpredictability, that may generate a serious discussion.

Health Reports

Once again, there is no standard for what belongs in the health screening portion of an assessment process, but nearly all courts and/or agencies require some sort of medical screening for the people involved in adoptions—adopters, birthparents, children to be adopted. At issue is how such tests are to be used.

> Wendy was raised in India and was exposed to T.B. there. In Ontario, where she now lives, the provincial agency, C.A.S., requires T.B. screening, a test Wendy will always "fail." Because there is no written standardized policy concerning what is to be done with the results of medical screening, Wendy's fear is that some uninformed "bureaucrat" will wipe out her chances for adopting a child with a stroke of his pen. While her fear may have no basis in reality, without written policy, her fear is logical!

Clients should feel assured that the agency understands and complies with health privacy rules mandated by the Health Insurance Portability and Accountability Act of 1996 (HIPAA). Furthermore, people who are involved in adoption have a right to be told in advance how the results of such screening could affect the adoption process for them.

> Cassandra and Craig applied to adopt a healthy Caucasian infant at an agency which had no written policies concerning health. They went through an initial group process with several other couples and then began to gather their "paperwork"—references, autobiographies, medical exams, etc. They expected to pass with flying colors and were shocked to find that they were not approved because the agency considered Cassandra "morbidly obese" despite her doctor's statement of her relative health. At the same time, a minority couple in the same study group was approved, despite what appeared to Craig and Cassandra as the husband's similar weight problem. Craig and Cassandra wondered:

is this an issue of health or an issue of cosmetics? Are health standards different for choosing the parents for children of different races?

Aside from medical issues about themselves, adopters have the right to know whether they will be given *all* available information about their children-to-be and about their birthfamilies. For many years traditional social workers resisted telling prospective adopters about birthfamily health issues that they feared would prejudice the adopting family about accepting the placement of a baby who appeared to the workers to be healthy. It's realized now that the appearance of health can be deceptive. Good agencies understand that it is important that social workers be better trained to understand the importance and significance of such items as APGAR scores, a history of ADHD or bi-polar disorder (BPD) in the family, etc.

As we come to know more and more about the damaging effects of in utero drug and alcohol exposure, about the effects of exposure to sexually transmitted diseases, about the genetic links to various learning disabilities and to heightened distractibility and hyperactivity, it has become increasingly important that parents be given all information about their child's birthfamily medical history, pregnancy and delivery history, and early experiences. This goes far beyond the issue of whether or not couples will say "no" more often to children they might have parented successfully had they been kept in the dark. Yes, some couples will indeed say no to certain risks. But more than this, parents cannot be expected to parent effectively if they are not given full information about the children they adopt. All of us deal more effectively with the known than with the unknown.

My own state, Indiana, conservative in many other ways, was the first in the nation to require the gathering and passing on of a relatively extensive non-identifying medical history which is to be presented to the adopting parents before finalization of both agency and independent adoptions, and a copy of which is to be placed in the court files. I was privileged to serve on the Attorney General's task force which drafted this document. But other states have been slow to follow suit. It remains the case that far too many agencies, through either ignorance and/or bad policy, do not pass on significant medical information to adopting families.

The bottom line, then, is that clients should know that agencies have no right to keep any information from prospective adopters. This is more than my personal opinion. It is emerging social policy. Several lawsuits contending that agencies, which deliberately or out of ignorance withheld medical data from prospective adopters, were guilty of social work malpractice are in progress and a handful have already been heard and decided—in favor of the parents!

Psychological Issues

A few nations require psychological testing of parent candidates who will be adopting internationally. Some other countries (notably China, at this writing) have set standards about under what circumstances they will accept or reject candidates for adoption who have used medications for conditions such as anxiety or depression.

No U.S. state requires psychological testing, but some domestic agencies have made such testing a routine part of their assessment process. Often used screening tools for this purpose include the Minnesota Multiphasic Personality Inventory™ (MMPI-2) and two newer tests, The Personal Assessment Inventory™, and—perhaps even more appropriate for candidates for adoptions—The Adult Attachment Interview[1] (developed by Mary Main, PhD and her colleagues at the University of California at Berkeley). In concept such tools have real merit. In practice, clients are often frightened by them.

> Rebecca and Bill had given birth to more than one child before deciding to expand their family by adoption. They were adopting out of preference rather than giving birth again. Well-respected in their community as involved and active parents, they were working on their third adoption of a waiting child when routine results of psychological testing suggested that Bill was a poor prospect for adopting due to apparent risk factors for substance abuse and impulse control problems.
>
> Bill and Rebecca were shocked and frightened at such a result. Their caseworker, however, simply decided to ignore the test. No confirming test was administered. No suggestion was made that Bill be screened by a mental health professional. The child—an unattached and character disordered 8 year old—was placed.
>
> Subsequently, Bill had many concerns about this situation. "How could she just ignore such results?" Bill asked. "It was almost as if we were talking about my horoscope and deciding that, while it was kind of fun to look at, it wasn't to be taken seriously. If this test was an important enough part of the adoption process to take up several hours of my time and add a significant charge to my bill, how could such results be dismissed so casually?"

Certainly if psychological screening tools are to become a standard part of any agency's homestudy process, the agency should establish specific policies regarding their use and application. To prevent misinterpretation and misunderstanding, such policies should be put in writing so that clients can read and reread them, ask appropriate questions, and refer to them as needed. This written information should include a thorough discussion of the strengths and weaknesses of the instrument being used, a statement about how the results will and will not be used, and an established route of appeal should applicants strongly disagree with the results of their testing. Beyond giving clients a copy of this written policy, every caseworker should be fully prepared to discuss this part of the assessment process in a thorough, encouraging, and supportive manner. Above all, agencies which do choose to administer such testing should do so consistently, and clients should be able to expect that their results will not be taken lightly.

If, as a client, you are asked to take a psychological test or assessment, remember that you have the right to know in advance the name of the test so that you can individually research this test's reputation among professionals, and learn the test originator's suggestions for how and by whom it is to be administered and scored. You also have a right to know the purpose of the testing and how its outcome might influence your pursuit of adoption; the qualifications of the person who will administer, score and write the test results, and whether those qualifications meet the standards of the test's developers; the results of the testing (you even have the right to read the psychological report itself); and to determine, through your signed release of information, who will have access to the testing information (interview information, raw scores, test reports) in your chart. You should know whether test results become part of a permanent record and, if so, who will have access to this information, how long will it be retained, and under what circumstances and to whom might it conceivably be released.

Criminal Background Check

Things have changed in 20 years. Dave and I were never fingerprinted before or after our three domestic adoptions. Now, clients of both domestic and intercountry placing agencies can expect to be asked to consent to a full criminal background check. Not that these checks often turn much up. Most would-be adopters are smart enough to know that people with a history of felonious criminality—especially domestic violence, sexual assault, or predation are not acceptable candidates for adoption. State, local, FBI, National Sex and Violent Offender's Registry and CPS checks have become mandatory. Agencies make clear to clients that the reasons for these checks are to try to assure the physical safety of their primary clients: children. Again, the expectation should be that your agency will keep the results of such background checks private.

Financial Statement

Tax documents, employment verification and other information, insurance information, a list of your financial assets (investments, 401Ks, your home equity, etc.) and liabilities (student loans, credit card debt, mortgages, car loans, etc.) and, in the case with hopeful parents who are single or who have health or ability challenges, a guardianship plan for your child-to-be are the kinds of paperwork that must be gathered in order to comply with the financial assessment portion of your homestudy.

If you have made careful choices about your adoption professionals, you should feel confident already that you can afford their services. Understand, then, that what social workers are looking for in this segment of your homestudy is not for how wealthy you are, but how well you manage what you actually have. If you are paring away at debt rather than accumulating it, and if you are clearly living within or below your means, so that it's a sure bet that you will be able to manage the added costs of having one more person and all of their needs added into budget, the financial assessment should not cause sleepless nights.

Approval Part Two: Training/Education/Support

Where service providers *really* differ from one another is in the amount and the quality of education, training, and support offered to both birthparent and adoptive parent clients. In some states, the rules require only the assessments we have already discussed, so you—and your child's birthparent—are actually at risk for getting little to no education, psycho-social counseling, and support if you are not using service providers who make it a required part of their services.

Licensed public agencies (and private agencies working under contracts with them) always require several hours of training for those who will be fostering and/or adopting children coming into care through child protective services. Continuing education is required in order for foster parents and foster/adopt parents to maintain their licenses.

Nearly all private agencies whose practice includes adoptions of infants born domestically also mandate several hours of education. Sometimes that education is done completely one-on-one with an individual caseworker while he or she is visiting your home for the assessment, and at other agencies these classes are offered to groups of prospective parents gathered at the agency or in some community meeting space.

The Hague Treaty guidelines mandate minimums in amount and content of pre-placement education and post-placement supervision, and support for prospective adopters. While these rules currently apply only to adoptions between two Hague-signatory countries, it should be expected that ethical U.S. agencies, recognizing the need for education for families, would require at least these education minimums for all client families, whether they were adopting from Hague compliant countries or not. Indeed, it should be expected that eventually the State Department and the United States Citizenship and Immigration Services (USCIS or CIS) may rule that Americans may adopt only from Hague compliant countries.

What Type of Education Is Supplied and How

Since my MS is in education and my first career was in teaching, I have some strong opinions about how to make adoption education effective. Most importantly because people have such a variety of learning styles, I think the best educational programs involve a combination of *all* of the following elements.

- Online learning modules. These can be good introductory tools—especially at stages where families have not yet made a commitment to a particular age, race, or ability child. At this time, however, the resources that are so far available provide more overview rather than in-depth materials. As an educator, I don't feel that any of these can take the place of in-depth reading and/or face-to-face training.

- One-to-one talking. Traditionally, virtually all education is supplied by individual caseworkers in the course of their meetings with individual client families. This remains the main way in which education is given at many agencies and one-on-one educating can be quite valuable. It allows it to be personalized; it provides the opportunity for individual follow-up to meet the needs of a particular client. But as the primary means of educating clients, this method is not optimal. It depends on expecting that each caseworker/educator will maintain the same quality, will be equally engaging, and will provide the same level of detail for every client.

- Classes. Many agencies provide their own classes, carefully customized to fit their own standards of education. These may be offered as full-day sessions, as two or more half day sessions, or as a series of evening sessions depending on what individual agencies find works best for their clients. Speakers may include agency social work staff (though keep in mind that many people who are very good one-on-one relationships are not effective in front of a group), "experts" from the community, or even "imported" educators. Agencies in some cities open their classes on special subjects or with special speakers to the clients of other agencies. This can be a fabulous way for agencies to cooperate with one another to achieve even higher standards in education. My only reservation about allowing clients to submit their participation in classes sponsored by others is directed not at the clients, but at the professionals. If you will be accepting these credits, you should be very aware of what information has been presented (most likely by attending yourselves) and you should follow up soon after with a "debriefing" for clients who do avail themselves of such classes for credit with you, since it will be important for you to have a clear sense of what they have learned (or not) and how they are reacting to this information.

- Required reading (or books on tape). The reading should be customized to the age of the child to be adopted (infant, toddler, middle childhood, teen), to the ethnicity and/or the country from which the child will come, and, if the adoption is to be open, to that as well. This reading needs to be followed by active discussion with the social worker—either one-on-one or in groups. There are excellent books available which focus on each of these issues.

- Homework. Adopting families need to learn about the resources available to themselves and their children within their particular communities before their children arrive. Families should understand the racial and socio-economic demographics of the community in which they intend to raise a child (and we are talking here about their local community, not the big cities nearby). They should investigate their school systems (early childhood offerings, educational testing, English as a second language resources, etc.). Intercountry adopters should be encouraged to learn about and plug into the closest international adoption medicine clinics and/or specialists. Adopters should know about the existence (or not) of attachment and adoption-literate therapists. They should be directed to local adoptive parent support groups, and be expected to attend a meeting or two and then talk about their experience there.
- Support and encouragement for an adoption expectancy (see Part 4).

Topics

So what topics make for solid education? Families need a foundation which introduces them to and supports their developing sense of entitlement; attachment and lots of practical advice about how to foster it; basic child development and how issues related to adoption (for example institutionalization) can affect it; how children learn in general and how they think, at various learning stages—about adoption, about race, etc.; cultural competence (that is, talking to children about adoption and choosing good resources such as books, TV programming, and movies to do so); educating family, friends, teachers, clergy and others who come in close contact with their families; respecting birthfamilies and culture of origin; and navigating an open adoption. I consider these minimal standards of adoption education.

Intercountry—Help with Dossier

The packet of documents required by a foreign country to approve an adoption is called a *dossier*. Dossiers are country-specific and sometimes even region-specific, as each geographic location may have different requirements. All dossiers include the finalized homestudy which demonstrates that the client is prepared and "fit" to adopt, and the rest of the documents include the I-171H form from the USCIS, medical forms that attest to your health, income statements and police clearances. Dossier documents are usually time-sensitive, which means they expire in a specific amount of time. They must meet internationally agreed-upon standards for authenticity (for example, apostilling or certification) and must be competently translated. Since countries do change and add to their dossier requirements, sometimes families will find that additional documents are requested even while they are in their child-to-be's country.

Agencies experienced in intercountry adoptions know just how to accomplish a dossier, and it is reasonable and logical to expect that your placement agency (which in some cases is not your homestudy agency) will assist you with this process, making what is by nature a complicated and usually frustrating process, more efficient and effective.

Domestic—Help with Profile and Marketing

If you are working with a full-service domestic agency, you will not be required to locate and make your own "match" with an expectant parent. Instead, you will create a profile which will be viewed by agency expectant parent clients. Full-service agencies will offer you clear guidelines about how to write and package this profile, as they will want them to follow a uniform style—attractive and easy to work through, but not something that stands out because of its packaging rather than because of who it describes.

When it comes to helping you make the match, adopting independently can be similar to or completely different from an adoption through a full-service agency. Some providers (attorneys, facilitators, etc.) pull together all of the resources you will need for advertising and making a connection into a nice, neat package. More often, though, an independent adoption requires that you do your own outreach to expectant parents considering adoption, perhaps by hiring a "coach" or a "consultant" to help you find places online and in newspapers to advertise, and put together a profile to be given to expectant parents who see your advertisement. (see Resources at the end of Chapter 11 for suggestions). While many people do feel that they gain an element of control in choosing independent adoption, this may come at the cost of having to find, evaluate, and then hire and depend on multiple service providers who are linked to one another only by virtue of being hired by you.

I encourage you not to avoid true parent preparation, yet instead to actively seek it out. If, for some reason, you are unable to connect with a modern-thinking intermediary and the agency or intermediary with whom you finally connect is not equipped to provide honest, competent, enlightening and even exciting parent preparation, please seek it out elsewhere. Read all that you can. Attend seminars. Find an infant-care class or take a parenting course. Learn CPR. Join a parents-in-waiting support group.

I have made clear throughout this book that I believe that adoptive families have far more in common with families formed exclusively by birth than they have differences from them. The differences, though, are significant, which is why I believe that education is vital. Frankly, I believe that good education—both before placement and as ongoing continuing education throughout a family's life—is the foundation of strong families. I have little respect for agencies and other service providers who provide only as little education as they can get away with, and I believe that families who avoid education by looking for opportunities to adopt with as little of it as possible are making *un*sound choices.

Embrace adoption's differences, so that you can relish adoption's similarities. Congratulations, Mom, Dad—a child is on the way!

PART FOUR
The Real Thing

While there has been much you could do to exert some control over how your *process* of adopting would work—choosing to work with an agency or without one, choosing the age, gender, race of your child and the country in which he would be born—other than having made very careful choices about the professionals who will take the lead in matching you to your child and in how his or her transitional care is managed, there's very little that adoptive parents can do about how their children will have been cared for before their lives are blended.

For many family-challenged people, this is one of the most frustrating elements and the most painful losses related to adopting a child rather than giving birth to him. As a would-be parent who feels that she would have done an especially careful job of making healthy choices throughout a pregnancy—abstaining from harmful foods, chemicals and environments, getting the best medical care, etc.—it can be frustrating to think of your child-to-be gestating in an alcohol bath, being neglected as a toddler by a depressed mother, or being abused in a caregiving setting. You may feel restless, powerless and angry at how slowly bureaucracies grind away before giving you paperwork that allows you to snatch your child from a short-staffed, over-crowded, sensory-deprived orphanage or to transfer him from a foster home across the city. This huge loss of control is something you can do nothing to change.

Precisely because you will have so little control over your child's experiences before he comes to you, your part in the list of responsibilities for helping to insure a healthy beginning for your lives together is to use this anticipatory period to learn, prepare, and become as flexible as you can be, so that you will be able to adapt to what your child brings to you when he comes to you—whether he comes as a newborn in a local hospital nursery, out of foster care in a nearby state, or from an orphanage half way around the world.

337

What you must remember as you prepare is that you, as parent, will lead the dance of attachment. How well you have prepared yourself for parenting, how fully you have listened to, fully processed and accepted as reality what you have read about and been taught by your service providers, how much you have learned about the particular issues that could come home with your child, how carefully you have researched the resources you may need, and how flexible you can prepare yourself to be as you become a parent are the things you *can* best control in your plan to form a healthy family through adoption.

This final section of *Adopting: Sound Choices, Strong Families* focuses on practical activities for making your transition to new parenthood a smooth and confident one. We will talk about getting ready through an adoption expectancy period in Chapter 13. Chapter 14 will focus on arrival issues for your child, his parents, and your extended family. Chapter 15 focuses on adjustment issues common to the first year of parenthood. The book ends with a chapter on moving out into the "real world" as a family formed by adoption.

Anticipation

The 1995 movie *Nine Months* draws an entertaining picture of a surprise pregnancy. In this comedy, Hugh Grant portrays a man whose long term live-in partner (played by Julianne Moore) becomes pregnant unexpectedly. He feels committed to her but not necessarily to being a parent. He doesn't want to change his life or his apartment. He doesn't want to lose his Porsche or his freedom. They split.

He's miserable without her and begins to explore parenthood in many of the ways described in this chapter. Throw in Tom Arnold as the epitome of a happy father and Robin Williams as an obstetrician who recently emigrated from Russia and whose questionable language skills lead to concerns about his medical abilities as well. Add a happy ending, and, well . . . you gotta rent this one.

Now, isn't it ironic for an infertility and adoption educator to recommend a movie about an unplanned pregnancy to a readership of people who are family-challenged? However, *you* need to be expectant too. You need to sort through all of those feelings of ambivalence, go through all of those ups and downs of life's changes while waiting for a new and very dependent person to be added to the family. You need to feel pregnant—by adoption.

Nine Months, More or Less

The time will come—after far longer than most prospective adopters hoped that it would, yet most often so suddenly as to render any adopter briefly shocked and somewhat panicked—when the reality of impending parenthood will suddenly hit. An agency will announce its approval and the staff expects that they can make a placement within a specified length of time. An attorney will say that a profile package has been selected by one of the expectant parents in her program. An international agency will actually send a photo and basic information about a particular child to consider adopting, along with information about how long it might take for the folks at both ends of the adoption to do the paperwork necessary for the child to travel to parents or for parents to travel to the child. A pregnant woman will respond to some piece of outreach and, after several conversations, she will tell a would-be mom that she's been selected to be the parent of her baby.

Expectancy has begun.

Writing it Out

First advice: write everything down—absolutely, positively everything—names (yes, of family members and friends mentioned too), descriptions and vital statistics, phone numbers or other contact information, background profile, needed paperwork—everything. Most simply that means keeping a pad by the phone and transferring everything you jot there to a journal or notebook. Some couples have found it useful to ask permission of the person on the other end of the line to record the conversation on their answering machine tape. Why record it all? Because someday you'll wish that you had! It's as simple as that.

You may believe that everything that is happening at this time is of such momentous importance (and it is) that you will never forget a word that is spoken. Unfortunately, the experience of most adoptive parents and most birthparents is that you may very well tuck some of those early details into the farthest reaches of your mind, expecting to be able to draw them up later, yet only to find that when later arrives, you can't seem to remember. Or you may discover later that you didn't ask about everything that you could eventually want to know.

> At 13, Treena and her friends became interested in astrology. One of the moms of the group had a friend who agreed, just for fun, to do everyone's chart. What they needed was the usual data—birthdates, times of birth, etc. Treena asked her mom, Karla, for the information she needed, but Karla just couldn't remember what time Treena had been born. Sure, she remembered that it had been dinner time when she and Daddy had received "The Call," and that the attorney had said the baby was born "that morning." It had never occurred to Karla that she'd need more detail than that. Of course not having this information was hardly life threatening, but for Treena, it was representative of how she was "different" from her friends. Once again she'd feel that she didn't "quite fit," and once again her friends would "feel sorry for her" that she was adopted and so didn't know anything about her "real" parents.

Some intermediaries may reassure you that they will be providing you with a detailed report of everything you'll be told, so that you can relax and just listen. But many parents have found that those reports, while wonderful to have, include some information not shared earlier while at the same time, seem to be missing other information that they "thought" they remembered hearing. Time passes, workers experience hundreds more cases, and their memories dim about "small" issues that somehow were not recorded in the permanent record, or they move on and are not accessible, or offices close.

> TiJuan's mom pulled out his agency report for him when TiJuan asked for it at age 11. TiJuan felt short; he wanted to know about his birthfather's adult height. He wanted to know if he had played basketball (TiJuan's passionate dream) in high school as had his six-foot-five dad. The information was pretty nonspecific: "African American male of 'average height and weight;' left school at 16; unable to contact for participation in agency counseling sessions; parental rights terminated by advertisement." What did that mean, "by advertisement?" TiJuan wondered. The report raised far more questions than it answered.

But, you think, *our* adoption will be open. We'll have access to our child's birthfamily directly and so will always have a way to find answers to those questions later. An important reality to understand about open adoption is that it involves fluid, changing relationships. In our increasingly transient society, even here there are no guarantees.

> For the first two years after the adoption, Marjorie's birthmother, Celia, was in frequent contact with Marjorie's family. They exchanged visits, letters, and gifts. But then Celia met and married Mark. The visits were less frequent. Marjorie's mom understood: Celia was busy settling into her new marriage and, besides, she was feeling comfortable that Marjorie was doing OK. Maybe Celia was moving on. Celia and Mark moved across the country and the letters came less and less often. A baby was born and a birth announcement came. A flurry of pictures and gifts were exchanged for about six months, and then all was quiet. Marjorie's mom understood: a new baby keeps one very busy. A first birthday card was sent and returned "Addressee Unknown." Marjorie's mom was surprised, but figured that the post office had just screwed up and they'd get this all straightened out soon. Shortly thereafter, Marjorie's family was transferred. Time passed. Five years later, when Marjorie was 11 and she really wanted some information, the connections had been broken. Attempts to contact extended family members were fruitless; nobody was where they had been eleven years before. Marjorie's dad hired a searcher. It took a bit of an expensive hunt, but it finally clicked. There had been a divorce, a remarriage, and surname changes. There had been several moves. Celia had attempted to make contact about some of this, but when she had called, Marjorie's family's phone number was disconnected and a letter came back marked "Forwarding Order Expired." She had remembered something about Marjorie's maternal grandparents living in Tampa, but she couldn't remember their last name.

Not enough written down!

If you enjoy writing, consider beginning a journal as you wait for your child to arrive. Journals can be used in several ways, both practical and personal. You might simply note your thoughts, or write poems or letters expressing your eagerness and the ups and downs of your waiting period. Such a journal, expanded from or in addition to the log suggested earlier (for jotting down all of the information imparted by conversations with intermediaries and birthparents), may someday be a treasured family record for your growing child.

Paula Acker, LCSW, an adoptive parent and clinical social worker with Oregon Health Sciences University's fertility practice, suggests to her clients that they consider a family scrapbook rather than a journal, one which will grow to be shared with future children. In addition to using the waiting time for practical readiness tasks and reading, Paula also recommends that waiting parents-to-be join an adoptive parent support group. "Couples should set aside a special time each week to discuss feelings about the ongoing process," says Acker. "A 'date' that will help them support one another's overlapping but yet differing feelings of stress."

The Adoption Expectancy

Mel and Lois decided that they wanted a baby, but they'd be darned if they'd do that dance with an agency. So they asked some people they knew casually how they'd done it, and then they called several doctors and lawyers whose names had come up frequently. They asked to be given a call if anything came up. Then they went right on with their lives and didn't give adoption another thought. They didn't attend any meetings. They didn't read any books, articles, or newsletters. They made no changes in the way they were living.

Six months later, when the call came, they'd almost forgotten they'd ever heard of the attorney whose voice was on the other end of the line. "Hey, sorry to call on such short notice, but the couple working with this expectant mother flaked out when they adopted from another source, another couple was on vacation, a third had gotten pregnant since I spoke to them last, and a fourth claimed not to be 'ready'—believe it or not. Meanwhile, this expectant mother had gone into labor a little early, and right now there is this real healthy little boy waiting to go home from the hospital tomorrow. Do you want him?"

How do you say no to an offer like that? You can, and some should, but Mel and Lois said yes (as most people would likely do). The next day they each called in to their employers with the shocking news that they wouldn't be in for a day or two, borrowed a car and an infant restraint from a surprised neighbor (both of their cars were two-seaters with no place for a car seat), appeared in court for a waiver hearing, rushed to the hospital, brought home a still nameless son, and then called their parents in distant cities.

The next several months were a blur of changes. The baby was colicky. Neither Lois nor Mel had any idea how to change, feed, or bathe a baby and they had no close friends who were parents to help them learn. They felt forced to move to a larger apartment after several weeks of tripping over one another and all the baby gear that began to fill their very neat, very adult world. They traded in one car, but in the rush, ended up with a minivan that they really didn't like. Lois' employer wasn't at all happy with her child care problems and she lost her job, cutting their income in half. Lois felt completely incompetent as a stay-at-home mom and soon sank into a depression. The court's designated social worker for their homestudy was both disapproving (of all independent adoptions) and unhelpful. And to top it all off, their families were shocked and not real happy about the adoption for what seemed like an awfully long time.

In earlier chapters I've referred a few times to the concept of experiencing a psychological pregnancy or adoption expectancy period: the process of allowing yourselves to wallow in an introspective series of changes, making the move from unhappily childless person to enthusiastic (and nervous) parent through a months' long journey involving fantasizing and dreaming about, and planning and making practical arrangements for a particular child (whether baby or older child) who will join the family. Much of this chapter centers on that process, which I consider to be one of the best ways to insure a smooth transition into parenthood for adoptive-parents-to-be, with lives already re-organized and slowed down to make space and time for a new person, parents already thinking in a child-centered way and prepared to seek help as needed, and parents ready to adapt quickly when the situation requires it. Experiencing an adoption expectancy is a busy, deliberate, yet calming and self-confidence-building process. It can help to inoculate against the possibility of post-adoption depression (Chapter 15) and offer solid preparation for dealing with the potential for attachment challenges.

But What about That Dragon over There?

A genuine expectancy doesn't come automatically. It has to be initiated and maintained quite deliberately. Often people who have experienced challenges in their family building are reluctant to allow themselves to fully experience the joyful anticipation of a psychological pregnancy. Even when they "know" that they'll eventually be adopting, because they have been approved and are waiting patiently in line at a traditional we'll-make-the-perfect-match agency, some adopters refuse to get their hopes up. Some of these folks have accumulated enough disappointments by this time that they may be experiencing a low level of undiagnosed depression. It's hard to believe in the reality of parenthood after those rollercoaster years of cycling through rocketing hope and crashing despair.

Increasingly, the movement to open adoption has meant that expectant parents considering planning an adoption and prospective adopters who have made a match spend significant amounts of time with one another during a pregnancy. They may speak on the phone; they may shop together; they may compare ideas about parenting practices and names for the baby; they may buy gifts for one another; they may attend medical appointments and prepared childbirth classes, and go through labor and delivery together. Traditional confidential adoption never offered such a concrete opportunity for adopting parents to feel expectant.

On the other hand, such openness puts both birth and adoptive parents at substantial emotional risk. Such closeness may sometimes allow adopting parents to feel too "entitled" to a particular baby and some expectant parents to feel reluctantly "obligated" to a would-be-parent with whom they have become close. Birthparent advocate Brenda Romanchik believes that unless expectant parents are completely honest with would-be adopters about what they are thinking and feeling, it can be easy for eager prospective adopters to forget that pregnant parents will need the opportunity to make the decision about adoption all over again after the baby is born . . . and that the decision may change.

This reluctance to feel expectant isn't limited to those who are expecting a domestic newborn. A birth-relative in Russia may step forward to claim custody of a child who has spent years in an orphanage while at that exact time you are waiting in a hotel room for a court appearance. A sick child may die before you can bring her home. A birthfather may come back into the picture and offer marriage and support. Fostered children whose birthparents seemed to be making no attempt at all to rehabilitate their lives may perform last minute hoop jumping that satisfies a judge that the children can be safely returned.

Many readers of this book have experienced challenges that have taught them not only that they are more likely to fail in family planning efforts than to succeed, but that reassuring professionals don't always deliver. Given the fact that our bodies were unable to allow us to do this parenting thing "right," sometimes it's even hard for us to believe in our own potential competence as parents. Yes, the agency has given us a Good Housekeeping Seal of Approval. But they don't really know us after all. We played the game well, hid all of our warts. We can't really be as perfect as that stamp of approval indicates. Guess what? You're right. You can't be that perfect. And, come now, did you really think that that social worker expected you to be? However, that very concern sometimes makes the stamp of approval a real burden for parents to carry. These risks are big ones, so it doesn't surprise me that so many consciously deny themselves the opportunity for a full-fledged expectancy.

In reality, social workers know that adoptive parents are normal people. They will become normal parents. They will do some things absolutely wonderfully. They will make some mistakes. They will be real, for sure parents . . . and so will you.

This time really is different. Physicians could go only so far in trying to assist your efforts to conceive. They couldn't guarantee a baby. But in family building by adoption, intermediaries really do have more power than the doctors did. If you have worked carefully to connect with reputable, caring professionals, then, barring some disastrous and *highly unlikely* possibilities—the agency, suddenly and with no warning, going out of business, leaving long lists of families approved and waiting; something entirely weird about a person's resume that makes him unappealing to any expectant parents despite the fact that an agency thought he'd make good a parent; a strange twist of fate that results in your being contacted by no expectant parents at all despite vast networking—couples who have committed themselves to adopting and have taken an active rather than passive role in pursuing adoption opportunities *will* become parents.

Why is it important to believe this? Because in being able to believe in the reality of impending parenthood, you will free yourself to begin the psychological journey to parenthood. Not that you can't become good parents without having had this pre-adoptive preparation time. You can. Many do. Mel and Lois eventually did. However, giving yourselves permission to experience this adoption expectancy begins the process of claiming, bonding, and attaching between parents and child earlier and tends to result in a less anxious transition upon arrival.

When?

Optimally, if you are working with an agency the expectancy period should begin at the point of approval. At a minimum, it must begin as soon as you receive the referral of a particular child from a state's resource book or an international agency's referral source, or the minute you have been "matched" with a woman confirmed to be pregnant and in the last half of her pregnancy who has chosen your profile. This expectancy is not going to be a predictable length, of course, and so you may (or may not) have reason to become a little impatient with it, but the lack of a specific "due date" is not a good enough reason to refuse to feel expectant.

Leaping Once Again

You've already made a substantial leap—away from other routes to parenthood and into adoption. And by now you've come pretty far along the path to adoptive parenthood. At some point, either you just have to give up and turn back, or you must leap, fully, into the experience. Making that leap means choosing—yes, making *an active choice*—to take the psychological risk and *believe* that parenthood will happen. Making that leap means fully embracing your own impending parenthood.

It also means taking off the emotional armor and letting go of options kept in reserve. It is impossible for most to experience a healthy, positive psychological pregnancy when enormous amounts of time, emotional energy, physical effort, and money remain committed to becoming pregnant biologically or in continuing the search for a just-in-case-this-doesn't-work-out alternative adoption. Every child deserves to be wanted for who he is, prepared for how he will arrive, and this means that when you've committed to a particular independent or open adoption or are approved and actively waiting for a confidential placement with a traditional agency, you should also be ready to put infertility treatment and alternative adoption options on the shelf for the time being.

You and your child-to-be—no matter his age at arrival—deserve to savor this same experience. Mary Anne Maiser insightfully described the difficulties for waiting adopters served by her agency, which does both domestic and international adoptions.

> "The international adopters served by Children's Home Society & Family Services of Minnesota have a fairly realistic time frame that they can depend on and so are inclined to 'get ready.' Domestic adopters, on the other hand, because they are served by a program in which expectant parents 'pick' them, may wait only a few days or may wait for many months. It is difficult to allow oneself to become emotionally involved in a 'promise' that comes without guarantees and fits in no absolute time frame.
>
> "Couples in this program cope in one of two ways after their homestudy/parent-prep is completed. Some confidently dive into a psychological pregnancy and make the most of the experience. Others, feeling such discomfort with the fact that they have no control over timing, self-defensively place their adoption thinking on a shelf while waiting. The trouble with this second approach is that getting a call to meet an expectant mother can send them reeling."
>
> Mary Anne described adoption's "wonderful/terrible issue of control—that, unlike parents by birth, adoptive parents have a choice. They don't have to do it, as it's not like you're on your way to a labor room and you *have* to give birth to this baby."
>
> One of her client couples had waited a long time and had "shelved" adoption after having been approved by the agency. Suddenly they were called to meet an expectant mother. "When they were finally selected," Mary Anne said, "they were so blown away and so frightened that they called me at home the night before the meeting to share all of the ambivalences and anxieties that having this ultimate choice brought

to bear on them . . . could they love this child enough, would they be good parents, etc."

This family was simply not emotionally ready, but their caseworker—a well trained and experienced adoption professional—knew what to do. She normalized their fears and feelings and delayed the meeting, giving them a weekend to do the work that they had not allowed themselves to do before. By Sunday night they were ready to go.

The tendency to avoid putting too much hope and effort into getting ready often means that people waiting to adopt find themselves trying to cram all the necessary practical preparations, as well as the unacknowledged emotional preparations, into a period of less than 24 hours. Couples working on independent adoptions are perhaps even more at risk.

Reluctance to dive into a psychological pregnancy is pretty normal, though. Let's think about what's going on here. This family building issue is something that has been very important to you—in many ways the center of your lives—for a long time now. And, despite how important all of this is to you, you're not in control. Furthermore, the process seems in many ways unpredictable. There may be delays in waiting to begin the preparation process. You may experience delays in your being "selected" by expectant parents or by the decision-maker inside an agency that matches babies with couples. When you are working on an international adoption you may experience delays with your own country's bureaucracy or delays with your child's country's bureaucracy. There's just an awful lot about this whole process of adoption that you can't control.

However, there are some things you *can* indeed control, and exerting that control can often make you feel better. Actively getting ready is one of the things over which you can exercise control. Sometimes, for couples who don't allow themselves a readiness stage, it's skipped completely, as it was for Mel and Lois. Try your best not to be a Mel and Lois or to be Mary Ann Maiser's family. Try to believe in adoption's reality for your family.

After attending one of my workshops in her hometown, Roni Breite wrote about her experience with a psychological pregnancy in the Resolve of Greater San Diego newsletter. She described her decisions to buy books for her child-to-be, to tell members of her family (especially nieces and nephews who, as children, tended to be much more positive than their more jaded parents). Roni collected potential names and cleaned out a room (but she wasn't quite brave enough to fill it up again). She wrote,

> "Sure, my expectancy is tenuous and invisible to most of the world—hidden, in fact, at work. It's tainted by the learned anticipation of failure. And *my* expectancy isn't really *our* expectancy. Sometimes I think it's just a mind game I play to keep my spirits up, a game my husband, my rock, my angel, doesn't need to or want to play . . . But I remind myself that it is a legitimate, important step in making the

transition from childlessness to parenting, so I continue to indulge, tentatively, cautiously.

"It helps me believe."

So *You're* Expecting, Too? That's Great!

Though most of us think only of the primary definition of the word *pregnant*—"carrying a developing fetus within the uterus"—the word has other usages as well. According to *The American Heritage Dictionary of the English Language*, the adjective *pregnant* also means "creative; inventive; fraught with significance; abounding; overflowing; filled; charged." Certainly, to be expecting a child—whether by birth or by adoption—is fraught with significance, charged with emotion, and necessitates creative and inventive thinking and actions.

That's why, if you have completed a parent preparation process and are awaiting a traditional agency placement or if you have been matched with an expectant family who has chosen you as the prospective parents for a coming baby for whom they are currently expecting to plan an adoption, you have every right to consider yourself pregnant in several senses of the word. And being pregnant is far from a static event. It's all about getting ready to take on an all new role—that of parent to a particular child who is going to be born and need the nurturing attention of at least one parent in infancy, through childhood and into adulthood, by a parent or parents whom he will carry within himself (even after their deaths) for all of his own life.

Parenting is not instinctual in humans nor does it come naturally with the flow of hormones that accompany pregnancy. Yet throughout time, humans have been given opportunities to learn to parent by being parented, by observation, and by being mentored. Even in today's transient society where women are less likely than in times past to live near their mothers, aunts, and sisters—a kinship system that has traditionally nurtured a pregnant family member and taught her, informally, what she needed to know to get ready to welcome a new baby—today's pregnant parents-to-be have many opportunities to prepare themselves for birth and for parenting. Through interaction with friends, natural or created kinship circles, and classes offered by hospitals, public school systems, the Red Cross, Y's, JCC's etc., throughout their pregnancies nearly all women and couples who wish to take advantage of preparation for childbirth or newborn parenting classes can, and are, encouraged to do so. Indeed, marketing various competing childbirth-related classes and support services has become a hallmark of medical center competition. Pregnancy-related services are everywhere.

The most significant differences between preparing for parenting by birth and preparing for parenting by adoption is the lack of a pregnancy— that pregnant belly which is visible to others and the physical condition which creates specific physical symptoms in the mother-to-be. That change in a pregnant woman visually triggers a completely unconscious change in those with whom she connects. Physical pregnancy is such a concrete state and such a visible period that it creates an opportunity not just for the mother-to-be, but for her partner, family and friends, work colleagues, and neighbors to anticipate, and to prepare emotionally and practically for the arrival of a new person in their circle. You will not have the visible pregnancy, so you will need to create the opportunity for others to think about you as expectant. You will need to bring your long-private journey out into the open, mentioning, for example, that you are taking an infant care class, or leaving a parenting or adoption-related book out on your desk. Ask coworkers their opinions about or experiences with child safety products or services providers. No longer will you couch appointments in secrecy.

Head Stuff

The psychological changes that take place for both mothers and fathers during a pregnancy are every bit as important as are the physical changes a pregnant woman experiences. During the nine months that biological parents wait for birth, both expectant mothers and involved expectant fathers become introspective, communicating with one another and with their baby in a rich and slowly growing joint fantasy, while sharing with one another common fears and anxieties. Waiting for a baby to arrive—no matter how carefully planned and no matter how much he was wanted—nearly always involves ambivalence for expectant parents. While they sort through this ambiguity, pregnant parents begin the practical steps of nest building: creating physical and emotional space in their homes and in their lives as they grow to love the particular child whose birth they are awaiting. These will become your tasks, too.

Childbirth educators have identified four emotional/psychological stages that all physically pregnant women and their active parenting partners need to go through in order to facilitate a healthy emotional experience (the preliminaries to solid attachment) between parent and child. They are

1. Pregnancy Validation. Accepting the pregnancy itself as a reality.
2. Fetal Embodiment. Incorporating the fetus into the mother's body image.
3. Fetal Distinction. Seeing the fetus as a separate entity from the mother in order to make plans for him.
4. Role Transition. Preparing to take on the parenting role.

According to childbirth educators, single women and parenting couples go through these steps all over again with every pregnancy, and the psychological shifts made during each transitional stage help the parents-to-be acknowledge, accept, and embrace the children conceived and born after each pregnancy they experience. These shifts, then, help them to form intimate attachments to one another as parents (in the case of couples), and to each particular child they will birth and parent.

Adoptive parents need to understand that a woman (and, we can hope, her partner) experiencing an untimely pregnancy needs to go through these steps too. For some birthparents, the pregnancy validation stage is a long one, extended by fear-driven denial of the reality of the pregnancy. Often it is psychologically easier for a woman to decide to terminate a pregnancy if she does so before reaching the fetal embodiment stage. A woman who transitions through fetal embodiment to the fetal distinction stage uses this time to decide whether or not she has the will, the support, and the resources to parent her child. If she decides that she does not, she must use the role transition stage to explore adoption options and to make adoption plans for her baby rather than living plans for the two of them together. For herself, a woman who chooses adoption must use the role transition stage of her pregnancy to help her prepare for the ambivalence of her status after giving birth to her baby: no longer a non-mother, she will not necessarily slip smoothly back into her former life (school, work, friendships, etc.). Yet as a non-parenting mother she may not feel accepted into the "sisterhood" of mothers either.

For those who will adopt, expectant parenthood is invisible. No increasingly cumbersome body signals to an expectant adoptive mother, and by default her partner, a need to slow down and get more rest. No heightening physical discomforts demonstrate the ticking away of a real clock, keeping track of how much time is left to prepare both concretely and emotionally for the arrival of a whole new being. No one offers to carry a package or rises to offer a seat on the subway for an expectant adoptive mother. There is no solicitous patting of the belly by one who presumes a community interest in a coming baby, and there are no water cooler questions about how the wife is doing. Parenting preparation classes for adopters are not easily found and routinely are not recommended, as are ubiquitous preparation opportunities for those who are physically pregnant.

Yet, childbirth educator and adoptive parent Carol Hallenbeck, RN, suggested as long ago as 1980 (in her curriculum guide *Our Child: Preparation for Parenting in Adoption—Instructor's Guide*) that there are stages comparable to those experienced by pregnant women and their partners in the "psychological pregnancy" of well-prepared adopters. They are

1. Adoption Validation. Accepting the fact that a child will join the family by adoption rather than by birth.
2. Child Embodiment. Incorporating this genetically unrelated child into the parents' emotional images of their family.
3. Child Distinction. Beginning to perceive of this child as real in order to make plans for him.

4. Role Transition. Preparing to take on the role of parents by adoption.

Of course, some of this work may have been accomplished during the course of a homestudy/parent-preparation process. If you were fortunate, the service provider who worked with you during that process was adoption literate, adoption sensitive, and had developed a well-rounded plan of parent education that validated your feelings of loss and lack of control (Chapter 1) as well as introduced you to the feelings of birthparents and adoptees. As discussed earlier, dealing actively with the losses which accompanied your journey to parenthood is an important part of beginning to build a sense of entitlement. This is the task of the adoptive pregnancy step Hallenbeck calls Adoption Validation. The adoption process itself continues the loss of control over aspects of life others take for granted, from family planning to privacy, and adds its own elements of lost control. In adopting, one cannot avoid the loss of the physical and some of the emotional expectations each partner had about being pregnant and giving birth. The loss of one's role in extending the family blood line and feeling personal genetic continuity cannot be resolved by adopting. While partners will share a parenting role with their children through adoption, they will not experience the intimacy of blending their genetic material to make a whole new person who grants them a kind of shared genetic immortality.

International adopters often talk about their experience with Child Embodiment. A grainy referral picture sent by fax is often described by parents as a bonding experience not unlike the experience of a pregnant couple's first view of an ultrasonic image of their fetus. Adopters' first glimpse of their child-to-be makes real all of the fantasizing and adds texture to the sidewalk glimpses at children presumed to be of the same ethnicity of the child they are expecting to adopt. Similarly, parents who become part of a physical pregnancy through an open adoption, while often nervous and feeling somewhat uncomfortable about their lack of control over an expectant mother's health, often reflect back with genuine pleasure about how meeting and knowing expectant parents enabled them to fantasize freely about how their coming child would look and sound, and what he or she would be like.

The leap of faith that allows adopters to believe that a pending adoption is real, and to experience fully the stage Hallenbeck calls Child Distinction, is a more difficult step for these parents-to-be than its corresponding stage—Fetal Distinction, in those who are pregnant. For the infertile, for example, months and months of treatments have resulted in no baby. For the single adopter who would have liked to be married, years of hoping to find the right partner with whom to share life and parenting have been fruitless. What is there to guarantee that adoption will work now?

Faith in your choice of professional advisors offers the next best thing to a guarantee.

I got a wonderful note via e-mail from a dad-to-be who had stumbled upon *Adopting after Infertility* on his own while in the midst of his home-study and was trying to read it sandwiched between the required reading from his agency. He wrote,

> "BTW, when I read the section on psychological pregnancy I got so excited that I wanted to redecorate the spare bedroom—at 11:30 at night. More and more, raising a child seems to be an immediate reality and not some nebulous event in the hazy future. I think we've taught ourselves not to raise our hopes, so it almost took someone else's permission for us to hope again."

Rituals such as nursery preparation, layette gathering, and baby showers are a routine part of Role Transition for those who are physically pregnant, and those who are preparing to launch a baby's adoption should actively create a similar situation for expectant adopters. If your agency doesn't sell the idea, do it yourself and look around for other service providers who will take the journey with you. Some hospitals, adoptive parent groups, and infertility support groups offer adoption "Lamaze" classes (often based on Carol Hallenbeck's curriculum guide). Such classes are a supplement to, rather than an extension of, a homestudy. They offer practical guidance and transitional emotional support in a kind of initiation ritual for prospective adopting parents. The classes cover such topics as choosing a pediatrician, bathing and other basic infant care issues, feeding (exploring both adoptive nursing and bottle feeding), product selection, managing the day-to-day, etc. If you can't find such a class in your community, consider asking an appropriate sponsor to offer one.

While waiting for Brandon to arrive, Denise was sometimes overwhelmed with frustration because there was no time frame. She wrote,

> "I found that knitting a baby blanket, working out on a treadmill, and nurturing myself really prepared me for my son. Interviewing a few pediatricians and taking an adoptive parenting class was really helpful too."

Adapting Your Life to Accommodate a Child

Making Space and a Place

> After Dave and I were approved at the agency, we knew logically that we would eventually become parents, but, after all the years of disappointments, our hearts refused to believe. On that logical level we accepted that we needed to get ready, but how? Slowly, tentatively, the spare room was emptied of boxes and the carpenter called to install another window. The walls were painted and the carpeting cleaned.

For weeks I would open the always closed door and look in, thinking about a nursery, but somehow not confident enough to really make this spotlessly clean white room into one.

The arrival of our best friends' daughter, Erin, via a completely out of the blue private placement, convinced me that adoption was real. Watching her mother, Linda, become her competent and loving parent, reassured me that Dave and I, too, could and would do this. We felt the need to do a little nesting, but it was still so cautious, so tentative. First, the rocker was moved into the empty room. A box of baby linens collected from friends went into the closet.

One Saturday morning I awoke early. It was time to do more. I spent the day designing and sketching the outline for a mural. A circus train was almost invisibly traced in pencil on the walls. I went out and bought paint—lots of paint, in bright, primary colors—and on Sunday afternoon began the process of filling in my coloring-book-outlined train. Every day for several weeks I'd come home from my teaching job and pick up brushes. Others got into the act. My parents came to help clean up the spilled enamel on the carpet one night. Dave's mother had the perfect idea for a circus tent window treatment. An old dresser was refinished, and its round, wooden drawer pulls painted to resemble clowns' faces.

The nursery became the focal point of our lives. The door was always open now, and as we passed, we walked in just to look. Visitors got "the tour" whether they wanted it or not, forced to smile and feign appreciation for my amateurish art. Early in the morning and late into the evening one or the other of us often sat in the empty room, rocking and dreaming.

The day after school was out for the summer, Linda called and suggested that we take Erin and go shopping. We stopped at a children's furniture store. In the window, stood the perfect bed for the circus nursery. We special ordered it and expected delivery in about two weeks—no rush, after all.

That evening, we got "The Call."

An excellent first step is to begin to plan your child's space in your home. While stories of babies cradled in bureau drawers are the heart of family legends, babies quickly need space and stuff. Before your child arrives you need to have given thought and begun to plan in advance for your family's future housing needs as they relate to living space, play space, safety, schooling, etc. A downtown condo may or may not work as well for a family with a toddler as it did for a dual-career couple. Your trans-ethnically adopted child must grow up in a neighborhood and school system where he will feel included and respected.

Do an honest appraisal of how your current space will work for the child you are expecting. Do you have space for the clutter of infant paraphernalia? Is there space to make a bedroom from an office or TV room to offer some privacy to the teen who is coming? Do you live in a school system that can offer the services needed for that school-aged child who doesn't speak English?

If your assessment convinces you that you are going to need to move within the next year or two, consider making that move before your child arrives rather than after. This child who is coming home to you has already experienced too many moves and transitions. Whether your child is a newborn, a toddler or even a teen, doing what you can to try to insure that he experiences as few moves and transitions as possible during his first months home will help the family with adjustment and attachment issues.

These days, stores like BabiesRUs offer expectant parents the opportunity to register their preferences, much like a wedding registry. Recently, I was in a BabiesRUs and was thrilled to note that those forms ask whether you will be adopting! Visiting a children's furniture store can feel strange at first, but you will soon begin to get caught up in the excitement generated by the pretty things, and obviously these stores expect you to! Your needs here are the same as those of parents expecting to give birth. Your baby will need a car seat, a bed, a place to store clothes, feeding and changing equipment. Selecting some of these things and having them placed in your home claims space for your child there. Yet of course, for those who simply can't make the leap of faith, the next best thing is to do the shopping and keep a list of where to find everything you want when you really need it.

If you are adopting an older infant or a toddler, keep in mind that under the stress of a move from familiar places to a new home and family setting, young children are highly susceptible to over-stimulation. In a later section we'll talk in detail about the role of the senses in promoting attachment, but no matter at what age your child will arrive, in thinking about space and "stuff," you may want to consider taking a minimalist approach for your child at first. Orphanages, for example, lack stimulation that is normal for a child in healthy one-on-one care settings. So allowing your child to adjust slowly to all that is so new and then adding the stimulating colors, textures, and toys slowly as he becomes adjusted to new caregivers is one of the things that you can do to lead those steps to the dance. Allowing children who are arriving at older ages to help in choosing colors, linens, wall decor and arranging furniture can help them to feel a sense of "ownership" about their new space, promoting a kind of "nesting behavior" on their part which can enhance the stirrings of new attachments as well.

Do only what makes you comfortable, but encourage yourself to stretch in making practical preparations. Browse in the toddler section at department stores. Look through the baby books and baby announcements at the card store. Allow a friend who wants to do so to give you a shower for your coming sibling group.

Schedules and Routines

Routine and scheduling—a child-led routine and schedule—will eventually become an important part of the safety and trust cycle that leads to attachment (Chapters 5 and 14). But you can't know your child-to-be's schedule and routine now. You can only know your own, and how it will need to be changed to accommodate the needs of a new person in your family. Now is the time to begin to pare away the extras that gobble up the average non-parent's time.

Women who are physiologically pregnant are more or less forced by their changing bodies to slow their lives down. They tire easily and, as time goes by, move more slowly. By association their involved partners tend to slow down too. This forced slowing down and paring back—working fewer hours, giving up some social and volunteer commitments, staying home more—makes space for the reveries of transition. Adopting parents must force themselves to make these choices.

Many non-parents keep irregular hours and often eat on the fly. Parenting changes all of this and more. Now is the time to begin to pare away at the extras you've been meaning to drop from your schedule. Establishing a sleep routine similar to those of children of the age of your coming child will not only help to make you healthier before you child arrives, but will help you to feel less "disrupted" by the new schedule she brings with her. Whether your child will arrive as a newborn or a teenager, plan now for a slowed period of cocooning after arrival.

In getting ready to become a parent—for the first or the second or third time—parents must readjust their lives. The waiting period provides the right time for making those adjustments. Couples who are pregnant-by-adoption and are caught up in the need to get space ready for a baby's arrival, or who are working on the paperwork needed to travel to another country, must give themselves permission to adjust their too busy lifestyles. Don't expect to dive right back in to your pre-child lifestyle a few weeks after your child comes home either. Children play havoc with adult schedules. Over time, things like "just window shopping" and volunteering become much more complicated and expensive when child-care must be arranged.

Respected neuropsychologist Ron Federici has adopted seven older children from orphanages and has built his practice around helping adoptive parents deal with difficult children from backgrounds of neglect, abuse, and trauma. He shared the following anecdote which emphasized his concern with how unprepared new parents often are for the realities of life-after-adoption that accompany children, creating a need for slow, thoughtful adjustments.

> Dr. Federicci received an emergency call from a family who had just come home from an Eastern European country with two school-aged brothers.
>
> "Help!" cried the father. "We're at our wits' end. Our sons are out of control and tearing the hotel room apart. Last night the older one threw shoes and fruit off the balcony. His brother peed on Mickey Mouse's shoe this morning. Our other kids are humiliated by their behavior and are acting out as well. What can we do?"
>
> "Mickey Mouse?" queried Dr. Federicci. "Where are you?"
>
> "Why, in Disney World," replied the father. "We had planned that our parents would have our other children in Orlando when we brought the boys home, so that we could all have a nice vacation together as a welcome home celebration."
>
> "What the hell are you doing in Disney World!" cried Dr. Federicci. "Of course these kids are acting out. They have been completely overstimulated by leaving the orphanage, by flying on a plane for the first time (for hours and hours), by a new language, and by new sights, smells, foods, and people. Take them home, shut off the TV and all video games and the computer, establish a predictable routine and don't break it, and don't go out for at least a couple of weeks!"

Learning What You Need to Know

If one is available, enroll in a hospital, Red Cross or Y's expectant adopter's class where you can learn practical infant or child care skills. If these are unavailable, consider whether or not you would be comfortable signing up for a general infant care class. Most hospitals have become much more sensitive to adoption than they were a generation ago, so it is not at all uncommon for these classes to include both expectant parents by adoption and expectant parents by birth. Other frequently available classes include infant massage (which can be especially helpful in encouraging attachment) and there are even Daddy Boot Camps offered just for men in some areas.

Those who are adopting toddlers or older children may want to consider taking a Parent Effectiveness Training course or some similar parenting issues classes. Take CPR and first aid courses. Karen wrote that when she was unable to find an infant care class designed for adopting parents available when her son arrived unannounced, she called the local hospital.

> "The childbirth educator there was thrilled to give us a private infant care class. She gave us lots of valuable information about newborns that we probably would not have known otherwise."

One of the complications common to international adoption is that children sometimes "age up" while red tape is sorted through. It is not unusual for families to receive a referral several months before the actual travel to unite parents and child. These delays can be particularly stressful, as families struggle with their feelings of powerlessness, fret about whether their child is receiving adequate care, and worry about possible complications. Among the practical things parents can do to make the best use of such a wait, and at the same time strengthen their sense of connection with their child, is to begin learning about normal development during each of the weeks and months until parents and child are together forever.

You might want to read books on parenting children of the age at which you expect your child to arrive. If you are adopting an infant, for example, an easy way to do so is to subscribe to the newsletter *Growing Child* from Dunn & Hargitt Publishers, West Lafayette, Indiana. Parents begin their subscription to *Growing Child* by supplying the publisher with their child's sex, name, and birth date. Beginning immediately, parents begin to receive monthly newsletters that correspond to their child's age that particular month. So that, for example, the newsletter received when the child is three months old will describe the kinds of physical, emotional, and cognitive development that is within the range of normal for children four months old. Each issue offers advice about problems common to that particular age and stage of development (sleeping through the night, using a pacifier, stranger anxiety, pulling up, or finding his fingers, for example) and offers suggested exercises and activities parents can try, and information about appropriate toys and games. *Growing Child* makes clear that the range of "normal" is a wide one, but will offer parents an opportunity for developing a relatively realistic picture of what their child may be like as he waits to come to them.

Now, while you are waiting, will be a more comfortable time to begin to read and learn about parenting—parenting in general as well as parenting by adoption. You probably will already have read several adoption how-to books, the best of which also include quite a bit of good information on parenting issues, too. You could buy some of the adoptive parenting books now (see recommendations in the Resource section), but it can be satisfying to focus now not on the adoption aspect of your transition to parenthood, but on the normal, everybody-does-it practicalities. If you will be adopting a very young child, look at the books of T. Berry Brazelton and Penelope Leach, and at the newest books you can find on infant care. If you will be adopting a child beyond infancy, in addition to the special focus books dealing with adoption issues, read the John Rosemond titles or Cline and Fay's *Parenting with Love and Logic*.

Getting Healthy to Stay Healthy

One of the things that adoptive parents worry about is whether their child-to-be's mother has had good prenatal care. Adopters' concerns are for the most part focused on the baby's need for a healthy pre-natal environment free of toxins, alcohol, recreational drugs, and unnecessary medications. One of the remnants of lost control that rises insistently to the surface while adopters wait for their newborn to come home to them is that they can do very little to ensure that he is nurtured by a mother's healthy eating, sleeping, and exercise regimen. However, many expectant mothers considering adoption have very strong feelings about taking good care of the babies for whom they are considering an adoption plan. They speak frequently about how powerful it makes them feel to know that, while they don't feel that they will be able to adequately parent their children over the long haul, they are able to do the healthy things that will get him off to the best possible start.

However, good prenatal care is not only about the needs of babies. New mothers by birth and yes, new adoptive parents, too need to be in the best possible physical condition when a new child arrives. The older you are as a first time parent, the more likely it is that you'll need to make this a priority. Babies are demanding little creatures whose needs for food, dry diapers, cuddling, and comforting rarely occur only during the day in the beginning. The arrival of a new baby (or toddler, or older child) is nearly always accompanied by weeks and even months of sleep deprivation as the caregiver dozes with one ear open for the sounds of a restless child and the newly arrived child deals with his change of environment, and establishes both trust with his caretakers and a familiar and comforting routine in his new home.

The inability to follow one's usual routine with any predictability adds to the physical and emotional stress of new parenthood. Meals may be skipped when a caregiver tries to meet a child's demands and then uses the child's quiet times to "catch up" with mounting laundry or cleaning, or to snatch a short nap. Even experienced parents may question their parenting skills with a child whose basic temperament is fussy and demanding.

New parents of toddlers often complain about strained muscles and unexpected physical exhaustion. Remember, a pregnant woman gradually adjusts to increases in the amount of weight she carries before the baby is born and her muscular structure changes with the growing baby, while adoptive parents are suddenly lugging a baby or toddler along with a grocery sack, or juggling a 15 pound 3-month-old in a front carrier while pushing a vacuum cleaner, or making more frequent trips up a flight of stairs with extra human baggage in tow.

> Marie was single and 45 when her daughter arrived from Guatemala at nine months of age. Never much for exercising, Marie was already dealing with arthritis in an area of her lower back injured in an accident many years before. Within days of Sofia's arrival Marie had badly strained herself, causing her doctor to recommend that she not lift her child for several weeks. This seriously complicated Marie's caretaking abilities; she needed the help of relatives. This confused her daughter's emotional need for consistent care from her only parent. Marie was grateful for help from her mother and her sister-in-law, but she was

disappointed by her own lack of preparation which had resulted in her less than full participation in her daughter's early adjustment. Marie was thrilled to be able to offer her experience as a cautionary tale for readers of this book and to recommend working out as a part of getting ready for parenthood!

Getting ready for a new child, then, involves getting oneself ready physically too. Your adoptive pregnancy should involve a regular exercise program that includes strengthening exercises for the lower back, arms, and legs. If you've never learned relaxation techniques before, consider taking a yoga class or a stress reduction workshop, or investing in some meditation tapes now so that you will be ready for one of parenthood's guaranteed experiences—needing to remain calm in the face of a crying child's refusal to be comforted for long periods of time.

Since non-parents are particularly adept at skipping meals, eating on the run, and treating their own nutrition lightly, use this waiting time to start new eating habits that will—probably to your amazement—make you feel better during the early months of your child's life with you, serve as a foundation for your learning to feed your son or daughter healthy foods on a regular schedule, and establish the healthy family ritual of mealtimes together.

Remember that you are under psychological stress during this waiting period and you will be again when your child arrives. Your body is particularly susceptible to the effects of poor health habits. So . . . stop smoking (it will be far easier now than during the stressful period of adapting to parenthood); eliminate alcohol; and eat less salt, sugar, and red meat and more fruits and vegetables.

If you were physically pregnant you would exercise good pre-natal care of yourself, so exercise good pre-adoption care now.

The Sympathetic Pregnancy

It's long been realized that over 60% of the male partners of pregnant women experience symptoms that seem to mirror some of those felt by their physiologically pregnant spouses. Expectant fathers report food cravings followed by weight gain, sleep disturbances, back pain, and even the frequent urination usually caused in pregnant women by the pressure of her growing uterus on her bladder.

In an interview, adoption educator Sharon Kaplan Roszia told me that in her 40+ years of experience with adopting couples she's often seen prospective adopters who appear to be experiencing a phenomenon she refers to as "sympathetic symptoms of pregnancy." One or both partners may experience repeated, and even predictably scheduled, episodes of nausea. Food cravings and significant weight gain are not unusual. One or both may complain of sleep disturbances, or emotional peaks and valleys.

When talking about expectant fathers with pregnant wives, counselors usually explain these symptoms as fathers' subconscious attempts to become part of the pregnancy. Of course, to a certain extent there may be some more concrete explanations, as well. For example, pregnant women usually try to eat more healthily and are even encouraged to eat more calories than before. The resulting change in Mom-to-be's diet may spill over via the menu of what's served and what's available to munch on to Dad. Changes in diet can cause changes in bowel and bladder habits. Nervous anticipation could cause an upset stomach. Natural ambivalence about the impending role change and its resulting responsibilities heightens emotional reactions. A restless partner in one's bed often disturbs one's own sleep.

But why would adopters experience sympathetic pregnancy symptoms? There are logical psychological and physiological explanations for prospective adopters' real physical symptoms of sympathetic pregnancy too. If a subconscious reason for a man whose partner is physiologically pregnant to experience sympathetic symptoms might be his subconscious yearning to be a part of the pregnancy, could this not explain why expectant adoptive parents feel similar symptoms? The tension of the wait, often exacerbated by worries that something will happen and/or a lack of support from family and friends—not to mention the suddenly heightened awareness that society in general doesn't have particularly positive attitudes about adoption—can create many physical problems. Nausea can be tension-related. Under stress people often snack more often, partake of "comfort foods," or experience cravings—all of which can lead to weight gain. Changes in weight often make us feel both physically uncomfortable (clothing too tight, pressure on the bladder, just not up to par) and psychologically stressed. Any of the above stressors may lead to sleep disturbances. The heightened anxiety of all of these pending changes and challenges sets many people on edge and triggers sudden emotional responses.

Just as one cannot predict with certainty whether a pregnant woman or her partner will experience any of these side effects of a physiological pregnancy, it is impossible to predict whether one or both partners in a pregnant-by-adoption couple might be prone to these symptoms. Knowing they could appear, though, allows one to see himself or his partner as "normal" if they do appear.

Even without actual physical symptoms, Sharon Kaplan Roszia's clients find it helpful to look at the many parallels between a physical pregnancy and being pregnant by adoption.

- Being approved is much like having a pregnancy confirmed, Sharon's clients learn.
- Just as an expectant mother's experience of feeling her baby moving for the first time triggers her ability to think more concretely about her child, so being given information about a particular mother's

pregnancy or the referral of a specific child helps adopting parents "feel life."

- All parents need to see their coming children as individuals, and parents by birth have the luxury of nine months to get to know their children, while for adopting parents this introduction often happens in just 24 hours.

- Labor and placement are each transitioning stages which concretely move a child into his family, says Sharon, leaving parents elated but exhausted.

- Sharon likens parents-by-birth's leaving the hospital and going out into the world to parent "on their own" to the feelings of relief, mixed with anxiousness about what lies before them in nurturing their children to adulthood, that most adopters describe as a part of their experience in going to court.

The idea of new parenting is wonderful and yet frightening; all parents feel eager and yet ambivalent as the journey begins.

Practice Makes Perfect?

While not everyone is able to do so, some waiting parents find it valuable to use their waiting time to "practice" some of the new routines of being parents. They may choose to live on one parent's salary and plunk the other partner's income into savings. They may adjust their schedules so that they establish a more predictable routine, staying closer to home and eating fewer meals out during their waiting time. This makes the transition to parenthood scheduling less of a shock, and it allows the family to save the money that might otherwise have been spent on eating out and recreation. Such a plan also gives them time to experiment with a new budget and style of financial operation.

As you begin to enjoy a psychological pregnancy you are likely to begin to feel less resistant to other people's children than you did when you were feeling child*less*. You will find yourself observing children more closely in public places, noticing different textures of hair, skin tones, body shapes, and personality types and fantasizing about how your coming child may look and behave.

Many expectant adopters actively trying to prepare themselves for the realities of parenting also find ways to practice with "the real thing." A transitional plan might begin with volunteering in your church or synagogue nursery for a couple of hours a week for several months, spending more time observing and interacting with your family and friends who already have children, and then moving to babysitting for nieces and nephews and the children of friends—first for short periods during the day, and increasing to an attempt or two at overnights or weekends. Including your family and closest friends in your process brings them with you in the same way that watching your sister's belly bloom brought the family along through-out her pregnancy.

Those planning an open adoption may have practical opportunities to involve themselves in a an expectant mother's pregnancy—visiting the obstetrician with her, watching her belly grow, feeling the baby kick, attending birthing classes. Many adopters find that a psychological pregnancy is much easier for them when the concrete evidence of a coming child provided by contact with his birthmother is a part of their everyday lives. Birthparent and advocate Brenda Romanchik, frequent contributor to the Internet's various adoption groups, has suggested a gift of *What to Expect When You're Expecting*, because it is written in language that everyone can understand, might be the single most useful gift prospective adopters could give a pregnant woman considering adoption, for whom getting good prenatal care is complicated both by a tendency to deny the pregnancy and the complications of finding affordable medical care. You could benefit from reading a good pregnancy guide, such as *What to Expect*, too. This will aid you in understanding possible mood swings and bouts of strong ambivalence, and offer you some concrete advice about how you can be supportive of your child's birthmother's pregnancy.

Financial Readiness

If it seems that we have talked an awful lot about money in this book, it's because family building is a pretty expensive business. If your family-building process has been challenged it can be even more so. After several years of supplementing patchy health insurance coverage of various medical treatments and then exploring the agency options, finding the loans or working the extra hours needed to finance adoption, many adopters have not given much thought to the financial realities of parenting itself. For those who have been unprepared, money matters in raising a child can contribute to the expected stress of adjusting to a new family configuration.

In the fall of 2006 the U.S. Department of Agriculture's Food, Nutrition and Consumer Service issued a report that predicted that in his first year alone a first child's two parents' costs for housing, food, transportation, clothing, health care, child care and education, and miscellaneous (but excluding his actual arrival costs—by birth or by adoption) would total $7,580–8,570 for families with annual incomes under $44,500; $10,600–11,660 for families with incomes between $44,500 and $74,900; and $15,490–16,970 for families with incomes over $74,000. In single parent homes, expenditures were about 7% less. Over eighteen years, the costs of raising that single child born in 2006 will range from $190,050 for singles to $381,050, and to include college, plan to spend over $120,000 more. And remember, these are 2005 and 2006 estimates. Additional children don't double the costs, but additions to the family certainly don't slide in without financial impact.[1]

Now, while you are awaiting your child's arrival, you should plan to spend time focusing on the family finances. This too can be considered "nesting behavior" on the part of a parent, like Ron Breite's husband, whose personal style focuses more on the practical and concrete than on the emotional. The following are some issues that need advance-of-arrival attention.

A Will

Many childless people have not drafted a will, but the arrival of a child complicates inheritance issues and necessitates planning for guardianship should parents die. This issue of guardianship may be more complicated than you expect, as occasionally the relative one assumes would be willing to say yes to accepting guardianship hedges in a way that makes both of you aware that he or she is harboring some adoption-related fears or prejudices. Obviously, this will hurt, but try, if you can, to keep in mind something we've already brought up: family members are often a few steps behind adopters in deciding about adoption and claiming a child into their hearts. Your patience and your willingness to educate and to be tolerant will usually result in successful resolution of any such misunderstanding.

The attorney assisting in your adoption may be able to help you draft a will or refer you to another attorney aware of potential adoption-related complications—and there are some in a few states and provinces. And while we're taking about wills, please tuck away for future reference that eventually you may wish to suggest to your child's grandparents (your parents) that they check with their attorney about whether there are any adoption-related complications in their own wills' wording as it relates to grandchildren adopted by the family rather than born to it.

Insurance Concerns

Contact your health insurance provider far in advance of your child's arrival in order to make the transition smoother. Only the state of Arizona decrees that adopting parents' insurance must cover an expectant mother's prenatal and birth expenses, and even that law is limited to those employers who are not self-insured and whose insurers are based in the state. Federal law does mandate the unreserved coverage of your adopted child under the same conditions as if he had been born to you, however claims staff are often poorly informed about this. You will find it much less stressful to anticipate their confusion and educate them in advance of your baby's arrival.

Singles, while often aware of a need for disability coverage, many times have seen no prior need for life insurance. Childless, two income couples may have felt that disability and life insurance were unimportant, but parents need to plan for their family's financial well-being should either parent become disabled or die, leaving the other with diminished family income and/or urgent childcare, health assistance, and homemaking needs over a child's growing up years.

The issue of adoption insurance is a controversial one. Several insurers do offer policies that are designed to reimburse families for expenses paid out for an adoption that does not come to be. Most of these policies come at a very high premium. Many of them can be purchased only by couples using insurer-approved intermediaries. Advice from those in the know varies as to whether such a policy is a good value. Be prepared to ask many questions and to seek more than one opinion.

Transportation

Children need car seats; car seats need their own seatbelts. Either parent must be able to safely transport a child at a moment's notice. That two-seater sports car may not be appropriate family transportation once your son or daughter arrives, and two-door cars can be particularly inconvenient when struggling to strap a little one safely into the car. Consult friends and family members who have recently parented babies about the pros and cons of various models of cars and car seats. Also utilize car seat inspections offered, often free, by hospitals and even some car dealerships. These inspections ensure that the car seat is installed correctly.

Employment and Income

While you are waiting, be sure to let your employers know that you are expecting. Among issues to consider and explore with your employer are

- What available leave time you have, and availability of a dependent care account (which lets you use pretax dollars to pay child care expenses).
- How to adjust your paycheck to reflect appropriate deductions.
- Do your employers provide for a family leave which is not part of the medical benefits plan (U.S. federal law mandates family leave for employees of firms with over 50 employees)? If so, it must be available to parents by adoption as well as to parents by birth.
- If parenting leaves are not possible and another form of leave cannot be arranged, will you at least be able to take your accumulated vacation time on short notice?
- Are there adoption reimbursement benefits? Increasingly, large corporations are adding this type of benefit, which is relatively inexpensive for them to fund yet very public-relations-positive both internally and externally.

If you are team parenting, can one parent stay home or work part-time? Two-parent families should seriously discuss and fully explore the possibility of one parent's leaving full-time employment to become a full-time parent, or both parents readjusting schedules or working less than full-time so that they can share full-time parenting. Not only is it in any child's best psychological and physical interests to spend his first year or more in the full-time care of his parent rather than the very best of nannies or childcare providers (no matter at what age he arrives), but for some families financial realities will determine that when the added expenses of a child (including his food, clothing and medical expenses as well as hundreds, and often thousands, of dollars in daycare) are added to the work-related clothing, food and transportation costs already there, one parent's job actually costs the family money rather than adding to its income. Single adopters have fewer options, yet some have found ways to accumulate extended vacation or leave time in advance, to work from home, or to budget for part-time employment.

How can you manage loss of income? I mentioned early that saving carefully during the year or two before your child arrives and living on just one income during the expectancy period is one way. Also, explore moving to smaller or less prestigious quarters for a while, driving less expensive cars, and reducing recreation and entertainment expenses. Short-term sacrifices may produce long-term gains for your child.

Setting up Short- and Long-Term Expense Funds

In the short-term, new babies are so expensive that it makes sense to change the family budget during the year before your baby's arrival to create an early-expenses savings fund to cover such unanticipated medical and adoption expenses, extended parental leave, or job changes, etc. Over the long-term you would be wise to plan from the beginning of your child's life to save small amounts steadily in anticipation of his possible post-high school educational needs.

Unanticipated Adoption Expenses

Some adoption-related expenses are difficult to predict accurately. A newborn's illness or a birthmother's medical complications may increase birth-related expenses. Foster care expenses may rise if birthparents need more time to be certain. Counseling sessions for expectant parents considering adoption are important and can't be predicted in advance. The need to stay longer than anticipated in order to deal with local bureaucracies may increase travel expenses. Increasingly, prospective parents may find that the money they have spent in anticipation of a specific adoption may be lost when a parent has a change of heart. In limited instances, adoption insurance (see above discussion) can be purchased to help with some of these unforeseen problems, and home equity or credit card loans may provide a cushion. While you wait, you would be wise to sock away into a special adoption account as much money as you can manage to save. Believe me, if you don't use it on the adoption, you'll find many opportunities to use such savings to your child's benefit as he grows.

Naming as Claiming

"What's in a name? That which we call a rose by any other name would smell as sweet." William Shakespeare, *Romeo and Juliet,* Act II, Scene 2

What shall we name this coming child? If you're honest with yourself, you'll admit that you've been thinking about this since you were a little kid fantasizing about being a parent. So now Mom-and/or Dad-to-be spend months and months pouring over a collection of names-for-the-baby books borrowed from the library or picked up in the check out line at the grocery story. You want one that's not "too ordinary." Your partner wants one that won't be "too different." It needs to sound right with the family surname. You try a few out on friends and relatives and watch their faces for reactions. "Oh, isn't that unUSual, dear." "How interesting!" "Cute." "Pretty big name for a little tiny person, isn't it?" "That's nice, and you can call him _____?"

Let's be honest. Naming is indeed a big deal for most families. Most of us carry our names with us from birth to the grave, we are identified by them, and they are a part of our own self identity. How we wear our names even directly influences how others come to feel about the name in general, not just us as individuals—a factor that influences what names we ourselves like when thinking about names for our children. For most parents, carefully choosing a name that has family or cultural significance, or sounds pleasing to our ears is an important way to claim our child and is seen as a "right" of parenting. In many cultures and religions around the world, the public calling out of a name shortly after a child's arrival carries deep religious significance.

For adoptive parents, however, the issue of naming a child should feel complicated, because in fact, it is. In adoption, a child has another set of relatives by birth and a genetic heritage different from that of his adoptive family, and that raises important questions and some important psychological facts should be considered.

Child development experts have presumed for years that babies younger than seven months old were not really aware of their own names. New research at the State University of New York at Buffalo, however, offers some interesting new data. Psychologist Peter Jusczyk and his team observed how long infants looked toward a stereo speaker that played four different prerecorded names. The results were that babies as young as four and a half months focused on the speaker an average of four seconds longer when their own names were played.

According to Jusczyk, when a baby learns to recognize her name it is the first intellectual sign that she is beginning to attach meaning to the sounds she hears. Name recognition is an important social milestone too. It is, says Jusczyk, "One main step on the way toward a child developing a sense of self."

Should the two sets of parents agree on a name in an open adoption, should they each contribute one name to a first and second pairing, or is the naming the right of one or the other set of parents? The movement toward open adoption has indeed complicated this process somewhat, as birthparents sometimes feel that they should be included in the naming process. This can in many cases become a wonderfully cooperative experience for birth and adoptive parents. But this can also become one of those awkward situations which critics of openness point to as one of the things which inhibit the new parents' ability to feel a sense of entitlement to their child.

The awkwardness can be prevented if the professionals are doing their jobs well. The counseling process of the expectant parents helps them to understand the value for their child and his parents in allowing them to choose the first name of the child who will be their own. The counseling process also helps the adopting parents understand how important it is for the birthparents to feel respected and included at this sensitive time. If appropriate counseling does not occur, adoptive parents, ultimately, will need to do their own adapting, compromising with the birthparents only to an extent that will not compromise their relationship with their child.

And what about culture? Should Kim Soon Hee or Marushka Wisc-znowski keep all or part of names that reflect the culture and ethnicity of their countries of birth, or should their names be Americanized? Professionals often encourage families adopting internationally to think about names carefully. While carrying an unusual or "foreign sounding" name can be awkward for a school-age child, it can be equally awkward for a child of an obviously Asian, East Indian, or South American culture to carry a distinctly non-ethnically-matching sounding name. The compromises may include choosing a first name which is as broadly "American" as possible, and embracing your child's heritage by including a name from that culture or country as part of the child's longer formal name. Or, choosing an ethnic or culturally reflective name from which an Americanized nickname can be drawn. Though a few parents continue to discard their internationally adopted child's original name, most now feel that, no matter what his age at arrival, it is important to celebrate and honor his ethnic background by keeping a portion of his original name as a first or middle name.

Might it be a burden or is it a blessing for a child not genetically related to his family to bear a name rich in family heritage—Reynaud Leviathan Fitzsimmons Curtis IV? It is important to consider that for a child who becomes a Junior or a III, this may be either a positive or a negative. Some children and their families experience this as a way to embrace one another. Other adoptees have expressed the discomfort of being so awkwardly and so obviously different from the person for whom they have been named. A recent exchange on this topic on an Internet adoption usergroup produced no consensus of a "right" answer.

What about the family, which already includes a son, who falls in love with a toddler in the photo-listing book and whose first name is the same? (George 1 and George 2? Hey, the Foreman family did it on purpose.)

For children adopted past infancy, the issue of changing a name has special significance that is unreasonable to ignore. Psychologists agree that unless a child is carefully prepared and follow-up is conscientious, changing the first name of a child of pre-school or elementary school age carries the risk that the child may subconsciously presume that the old name and the person who bore it were "bad" and "rejectable" and thus struggle to be "good," bearing a new name that makes him feel like an imposter. Far too often adoptive parents aren't told this—or is it that they don't hear it?

On the other hand, some older aged adoptees may specifically request that their names be changed in order to make them feel less different in their new environments or to facilitate their own feelings of entitlement toward the family.

Adoption grows families, and in child-centered adoptions what's best for the child must take precedence over the wishes and needs of the adults in his life. The issue of naming your child is one of the significant differences in parenting by adoption that deserves careful, well-informed thought and action.

> "What's in a name? That is what we ask ourselves in childhood when we write the name that we are told is ours." James Joyce, *Ulysses*

Making Caregiving Choices

Choosing Your Baby's Doctor

Choosing the "right" physician to meet your baby's medical needs is an important issue no matter how your family was formed. Many of the most important issues for families formed by birth are the same as for those expanded by adoption. For example, the question of whether you can choose at all (those whose health coverage is provided through an HMO often have limited choices) is universal to all families. Whether to choose a physician in a group or partnership practice, or a solo practitioner is common to all families. Deciding between a family practitioner and a pediatrician is something all families must do. Predicting your "fit" with the physician's practice protocols and style (hospital affiliation; use of nurse practitioners; rotation among partners; office hours and location; office atmosphere; the way in which phone queries, emergencies, scheduling appointments, or length of waiting times are handled) is something all families do. All families must feel that there is a philosophical match between patient and practitioner regarding issues as varied as rigidity vs. informality in personality, partnership vs. paternalism between doctor and patients, attitudes about nutritional issues ranging from breast-feeding to vegetarianism, overall beliefs about preventive medicine and/or how medications and other interventions contribute to well being, etc.

Adoption issues can, however, contribute to the feeling that a partnership between family and physician is just not right. Parents need to feel assured that their physician and staff value adoption as a positive way for families to be formed and as a positive alternative family planning choice for one who is dealing with an untimely pregnancy.

According to Dana Johnson, MD, parent-by-adoption and director of the very first International Adoption Clinic which is located at the University of Minnesota, one cannot presume that a medical practitioner is adoption-literate or adoption-sensitive. Adoption issues are not a part of standard training for most medical professionals. Dr. Johnson is pessimistic about the likelihood of most physicians who are not personally involved in adoption being "in tune" enough with adoption-related problems to be relied upon as a first source of referral if and when adoption-specific problems arise.

This means that unless they are fortunate enough to have access to a local adoption medicine clinic or a doctor in private practice who is part of the American Academy of Pediatrics adoption medicine interest group, parents will need to become assertive advocates for their families. You will want to know that the medical practitioners you choose are realistic in their adoption knowledge, and that they are open to learning more about developing adoption issues or to helping you to do so as your child grows. Over time you may want to offer your medical team information on positive adoption language and imagery, or suggest that *Adoptive Families*, *Adoption Today*, or *Pact Press* be added to their list of waiting room periodicals. If you are adopting transethnically or transracially, you and your child deserve to feel confident that your physician and his staff harbor no racial biases that may come across in subtle ways—in the staffing pattern, in the diversity (or lack of) in the waiting room, in comments directly made or overheard from staff.

Most physicians would welcome your making one or more (paid) consultation appointments in advance of your child's arrival. Once you have settled on a good match between your family and the baby's doctor, you can use these times to ask your physician for his advice and support as you make decisions about feeding, about circumcision, etc.

Enlist your pediatrician's support in analyzing the data you receive about a child referred to you domestically or internationally, but be aware that you may need to be a little pushy about this. For families adopting a child with "no known medical problems" domestically, sparse or unknown medical history should not be allowed to be interpreted as a clean bill of health. Assumptions about the educational level or financial status of birthparents or adoptive family may cause some physicians not to automatically screen for some important problems. Dr. Johnson recommends, for example, that all new adoptive parents specifically ask for testing that could reveal Hepatitis B, exposure to sexually transmitted diseases such as syphilis or HIV, or to drug and alcohol exposure during gestation, which can lead to serious problems, including fetal alcohol effect or syndrome. With increasing numbers of children having spent significant time in orphanages or shuttled between foster homes, parents and physicians need to be aware that the greatest period for learning and brain growth in children is in the first year or two of life. Children who may have been neglected (or possibly abused) in previous settings are at significant risk for speech and language disorders and other learning problems that physicians may not expect unless prodded to watch for, even though parents may not have the social history available to realize that these risks exist.

If your child will arrive with known medical problems, a physician's familiarity with or expertise with those problems must become a part of the data you use in choosing a doctor. In these cases, families might contact the department of pediatrics at the nearest major medical center or teaching hospital for a referral.

Those adopting internationally should make their child's physician aware of the International Adoption Guidelines published by the American Academy of Pediatrics. These guidelines will provide information about the need to test for various medical problems less common in the U.S.

Dr. Johnson points out that a country of origin's growth charts are only helpful at the time of the initial screening. World Health Organization growth charts available to all physicians take into account ethnic diversity in well-nourished children worldwide and so serve as the standard to which children should be compared in the months and years after placement.

The Yellow Pages should be the last of several likely places in which parents begin their search for their child-to-be's physician. Parents who know and are already a part of a community use many sources of referral in narrowing their search for the right doctor, including advice from their own medical care givers, the practical experiences of family and friends, and suggestions from an adoptive parents group. When moving to a new community where one has few connections and prior medical caregivers have not been able to provide a referral, this search can be more challenging. Adoption agencies and parent groups in the new city may be a good source of referrals. Choosing medical care givers wisely is, for many parents by adoption, the first step in becoming their child's loving and supportive advocate.

My own bias would be to suggest in the strongest way possible that, while of course it will be best to have your child's primary care physician be local, your referral information—whether domestic or adoption—would best be examined by an adoption medicine clinician. This may mean consulting over the telephone or by email, fax, and letter with a clinic located outside of your city. In nearly every case, this is a normal scenario for such clinics, who welcome the opportunity to do this, and to later serve as mentors and consultants to primary care physicians of your children.

Diapering

Some readers of this book were babies in the pre-disposable-diaper era. They may remember those days of smelly diaper pails, bleach soaks, and cloth diapers flapping on backyard clothes lines. However, since the late '60s disposable diapers have become major convenience items for busy families. There's no adoption angle to the debate about whether to use cloth or disposable diapers, but the wait for baby's arrival will provide parents with plenty of time to solidify their thinking about diapers in the context of both the world's ecology and their family's economy, to investigate their options (shopping for prices at various discount stores and comparing with commercial cloth diaper services) and to consult with their pediatrician, prospective daycare providers, and with more experienced parents for their views.

In many areas of the country commercial daycare providers are required by health department regulations to use disposables. Additionally, it is possible that once your child arrives, a skin condition, allergy, or some unforeseen issue of convenience may cause you to change your plans. Yet, having given the issue of diapering some careful thought and investigation will at the very least give you a head start and some relatively painless experience in making parenting decisions and wearing the role of parent as decision maker.

Circumcision

Whether or not a baby boy should be circumcised is another highly personal decision usually left to parents to make . . . but not necessarily in adoption. While cultural and religious convictions, health attitudes, "claiming" feelings about the boy's being "like Daddy," and even politics can influence your own decision about whether to have this done, prospective adopters should know that in order to have a say in the decision, they may need to speak out loud and clear to their adoption facilitators and, when they can, to expectant parents way ahead of time. Though circumcision is not quite as routinely performed as it was a generation ago in U.S. hospitals, it is still widely practiced. In other countries, standard practice varies. You need to ask.

For couples whose religious traditions mandate ceremonial circumcisions, it is possible to "re-circumcise" a boy who has already been through the procedure. Contact your clergyperson. Through plastic surgery, a reconstructive opposite procedure is also possible, though rarely recommended for or performed on children.

Umbilical Cord Blood Storage

So much medical research focuses on genes, and we have yet to discover the extent of this new knowledge. The process involves umbilical cord blood being saved when a baby is born, cryogenically stored, and then available if your child later becomes sick and needs a bone marrow transplant. This type of transplant would be autologous (coming from the self) and is different than the more common allogenic (species related) transplants that might be done from a sibling, other relative, or an unrelated donor.

Cord blood storage is a growing trend among parents by birth, who know that the material there can, in those now-rare instances like leukemia and some other cancers, hold hope for medical miracles. Who knows what else such access might do in the future?

In birth families, where access to DNA matches is statistically high, the expense of cord blood storage may not be worth it. The American Academy of Pediatrics has said that costs do not yet make it sensible for them to recommend this as a routine procedure at this time. But for adoptive families of newborns, whether the adoption will be an open one or not, making prior arrangements for storing cord blood at birth may make good financial, physical, and emotional sense.

So what are the costs? As I write, in 2007, this requires an upfront investment of something in the neighborhood of $1500, depending on the service provider, for retrieval and initial cryopreservation. The blood can then be stored for up to 21 years at an average cost of about $95 per year—for a total investment of about $3500.

I must emphasize that this is *not* a routine perinatal service at most hospitals at this time, so this requires several weeks of advance research and preparation. Thus it is only available to those adoptive families who will be matched with an expectant parent several weeks before a child is born. Speak with your agency first about their experience with this. Speak with your physicians (pediatricians, ob-gyns, etc.) as well. If this becomes something for which you are prepared to pay, speak with the expectant mother with whom you have been matched (or ask her counselor to do so). If she agrees, you may proceed to make all of the practical arrangements that must be made by working with her obstetrician and the hospital where the child will be born.

Breast-feeding and Adoption

Until recently the issue of how to feed a baby was not much a part of adoption practice—either in advising expectant parents or in preparing prospective adopters. But that is changing.

Nowadays, few dispute the physical and emotional benefits of breast-feeding—both for infants and for their nursing mothers. Under most circumstances human breast milk is the best possible food for a human baby. It is custom formulated for proper nutritional balance and is allergen free. For those who give birth to their children, breast milk is readily available, convenient, and free. What's more, antibodies passed from a newly postpartum mother to a newborn child in colostrum provide babies with a valuable immunologic boost. It has even been theorized that breast feeding leads to subtly different facial musculoskeletal development in babies, so that children who are fed at the breast rather than from a bottle may have lower incidences of ear infection, better aligned teeth, and perhaps even enhanced speech development. Furthermore, breast-feeding can contribute to the postpartum physical recovery of a birthmother and seems to lower the statistical odds for her later development of breast cancer.

In addition to these physical benefits to birthmother and child, proponents of breast-feeding claim a single overriding psychological benefit for nursing couples who breast-feed: enhancement of bonding. And because the very word *bonding* has become so disproportionately significant in the world of birth and family formation (spawning new businesses and being used as a marketing gimmick by hospital birth centers), breast-feeding has become a cause celebré.

These sections which follow are not meant to be a comprehensive how-to on the subject of breast-feeding the adopted child. The recommended resources will serve that purpose. Instead, these sections are meant to raise some issues for adoptive parents and adoption professionals to consider when trying to make a decision about breast-feeding and adoption.

Adoptive Nursing

For well over thirty years now, relatively small but stable numbers of adoptive mothers have been nursing their babies. Early on, the decision to try adoptive nursing was made more or less "underground," passed from adoptive mother to adoptive mother almost entirely outside the agency's knowledge. This "secret" nursing happened because many social workers found the concept of adoptive nursing troublesome. During the same period of time when they were universally worrying that a birthmother who wanted ongoing information about her child would never resolve her loss, social workers then worried that adoptive nursing was an attempt to deny or reject adoption's differences and represented unresolved infertility issues. However, the cultural embrace of breast-feeding, combined with increased access to information in parenting and infertility-related emotional issues, have brought new attention to adoptive nursing as a part of the breast vs. bottle debate.

Breast-feeding is, for many women, an expected and central part of being a mother, so that for some women breast-feeding may be as important a potential loss accompanying infertility as are genetic connection and pregnancy. But just as the loss of the opportunity to parent can be avoided by choosing to parent through adoption, it is also possible to avoid the loss of the breast-feeding experience. No, it won't be easy, and no, just as parenting in adoption is not "just like" parenting by birth, adoptive nursing is not "just the same" as breast-feeding after giving birth. It is, however, possible, and worthy of consideration by those to whom it appeals.

Let's begin with a brief discussion of the mechanics of adoptive nursing. The production of milk is the body's response to the ebb and flow of hormones during pregnancy, and at and after birth. However, it is possible to stimulate the body to produce milk without a pregnancy. Regularly pumping the breasts mechanically or establishing frequent and regular suckling may stimulate the production and flow of milk. Additionally, a physician may prescribe various drugs which can stimulate the pituitary gland's production of prolactin, which induces lactation. There are, though, at least two bottom-line realities about adoptive nursing to consider: First, few women who have never been pregnant are likely to produce enough breast milk to provide all of their babies' nutrition. Second, adoptive nursing is likely to be most successful with newborn babies since they have not yet become used to an artificial nipple and bottle, and is less likely to be successful with babies who have already become used to bottle feeding. The underlying problem with trying to introduce the breast to older babies who have been bottle-fed is what is called nipple confusion, which can also be a problem for nursing mothers whose children are occasionally bottle fed.

Because many women see breast-feeding as an important component of attachment between mother and child, the issue of whether adoptive nursing provides all of the baby's sustenance, however, is relatively unimportant. Whether or not lactation is fully induced, proper nourishment and nutrition can be virtually guaranteed in the adoptive nursing couple with the use of a supplemental nursing system (SNS). Several brands of SNSs are now available. All work on the same principle: a thin plastic tube is attached to a plastic pouch or bottle containing a physician-recommended baby formula. The pouch is suspended around the neck of the nursing mother and usually hangs between her breasts. Very thin tubing runs from the bottom of the pouch and is taped (surgical tape works best) next to the mother's nipple. As the baby sucks on the mother's nipple, the breast is stimulated (encouraging production of milk) and at the same time formula is pumped from the pouch at about the same rate that it would flow from a nursed breast.

> Jane Anne wrote that Leah's birthmother was perfectly comfortable with her nursing Leah. "In fact, she was merrily chatting on the telephone to her friends as I gave Leah her first meal, right in the birthing room. I nursed after our birthmom went home, throughout our hospital stay, and for the next ten months of our daughter's life. . . . I know I'm doubly blessed with a lovely, healthy child and a birthmother who went along with my plan to nurse.

Catherine's experience was positive, too, though with a different twist . . .

> Despite her home province's rule that babies needed to stay in foster care for ten days to give birthmothers time to consider changing their plans, Catherine was determined to try breast-feeding. For Cath-

erine and Michael their open adoption provided a particularly positive start for Catherine's wish to breast-feed, since the baby's birthmother nursed him in the hospital. Catherine wrote, "Our son's birthmother wanted to give him every advantage she could—so this way he was held and nurtured, cared for and loved by her while in the hospital, and as a side effect, received the benefits of all her antibodies. How could we have denied her this time, if she wished it? . . . We all felt that it was important for the two of them to do this—even though we knew this was hard for her. We were fortunate that our son's birthmother was making a clear adoption plan for him—she was not 'giving him up' out of desperation, but choosing to place him with us."

An important adoptive nursing benefit to his birthmother's decision to breast-feed was that Catherine's son had already learned to nurse by the time he went to be fostered in Catherine's sister's home, where social workers were supportive of her breast-feeding her baby and agreed that it offered her a legitimate reason to be in his foster home at any hour of the day or night. Since Catherine had been using a breast pump for several weeks, she was somewhat prepared. Despite cracked nipples, Catherine found that with the support of her husband, fostering sister, son's doctor's careful attention and support (she had changed doctors before her son was born in order to find one who was supportive of this option) and, most importantly, her son's birthmother, adoptive nursing was completely successful. Catherine's only regret? That she hesitated to ask for help from La Leche League, and didn't reach out earlier to other expectant and new mothers-by-birth, whose problems and concerns, she now realizes, weren't very different from her own.

Lest you feel pressured, let's be clear that it is not my intention to advocate for adoptive nursing. This is not for everyone. Some women—and some partners—are "grossed out" by the idea and/or the paraphernalia of adoptive nursing. Feeling pressured to make such a choice is a very negative way to begin a relationship with a new family member.

Others are offended by an implication they hear, that without it their children will not attach properly. Indeed the "bonding issue" and the breast-feeding connection deserve a bit of discussion.

A nursing mother becomes her child's near exclusive source of food and more. In her provocative and insightful book *I.D.: How Heredity and Experience Make You Who You Are* (New York: Random House, 1996) science writer Winifred Gallagher writes

"For adults the basic point of eating is getting adequate nutrition. For babies, however, the mouth is the major sense organ and gateway to the external world, and feedings are a perceptual and social as well as gustatory feast. Mealtimes provide them not only with calories but with an opportunity to engage with their mothers, fathers, and other affectionate parties in delicious emotional and sensory exchanges—visual, tactile, olfactory, auditory, and vestibular. This complex physiological and social experience, which Lynn Hofer calls a 'dance of attunement' is a cornerstone of a baby's physical, emotional, and cognitive development."

Gallagher writes this not in support of breast-feeding, rather as an introduction to a segment in which she describes how the parents of children born with gastric problems which require that they be fed through a stomach tube can be trained to provide a successful substitute for the benefits of nursing/bottle feeding experience.

Most experts feel that it is the nursing environment, much more than the physical act of breast-feeding that enhances bonding, and a parent can come very close to replicating this environment without breast-feeding. A baby's face and his parent's are the precisely correct distance apart when he is at the breast for Baby to be able to focus and gaze into his parent's face. A baby held in the crook of his parent's arm while offered a bottle is in the same position. The skin-to-skin warmth can be replicated, if desired, by dressing to insure that the baby's face makes skin contact while feeding. If desired, parents may decide that in order to enhance his attachment to one of them, one of them will become Baby's primary source of a bottle for a few weeks. That parent can, with about the same difficulty as a nursing mother, even arrange to leave work for a nearby or on-site child care center for Baby's feeding time.

Most important to protecting the bonding benefits of feeding time is to insure that Baby's bottle is never, ever propped, that he is never left alone in a crib with a bottle while parents or child care providers use this quiet time for another purpose. Some of our children have already experienced far too much of this in orphanage care.

Some adoptive fathers are distressed when their wives begin to talk about adoptive nursing. They may fear that their own opportunity to interact on a level as intimate as feeding may compromise their own ability to claim the child or may give their nursing partners more "power" in a parenting relationship that they had come to look forward to as being "more equal" than the circumstances which often surround new parents-by-birth.

Deciding whether or not to breast-feed your adopted child is a highly personal decision. While many sources of information are available, your own instincts and open communication with your partner will help you to make the decision that is best for you and your child.

Since adoptive nursing can be done, the issue for individual parents to decide is should it be done. Here are some issues for mothers-to-be and their partners to consider.

- Do you want to do this? Don't succumb to pressure from others about what defines a "good" mother.
- How patient can you be? Inducing lactation and/or nursing with a nursing system is time consuming, often sloppy, and demands consistency and dedication. Establishing comfortable accomplishment on the first day or in the first week is rare, so that adoptive nursing is unlikely to be successful unless you are committed to doing it 100% of the time over several weeks and, perhaps, months.
- Will your spouse, your family, and your child's pediatrician support your efforts in adoptive nursing? If not, what stress does this add to your relationships with them and with your new baby? Be particularly sensitive to your husband's feelings here, since in many couples one of the perceived benefits of adoption is that parents can be equally involved with the newborn in a way that is less expected when the mother has given birth to the child.
- If your adoption is to be an open adoption, how does your child's birthmother feel about your nursing the baby? Don't even consider not telling her.
- What would define success for you? If you are dedicated, the emotional connection between mother and child, which is a hallmark of nursing couples, can almost assuredly be yours. Other presumed benefits of nursing may be more elusive. Be especially careful not to expect this to be a substitute way for you to prove that you are a "real woman" after attempts to become pregnant have been unsuccessful. Unless you can be satisfied successfully using an SNS but producing little or no breast milk, your odds of feeling that you have failed are high. How might such a "failure" affect your relationship with your child?

Written sources of help for those considering adoptive nursing are listed in the resources section. The manufacturers of several slightly differing nursing systems produce written educational materials and offer some telephone support for their products, which can also be helpful. Don't ignore the parent education department of your local hospital or its childbirth educators who can refer you to a nursing consultant.

Breast-feeding and Birthmothers

Other breast-feeding issues may also arise for you and your child. Even more than they once discouraged adoptive nursing, social workers once strongly discouraged birthmothers from breast-feeding their newborns. But some birthmothers refused to listen to this advice.

> Sharon nursed her daughter for three days in the hospital, against all wishes of her doctor and her parents. She wrote that it was a difficult decision, but that "even at 14 I had read enough to know that

breast-feeding was best, and the first few days of colostrum the most important. (The baby) was given bottles as well, as the adoptive mom would not be nursing her. I felt better knowing that I had done what little I could to help her get a good start in life. To me, it was on par with getting good nutrition while pregnant."

Recently, a small but growing number of birthparent counselors have used reasoning like Sharon's to begin to encourage birthmothers to breast-feed their newborns for a few days before the babies are transitioned to their adoptive homes. Like most other changes in adoption practice over the years, this change has not come about as a result of formal research, nor has the issue been discussed in any professional or advocacy forum. Little has yet been written about the concept. Instead, it has been introduced experimentally by extraordinarily well-meaning practitioners, most of whose positive experiences with breast-feeding have been outside the model of adoption-expanded families.

Given the widespread acceptance of the physical and medical benefits of breast-feeding, one might conclude that encouraging birthmothers to breast-feed their infants before placement creates a win-win situation for all: Babies receive the best possible food, an immunologic boost, and potentially fewer allergies. Birthmothers speed their physical recovery. Adoptive mothers wishing to nurse increase their likelihood for success.

It is the psychological issues surrounding breast-feeding, however, which should give those planning a baby's adoption pause before encouraging birthmothers or adoptive mothers to nurse their babies. Virtually all enlightened adoption advocates and mental health practitioners agree that parenting by birth is not the same for mothers who subsequently plan an adoption, and that adoptive mothering is not just like parenting by birth. Thus, the bonding experience in adoption may be different too. (Note that I said *different from*, not *lesser than* parenting and bonding in families formed by birth.)

If there are differences, then the claim of enhanced bonding through breast-feeding is not necessarily transferable to babies to be adopted and their adoptive parents, and promoting anything which encourages post-birth bonding with birthparents has the potential for creating problems for birthparent, baby, and adoptive family.

I believe the most important elements in making decisions about adoptive nursing and birthparent breastfeeding are full communication and agreement between *all* parties to the adoption—birthparents, adopters, and their counselors and intermediaries.

Roberta's son's transition to home was far different from the smooth transition described by Catherine and Jane Anne. Melanie spent two months with her son Roger in a residential facility before he was placed with Roberta. Without bothering to tell the agency (she felt it really wasn't their concern and she was already resenting their intrusions into her life), Melanie breast-fed Roger during these weeks in addition to offering him bottles. By the time of his placement, he was a healthy, strapping boy.

But the lack of information and communication between counselors and two sets of parents worked to Roger's disadvantage. His adoptive mom, Roberta, had no idea why he cried inconsolably for long periods all day and seemed to be comforted only by a bottle—and then not fully comforted. Obviously he missed his birthmother, and she had expected that a move might be difficult at first. But Roberta didn't know all she needed to know—she didn't know that he had been breastfed—and she felt increasingly guilty about her apparent "incompetence" as a mother. Had the two mothers and the agency considered the issue of how the baby would be fed over the continuum of his first year, an issue to be discussed among all of them, Roger and Roberta's transition could have been greatly enhanced.

Before the trend to encourage birthmothers to breast-feed their babies becomes a new practice standard, careful consideration must be given to all potential ramifications. To be useful, the ongoing discussion should grow to include responses from adoptive parents, birthparents, adoption professionals, and even adoptees when possible. What is difficult about gathering such input is that there is a tendency for only those who have had extreme experiences of resounding success or abysmal failure to participate. The great center of experience of people who have had mixed experiences with an issue often don't report. In fact, the confidentiality rules which demand that all adoption studies be done on people who self-select rather than be performed on universal pools has made adoption as an issue nearly infamous among researchers. Furthermore, the issue may, for many people, be emotionally charged, so that it will be important for those involved in the discussion to make a supreme effort to be respectful of differing points of view.

Darilyn Starr has written several magazine and newsletter articles, and contributed to Debra Peterson's book about her experience with breast-feeding all four of her adopted children. While supporting a birthmother's right to breast-feed of her own volition, she feels strongly that birthmothers should not be pressured, "There is already so much that we ask of birthmothers out of necessity, I don't think we should ask more," she writes. About whether birthmothers should require this of adopting mothers, she says, "I think the birthmother has the right to seek an adoptive mother who is interested in breast-feeding, if that is important to her. However, I don't think asking it of a prospective adoptive mother who was not interested would be good. With all of the dedication that adoptive nursing requires, I doubt that it would result in anything but added stress for a woman who was only doing it because the birthmother wanted her to."

Nursing by Foster Parents

My youngest daughter was breast-fed by her first foster mother for the first eight weeks of her life. Neither the agency nor the foster mother even considered asking Lindsey's birthmother's permission before beginning this. Dave and I had not yet been identified as her parents, so we were not consulted either. The agency's decisions were based on several pieces of poorly thought out rationalizations based on inaccurate information that this had to be "good for" our daughter-to-be, but the result was a baby who was cold weaned from one day to the next, and disrupted a total of three times before she was placed in our home. Needless to say, her adjustment was difficult. Had we been first-time parents or experienced parents who had allowed ourselves to stay adoption illiterate, I am certain that we would have blamed ourselves for our baby's unhappiness.

And the Answer Is . . .

Input from adoptive parents, birthparents, adoption professionals, and even adoptees is needed to determine what, over the long term, is in the best physical and psychological interests of most babies. Only by respectfully sharing and listening to differing points of view can we help adoption practitioners understand how to help birthparents and adoptive parents make healthy, fully-informed choices about the place of breast-feeding in the lives of their babies. Here are some questions you may wish to discuss with your own and your child's birthmother's counselors in making your own decisions about the place of birthmother breast-feeding in the life of your child.

1. Since new mothers are in a highly vulnerable emotional position, how do prospective adoptive parents and professionals avoid allowing their personal values to pressure a expectant mother to get a baby for whom she is going to make an adoption plan "off to a good start" by breast-feeding him for a few days or weeks? Have we any concrete evidence about whether the choice to breast-feed makes it more or less difficult for a new mother to separate emotionally and begin to resolve her loss? Are there ways to predict in advance how a particular mother may react?

2. Should prospective adopters have any role to play in the decision about whether their child-to-be is to be breast-fed by his birthmother?

3. If nursing enhances attachment, might a baby who has been breast-fed by birthmother for a few weeks have a harder time moving to adoption? If breast-feeding could cause attachment confusion, but if the physical benefits of being breast-fed appear to outweigh these risks, what suggestions can we make that will help birth and

adoptive parents to help their babies' transition as smoothly as possible?

4. Might an attempt to prevent a troublesome transfer in such a situation put excessive pressure on an adoptive mother to attempt adoptive nursing and thus disempower adoptive parents when it comes to choosing how to feed their child? How can this be predicted and addressed?

5. Similarly, does an adoptive mother's interest in adoptive nursing pressure a birthmother to breast-feed her baby at birth in order to "get him going" with breast-feeding?

6. What is the role of foster mothers in the discussion of breast-feeding and the adopted child? Should lactating foster mothers be allowed or encouraged to breast-feed babies in interim care? Under what circumstances? What about the concept of a wet-nursing foster mother serving as a mentor/lactation counselor for an adoptive mother who wishes to try breast-feeding?

7. Because breast-feeding sometimes creates issues of fathers feeling "left out" among couples who give birth to their baby (a common situation routinely addressed with practical strategies for coping in all of the literature supporting breast-feeding after birth), does adoptive nursing eliminate a potential strength/benefit in adoption: equalizing relationships between mothers and fathers and their babies? Could adoptive nursing add to adoption's attachment challenges for adoptive fathers? How can this best be addressed?

Since nearly everything which can be shared is currently anecdotal rather than formally research-based, there is little likelihood of a clearly right or wrong answer emerging yet. What we can hope for is that by talking about these issues aloud, we encourage a large enough response to help those who are guiding practice to understand how to help birthparents, foster parents, and adoptive parents make healthy, fully informed decisions about the place of breast-feeding in the lives of their babies.

Daycare Decisions

If you will be returning to work shortly after your child's arrival, begin to think about child care long before baby arrives. Many infant care centers and family daycare providers have long waiting lists. While it may be impossible for you to predict exactly when your child is "due," some centers will be flexible about trying to provide a space for you if they know about your pending adoption.

The issue of consistency of care can be an important one for a child whose adoption was preceded by several changes in care providers or living arrangements. Parents who offered comments about this provided logical arguments for and against both in-home or private-home care and larger, multi-caregiver commercial facilities. Ask family and friends to share their experiences and opinions, but reserve final decisions for you as parents.

An important attachment-related reality check for those adopting older babies and children who have spent time in orphanage care: Having his parent available full-time during an extended adjustment period may be especially important for a child who has been institutionalized before placement and has not had the experience of attaching to a single caregiver. If such a child spends a significant amount of his day in a large daycare center—an environment which may feel very much like the orphanage or group home from which he came—he or she may have a difficult time learning to attach to Mom and Dad.

Preparing Siblings-to-be

More and more of the family-challenged are those who have secondary infertility problems, second marriage relationships where one or both partners have children from previous relationships, or in other ways involve one normally developing child already in residence in the family. Waiting adopters who are already parents of one or more children—whether by birth or by adoption—will need to use some of their getting-ready energy on preparing these soon-to-be siblings.

Age of the resident child is a factor, of course, and much of the written advice and many of the children's books available for preparing children for a sibling coming to them by birth can be useful. You can count on your older child to be wildly ambivalent about his finally-arrived sister or brother, and behavioral regression is not unusual. After all, becoming a big sib sounds so great in theory . . . but then The Kid is there, and he can't really play, and he's getting all the attention.

What's different in adoption? For one thing, there is the lack of a completely predictable timeline. Kids are so much more comfortable with time that can be visibly measured on a calendar. That's rarely possible in adoption. Yet one of the things we think we know about getting older children ready for the arrival of a new sibling is the importance of specifically letting children in on what's up fairly early in the expectancy period. Why? Not because they need that much time—in fact long waits can become difficult—rather because children almost always know that something is afoot in a family and when they don't know what it is, they tend to speculate strangely, feel left out, and to a certain extent feel abandoned. So it's always a good idea to bring an older child up-to-date on his parents' decision to adopt again.

Another difference about adoption is parents' worries about how to handle a pre-placement change of heart, and this correlates with the unpredictability problem. My advice is to speak with your child in terms of "hoping" and "trying" to adopt before a match has been made.

When they decided that they were ready to expand their family, Renee and Maurice began to respond to Dion's questions about the possibility of a baby sister with comments like this: "Mom and I think it would be great to have another baby, too, Dion, and we've decided to work on it. But you know, lots of people would like to be as fortunate as we have been and adopt a baby like we adopted you. It may take a while."

Soon they were matched with Stephanie, a young mother-to-be who was considering entrusting her coming baby to their family. The discussions with Dion continued . . .

"You know, Dion, Stephanie is thinking very hard about whether or not she is ready to be a parent to her baby. She loves her baby, but she would like her baby to have a mother and a father to take care of him—just like you do, and she's worried that she isn't finished growing up herself yet. She wants to do what she thinks is the very best thing she can do for her baby, and that's why she is talking to us and visiting with us, and talking with Mrs. Ryan [a social worker]. If she figures out that she is not ready to be a mother yet, she might ask Daddy and you and me to be her baby's family. She's thinking about this a lot because she has a lot of things to figure out. We won't know for a while."

Stephanie decided to parent, and Renee and Maurice talked to Dion about that decision like this

"By the time Stephanie's baby was born she had figured out the things she needed to figure out in order to be a good mommy to her baby. We like Stephanie, and so we are happy for her, even though we are feeling a little sad that our family doesn't have a new baby yet."

Beyond these issues, expectant adoptive parents will want to follow the typical advice offered to parents-by-birth in preparing older children for a new baby: involve the sibling in preparations like decorating a nursery and getting out the old baby clothes; use these opportunities to reminisce about his own homecoming and how exciting it was; make any major life changes—like a new house or a changed bedroom or moving out of a crib—well in advance so Older Sibling doesn't feel displaced. Create opportunities for your older child to get used to the fact that she may have less of your time than before. Just as it's a good idea to take an older sibling along to an appointment with the obstetrician, plan an opportunity for the child to visit the agency or get ice cream with expectant parents you've committed to, etc. "Get into" babies at your house: talk about how old the babies you see at temple or at friends' houses are and look at pictures of babies of the approximate age and ethnicity of the baby you are expecting that you may bring home (making clear, of course, that these are not pictures of your family's baby). Check at your local hospital for the availability of a new sibling class and speak with the teacher about whether or not she feels it would be appropriate for an expectant adoptive brother or sister.

> Oh, and Dion? He eventually became a big brother to Aimee. It was particularly exciting to go with Mom and Dad to pick her up, because they had to fly on a plane to get there. Brother and baby are doing fine.

When the Coming Sibling Won't Be a Baby

As more and more families add toddlers, preschoolers, school-aged kids, and even teens to their family through adoption we are becoming more aware of the impact this has on the normally developing children already residing in the family. Not enough, however, is being done to prepare families for what it can mean to add children who are not on a normal developmental schedule—because they have been institutionalized; because they have experienced some level of trauma or abuse or neglect; because they have been exposed, prenatally, to toxic substances that have changed their brains.

The addition of any new person—newborn, step-sibling, step-parent—to any family changes the context of that family forever. Adding children from difficult backgrounds guarantees compromised adjustments. Families who either have not been properly prepared for what these things mean in the context of family life, or have simply refused to accept what they have been told, are often shocked to find their world rocked and their other children actually suffering from what had started out as such a positive and hopeful decision.

Families who find themselves here have options, but they are sometimes difficult to find. I would love to say that the answer is just a phone call away to the placing agency, but that is often not the case. Check out the Resources section for some recommendations.

When the Adoption Styles Are Different

Not-yet-parents and parents-of-onlies often worry about whether the adoptions of each of their children need to be alike. If the first adoption is open, must the second one be too? If one child is adopted internationally and confidentially, wouldn't an open domestic adoption make two children jealous of one another? I usually begin to answer this question with a story.

> When I was a child, my parents tried to be "fair" about everything. We all got new shoes at the same time. If Daddy brought one of us a present from a trip, he brought all of us presents. If there was one piece of cake left, there were two ways of handling that Mama defined as "fair." One was to cut it into tiny equal pieces—one bite for each of us. The other was to let Daddy eat it. That was fair too.

> I grew up believing that life would be fair and equal like that. For me, that expectation of fairness, of equitability in life, of just rewards, made facing infertility particularly difficult. Infertility wasn't "fair." People who didn't want babies or didn't deserve babies had babies, but I, who had worked so hard, had prepared so well, had so much to give, couldn't have a baby. This experience led me to make an important decision about parenting: life is not fair, and it's not a good idea to let children think that it is. South Carolina adoptive parent and social worker June Bond has the right answer to this one. "Not fair, honey?" she drawls to her kids. "You're right. Life's not fair. The fair's in August. We'll go."

An important fact of parenting life is that no two children are ever parented "the same." Not even twins. Many factors, including age, sex, personality, and birth order influence the way children interact with each of their parents. Even when the styles of two adoptions are the same, or the agency or country source of two adoptions are the same, the children will not be the same. While small children may experience this as being treated "fairly," *fair* doesn't necessarily mean *equal*. Equal treatment is not the issue so much as is children's perceiving that communication in the family is open, that their parents respect their individuality, and that parents meet their needs.

> My family consists of three children: a son whose 1975 adoption was confidential; a daughter whose 1981 adoption was identified, but has been, by her birthparents' choices, entirely non-communicative; a daughter whose 1984 adoption is communicatively open with both of her birthparents. Each of these adoptions has its own complexities. My son and daughters are well adjusted and comfortable with both their adoptive status and their places in our family, and none of these adoptions has, to date, proven any easier than the others based on style. Our children have been interested in talking about one another's adoptions, and about the circumstances and the times that led adopting parents, birthparents, and professionals to plan each adoption as it was planned. They are aware that the style of each of those adoptions really had very little to do with who they themselves are. They have experienced no feelings of jealousy, competition, or sadness about the differences in their adoption. What each of our children knows well is this: Mom and Dad love us and are on our side. They would do their best to help us get any need met.

Preparing Family and Friends

As we discussed in Chapter 2, the truth is that, you probably knew little about adoption before you began to consider it for yourself. Adopting can sound like pretty scary business to those who have not pursued it. Before you were well informed, you, too, read the same kind of articles, watched the same kind of movies and talk shows and so were likely to believe some of those old myths that have now come to be oh-so-much-more-than annoying:

> You have to wait *how long?*
>
> But you have such a nice family. Wouldn't you rather have *another of your own?*
>
> It'll cost *how much?*
>
> He's been in *how many* foster homes?
>
> Oh, honey, *how much will you know* about his background?
>
> *What kind of person* would give up their own flesh and blood?
>
> You actually have to meet the *real mother?*
>
> What if *his people* want him back?
>
> They're abandoned on the streets in slums in *what country?*
>
> Adopt from *that culture?* You know what they say *about those people.*

Education changed your view of adoption, and it is the answer for your friends and family, too. What I hope you've done is work on this gradually, from the time you began to consider adoption seriously. I hope that you listened in Chapter 2 and that you have already taken the most receptive member of your circle with you to a conference, later enlisting that person's help in serving as your advocate with persistently snoopy and insensitive others. Your advocate may already have had quiet heart-to-hearts with the potentially offended or offensive among your family, enlisting them to become part of your sensitivity team too. If you haven't been working on this all along, however, it isn't too late to start on this project as a part of your waiting routine—but it's going to need to be a crash course at this point.

At first most others won't be interested in reading full books on adoption. Start by sending short things—Pat Holmes' *Supporting an Adoption* or Linda Bothun's *When Friends Ask about Adoption*, or my book *Adoption Is a Family Affair! What Relatives and Friends Must Know.* Offer them CDs from conferences. Include a subscription to *Adoptive Families, Fostering Families Today, Adoption Today* or *Pact Press* on your holiday shopping list. Perhaps you could subscribe to several of these for yourself and pass each along to a different relative. When things are definite, ask those closest to you to read some of the books that you have found most helpful. Plug your family members into the Internet and send them to your favorite sites or suggest that they susbcribe to some listservs you've found helpful.

Your family may find some aspects of adoption (openness, for example) threatening at first. They will need help in fielding the unwelcome or insensitive comments and questions from their own peers. They will need to learn to use respectful adoption language (Chapter 16). They will want to learn, and they will, with your help.

If you were pregnant, the family would be very involved in the rituals that welcome a child—baby showers, gathering a layette, preparing a room. As I hope you've learned in this chapter, such waiting behavior is an important part of the psychological preparation process of pregnancy, and you and your family need to create the environment of a psychological pregnancy. Take family members on shopping trips to look at children's furniture. Encourage garage-salers to pick up special bargains to put aside. Have Grandma- and Grandpa-to-be help you sort through children's books about adoption or about your child-to-be's culture to find one or two extra special ones just for the grandchildren's shelf at their house.

Give nieces and nephews adoption-informative and adoption-sensitive books as gifts. *Tell Me Again about the Night I Was Born*; *More More More, Said the Baby*; *Love You Like Crazy Cakes*; *The Velveteen Rabbit*; *Kids Like Me in China*; *Love You Forever*; *People*; *Something Good*; *Borya and the Burps*; and *When You Were Born in Korea* are among my favorites for these cousins- and best-friends-to-be. On the flip side, you might suggest that certain commonly owned adoption-insensitive books should be snatched from family shelves. Birthparent-insensitive Dr. Seuss' *Horton Hatches the Egg* might be replaced by Anne Brodzinsky's *The Mulberry Bird* and P.D. Eastman's *Are You My Mother?* exchanged for Keiko Kasza's *A Mother for Choco*.

While it's true that your extended family may be slightly behind you in accepting and embracing adoption, the actual arrival of a wonderful little person is hard to resist. Extended family can become involved in the claiming process through the selecting of names. Choosing a name which honors an ancestor or a willing grandparent, aunt or uncle can publicly proclaim a child as a member of your clan.

Claiming, you'll remember, is something members of families do over and over in both subtle and obvious ways whether the children were born to or adopted by the family. Having our children claimed by their grandparents, aunts, uncles and cousins is important for them, but sometimes we don't consciously recognize that it is important for us too. When we claim the children of our family's new generation, we reaffirm our own connections to the current and prior generations. When this claiming doesn't happen, those old feelings of inadequacy can be stirred again. The more important the loss of genetic connection is to you, the more likely it is that you will find it especially important for your family to claim your children.

Try to be patient with the laggers-behind, but through the years look for ways for them to claim your children. Encourage your parents to spend as much time as possible with these grandchildren. Educate them about some of the ways in which adoption is not like connections by birth (for example, in some states, unless adopted grandchildren are either specifically named or the inclusive terms "by birth or by adoption" are added to a will, adopted children will not automatically inherit from their grandparents). Allow them the silly comparisons which have no basis in fact ("Why, he looks just like Uncle Ralph!").

> Pam and Dick were able to laugh about it all much later, but when their biracial baby Larry first arrived, and Dick's parents exhibited some uncomfortable reluctance to introduce their new grandchild to their friends, it hurt. Pam and Dick knew that the problem was their fear of their friends' racial intolerance.
>
> They tried to be patient, and so to encourage their parents to come to love Larry for who he was, they made the eight hour round trip to their parents' city every weekend for several months. It worked. Who could resist such a beautiful, smiling, bouncing, loving boy?
>
> One weekend many months after Larry's arrival, Dick's father rushed eagerly to the car upon their arrival to grab his grandson from the car seat. "You know," he observed as he covered Larry's face with his kisses, "I think he's looking a little lighter." The next morning, at Grandpa's suggestions, the family went to church together for the first time.
>
> Now, Dick could have been offended on his son's behalf by his father's bias. In reality, Larry's skin was darkening and his hair becoming coarser and curlier as he matured. But Dick was wise. He recognized that his father was still playing catch up. He was working to claim this boy in the ways he knew how. Eventually he would make it. And he did, leaving behind most of the bigotry that he had learned growing up along the way.

When adopting parents find certain family members or friends unwilling to consider their child one of the family they may feel hurt or resentful. Openly discuss your concerns and your hurt feelings with these relatives. While no one wants to perpetuate family rifts, the decision to distance oneself from a stubbornly unsupportive relative is a sign of a strong need to protect one's child and indicates the development of a healthy sense of entitlement between parents and child.

Yes, you deserve to have your friends and family support your family planning decisions, but no matter how carefully you try to educate them, a few people may remain insensitive. Don't continue to beat yourself up about this by trying over and over again. After they have been given the opportunity to learn, to change, and they have not, no matter how closely they are related to you, the best method for coping with these rare few is by avoiding them. That will be hard and perhaps painful to do, yes, but you must do this for your child. Don't just "disappear," however. Make clear to this person—very privately, but very firmly—why, as a good parent, you need to do this: because you can't allow your child to be subjected to adoptism or racism or any other bias which affects them and will cause them pain.

Parallel Expectancies

If you will be adopting a newborn from the U.S., the chances are very good that you will be in direct contact with that baby's first mother (and perhaps other birth relatives) during the last several months of her pregnancy and your expectancy period. This is going to be hard.

Frankly, I consider this one of the few real negatives in open adoption—for everyone. Why? There are three reasons.

To begin with, there are far too few really well-trained, experienced, and fully competent adoption counselors who can work effectively with these two client sets with such different needs and expectations, supporting the needs of both, and helping each to maintain enough emotional distance to retain their objectivity. In the 25 years that openness in adoption has been growing to become the new normal, I've not seen this changing as much as it should have. Schools of social work and psychology are not offering more courses in adoption counseling. No professional association has set any real standards for this kind of counseling. Open adoption has not become a common continuing education topic.

Second, pregnancy is such a sensitive period to begin with—loaded with hormonal shifts—and an untimely pregnancy is especially difficult emotionally. Ambivalence should be expected in these last weeks and thoroughly experienced, without embarrassment or guilt. That's hard for an expectant mother to do when she's being hovered over by eager would-be adopters she's come to like very much. How dare she disappoint them?

And while it's important that adopting parents understand and appreciate the extremes of ambivalence experienced by a pregnant woman considering adoption, it's also very important that they allow themselves to feel excitement and joy in their own anticipation period. That's very hard to do when faced with another's looming loss and grief and one's own possible bitter disappointment.

I see no imminent solution to these three concerns.

So it remains that readers of this book—prospective adoptive parents—must walk a tight rope, urging themselves to feel expectant, but accepting that the child they are anticipating has only one set of parents—parents by birth—until after he has been born and a final decision has been made. Careful and realistic language is part of the respect due families facing the difficult choice to plan an adoption and using this language helps to support this factual state of limbo. An expectant mother should *never, never, never* be thought of or described as "a prospective birthmom (PBM)" which seems to describe her as a commodity. Nor should she be described or thought of as "our birthmother," which seems to imply that prospective adopters possess her in some way. She is, plainly, simply, and realistically "an expectant mother considering adoption." After delivering her child, she will be, simply and realistically, "a mother." Finally, she will need to make a decision about whether she can parent her baby herself. If she cannot and she chooses adoption, then, and only then, may you say that she is "our child's birthmother."

When Everything Changes

What if a much prepared for arrival doesn't happen? Three things might happen to change it all before an expected baby comes home through adoption: an expectant mother or expectant father might realize before the baby is born or immediately thereafter that adoption is just not the right plan; the baby may be miscarried, stillborn, or die shortly after birth; the referred child or the expected baby may be decidedly unhealthy and adopting parents may find that they need to say "no" to the plan to adopt. Any of these options can be devastating.

When a Mother Changes Her Mind Just before or Just after Birth

Of these three possibilities, the first is the most likely to happen in domestic adoptions, and with the advent of open adoptions, this kind of loss is happening to more and more would-be parents. Not only do fewer men and women dealing with an untimely pregnancy consider adoption today (fewer than 5%), but those who do explore adoption very often don't follow through. The fact that through open adoption more birth and adoptive parents come to know one another before the baby is born means that more adopting parents are directly exposed to these situations, creating bitter disappointments for which they feel a need for much support and for which there is little routinely offered. Though pre-placement changes of heart may be less traumatic than reversals after placement, they are bitterly disappointing. These situations can be compared in some respects to miscarriages—which are themselves poorly supported in the larger society—though much of the time those who might offer comfort after a miscarriage may not even be aware that the prospective adopter is feeling expectant.

In a few countries, it is possible that international adopters can experience a similar loss. When that country's policies dictate that birthfamilies may reclaim their children any time up to the time a court grants parental rights to another family, or that in-country adopters have first claim when it comes to adopting a child of their own nationality, sometimes families who have traveled from across the world expecting to bring that child home will go home empty-armed or will be asked to consider a new referral on the spot. How difficult it can be to be asked to choose a "replacement" for a child one has already grown to love!

When a Child Dies before Placement

If a mother miscarries or gives birth to a stillborn or fatally ill child, the grief is doubled. Two families will mourn this loss. Because both are grieving differently—the adopting couple feeling very disappointed and the new mother feeling guilty for disappointing them—these families may have a difficult time supporting one another. Adoption intermediaries have an important role to play in these losses.

Similarly, it is sometimes the case that a baby or toddler dies in an orphanage before the parents who have his photo posted on their computer screens and refrigerators, and his description written on their hearts can reach him. Far too often, theirs is an invisible and unsupported grief.

When the Prospective Adoptive Parent Says No

A third, and perhaps the most traumatic, change of heart occurs when, without warning something about the child met at an orphanage or born at a local hospital seriously jeopardizes the adoption. He may be of a different race than expected. More often the case is the existence of a serious medical condition that is not life threatening but does create a significant parenting complexity.

> Sabra and Shmuel flew "blind" to a region of Russia where it was required that they appear before local officials to receive a referral. They arrived confident that any referral would work because they had been so completely clear with their agency about their expectations about age, race, gender, and health issues for the child they wished to adopt. Imagine their shock when their guide and translator informed them that the paperwork being offered them described a girl, not a boy, and a child of Asian heritage rather than European genes. They argued, but finally agreed to see the child.
>
> They felt no connection. Indeed, so much about this little girl felt so "wrong" when compared to their expectations that they weren't able to stay for the entire expected length of the visit.
>
> The next day they visited the Ministry of Education again, and the translator announced that no boys under two were available. Sabra and Shmuel went home disappointed and angry. How could their agency have allowed this to happen!

However, this wasn't the agency's "fault." In nearly every international adoption, agencies make clear somewhere in their information that they do not have the ability to pick and choose referrals in most countries. The problem is that too many adopters don't "hear" this. Would it have been possible to avoid this? Yes. This family could have insisted on going to a country, or to a region within a country, where referrals are sent before a family travels. In doing so, they would perhaps have had to have made some "trade-offs"—in time waiting, in money spent, in some descriptive element about what constituted "acceptability" for them to parent a child, but they wouldn't have wasted resources or been disappointed.

> LuAnne became very involved in Sheila's pregnancy. She had accompanied her to medical appointments, spoken to her on the phone daily, and provided much of the emotional support missing when her family refused to offer their support during her pregnancy. There had been no reason at all to believe that Sheila's son, Stuart, would not be a bouncing baby. But he was not. Stuart was born with severe spina bifida.

> LuAnne was shocked, verging on panic. She had made careful plans about this adoption. She had been entirely aware of her limitations and felt that she had been honest with the agency and with Sheila. LuAnne contacted a pediatric specialist, who told her that Stuart's life expectancy was relatively normal, but that his condition was serious enough that he would probably be confined to a wheel chair throughout his life. LuAnne and Sheila were both devastated.

> After several days' reflection, despite the fact that she loved and respected Sheila, LuAnne decided that she could not adopt Stuart. Though she really didn't want to do so, her case worker insisted that she face Sheila and tell her herself. After much soul searching, LuAnne complied, and the case worker served as a supportive mediator in the meeting. Though Sheila was furious and hurt (which only added to the guilt she felt about Stuart's condition), the mediator was able to help these adults come to some sense of closure.

> The agency found foster parents for Stuart, and several months later he was adopted by a family quite ready for this little boy's bright mind and physical challenges, but not ready for an open adoption. Sheila was disappointed about the lack of openness—yet hopeful that this might change later. In the meantime, her social worker did an admirable job of helping Sheila to work through her bitterness about LuAnne's change of heart and her feelings that perhaps Stuart's disability was a punishment to her for having become pregnant outside of marriage.

> LuAnne took the time she needed with a therapist to work through her guilt in not following through with Stuart's adoption and sorted through her need for control. She entered infertility treatment with donor sperm and eventually gave birth to a daughter.

Things like this don't happen very often, but since they can happen, we can't close this section without addressing whether or not LuAnne, and Shmuel and Sabra were "wrong." Should prospective adopters be willing to accept any possible challenge? Certainly it is vital that prospective adopters understand and accept that there are no guarantees in adoption any more than there are in giving birth. My personal view is that it would be immoral to say "yes" to an adoption and then attempt to "exchange" a baby as "damaged goods" after he had become a part of one's home and a family. I think that a carefully considered change of mind is acceptable and probably represents a decision made in the best interests of a baby.

To those who might respond to this by saying that if people who give birth to handicapped babies sometimes make a later adoption plan, adopting parents should be able to change their minds after placement I remind you of this: parents who give birth to a baby have almost never had the opportunity for self-reflection and education, or been offered as many choices about who and how to parent as have prospective adopters. That opportunity for advance control that adopters are given—about what sex, age, race, or physical condition their baby might be—seems to me to be a tradeoff for the reproductive control that they have lost. Making those choices before taking custody of a child one agrees to parent is a fair trade. Yet from that point forward, I believe that the parents of babies should plan to be committed. Adopting older children, on the other hand, is a different situation.

Adoption is different enough in so many ways that I believe it is just as unreasonable to expect that before a placement is actually made adopters have to follow through no matter what. The same can be said for expecting that expectant parents should have no option of changing their minds about adoption once the baby has been born. Agencies, adopters, and birthfamilies in both confidential and open adoptions enter into relationships of good will in which each promises the others to listen carefully, to think hard, to accept education and counseling, and, once a baby is born, to think carefully about whether his adoption is in their best interests as well as his. Since every child deserves to be wanted for precisely who he is, well-informed and educated birthparents need to have the right to say no to adoption once their child has been born, and well-informed and educated adopters need to retain the right to change their minds about accepting a baby for adoption.

waiting for The Call[2]
by Shelia Stewart Darst

every time the phone rings now
my blood pressure soars
my heart drops to my left foot
and my scalp starts to tingle
and with all the serenity of a hungry cat
I say hello in a voice three octaves too
    high.

I unconsciously hum cradle songs
and review old nursery rhymes
because in my bones
I feel the time nearing
as I study spring's calendar
musing on days and dates

I sit by a green sunny window
in my great-grandfather's rocking chair
and am pleased as I look around
the new calico walls that everything is
    ready
and it reassures me and makes it real

the calico dog and calico cat
chase one another on a bright field
of yellow and green and orange and blue
and I try to imagine our child, our
    children

distant laughter circles the hall
and tiny feet run to me
in my imagination as I
sit and rock and write
and wonder and dream and plan

the old rocker squeaks a
comforting old song
and I think of all the children
rocked to sleep in its arms over a century
of all the stories it could tell
of all the family ties that it has bound,
and I am calmed by the infinite cycle of
    time
and the continuity of life

until the phone rings

Resources

Preparing to Live Adoption

Adoptive Families magazine, the premier periodical for new and growing adoptive families is published six times annually by New Hope Media. www.adoptive-families.com

Adoption Today magazine is devoted to international and transracial adoption. It is published four times annual by Louis & Co., which also publishes *Fostering Families Today*. www.adoptinfo.net/

Pertman, Adam. *Adoption Nation: How the Adoption Revolution Is Transforming America*. (New York: Basic Books, 2001)

Getting Ready for Parenthood

Belsky, Jay & Kelly, John. *The Transition to Parenthood*. (New York: Dell, 1995)

Bowden, Melanie. *Why Didn't Anyone Tell Me? True Stories of New Motherhood*. (Nashville, TN: Booklocker.com, 2006)

Brott, A.A. & Ash, J. *The Expectant Father: Facts, Tips, and Advice for Dads-To-Be.* (2nd ed) (New York: Abbeville Press, 2001)

Luminaire-Rosen, Carista. *Parenting Begins Before Conception: A Guide for Preparing Body, Mind and Spirit For You and Your Future Child.* (Rochester, VT: Inner Traditions, 2000)

When You Know that Your Child Will Have Special Needs

Babb, L. Anne and Rita Laws. *Adopting and Advocating for the Special Needs Child.* (Boston: Bergin & Garvey, 1997)

Keck, Gregory and Regina Kupecky. *Adopting the Hurt Child: Hope for Families With Special-Needs Kids: A Guide for Parents and Professionals.* (Colorado Springs, CO: Pinon Press, 1998)

Klein, Stanley and John Kemp. *Reflections from a Different Journey: What Adults with Disabilities Wish All Parents Knew.* (New York: McGraw-Hill, 2004)

Winter, Judy. *Breakthrough Parenting for Children with Special Needs: Raising the Bar of Expectations.* (New York: Jossey-Bass, 2006)

Financial Readiness

Bauer, Jean W. and Kathryn D. Rettig. "The Costs of Raising a Child." (St Paul: University of Minnesota Extension, 2002) www.extension.umn.edu/distribution/businessmanagement/DF5899.html

Lino, Mark. *Expenditures on Children by Families, 2006.* U.S. Department of Agriculture, Center for Nutrition Policy and Promotion. Miscellaneous Publication No. 1528-2006 (2007) www.cnpp.usda.gov/ExpendituresonChildrenby Families.htm

Breastfeeding

Adoptive Breastfeeding Resources Website fourfriends.com/abrw/

La Leche League (www.lalecheleague.org/NB/NBadoptive.html), and its local chapters, can provide support and information, written materials on adoptive nursing (including the classic guide *The Womanly Art of Breastfeeding*), help you find a supplemental nursing system, and can often put you in contact with other adoptive mothers who have breast-fed.

Newman, Jack, MD and Teresa Pitman. *The Ultimate Breastfeeding Book of Answers Revised and Updated: The Most Comprehensive Problem-Solving Guide to Breastfeeding from the Foremost Expert in North America.* (New York: Three Rivers Press, 2006)

Peterson, Debra Stewart. *Breast-feeding the Adopted Baby.* (San Antonio: Corona, 1994)

Smith, Anne, BA, IBCLC. "Relactation and Adoptive Nursing" on the Breastfeeding Basics web site. www.breastfeedingbasics.com/html/Relactation.shtml

Preparing Siblings

"Siblings and Adoption" a collection of links to articles from the *Adoptive Families* magazine archives. www.adoptivefamilies.com/siblings

James, Arleta. (Title yet to be finalized). Indianapolis: Perspectives Press, 2008 (Therapist Arleta James is working on a book specifically designed to help parents understand the impact of the arrival of a child from foster care or orphanage care on the typically-functioning-and-developing children already living in the family.)

Mason, Mary Martin. "Preparing the Sibling-in-Waiting Before Adoption Occurs." Adoption.com library.adoption.com/counseling/preparing-the-sibling-in-waiting-before-adoption-occurs/article/3397/1.html

Petertyl, Mary Ebejer. *Seeds of Love: For Brothers and Sisters of International Adoption.* (Michigan: Folio One Publishing, 1997)

Preparing Family and Friends

Coughlin, Amy and Caryn Abramowitz. *Cross Cultural Adoption: How To Answer Questions from Family, Friends & Community.* (Washington, DC: Lifeline Press, 2004)

Johnston, Patricia Irwin. *Adoption Is A Family Affair! What Relatives and Friends Must Know.* (Indianapolis: Perspectives Press, Inc., 2001)

Changes of Heart

"Saying 'No' . . . Thoughts on Declining a Referral" on AdoptKorea.com www.adoptkorea.com/Referral/Referral.htm

Craft, Carrie. "Saying 'No' to A Child Referral" on About.com adoption.about.com/od/international/a/declinereferral.htm

Russell, Marlou PhD. "Hello Before Goodbye." Adopting.org www.adopting.org/adoptions/hello-before-goodbye-domestic-infant-adoption.html

CHAPTER 14

Planning for a Happy Homecoming

It comes—that call, that email, that FedEx package—and suddenly, it's real. You are about to be a parent. Now all of the anticipation, all of the preparation comes down to one thing—a round of last minute panicked planning to get details in order before your child comes home.

Warning: parenting is not what you have fantasized that it will be. It's much better. It's also worse. Parenting—more than any other "new" situation you have had in your life—is a transformative experience, guaranteed to change your expectations, your plans, your opinions, your politics, your priorities, your relationships—everything!

Traveling to Meet Your Child

More and more adoptive parents of children born both in-country and abroad are finding that their child's arrival will not be on the parents' home turf. Whether it's traveling to another country for several days or weeks (and occasionally for months) in order to meet that country's requirements for adopting parents, or whether it's flying to a city across the country to be in the labor room in a birthmother's home town and then waiting several days for Interstate Compact paperwork to be done, traveling to adopt has become common. Following are some practical tips experienced parents offer parents-to-be who will travel.

- Parents of internationally adopted children strongly suggest that you use various Internet chat groups (e.g. FRUA, FCC, EEadopt, Guatemala-adopt) to connect to families who have traveled within the last six months to a year, at most, to the region from which you are adopting. Recent travelers will be able to offer practical suggestions for availability and reliability of cell phones, email, and faxes; lodging options; shopping; transportation; sightseeing; and more.

- Use those same groups to determine before leaving home whether the area to which you will need to travel is remote enough that you should buy diapering and feeding supplies, or toilet paper, soap, bug spray, or something equally important and geography-, culture- or climate-specific before heading out of the "big city" where you landed.

- Think about insurance. Review your health policy to determine how to obtain care when away from home or out of the country. Do your health or homeowner's policies offer the option of evacuation coverage should you become seriously ill and in need of medical transport home? Since dates may well change, you would be wise to avoid "bargain" plane tickets and to consider trip insurance for your flight plans.

- In addition to connecting ahead of time with an adoption medical specialist to whom you can email or fax back information about your referral, be certain to contact your own doctor or ask him to refer you to an infectious disease specialist who can help you to determine what inoculations would be wise to have (if not required) and what medications to take with you to help you with certain predictable travel problems or illnesses.

- Pack as lightly as possible, many parents suggested. Take mix and match and layer-able clothing designed for traveling that, when laundering facilities are not available, can be easily washed out and hung in a hotel room to dry. The less luggage you have to keep track of the better.

- Karen wrote that because she had to spend several weeks in another state in order to accomplish her baby's adoption, she chose to care for her baby in a suite-style hotel, with a sitting room and kitchenette, rather than in a normal bed and bath hotel room. The nearer-to-home-like atmosphere allowed her to eat most meals in and stay "cocooned" with her son for nearly two weeks before she brought him home. "Although nothing can compare to home," she wrote, "suite-style hotels are nice. We treasured this time alone with our baby and the opportunity to bond in privacy. Once we returned home, our house was like Grand Central Station for the next several weeks."

- Alana's husband stayed at home with their older children, so she took an older family friend along with her to the country where her child waited. An experienced traveler, this "surrogate grandma" was of invaluable assistance to a stressed out mom in handling the logistics of flagging down taxis, seeking help in finding a pharmacy, keeping track of tickets, etc.

- In addition to taking contact information with you for how to reach your adoption doctor or your pediatrician back home, know the name of a pediatrician in the area. (If you are outside your homeland, make sure that this person speaks English.)
- If you are bringing a child home from the hospital, take down the number of the newborn nursery at the place where your child is born. "I called that number in the middle of the night, since I was away from home without Grandma!" Denise wrote. "The nurses were wonderful!"
- Many parents emphasized the importance of using any travel opportunity to take videos and photographs of the place where your child was born and any and all buildings of significance—the hospital, the orphanage or the adoption agency; the spot where the child was left.
- Remember, as well, international parents suggested, to bring home samples of local art and crafts. Visit a bookstore and stock up on books about the country, and its foods and culture. Buy children's books in the native language (especially fun are translated copies of universal classics like *Goodnight Moon*). While waiting to fly home from another country, experiment with local foods and buy tapes of local music. Many of these items can later become the core of your child's life book or arrival box.

Dr. George Rogu's adoptiondoctors.com site has an especially helpful article on health and safety issues for families and children traveling abroad, that is applicable to domestic travelers as well. Find the link to this in the Resources section and be sure to read it.

Transitions

Though you can do little to influence your child's experiences prior to his coming home to you, you *can* make an impact on his having a child-friendly transition to you. For example,

- No matter the age of the child you will be adopting, you can ask those who are working with your child to make a transitional plan that is adoption-friendly for his age. While every social worker *should* have received careful training about child-friendly steps in transitioning children between homes, many have not. Excellent suggestions for designing and implementing age-appropriate child-friendly transitions can be found in two books in the Attachment section of this chapter's Resources. Dr. Vera Fahlberg's book *A Child's Journey through Placement* and Deborah Gray's *Nurturing Adoptions* both offer step-by-step suggestions for transitioning infants through teens.

- If you will be adopting an infant domestically, you can hope that interim care will be used only as a last resort and, thinking in that child-centered way, perhaps you will have made the choice to foster this child during any interim period before a firm placement can be made, putting *yourself* (an adult) at risk for emotional pain if he were to be moved back to his family of origin rather than putting the *child* you hope to adopt at risk of an unnecessary move.

- In a domestic adoption, you can ask to be involved in the interim care planning when it comes to making selections about types of bottles, brand of formula, or pacifier to be used with a baby. At the very least, if you can't contribute to the decisions, you can make sure that you know what these choices were so that you can follow them too—an important way to keep as much continuity as possible in your child's transition to you.

- You can offer to provide the foster parent or orphanage caring for a young child with sheets, blankets, a pacifier, and a music box, which will come back to you with the child.

- In an international adoption, on a first trip to his home country you can leave a scrapbook with pictures of your home, your family, and your pets with the child to whom you commit, hoping that workers will find time to look over them with him before you return.

- You can encourage an attachment-friendly transition by learning your child's care from his prior caretakers, and through back and forth visiting over a several day period between you and the foster home or between your hotel and the orphanage.

- You can do the research necessary to plug you in, in advance, to potential sources of help and support—from professionals, from family support groups, and more.

Entrustments and Other Rituals

Many families wanting to contribute to this book and the two it replaces contacted me about the issue of ceremonial starting points for their adoptions. Some of those who weighed in on this did so because they felt sad that they had not had this kind of formal beginning experience and hoped to encourage others to plan for them. Others wrote to express their retrospective gratitude that the intermediaries involved in helping in their adoptions had indeed arranged for such a ritual when they themselves would not have realized that there might be a need for one.

Many have compared adoptions to marriages, in that they involve the deliberate choice to take an unrelated person into a family and so necessitate making sure that the extended families develop working relationships. My own resistance to such an analogy rests on two important differences between adoption and marriage. The first is that in modern Western world marriages the principal parties all make their own personal choices rather than having marriages "arranged;" while in infant adoptions, the central party—the child—is quite powerless, and in fact, is at the mercy of a number of adults who purport to have his best interests at heart but don't always. The second is that the blending of families in a healthy marriage, while often tinged with a bit of sadness and apprehension on the parts of the parents who are "losing" a child in order to "gain" another, are rooted in joy. Adoptions, on the other hand, nearly always involve a basic imbalance: joy for the adopting family, and grief and loss for the birthfamily. These reservations taken into account, one thing about the marriage analogy that does work is its dependence on a ritualized and often very public ceremonial beginning that involves the participants making pledges to one another before family and friends, who in turn celebrate the launching of the new family into what all will hope are happy lives.

A few agencies—especially agencies with religious affiliations—have been using adoption rituals for many years. When adoptions are confidential, these ceremonies usually involve some members of the agency's staff, the adopting parents and sometimes members of their families, the new child, and perhaps a clergyperson. Though serious, these occasions have been celebratory rituals. As adoptions have become more communicative, letters from birthparents have been included.

The advent of open adoptions has led to the participation of birthparents and perhaps their extended families in a ceremony designed to give two sets of parents a formal opportunity to acknowledge their responsibility for the adoption plan, as well as their separate yet cooperative roles in the life of the child whose adoption is being launched. Often these dual family rituals in open adoptions are called *entrustment ceremonies* and involve the formal, concrete, handing over of a baby by a birthmother to adopting parents.

> Mary Anne Maiser is a social worker at Minnesota's Children's Home Society and Family Services, an old and large agency which has facilitated both domestic and international adoptions for years. Originally the adoptions were only done confidentially, but now include open adoptions as well. Mary Anne advocates on behalf of the need for entrustment ceremonies in all kinds of adoptions—confidential and open, domestic and international—and suggests that, while such rituals always have many things in common, each needs to be personalized for the particular circumstances of one baby and his families. Professionals always seem to understand that such a ceremony will likely trigger a birthparent's grief and loss, resulting in the need for strong and effective support, says Mary Anne, but she believes that many professionals have not done as effective a job preparing adopting parents for facing this surfacing loss. When adopters aren't well-prepared to face birthparents' grief firsthand, they may be overcome with guilt, which

has the potential for interfering with their ability to claim and attach
to their new baby.

Though less common, a few agencies focused on moving fostered children to permanency have also used planned rituals. These rituals may not
include birthparents, but they should involve foster caregivers and perhaps
any extended family members with whom the child remains in touch. These
current and past care providers are charged with sending clear messages
to the child that the move is permanent, that it is positive, and that those
who have cared about him want him to do well in his new home. Especially
with these older children, who have a store of very real memories of and
commitments to former families or caregivers, it is important to involve
adoptees themselves in planning these events, which can give them hope
and a sense of claiming their new families.

Such a climate is a far cry from the situations that occur for far too
many older children, who are sometimes told by orphanage workers or
roommates that they can expect to become organ donors in their new country, or by foster care providers that their behavior will get them thrown out
of the next home too.

In child-centered adoptions—whether open and communicative or
confidential—professionals and those they are counseling must understand
that entrustment rituals represent both endings and beginnings. They have
in common some of the emotional responses of both marriages and funerals. This requires that professionals, too, make a commitment in an entrustment—a commitment to ongoing support of the child and his birth and
adoptive parents—rather than allowing the ceremony to represent an end
to professional involvements.

Poetry, prayers, music, essays, pledges, and gifts are elements of many
adoption rituals. Many families take great pleasure and pride in fully cus-
tomizing their event. Others look for existing structures within which to
work. Though the Catholic Church, Judaism, and several denominations
of protestant Christianity have some formal rituals that can be effectively
adapted, and many agencies have gathered materials used by previous families, those who are planning an adoption ritual may also find helpful some
of the books, Internet articles, and other materials listed in the Resources
section.

Adoption entrustments don't take the place of other cultural symbols
and practices families use to celebrate their children's arrivals. Jewish families will still want to have formal conversion, complete with mikvah for
older children, a formal bris for their infant sons, and a naming for their
daughters; Christian families will still christen, baptize, or dedicate their
children, yet an adoption ritual provides one way for parents and their
extended families to acknowledge adoption's difference, to express their
support for a baby's full cultural heritage of origin, and to promote attachment between new parents and child.

Home at Last

Karen's Grand Central Station image at the beginning of this chapter rings familiar to many adoptive parents. One of the most challenging aspects of the actual arrival of your long-awaited child will be coping with the tumult! After months of being oh-so-ready, arrival can sometimes become mass confusion. The excitement of others often tends to produce too much of a good thing. It is not uncommon for adopting parents to experience what I've come to call Cinderella Syndrome, finding themselves cooking and cleaning for visiting guests who are delighted to come, visit and play with the new child, but who have overlooked or forgotten how much of new parents' exhaustion after a new child's arrival has to do with the lack of sleep and adaptation to massive change as much as it has to do with the physical recovery from having given birth, and so they behave as guests. There are several things you can do in the months in advance of your child's arrival to prepare to deal with or prevent Cinderella Syndrome.

- Speak to your child's prospective grandparents, aunts and uncles, and to family friends about your needs for the first weeks after arrival, finding ways to include them which will not deplete your energies. Obviously you want your extended family to claim your child as their own, but you may find it awkward to encourage this while at the same time dealing with your nuclear family's needs to cocoon and attach. If your family members live nearby, this may be easier to accomplish than if they live in other cities, as you will be able to limit and stagger visiting times. If they will be visiting from out of town, discuss with your family before arrival time what arrangements will need to be made. Would you prefer that they stay in a hotel this time? Can they be helpful to you in other ways as you attend to your new baby's physical and emotional needs? Would it be better to send snapshots or videotapes for them to view on arrival day and to speak frequently by phone for the first week or so before planning for them to come for a visit?

- In advance of the placement, advise local friends, co-workers, and neighbors of your family's need to have quiet, private time together for a few days before opening yourselves to visitors. A practical way to handle this is to let everyone know that you will be holding an open house on a weekend afternoon a few weeks after your child's arrival. Suggest to some that arranging for refreshments and/or helping with preparation and cleanup for this open house would be a welcome and much appreciated baby gift.

- Arrange for your telephone to be answered by machine for a week or more. The message might announce your news and explain that the chaos of settling in prevents you from taking phone calls or visits for a few days, thank them for their congratulations and good wishes, and promise to return their calls as soon as possible.

- Prepare and freeze some microwaveable main dishes or collect restaurant take-out menus and set aside budgeted money for extra help with meals—or suggest prepared meals as a welcome baby gift.

- Consider budgeting for professional assistance with housecleaning during the first weeks after arrival (you might mention this as a welcome baby gift from grandparents-to-be).

- If you are adopting a newborn, you might find the assistance of a doula helpful. Doulas are trained and certified to help and support new mothers. Post-partum (after birth) doulas offer support, information and education about baby care, help new mothers learn soothing techniques for their babies, and work with siblings to introduce the new baby and teach about his safety needs. Some doulas do light housework or meal preparation while new parents are adjusting to their roles.

When parents give birth there are certain expectations related to the physical process of giving birth which trigger much needed support for the family. The physical experience of labor and delivery has been a strain, so there is the expectation that Mom will be sore and tired. She is usually given some resting space. If she births in a hospital setting, visiting hours may mandate that visitors be limited. Traditionally, in many families, grandparents arrive to help with housekeeping so that Mother and Baby can have time alone. As times have changed and extended family members have become more and more likely to have jobs which make their participation difficult, some families have hired doulas for this purpose. Friends bring or send in meals, or offer to run errands.

When families adopt—and even more so when they adopt a child who is not newborn—traditional supportive steps are often left out. They shouldn't be! If you had given birth, would your mom have expected to come and help? Why? Not just because you would be recovering from a physical trauma, but also because this is a way that families claim new members. Mothers and mothers-in-law teach their sons and daughters about parenting—in the past, these women took on the role of doulas. Don't deny yourself, your mother, or your child this same experience just because you're adopting. And whatever you do, don't risk being disappointed that your mother may not figure this out on her own. Tell her in advance that you'll need her help when the toddler arrives. Pull her into your joy.

Circling the Wagons

But there is a balance to be achieved here. We want to encourage family members and close friends to help us "claim" our new children, but part of the process of claiming a new family member and forming attachments involves behaviors that I call *circling the wagons*. Others refer to this as *cocooning*. By any terminology, the point is to create an almost ritualized time and space for shutting off the outside world and allowing only immediate family members access to the child and his parents. Nearly all families do this to some extent or another, but for adoption-expanded families it can carry more significance, whether the new child will arrive as a newborn or at an older age. The intimacy of such a cocooning time produces fewer distractions and lessens the risk of over-stimulation as new parents, siblings, and children come to know one another in the privacy of their home. Wagon-circling is healthy behavior, and it is rarely questioned—or even noticed—by most non-family members, who seem to take such behavior pretty much for granted.

Yet cocooning can be misinterpreted by two groups of people who are important to adopting parents and their child. One group consists of friends whose bond with the adopters is constructed out of the shared experience of waiting to adopt. If you are "first," you may find that still-waiting friends are particularly sensitive to anything that makes them feel you've "forgotten" them. Also sensitive to the feeling of being slighted by wagon-circling behavior are birthparents in open adoptions who have most often been completely unprepared for this possibility (as have most adopters). Since cocooning usually happens very soon after a baby's arrival, birthparents are likely to face this from their baby's adopters at exactly the same time that they are struggling with ambivalence about their adoption plan. They have just begun to react to adoption's grief and loss, when they suddenly feel held at arm's length from the baby and his family. Birthparents may feel some initial panic that the plan isn't going to work—that they have lost not just the baby, but the adopting parents to whom they had become attached and on whom they may have become emotionally dependent as well.

What to do about these two groups' reactions as you need to circle your wagons is easier said than done, yet to suggest that an entrance be broken open in that circle. This brief window of defensive intimacy can be an important part of your family's attaching. Adopters need to be aware of this necessity so as not to surprise themselves with it or feel guilty about it. They also need to figure out ways to deal with still-waiting friends and with birthparents. A solution to the problem is to have discussed this phenomenon in advance, and to expect other friends (perhaps other experienced adopters) to provide support to still-waiting adopters and the adoption intermediary to provide support for the baby's birthparents during this family time.

Family and Friends

Claiming is something members of families do over and over in both subtle and obvious ways whether the children were born to or adopted by the family. Having our children claimed by their grandparents, aunts, uncles and cousins is important for them, but sometimes we don't consciously recognize that it is important for us too. When we claim the children of our family's new generation, we reaffirm our own connections to the current and prior generations. When this claiming doesn't happen, those old feelings of inadequacy can be stirred again. The more important the loss of our genetic continuity was in our infertility experience, the more likely it is that you will find it especially important for your family to claim your children.

With the trend toward openness between birthfamilies and adopting families, it has become even more important to try to get family members prepared along with parents-to-be. Several families whose adoptions involved ongoing contact with their child's extended birthfamily have written to tell me of the unexpectedly difficult time they had with their own parents' ability to claim this new grandchild. The problems seemed to be of several types: fears that the frequent contact would result in a change of heart and the loss of the baby; the awkwardness—and to some degree competitiveness—these new grandparents felt towards the baby's grandparents by birth; discomfort having to do with relative ages of the members of the birthfamily; and awkwardness with the differences in socioeconomic and educational backgrounds.

> Micky's grandparents were aloof and cool when introduced to Micky's birthfamily on his naming day. "Why, we have almost nothing in common with 'those people,'" cried Grandma. "And that birthgrand-mother is closer to your older sister's age than to mine, Seth! What am I supposed to say?"

> Because they lived several hundred miles away from their son and his family, these grandparents had not had the opportunity to meet the birthfamily gradually over several months. What's more, that distance would also mean that their opportunities to interact with them—not to mention with their grandchild—would be limited in the future.

Experienced families suggested several possibilities for preventing or dealing with "grandparent problems."

- Helpful for the families of long distance grandparents was the realization that the difficult, and therefore infrequent, visits had become such special occasions that they had fallen into a trap of using them as an excuse to draw the larger extended birth and adoptive families together. Doing so had produced two negative side effects to bear upon their parents' claiming abilities. First, it prevented the adopting grandparents from having enough intimate, private time to form their own bond with their grandchild. Second, these very "public parties" at which the baby's adopting parents and birthfamily members displayed increasing comfort and intimacy with one another while the grandparents were making little forward progress in this regard, seemed to create jealousy and competition—especially in grandparents who had already been especially sensitive about the geographic distance between themselves and their children. Those families who were able to identify these problems (and it was sometimes the birthfamily members who were helpful in quietly pointing them out and offering suggestions), found it useful to change their habits. They suggested using grandparent visits for more focused family time.

- Families who had worked with service providers or who belonged to parent groups which did periodic "Grandparent Prep" programs were especially pleased with these pre-adoption opportunities for their parents and other extended family members to have the process of adoption demystified and the myths they believed corrected. They recommended them highly! Designing such programs to include time spent with the adopting parents and time spent without them in attendance allowed both interactive preparation and the opportunity to have private—and possibly embarrassing or hurtful—questions or thoughts addressed.

Adoptions of Indiana, an agency in Indianapolis, offers extended family sessions for families waiting to adopt transracially. While not required, in these sessions grandparents, aunts, and uncles are offered the opportunity to explore their (sometimes subconscious) biases in a safe environment before the new family member arrives. Additionally, AdIn welcomes grandparents-to-be to their adult children's preparation classes.

- Another way to encourage grandparent-claiming is to find ways to visit longer distance Grandmas and Grandpas with your child rather than having the grandparents come to you. Using frequent flyer miles to "alternate" who travels and when can offer distant grandparents the opportunity to introduce their new grandchild to their own friends and neighbors, adding themselves to the local grandparent "club."
- "Budgeting" conversations about, and sharing pictures of, birthfamily members was another suggestion. This careful attention to your own parents' needs helps them to establish their own relationship with their grandchild and lessens their predictable fears about what open adoption really means. As confidence grows, experienced adopters suggest, grandparents become more accepting of and comfortable with the openness in the adoption.

How our families feel about our children who have been adopted is important to us, as well as to the children, and it is worth our concentrated efforts to facilitate those attachments when we can. It is not unusual, however, for adopting parents to find certain family members or friends unwilling to consider a certain child one of the family. This apparent rejection may reflect general adoptism, be rooted in racism, or reflect intolerance for certain behaviors often seen in previously institutionalized, abused, neglected or otherwise traumatized children. Rejections like this can create strong resentments which may result in rifts. You will want to do all that you can to openly discuss your concerns and your hurt feelings with this relative before this becomes unresolvable.

Yet, while no one wants to perpetuate family rifts, the decision to distance oneself from a stubbornly unsupportive or critical relative reflects a good parent's strong need to protect her child and indicates the development of a healthy sense of entitlement between parents and child. Sometimes, we simply have to take a stand that alienates another but protects our child and our own family.

Getting the Info You Need to Begin Attaching

It's important that you have access to as much information about your child's previous life as possible. But what is it that you need to know? We all seem to know that it's important to find out about eating and sleeping schedules, or that favorite blankets, toys or a pacifier must be moved with babies. Sometimes, though, adopters are not taught that other familiar patterns contribute to the feeling of safety that leads to attachment.

Insist that you learn as much as can be gathered about each of your baby's previous environments and the routines there (see list which follows).Was his bottle propped or fed? (For example, drug exposed and preemie babies may have been fed in their isolets, often with their heads turned to one side, and so may not have learned to make eye contact.) Were there kids around or was it a quiet house? Did she experience just one or two caregivers, or was she cared for by staff members taking institutional shifts? If in family care, what was the family schedule? (For example, a child whose foster father worked a night shift has become used to an entirely different routine of when the house hums and when it is at rest than one who has spent time with day shift families.) Did the baby spend time in a daycare facility? What kind of car seat has been used with this child? Did they use a stroller, buggy, or personal carrier? A cradle, crib, hammock, or mat?

> In an article reprinted from New York's *Families with Children from China* newsletter in the Summer 1996 issue of *Roots & Wings*, Katherine Cobb described the way in which she and her husband Eric used their trip to China to pick up their daughter, Emily, to gather information they felt she would probably need in the future. In advance they had prepared an extensive list of questions about all of the known

circumstances surrounding her arrival in the orphanage, any known sociological background information, her physical and health history, her routine and eating and sleeping schedules at the orphanage, names of crib mates and nurses and the orphanage director at the time of her stay there, and more. As has been emphasized earlier, everything was written down. They made photocopies and took photographs of the written material that had been left with their daughter. Then the family visited the place in which Emily had been "abandoned' and took more pictures, noting other nearby landmarks that might help locate this place should its surroundings or use change in subsequent years.

Emily's family prepared themselves well for her longer term future needs, and you can prepare well too. But in her article, Emily's mother goes on to point out that they had been more fortunate than other members of their travel group who were adopting from different orphanages. In this case the staff of one particular orphanage, offended by a recent documentary on conditions in their country's orphanages—a documentary which had been made using concealed cameras by journalists posing as tourists—would not allow parents to visit the orphanage and sent a business person who knew little about the children's background as representative rather than a caregiver. These parents were denied the opportunity to explore their daughter's far and recent pasts in anticipation of her future needs. I share this because it emphasizes once again how important it is that all prospective and recent adoptors respect the law, rules, customs, and motivations of the people who have been caring for their children. The only way to support open communication between governments and U.S. agencies, between social workers and clients, between past caregivers and new parents is to behave respectfully.

For example, if, despite your wishing to have a smooth and child-friendly transition for your child, you are instead handed the child quickly in a single moment's transition (as is true for far too many parents) recognize that you will find yourself parenting a suddenly moved, frightened and confused child, but that all is not lost. The key will be flexibility on your part. Have a list ready of questions you would like to have answered, and pose them respectfully. Personalize them to the age, culture, and circumstances of your particular child.

1. Sleep: Did my child sleep in a crib or a bed, or on a mat? Was he alone or with other children? Was the room lighted at night? Did my child nap during the day? How often and for how long? Alone or with others? May I see the sleeping area?

2. Food: What foods is this child used to eating? Has he or she expressed any preferences (favorites and really disliked)? How is eating handled here—predictable schedule, on demand, or eating in groups? Does my child feed himself? (Especially try to determine

whether, if the child is using a bottle, it is propped.) What eating implements does this child use? Have any food allergies been noticed? Are there any allergies common to children of this ethnicity?

3. Name: Is the name this child is using the one given him by his birthfamily, or was it assigned by an orphanage, a foster care provider, a social worker, etc.? If this is not the first name that would have been listed on his birth record, may I know what that first name is?

4. Comfort Sources: How was this child comforted (held in arms for carrier, rocking, swinging, singing, pacifier, or left alone to cry it out)? Does this child self-stimulate for comfort (thumb sucking, rocking, head banging, singing to self, etc.)? Does he have favorite toys, or a blanket or pillow that can come with him if I replace it with new ones one for you? If the child has been cared for by a single care provider, ask for a shirt, sweater or smock that this person has worn and replace it with new.

5. Environmental History: How long has my child been living in her current situation? Where was she before and for how long? Has this child ever lived with birthfamily or extended family? What were the circumstances of her prior moves? Were they transitioned or sudden and done in an emergency? Was she abandoned (where)? Did the family bring her in voluntarily? If this is a domestic adoption, ask whether you might be able to speak with prior caregivers. If the child is being moved from the foster care system, ask for a copy of her lifebook. If there is no lifebook, get the caseworker's commitment to helping you build one.

6. Health: Please provide the health file on this child in which health milestones (height and weight, immunizations, outcome of all medical educational testing, etc.) have been recorded. Is there any physical and mental health or social history information on this child's birthfamily? Does this child have any allergies? Have children here been recently exposed to any illnesses, infestations, or infections that I should watch for?

7. You know this child so well, Caregiver. What else can you tell me about my child that will help me understand how he thinks, how he reacts, how he behaves? What are some things about this child—both positive and negative—that make him himself?

Pre- and Post-Arrival Strategies for Promoting Attachment

Before we get to some practical pointers for promoting attachment, I want to reiterate that I am not a therapist, nor am I an attachment expert. What I am is an adoption educator and an adoptive parent. What I have learned—and therefore am able to share with you—is based on three generations of Johnston family personal experiences and the intensive efforts we have made to learn more about our own situation. In addition to my personal experiences, I am able to share learned knowledge from attachment literature mostly focusing on older children, and confirming anecdotal evidence shared with me by literally hundreds of adopters. These adopters have seen themselves and their family's experiences reflected in the anecdotes I have shared in the trainings I have been doing throughout the U.S. and Canada over many years. After every session I have conducted on claiming and attaching in which I shared personal family anecdotes, at least one or two parents (and usually many more) approach me to exclaim that they never realized what it was they were dealing with—when, riddled with guilt that their babies didn't seem to fit smoothly into their families and their lives, they lived with a grieving infant.

I've said before, but I think it bears repeating, that the younger the child at arrival, the more likely it has been that these families have not shared their stories with anyone before telling them to me—not with their caseworkers, not with their families, not even with other adopters. Why? Because no one had ever mentioned the possibility of attachment problems with an infant to them before (especially during their parent prep process). They had assumed—for over 40 years in three separate cases about which I know—that the only possible reason for their awkward beginnings with their babies had been because they were not "good enough" parents. Having been given the equivalent of a Good Housekeeping Seal of Approval as perfect prospective parents upon completing a homestudy, these adopters were afraid to go to their adoption workers to ask questions about what they were experiencing. They feared that in doing so they could risk losing their child by admitting to their caseworker—the most powerful person they had had contact with in their family-building experience—that there were problems. Do *not* follow this model! Reach out if you suspect that you need help!

No matter his age at arrival, as soon as he arrives, plan to take full advantage of whatever opportunities you have for private time with your child to learn what makes him unique and to allow him to get used to you as well. Family therapist Michael Gurian (*The Wonder of Boys* and *The Wonder of Girls*) calls this process nurturing the nature of your child. His practical book *Nurture the Nature: Understanding and Supporting Your Child's Unique Core Personality* (John Wiley & Sons, 2007) would be an excellent book to read while in the late stages of anticipation—perhaps on a plane ride to an internationally adopted child's country. You can then take advantage of what you have learned during those frustrating days (or weeks) in temporary quarters waiting for bureaucracy to grind away. Parents who travel out of state or out of country often rush to return home, where they are initially thrilled by the welcoming celebration, but most adoptive parents have found that taking advantage of a few days or weeks of privacy has its advantages.

For children who must move from an environment in which they feel secure, transferring attachment to a new parent will be enhanced by efforts to avoid overstimulating them and to maintain as many familiar sensory elements as possible. It's a poor idea to flood an older child with a vacation, special events, new toys and games, etc. in his first weeks at home. Keep him close to you—don't start school yet—as you allow him, and yourself, to adjust to an entirely new environment.

Children (and especially babies) are highly sensory beings. Because their primary intellectual task during the first few months involves learning to use all of their senses and developing motor skills, each of a baby's senses is finely tuned and he is acutely aware of changes. His environment is defined by all of his senses: how things look, taste, smell, feel, and sound. Preschool-aged children who have experienced several moves between caregivers and those who have been cared for in institutional settings are frequently emotionally and developmentally delayed, so that thinking of them as infant-like while helping them to develop attachments makes sense too.

Families adopting internationally and the professionals working with them seemed to acknowledge these needs earlier than have those working with domestic infant adoption. Magazines such as *Adoptive Families* (and its predecessor *Ours*) and *Roots & Wings* have through the years featured articles on the adjustment difficulties common to children arriving from India, Asia, and South America. The symptoms discussed are the symptoms of grieving, as these children dealt with the loss of the familiar—familiar caretakers, familiar food, familiar sounds, familiar smells, familiar voices and language, familiar culture—and were forced to make a transitional adaptation. In a powerful example of David Kirk's Shared Fate theory in action, it has been those adopters who were, by virtue of the obvious in their family, unable to reject or deny difference and instead were forced to acknowledge it, who have led the way in dealing with this important adoption-related issue.

Being asked to maintain the familiar for the baby's sake is sometimes a difficult thing for new adopters to hear. In finally claiming for themselves the title of parent, new adopters had expected that it would be their role and their unquestioned right to make all of the decisions that new parents make—decisions about nursery decor and wardrobe, about feeding, about a comfort cycle, about family routine, etc. Now being asked to "adapt" to a parenting style and routines already established by birthparents, foster parents, or group home workers may remind adopters once again that their family's beginnings are different from the beginnings of families built by birth. They may balk at feeling out of control once more and vow to do things their own way despite suggestions from others.

Promoting attachment, however, lends itself to a whole style of parenting in which parents promote intimacy by responding to the child's cues rather than imposing their own will upon her. The pediatrician and author William Sears, MD, actually calls this style "attachment parenting." Dr. Sears writes for the general population of parents, so his focus is not adoption and some of the things he writes may not feel particularly sensitive to adoption. On the other hand, Sears believes this "tuning in" approach to parenting carries over into closer relationships between parent and child that will lead those children to become better parents themselves.

Similarly, the brilliant books of the neuropsychiatrist Dr. Daniel Siegel (see Resources) synthesize "neurobiological research and clinical expertise (and) should forever lay to rest the mind-brain dichotomy . . . including highly readable descriptions of brain development, information processing, models of memory and narrative, and the importance of attachment in human development."[1] Siegel uses the concept of *mindsightful awareness* to suggest that attachment is an attunement-based link between any two human brains.

The older your baby is at placement, the more significant transition issues may be for him. Please try to recognize your resistance to being told how to parent as a leftover loss-of-control issue and attempt to be flexible here. Over the long haul, your willingness to compromise during transition, to allow your child's reactions to prior experiences both bad and good to lead you as his parent so that you gradually introduce your child to the new sensory experiences and routines which reflect your own preferences, may result in fewer adoption-connected problems or differences later.

The following pages offer you suggestions for addressing ways to incorporate the familiar into your baby's routine. Some of the suggestions are proactive. They are things you can do to try to put your "personal stamp" on the environment in which your child will spend his time before he comes to your home. Parents whose children will continue to live in an orphanage or in foster care in another country after they've already been "assigned" may find some of these tips useful, as may those whose children will move temporarily after birth to a domestic foster home and those whose children will need to spend time in a neonatal nursery. You may be able to send ahead some items that can help your child adapt to his family-to-be such as blankets, toys, pictures and posters, and cassette tapes (nothing of heirloom quality or irreplaceable family significance). Even if this adoption does not come to be, what will you have lost by providing these inexpensive items? Other suggestions are reactive. These are some ways that you can adapt and retrofit your home's environment to include some of the familiar comforts of the place in which your child lived before he came home to you.

Keep in mind what we've said about overstimulation. Babies are individuals, and some babies are hypersensitive to stimulation. Some babies are able to handle only one source of stimulation at a time—visual, tactile, auditory, etc. If your baby seems to have difficulty calming even though his expressed needs appear to have been met, be especially gentle. Don't bounce, rock or swing, for example. Perhaps don't pat or sing. Try swaddling her and holding her close in a still, darkened room. Watch and listen for your baby's cues, but cut yourself a little slack about how quickly you are able to interpret those cues.

Visual Connections

Consider your child's sense of sight. His move has brought him into an entirely different place. If he has spent several weeks, or even months or years in another location, sights there have grown familiar. Consider your home from his visual perspective. The lighting is different now, the wallpaper or paint is different, new faces appear above his crib (and, for children adopted internationally or trans-ethnically, these faces may be shaped and colored differently from those he is used to). Even the view outside his window—perhaps at a different latitude and possibly a different climate—may seem brighter or more dull, greener or less green that the familiar place in which he has spent most of his time to now.

In situations where you know about your child from before or at birth but he must go to temporary foster care (sometimes called cradle care), you may be able to request that when possible your child's caregivers consider your wishes about light. You might even give the foster caregivers a particular night light and ask them to plug it in the baby's room, or a particular poster to hang on the wall or ceiling around his crib. More often you will need to borrow from the earlier caregivers' leads, in acknowledgment of the fact that moved babies are susceptible to overstimulation, perhaps leaving the walls neutral for a while and then slowly adding in the visual stimuli—mobiles, colorful borders—that you want for your child.

The older your child is at arrival, the more likely she is to be in tune to the body language of others. Making eye contact is an important part of human connection, and it becomes even more important that you work to make eye contact if your older child does not understand your words, spoken in a language he does not yet understand.

Older children may benefit from having seen pictures of new parents, their pets, and their home arranged in an album to be shared with them over and over before new parents come to take them home. They may have strong preferences that they can express about light, color, and other visual stimuli. Reactions to some of these visual cues (e.g. men with beards, large animals, women with long fingernails) may even help you to decipher prior traumatic events that will eventually need to be worked on in therapy.

Whenever possible, try to see and photograph or videotape the place or places where your child has been living. Why the pictures? Not only will they come in handy in later years for helping your child understand his personal story, but right now, in the excitement of arrival, you are particularly prone to "forget" details that may be helpful to you in the next weeks. Note the colors on the walls and floors, the posters and pictures, the plants and animals. How is the room lighted? What might you be able to do to simulate sights with which your child is familiar?

Lighting, for example, is one thing that can be fairly easily replicated. Will the room have darkening shades or not? Has a night light been in use? A child who has spent significant time in a hospital nursery or in some orphanages may have been exposed to bright lighting overhead both day and night. You can adapt the lighting in your child's new room to approximate the kinds of lighting he may have grown used to. If that lighting is not comfortable for you, by using a dimmer switch, you can very gradually adjust the amount of light as your child adjusts to his new home.

Scent and Fragrance

A youngster's sense of smell is stimulated by a variety of odors in his environment, and humans store the odors they know in long-term memory. Every habitat, every workplace has an odor that is its own. When you go back to your parents' home today, do you notice upon entering that it "smells like home?" When you open your partner's closet, do you smell him or her there? When you enter your workplace, do you notice a familiar odor comprised of the product of that workplace (e.g. paints, toners, fabrics, papers, chemicals, the carpeting, the smoking or non-smoking)? Your favorite restaurant is permeated by, among other things, the cooking smells associated with the herbs, spices, and other foods that draw you back there again and again. These kinds of "friendly" fragrances create emotional responses, but so the odors we subconsciously associate from a frightening experience in our pasts. What distinctive odors are part of your home—your baby's new home?

Observe or ask about your baby's previous environments. Did incense scent the room? Use candles in your home. What colognes, soaps, powders, deodorants, detergents, fabric softeners, cleaning products, and cooking odors were a normal part of your child's prior environment? Sheets and blankets washed with the same detergent or tumbled with the same fabric softener strips as those used by a foster mom can make a new bed seem more like home. If you will be traveling to another country, you may wish to purchase local soaps or detergents to take home with you. Might you and your partner use some of those earlier-known scents for a while in order to give your baby a sense of the familiar? If not, then be sure, at least to be consistent with the scents that you yourself use, waiting a while to try a new aftershave or cologne. Your child will appreciate the consistency.

Whenever possible, ask to take actual blankets or clothing with which the baby may be familiar home with you. Frequently those adopting internationally will find that the foster parents caring lovingly for their child are so poor that they are hesitant about allowing the adopting parents to keep anything. Mary Hopkins-Best, in her book *Toddler Adoption: The Weaver's Craft* (Perspectives Press, 1997) suggests planning ahead for this eventuality. Most foster parents and nursery supervisors are more than willing to trade old linens and clothing for new, she suggests.

Research seems to indicate that newborn babies quickly come to identify their birthmothers by smell—both through the pheromones generated by their bodies and the unique fragrance of their breast milk. If your adoption is an open one and your child's birthmother will have cared for him for a time, you may wish to ask your baby's birthmother to give you a tee shirt she has worn which you can wear (without washing her smell out of it) for several days at home as your baby gets used to you. If your child has spent several weeks with a single foster caregiver, you might make the same request of that person.

> Therapist and open adoption expert Sharon Roszia observes for both parents and professionals that supporting and encouraging these kinds of interlinks in transitioning between birth and adoptive (or foster and adoptive) families can offer benefits to the adults, as well as the child, diminishing any possible feeling that one is "taking something away from" or "beholden to" the other and helping each feel that together they are a "team" working on behalf of a baby they both love.

The Taste of Home

Food provides both nourishment and comfort. The taste of his mother's breast milk or of the formula he is used to drinking are a part of the familiar. Cultural staples—from potatoes to kimchee—are familiar and comforting. If your newborn has been breast-fed by his birthmother, you may wish to consider asking her to freeze some milk for your later use. If the child has been breast-fed and his new mother intends to try adoptive nursing, keep in mind that skin "taste" will change and may occasionally cause initial confusion for baby.

Formula brands and formulations are different between countries. When traveling to another country, it would be wise for you to purchase and take home with you a supply of the local formula to help in transition. If a change of food is absolutely necessary, ask your doctor for directions about mixing the formula originally used with the new one in order to transition for several days or even weeks.

All of us associate the tastes, temperatures, and textures of certain foods with comfort. Older children have surely developed certain preferences in taste. Ask about the favorite menus in your child's foster home or orphanage. As you offer new foods, be aware that many of the things most familiar and common to you may not be familiar to your older child. Perhaps he has never tasted strawberries, eaten macaroni and cheese, or been introduced to peanut butter and jelly. He may acquire a taste for these things, but you must also consider acquiring a taste for some of the foods with which he is already familiar, as they may be a part of his cultural identity.

As time goes by, your child's identity as a part of your own family will be reinforced with memories related to taste and to other senses. It can be important—especially when your child arrives at an older age—that you very deliberately develop and reinforce sensory-related memories that help them claim their home with you.

> Among the local cousins in my children's extended family, we have established a holiday routine that is over 25 years old now, and is following these kids—ranging in age from 16 years and older—as they grow to adulthood, into their own homes. It revolves around holiday baking, an all day event. Daddy (Dave) loves the iced raisin-filled cookies that he associates with his grandmother, Ella Brisbee Rohrer and the other cousins' dad (Uncle Erv) loves them too. This is a complicated recipe—the dough made the night before and chilled; the filling cooked on the stove top and then cooled; the cookies rolled, cut, filled, topped, baked and then finally iced before quite cool. I love the much simpler pecan crispies made by my grandmother, Nina Short Irwin, but there's no getting away with not making raisin cookies at least once a year. We add to these holly berry treats—an adaptation of Rice Krispy treats made with corn flakes and cinnamon imperials.
>
> So on a Saturday in December, we all gather in Aunt Patty's kitchen with holiday music playing in the background. When the "good" cookies are completed, the fun part begins: out come the Chanukah and Christmas shaped cutters and the "leftover" dough is rolled and cut, and then iced in riotous colors and sprinkled. The kids laugh that they don't even like these end of the session cookies—but Uncle Bud does! The cookies are packed and hand-delivered or sent off to anyone who can't make it "home" for the holidays.
>
> One cousin has lived away for almost ten years, but he expects those cookies. Now, two of the cousins are married. Next year this may move to a different kitchen, but I really can't imagine that the tradition will not carry on.

Touch, Shape, and Texture

Your child's tactile senses quickly help him respond to the shape of a trusted caretaker's body, the touch of her fingers, her rough or gentle handling, to a manner of being carried and cuddled (arms, backpack, frontpack, sling, rocking chair, hammock, etc.), to the softness of a particular mattress or the firmness of a sleeping mat, to the texture of clothing and bedcoverings, or to the shape and firmness of a particular latex nipple or pacifier.

In some situations you may be able to send blankets and clothes, and/or a supply of a particular brand of nursers and nipples to be used for the baby who will be yours. In other cases you may be called upon to adapt to the textures your baby has already grown used to. Though you can't change your body shape, understanding that a baby may be missing the soft shape of his plump foster mother as he struggles to get comfortable against a new dad's flatter and more athletic frame will help you to understand what he's working on.

Pay attention to how your child comforts himself. Perhaps he feels more secure when wrapped up. He may have been swaddled in his early days. You can recreate that sense of comfort for a toddler by wrapping him in a soft blanket and taking him up onto your lap for a story.

Make time and opportunity for quiet skin-to-skin contact, perhaps taking a young child into bed with you for a while late at night or early in the morning, for example. Some parents swear by the positive effects of a Family Bed routine (which works especially well with adoptive nursing), while others feel strongly that everyone in the family benefits from separate sleeping spaces. Those adopting internationally may find that their children have slept in crowded rooms or shared bedding with others and so may be comforted by the warmth, touch, and sounds of similar sleeping arrangements, at least in the beginning. Tuning in to your child, as well as yourself and your parenting partner, will help you decide what is best for your family.

> Once after my children were long past babyhood I sat looking through photo albums of those years. Interesting, I thought, how many of those first-year pictures of Mommy and Joel, Mommy and Erica, Mommy and Lindsey were of Mommy wearing Baby—in a Snuggli™ or in a hip sling, and eventually in a backpack, at the kitchen counter, in the backyard, on a bike, on a mountain trail. Why, I remembered, for four years my driver's license photo had shown the back of Lindsey's fuzzy five-month-old head rising beneath my chin. I had indeed enjoyed having my babies close to me, and, for the most part, they had too. In retrospect I think that my tendency to "wear" my babies for six months or so was my subconscious substitution for the months I wasn't pregnant with them. I wore them to make up to myself and to them what we had missed together.

Many believe that bathing with Baby or taking him to a heated swimming pool and walking slowly through warm water with his head on your shoulder, and speaking or singing softly into his ear recalls for him the security of floating in the amniotic pool of his birthmother's womb and relaxes him, tuning him in for the opportunity to bond. (Indeed, this exercise and its continuation through Mom and Baby swim-n-gym classes was part of what was helpful for our unhappy daughter, who now—coincidentally or not—is a competitive swimmer.)

Older children—especially those who may have been abused—may want very much to avoid touch that seems perfectly friendly to you. Find ways to win "touch-trust" with your child gradually. A little girl may like having her hair brushed or her nails painted. Eventually such a routine can lead to a shoulder rub. Congratulate that tough guy on his good test result with a pat on the back. Offer to put lotion on his sore muscles.

Some children are born with—or develop in an institutional setting— special sensitivities to texture and taste. This is more than just a preference for soft or scratchy. Instead it is a strong preference for or avoidance of certain textures. Such a kid may be hyperstimulated by labels on shirts (cut them out) or may refuse to wear scratchy sweaters (sorry, Grandma, we appreciate the effort, but a sweatshirt is needed here). Mention these sensory sensitivities to your child's doctor. They could be—but often are not—signs of a sensory integration disorder that can manifest itself in other ways as well.

Sound and Silence

From before his birth, noises have surrounded your child, and even as a newborn his sense of hearing is acute. Babies hear their birthmothers' voices, and research has shown that they can be calmed both in utero and after birth by music they have grown accustomed to hearing before their births. From a bustling city's teaching hospital's echoing, uncarpeted intensive care nursery or a rural orphanage in a country far away, your child may now be moving to your quiet, lushly carpeted, suburban, previously childless home. He may have lived in a group facility where ethnic music, American country or classical jazz played in the background, or in a tiny apartment where bustling traffic filtered constantly from the streets outside, or where television provided background noise throughout the day and evening. A fan or a humidifier may have hummed day and night. He may have been surrounded by the voices of many children and the vocalizations of pets, or he may have spent time with a single, childless foster mother. The voices this baby, or older boy or girl heard had a particular rhythm, tone and timbre, and those voices may not have been speaking your language.

If you are observant and creative you can duplicate many of the sounds to which your baby has grown accustomed. Ask whether his birthmother or his foster caregiver would be willing to record stories or songs to be played for him at quiet times. If your adoption will be open, discuss whether your child's birthmother would consider regularly playing a tape of the voices of his parents-to-be, or a CD of a particular lullaby or relaxation music for her unborn child. If traveling to another country to adopt, purchase audio tapes of native language children's lullabies, songs or stories.

Both because the sound of a voice is comforting and because talking to a child encourages his verbal and cognitive development, no matter what his age at arrival, and no matter whether he understands your language or not, talk soothingly to your child while you feed, dress or walk with him. By all means learn some comforting words or songs in your child's original language. The older he is at arrival, the more important it is that you find a way for him to use the language skills he has to communicate with you. Find an interpreter if you cannot become fluent.

> Music can become a "family thing." My kids all remember singing in the car. They learned the words to oldies, and to Rodgers and Hammerstein musicals. When we moved back "home" to Indianapolis from Fort Wayne, their cousins were frequently packed into the car, too. At holiday time we used holiday music tapes—Chanukah songs for the cousins, Christmas tunes for the Johnstons. Everybody sang everything.

As mentioned above, some children are sensorily sensitive—they may crave or need to avoid music, loud voices, or specific sounds. Other children have learned to associate certain sounds (slamming doors, a human's whistle, a panting dog) with past traumas. If it is comfortable for your child, make gentle rocking or swinging, reading and singing to Baby a part of your routine.

Routine

How has this child learned to comfort herself? Has she been rocked? Was she swaddled? Did she nurse, use a pacifier, or find her thumb to suck? Does she have a comfort object such as a stuffed animal or a textured blanket? Has a mobile, music box, or lullaby sung to her helped to lull her to sleep? Is this boy's masturbation his method for coping with unwelcome stress?

Comforting routine is another place where, if you are adopting a very young child, you can try to be somewhat proactive. Speak with your agency staff about how they have trained their foster parents to provide portable comfort agents which move with the babies for whom they care. Are babies helped to "attach" to a pacifier, blanket, or stuffed toy? Are foster parents willing to accept blankets or stuffed animals, music boxes, or tapes from prospective families? If so, your child will have an opportunity to become familiar with some of the surroundings that will move with her new home.

Children benefit from and are made to feel safe with a predictable routine—especially when adapting to a new environment—so plan in advance to establish one, even if you have been rather relaxed about personal schedules before becoming parents. If your baby is several weeks or months old and you have been able to learn anything about her previous routine, pattern your own on that one to any extent possible. If your child is a newborn, you may have more flexibility in establishing the routine, but be aware that babies tend to set the schedule for a family rather than to fit nicely into a previously configured one!

A mother I met at a conference in Saskatchewan described her baby girl's arrival at age 3.5 months. The new family felt especially pleased that the baby's foster parents were able to meet with them and give them a detailed report about the baby's schedule, likes and dislikes, and the atmosphere of their home (noise level, routine, etc.). For the first two weeks the baby seemed sleepy all the time. Though at first the new mom counted her blessings, she later realized that sleep is a common escape mechanism for depressed or stressed people of any age. A crisis came when the family left the new arrival with a baby-sitter. From that point on, the little girl began waking frequently in the middle of the night and wailing inconsolably. Mom tried everything—a bottle, rocking, a music box, a lullaby—with no success. Finally, she hit upon an idea. At three and a half months old, this baby understood quite a bit of language. Her mother decided to try an experiment. She picked her up and carried her through their house, turning on lights in each room and talking to her softly, "This is our house. Nobody up here, because everyone goes to sleep at night. . . . This is our kitchen, but no one is eating dinner here, because everyone goes to sleep at night. . . . This is our rocker, just where it was before you went to sleep." She moved from room to room, whispering to her daughter, and turning lights out as they moved to the next room. After just a few nights of going through what Mom termed a reassurance ritual, the baby was able to sleep through the night peacefully and awake without being afraid.

Playing floor games with your child, laying him on his back and kneeling over him to sing and laugh, and move his arms and legs in "baby calisthenics" motions, or playing pat-a-cake as he is seated in an infant seat gives the two of you opportunity for making eye contact in an entirely different set of circumstances from the intimacy of feeding.

Try your best to arrange your lives so that one of her parents can become your new child's primary caretaker for as long as you possibly can. Six months is the optimal minimum. Plan to take maximum advantage of your right as adopters to parental leave under the Federal Family and Medical Leave Act. The older your child is at placement, the more she will be aware of the newness of her situation and so the longer she may take to adapt to the change and begin to attach comfortably. In such circumstances you will find it beneficial to her attachment not to confuse her growing trust in you by putting her in daycare or leaving her with a baby-sitter. If your child is a newborn, two parents may comfortably share primary care duties, but it is often helpful to older babies' attachment for one parent to take principle responsibility for the more intimate aspects of childcare (particularly feeding and comforting) until attachment to one parent is secure and can then be "shared" with the second parent and older siblings.

Unfortunately, in most international adoptions and with the domestic adoptions of a great many children older than the newborn stage, you are likely to find that agencies or institutions remain uninformed about the value of these transitional aids and processes, and will not be willing to co-operate with your requests about transitional preparation. Some don't want to offend orphanage workers or foster parents. You may even find some professionals apparently afraid of and resistant to your questions about the details of your baby's sensory and experiential life before adoption. If this is the case, all is far from lost. As parents, your willingness to reach out for help if needed and, even more so, to be flexible and adaptable as you search for what seems to "feel" right between you and your baby is perhaps the most important element in building your attachment to one another.

More Tips for Encouraging Attachment with the Youngest Children

Take into consideration that your own emotional ability to give your-self completely to your child may be inhibited somewhat during any limbo period between placement and finalization—another reason why extended periods of limbo, like California's longest-of-all-states'-and-provinces', are not baby-centered. Despite assurances from family, friends, the agency, or one's spouse that everything will be all right, many new adopting par-ents—especially those who have experienced the repeated dashed hopes of the infertility roller coaster and those who have previously experienced a birthparent's change-of-heart—may feel like imposters in the parenting role at first, finding it difficult to believe that a birthparent won't change her mind or that an agency won't change their opinion, bursting the new family's bubble of joy. Though statistically such after-placement disappoint-ments are highly improbable, doubts are common. They are best dealt with when voiced aloud within a support group, or to a social worker or mental health professional.

For those concerned about it, bonding is more easily identified by its absence than by its presence. Among younger children there are a variety of behaviors which may be symptoms of insecure attachment.

- The baby may appear reluctant to express needs at all. In psycho-logical jargon, the term that describes this is *flat affect*.

    In a documentary on children in Chinese orphanages excerpted on CBS' "Eye to Eye" a British reporter demonstrated on film that infants and toddlers new to an orphanage cried often, loud and long, when they were wet, cold, hungry, or in need of comfort. Their cries sought help. Children who had been residents of even the best nurser-ies for a few weeks, however, seldom cried at all. These babies had already learned that their cries would not be dependably responded to and had given up asking for help in this way. Most of these babies had already learned that their caretakers could not be trusted to meet their needs.

Parents of quiet, undemanding babies are seldom taught that such children need to be aroused and to learn again to express their needs. As a result their parents sometimes reinforce their unexpressive behavior by learning to read their babies' needs before they are felt, since the babies seem so reluctant to express them. Ultimately these children do not have an opportunity to participate in an arousal-relaxation cycle. Allowing babies to fuss some reinforces their learning that if they will do so, a reliable person—Mom or Dad—will help them.

- The baby may avoid the person who tries to meet needs once expressed and refuse to make eye contact with the person holding him—or even with all humans. There may be body stiffening and arching the back away from the caregiver when being held rather than molding to the "shape" of the parent.

Jennie described her experience with her son Tomas as a wrestling match. He had come to them presumably at about nine months of age after having spent six months in a "good" South American orphanage, into which he was taken after having been abandoned at their gates at what the orphanage doctors assumed to be about three months of age. Nothing was known about his earliest weeks and months, but he had seemed to adapt well to the group home and had been described as a "good natured baby." Jennie's own fantasies about mothering had included rocking her baby as she fed him, and so she was eager to cuddle Tomas in the big rocker in front of his nursery window. Tomas would have none of it. Though really hungry, he steadfastly refused to be held to be fed—arching his back, flailing his arms, screaming, and refusing to make eye contact with Jennie. Only when she laid him on his side in his crib and propped his bottle would he soothe himself to sleep. Yet Tomas enjoyed some kinds of interaction. He sat comfortably in his mother's lap—back to her chest and face out—and made steady eye contact with Daddy, laughing at peek-a-boo and pat-a-cake games. It was quite some time before Jenny figured out through a casual support group conversation about sleeping patterns in various countries that perhaps Tomas' struggles with being fed were not a rejection of her as his mother-figure, but simply his way of demanding that his own familiar comfort-cycle be maintained. Jennie stopped trying to lead the dance. She decided to meet Tomas' needs as he needed her and to experiment with other ways to get him to meet her needs. They could rock with a story book. He would make steady eye contact with her from his infant seat.

- Baby may show no preference at all for one primary caregiver, or will accept care and affection indiscriminately from anyone.

> Lee had been passed around from family member to family member for care in his birth home and then in his large foster family, so why was it a surprise to Lee's single dad that Lee simply didn't care who it was who fed, diapered, or bathed him? There were no problems settling in at daycare at all, so Lee's dad took only a couple of weeks off work. Yet by the time Lee was a toddler this apparent adaptability had become a problem. Lee was willing to wander off with anyone who extended his hand in a store and, while seemingly content with his dad, Dad felt that the two were not emotionally connected. An attachment therapist recommended that Lee's dad reclaim the several months available to him for parenting leave in order to spend intensive one-on-one time with Lee without the distractions of daycare providers. During this period they entered short-term therapy together as well.

- The baby may emit a high-pitched wailing cry and cry even at times when he is not sick, hungry, wet, or cold. Over time such a cry may "feel" to the parent like an expression of grief rather than a request for food, clean diapers, or cuddling.

> Several years ago, in a now out-of-print publication for those adopting from the International Mission of Hope, Holly Van Gulden wrote eloquently about the unusual high-pitched cry common to Indian adopted infants, and about the standard comments from strangers about these newly arrived babies' enormous eyes. Observing that within a few months these babies' eyes seemed no larger proportionately than the eyes of other babies, Holly pointed out something that no one else had bothered to consider. Upon arrival, these babies were terrified, looking up into pale and unfamiliar white faces for the first time. Their eyes were round with fear. Their cries were cries of grief and fear.

- Babies may seem to prefer to be alone. They may isolate themselves by expressing no needs at all, not tracking human movement with their eyes, or vocalizing infrequently. Such a baby may appear to be content lying in a crib or on a blanket on the floor, or propped for hours in a car seat rather than expose herself to new people who frighten her or who remind her of formerly abusive caretakers.

It's important to recognize, however, that there are other issues which may produce some or all of these behaviors. Children who have vision problems, for example, may not make eye contact. Children who have been drug exposed, are hyperactive or are affected by autism may respond badly to touch and to cuddling, and may be difficult to calm. Similarly, babies who are colicky, who are experiencing allergic reactions to their formula, or who are drug or alcohol exposed may also cry strangely and inconsolably.

More Tips for Attaching with Toddlers and Older Children

Don't underestimate your older child's feelings about his "home" and his culture. He has brought these with him in sensory memories both conscious and unconscious. Even if you need a translator to do it, begin early to get your child to talk about what kinds of sensory-related things he misses and then try your best to provide them for him.

- Perhaps it is a particular type of music. Find a CD in a good music store.
- Perhaps it is a spicy comfort food for which you can find a recipe. Have your child help you make it; let her teach you how to shape those dumplings correctly.
- Perhaps it is a game played in the yard. Have your child teach it to you.
- Is it a bedtime routine or a Sunday afternoon routine? Try it out!

Let your child comb or brush *your* hair, paint *your* fingernails, feed *you* small bites of cheese or fruit. Soon he or she will be ready to reciprocate. Find games that encourage comfortable closeness to encourage comfortable touch.

> In her trainings, Sharon Roszia shares a food-related attachment game that she played with her own children. It involves a meal made up of finger foods—cut up cheese, meat, and fruit (have everyone involved in preparing the feast!). Then seat everyone around a table (even a coffee table with seating on the floor will do well). The challenge is that no one can feed himself. In order to get a bite of a preferred food, each individual (taking turns) must make eye contact with another family member, look at the food, and then make eye contact again. As soon as the other person "gets the message" he or she hand feeds a nice bite of that food to the person making contact. Then the next person gets a chance. The game can be messy (part of the fun), but it invites practice with eye contact, attunement, touch, and reciprocity.

If you suspect that attachment is a problem for you and your child, trust your instincts and reach out for help. One way of dealing with concerns is to give them voice. Begin by sharing your concerns with your child's pediatrician and asking for a particularly thorough examination. Once health issues (including those mentioned in the paragraph above) have been ruled out, reach into the adoption community. If you are confident in your relationship with your social worker, start there. If you feel unable to confide in your social worker (yes, I understand the fear—usually unfounded—that the social worker will brand you a bad parent and/or take the baby away), or if your social worker dismisses your concerns (does "Relax, you're trying too hard" have a familiar ring to it?), contact your local adoptive parent group (or Adoptive Families of America for a referral to one) for a list of books and articles to read, experienced parents to provide support and encouragement, or for referral to a specific adoption-literate counselor.

Above all, don't panic. Difficulty in attaching does not mean that you are a bad parent or that your child is destined to become a sociopath. Families who are feeling anxiety about bonding should know that those who do experience difficulties with attachment with babies can, in nearly all instances, be helped. I know. I've been there.

Resources

Travel Tips

Mother Goose Adoptions. "10 Domestic Adoption Travel Tips" www.adoptive families.com/pdf/DomesticAdoptionTravel.pdf

Rogu, Geroge, MD. "International Adoption Travel" on adoptiondoctors.com www.adoptiondoctors.com/articles/Article/International-travel-tips/66

St Martin, Michele. "10 Adoption Travel Tips" on iVillage.com. parenting.ivillage. com/baby/badoption/0,,adoptivefamilies_94j0ggsx,00.html

Entrustment Resources

Krista, 2ofus4now Host. "(Mormon) Temple Sealing" www.2ofus4now.org/Article. asp?ArticleID%3D20

Konick, Lisa. "Adoption Rituals." belief.net www.2ofus4now.org/Article.asp? ArticleID%3D20

Leiberman, Cheryl and Rhea Bufferman. *Creating Ceremonies: Innovative Ways to Meet Adoption Challenges.* (Redding, CT and Phoenix, AZ: Zeig, Tucker & Theson, 1998)

Mason, Mary Martin. *Designing Rituals of Adoption: For the Religious and Secular Community.* (Minneapolis: Resources for Adoptive Parents, 1995)

Morris, Margaret. "Adoption Celebrations: Welcoming Your Child with an Adoption Ceremony." Suite101.com adoption.suite101.com/article.cfm/ adoption_celebrations

"Open Adoption Ceremonies." Adoption Media LLC www.openadoptions.com/in-formation/open-adoption-ceremonies.html

"Planning a Ceremony." BirthparentForum.com www.birthparentforum.org/ modules.php?name=News&file=article&sid=37

Raphael, Simcha and Geela-Rayzel "A (Jewish) Ceremony to Welcome Our Daughter." www.jewishfamily.com/jc/lifecycle/a_ceremony_to.phtml

Roseman, Ellen. "Rituals and Ceremonies in Celebration of Adoption." library. adoption.com/hoping-to-adopt/rituals-and-ceremonies-in-celebration-of-adoption/article/1699/1.html

Smith, Deborah Goldstein. "One Family's Jewish Adoption Rituals." StarsofDavid. org www.starsofdavid.org/stories/ourfam.html

Music

Adoption.com has produced and/or markets several CDs of music inspired by or inspiring to those touched by adoption. adoptionshop.com/adoption_categories/audio-&-video-music-other-cds/ Titles include: *Adoption . . . The Songs You Love, Vol.1, Chosen-Songs of Hope Inspired by Adoption, Do You Have a Little Love to Share?, The Spirit of Adoption, and more*

"From Infertility to Family: A Musical Journey." www.perspectivespress.com/infertilitymusic.html Lyrics to popular songs providing comfort and empathy through the infertility journey.

Poetry

Johnston, Patricia Irwin, ed. *Perspectives on a Grafted Tree: Thoughts for Those Touched by Adoption.* (Indianapolis: Perspectives Press, Inc., 1981) An anthology of poetry by birthparents, adoptive parents, adopted adults, and professionals.

"Adoption Poetry" www.comeunity.com/adoption/adopt/poetry.html

"Inspirational Quotes, Poems, Verses and Links for Adoption" www.karensadoptionlinks.com/inspirat.html

Attachment 201

Babies & Toddlers

A4everFamily.org www.a4everfamily.org is a website devoted to providing excellent practical attachment tips for babies and toddlers.

Hopkins-Best, Mary. *Toddler Adoption: The Weaver's Craft.* (Indianapolis: Perspectives Press, Inc., 1998)

Karen, Robert. *Becoming Attached: First Relationships and How They Shape Our Capacity to Love* (New York: Oxford University Press USA, 1998)

Trout, Michael. *Gentle Transitions: A Newborn Baby's Point of View About Adoption.* VHS or DVD (Champaign, IL: Infant-Parent Institute)

Trout, Michael. *Multiple Transitions: A Young Child's Point of View on Foster Care and Adoption.* VHS or DVD (Champaign, IL: Infant-Parent Institute)

School-Aged Children

Gray, Deborah. *Attaching in Adoption: Practical Tools for Today's Parents.* (Indianapolis: Perspectives Press, Inc., 2002)

Keck, Gegory and Regina Kupecky. *Adopting the Hurt Child: Helping Adoptive Families Heal and Grow.* (Colorado Springs, CO: 2002)

CHAPTER 15

Adjustments in the First Year Together

Probably the most frequently asked question prospective and new parents ask is, "How do I know what's an adoption-related issue with my child and what's not?" Actually, I cleaned that question up a bit for presentation here. The advocate in me cringes at the more common wording—"How do I know the difference between what's *normal* and what's *adoption*?"—because of my belief that unless we ourselves see adoption as a completely normal, healthy and positive way for families to be related to one another, we can't expect others to do so. (But that topic is another segment of this book.)

My answer to that question is that most of what happens within an adopted child's first year at home (and most of what happens in the future as well) will not be adoption-related. It is far more accurate to say, and to understand, that some difficulties in the first year and some later on will absolutely be influenced by your child's prior experiences (as well as by yours)—all of which led up to the fact that you became connected to one another by adoption.

All new parents worry about whether their child's growth and behavior falls within the wide range that is defined as *normal*. Why should adoptive parents be any different? In order to feel more confident in general, it's a commendable idea for parents to want to learn as much as possible about how children develop physically, cognitively and emotionally, so that they can offer their little ones appropriate stimulation and encouragement.

But Adoption's Different, Right? You Already Said So!

In his article "The A.D.D. Epidemic," excerpted from "Reasons and Significance of Societal Mayhem and Severe Disturbances in the Population" (for the Summer, 1995 issue of *Attachments* newsletter from the Attachment Center at Evergreen), psychiatrist Dr. Foster Cline wrote,

"The importance of the first year of life simply cannot be overemphasized. The first year lays the foundation for four essential and related human thought and personality traits:

- causal thinking
- conscience
- basic trust
- the ability to delay gratification

"Upon these variables, civilization is built. If we meet a person walking the streets at night without them, we're dead. Without them, civilization as we know it is lost!"

Yes, adoption is different from parenting by birth in those significant and unavoidable ways mentioned when we talked about entitlement and about Kirk's Shared Fate theory in Chapter 4. This difference, which is likely to have the longest-term impact on many children who join their families by adoption, is the sheer fact that they will not have joined their families early enough in their lives to avoid having been exposed to prenatal stressors such as poor nutrition and/or drug or alcohol effects, or to prevent their having experienced abuse and/or neglect in prior caregiving settings, or to ensure that they won't experience the trauma of multiple changes in caregivers. Those are things that come with the territory that is adoption. As a parent, your tasks are to accept that they are there and to address them.

Foster Cline's adoption-sensitive and adoption-informed work on attachment and parenting is another chunk of the best stuff I've learned from over the years, which should explain why I feel that normal, predictable developmental issues are just too important to be condensed into the space of a short chapter in this book. Please read one or more full books on normal child developmental issues in the first year of life. At the end of this chapter, I've included a short and selective list of current reading material that I particularly recommend. Using books like these by recognized experts in infant, toddler, and child development will do a much better job of teaching you about month-by-month milestones and general parenting issues than could I, and they will do so in an adequate space—rather than a severely condensed, single chapter in a book designed with a different focus.

Additionally, the sheer act of going to the general parenting bookshelf is important in learning to see oneself simply as a *parent*, rather than continuing to qualify your relationship by focusing on how your family came together. This will help your family build confidence and begin to feel that you fit into the very large corner of the world occupied by parents and children. To stay up to date, subscribe to magazines and newsletters such as *Parents*, *Parenting*, and *Growing Child* as well as *Adoptive Families*, and have lists of questions ready for your pediatrician at your routine well-baby visits. Most of your questions about your baby's growth and development issues can be handled in this way.

I intend to devote this chapter to the issues in your first year together as a family that are indeed related to the fact that your child has not been with you from his conception. Yet before we begin I must harp at this pre-adoptive audience one last time with my strong bias as an adoption advocate, an adoptive parent, and a parent educator. I am offended by what I see as a growing phenomenon among some prospective adopters who seem to be embarked on what I've come to call "The Search for the Good Enough Baby." In my writing and training I offer advice about "problems" that may arise during the parenting experience because I believe that well-informed parents can do the best job for their children. But if a perfect match to what you believe your birth child would likely have been, or if rock-solid assurance that an agency has found for you a baby who carries something akin to a *Consumer Reports* Best Buy is what you are expecting, instead of saying yes or no to adoption in general or to a specific child offered to you, *please don't adopt at all*. Parenting doesn't come with a guarantee or a warranty, and if you expect one, you are bound to be disappointed. Any child deserves more than that. Every child deserves to be valued for who he is, rather than as a substitute for what might have been.

On a more positive note, you will surely find it supportive and encouraging to know that research focusing on adjustment of new babies and their families (much of it done in England, and including families expanded via assisted reproductive technologies as well as families expanded through adoption) seems to indicate that adoptive families look even better on adjustment scales than do non-adoptive families. Why? After first cautioning us that over-generalization is not a good idea, David Brodzinsky has suggested that because adoptive parents are highly motivated with a desire and will to succeed, tend to be well-prepared, are more mature on average, and become parents out of a sense of deprivation and so rarely take it for granted, they experience parenting with a "level of joy that . . . overshadows almost anything else."[1]

Settling In

As you read the recommended parenting materials you'll come to see that adjusting to parenthood is not exclusively an adoption issue. All parents need time to learn to attune themselves to each baby's unique personality, temperament and style, to adjust to a change of pace and routine in their lives, and to readjust their relationships with their parenting partners, other children, family and friends, and employers and coworkers. Things that might be different about adjusting for adopting parents include the possibility that you will not have been your child's only caretaker, the increased likelihood of a mismatch in innate temperament or personality between you, inappropriate expectations about self and partner as parents, and inappropriate expectations and reactions from the rest of your world.

If you've taken the advice of the first several chapters of this book, one thing that won't be different is your preparation for parenting. Having allowed yourselves the privilege and the opportunity to fantasize about your child-to-be and talk with your parenting partner and other intimates about what your growing family will be like, and having taken the practical steps of getting ready in your heart, home, job and bank account, you can expect to be just as "ready" for parenthood as is any parent who's arrived there through pregnancy and birth—probably more so than the average parent by birth.

Yet there's something about parenting that you may not expect and that parents by birth don't seem to know in advance either. Parenthood seldom matches our expectations. Just as high school was different than you expected it to be, and marriage was different than you expected it to be, and that dream job was different than you expected it to be, parenting will be different from your expectations. In some ways parenting will be disappointing and in other ways it will be more wonderful than your wildest dreams. You'll learn a whole new way of looking at yourself and your partner, if you have one. You'll discover both that eau-de-spit-up can be an aphrodisiac when you peek into a room in the wee hours of the morning and find your proper and sophisticated partner talking goofy baby talk and making silly faces in an attempt to soothe and cheer up a fussy baby, and that staying out late in those ways you both used to enjoy loses its appeal when the prospect of 2:00 am feedings looms.

Needing to find ways to soothe a relentlessly fussy baby is probably not an adoption thing (though a recently moved baby who misses a familiar first home will certainly cry in grief) . . . but on the other hand it's such a trying experience to try to comfort a fussy baby that it's worthwhile to list some possible solutions here anyway. If a soft voice and a few words of comfort don't work, check the diaper, the temperature of the room (too hot? too cold?) and the temperature of the baby, the presence of erupting teeth, and verify that Baby isn't hungry (or needing to suck whether he's hungry or not). Cuddle and rock for a few minutes. Sing softly or play a favorite tape. Put the baby in a swing. Carry him (in your arms or in a baby pack) and move—walk through the house or take a walk outside. Try swaddling. Give Baby a massage or a bath. Go for a ride and hope he falls asleep in his car seat.

There won't always be an answer. Your child may continue to fuss and fume. But it isn't likely to be an adoption thing. These experiences of frustration are the places where parents can use some of the relaxation techniques for themselves that they learned during the course it was suggested they take while they were expecting. Hand Baby off to co-parent (or call for help) and then take a warm bath, take a brisk walk, play a computer game, listen to soothing music over noise-reducing headphones, do some yoga stretches, try controlled breathing exercises—whatever works to ease the tensions of being a parent is an earned respite.

What we sometimes forget is that each human has an individual style. Some people are quiet and some are active, some enjoy touch and others find it annoying. Some people are very intuitive, and some are concrete and literal. Sometimes parents' and children's styles of interaction just aren't in tune. It then becomes the parent's responsibility, as the more experienced and sophisticated of the pair, to figure this out and to change the steps to the dance—the dance of attachment. A mom who had contacted me about what she was experiencing as an attachment problem after attending a workshop I gave on attachment wrote to me again many months later after seeing a well-regarded specialist on infant psychology to whom I had referred her, reading more, and focusing special attention on this issue.

> "I think the heart of what I was struggling with was communication with my son," she wrote. "Don't you think that that's (communication) the foundation of attachment? I think the little diagram with the arrows going around and around (attachment cycle) is a powerful representation of what goes on between parent and child. The child has to be able to accept what the parent is giving, and the parent has to be convinced (through the child's own signals, which are then interpreted through the lens of the parent's experience and expectations) that the child is receiving them. With (my son) and me, we had channels on which we did communicate, but we also had those on which we had a hard time communicating. The way we did communicate was through touch, but it really threw me when he avoided eye contact. Maybe I wanted more from that particular channel than I needed to worry about, but it did act to inhibit our communication and my confidence that I was 'getting through' to him.
>
> "What narrowed the communication gap for (my son) and me was language. When I could ask him what he wanted and he could point and understand, and especially when he began to use words, I felt like we were finally really beginning to communicate. When he could ask for me, when (at about age 15 months) he started (for example) objecting to my departures, my confidence soared."

When a parent's temperament and a child's clash in some way, producing a mismatch between the parent's expectations, hopes, and needs from the parenting experience and the child's needs for parenting, the result is likely to be that the parent feels somewhat insecure.

> When Kirk brought his son home from an orphanage far away, the five-year-old's frustration about all of the changes in his life and his ability to express himself in a language his new father could understand resulted in huge tantrums. Micah would scream and curse (Kirk recognized those words), kick the furniture, and throw toys and pillows. His dad's attempts to hold him closely until he calmed prompted hysteria,

with biting, kicking and clawing. Before Kirk found the intercountry adoption-literate therapist who would ultimately become their guide to a positive relationship, all Kirk could do was make one room in their apartment tantrum-safe and let Micah rage away while he sat in the doorway muttering soft reassurances.

Jenny knows what this feels like, and she offered an affirmation or prayer that she's found helpful in such situations.

Thank you, Lord, for my beautiful son. Thank you for the privilege of being his mother. I'm glad he is he and not another child.

He depends on me and I am here for him. Forever and through anything I am here for him.

I can't be everything for him. I didn't give birth to him. I can't protect him from the pain of growing up or the pain of losing his birth family.

Not only that, but I'm not even a perfect adoptive mother. I make mistakes! But here we are, mother and son, together in this imperfect world, and the only way to go is forward.

Help me to know my son and his needs; help me to be patient and persistent in the places he is hard to know.

I pray for help where I lack, Lord. I trust that I will learn from my mistakes. Help me to open doors for my son, even to let others give him what he needs if I can't.

Adjustment Issues Caused by Prior Experiences

Attachment can be one-sided. For example, parents can be firmly attached to a child whose physical or mental condition makes it difficult for the child to form attachments. Children who have been institutionalized, traumatized, or who have experienced breaks with multiple caretakers and thus do not "trust' parent figures may have difficulty attaching. Similarly, children with autism, kids who have been abused or neglected, those who have been prenatally drug or alcohol affected, or those whose physical problems create chronic pain which goes unrelieved despite parents' best efforts may be candidates for bonding problems. Conversely, certainly children can actively seek approval and love from and attach to parent figures who, for a variety of reasons revolving around their own dysfunction, are unable to reciprocate by attaching appropriately to the child. These last aren't healthy attachments, of course, but they are attachments.

Attaching as a Family

For weeks Jaimee and Steve looked at that wonderful little fat face posted on their refrigerator, their bathroom mirror, and the dashboards of their cars. Soh, Min Jung (soon to be Mindy) was to arrive from Korea via O'Hare International Airport two months after the letter inform-ing them of her assignment to them. They were so ready by the time the day came—packing the camera, the diaper bag, the stroller, and Grandma and Grandpa into their car for the two hour drive, that they thought they might split from excitement!

The gate area was crowded with waiting families from a several state area. There were banners, balloons, laughter, and tears. The plane was delayed. But at last the announcement came.

The babies and their escorts would be last off the plane, but all of the other passengers who filed off first knew that waiting families would meet the plane at the gate, and many couldn't resist just hanging around to watch the joyful arrival of these children into their forever families. For Jaimee and Steve it was the most beautiful chaos that had ever been! Grandpa took the video. Grandma remembered to thank the escort. Steve and Jaimee fumbled with diapers and heavy winter clothes. Mindy stared in wide-eyed terror.

In Chapter 5, I offered an attachment primer, giving readers still not sure if adoption was a good choice for them an overview of how attachment works and how it can be challenged. In that section I did my best to affirm that, while families built by adoption should expect that their families are at risk for attachment challenges, parents who are well-prepared and are able to access good professional assistance should feel confident that they and their children can meet these challenges. In Chapter 14 I presented some practical ways to initiate and foster attachment. The next section provides a very personal look at what challenged attachment—with a small baby—can look like. My hope is that sharing it will help readers under-stand that there's no such thing as learning too much about attachment. It's always better to come to a new situation highly-prepared rather than under-prepared.

What Challenged Attachment Looks Like

In talking about how parents' unresolved losses can influence their own attachment and entitlement experience, I wrote a bit in Chapter 5 about the arrival of Dave's and my third child, Lindsey, and how this sad baby triggered my mother-in-law's unresolved infertility-related losses after they had been stuffed down for over 40 years. Let's talk more about Lindsey, and about her own challenged attachment.

Lindsey, a child probably just genetically programmed to be less resil-ient than another baby might have been, had not been abused or neglected. Her birthmother had a healthy pregnancy and planned her baby's adoption over many months, never wavering that adoption was in her child's best interests. This was to be a healthy baby, and the only things that challenged this experienced agency in making her placement plan should have been readily accomplishable in six months. This baby would be biracial—African American and Latina—and her birthmother wanted to meet the family that the agency selected to parent her. So there was nothing about her prenatal environment or her birthfamily's choices that created her adjustment issues. It was the choices made by the adoption professionals responsible for her placement that created the trauma at the root of the challenges Lindsey faced. Unfortunately, this is not unusual, which is the main reason that I share the story.

> She was ten weeks old when she came home, and Lindsey had already been in two foster homes, the first for eight weeks and the second for two. We knew that, but we had no idea at all what that might mean, short-term or long-term. Dave and I had parented two other children from the newborn stage. Our son came to us from a preemie nursery at 10 days old and was now a bright, healthy, handsome, robust 9-year-old. Our older daughter, now not quite 3, had arrived from the hospital five days after her birth and was thriving. We felt fully prepared to parent a healthy baby.
>
> We were immediately aware that something was wrong about this beautiful, healthy little girl. She cried nearly nonstop, in a high-pitched, nearly hysterical way that was very different from any of the variety of cries that we had learned to interpret in our older two children. The daytime crying created a good deal of stress for me, a stay-at-home mom. I spent most of my time trying—unsuccessfully—to figure out a way to comfort her.
>
> My older two children soon began to feel a bit neglected and resentful though, because I was distracted, it took me a while to see this. After all, I was feeding them, washing their laundry, taking them where they needed to go. What was missing was the calm and quiet story before nap time, the game of Boggle on a summer afternoon, the Mommy with an empty lap or a ready ear. I was exhausted.
>
> Lindsey was so worn out by the end of the day that she easily slept throughout the night. Thank goodness for this! It allowed me to recover (some) from the stress and tension of long days as Lindsey's full-time caregiver. It didn't help me feel better about how hard it was to parent three, rather than two, children.
>
> Chubby Lindsey wanted to suck constantly, yet she could not be consoled by a pacifier, her thumb, or anything other than formula offered from a bottle. She panicked when alternatives were offered—stiffening and raging. She craved the warmth of body contact, but not if it involved making eye contact; instead she would stiffen her body, arch her back and avert her eyes when held to her parent's face or shoulder. She would be held only in a feeding position, and then, only if being

fed. Otherwise, holding was comforting only if Lindsey sat with her back to her parent's front, facing out.

Suspecting colic or milk allergies—or could she have chronic earaches?—Dave and I had Lindsey thoroughly checked by her pediatrician, who pronounced her healthy and overfed. We were at a loss. We knew that something was wrong. We had successfully experienced what we now looked back on as absolutely blissful infancies with our older two children. Since we were confident in our parenting abilities, when Lindsey had been with us for two months we approached our social worker, who promptly pooh-poohed our concerns and suggested that we relax. (Where had we heard this suggestion before?!) The social worker offered absolutely no information, referral, or support.

Indignant and undeterred, we first contacted the foster parents from whom we had picked Lindsey up. This older couple, who had fostered babies for many years from their farm, confirmed that the baby had been "fussy" and "difficult" during her two weeks with them as well, but they could offer no reasons and no solutions.

We then contacted the first foster parents, whom we had never met, and from whom we had received no transitional reports. During the course of a lengthy conversation, this foster mom casually dropped in an important nugget of information—she had breast-fed Lindsey, "Oh, not enough to really *feed* her, since my oldest is three now, but it was an easy way to comfort her, and of course there were those immunities I was passing on." Did the agency know? Sure! This foster mom had breast-fed several fostered babies over the last couple of years. Had the next foster parents been told? No, after all, Lindsey's primary food came from a bottle. She had eaten well.

Finally we had one answer to our baby's sadness. For her first eight weeks of life, Lindsey had been firmly attached to a non-portable pacifier! Lindsey had not even been weaned.

But that wasn't the only trauma—or even the biggest one—and this was the one that we didn't initially understand. Lindsey had been suddenly moved, cold-weaned and with no transition, to new caregivers when her foster family left for vacation. Then, barely given time to begin to adjust in just two weeks with a second set of very good, very committed—but very different—caregivers. Then—BAM!—two weeks later she was passed off again to our excited family.

Think back to Chapter 14's discussion of infant attachment, which is mostly sensory. Twice in her short life (three times if you consider—and you should—that she had also lost the familiar environment of the womb, through which her birthmother spoke to her and provided a routine), Lindsey's life had been turned upside down.

She moved from being held in her birthmother's arms and listening to her already-familiar voice in a hospital setting to the arms of another woman, whose body shape, voice and scent were different, and who was mothering other children. The family had a dog and lived in a child-filled subdivision where open windows brought in kid-noises and the TV was tuned to cartoons. The dad worked at night, and so the routine was to stay relatively quiet during the day and then have rowdy play with Daddy after dinner and before he went to work. Children loomed over the crib in the room the baby shared with another child. They interacted with the baby. Cooking odors from kid-friendly foods were in the air. When Lindsey needed comforting, a mother came and offered her breast. It was a good place. She was well-cared for and felt loved.

One day, everything changed. For several days there had been excitement in the air as the family packed and got ready for vacation. On this day, the social worker came. She lifted the then 8-week-old baby from the foster mother's arms, put her in an unfamiliar car seat in an unfamiliar car, and drove for a while. When the car stopped, they were in the country. No neighborhood noises here, just farm equipment engines in the distance and occasional animal noises. The air smelled different from the subdivision. The caretaker smelled different too, and she was shaped differently than the fit young mother. Hers was a grandmotherly shape, and a grandmotherly face that was unfamiliar. She had a calm voice, but one that she didn't know. There were no children here and no dog, but instead cats roamed, even investigating the baby at face level as she sat in an infant seat on the counter. The man here spoke differently than the father-figure before. Retired, he was more involved in childcare. The routine was different too, as this was a family which had arisen with the sun and the rooster for many years. The radio was tuned to farm news and country music. It was much quieter here, and the cooking odors were different. The nipple on the bottle was a different shape, though the formula tasted the same, but when the baby needed comfort and a pacifier was stuck in her mouth, she didn't understand it and spit it out. She liked the rocking motion, but she didn't like this face, and no breast was offered. She was frightened.

Two weeks later there was another sudden change. A different looking and smelling family with two children came. While the woman dressed the baby in new clothes that smelled different, the caregiver went to another room. Two children, but not with familiar faces, hovered over her and touched her. Within minutes she was in a car in yet another unfamiliar car seat, children on either side waving toys in her face to try to get her to smile. When they arrived "home" the room was filled with well-wishers—friends from an adoptive parent group and within minutes a grandma, aunt, uncle, and cousin arrived from a city two hours away to greet the newcomer. A couple of hours later, everyone left, the older children were put to bed, the dad and the mom looked at the quiet baby's confused face and examined her toes and arms, and changed her into an unfamiliar-feeling diaper and nightshirt. They brought a bottle with yet another unfamiliar nipple and the woman rocked her in a darkened room before putting her into still another unfamiliar crib. The world had changed again. The frightened, sad baby knew that screaming wouldn't help, but her grief came out in the form of a low, mourning cry that was almost constant for weeks.

At ten weeks old, Lindsey had learned an important lesson: Don't trust mothers to meet your needs; they disappear.

Let's stop here in Lindsey's story and evaluate. Lindsey (and Dave and I, and her siblings) was the victim of poor professional practice in several ways:

1. **There was inadequate training for every person involved with this adoption.** Lindsey's first foster parents were completely unfamiliar with important attachment issues (though well-meaning), and they had provided inappropriate care based on inaccurate information. The second foster parents, too, did not understand attachment well enough to ask for the information they needed to take over Lindsey's care. They just "loved her up," as they had done with other foster children for at least a generation. Three years before, this agency had prepared us well for the issues of transracial adoption we would face in adopting a Latina/African American baby, but certainly we, as a family, were given no preparation about potential attachment issues in infants then, and the update that came before Lindsey came home was pure paperwork. Evidently, Lindsey's caseworker (who had several years of adoption experience and later went into private practice as a family therapist) had no infant attachment training either, as neither this nor what happened subsequently raised any red flags for her. She was not even with us when we went to bring Lindsey home!

2. **There were multiple changes in caregiver, all unnecessary.** Lindsey's birthmother had been ready for adoption for months, and she had not wavered after the birth of her child. Still, knowing for over six months that they were expecting a baby of color and that the birthmother wanted to meet the adopting family that the agency would choose, the agency had not pre-selected parents for a perfectly healthy newborn baby by the time the baby was born. Foster parents were an unnecessary way station in Lindsey's life to begin with. She should have gone straight home from the hospital to a permanent family. Then, given that the first fostering family

had let the agency know from the day they were asked to take this baby that they were going on vacation in eight weeks and would not be taking a baby, the agency was still not ready for a placement when the family left. We had not even been contacted about Lindsey until she was about seven weeks old and the first foster family was getting ready to leave. We said yes immediately, but the agency then needed two weeks to update our expired homestudy. The second foster parenting situation could and should have been avoided.

3. **Transitions were completely inadequate.** No written information about Lindsey's schedule or first eight weeks of history was passed along either to her second interim caregivers or then to Dave and me. It was as if that first eight weeks in a breast-feeding foster home were inconsequential. A social worker carried Lindsey from first fostering home to the second, and stayed at neither place more than a few minutes. At ten weeks, Lindsey came to us in a twenty-minute pass through. We were offered little information, and we didn't know that there were questions that we should ask.

Now, Dave and I—and therefore Lindsey—were lucky. Experienced parents and active in adoption issues already, at least we knew where to turn for help. Back to Lindsey's story.

> In Chicago, at the North American Conference on Adoptable Children, with 14-week-old Lindsey in tow in her Snuggli™, I made contact with several nationally-known attachment experts as well as with La Leche League. Except for the La Leche League trainer, this handful of people were in the forefront of the "new" (it was 1984) focus on attachment in older adopted children, and of course they knew Bowlby, whose work years before had been with babies. I interviewed these experts as they watched me interact with my baby, made notes on the suggestions of each and went home to devour Bowlby.
>
> Then, on my own, I made up the steps to a routine that I hoped would enhance our attachment. The plan seemed complicated then, but it feels rudimentary to me now—the difference between a box-step waltz and a tango. It looked like this.
>
> 1. We needed consistency, and it began with feeding. One parent (in this case, it was me) was to do all of the feeding until attachment was more secure. Knowing that Lindsey had been breast-fed, I tried a Lact-aid (a supplemental nursing system) for a couple of days, but it was too late for Lindsey to remember how to nurse, so she was just further frustrated.
>   - Daddy and siblings interacted with Baby through play, not through caregiving in those early months. It was simply

vital that she come to believe in and trust one consistent caregiver before transferring and broadening her family attachments.

- For many months we didn't use a babysitter unless Lindsey was soundly asleep when we left and we knew that we would get back without her waking.

2. She needed dependable comfort and closeness if she was to learn to trust adults. Sucking gave her comfort, but only if formula was involved.

    - With the support of our pediatrician, we carefully measured Lindsey's formula for the day and let her eat as often as she wanted, watering it down during the early part of the day and moving to full strength as the day wound down to ensure that she ate enough calories but not too many.
    - I "wore" Lindsey most of the time in the Snuggli™ baby carrier. She resisted at first, but eventually she liked it.
    - We held her a lot, but did not force face-to-face contact this way, letting her sit with her back to the chest of the person on whose lap she sat, making eye contact with others.
    - It was summer, so for weeks the children and I went daily to a pool, where Lindsey and I floated quietly together in the warm water (simulating the amniotic fluid of the womb) while I sang and spoke soothing words into her ear.
    - In the fall, with Erica in preschool and Joel in grade school, Lindsey and I enrolled in a two mornings a week Swim-and-Gym class at the local Y, where we continued our water experience and our fun and games.

3. We needed a routine, because the familiar becomes comforting to children. I'm good at predictable routines (we'd had one before Lindsey came home), so with the exception of letting the baby eat whenever she wanted to, we stuck to one—getting up, napping, and going to bed at the same time each day.

    - Mommy was back for one-on-one time with older siblings.
    - Lindsey spent lots of time in the Snuggli™.
    - For the summer, there was the pool after lunch and before nap.
    - Lindsey sat in a swing looking on while Mommy played a game with bigger sister.

- Big brother entertained Lindsey with peek-a-boo and baby toys while Mommy worked on dinner.
- She sat at the table while everyone else ate dinner.
- Bath time with big sister came soon afterwards.
- She was on Daddy's lap with her sister for a story book after the last bottle, before two little girls went to bed . . . and to sleep.
4. We all needed some fun and some respite.
   - When going out to dinner was uncomfortable with a moaning baby, Daddy began to take the older children to McDonalds, for walks, or for ice cream while Lindsey and Mommy stayed home.
   - My good friend Becky came to sit at the house while Lindsey napped so that I could take a quiet walk.
   - We played floor games—baby calisthenics—where Lindsey lay on her back and Dave or I knelt over her, singing, laughing, holding toys for her to grab, stimulating Lindsey to make unwanted eye contact.

It took months, but when Lindsey was about eight months old, Dave and I realized that the transition had been made. Lindsey had decided that we were "hers," and she responded warmly to our contact with her.

It was at this point that my mother-in-law, Helen Johnston, and I had our amazing conversation about her children's arrivals in the 1940s (Chapter 5, talking about how unresolved loss can color our future lives and parenting). Let's revisit that from another perspective too—her children's.

Best practice standards from the 1930s into the 1950s deemed that babies who would not be parented by their birthparents should spend their first several months (most often four to six months) in a baby nursery staffed by shifts of caregivers supervised by registered nurses in their white uniforms and stiff white caps. Often these nurseries were on the adoption agency's premises. It was assumed that this time would provide the caregivers and the social workers time to determine that these actually were healthy children (didn't want to give these poor infertile adopters unhealthy ones. Better to put those kids and the older ones in foundling homes or children's homes). It also provided time to observe the developing babies' personalities and intelligence, hopefully allowing social workers to make custom matches to adoptive parents.

Dave and Mary Jane Johnston (as well as two of their four cousins) each spent their first six months in just such a baby nursery, cared for by committed shift workers who loved babies. Their would-be parents were then sent into a room where one to three babies sat in cribs, pre-selected as "good matches" for these parents-to-be. A child was selected, dressed in new clothes, caregivers (from at least that shift) said their goodbyes, and the child was driven off to live in a house—to sleep in a room alone, in a larger crib, and in a differently decorated room. These caregiver parents wanted to cuddle, expected to hold the baby while he or she drank a bottle rather than prop it familiarly. The sounds were different (this wasn't a busy office, after all) and so were the smells (people cooked here). The formula changed, and so did the routine. The babies mourned. The mothers felt guilty—not good enough.

Interesting, isn't it, that these U.S. "best practices" of 45–70 years ago are almost exactly like those of social welfare systems in the majority of countries sending their children to others for adoption today? (Though today's rationale for these practices is usually justified by an interest in cultural-face-saving in trying to find local adopters.) We are beginning to recognize the negative effects of institutionalization on children today, but we didn't "get it" then and so at least one generation of U.S. adoptees were "institutionalized."

Reading the memoirs and blogs of many adult adoptees of this era tells me that these people, placed in unprepared families with varying degrees of skill and intuitiveness continue to deal with the aftermath of such beginnings in their own personal lives. I have yet to see this addressed at a conference for adoption professionals.

And my daughter?

Now an adult, Lindsey is a poised and sensitive young woman who is definitely attached to her family. Initially shy, tentative about new relationships and basically a pessimist (her life's proverbial glass is always half empty, while her sister's is always enthusiastically half full), she is slow to adapt to new situations and reluctant about establishing trust with new people. It is still easier for her to trust men than women. How much of who Lindsey is, we wonder, is due to Lindsey's inborn traits (undoubtedly hers is a relatively inflexible personality) and how much to her unnecessarily negative beginning (having learned early not to trust caregivers, who disappear—two or three times—taking your comfort with them)? We can't know. This is the point. *We can never know!* Children deserve permanency from the earliest possible moment. Their needs simply have to supersede the needs of either birthparents or of agency administrivia!

As I speak with those adopting infants or toddlers, I hear many stories like those in the two generations of our adoption-expanded family, with one important variant—in most cases these babies are placed with first-time parents who have no experience with normal infant adjustment or behavior. Consequently, most of these parents experience a kind of horror which they are often reluctant to share even with a parenting partner (my mother-in-law never had). Since attachment is a reciprocal relationship—baby responding to parent, parent in turn responding to child, which provokes more response from baby—oftentimes parents of awkwardly attaching babies wonder if indeed they are attaching to their children. The rejecting behavior of a baby like this makes it very difficult for a new mother or father to feel drawn to him. As a result, sometimes parents subconsciously distance themselves to a certain extent from such children, meeting basic needs, but feeling little inclination to force unwanted cuddling or play. This, of course, reinforces the poorly attaching child's sense that parents aren't for trusting, and a negative vicious cycle is reinforced.

Most parents (and professionals) involved in the adoption of newborns don't need to be experts in attachment theory, because most of those parents and children will find that their families attach normally. The primer provided most of the theory that these families are likely to need: how attachment develops and how it can be damaged, so that they are able to recognize some of the symptoms of possible difficulty in this area and, if they find themselves dealing with problems, then can acknowledge them and seek out the help they need as early as possible.

Those adopting older children—babies beyond a few weeks old, toddlers, school-aged children and teens—however, do need to be more attachment educated. Far too often they are not. Sometimes their apparent lack of information is because the social workers who completed their homestudies simply didn't do a good job of teaching about attachment and separation issues in children or may not have taught about it at all. Just as often, however, the lack of knowledge is because parents-in-waiting themselves were playing ostrich, simply refusing to believe that attachment challenges could or would be part of their experience in adoption. The truth is—please hear this—that adoption has changed enough in the last generation that preparation and expectations need to change too, if families are to be realistic and to get off to the best start.

Lacking appropriate education, misinformation continues to run rampant among the public at large and even among some professionals. Despite twenty-five years of talking a lot about supporting bonding, even the courts seem to have misconstrued what "bonding" means. Often, this is misconstrued to the extent that most courts are resistant to terminating the parental rights of birthparents even when guilty of abuse and neglect—and often prefer instead that babies bounce from foster home to foster home as workers are ordered to attempt to reunify the family of origin.

> Tina, an experienced and well-read foster mother, had an infant placed with her on an emergency basis after the mother abandoned her and could not be found for two weeks. The baby arrived unresponsive and listless. Tina held and cuddled her during every waking moment,

seeking eye contact as she fed her. On the day of the court hearing three weeks later, the baby's grandmother looked at the baby with tears in her eyes and commented that the little girl, now alert and responsive, was a "totally different child" than she had been just three weeks before. All waited in the hallway to be called to testify, but the judge heard no testimony. Minutes later a social worker appeared and announced that the baby was to be sent home with her birthmother, who promptly deposited her in the frightened grandmother's arms and walked away.

This baby may well come back into care—in a few months, in a few years. She may or may not have a foster mother as knowledgeable as Tina. She may or may not be adopted by those second foster parents.

She may become your child!

There really is a large and convincing body of evidence-based information about attachment available to those who want it or need it. I've included a list of more reading materials on attachment at the end of this chapter. What it says to families built by adoption is that while it is possible for families to build secure attachments to one another at any time, and that it is probable that well-supported, well-informed families will do just that, it won't happen in a vacuum. Full and accurate information about a child's prior experiences and environments, adequate education for dealing with the missing or problematic elements in that environment, and emotional support for the family are indispensable parts of this recipe for successful attachment.

Occasionally, parents become so frustrated at being rejected by the child they have waited so long to love that they are horrified to find themselves on the verge of abuse—tempted to shake the baby into response, to hit a constantly crying child. Such situations promote enormous guilt in the parents, of course, most of whom feel that they cannot possibly share such terrors with their spouse, friends, parents, or caseworker and simply stuff it down inside to fester over years—or let it explode into tragedy. The horror stories we have read in recent years about adopting parents killing their internationally adopted children often fit this mold. These were not bad people, rather they were people put in bad circumstances. Poorly prepared, poorly screened, matched with children with unrevealed serious problems and offered little to no support, these families became ticking time bombs. Every one of these tragedies could have been prevented, with the family remaining intact and growing healthy. Families and professionals alike needed more information, more education, more support. They needed to make choices that were more sound, in order to build families that were stronger.

Everyone who has even a little knowledge about adoption seems to be able to acknowledge that when families adopt older children there is a significant risk for attachment difficulties. More often than not, older children who are available for adoption have been victims of multiple breaks in attachment or have been attached to people who have hurt them in some way and so have great difficulty in learning to trust parenting figures. Everybody seems to acknowledge that the process of building transferred attachments with a much older child is complex. It involves parents and child each being well-prepared for a transfer and coming to clearly understand that adoption is an add-on rather than a replacement experience.

Older children must be supportively disengaged from earlier attachments and allowed to grieve for them, and must be encouraged to open themselves to their new parents. Goodbye meetings or rituals with former caregivers and family members can serve this purpose, especially if the adoption professionals have encouraged those caring adults to tell the child quite directly that they want him to have a good life with his new family, that he has their permission to move on. Their new parents, at the same time, can be taught to find ways to stimulate an arousal-relaxation cycle with their new child that will encourage the child's coming to trust his new parents, so that the family begins to build attachments to one another. Building attachments with older children is complicated enough that I would not begin to try to deal with it in any definitive way here. The books on older child attachment in the Resources section provide many practical strategies for encouraging this reciprocal process.

When children do not learn to trust at an early age, they experience the world as an unsafe place and they may have a hard time learning to trust. Moreover, untrusting, unbonded children often do not develop a conscience. Yet, when children receive quality care and develop secure attachments to a dependable early caregiver, with competent assistance, that attachment can be successfully transferred to another parenting figure.

A number of well-respected authors and trainers have provided valuable material about serious attachment problems and solutions for families adopting older children. If you have adopted or are considering adopting a child older than infancy, do not pass Go and collect your child without reading or hearing Vera Fahlberg, Claudia Jewett-Jarratt, Foster Cline, Kay Donley, Barb Tremitiere, Jim Mahoney, Gregory Keck, Deborah Hage, Janelle Peterson, and others. Your knowledge about these folks and their expertise will prove irreplaceably valuable to you and the local professionals you work with as you parent your older-adopted child.

I think that it's important, however, to direct some specific information to those who will adopt very young children—babies under a year of age—and little has been written for these adopters about attachment. It is my impression that this gap exists because there has been a basic assumption among adoption placement professionals that there is nothing special to discuss. When well-prepared parents adopt healthy newborns and take them straight home from the hospital, the odds are very high that their attachment to one another will be relatively uncomplicated, and so, the reasoning goes, filling new parents' heads with too much "stuff" about attachment problems could become a self-fulfilling prophecy.

Human babies are not like lumps of Playdoh™ that can be moved about at will for some predictable length of time before exposure to the air results in hardening. Still, it remains the exception, rather than the rule, for the parent preparation process of those adopting in-racially and in-country to include any specific information about the possibility of awkward attachments in children younger than one year old. While it is more common for there to be some discussion of these issues for those adopting babies from other countries, such preparation is still inadequate in most cases. This section of this book is an attempt to partially fill that important gap. Families like Sam's need better preparation themselves, and the professionals who come in contact with them need more education too.

> Marv and Eleanor's long-awaited son arrived at age 14 months. Sam was the proverbial apple of his father's eye. After a period of adjustment, Sam did well at home, but something seemed to go askew when Sam was in a group environment in a Parent's Morning Out program or religious services child care situation. When he went to nursery school at age four, Sam began to terrorize other children, and his behavior led his frightened parents to seek a full neurological/psychiatric evaluation at a respected hospital. The first diagnosis? His parents must have been abusing him.
>
> Months of being their own advocates (the full story of how they went about this is too long to share here) unearthed suspicious circumstances about Sam's first months. He had been cared for in an institution where the caregivers were largely poorly supervised teen girls, themselves living in an institutional setting. It was known that many of the other children there had been neglected, and physically and sexually abused. No one could be certain that Sam had been, and his own memories of this pre-verbal period in his life could not be retrieved and explained. And yet, upon closer examination by attachment experts, it was apparent that Sam's problem was that he felt such danger in group settings that he went into a self-protective mode often called "fight or flight."
>
> Sam's whole family needed help, and, on their own, they found it. Marv reports, though, that an enduring side effect of his family's attempts to find sensitive help, which resulted in the system's trying to blame these victims, is Marv's own fear about being physically close to his children after this experience. Marv is afraid to risk being accused again of child abuse.

Parenting with a Partner

Nearly all of the books about first year parenting point out that one of the biggest areas of adjustment for those who are parenting as partners is a readjustment in the relationships between the adults. Among the issues: negotiating a division of labor, balancing an emotional triad, and feeding the sexual and emotional relationship between the adults. Are there adoption angles to some of these issues? Probably.

Let's look at the overall issue of balance. Certainly today's parenting partnerships involve more balanced involvement of parents with their children than was typical of baby-boomers' parents. In my own relatively typical 1950s upbringing, my dad was The Provider and my mom was The Caregiver. This clear division of roles began during the pregnancy. During the 1940s and 1950s and into the early 1960s, fathers were not involved in prenatal care or in labor and delivery. Their role was to rush Mom to the hospital and then wait in a congratulatory, cigar smoke-filled room with a role of coins to be used at the pay phone to notify the relatives. Dad's first glimpse of Baby was through a glass window, and in general his relationship with his children from that point forward was with babies who were clean and sweet smelling, and not hungry. There wasn't a lot of baby bathing, feeding, or diaper changing among '50s dads. The exception to this is that those of you who have known adoptive families of that era may have noticed an unresearched, but anecdotally broadly noted, phenomenon: adoptive fathers tended to be especially involved with their babies and their growing kids.

Fast forward to today. Dads by birth in the 21st century are fully expected to be intensely involved with pregnancy, labor coaching, the delivery room, and the active and hands-on parenting of their children. Today's dads, beginning with the very conception of their children, have "caught up with" adoptive fathers, who have for years been experiencing a relationship with their infants that is relatively "equal" to their wives' relationship with the babies. Furthermore, adoptive dads have long expressed pleasure about this.

> Daniel pushed for the choice to adopt as an alternative route to parenthood. Long before his wife was ready to let go of her dream of becoming pregnant, Daniel knew that adoption felt good to him. He wanted to be a parent—an active, involved parent—but the infertility was his. Daniel liked the equitability of adoption as a route to parenthood—the fact that it would bring the relationship long torn by the pain of infertility back into balance again. He and his wife would have an equal relationship with their child by adoption, just as without the infertility, their connection to a child by birth would have been equal. Until he became involved in an infertility support group, Daniel had not mentioned this particular angle of his motivation to adopt before.

But a local infertility support group sponsored a conference at which couples were encouraged to explore all of the paths to parenthood. At lunch one of the women at their table brought up the fact that she and her partner, another woman, had already adopted their first child and were hoping for a second adoption. A great thing about adoption, she had said, was how very easy it had made it for them to claim their daughter equally.

So perhaps adoptive parent couples, more than parents by birth, start with their babies on more equal footing. Each can diaper and feed Baby (though with adoptive nursing, just as in traditional breast feeding, special attention must be paid to retaining the balance). Baby doesn't "need" either parent more than the other (though when dealing with a possible attachment difficulty it makes sense to agree to forge a particularly close bond with just one parent that can then be transferred to include the other). Neither parent is any more deserving than the other of the special treatment that one recovering from a medical experience may need. Neither adoptive parent will be eligible for a medical leave, but both should be eligible for parenting leave, making it less clear about which one might be home for a while with baby—or, on a more positive note, encouraging both of them to be.

On the other hand, sharing a child, and each other, with one another, brings all new parents challenges. Babies create a love triangle where once there was a twosome. No matter how babies arrive, this factor of parenting life needs acknowledgment and attention. Effective communication is an important tool, of course. Whatever you do, don't stifle your frustrations or stuff your annoyance. Think back to what you have learned before in this journey toward parenthood about how differently any two people may communicate with one another and how easy it is to draw inaccurate conclusions. Nurture your relationship by taking walks together with that stroller (a side benefit is that exercise will relieve tension and help you to sleep), getting out for or renting a movie (a funny one, which can nudge your senses of humor), and engaging your partner with a reward he or she will appreciate (a comfort food? something new to wear? outside help with an overwhelming task?).

As for retaining and nurturing the sexual relationship of the parenting couple, it isn't recovering from an episiotomy and delivery that may disrupt the sex lives of new adoptive parents, but adoptive parents should expect that their intimate lives may indeed be disrupted. Tension in new roles, discomfort about the "invasion" of a third person into intimate physical and emotional space, change of routine, sleep deprivation, anxiety during any limbo period during which a birthparent could have a change of heart—all may contribute to a need to look at ways to preserve, reconfigure, or rebuild both the socially and emotionally intimate and the sexually intimate aspects of parenting couples lives.

Furthermore, the sex lives of infertile couples may have been stressed for a very long time. It is not unusual for infertile couples to feel sexually "burned out." After years of having sex on command and by calendar (with technicians and physicians theoretically, if not actually, looking in at them), couples often stop making love for a while. If they begin to pursue adoption vigorously and immediately, they may not have given this aspect of their lives time to heal. At the same time, this mostly goes unspoken about. The arrival of a long-awaited child after the deprivation of infertility, may, as David Brodzinsky has said, "fill a void that has been felt." What was injured or empty may now feel whole, and the result, for many couples, is the rediscovery of their romantic relationship on a whole new plane.

Parenting without a Partner? Not Really!

The longing to be called "Mom" or "Dad" exists with or without a marriage certificate. Single parenting as a *choice* stepped out of the closet and into the light of public awareness in the early eighties. For the most part, it was women who opened that door and led the way. I've asked my long time friend Cynthia Van Norden Peck, who was one of those women and who has parented eight children of various ethnicities, nationalities, age-at-arrival, and abilities to adulthood (and fostered several more), to share her thoughts about adjustment for those parenting without a partner. Cindy writes,

> "In increasing numbers, single, well-educated career women on the path to social and financial independence turned to international adoption and artificial insemination to fulfill their deep longing to hold and raise a child. Privately arranged adoptions by singles, often within extended families, certainly were not new. These women of the eighties, however, were actively seeking to become parents on their *own* terms. Friends and family replaced a married partner through a pregnancy, labor coaching, and the delivery room, or the "invisible pregnancy" of one waiting-to-adopt. *Choice* was key; options existed as never before. By the end of the decade, men openly joined them in expressing their desire to become single parents through adoption or surrogacy.
>
> "The rising divorce rate of the eighties and nineties collaborated in some ways to 'normalize' single parent families. Both men and women who had never planned on raising a child or children on their own found themselves thrust into the role of primary caregiver and provider. To the benefit of all, singles-by-choice challenged studies that pointed to distinct social, emotional and psychological disadvantages of children of single parents living at or below the poverty line. Tradi-

tional parenting definitions, standards and attitudes began a subtle and perceptible shift."

Different and the Same

"The issues of achieving balance, equality and stable relationships are as important for those choosing to parent without a partner as they are for couples. Balancing home and work responsibilities may involve job-sharing, telecommuting or flex-time scheduling or a new career path altogether. For some singles, extended family members fulfill the role traditionally held by one's marital partner. Others are choosing live-in help, daycare and part-time babysitters to support the necessary hours they spend at work. Childcare can be costly, especially when only one income is available, but many single parents will tell you that the sacrifice is small compared to the joy of parenting and the love they feel for the child they have chosen to bring into their lives.

"How does life change for a single choosing to parent a child, whether through a planned pregnancy or adoption? In many significant ways, life does not much. Men and women who make the deliberate choice to build a family on their own tend to be dedicated, strong-minded, independent thinkers in most areas of their lives already. As creative problem-solvers, they have forged strong connections among friends, family, mentors and the community-at-large and actively participate in many areas. They have experienced success at work and in their communities, and while traditional marriage and parenting with a partner may have been part of their original plan, the absence of a partner does not automatically put parenting out of their reach. The skills these single-parents-by-choice bring to their children-of-choice serve them well as they make changes to accommodate to the needs and schedules of their new children. The emotional joining, separating, expanding and rejoining that characterize growth in any new relationship can be more intense between a single parent and single child. Yet, the strong connections already established before a child arrived stand ready to support and draw that child to new connections among friends, family and mentors and strengthen the family. These relationships provide love, acceptance, validation and success—for both parent and child.

"One irony worth noting is the fact that at times, single parents seem held to a higher standard than their married counterparts. *Higher standard* sounds to this writer (a single parent for over 30 years of a large number of youngsters adopted at many different ages) like a fancy way of saying *judgment*. Some of my peers questioned my judgment with a roll of their eyes or a 'harrumph!' Others took pains to let me know that if I chose to stop at one, I wouldn't have to deal with a cold that started with one child in the fall and got passed around from one to the other until sunny and warm May returned. Clearly the so-called *higher standard* meant having the good sense to adopt just one child— *good judgment*. I'd lowered the standards and shown dramatically poor judgment to add five, six, seven then eight to my family!

"For my first fifteen years as a single parent from the mid-seventies through the eighties, I felt I was constantly defending my right to build my family through adoption. By the early nineties, however, all that changed when singles by the thousands brought home international children, primarily from China, Russia and Guatemala, and single parenting was no longer seen as an oddity. These were strong, successful parents communicating love, support and a strong sense of identity and future direction to their children, and as we entered the new millennium the great diversity found in young families was something to celebrate."

Sex, Relationships and New Social Networks

"Singles who choose to conceive or adopt and bring a child into their lives to expand on a life that is already relationship-rich and functional are inviting that child to settle in and to seek a place where he can grow by experience and example in love and security.

"Those who chose pregnancy or adoption to fulfill a need for the exclusive love and companionship of a child at the exclusion of regular adult social and sexual relationships set themselves—and their child or children—up for disappointment. An adult/child relationship is best nurtured with many examples of how families "work." The parenting adult needs to be seen in a variety of other adult relationships, friendly and more intimate.

"Once the decision is made, regardless of the motivation, the successful single parent wisely monitors and adjusts to the demands of the newest member, relishing the task, sometimes at the point of exhaustion, but understanding that *choice*—his or her own choice—created this new constellation, and *responsible choices* will create a new reality and stable future for the child you dreamed would one day call you 'Mom' or 'Dad.'"

No one could say it better than Cindy, a long time adoption advocate (Angel in Adoption, 2005), niche newsletter editor (the fabulous *Roots & Wings*, followed by *Adoption Today* and founding editor of *Fostering Families Today*), and author of *Parents at Last: Celebrating Adoption and the New Pathways to Parenthood* (New York: Clarkson Potter, 1998).

Arrival Adjustment
and the Post-Adoption Blues

Post-arrival confusion, anxiety and minor depression is relatively common among parents. Some sources claim that at least 50% of parents—both fathers and mothers—suffer from the Baby Blues. Unlike the more serious medical condition known as postpartum depression, Baby Blues are not necessarily influenced by hormonal fluctuations. That's why it's just as likely that dads as well as moms may experience Baby Blues whether they become parents by birth or by adoption.

Many factors contribute to the Baby Blues, no matter how the child arrives. Becoming a parent is in itself a major life change. Many parents—including those who have prepared themselves well—initially feel inadequate for such an enormous responsibility when a real baby is finally in their arms. No matter at what age the new child arrives, new parents' sleep patterns are usually interrupted as they doze with one ear tuned to the needs of a small person in unfamiliar surroundings. Parents may eat differently or even skip meals entirely when distracted by a needy small person. Schedules and routines fall by the wayside and life begins to feel out of control. A child who is particularly fussy or anxious, who is experiencing some attachment difficulties, or who is medically fragile may create an early parenting experience far different from the idyllic one dreamed of for so long.

Issues specific to adoption may contribute to post-arrival depression too. Enormous excitement surrounds the arrival of a new member of the family, but what if you're worried that grandparents or aunts and uncles won't accept this child? And what about the insensitive comments that ignorant but usually well meaning others throw about? And what if it doesn't feel the way you expected that it would? And what if you're finding that this new experience is re-triggering old memories? And what if you are feeling consumed with worry or guilt about your child's birthparents' loss?

New parents usually take time away from work. But despite recent U.S. federal laws which support the need for adoptive parents to have leave, some employers may be less than cooperative if they see post-arrival leave as a medical issue for those who give birth rather than as a parenting issue. Depending on whether you were able to plan this well in advance or were surprised by the timing of the adoption, being away from the job can produce anxiety and even guilt—both of which may be enhanced by the parent's berating of self for not being able to forget the job and focus exclusively on the longed-for new arrival. For some people personal self-image is so intrinsically tied to their jobs that becoming a full-time parent, whether on temporary leave or as a change in lifestyle, can be difficult to adjust to.

Some new adopters find that infertility issues resurface briefly when their new child arrives, so that they feel some (usually temporary) sadness that this child is not connected to them genetically. Other adoptive parents are overwhelmed by feelings of sadness for the losses experienced by their child's birthfamily and find it difficult to allow themselves to feel joy rooted in another's grief. Still others find it difficult to let themselves fall unconditionally into love with a child during any period of time when a birthparent's decision may be revoked.

To help yourself or your partner in staving off or coping with post-arrival blues, try these tips, some of which have been offered before as general arrival tips:

- Acknowledge that you're only human. That approved homestudy may have felt like getting the Good Housekeeping Seal of Approval, but it didn't grant you status as Super-Parent-To-Be. Don't beat yourself up!

- The stay-at-home parent should shower and dress before the other parent leaves in the morning. Not only is it hard to find time for this later, but getting off to this kind of "fresh start" can set a tone for the day.

- Eat a balanced diet. (Those pre-arrival prepared foods suggested earlier can come in handy now, or suggest to friends who want to know what they can do to help that a carried-in meal would be welcomed far more than would "holding the baby.")

- Be kind to your head and to your soul. Hire a sitter (or recruit a friend or your partner) to give yourself a few minutes each day just for yourself—to take a leisurely bath, to read a book, to meditate, to make a phone call, etc.

- Relieve stress by remembering to exercise regularly . . . yoga stretches during nap time, a brisk walk around the block while pushing a stroller, new parent aerobics or swimming classes (with daycare provided) at the local Y.

- Don't allow yourself to feel "trapped." Take the baby with you to the mall or a museum. Have lunch at Wendy's with a friend. Contact a parents' group.

- Feed your marriage. It's easy for new parents to forget that the marriage came first and for parenting partners to feel cast aside by a devoted new parent.

- Be your own advocate for quiet time with your family as you adjust to one another and the changes that accompany this new experience. Well-wishers often forget that it isn't just the physically demanding experience of giving birth that puts new moms in need of help and rest, many birthfathers and adoptive parents experience "Cinderella syndrome" in the days following an arrival as they struggle to keep up with entertaining a constant flow of visitors.

The Baby Blues are normal, but that doesn't make them seem less scary. Seek help—from your parent group, from your child's pediatrician, from your social worker, from your family doctor—if the "down feelings" don't begin to dissipate in just a few weeks.

Common "Differences" in an Adopted Child's Early Development

Interrupted or Unexperienced Stages of Development

Your baby may not join you at his birth. That's an adoption thing. That may or may not result in adjustment problems for either or both of you, but if your baby has a hard time adjusting to change, or if you find it difficult to help her adjust, many tools for dealing with those potential problems were offered in the last chapter. If those don't work, more may be available if you are willing to make contact with an adoptive parent group about your concerns.

Psychiatrist Justin Call's research concerning how babies can be expected to react at certain vulnerable stages of development during their infancy is, unfortunately, not well known among those who are arranging placements. In a 1974 article called "Helping Infants Cope with Change" published in the January issue of the journal *Early Child Development and Care*, Dr. Call describes how babies of various ages may feel and express distress about a change in environment and caretaker. For example, newborns to three-month-old infants are described by Dr. Call as being most concerned with having their needs met. One might assume, then, that if needs continue to be met consistently, babies might not be particularly distressed by changed surroundings. Perhaps, writes Call, this is true of newborns. But it's also true that by age one month, babies are alert enough to respond to stimuli but are not sophisticated enough to modify them, so that until they are over three months old they are particularly susceptible to overstimulation and overload. Call believes that babies who are between four and twelve weeks of age are highly likely to be distressed by a change in environment and caretaker.

A more adaptive time for change is when babies are between three and six months of age. These babies, Call says, are more able to respond to and modify stimuli and are physically sophisticated enough to respond more easily to a changed diet. But a particularly vulnerable window again appears for the child between six and twelve months of age. Children who have been given the opportunity to do so have usually formed an intense attachment to a caretaker by this time, and if moved they are likely to experience a full range of typical grieving behaviors, including shock and denial, anger and despair, depression and withdrawal. It's important to keep in mind that because these devastating losses are occurring before a baby has language with which he might be able to communicate more directly and more successfully, it is particularly hard for him to resolve this kind of anxiety.

If you are adopting a child who will not arrive home until he is several weeks or months or a year or more old, I recommend that you use the time before his placement to try to get a sense of what milestones he may have passed and what growth experiences he might be expected to have had before he arrives at home. One way to do this is simply to check out the growth and development books and read the chapters for the weeks and months you will have missed as your child's parent. If you miss time together not because you didn't know about the existence of one another but because you are waiting for some bureaucracy somewhere to free your already identified child to his family, the newsletter *Growing Child*, which arrives on a monthly basis planned to coincide with your child's age, provides an even better way to "keep up" with your child.

It's important to be prepared for the possibility that your later-arriving infant—even if very healthy—may not have achieved all of the milestones the books have described as "average" or "normal" when he arrives home. Sometimes those delays are a result of the child's not having had enough one-on-one stimulation in previous environments. In orphanages, babies often have many caretakers in one day (and some of these caretakers may be older children rather than adults). Orphanage kids may have come to expect few interactions each day and may not have learned that there can be a cause/effect relationship between expressing a felt need and having it met. Some later-arriving infants may never have experienced comfort and so do not know how to. If he has never felt full of food before, never felt comforted by cuddling, your child may have real difficulty understanding these new feelings and accepting them. And if he has been deprived of this kind of early caregiving, he may be operating mostly in "survival mode," having become so fearful and stressed as to be hyper-vigilant. Sometimes developmental delays are traumatically induced regressions that have to do with Baby's fear and discomfort about this move or a series of moves.

Every parent wants her child to be as smart as he can be. Adopting parents often worry that the things they've had no control over—a birthmother's poor diet or ingestion of toxins such as chemicals or alcohol during her pregnancy, poor nutrition or a lack of stimulation during the period before we become his caregivers, trauma from neglect, abuse or separation—will affect his intelligence. Though basic intelligence is innate, parents who provide appropriate stimulation can offer their babies optimal intellectual support.

In the first year babies' brains develop more synapses (electrical connections) than at any other period in their lives. The first year of life is a crucial one for cognitive development. It behooves you to learn as much as you can about where a well-cared-for baby might be expected to be by the time he is the age of your baby at arrival, and to learn as well just how much stimulation a baby of that age can handle. Then use this information as you interact with your baby.

Because babies are so sensorially focused, stimulating all the senses will help the baby learn. New sounds, tastes, touches, and sights when offered by a trusted caregiver engage a baby's brain. Mobiles that flutter above a crib, fathers who talk while they change diapers or give baths, songs sung while the bottle is being warmed, a variety of textured items placed on a tray all help Baby to learn. In order to learn, babies need to do things over and over again, and yet intellectual growth requires a balance between familiarity and novelty. So change those mobiles occasionally, find new songs to sing, give baby different textures, and set his chair so that he has a different perspective on the room.

By the middle of the first year of life, babies who have been well-stimulated yet not over-stimulated and who have experienced consistency while being exposed to new things, have been steadily growing cognitively and are able, on a rudimentary level, to understand that their actions have an effect on the world. At about age eight months, children have sophisticated enough motor control as well as cognitive ability to deliberately reach out to ring a bell on a toy and understand with real delight the cause and effect relationship in a game of peek-a-boo.

By the end of the first year, most children who have experienced a steady relationship with a trusted caregiver are communicating very well with signals, body language, coos and grunts, and most have begun to use a few words. Cultural differences and changes of language can create interruptions in this growth, and sometimes these interruptions can trigger regressions. If you child is not with you during some or all of this first year, his progress in these developmental stages may very well be delayed.

Progress in motor skills can be delayed as well. Babies whose early months are spent in group care facilities have few of the opportunities for developing motor skills that children cared for by skilled foster parents or reared from the beginning in their adoptive home have. Babies must be unswaddled and given space in order to learn to kick and to roll from side to side. Children who spend little time being carried—spending hours in a crib and then strapped in a seat—have few opportunities to test their motor skills. If there is nothing colorful or interesting to bat at or try to pick up, a child may not have learned to grasp a rattle.

Developmentally interrupted babies who are given consistent, careful and attentive care, love and stimulation should be expected to catch up within a matter of weeks or months. If your child does not catch up within a half year of his arrival, talk with his doctor about your concerns and elicit help in screening for less common health problems which may have gone unidentified. These could include fetal alcohol syndrome or fetal alcohol effect, lingering effects of institutionalization, or undiagnosed post traumatic stress syndrome. You may also find helpful advice from your adoptive parent group.

Low Birth Weight Babies

Parenting is fraught with risks, no matter how children join their families. Among the few extra risks adoption may carry are those that arise for a child born earlier and/or smaller than average. Mothers whose circumstances aren't conducive to parenting their babies themselves and so plan adoption for their children are often at substantial risk for the circumstances that lead to low birth weight (LBW) babies. A birthmother may have been ill or poorly nourished herself due to monetary and social circumstances. Women under seventeen and those who do not receive early prenatal care are at increased risk for delivering pre-term. A birthmother may have been under extreme emotional pressure or have denied her pregnancy and attempted to control her changing body shape by dieting—starving both herself and her baby. Smoking, drinking and using drugs of any kind—over the counter, "recreational," or prescription medication—during pregnancy contributes to the births of both pre-term and low birth weight babies. Many of these factors may be a part of the lives of women whose children become available for adoption.

In North America, babies who weigh less than 2.5 kg (5 lbs 8 oz) at birth—whether born at term (37–42 weeks gestation) or pre-term—are said to be of low birth weight. The reason for the low birth weight—that is, whether the baby was born too early (pre-term) or arrived at term but was considered small for his gestational age (SGA)—can signal different problems with different long-term outcomes.

On the other hand, what is considered average birth weight in North America and Western Europe is not necessarily average in South America, Asia, India, the Philippines, and other countries. It is important, then, for pre-adoptive parents and the pediatrician they have chosen to care for their coming child to be familiar with the size and weight norms of the ethnic group and/or country of origin of the child they are preparing to adopt when evaluating any information given to them about the child's prenatal history, birth history, and early weeks or months of life.

The most reassuring thing you can know about LBW is that, while it requires special attention and care, most children who are born otherwise healthy and without the complications of some of the more serious factors contributing to LBW (such as a pregnancy awash in alcohol or drugs, or severe maternal malnutrition) overcome their low birth weight and "catch up" with their peers. On the other hand, parents should be aware that LBW babies seem to be at slightly higher risk for developing learning disabilities, hyperactivity and attention deficit disorder, and sleep disturbances. Because of the wide variation in outcomes, there are no guarantees that an LBW baby—even one who receives the best interventional medical care and loving nurturing from permanent parents right from the moment of birth—will grow to be healthy and "normal." Furthermore, when adopting, one cannot be assured that an accurate birth and prenatal history can be obtained.

Pre-term (you may be more familiar with the older term *premature*) babies have not had a full in-utero gestational period, and so tend to be susceptible to problems having to do with being ready to live outside the womb. They have a limited ability to keep themselves warm, and may have poorly developed sucking reflexes and underdeveloped bowels. The immaturity of their lungs may cause breathing problems, making them more susceptible to apnea. They are often anemic, due to the fact that most of the iron storage a baby needs to make healthy red blood cells is transferred from his birthmother during the last three months of pregnancy. Babies who are severely pre-term (usually weighing less than 3 lb 8 oz or 1.5 kg) are significantly more likely to have seriously disabling conditions such as cerebral palsy, blindness or deafness. Among U.S.-born babies, two-thirds of LBW babies are pre-term.

Many of the factors that lead to pre-term birth can also lead to the full-term births of babies who are small for gestational age. SGA babies are most often LBW not because they were born too soon, but because they and their birthmothers did not receive proper prenatal care. These babies usually have experienced some degree of intra-uterine growth retardation. SGA babies are often of average length, but are very thin, so that they too have problems with retaining heat and need to be kept warm. They need fortified formula and vitamins, and while they are less often in need of intensive care at birth than are premature babies, they are indeed in need of special care.

For many years studies of the outcome of babies born small did not try to distinguish the differences between pre-term and small-for-gestational-age babies, so that the older the infant care book to which you are referring for information, the less likely you are to see these described separately. Now, however, some studies have begun to separate pre-term and small-for-gestational-age babies into two distinct groups, and these newest studies indicate that long-term outcome in terms of learning abilities seem to be better for those children who are LBW because of prematurity (except for those who are severely pre-term) than for those who were small for gestational age and may have experienced intra-uterine growth retardation.

Parents of babies suspected of, or known to have been, LBW should attempt to acquire as full a health history as possible of their child and his birthparents, and should make their concerns clear to their pediatrician and seek her help. While LBW children are sometimes easily overstimulated, it is important to give LBW children plenty of nurturing stimulation, both physically (games and exercises) and intellectually (conversations and lots of being sung and read to). Of course this is what all children need, and one would assume that parents who have run the gantlet of adoption would be more than eager to engage in active parenting.

> My oldest child was born pre-term and came home to us at ten days old weighing just 4 lbs, 8 oz. My husband and I were just as anxious about the health of our pre-term son as any parent can reasonably

be expected to be. The good news is that, just as do most actively parented preemies, he turned out great and is now, in adulthood, normal both in size and in intelligence.

Contact your local chapter of the March of Dimes for referrals and fact sheets on low birth weight and disabilities, and local hospitals for the names of support groups in your community for parents of low birth weight or pre-term babies.

Speech Delays

During the first six months of life, language development is identical in babies of every nationality. Since the purpose of language is not to make noise, rather to communicate, the first gurgles of the six week old are communicative. This leads to the babbling open vowel sounds of the three month old, with consonants following. Usually from about six months onward the babble becomes increasingly elaborate and expressive, until somewhere between the 10th and 14th months when your baby will start to use specific sounds to identify particular objects. By 18 months the average toddler will have a spoken vocabulary of up to 20 single words (he understands far more words spoken to him), and by two years he has developed over 50 single words and is using the two-word phrases that lead to the full sentences (including verbs, prepositions, and chanting of rhymes) of three-year-olds.

Universally, children learn to speak a language from hearing it spoken, so that it is through immersion in the stimulation of spoken words that children become fluent in a language by the age of three. As is typical of all new language development (whether with babies just learning to speak or adults learning a second language), one understands language spoken to him more rapidly than one can fluently speak a language. This principle of learning language through immersion is so widely understood that it served as the basis for the development of the Suzuki method of teaching very young children to play violin, flute, and piano. In this program, parents are encouraged to think of music as a language and to play a series of simple recorded songs over and over for their babies and toddler, leading eventually to their early "playing by ear."

There are some things that can get in the way of language development. The most common reason for speech and language delays is mental retardation, followed by hearing impairment and learning disabilities which can include disturbances in receptive or expressive language. The observant parent who notices symptoms such as failure to respond to noises from outside the field of vision, disruptions in her child's language development (for example she was cooing and babbling at 3 months and then stopped a few months later) might suspect a hearing loss. Children who begin speaking normally and then stop could be autistic. These kinds of language delays, of course, demand expert diagnosis and ongoing professional assistance.

Adoption per se does not put children at higher risk for these kinds of problems, but adoptive parents who do not have a complete or reliable health history for their children may need to be especially observant.

Some children's language delays are due to environmental or stimulation deficit problems. For example, a child being cared for in an overly crowded daycare situation where he gets little one-on-one attention or a child alone all day with a daycare provider who talks very little or who speaks a different language than the one he hears from his parents is at increased risk for stimulation deficit. Still other children have emotional difficulties which can lead to speech delays. With proper intervention, these more easily remediable types of delays represent only short-term problems and are not disabling.

Some groups of babies who have been adopted are more at risk for these emotional and environmental kinds of speech and language delays. Children who experience breaks in attachment during the crucial first 24 months of language development may experience stalls in their acquisition and use of language, as may children who have been cared for by overworked and frequently changing caretakers in group settings and institutions, who therefore have been stimulation deprived. Children who experience the confusion of moving from one culture and language environment to another are also more likely to experience some speech and language delays.

Several authors have written about the language issues of older internationally adopted children. According to Holly Van Gulden and Lisa Bartels-Raab in *Real Parents, Real Children*, youngsters adopted internationally beyond toddlerhood may temporarily refuse to learn English as a way to protect themselves from a frightening alien culture. Some parents have felt that their internationally adopted children used refusal to learn a new language as a control issue. In *Are Those Kids Yours?* author Cheri Register relates the experience of several families who found that their internationally adopted older children experienced a pattern of speaking fluently in their first language, followed by several weeks or months of not speaking at all, which were followed by the fluent use of English. In her book *Toddler Adoption: The Weaver's Craft*, Mary Hopkins-Best shares similar anecdotes describing much younger children.

The single most important factor in stimulating a child to develop language—whether he is with you from birth, has come to you through foster care or from a group home, or has been adopted from another culture—is to let him hear language used in a loving and positive way. According to many child development experts, children with speech delays are more likely to be helped by speech stimulation at home than from speech therapy during the pre-school years. In fact, many speech professionals find that when their professional services are sought out, the best thing they can do for very young children is train their caregiver to be "therapists."

From earliest infancy read to your baby, sing to him, and talk to him. Talk to your child as you dress him on the changing table. Carry on a one-sided conversation in a soft, simple patter throughout your day together. Recite nursery rhymes and play pat-a-cake and peek-a-boo. Identify objects you notice while going about your daily routine . . . "Pretty flowers!" and "Soft bunny;" "Mmm, applesauce" and "Hot stove;" and "Kitty—meow," "Cow—moo." It really doesn't matter to your child whether you can carry a tune; sing simple nursery songs as you drive in the car and sing lullabies with words rather than simply playing wordless music as he goes to sleep. The added element of frequent close body contact while reading to your child enhances not just language development but attachment as well.

Choose daycare providers carefully (even more so for the child with attachment breaks or the one who has changed cultures and language), being certain that your child will be in a language-stimulating rather than language-deprived or over-stimulating environment. Beware the crutch of playing records or tapes, or having the TV going in the background. These more complex mixtures of language and sound effects and orchestration can be too complex and over-stimulating for some infants and toddlers, who may, in fact, learn quickly to tune them out.

The less complicated sound of your child's family's loving voices spoken directly to him is by far the best stimulation for his acquisition of language—not to mention for his emotional development.

Adoption and Stranger Anxiety

As parents will have learned from reading almost any of the many good books available on parenting infants and toddlers, stranger anxiety (also called separation anxiety and defined as the tendency of children to react with fear when left by parents with anyone other than their primary attachment figure) is a common, though not universal, occurrence among babies from about eight months of age until about two years. While most parents are wrenched and guilt stricken by the experience of leaving a screaming little person reaching out for Mama from the arms of a loving grandma, or peeling off clinging fingers from around Daddy's knees in order to make it to work on time from the familiar daycare provider's home, the fact that this anxiety occurs is really a pretty good thing. Its appearance indicates that one of the most important tasks of infancy—attachment to a parent—is working.

Well-cared for and well-loved babies younger than 8 months most often are indiscriminately social, no matter how they arrived in their families. From around age 4 months when they begin to smile spontaneously and to engage in social exchanges with others, as long as their needs for food and comfort are being reliably met when they are expressed, most babies are trusting. But slowly, over the course of day-to-day living, children come to realize that they are separate people from their caregivers and that not only must they be able to trust that their needs will be met, but that there is a specific someone—most often Mama or Daddy—who meets those needs when they are expressed. It is Daddy who quickly brings the bottle and satisfies the pain of hunger. It is Mama who changes the cold, wet diaper or pulls up the kicked-off blanket.

For babies (as for adults), that consistently repeated cycle we've referred to so often in this book of expressing a need, having it met, feeling comfortable, and associating that comfort with nurturing by a specific person creates the bond of trust that leads to secure attachment. For children adopted as healthy, non-drug-exposed newborns by well-prepared and responsive parents, the likelihood of secure attachment is very high, and most adoption professionals agree that the experience of separation/stranger anxiety, while likely to occur, is unlikely to be colored by the fact of adoption.[2]

Yet not all babies join their families at birth and not all children are healthy. For those young children, a series of changes in caretakers and environment can make it difficult for them to learn to trust. Symptoms you'll recall from the earlier discussion range from anxiousness about everybody (parents included) for many months, to an apparent willingness to go to anyone and everyone right from the beginning. It is for these insecurely or anxiously attached babies and toddlers that adoption becomes an element in the appearance or lack of separation anxiety.

While it is may seem obvious why children who have been abused and neglected in previous homes would have a difficult time learning to trust and would be slower to attach, many people presume (inaccurately) that older babies placed from secure environments (stable, loving foster homes or well-staffed group care facilities) will automatically attach smoothly. And certainly some babies do make amazingly smooth transitions. But for other children a change in environment can be very difficult.

As we have discussed before, in-born personality traits—including adaptability, stress tolerance, and a tendency toward low or high emotionalism—add important elements to the attachment formula, as do the relative health of the child and his exposure, or lack of, to drugs and alcohol in-utero. For those who have had more than one caretaker, the routine of knowing one can depend on one consistent adult to be there—to meet needs, to provide love, to care—must be experienced for a long enough period of time to be internalized. This must occur before a child can be expected to care about, trust, and therefore miss the presence or fear the disappearance of a particular adult.

Parents may have cause for some concern if their children do not express normal stranger anxiety after several months in their new homes. Not caring who one goes to and not appearing to miss a primary caregiver can lead to a toddler's indiscriminately wandering away from parents or putting himself in danger at the hands of strangers. While these are practical concerns for parents, they may also carry with them the underlying message that attachments have not yet formed and signal a need for help.

Yet other adoptive families may find that once attachments do begin to form, separation anxiety may be particularly intense. Parents of these youngsters must then be carefully attuned to the child's need for very short separations and the fewest possible number of caretakers as infrequently as possible for a while. Some working-parent adopters may find it useful to save up some of the leave time they plan to use for the arrival of their child for possible use several months later when newly forming attachments may lead to a short period of particularly difficult separation anxiety. For these families, the appearance of a good dose of "normal" stranger anxiety can be a cause for celebration.

Birthparent Relationships

Even if the adoption is a traditional, fully confidential adoption involving no communication between birth and adoptive families rather than a somewhat communicative or fully open adoption, the reality is—and you know it—that your child has two sets of parents. You have a relationship with that birthfamily, whether you ever meet them. Birthparents provide their children with prenatal experiences, genetic connection, and their ethnicity. Birthparents connect their children to a culture, though you may connect them to an additional culture. In a workshop we presented together in the San Francisco Bay area in California, attachment therapist Vera Fahlberg pointed out that birthparents have great power over their children's lives. If we acknowledge the things that birthparents provide (a part of practicing acceptance of difference behavior, don't you think?), we give children the power to decide how those factors will impact their lives. On the other hand, said Dr. Fahlberg, if we don't acknowledge birthparents' influences on their children (practicing rejection of difference behaviors) these factors will still influence children, but the children will not be in psychological control of them.

If your adoption is an open adoption this other family will be a concrete part of your life. Yet even if you have never met your child's birthparents and never expect to, you have a relationship with them. You will think about them; you will wonder or worry about them. This is an adoption thing too.

The first year of parenting is crammed full of adjustments, and settling into a comfortable relationship with your baby's birthparents—either a concrete one in an open adoption or an imagined one in a confidential adoption—is another of the necessary additional adjustments in adopting.

Open adoption is most certainly rooted in reality rather than in imagination, and reality has its advantages and drawbacks. Possible advantages to open adoption in the first year after placement? Well, there is no "unknown" to be afraid of; you know what it is and who it is that you are dealing with. Parents also have ready access to information should the need for it arise. But even if everyone had good preparation and good quality post-placement support services are in place, adjusting relationships in open adoption can be difficult.

Marilyn Shinyei, social worker and adoptive parent from Adoption Option in Canada, describes her role as a professional working in open adoptions as akin to that of a midwife standing by as a birth unfolds. In workshops for adoptive parents, Marilyn describes several issues of open adoptions that are short-term (occurring during the first two years or so). First is establishing trust between the two families. Recognizing that the first six months of grief are probably the worst for a birthparent and may well feel "in your face" can produce adjustment challenges. Marilyn finds that these issues can produce bonding and entitlement problems for adoptive parents, since the closeness between adopters and birthparents sometimes makes it very hard for adopting parents to feel that it's really okay to have this baby. Shinyei suggests that the only way to deal with this problem is to be absolutely certain that adoptive parents not be allowed to become a child's birthmother's primary source of support.

During the first year of an open adoption, Marilyn finds that most connected families tend to renegotiate the "contract" as they establish boundaries. The naming process can go smoothly or with some conflict, for example. Families often need to establish limits or negotiate gift giving—especially when it comes to purchases of items of special significance (a Christening dress, for example). During the first year, families need to make decisions about how visiting and phone calls will work. Whether birth families will be a part of special events must be worked out (and as was mentioned before, these negotiations can be affected by how the adopter's family of origin reacts to the openness). Of course since all relationships are fluid and change over time as circumstances and needs change, families shouldn't expect that all of the "agreements" or "decisions" made before and in the first year of an open adoption are set in stone. The first year, however, provides an opportunity to set a positive tone for a relationship that should last throughout the families' lives.

Families whose adoptions are confidential have none of these negotiations to consider. On the one hand this may sound pretty good—or easier, anyway. On the other hand many families in confidential adoptions allow themselves to deny that there even is a relationship with birthfamilies, a mistake that open adopters cannot make. With no real information to process in confidential adoptions, imagination tends to take over, sometimes spawning fear, or alternately resulting in a pedestalizing of birthparents. Parents may find themselves worrying that an unknown birthparent may appear out of nowhere with a change of heart. A parent may feel guilty imagining her child's birthmother's grief and loss which seems to be rooted in her own joy. Parents in confidential adoptions have often admitted that the whereabouts and the unknown, and therefore unexplored, feelings of their child's anonymous birthparents hung like a sword over their heads, preventing them from giving themselves fully to their baby until the adoption was actually finalized several months to a year after his arrival.

What If??

Sometimes what starts out to be an adoption just doesn't end up that way, and this seems to be happening proportionately more frequently than it did in the days of entirely confidential adoptions. Several adoption professionals who are among the staunchest of advocates of openness, and the benefits and opportunities it offers to all touched by adoption, describe the risk of reversal and its resulting emotional devastation as the single greatest negative change that has accompanied the practice of open adoption.

Please understand that while statistically the overwhelming majority of those entering counseling about an unplanned pregnancy don't plan an adoption, among those who do, reversals of actual placements remain the exception rather than the rule. With frustration, professionals say that they are learning that there is little they can do to predict reversals. Despite cautions from intermediaries, adoptive parents often believe that because the open relationship is wonderful birthparents won't reverse their decision. But, no matter how open, trusting and wonderful the relationship has been between adopting parents and birthparents there is still a risk of a change of heart. Several social workers interviewed said explaining why a reversal happens very often comes down to a birthmother's extended relationships—her parents (especially the birthgrandmother) wanting her to "keep" the baby, a previously uninvolved birthfather promising a resumed relationship. Over the past several years the issue of adoptions which are uncompleted because a birthfamily member reclaims a child has received so much media attention that it has become nearly as large and looming a worry for prospective adopters as is the bonding issue. Avoiding the possibility of a birthparent-initiated adoption reversal is often cited as the primary reason families choose intercountry rather than domestic adoption.

The issue is a tough one. Even figuring out what to title this section was difficult. Why? Because point of view makes all the difference. In the call for participation letter I circulated as part of writing *Launching a Baby's Adoption*, I referred to the issue as "When the worst thing happens." I was thinking as an adoptive parent, of course, about how painful it would be to have a child already in my home taken away. Birthparent Brenda Romanchik rightfully took me to task, indignantly but quite correctly pointing out that a birthparent's choice to parent her baby has to be supported as reflecting all parents' interest in doing what they think is the best thing for Baby.

Deciding that a baby will be adopted is an enormous responsibility. Birthparents have to be certain. To be sure they need time . . . but how much? Given that every human is unique, is it possible to identify completely reasonable timing for making such a final decision? Everyone seems to agree that decisions made during pregnancy must be made all over again once birthparents have seen and held a real baby. Yet whether the decisions made during pregnancy or after birth are likely to be best is certainly an issue for debate. It is argued that birthparents in open adoptions can be easily coerced by adopting parents they've come to know and like. Just as logical, though, is the argument that it is the knowing of the parents-to-be and feeling confident about them that makes planning an adoption possible at all in today's social climate. Some claim that it's the pregnancy itself that creates hormonal chaos, and that making a decision at birth allows for greater clarity. Others argue that mothers need many hours or a few days after birth for the effects of medications to wear off and for what they see as much more significant post-natal hormonal shifts to calm in order to make a rational decision. Still others lobby on behalf of a much longer wait, arguing that it takes many weeks or months for physical recovery to occur, extended family to rally, and practical strategies to be set in motion. State and provincial statutes about when irreversible consents may be taken range from allowing them to be taken immediately after a baby has been born to ensuring that a preliminary consent to adoption may be reversed without question as long as a year after a voluntary placement. Agencies often establish their own guidelines and policies which offer birthparents more time for finalizing their plans than does local law.

State and provincial laws and agency policies include a variety of approaches to making certain that a birthparent is sure about adoption. Once it was common for agencies to arrange for babies to be cared for in large nurseries for the days or weeks until birthparents' options for changing their minds had passed. Sometimes birthparents were among their children's caretakers in such settings. This approach gave over to putting birthmothers and their babies in residential settings or foster homes together, so that a birthmother might personally care for her baby with mentoring support while making her final decision. More recently agencies attempting to give birthparents some emotional distance in which to make their decisions but unwilling to submit adopting parents to the risk of a reversed placement have used foster parents to care for babies in what they call cradle care for several days, weeks or months, giving birthparents—and often prospective adopting parents—frequent access to the baby. Today most agencies recognize that babies need permanency and that they should be exposed to as few moves as possible, so adoption professionals increasingly encourage adopting couples to serve as legal-risk foster parents to the babies they are likely to adopt. In these situations, couples offer direct care to a baby they hope to adopt for the days or weeks—or sometimes even months, depending on the status of the birthfather and the law in their locale—during which birthparents have the unquestioned option to decide to parent before an adoption could proceed without risk.

Mary Anne Maiser calls the period during which adopting parents have physical custody of a baby but birthparents still have absolute parental rights "murderously difficult" for everyone, but especially for adopting parents, who are consistently advised of their own and their babies' need to bond to one another immediately, but who, for emotional safety's sake, may be inclined to keep some emotional distance "just in case." Many workers interviewed worried about the long term impact on attachment between adopting parents and children that extended periods of risk create.

And, really, when asked to focus on the needs of the baby, few disagree that what babies need first and foremost and whenever possible, is permanent, consistent, loving, and competent care from the very moment of birth. Ideally, in child-centered adoption practice, these movements back from adopting parents to birthfamily members—movements called reversals, reclaimings, changes of heart, birthfamily disruptions, etc.—would never happen. Theoretically, if birthparents were well-counseled they would either parent from the beginning or plan a firm and final adoption. They wouldn't change their minds. But birthparents aren't theories; they are real people coming at all of this in the midst of a crisis. Whatever their reasons for considering adoption for the child they conceive and birth, the choice to parent or to entrust a child to adoptive parents cannot be cut and dried.

To begin, one must first ask, if a birthparent asks for the return of a child a few days or weeks after the placement, should we comply? My answer is unequivocal, as stated in Chapter 7 on Ethics. This isn't a question of possession and legal claims. This is a moral question. Once parents have assured themselves that competent counselors have worked with the birthparent, advising of the consequences for self, adoptive parents and—mostly especially—baby, and helping him or her work out a practical parenting plan and a plan for the baby's smoothest transition, the answer, of course, is yes. The baby must be returned. And then the grieving must begin.

My friend Wendy Williams, an adoptive parent from Ottawa, wrote an especially poignant essay about her family's experience with a reversed adoption. She titled it "The Unfinished Symphony."

> *"A memory is what is left when something happens and does not completely unhappen."* (Edward de Bono (b. 1933), British writer.
>
> I wonder why it is so difficult to talk about this? Why do I feel so much ambivalence about the memories? They are no longer painful, and it is not that I want to forget. Maybe it is just because there isn't a place to put them. I doubt there ever will be.
>
> The loss of a son was devastating enough, but that is not what lingers in my day-to-day life. I can think back over the whole experience and still touch the happiness, warmth and innocence of each one of those golden days with my son. It is a gift and a miracle that I turn over and over in my mind, once something brings the memories unbidden to the surface, although it is not a place I seek out on my own.
>
> I sometimes wonder if it would have helped to fight. By doing nothing, we have been reassured that we have done the best we could. I have come to know this was wise advice. But it cannot penetrate the

void of not even being allowed to struggle. How can one find completion in a vacuum?

Mostly there is the senseless waste of it all. The lost happiness. The lost love. Lost ownership of the past. A lost future. And the lost present of living with an empty nursery until the time when we could take up our lives and begin moving forward once more. To go forward past this impasse, we would have had to change the definition of who we were and where we were going.

This waiting was like no other waiting I have ever known. We waited ineffectively, marking off our sentence as time moved backwards to the pivotal point where we had been before. Only then could we begin to move forward once again with a new future.

By bringing us a daughter, the future rediscovered our present and built a new timeline for us to follow. It was not a continuation or replacement timeline. It was a glorious new beginning, bringing the opportunity to choose between bitterness and gratitude. I no longer feel victimized or powerless. My life and that of my family is full and good. I am grateful and content.

Yet I will always live with a shadow child, and one foot in the twilight of that disrupted timeline that once was, but never will be for me. My life flows in and around the holes left behind in my daily experiences. This has become a familiar and comfortable, rarely demanding conscious thought. But the aspects of my loss remain in the present, because I know that the original timeline continues to exist for my son. I am always aware of the other timeline, shimmering on the distant horizon of my unconscious thought.

The strangest aspect of this loss is that the past and current timelines of my life are not parallel. Instead, they weave in and out about each other, sometimes crossing when I least expect it, distorting the boundaries between past and present. Sometimes, for an instant, I am pulled unexpectedly into that other timeline to experience what-might-have-been. This blurring of reality occurs most often at pivotal moments in my son's life, as if some inexplicable force continues to draw our lives together.

These moments are less and less painful each time, despite the jarring shock of the return journey. The blurring of reality brings a new clarity of perception in its wake that highlights the infinite value of the present moment, the relationships that are now and the constant blessing of gratitude.

For better or for worse—no, for better—I am the mother of three children. One is always distant, but he is no less my son.

The pain and loss of a reversed adoption needs expression, acknowledgement, and support. Of course we all know that, but finding the best way to offer that is challenging. Several parents who had suffered adoption reversals expressed frustration at the attempts of professionals and caring others to comfort them by suggesting that this loss was like some other, more commonly experienced parenting loss.

"No!" these survivors say, experiencing an adoption reversal is not "like" a miscarriage or stillbirth. This baby lived and was a concrete part of a family's day-to-day lives for some time. No! This is not like a sudden infant death or losing a baby to illness. This baby lives on in another's arms. And yet one feels a need to find something in common with other parents who have lost children, and so adopting parents seek comparisons too. A few parents expressed some identification with birthparents, whose children's involuntary terminations led to confidential adoptions, cut off from their still living children. However, these disappointed adopters are not "like" voluntary or involuntary birthparents who struggle for months to do the right thing for their children. A reversal has been compared to a forcible rape of a victim afraid to struggle against the outcome for fear of killing her future dreams of adoption. Many parents likened adoption reversal to surviving the murder of a child. Why? Because of the sudden and violent nature of their loss; because their experience was that someone (for some blame lay with the birthparents who changed their minds, for others blame lay with agencies that hadn't done an adequate job) was responsible for a loss that seemed avoidable.

For Corinne and others, the reversal seemed analogous to being raped. They felt victimized and were recognized as victims, and yet there was a tendency for others to blame them for their loss. (At least he's with his birthfamily. It's for the best.) As the reversal happened, Corinne had a sense that she was being held with a knife to her throat. She wanted to struggle, and yet to struggle carried the risk that her adoption hopes would be killed— that The Social Workers would never make another placement with her.

Wendy Williams notes that this loss has all the traditional stages of grief, but that there are unique components as well.

- Ultimately there is no frame of reference for this unique loss. Along with the burden of grieving there is the constant struggle to find the right words to describe this, even to yourself.
- Grief for your lost child has nothing to do with loving the next one. After the initial shock, time is not a factor that trades off between grieving one and loving another. The processes will be forever intermixed.
- There is no closure on the grief for an ongoing loss. Your child is growing up somewhere, in another home, with another name. You will continue to be aware of the milestones as time progresses. It will hurt less as time goes by, but you will not forget or lose any of the intensity of the love you felt for your child.

- There is a unique and terrible violence in being forced to stand by and watch your child being taken from you against your will. This is an infinitely dark and angry thing and it will consume you if you get drawn into it. You cannot get past this experience by force.
- After grieving the losses of parental rights and control for while, one must consciously choose between gratitude and bitterness. This step is not easy, nor is it a passive decision. It is hard work to decide to let go, and even harder to begin to forgive.
- In the end, adoption reversal is like no other parenting loss. It is its own uniquely painful experience. Families seek ways to move on. They look for practical advice.

Much of the following comes from Wendy Williams and her husband, Rob.

- Understand that while this loss may not be recognized or validated by society in general, this is a significant loss.
- Have someone else make all those first calls to friends and relatives, and field the initial questions and reactions. You can talk to everyone when they call you to offer support and when they are ready to listen to you.
- Have someone call your employer to explain the situation and pass along news to co-workers. Let this person include suggestions on how you want to be treated when you return to work.
- If possible, arrange for a bereavement leave from work—a week or two or three, if available. When you do return to work, try to do so gradually—an hour or two the first day, which will be the worst.
- Remember that people grieve differently. One partner may need to cry and talk a lot, while the other needs to withdraw and be alone. Try to compromise and find ways to let each of you get what is needed.
- If you already have children in your home, try to find a way for them to feel safe and comfortable while you get time together as a couple. Trying to "hold it together" while comforting a grieving, confused child is brutally draining. If your child is too traumatized to let you leave, plan for special times together after they are asleep.
- Hug one another a lot. It may be sadly and quietly, but it builds a pathway back to the future.
- Ask for help wherever you can find it. Because you don't want to overload your spouse or members of your friends and families, a good counselor is recommended, especially when you feel a lack of validation and understanding from the people around you.

- Find someone who has been through this experience who is willing to talk to you. This is the place to be yourself without explanations or guarding of feelings.

- Make use of the Coach Model. A personal contact/phone call from someone every day for about fifteen minutes for the first few weeks, then moving to weekly for as long as you find this helpful. These talks should be structured, beginning with a discussion of how you are and how you are feeling, a report on how you've done since the last call, and a setting of new goals for the next day (which may be as simple as making dinner or taking a walk).

- Getting the nursery packed up can help you to say goodbye and to admit the finality of your loss. It can also give you a brighter, fresher place to begin when it is time to prepare for another child. You may feel that this is something that you should do by yourself, but if it would be helpful, ask friends to do this or to come and help you do it.

- Your home may be painful for a while. Find some safe places that aren't full of constant reminders. This may be a friend's home, a favorite restaurant, or any place where you feel that you don't have to "perform" before others.

- Don't take on any new challenges (work travel, a new job, a move) for a while. This is not the time for big decisions and new stresses.

- Look for activities that aren't full of constant reminders of loss. Choose books, movies, TV programs and social activities that give you a break from the constant emotional strain.

- Take care of yourself physically, eating healthy foods and exercising often, avoiding alcohol. Grieving often makes sleep difficult, but healthy practices can alleviate this, aiding in emotional healing and keeping you fit for your ongoing or next parenting experience.

- Allow yourself to tell your story over and over to those who will listen. Write a journal and letters to friends.

- Writing letters to your lost child can be helpful too, but have a concrete plan for what you will do with them—a symbolic action such as burning them in the fireplace and sending your love up the chimney—to prevent yourself from using them as something over which to brood.

- Find concrete ways to say goodbye and express ongoing feelings— plant a tree, make a donation to a charity for children, buy a plot of rainforest in your child's name. Choose a favorite photograph of your child to place in a prominent place in your home. People may be surprised, but most will respect your grief and be glad for an opportunity to express their concern and support for you.

- Of crucial importance is to find ways to rebuild your self-worth by expressions of self-affirmation. This can be a private project or habitual act (such as lighting a candle at special times, or wearing a favorite piece of clothing or jewelry regularly), or the process of creating a concrete object that is symbolic to you.
- Prepare for major holidays and family celebrations. If you need to, avoid gatherings such as baby showers or christenings that might be difficult, participating only as much as feels right and safe.
- After the initial time of grieving, gradually start to reclaim control over your life. Look for laughter; acknowledge what is good in your life daily.
- Consider rituals to help with various stages: saying goodbye, dealing with the sadness, moving on to considering another adoption. If you belong to a faith community, consider some kind of service.
- Quietly celebrate the people you have in your life as a way to build a pathway back to the future.
- After the initial shock is over, consider taking a trip or vacation. Delay this until you feel that you are strong enough to walk back into the house, with all its memories, when the trip is over.
- If or when it feels right, become an advocate to explain this loss. This can help others as well as yourself as you deal with your own anger and sense of helplessness.
- If and when you are ready for another adoption, the waiting can seem excruciating. Plan an absorbing activity designed to give you plenty of rewards and success to keep you busy.

Wendy writes, "There is no fairness here: there will never be reunion registries for adoptive parents who lose their children and no legal system will ever recognize the connection between you and your child. You don't have to like it, but the only victory comes with acknowledging the injustice and refusing to be drawn into fighting it emotionally or continually brooding. Save your mental energies for more hopeful things: your future family, for instance."

And as for the final stage of moving on—the arrival of another child, Wendy found that "The adoption loss experience steals the last vestige of innocence left after infertility. The arrival of your next child cannot be the same. There will be less spontaneity and much more fear, and you will become acutely aware of the vulnerability that comes with parenting.

"There will be painful memories and associations. Your body and mind will try to protect you from being hurt again. All parents compare child-arrival experiences. This is instinctual, parental behavior. However, loss changes people, and you are not the same person you would have been. Remember that parental love is not competitive, and it does not rely on erasing the past to make room for the new.

"Becoming parents again brings special healing. There is a fine, but critical, distinction here that is often misunderstood: while seeking healing for your loss may not be the cause for choosing to parent again, it is the effect. Your empty arms are full again. That brings its own special blessing. Of course it feels wonderful. Would anyone really want it to be otherwise?"

The Grief of Siblings Left Behind

About three months after the loss of their baby, Terry, Wendy went in to check on her older son, Jamie, and found that he wasn't in his room. She found him in Terry's room, holding a pillow from the crib and rocking quietly in the dark, completely ignoring the piles of Christmas gifts that were in various stages of wrapping. When Wendy asked Jamie what he was doing, he began to cry. "I miss my baby, Terry." Resisting a first impulse to distract him and get him out of the room, Wendy took him on her lap. They stayed awhile and rocked and talked about Terry. A few minutes later he went back to bed quite willingly.

It's important to remember that children are individuals too, and so will find their own triggers to and pattern of grief. This means that some of the members of your family may be ready for laughter when others aren't or may dissolve into tears with little warning. Encouraging full expression of feelings is invaluable, and children need to see their parents' sadness, though they may need help in understanding that they are not responsible for it. Children cannot think abstractly as adults do, and so they are likely to experience loss personally, perhaps even blame themselves in some way.

It is quite common for children to become fearful of their own adoption's permanency after the reversal of a sibling's adoption. Grieving children need a safe, predictable, routine-filled environment and lots of family time. Their need for concreteness also makes it important that children have access to visible reminders of their lost sibling—a picture on the wall, toys or blankets in their own room, etc.—and that they have absolute control over what happens to these pieces of memorabilia, to whom they are shown and whether they are shared.

In children, anger is often fully externalized. While setting limits that prevented his hurting himself or others, Wendy and Rob found it helpful to allow Jamie to scream, yell and trash his room with little reaction to these outbursts from his parents until after the anger had let up, at which time there were hugs and reassurances all around. Because children will often feel especially powerless and out of control in reaction to loss, it may be helpful to offer them lots of choices over which they can feel control. Children can find goodbye rituals as important in resolving loss as do adults, and may develop their own.

As with adults, the grief of children is often retriggered by new insecurities, additional changes, or new experiences of unrelated loss, yet families who are able to see their experience as the family's loss and include their children in the grieving and the healing will find that the family becomes closer by having worked together on grief and loss.

While decorating for Christmas, Jamie was thrilled and excited. He would hang one ornament and then run around the dining table for a while, blowing off steam, before rushing to find another bauble to hang. But taking the brass creche out of its box quieted Jamie. He played with it for awhile, fingering the tiny baby lying in the manger, and finally tucked the baby gently back into the manger, asking him to "take our love to Baby Terry."

Finalization

Arrival day is a momentous occasion, and for those whose adoptions' finalizations are marked by the ritual of going to court, there is incredible joy and relief. Wouldn't it be wonderful if every judge or referee could acknowledge the special nature of such an event with every family? Most do, often sharing with families a special poem such as Fleur Conkling Heyliger's "Not Flesh of My Flesh" or Carol Lynn Pearson's "To an Adopted." Many jurists enjoy these occasions of what they call "happy law" and ask siblings to join in, invite grandparents to the bar, and give plenty of time afterwards to families for pictures. But even if you are among the unfortunate few whose adoption proceedings seem to be perceived by court staff as one more bothersome interruption of routine, make your finalization day a joy-filled occasion for your family, complete with special outfits and a meal out. And, whatever you do, don't make the mistake the Johnston family made in finalizing our middle child Erica's adoption. In our excitement, we forgot to check, and found out a week later that there had been no film in our camera!

Resources

Post Adoption Depression in Parents

Bond, June. "Post Adoption Depression Syndrome" on Adopting.org from *Roots & Wings Adoption Magazine*, Spring, 1995. www.adopting.org/pads.html

Foli, Karen J. and John R. Thompson. *The Post-Adoption Blues: Overcoming the Unforseen Challenges of Adoption.* (Emmaus, PA: Rodale Books, 2004)

Fontaine, Nancy S. PhD. "I am Not Supposed to Feel This Way—Post Adoption Depression" www.chinesechildren.org/Newsletter/Professional%20Corner%5 CPC_07_2003.pdf

McCarthy, Harriet White. "Post Adoption Depression—the Unacknowledged Hazard." from International Adoption Articles Directory. www.adoptionarticles directory.com/Article/Post-Adoption-Depression---The-Unacknowledged-Hazard/53

McLeod, Jean. "Baby Shock: Dealing with Post Adoption Depression" on Baby Center.com from *Adoptive Families* magazine. www.babycenter.com/refcap/baby/adoption/1374199.html

Steinberg, Gail. "Bonding and Attachment: How Does Adoption Affect a Newborn?" from *Pact Press*. www.pactadopt.org/press/articles/attach-infant.html

Tarken, Laurie. "Even Post-Adoption, the Blues Can Lurk." *The New York Times*, April 26, 2006.

Normal Child Development

Ames, Louise Bates and Frances Ilg. A classic series of age-specific books on child development from researchers at the Gesell Institute: *Your Three-Year-Old: Friend or Enemy*; *Your Four-Year-Old: Wild and Wonderful*; *Your Five Year Old: Sunny and Serene*; *Your Six-Year-Old: Loving and Defiant*; *Your Seven Year Old: Life in a Minor Key*; *Your Eight Year Old: Lively and Mysterious*; *Your Nine Year Old: Thoughtful and Mysterious*; *Your Ten-to Fourteen-Year-Old* (New York: Dell, 1980s)

American Academy of Pediatrics. *Caring for Your Baby and Young Child.* (New York: Bantam, 2004)

Eisenberg Arlene, Heidi E. Murkoff and Sandee E. Hathaway. *What to Expect the First Year* (2nd Edition). (New York: Simon & Shuster, 2004)

Eisenberg Arlene, Heidi E. Murkoff and Sandee E. Hathaway. *What to Expect The Toddler Years.* (New York: Simon & Shuster, 2007)

Sears, William, Martha Sears and James Sears. *The Baby Book: Everything You Need to Know About Your Baby from Birth to Age Two* (Revised and Updated Edition). (New York: Little, Brown & Co., 2003)

Parenting

(See also Resources for Chapter 5)

Bailey, Becky. *Easy to Love, Difficult to Discipline: The 7 Basic Skills for Turning Conflict into Cooperation.* (New York: Harper, 2001)

Cline, Foster, MD and Jim Fay. *Parenting with Love and Logic* (Updated and Expanded). (Colorado Springs: Love & Logic Press, 2006)

MacLeod, Jean and Sheena Macrae. *Adoption Parenting: Creating a Toolbox, Building Connections.* (EMK Press, 2006)

Siegel, Daniel MD and Mary Hartzell. *Parenting from the Inside Out.* (Jeremy Tarcher: 2005)

Siblings

Brazelton, T. Berry, MD and Joshua D. Sparrow. *Understanding Sibling Rivalry: The Brazelton Way*. (Cambridge, MA: DaCapo Lifelong Books, 2005)

Faber, Adele and Elaine Mazlish. *Siblings Without Rivalry: How to Help Your Children Live Together So You Can Live Too*. (New York: HarperCollins, 2004)

Attachment 301

Attachment disorder is a treatable condition characterized by problems with the formation of emotional attachment to others. Children with this condition have had problems or serious disruption in early childhood parent-child relationships. These problems have affected the child's social, emotional, and behavioral systems.[3]

(See also books on Attachment listed in Resources for Chapters 5 and 14.)

Association for Treatment and Training in the Attachment of Children (ATTACh) www.attach.org

Attachment and Trauma Network www.attach.org/faq.htm

Cline, Foster, MD. *Can This Child Be Saved? Solutions for Adoptive and Foster Families*. (World Enterprises, 1999)

Gray, Deborah: *Attaching in Adoption: Practical Tools for Today's Parents*. (Indianapolis: Perspectives Press, Inc., 2002)

Gray, Deborah. *Nurturing Adoptions: Creating Resilience after Neglect and Trauma*. (Indianapolis: Perspectives Press, Inc., 2007)

Hughes, Daniel A. *Building the Bonds of Attachment: Awakening Love in Deeply Troubled Children*. (Lanham, MD: Jason Aronson, 2006)

Hughes, Daniel A. *Facilitating Developmental Attachment*. (Lanham, MD: Jason Aronson, 2000)

Keck, Gegory and Regina Kupecky. *Parenting the Hurt Child: Helping Adoptive Families Heal and Grow*. (Colorado Springs, CO: 2002)

Thomas, Nancy L. *When Love Is Not Enough: A Guide to Parenting Children with RAD*. (Glenwood Springs, CO: Families by Design, 2005)

Trout, Michael. *The Jonathon Letters: One Family's Use of Support as They Took in, and Fell in Love with, a Troubled Child*. (Champaign, IL: Infant-Parent Institute, 2005)

The Brain and Relationships

Siegel, Daniel J., MD. *The Developing Mind: How Relationships and the Brain Interact to Shape Who We Are*. (Guilford Press, 2001)

Siegel, Daniel J., MD. *The Mindful Brain: Reflection and Attunement in the Cultivation of Well-Being*. (New York: W.W. Norton, 2007)

Siegel, Daniel J., MD. and Mary Hartzell. *Parenting From the Inside Out*. (New York: Jeremy Tarcher, 2004)

Medical Problems You Might See

This section provides initial resources for a variety of learning and behavior problems that are not necessarily common in children who join their families by adoption, but are frequent enough (especially among children adopted at older ages or from institutional settings) that families may find it helpful to be aware of their existence in case they see symptoms of unusual or difficult to diagnose behaviors in their one year or older-arrived children.

Alcohol-Related Neuro-developmental Disease aka Fetal Alcohol Syndrome or Effects (ARND, FAS, FAE)

The range of neurological impairments that can affect a child who has been exposed to alcohol in the womb. A number of factors, including how much the mother drank and at what point during the pregnancy, can influence the severity of the impairments and what functions they most affect. Children with FASD can display symptoms of ADHD, autism, Asperger syndrome, Tourette's syndrome, epilepsy, mental retardation and various psychiatric disorders, but will often not respond to traditional treatments for those disabilities.[4]

Centers for Disease Control Fetal Alcohol Spectrum Disorder www.cdc.gov/ncbddd/fas/default.htm

National Organization on Fetal Alcohol Syndrome www.nofas.org/living/

Kleinfield, Judith. *Fantastic Antone Grows Up: Adolescents and Adults with Fetal Alcohol Syndrome.* (Fairbanks: University of Alaska Press, 2000)

McCreight, Brenda. *Recognizing and Managing Children with Fetal Alcohol Syndrome/Fetal Alcohol Effects: A Guidebook.* (Washington DC: CWLA Press, 1997)

Streissguth, Ann Pytkowicz. *Fetal Alcohol Syndrome: A Guide for Families and Communities.* (Baltimore: Brookes Publishing Co. 1997)

Attention Deficit Disorder or Attention Deficit Hyperacticity Disorder (ADHD/ADD)

A common developmental and behavioral disorder characterized by poor concentration, distractibility, hyperactivity, and impulsiveness that are inappropriate for the child's age. Children and adults with ADHD are easily distracted by sights and sounds in their environment, cannot concentrate for long periods of time, are restless and impulsive, or have a tendency to daydream and be slow to complete tasks.[5]

Children and Adults with Attention Deficit/Hyperactivity Disorder (CHADD) www.chadd.org, 8181 Professional Place—Suite 150, Landover, MD 20785 (301) 306-7070

Hallowell, Edward M and John J. Ratey. *Driven To Distraction: Recognizing and Coping with Attention Deficit Disorder from Childhood Through Adulthood.* (New York: Touchstone, 1995)

"50 Conditions that Mimic ADHD" www.incrediblehorizons.com/mimic-adhd. htm

Auditory Processing Disorder or Central Auditory Processing Disorder(APD/CAPD)

The reduced or impaired ability to discriminate, recognize, or comprehend complex sounds, such as those used in words, even though the hearing is normal.[6]

National Coalition on Auditory Processing Disorders www.ncapd.org/php/index. php?menuoption=Professional%20Listings

National Institute on Deafness and Other Communication Disorders www.nidcd. nih.gov/health/voice/auditory.asp

Bellis, Teri James. *When the Brain Can't Hear: Unraveling the Mystery of Auditory Processing Disorder.* (New York: Atria, 2003)

Foli, Karen J and Edward M. Hallowell. *Like Sound Through Water: A Mother's Journey Through Auditory Processing Disorder.* (New York: Atria, 2003)

Autism Spectrum Disorder or Pervasive Developmental Disorder

A range of neurological disorders that most markedly involve some degree of difficulty with communication and interpersonal relationships, as well as obsessions and repetitive behaviors. As the term "spectrum" indicates, there can be a wide range of effects. Those at the lower-functioning end of the spectrum may be profoundly unable to break out of their own world and may be described as having *Kanner's autism.* Those at the higher-functioning end, sometimes diagnosed with *Asperger Syndrome (AS),* may be able to lead independent lives but still be awkward in their social interactions. Other, more rare autism spectrum disorders include *Rett Syndrome (RS),* which affects mostly girls, and *Childhood Disintegrative Disorder (CDD),* which affects mostly boys; in both cases, there is a period of normal development before the onset of autistic symptoms.[7]

Koegel, Lynn Kern and Clair LaZebnik. *Overcoming Autism: Finding the Answers, Strategies, and Hope That Can Transform a Child's Life.* (New York: Penguin, 2005)

Lockshin, Stephanie B, PhD, Jennifer M. Gillis and Raymond G. Romanczyk. *Helping Your Child With Autism Spectrum Disorder: A Step-By-Step Workbook For Families.* (Oakland, CA:New Harbinger Publications, 2005)

Post-Traumatic Stress Disorder

Post-Traumatic Stress Disorder, PTSD, is an anxiety disorder that can develop after exposure to a terrifying event or ordeal in which grave physical harm occurred or was threatened. Traumatic events that may trigger PTSD include violent personal assaults, natural or human-caused disasters, accidents, or military combat.[8]

National Center for PTSD www.ncptsd.va.gov/ncmain/index.jsp

National Institutes of Mental Health www.nimh.nih.gov/healthinformation/ptsd-menu.cfm

ThinkAnxiety.org www.thinkanxiety.org/article-2996101.htm

Gray, Deborah D. *Nurturing Attachments: Creating Resilience after Neglect and Trauma.* (Indianapolis: Perspectives Press, 2007)

Sensory Processing Disorder or Sensory Integration Dysfunction (SPD/SID)

Sensory Integration Disorder or Sensory Processing Disorder is a neurological disability in which the brain is unable to accurately process the information coming in from the senses.[9]

Sensory Processing Disorder Resource Center www.sensory-processing-disorder.com/index.html

Sensory Processing Disorder Network www.spdnetwork.org/

Kranowicz, Karen Stock and Lucy Jane Miller. *The Out-of-Sync Child: Recognizing and Coping with Sensory Processing Disorder*, Revised Edition. (New York: Perigee Trade, 2006)

Smith, Karen A. *The Sensory-Sensitive Child: Practical Solutions for Out-of-Bounds Behavior.* (New York: Collins, 2004)

Relationships with Birthparents

Bailey, Julie Jarrell. "Overcoming Birth Parent Prejudice for the Best Interest of the Child," *Fostering Relationships* Vol. 6, No. 2, May 2002.

Duxbury, Micky. *Making Room in Our Hearts: Keeping Family Ties through Open Adoption.* (London; Routledge, 2006.)

Gritter, James L. *The Spirit of Open Adoption.* (Washington, DC: CWLA Press, 1997)

Melina, Lois Ruskai and Sharon Kaplan Roszia. *The Open Adoption Experience—From Making the Decision Through the Child's Growing Years.* (New York: Harper Perennial, 1993)

Ruprecht Katie. "Building Healthy Relationships" *Open Page Newsletter* (Open Adoption and Family Services), Winter, 2002. www.openadopt.org/newsletter/2002/winter.php#building

Tana W. "Why to Facilitate Relationships with Birthparents." LDS Adoption Blog lds.adoptionblogs.com/index.php/weblogs/why-to-facilitate-relationships-with-bir

CHAPTER 16

Adoption in the Big Wide World

Though things are certainly better than they were as recently as a generation ago, people touched by adoption almost daily experience the mixed messages of a larger society which continues to find adoption strange, somewhat threatening to the integrity of their own families and senses of connection, and most assuredly second best as an alternative for everyone involved. On the one hand parents hear the "Aren't you people wonderful" messages, and on the other they are told, "Too bad you don't have any kids of your own." Birthparents hear that they have been irresponsible for having practiced unsafe sex, and that children raised in single parent homes are at great risk for all kinds of awful things, but on the other hand they also hear, "How could anyone ever give up their own flesh and blood?" Adoptees are told that they are "lucky" that someone as unselfish as their adopters took them in when those birthparents "who loved you very much" made the choice to "give you away." They are urged to feel "grateful and loyal" to their adopting parents, while at the same time they see the overwhelming curiosity that society has about the "real" genetic relatives who meet one another—often for the first time—in media-spotlighted "reunions." Despite high profile adoptive parents among politicians and entertainers, and more and more people in the general population delaying parenthood until adoption becomes the most viable choice, adoption continues to be an oddity.

Those of us who are adults could make the indignant and idealistic claim that the reason we want to change this view is "for our children." This is true. Child advocates could claim that they wish to change the pervasive view of adoption as second best in order to promote and preserve adoption as a viable option for children born at risk to families which perhaps should not be "preserved." This is true too. But the reality is that we as adoptive parents want and need to change this view for ourselves as well. It hurts to be thought of as out of sync, unusual, or incomplete. It's painful to know that many of the people who interact with us on a daily basis view our relationships as inauthentic and, to a certain extent, feel sorry both for us and for our children.

How people develop negative views is a complicated stew blending many years' worth of truth and misunderstanding, fact and fiction. Personal experience with friends or relatives; media exposure through news stories, talk shows, and television shows; word choices; and advertising gimmicks are all seasonings added to the pot. In this chapter we will look at that stew and examine ways to "adjust the seasoning" to make adoption a tastier dish for the world at large.

The Language of Adoption

Those who are native speakers of English are sometimes unaware of how unusually colorful and diverse our language is when compared to others. Through centuries of borrowing liberally from the languages of the people who have conquered and been conquered by English-speakers, our lexicon has been remarkably expanded. No other language has as many synonyms as does English. Why, we have entire books, called thesauruses, which focus on nothing but synonymity. Thus, in no other language does word choice result in such subtle nuances of difference.

English speakers use this variety to remarkable advantage, understanding clearly how word choice affects marketing, friendships, and politics. Poorly chosen words can lose sales, incite debate—and even start wars! People who work with the public at large understand this. Language choices both drive and reflect stereotypical thinking. Authors create naive and innocent characters who come from Iowa or Indiana, and name their not-too-bright characters "Bubba." Chrysler sells New Yorkers rather than Podunkers and Ford offers Mustangs rather than Tortoises.

Word choice can affect bias and discrimination. Beginning with the civil rights movement of the 1950s and '60s and moving right through the sexual revolution, the women's movement, and the gay rights movement, minority groups have used language as a battleground for promoting understanding of their unique issues. The pressure to use these more politically correct (P.C.) terms has produced, over time, subtle changes in understanding as well.

As one who has made a career in the field of words—as an English teacher and librarian, then as a writer, public speaker, and publisher—I am fascinated with the nuances of language. It was exciting for me to contribute to and then use Rosalie Maggio's *Talking About People: A Guide to Fair and Accurate Language* (Oryx Press, 1997) in writing this and other books. I'm quite sure that if you look carefully, you'll catch me in a number of errors in political correctness, but I'm trying. The time has come to insist on a P.C. language of adoption as well.

The concept of Positive Adoption Language (PAL) was first introduced in the 1970s by Marietta Spencer, a legendary social worker with the Children's Home Society of Minnesota (now Children's Home Society and Family Services) who was also a pioneer in the push for post-adoption services. During the 1980s, several adoption activists and advocates—myself included—became missionaries for the use of more positive language. Eventually, however, most of us came to see that what felt "positive" to one member of the adoption circle sometimes was felt negatively by another. Eventually I began to think in terms of trying to use *Respectful* Adoption Language.

Respectful adoption language is vocabulary chosen to offer maximum respect, dignity, responsibility, and objectivity to the decisions made by pregnant women and their partners, birthparents, and adoptive parents concerning their family planning. By using RAL we can hope to eliminate the emotional overcharging that perpetuates the myths society holds about adoption. The use of this vocabulary shows those involved in adoptions to be thoughtful and responsible people, gives them both authority and responsibility for their actions, and, by eliminating the emotion-laden words which sometimes led in the past to a subconscious feeling of conflict or competition, helps to promote understanding among members of what has come to be called the adoption circle (as opposed to the older term *adoption triangle*, which seemed to imply "sides").

In learning to use RAL, one begins with the concept of what it means to be a family. In our society, historically people have been considered to be members of the same family when one or more of four conditions are met:

- They are linked by blood (as are birthfather and son).
- They are linked by law (for example husband and wife).
- They are linked by social custom (as would be a woman and her husband's sister).
- They are linked by love (so that by the end of the 20th century it was commonly agreed that a married couple who has chosen a childfree lifestyle, a same-sex partnership, and a single parent with children are families—just as is the married couple who have conceived and birthed six children together).

Yet while things are changing, adoption continues to be seen as "different." If it were not, the parent and child linked both by love and by law would not be exposed to questions about their lack of a blood connection. People who think like this ask questions such as, "Do you have any children of *your own*?" or "Are they *natural* brother and sister?" or "Have you ever met your *real* mother?" and assume that adoptions are tentative ("Will the agency take him back now that you know he's '*handicapped*'?" or "What if his *real* mother wants him back?").

Perhaps we could let comments like these go if they were made only to reasoning adults who could pretend, at least, to "know what I mean."

But the stereotype of adoption as not genuine is so deeply ingrained that many adults think nothing of making such comments within earshot of our concrete-thinking children. We must effect change!

A commitment to using respectful adoption language can sometimes result in longer than usual sentence constructions and demands that we change very old habits. With practice, however, it is doable. You'll make mistakes and sometimes, for the sake of clarity it will be necessary to use the qualifiers you have worked so hard to eliminate, but the effort is worth it.

The message those using RAL are trying to send is this: Adoption is a method of joining a family, just as is birth. It is also a method of family planning, as are birth control pills, condoms, and abortion. Adoption is life-long, but it should not be thought of as a "condition." In the limited instances when it is appropriate to refer to the fact of adoption at all, RAL suggests that you say "Kathy was adopted" (referring to the way in which she arrived in her family) rather than phrasing it in the present tense ("Kathy is adopted"), which implies that adoption is a disability with which to cope. In an article or situation not centering on adoption (for example during an introduction, in an obituary, or in a news or feature story about a business person or celebrity), it is usually inappropriate to refer to the adoption connection at all.

It's also important to listen to others touched by adoption when deciding what words to use. For example, over time, the use of RAL has evolved in response to birthparents, who prefer to see this term reserved for themselves, used only to designate people who have already given birth and planned an adoption or had their parental rights removed involuntarily by court order. In other words, we don't all have birthmothers, even though each of us has been birthed by a mother. Women who are pregnant with an untimely pregnancy are not *birthmothers*, they are *expectant parents* until the child is born and legally adopted either because the birthparent chose to plan an adoption or her parental rights were terminated involuntarily by court action. Another term claimed for themselves by many birthparents, and so used by many adoptive parents, is *first mother.*

Children who were adopted (sparingly referred to when necessary for important clarification as *adoptees* or *adopted people*, but preferably referred to only as *sons* and *daughters, children*, and *humans*) will always have two sets of parents. Their birthparents have given them their genetic heritage of gifts and deficits, and the people who adopted them—who become their social, legal, psychological, cultural parents—support and encourage those gifts. These are their *parents: mother, father, mom, dad.*

It's a good idea to avoid terms like *real parent* or *real family, natural mother* and *natural father*, since these terms imply that adoptive relationships are artificial, tentative, less than whole, and less enduring than are genetically-linked relationships. Using a phrase such as *children of your own* reflects old style thinking of children as chattel. The poet Kalil Gibran, writing "On Children" in his collection *The Prophet* summarized best the relationship between parents and their children, no matter how the connection began.

On Children

And a woman who held a babe against her bosom said, speak to us
  of children.
And he said:
Your children are not your children.
They are the sons and daughters of life's longing for itself.
They come through you but not from you.
And though they are with you they belong not to you.
You may give them your love, but not your thoughts,
For they have their own thoughts.
You may house their bodies, but not their souls,
For their souls dwell in the house of tomorrow, which you cannot visit,
  not even in your dreams.
You may strive to be like them, but seek not to make them like you.
For life goes not backward nor tarries with yesterday.
You are the bows from which your children as living arrows are sent
  forth.
The Archer sees the mark upon the path of the infinite and He bends
  you with His might that His arrows might go swift and far.
Let your bending in the Archer's hands be for gladness,
For even as He loves the arrow that flies, so He loves also the bow that
  is stable.

Though it was once true that birthparents were given few choices in dealing with an untimely pregnancy, and that in years past they may well have *surrendered*, *relinquished* or *given up* their children to adoption, today those terms are rarely accurate, and certainly only when children are involuntarily removed from parents whose children's safety is at risk due to their own problematic choices, addictions or mental health problems. Expectant parents today have a different experience than did those of the '70s and before. Empowered to make the best choices possible in an overwhelmingly difficult situation, these men and women truly make *adoption plans* for their children—reading resumes, interviewing people, and negotiating expectations about openness and communication or confidentiality.

RAL speakers would encourage you to keep this in mind as well in speaking about women who do not choose adoption. These women, when well-counseled and offered opportunities to carefully consider their options choose to *parent* their children rather than to have an abortion or to make an adoption plan. They do not *keep* their babies, because babies are not possessions, they are children in need of 24/7 care for a minimum of eighteen years.

Unlike it was in the orphan train era of the 1800s, children are not *put up for adoption* on the station platforms of towns along the way. Their parents or court systems *plan adoptions* or *make adoptive placements* for them. Should these children spend time in care between their birthparents and the home of their adopters, RAL speakers prefer that we refer to that care as *interim care* by *interim caregivers*, since the older terms *foster parents* and *foster care* don't make clear that this substitute care is not considered permanent, but temporary, until permanency can be planned. The terms *foster parent* and *adoptive parent* have become so misunderstood that most people use them nearly interchangeably.

Hopeful parents-to-be once submitted to *homestudies* so that inappropriate prospects could be weeded out, but today's prospective adoptive parents participate in a *parent preparation process*, which, as has been made clear earlier, is really much more about education than it is about gatekeeping.

In choosing a style of adoption, some couples do not adopt in their country of citizenship, but rather arrange an *intercountry* or *international adoption*. We no longer use the term *foreign adoption* because the word *foreign* carries such negative connotations in the English language.

Parents who choose to be in direct contact with their child's family of origin can arrange *open adoptions*, most of which are also *communicative adoptions*. Those who prefer privacy may instead choose a *confidential adoption* (as opposed to the more negative label *closed adoption*). When parents choose to parent children facing the challenges of *special needs*, we no longer label these children *handicapped* or *hard to place*.

Perhaps the most difficult situation for which to find a respectful term is the one wherein adopted people meet members of their birthfamilies. This is often referred to as a *reunion*. To birthfamily members who have had some contact with the adopted person over the years, the idea of *reuniting* may seem accurate. Many adoptive parents and nonsearching adoptees, however, find this term difficult—charged as it is with associations of class reunions, family reunions, and other such special events between people who have years of shared memories and events about which to reminisce. In fact, most adoptees join their cultural families as babies and have no such memories in common with their families of origin. Some therapists have suggested that the use of such an emotionally overpowering word as *reunion* has been responsible for setting up unrealistic expectations for both birthparents and adoptees who have initiated contact with the other. A suggested alternative has been the simple term *meeting*, though some searching birthparents and adult adoptees find this term cold and emotionless. We continue to look for just the right term here.

You get the idea, by now I'm sure, that carefully choosing the words we use in talking about adoption does make a difference. Learning to use respectful adoption language, and encouraging our friends and families, our clergypeople, and our children's teachers to do so will help over time to exert a subtle shift that will have a positive effect on adoption in general.

The Image of Adoption

Yes, adoption has an image problem. From the musical *Annie* (spun off from the cartoon series "Little Orphan Annie," which in itself was a spinoff of a popular 1800s poem by the colloquial Hoosier poet James Whitcomb Riley) to sitcoms and soap operas, pulp fiction and serious literary fiction, adoption has often been misrepresented and misunderstood. Even worse, adoption gets a bum rap in the non-fiction world of journalism as well, as far too many journalists (with a few notable exceptions where a publisher's stylesheet does not allow it) note adoption inappropriately in news stories, obituaries, and more. This results in an almost obsessive need to attach inappropriate qualifiers ("This is Bill's adopted son, Mark") in situations where one would not dream of doing so in a non-adoptive family.

When, for example, have you heard an introduction like, "I'd like you to meet Bill's birth control failure son" or "Allow me to introduce Mary's caesarean section daughter, Jill"? When reporting the murder of a parent by his child, have you ever seen a sentence like "Humboldt, 33, confessed to killing the mother to whom he was prematurely born in a fit of rage"? Yet I know that you could list a number of famous criminal adoptees—including David Berkowitz (Son of Sam) and the Hillside stranglers.

Society at large holds some widespread negative assumptions about adoption, and this widespread mythology produces a number of significant negatives. Not only do such negatives compromise our own attempts to build positive self-esteem in our children and to encourage our families and friends to see our relationships as authentic, but they overflow into the much broader public policy arena. Dorothy DeBolt, the mother of a large family of children with special needs who were brought together through adoption, has referred to what she calls "a worship of the womb," which she believes results in too many social workers and judges placing children at further risk by refusing to terminate the parental rights of absent, abusive, or incompetent parents by birth.

Counselors have noted for years that pressure from peers leads many young parents not ready or able to parent competently to refuse to consider the adoption option in dealing with an untimely pregnancy. In fact, it is the most cognitively mature birthparents and often the oldest ones—those who might have the best chance of pulling together the resources needed to parent a child born of an unplanned pregnancy—who do make adoption plans. The result is that too many children born to very young mothers are at significant statistical risk for abuse, neglect, failure to thrive, educational impoverishment and poverty, and many of these children find their way into the adoption system years later, no longer healthy infants easily placed, but older children with very special needs.

Adoption Is Entirely Exploitable

As soon as I picked up the urgently ringing phone, the voice on the other end cried, "I've had it!"

"First it was those crazy Cabbage Patch dolls. When they were so popular that a black market developed, everybody got on the cutesy adopt-a-reject bandwagon. The state wanted me to adopt-a-highway and the city a park, my local zoo has an "adopt-a-wild-child" campaign, the Intercountry Wildlife Coalition wants me to adopt a humpback whale, the Save-The-Redwoods League recruits adoptive parents for trees. All of them come with adoption certificates. All of them make me a parent to the object I'm sponsoring. Meanwhile, I've had to deal with the aftermath of that horrible movie *Problem Child*.

"I've tried to be patient, really I have, but yesterday when I walked into the video store and saw a stack of dusty used videos piled under a sign that read "Adopt-a-video" I reached my saturation point!"

People who are involved with adoption issues on a daily basis are becoming increasingly concerned about the negative adoption imagery besieging our families today. Of special note because they seem to be spreading are programs taking an adopt-a theme which have proliferated since the Cabbage Patch doll craze of the early 1980s. These programs range from those mentioned by my friend Susan in the anecdote above to silly not-for-profit fundraising ideas (such as Adopt-A-Rubber-Duck river races sponsored by a local radio station to benefit a food bank), city adopt-a-park and adopt-a-pothole programs, commercial adopt-a-product promotions, ecological and wildlife education programs, and Humane Society animal placement programs.

Granted, the English language is a complex and varied one, and the words *adopt* and *adoption* have more than one meaning. In addition to the primary definition ("To follow a legal and social process permanently transferring parental rights from a set of birthparents to a set of adoptive parents"), the second and third definitions of the verb form ("To take and follow by choice or assent" or "To take up and use as one's own") have non-family-related meanings, describing the processes by which schools adopt textbooks, campaigns adopt themes, and so on.

The adopt-a projects, though, trade not on the secondary definitions, but on the family building definition of adoption, conjuring up a quick and clear picture which then produces a marketing advantage. Every marketing person I've ever spoken to about my concern about this admits that it is the immediately recognizable image of sheltering an otherwise unwanted "orphan" that makes such a theme attractive and successful. That's why these exploitive, tug-at-the-heartstrings programs always include an adoption certificate naming the sponsor as "parent" as a premium.

Those of us who are parents by adoption and adoption activists, however, believe that such programs trivialize a very serious topic and that they further myths and misconceptions about this family planning method to yet another generation of children. Unfortunately, they turn upon a kind of "save the rejects" image that may seem cute and harmless to grownups, but confuses concrete-thinking children—be they adopted or not.

Those who are skeptical about the very existence of adopt-a confusion argue that it is up to adoptive parents to work with their kids to explain the realities of adoption. They are absolutely right, of course. And as adoptive parents we do work with our children (and with the children of friends and relatives) to help them sort through the differences between adoption of people and adoption of animals or adoption promotions. Yet because children are not abstract thinkers, this is not an easy task. Besides, we can only reach the children closest to us, not the children who use their own and their parents' misinformation to throw playground barbs at our kids. We wonder, then, why we adoptive parents should have to spend all this time explaining a confusion, when, by just sensitizing the good people responsible for developing marketing programs, we could instead eliminate this particular confusion entirely.

Adoption is difficult enough an issue for young children without adding to the confusion through commercial projects. Research by David Brodzinsky at Rutgers University has shown that children who were adopted are really no quicker to understand the complex social issues which underlie adoption than are their non-adopted peers, though children who were adopted do learn to parrot the terminology much earlier.

Perhaps you have not experienced adopt-a confusion in your own family (or at least you may not be aware that such a confusion is at work), but such misconceptions are widespread among pre-school and elementary-aged youngsters. Three examples of adopt-a confusion among children under 10 (who are almost universally too intellectually immature to reason logically) typify those I hear about as occurring regularly in cities across the continent.

A 5-year-old friend (adoptee) was "given" a giraffe by her grandparents through their much-loved zoo's Adopt-An-Animal program. Over the course of several months the child was very upset to learn that not only could she not take "her" animal home or care for it directly, but she also could not consider it "hers" after the year had passed, when a different animal was substituted for "her" giraffe in the next year's campaign. In another city, another child learned that an acquaintance had been assigned the same specific animal as he had! A third child was told by a non-adopted friend who had participated in such a program that if his parents wanted to, they could trade him for a "better" child next year, as his family had in "upgrading" their zoo adoption. Children waiting in foster care for permanency have been teased by peers with taunts such as, "We adopted a giraffe. Nobody wants you!"

Each of these children has become confused and concerned about his own situation. In each case parents had no idea before this experience that they were participating in a program that would lead to such stress for their kids or others' children. That's because all of the adults involved—zoo administrators, parents, etc.—could think abstractly and thus were able to see clearly the difference between adoption of people and sponsorship of animals sold as adoption. These adults simply forgot that children are incapable of following a line of reasoning this complex to a clear conclusion and that they take everything very personally.

> My son, who was 8 or 9 at the time of the first round of Cabbage-Patch-mania, watched an evening news feature story on the black market developing with these ugly little creatures who spring from the dirt accompanied by adoption papers. He turned to ask, "Mommy, is that the way adoption really works? Do they give babies to the people with the most money?" Ouch!

Similarly, school-aged children who look at the offerings of programs such as most zoos', with different "prices" for different varieties of "wild children" are often led to ask their parents how much they themselves cost, and whether a brother or sister was more or less expensive and why. The issue of money and adoption is certainly a part of our helping our children understand the process, but not at eight! No amount of explanation about how adoption fees work and how they are disbursed can be absorbed by a non-reasoning small child.

I've heard from several families who have "adopted" an animal from Humane Societies. In contrast to other "adoption" projects, on the surface these seem "like" human adoption, in that there actually is an investigation and approval process, the animal is the family's to take home and nurture, the Societies stress the permanence of the relationship, and thus participation in the program seems a good "lesson" for children in what adoption is about.

Because of their more direct connection to human family adoption, I find these animal companion programs far less objectionable than adopt-a-wilderness-river programs. (And please note Humane Society of the U.S., that I am using your preferred term *animal companion* instead of the more familiar term *pets* in an attempt to follow your line of P.C. reasoning.) Yet despite good intentions, these too can be confusing. In several cases problems have started when animals brought home turned out to have serious problems—biting, failing obedience training, etc.—and the family has come to the realization that they would have to find the animal another home or return him to the Society. Soon after, their children began to experience nightmares or other acting out behavior. Upon investigation it has been discovered that these kids were afraid that if they were "bad," they too would be "returned"—or even "put to sleep."

The way to prevent these confusions is really quite simple. Adoption is a process by which families are planned and formed. To trivialize it in a commercial way insults the birthparents, adoptive parents, and adoptees who have been personally touched by this process. We no longer find it acceptable to trivialize other minority groups in this society. The proliferation of adopt-a-promotions has become about as humorous to many of those personally touched by adoption, as are shuffle-footed pickaninny humor or Pollack jokes to the minority groups they deride. For the sake of children waiting for adoption and those who have already found their permanent families in adoption, we adults must insist that adoption be treated in a dignified manner.

How to proceed becomes the challenge. I've been an anti-Cabbage Patch campaigner for years. I have carefully penned indignant letters, made articulate but annoyed phone calls to people in high places, and have had some, but few, successes. People either get so defensive that they dig in and refuse to admit they are wrong or they get it but don't care what "the crazy adoption woman" thinks.

Sometimes I have even been embarrassed by the response I got. For example, once I wrote an indignant letter to the editor of a small newspaper in response to a "humorous" article on environmental adopt-a programs as alternative gift ideas for infertile people tempted to spend money on unproductive high technology. I put on my very official sounding title as then chairman of Resolve's national board of directors and waxed on about how tough infertility was, how offensive this joking was, and then shared the examples of adopt-a confusion cited above. My letter was printed all right—along with a direct response from the editor, who pointed out that he thought I was some kind of a nut who couldn't take a joke. The lessons learned? There were two: 1. The editor had felt defensive about being attacked and had thus dug in, and 2. Since adults are supposed to be tough and to be able to take a joke, leaving out the insult to adults and focusing only on confusion to children might have been more productive (though in this case the article was really an adults-only piece).

There are other approaches. My own year-long experience with the Indianapolis Zoo and some national reactions to it serve as an interesting example of what works and what doesn't. In 1992, the Indianapolis Zoo became the first zoo in the country to change the name of their animal "adoption" program, publicly announcing that the change was out of sensitivity to concerns raised by adoption-touched people. The new program, Animal Amigos, may not be transferable to your zoo, because it was chosen to allow the Indy zoo to take advantage of their relationship with a licensed cartoon character (a parrot named Amigo who had been the official mascot of the Pan American Games held in Indianapolis a few summers before), but there are alternatives for your zoo, your highway department, and your local merchant to consider.

I dropped my indignation and annoyance and began with compliments about everything there was to like and admire about the zoo. This was easy to do, because there is lots to like about our zoo—we have a gorgeous one here, and we'd love to have you visit it and our beautiful city. My approach presumed that the zoo staff were good folks who had likely made an honest mistake in that they simply didn't know that anyone might be confused or offended by their program.

I centered my information about confusion in children. It really doesn't matter what adults think if children are confused by it. For an institution for whom children are a major audience, how children react to a program is very important. This may mean that you are likely to be more successful effecting change in adopt-a programs which are child or family focused (and most are).

I kept in mind at all times that I was dealing here with marketing and development people. What would make sense to them was how their mistake might be affecting their pocketbook. In the case of this family-sensitive institution, I could point out that adoptive parents, who tend to be slightly more affluent on average than families in general are also very motivated as parents to provide educational and cultural experiences for their children and thus probably belong to libraries, zoos, museums, etc. in proportionately high numbers. As an educational program, animal sponsorship might be attractive, but when this highly visible program was marketed as adoption, it provided enough offense or danger of confusion to make these families decide to avoid it—and in some cases zoo membership as well—and that sometimes they took their extended families with them. I offered my help not just in brainstorming about possible alternatives, but in publicizing and fundraising for the new program.

In general, I made certain that I was a positive, non-threatening, cooperative person with whom to work (I really am anyway most of the time). In response, I found that the Zoo staff was equally pleasant and positive. They never needed to find themselves on the defensive. Contrary to one very well-meaning but unfortunately worded article written in a midwestern newspaper during Adoption Awareness Month, the Indianapolis Zoo and I did not do battle. We didn't need to. We worked together to bring about change that would work for our mutual benefit.

The result of this effort was amazing. The Indianapolis Zoo got well-deserved attention from the media and the community at large. Local memberships increased. Several national organizations wrote letters of support and honored this zoo in some visible way. Throughout the country people touched by adoption sent checks from $5.00 to $100.00 to show their appreciation.

Eliminating adopt-a confusion, and using respectful language and imagery, are important goals for adoption advocates. Because we care about adoption, about waiting children and most of all about our own kids, most of us understand that at times we will feel called upon to become advocates of adoption sensitivity. Some of us are letter writers, some of us are public speakers, some of us are lobbyists or sales people, some of us are one-on-one conversationalists. Still others of us find it uncomfortable to take a personal public stand, but we want to support those who are willing to speak out on our behalf, so we become members of organizations and donors to campaigns that such organizations, with their strength in numbers, can make successful. Each of these types of advocates is an important link in the advocacy chain—and one of these links is you.

Those Caring Others Close to Us

Sometimes it is the people who touch us most directly who need our attention first—the grandparents who feel a need to introduce their much-loved grandchildren with qualifiers ("Judy and Tyrone adopted Tawanda, you know."), clergypeople who forget that in speaking to one family in a post-service reception line they are speaking to those all around, teachers who mean well but just can't get it right.

> Even after I had spoken to her teacher about it once (see earlier chapter), Erica came home from school on the very day several years ago that I was writing on this topic yet again. She had a beautiful report card, and on the bottom of it, her teacher, who absolutely adored her and made no bones about it, had written, "Erica, always know that I'd take you as my own, any time, any day. You are a peach. Love, Mrs. H."

Now, I knew very well that Mrs. H. meant this as the highest compliment to my daughter and to us, her parents. What she had forgotten was that Erica joined our family by adoption. For many children at Erica's age (fifth grade) such a message could be very confusing. Just like all other fifth graders, she was experiencing days when she'd like to trade her parents in for any other convenient set. But for children who were adopted, as was Erica, the fact is that the normal fantasizing about having a better set of parents was complicated by the fact that she very likely could have had a totally different set. It could set her up for conflictual grieving. In fact, it did, as I shared earlier. The year before when this same teacher made similar comments in class, Erica had several bad days which finally produced a long discussion between us of why birthparents make adoption plans and how hard it is sometimes to be adopted.

As a former teacher I am well aware of the mixed perceptions of adoption among teachers in general. Some teachers single these children out as "special" and especially admire their "wonderful, selfless parents." Other teachers believe that children who were adopted are at risk for problems and, if they know that one of their students was adopted, seem to wait for the proverbial shoe to drop. In reality, teachers are very normal people, with the same mix of fact and fiction to deal with as has the rest of the world. But with teachers, parents can find an advantage. These are people who truly care about kids, who understand how kids learn and care about educating them, who are themselves usually omnivorous learners. Teachers and school counselors will soak up information you are willing to provide them. Make certain they have copies of articles and booklets you have found helpful, and engage them as your allies in helping your children deal with their adoptive status.

> "It's too bad that there have been *no children of your own*, but it's wonderful of you to have taken her in," commented the smiling clergyperson as he patted the head of the brown toddler who clung to the skirt of the blond, blue-eyed woman he addressed. "Do you know anything at all about her *real parents? How could anyone give up such a beautiful child?*"
>
> In the line behind them I cringed as I heard her words. The pastor was well meaning, of course, but I knew that his words stung the family for whom they were meant. No children of their own? Real parents? Did the years they had spent working to build a family, the weeks they had spent consoling a terrified grieving baby, who, for the first time in her short life looked up into white face and blue eyes, the nights they had walked the floor with a baby wracked with the pain of a parasite that had accompanied her from the land of her birth count for nothing? Wonderful people who had rescued a waif? Did he not know of the thousands of others who waited for babies, could he not realize how lucky *they* felt to have been given the privilege of parenting this beautiful child? And their daughter, tired and cranky and ready to go home, yet listening to the words of the adults over her head . . . what did she take in from this exchange? What message about herself and her family was added to her internal tape?
>
> Between me and the adoption-built family waited another family—mom, dad and daughter. The daughter was fifteen, a freshman in high school, bright and popular, and—unknown to the pastor—pregnant. They too heard her words. *What did they think?* I wondered. How did this caring professional's subtle prejudices weigh upon their minds and contribute to their thinking as they worked so hard to sort through a maze of options—parenting, abortion, adoption?

Can you let instances like these go? I think not. It's about entitlement again—your child's!

Each of us must find ways that will allow us to become adoption educators at the level we find most comfortable. Perhaps it is a private telephone conversation or a note. Of course you can pass along the brochure describing an adoption educational event you think might help. Perhaps you are braver than that. Can you volunteer to do a brief in-service training for staff at the schools, doctors' offices, scout leader training, or houses of worship which touch your family's lives?

The Myths Still with Us

Myth: Now you'll get pregnant! They always do!

Fact: Adoption is neither a "relaxant" nor a "fertility treatment," let alone a sperm donor! Fewer than 5% of people who adopt become pregnant without intending to or without further fertility treatment—the same percentage of spontaneous pregnancy among family-challenged people who do NOT adopt.

I could not resist adding this. It's the most commonly held myth about adoption and adoptive parenting. It was right at the top of the list of Five Hot Buttons Not to Push—a list of the five most insensitive things adoptive families hear that is part of the book *Adoption Is a Family Affair: What Relatives and Friends Must Know*, which I wrote with the participants of the adoption chat boards I moderate for INCIID.org. Here are all five.

5. "What about the money?"
(Didn't your mother teach you it was bad manners to talk about money, politics and religion?)

- From my mother-in-law when we first told her that we were going to adopt, 'You know, you can get a Mexican baby for $250!'

- Friends of mine adopted, and shortly after adopting the husband was telling a client about it and the client asked, "Oh, well how much did she cost you?" No this was not a blundering idiot like most, but a social worker!

- Q: "Why would you spend so much money on adoption after spending so much money on infertility treatment?"
  A: "Well, didn't you just buy that nice $35,000 SUV? This is our family we are talking about. Priceless!"

- My brother-in-law told his kids that we were "going to Korea to buy a baby!"

- Someone asked me if adopting babies from China was like a black market. I had to explain how they take good care of the babies and rigorously screen who they will allow to adopt and that the fee is used to keep the orphanages running and take care of all the kids, including those who won't be adopted. I sure don't ever want my kid getting the idea that she was bought on the black market.

■ An acquaintance who heard about our plans asked us "How much will your child cost?" (ARGHHHHHHHHHH) No further comment with this one. On the other hand, yes, my husband and I have had this question numerous times. Some people who have inquired are very sincere, as they too, are weighing the decision to continue infertility treatment, live childfree, or move to adoption. That is very understandable, and I respect that question from them.

4. "Adoption connections aren't real connections anyway!" (Do you really want to say "You can do better than this"?)

■ Are you sure you tried hard enough?" (to conceive)

■ Q: "Does it bother you that they won't be your own?"
A: "My favorite comment to this one is what I read from the INCIID Adoption Waiting Room bulletin board earlier this summer: 'I gave birth to them through my heart' . . . that is the shorter version I use with this stupid question. It makes people think about how ignorant they were for asking in the first place."

■ I mentioned to my sister-in-law that I wanted to name my future adopted son Truman, nickname Tru. She said "You can't call him Tru Kingsley, because he is not a true Kingsley. He will not be related . . . umm, I mean by blood." I was appalled and since then have refused to tell anyone the names I am considering for my future children.

■ My husband adopted his first wife's daughter at the age of 9 months (she is now 22) and adopted my son at the age of 3 (he is now 10). Much to our surprise, I am now 30 weeks pregnant. On New Year's Day we went to my husband's mother's house. His sister (whom he has never really liked and hadn't seen in over a year) comes swooping in the door and hugs him and loudly exclaims, "I want to hug you before you get to become a real father." My husband said very angrily, "I've been a real father twice now, but thanks." He was so angry, and I was so angry, especially because both his son and his daughter heard her comment. I couldn't believe how stupid, totally insensitive and wrong her comment was.

■ Q: "What's her mother's name?"
A: "My name is Lisa."
Q: "No, I mean her real mother's name."
A: "I'm her mother."
Q: "NO, I mean her real mother."
A: "What do you think I am? Polyester?"
And then, as if I must be some sort of an idiot, I said, "Ohhhh you mean her birthmother!"

Q: Then she said, "Well you knew what I meant all the time."
A: "No I didn't. I'm her real mother and I always will be. What do you think Sara will go through if she heard you say that I'm not her real mother and she is too young to understand?"

■ From my brother who has a master's and a PhD in theology when my mom told him over the phone that we were going to adopt: "Why don't they just have their own kids?"

■ "Too bad you have to adopt . . . your real kids would have been real cute."

■ Q: "What does her mom look like?"
A: "You tell me you are looking right at her!"
Q: The nerve of this woman She kept prying she said "Come on you know what I mean."
A: I said "No, I do not!"

■ "She looks like she could be yours!"

■ "Can they get her back?"

■ "What are you going to do when he's 3 or 4 and the birthparents want him back?"

■ "Can you give him back if you find out he's retarded or something?"

■ An adult adoptee asked me, "If you and your husband get divorced, will you have to give him back?" I was so dumbfounded I didn't respond how I really should have, which would have been to ask if her parents would have had to "give her back" if they had ever divorced.

3. "Adopted people are 'flawed.'" (The Bad Seed myth, or is it Racism?)

■ My reproductive endocrinologist said, "You might not want to adopt . . . you never know what you're going to get." As if you know with a biological baby!

■ "Adopted kids are always so stupid!"

■ I was talking to my sister, who by the way, is very well educated and is currently in a high-paying, high-profile job working for an African-American man. I was mentioning to her about our long wait for our child. She (once again) asked what my "criteria" was for our child, meaning, had we requested a newborn, toddler, what race, etc. I told her that all I asked for was that the child be under age 3. To which she said, with much surprise, "Even a black child?" "Yeeeeessss" I replied. "But you don't know how to cook collard greens, or how to comb their hair!! . . . and Desiree (the daughter born to us) will *know* that s/he is not her real sibling!!" she says, totally serious. Funny thing is, (and I also told her this) that I am hispanic (Colombian), yet I have *never* cooked a Colombian meal for my daughter!

- "I never knew Adopted Children could be so cute"

- An old friend of the family said "I think if someone is stupid enough to get pregnant and doesn't want the baby, she should turn around, walk the other way, and never look back." I thought that was so cruel. As if he is so superior that he never has made a mistake, and as if a birthmother could ever forget her child. This experience taught me not to tell many people about our open adoption. It's really no one's business.

- A co-worker of my husband said "I wouldn't adopt, you will never get a perfect child." I was stunned when he told me. She has a toddler who I am sure isn't "perfect" and I think anyone who expects any child to be "perfect" is setting that child up for a life of misery!! My husband told her we were hoping not to have a perfect child, because it wasn't going to have perfect parents. GO husband!!

- When I told my friend (a woman who was aghast that there was another girl in her play group with the same name as her daughter—she wanted hers to be the only one with that name) that if I had a boy, I'd name him Noah, she exclaimed "Yikes! Why would you name him something so unusual, he's going to stand out enough as it is. Why not name him something normal, like Larry?"

- Q: "Why don't you just try to get a healthy Caucasian baby?"
  A: "HELLO!!!!! We want a baby from another country. That is our choice."

- Q: "Why on earth would you want to adopt a black baby? They are ugly, have kinky hair and are always boarder babies. No black baby is ever given up for adoption without drugs and alcohol. Could turn out to be a criminal too."

- Apparently everyone born in Asia speaks an Asian language because it's a genetic thing. People are forever asking me if our toddler son Cameron (who was born in Vietnam) can speak English. Just for fun, I told one person he was bilingual. After all, he was just a baby and saying only *ma*, which happens to be Vietnamese for mother and *ba*, which is Vietnamese for grandmother. I suppose he's as bilingual as the next baby!

- Our Latina daughter was born in Alabama, but people are always asking me, "Do you think she will have an accent?"

- "Why not just adopt from Russia? At least they'd look like you."

■ A girlfriend who told me during my infertility treatment, "Why not just get a dog, it's a lot easier" (probably should have ended the friendship right then) noted the other night that "It's a good thing you are adopting an Asian kid, because he'll be short like the two of you." When I informed her that Koreans come in all different sizes like Americans she said, "Well we all know that Asians are generally shorter than Americans."

■ I am 6′ and my husband is 6′3″. We have had two people tell us we shouldn't be adopting from Guatemala because our daughter will be short. Who cares!!

■ "Oh, no! You're going to adopt a Mexican?"

2. "Didn't you know that . . ."
(Ignorance isn't bliss in personal relationships)

■ "Why don't you just go and pick one out?" Gee, where's the closest Babies-R-Us store?

■ "Will you tell her she's adopted?" Duh . . . our Chinese daughter and we won't exactly look alike.

■ We adopted our daughter from China in Dec. 1999. A few months ago we went out to dinner with my father- and mother-in-law. Our daughter was eating rice and getting it everywhere (she was 16 mos. old). My father-in-law said, "If she were home she would know how to use chopsticks by now." I just gave him a weird look and said "She is home and what does chopsticks have to do with it?" I know he did not say it to be mean; he is just clueless. He loves his granddaughter to death.

■ "If God intended for you to have children, you'd be pregnant by now."

■ We are African American, and we have been asked more than once, "What's taking you so long. Aren't there piles of African-American babies that need homes? You must be doing something wrong!" I think that her comment does kind of reflect this notion that there are a lot of African-American infants to be adopted—and this is in part supported by agencies and other adoption professionals. There isn't a "surplus" of African-American babies out there. What is closer to reality is that there are a lot of older children of color in the foster care system, many of whom are adoptable.

■ At Christmas my sister-in-law asked about the progress with the adoption, commenting that it is taking a long time. I told her our homestudy is being reviewed by the Immigration and Naturalization Service and this time frame is about what the agency projected. She responded, "Well, if it doesn't work out you can always go for artificial insemination." Was she really paying that little attention during all the years we struggled with infertility??

■ Q: "Do you get to name her?" She was still a baby, and had only the name the Chinese government assigned to her. Should I have answered "No, I have to call her Rover for the rest of her life"?

■ "Well, you should know adoption is expensive" . . . Hmmm, well thanks for telling us that. Those hours researching adoption must have done us no good.

■ "You mean you can still adopt within the United States?"

And last, but not least,

Sad-but-True variations on the Number One Insensitive Comment Made to Those Who are Adopting— "Now you'll get pregnant! They always do."

■ "Adopt and then you'll get pregnant at last!" Does that mean the adoption won't have any meaning then if a woman becomes pregnant?

■ Everybody in my life knows that my significant other is a woman and that we want to be mommies. So when I told my oldest sister that we were planning on adopting, she delivered the usual line about getting pregnant now that we've decided to adopt. So I told her no, we've stopped all treatment. We're building our family through adoption. She insisted, "Oh no, you won't need treatment. You'll get pregnant now that you are going to adopt." I finally just said, "Do you know how babies are made?"

■ "Once you adopt you will soon become pregnant!" That is impossible since I had a complete hysterectomy. These people who say this to me, knowing I had the surgery, are down right mean. How cruel!

■ My mother and my mother-in-law both really believe that once I adopt I'll get pregnant. In fact, I hear this from everyone I tell that I am trying to adopt. Sheesh, pregnancy after adopting only happens in about 5% of the cases and who knows what their fertility problem was.

■ My mother-in-law added the best comment to this one. "If you adopt and get pregnant I am not coming to Ontario to help you with babysitting!" My response is "**Thank goodness!**"

Someone needs to compile a top-five list of insensitive comments made to teen adoptees! You are an activist now. Is that *your* job?

The Politics of Adoption

Cynthia Martin created a stir many years ago when she authored a how-to book on adoption which she titled *Beating the Adoption Game*. The title certainly caught the attention of many—prospective parents who immediately sensed that here was a book that was written by someone who understood where they were coming from, as well as outraged traditional practitioners who felt that such an image trivializes a dignified service to children and families.

The image—adoption as a game to be played—may not be a pretty picture, but many touched by this process would say that the analogy certainly works. Over the last few decades it's been used more and more frequently, and we'll use it again here to talk about the key organizations which impact society's view of adoption—the players in the game.

The world of adoption is a rapidly changing one. Beginning in the early 2000s, adoption, once thought of as a family building option only for white, middle class, infertile couples looking for a healthy baby became—in principle—amazingly diverse.

I emphasize the phrase *in principle* because the fact is that minority families continue to be both poorly recruited and insensitively treated by far too many agencies who have placement responsibilities for large numbers of children of color. Couples who have more than one child by birth and single prospective parents are rarely seen as "families of choice" except in the placement of children with special needs, and working class and poor families often find themselves challenged in their quest to build families by adoption. Women facing an unplanned pregnancy find it extraordinarily difficult to get the truly objective counseling that will allow them to make unpressured choices about options so that, on the one hand, far too many children for whom adoption might be an appropriate option are aborted or born only to remain with unprepared and possibly neglectful birthfamilies, and on the other hand far too many women continue to feel that they have been pressured to choose adoption.

As we discussed in earlier chapters, the menu of options for building a family by adoption ranges from public and private agency adoption and adoptions arranged by the more traditional non-agency sources (doctors, lawyers, clergy) to entrepreneurial independent services which offer consultations on self-marketing, provide education, and refer to counseling as requested. Birthparents and prospective adopters of infants and older children can put all the control into the hands of professionals, or may choose to retain personal control over all decisions in finding and choosing a family. Adoptions vary on a spectrum ranging from the traditional confidential form in which no or very little identifying information is shared, to those which involve close, ongoing communication and/or visitation between birth and adoptive families in a kind of extended family form. Intercountry adoption continues to occur, though the countries from which children arrive seem to change nearly annually, with each country establishing its own procedures and requirements. Old social service agencies abandon the practice of adoption and new agencies form every year. Consumer groups begin and old ones die. Legislation is introduced, and passed or defeated.

The game is confusing, and the rules are constantly changing. No matter how idealistic we are in talking about recent positive changes in adoption, healthy babies—no matter what their racial status—are, more often than not, adopted (after payment of large fees) by white, upper middle class families; far too many children linger in foster care rather than finding permanent families in adoption; children around the world continue to be stolen from their birthfamilies and sold into adoption; and birthparents continue to feel improperly served. These continuing inequities have resulted in strongly negative reactions to adoption "as practiced" from groups as diverse as the National Association of Black Social Workers, Concerned United Birthparents, American Adoption Congress, and National Council on Adoption. And everybody seems to have an answer to how to "fix" adoption's problems.

Becoming informed and staying informed is not an easy task. But doing so is worth it. A recurring theme throughout this book has been David Kirk's premise that it is families who fairly consistently acknowledge the differences in adoption (rather than deny them) who are best able to build the kind of empathic communication with their children (acknowledging that each of them has experienced both significant losses and significant gains in adoption) which fosters healthy attachments between parents and children. To practice this kind of acceptance of difference is possible in adoption only when we keep ourselves in touch and informed—when we know the "players on the field."

Resources

National Level Political Activist "Players" as of 2007

I have chosen to define organizations as they define themselves, which is why I have used quotation marks around the explanatory paragraphs. Readers should not assume, however, that all of these organizations "play nicely" together. Each has its own political agenda. A few are, in general or quite specifically, opposed to the very concept of adoption. It is important, however, to include them all, since each of those listed, through their financial distributions, their lobbying efforts, or extensive media work has had or continues to have a major impact on how adoption is perceived by the world at large, how it plays out for children in need of permanency, and how it is legislated, both state-by-state and nationally. Please visit and read the websites and form your own opinions about whether your own philosphy

Adopt USKids (est. 2002)
8015 Corporate Drive Suite C
Baltimore, MD 21236
(888) 200-4005
www.adoptuskids.org
"The Children's Bureau is part of the Federal Department of Health and Human Services. In October 2002, The Children's Bureau contracted with The Adoption Exchange Association and its partners (the Collaboration to AdoptUsKids) to devise and implement a national adoptive family recruitment and retention strategy, operate the AdoptUsKids.org website, encourage and enhance adoptive family support organizations, and conduct a variety of adoption research projects."

American Adoption Congress—AAC (est. 1978)
PO Box 42730
Washington, DC 20015
(202) 483-3399
www.americanadoptioncongress.org/home.htm
"The American Adoption Congress comprises individuals, families, and organizations committed to adoption reform. We represent those whose lives are touched by adoption or other loss of family continuity. We promote honesty, openness, and respect for family connections in adoption, foster care, and assisted reproduction. We provide education for our members and professional communities about the lifelong process of adoption. We advocate legislation that will grant every individual access to information about his or her family and heritage."

American Academy of Adoption Attorneys—AAAA (est. 1990)
P.O. Box 33053
Washington, DC 20033
(202) 832-2222
www.adoptionattorneys.org/
"The American Academy of Adoption Attorneys is a national association of approximately 330 attorneys who practice, or have otherwise distinguished themselves, in the field of adoption law. The Academy's work includes promoting the reform of adoption laws and disseminating information on ethical adoption practices. The Academy publishes a newsletter, holds annual meetings, and hosts educational seminars."

Annie E. Casey Foundation (est. 1948)
701 St. Paul Street
Baltimore, MD 21202
(410) 547-6600
www.aecf.org
"Founded in 1948 by Jim Casey, founder of UPS and his siblings in honor of their mother, the primary mission of the Annie E. Casey Foundation is to foster public policies, human-service reforms, and community supports that more effectively meet the needs of today's vulnerable children and families. In pursuit of this goal, the Foundation makes grants that help states, cities, and neighborhoods fashion more innovative, cost-effective responses to these needs."

Bastard Nation (est. 1996)
P.O. Box 1469
Edmond, OK 73083-1469

Phone / Fax: (415) 704-3166

www.bastards.org/

"Bastard Nation advocates for the civil and human rights of adult citizens who were adopted as children. Millions of North Americans are prohibited by law from accessing personal records that pertain to their historical, genetic, and legal identities. Such records are held by their governments in secret and without accountability, due solely to the fact that they were adopted."

Child Welfare League of America—CWLA (est. 1920)

2345 Crystal Drive, Suite 250

Arlington, VA 22202

(703) 412-2400

"CWLA is an association of nearly 800 public and private nonprofit agencies that assist more than 3.5 million abused and neglected children and their families each year with a range of services. Our highest mission is to ensure the safety and well-being of children and families. We advocate for the advancement of public policy; we set and promote the standards for best practice; and we deliver superior membership services."

Concerned United Birthparents—CUB (est. 1978)

P.O. Box 503475

San Diego, CA 92150-3475

(800) 822-2777

www.cubirthparents.org/

"CUB is a national organization serving those separated by adoption and others who are concerned about adoption issues. "Although our focus is on birthparents, long the forgotten people of the adoption community, we welcome adoptees, adoptive parents, and professionals. We find that we all have much to learn from each other and that sharing our feelings and experiences benefits all of us."

Dave Thomas Foundation for Adoption (est. 1992)

4150 Tuller Road Suite 204

Dublin, Ohio 43017

(800) 275-3832

www.davethomasfoundation.org/contact.asp

"The Dave Thomas Foundation for Adoption is a nonprofit public charity dedicated to dramatically increasing the adoptions of the more than 140,000 children in North America's foster care systems. Dave Thomas, founder of Wendy's, created the Foundation in 1992 to assure that every child has a permanent home and a loving family."

Ethica: A Voice for Ethical Adoption (est. 2003)

8639-B 16th St. #156

Silver Spring, MD 20910

(301) 650-0649

www.ethicanet.org

"Ethica is a nonprofit corporation that seeks to be an impartial voice for ethical adoption practices worldwide, and provides education, assistance, and advocacy to the adoption and foster care communities."

Evan B Donaldson Adoption Institute (est. 1996)

525 Broadway, 6th floor

New York, NY 10012

* (212) 925-4089

www.adoptioninstitute.org

"The Evan B. Donaldson Adoption Institute, founded in 1996, is a national non-profit organization devoted to improving adoption policy and practice. In order to achieve its goals, the Institute conducts and synthesizes research; offers education to inform public opinion; promotes ethical practices and legal reforms; and works to translate policy into action."

Joint Council on International Children's Service—JCICS (est. 1976)

117 South Saint Asaph Street

Alexandria, VA 22314

(703) 535-8045

www.jcics.org

"Joint Council on International Children's Services is the lead voice on intercountry children's services. With a mission to advocate on behalf of children in need of permanent, safe and loving families, Joint Council promotes ethical child welfare practices, strengthens professional standards and educates adoptive families, social service professionals, and government representatives throughout the world. International child welfare agencies, child advocacy groups, parent support groups and international medical clinics choose membership in Joint Council as a means to address the critical issue of parentless children and create permanent solutions."

National Council for Adoption—NACAC (est. 1980)

225 N. Washington Street

Alexandria, VA 22314-2561

(703) 299-6633

www.adoptioncouncil.org

"NCFA has been a champion of adoption since its founding in 1980. Whether as an advocate for state laws that promote sound adoption policy, a resource for federal officials and policymakers about appropriate federal adoption initiatives and reform, a diplomat for sound international adoption policy, or a source of adoption facts and education, NCFA is devoted to serving the best interests of children through adoption. NCFA works to promote the positive option of adoption."

North American Council on Adoptable Children—NACAC (est. 1974)

970 Raymond Avenue, Suite 106

St. Paul, MN 55114

(651) 644-3036

www.nacac.org

"NACAC promotes and supports permanent families for children and youth in the U.S. and Canada who have been in care—especially those in foster care and those with special needs. To achieve this mission, NACAC focuses its program services in four areas: public policy advocacy, parent leadership capacity building, education and information sharing, and adoption support."

Spaulding for Children (est. 1968)

16250 Northland Drive Suite 100

Southfield, Michigan 48075

(248) 443-7080

www.spaulding.org

"This multi-faceted organization provides help to children who wait the longest for permanency and support services for their adoptive, foster and kinship families. Nationwide, Spaulding's Resource Center provides training, consultation and informational materials for professionals, organizations and parents. Included is the **National Child Welfare Resource Center for Adoption** (NCWRCA) which assists States, Tribes and other federally-funded child welfare agencies as they work to ensure permanency for abused and neglected children. The Center specializes in providing technical assistance, with a focus on program planning, policy development and practice through consultation, training, information/research and resource materials aimed at supporting organizations in their efforts for continuous program improvement. Additionally, the Center offers resources to assist with every phase of the Federal Child and Family Services Reviews."

Books on Adoption Activism and Politics

Babb, L. Anne. *Ethics in American Adoption.* (Westport, CT: Bergin & Garvey, 1999)

Carp, E. Wayne. *Adoption Politics: Bastard Nation and Ballot Initiative 58.* (Kansas City: University Press of Kansas, 2004)

Gritter, James. *The Spirit of Open Adoption.* (Washington DC: CWLA Press, 1997)

Pertman, Adam. *Adoption Nation: How the Adoption Revolution Is Transforming America.* (New York: Basic Books, 2000)

Shaw, Randy. *The Activist's Handbook: A Primer.* (Updated Edition with a New Preface) (Berkeley: University of California Press, 2001)

Sollinger, Rickie. *Beggars and Choosers: How the Politics of Choice Shapes Adoption, Abortion, and Welfare in the United States.* (New York: Hill and Wang, 2002)

Zelizer, Viviana. *Pricing the Priceless Child: The Changing Social Value of Children.* (Princeton, NJ: Princeton University Press, 1994)

Periodicals for Adoptive Families

See Resources for Chapter 5.

Adoptive Family Support Organizations

See Resources for Chapter 5.

An After Thought

Sweet Beginnings

by Jennifer L. Schuler

In the beginning, I was loved. I was loved before I ever came to see, before my time was to be.

This great love came from my mother who, before she had ever met me, had thoughts of me. Oh, she'd try hard to ignore them, but rarely did she succeed; the feeling of me always had a way of creeping into her mind, butter-flying in her stomach, and pounding in her heart.

Mommy thought of me when she was a little girl, playing with her dolls. She thought of me when she was growing up, wondering if she would ever know a happy family. She thought of me when she was a young woman, believing that she might never know me.

But she did know me. I was always there. Swirling around her very existence.

I say I know this because I could feel that love long before I came to see, before my time was to be. I think, though, that this is what all children, regardless of their age now, regardless of how they come to their families hope for, isn't it? That they were loved and wanted, and treasured long before their mother held them in her arms?

This is what I hope for. And this is what I feel for my little one. I love her now. I will love her then. My love for her will always be there, just as it was for me.

In the end, it must be less about connections by blood or by law or by social custom. It must be less about rights and entitlement and myth and misunderstanding.

In the end, it is *all* about love. About families—birth and adoptive—who deeply love their children. Some families understand that their children can't wait for the temporary crises of youth, inexperience and lack of resources (emotional, temporal, financial, physical) to be resolved. They plan adoption, with a mixture of grief and hope for their beloved sons and daughters. Some families have problems—substance abuse, mental health issues, criminal involvement—that run too deeply and manifest themselves too dangerously for society to allow them to continue to struggle at parenting children whom they love, but whom they can't keep safe. They submit, with grief, and anger, and still with hope, to a termination of parental rights. Some are family-challenged—infertile or with genetic issues, partnerless or partnered with a person with whom they cannot "make" children—and, looking for ways to bring children into their fully-prepared lives, they adopt and raise, with great love, the children of those grieving birthfamilies.

And in the end it is also about those birth and adoptive families loving one another—whether close or at a distance—respecting the role each has in the lives of the person at the center of it all—a child. May that child love and be loved, twice over.

Acknowledgments

Writing a book is never a solo project, and this book, which summarizes a 30 year career of learning and practicing in the fields of infertility and adoption, involved thousands: those who mentored me; the members of support groups I helped to lead; the members of boards of directors and committees on which I served; the consumers and professionals who attended my workshops, read my books and followed up with questions—all are reflected in these pages. Each and every one remains in my mind and in my heart, and will, throughout my life. Thank you for teaching me so much.

Thank you to INCIIDers who offered to read and react to drafts of this material—Annie, Erin, Rebecca, Julie, Julia, Jennifer. Thank you to Cynthia VN Peck, Emily Perl Kingsley, Shiela Darst, and Arthur Dobrin for invaluable additions. And thank you to my patient editor, Erica Marchetti, and to the final proofing wizard, adoptive-mom-to-be Jennifer Schuler. Mayapriya Long at Bookwrights has made this and several other Perspectives Press, Inc. books both readable and beautiful for nearly a decade now.

Thank you as well to the adoption and infertility experts who graciously previewed early drafts and caught factual errors. Dr, Greg Keck, Dr, Jeff Deaton, Mark McDermott, Kathie Stocker, Carole Lieber-Wilkins, Jayne Schooler, Jane Page, Courtney Lewis, Dr, Deborah Borchers, and Meg Sterchi, gave huge chunks of their valuable professional time to read through these 500+ pages, and I am ever grateful for their comments, which vastly improved the final product.

And, finally, serving as sounding boards and support system, fodder for so much of what I say and write, my family has been patient—and, obviously, involved! Thank you to each of them for agreeing that we had something to say that could be of value to others. Most especially, I thank my husband, Dave, who over 32 years of kids growing up and leaving the nest gave me the priceless gift of being a business person who could also be a stay-at-home mom!

Patricia Irwin Johnston
Indianapolis
August, 2007

Endnotes

Endnotes to the Introduction(s)

1 Nigeria, in the early 21st century, has, more than any other country in the world, become a hub for various Internet-based financial scams, beginning with the one which gave this kind of scam its country's name. The first versions were letters from persons claiming to be the widows of wealthy men who had died with their money tied up in banks which did not respect widows' rights, offering a part of the loot for financial assistance in getting the money out. By 2007–08 almost all adoptive parents whose profiles appear on the wanting-to-adopt sites which are proliferating on the Internet had received several versions of a similar plea—"I'm a poor widow/widower in X country unable to care for my child/children. I've seen your profile and want you to adopt my children. Help me get this started by sending money to . . ."

Endnotes to Chapter 1

1 This scenario has been borrowed and then significantly adapted and embellished from the 1976 version of *How to Survive the Loss of a Love*, by Melba Cosgrove, Harold Bloomfield, and Peter McWilliams. While in today's completely connected society (answering machines, busy-signal voice mail, call forwarding, pagers, cell phones, etc). scenarios like this one are less and less likely to happen, this anecdote continues to be the best analogy I've found for helping people to understand the loss reaction as more than a "death and dying" phenomenon. The 1991 revised version (Bantam Books) no longer contains this clarifying anecdote. Too bad! But the book remains a good resource for those dealing with loss of any kind.

2 In writing her classic book *Infertility: A Guide for the Childless Couple* (Prentice Hall, 1976; revised in 1988) Barbara Eck Menning was the first to tie the emotional reaction to infertility to the grief pattern (surprise, denial, anger, isolation, bargaining, depression, and acceptance) first identified by Elisabeth Kubler-Ross in her book *On Death and Dying*. Ms. Menning wrote that couples experiencing infertility were experiencing a kind of death—the death of a child never conceived or never born. This theory has been helpful to thousands of couples, but it has been my experience that many couples cannot identify with this specific loss. This is why I have found it more helpful (first in *An Adoptor's Advocate* (1984), then in *Adopting after Infertility* (1992) and in *Taking Charge of Infertility* (1996), and now here) to identify for couples a broader spectrum of loss, from which they can then identify the losses most meaningful to themselves

3 Mason, Mary Martin. *The Miracle Seekers: An Anthology of Infertility*. This and Mary's other valuable book *Designing Rituals of Adoption: For the Religious and Secular Community* are available as used books through Amazon and other Internet sources.

Endnotes to Chapter 2

1 Tannen, Deborah, Ph.D. *You Just Don't Understand: Women and Men in Conversation* (New York: Ballantine, 1990) p. 73.

2 Tannen, Deborah, Ph.D. *op. cit.*, p. 26–27.

3 Carter, Jean W. and Michael. *Sweet Grapes: How to Stop Being Infertile and Start Living Again*. (Indianapolis: Perspectives Press, Rev 1998) p. 132

Endnotes to Chapter 3

1 The first time I presented the decision making model in this chapter, in the 1992 book *Adopting After Infertility* which *Adopting: Sound Choices, Strong Families* replaces, I was writing for an infertile audience. These folks had not been given the opportunity to think about strategic planning as a way to look at, and exert some control over, infertility treatment. So that book included a great deal of material about making choices within infertility and looking at other family building options in addition to adoption. Because *Taking Charge of Infertility* now offers that material to those still in treatment, I've chosen to remove most of the discussion about making treatment decisions from this book, retaining only discussion of classic adoption and, to a lesser extent, the "quasi-adoption" options involving collaborative reproduction. Those who are still in infertility treatment and counseling professionals who have not seen the infertility portion of this process can find it in *Taking Charge of Infertility*

2 Those who are using this process while in infertility treatment would, of course, not limit themselves to personally reflecting on adoption, rather on various treatment options, as well as alternatives from adoption to collaborative reproduction to childfree living. Having given some thought in advance to these issues will help each partner to clarify his or her concerns when the time comes to share.

Endnotes to Chapter 4

1 "Gay Adoption Basics" about.com adoption.about.com/od/gaylesbian/a/gay-adopt.htm

2 "Nolo Parenting Issues for Unmarried Partners" Nolo.com www.nolo.com/article.cfm/objectID/893B37A0-D0E8-4B7D-9FD90CE5DCBC3BE7/118/304/145/FAQ/

3 "Single Parent Adoption: What You Need to Know" Child Welfare Information Gateway www.childwelfare.gov/pubs/f_single/index.cfm

4 ©1987 by Emily Perl Kingsley, All rights reserved, Reprinted by permission of the author. Do NOT reprint from this book without permission from Emily Perl Kingsley.

5 Brodzinsky, David M. "A Stress and Coping Model of Adoption Adjustment," *The Psychology of Adoption*. New York: Oxford University Press, 1990, p. 20.

Endnotes to Chapter 5

1 Gray, Deborah. *Nurturing Adoptions: Creating Resilience after Neglect and Trauma.* Indianapolis: Perspectives Press, Inc., p 262.

2 Siegel, Daniel J. The *Developing Mind: How Relationships and the Brain Interact to Shape Who We Are*. New York: Guilford Press, 1999. p140.

3 Brodzinsky, D.M., Singer, L.M., and Braff, A.M. "Children's Understanding of Adoption." *Child Development*, Volume 55, pp. 869–878.

4 Brodzinsky, David M. "A Stress and Coping Model of Adoption Adjustment," *The Psychology of Adoption*. New York: Oxford University Press, 1990, p.7.

5 The organizations listed here are self described, which is why those descriptions have been placed within quotation marks.

Endnotes to Chapter 6

1 Published in *Perspectives on a Grafted Tree: Thoughts for Those Touched by Adoption,* edited by Patricia Irwin Johnston, Perspectives Press, Inc, 1982. Please contact Perspectives Press for reprint information at info@perspectivespress.com.

2 The Adoption History Project, University of Oregon darkwing.uoregon.edu/~adoption/index.html offers a fascinating introduction to adoption's evolution and how it has been studied and changed over time.

Endnotes to Chapter 7

1 Mitchell, Mary. "Utah's adoption laws ensnare poor parents here" *Chicago Sun Times*. January 15, 2004.

2 "The Commitment" first appeared as an article in *Adoption Today* magazine's January, 2001 issue.

3 "Instant Family? A Case against Artificial Twinning" appeared in articles in *Adoptive Families* magazine, Pact Press, and Serono Symposia USA's newsletter *Insights into Infertility* before becoming part of *Launching a Baby's Adoption* and then this book.

4 According to the 2004 Child Information Gateway article "Adoption Disruption and Dissolution Numbers and Trends" (www.childwelfare.gov/pubs/s_disrup.cfm), the term *disruption* is used to describe an adoption process that ends after the child is placed in an adoptive home and before the adoption is legally finalized, resulting in the child's return to (or entry into) foster care or placement with new adoptive parents. The term *dissolution* is used to describe an adoption that ends after it is legally finalized, resulting in the child's return to (or entry into) foster care or placement with new adoptive parents.

5 www.childwelfare.gov/pubs/sdisrup.cfm

Endnotes to Chapter 8

1 MacDonald, G. Jeffrey. "For Single Guys, More Hurdles to Adoption." Christian Science Monitor, June, 2004 www.csmonitor.com/2004/0618/p11s01-lifp.html

2 Islamonline.net www.islamonline.net/servlet/Satellite?pagename=Islam Online-English-Ask_Scholar/FatwaE/FatwaE&cid=1119503544668,

3 Freundlich, Madelyn. "The Americans with Disabilities Act: What Adoption Agencies Need to Know" www.adoptioninstitute.org/policy/ada.html

4 www.cnpp.usda.gov/Publications/CRC/crc2006.pdf

5 The cap figure changes annually. See www.irs.gov/formspubs/article/0,,id=109876,00.html#adopt_2007

Endnotes to Chapter 9

1 Bartholet, Elizabeth. "Where Do Black Children Belong? The Politics of Race Matching in Adoption." *University of Pennsylvania Law Review*, Law Review, Volume 139, Number 5: May, 1991, pp. 1172–73.

2 North American Council on Adoptable Children. *Adoptalk*, Winter, 2007, p.4

3 Gross, Gregory. "Banana Splits: A Biracial Family in Paradise." *Interrace*, Volume 3, No. 2. March/April, 1992, pp. 19–20

4 "Life Expectancy at Birth, Table 27" www.cdc.gov/nchs/data/hus/hus06.pdf#027

5 "Aging and Life Expectancy" *World of Genetics*. ©2005–2006 Thomson Gale, a part of the Thomson Corporation

6 www.acf.hhs.gov/programs/cb/stats_research/afcars/tar/report13.htm

Endnotes to Chapter 10

1 Huda. "Adopting a Child in Islam" About.com islam.about.com/cs/parenting/a/adoption.htm

2 Grotevant, Harold D. and Ruth G, McRoy. *Open Adoption: Exploring Family Connections* (Sage Publications, 2000)

3 McRoy, Ruth G. and Harold D. Grotevant

4 Critics prefer to use the more negative term closed adoption. In a parallel action, opponents of open adoption refer to it as experimental adoption. In this book, in both this instance and elsewhere, I have tried myself to use whichever language the proponents of a system prefer. I believe this is the fairest way to promote communication and discussion of an issue. In the same vein, were I writing about abortion, I would use the terms pro-life and pro-choice as the terms self-selected by those sharing each of these philosophies, rather than to label groups anti-abortion, anti-choice, or anti-life.

Endnotes to Chapter 11

1 The American Heritage® Dictionary of the English Language: Fourth Edition. 2000

2 Nelson, Betty "For-Proft vs Nonprofit" for Greater Knoxville SCORE www.scoreknox.org/library/versus.htm

3 Andringa, Robert, PhD. "Profit vs Nonprofit Boards" www.cccu.org/resource center/resID.1937,parentCatID.162/rc_detail.asp

4 While describing children as commodities is entirely offensive, this is the reality of what we are discussing!

Endnotes to Chapter 12

1 "The Adult Attachment Interview contains 20 questions that ask the subject about his/her experiences with parents and other attachment figures, significant losses and trauma, and if relevant, experiences with their own children. The interview takes approximately 60–90 minutes. It is then transcribed and scored by a trained person (who has undergone two weeks of intensive training followed by 18 months of reliability testing). The scoring process is quite complicated, but generally it involves assessing the coherence of the subject's narrative." (www.daniel-sonkin.com/attachment_psychotherapy.htm)

Endnotes to Chapter 13

1 www.cnpp.usda.gov/Publications/CRC/crc2006.pdf

2 Darst, Shelia Stewart. "waiting for The Call" in *Perspectives on a Grafted Tree: Thoughts for Those Touched by Adoption*, by Patricia Irwin Johnston. (Indianapolis: Perspectives Press, Inc., 1981)

Endnotes to Chapter 14

1 Kestenbaum, Clarice J. MD. Amazon.com review

Endnotes to Chapter 15

1 Brodzinsky, David in an interview in *FACE Facts*, November/December, 1994, pp. 6–11

2 Nancy Verrier's Primal Wound theory from her book of the same name alleges that an adoptee "separated from its mother at the beginning of life, when still in the primal relationship to her, experiences what I call the primal wound. This wound, occurring before the child has begun to separate his own identity from that of the mother, is experienced not only as a loss of the mother, but as a loss of the Self, that core-being of oneself which is the center of goodness and wholeness. The child may be left with a sense that part of oneself has disappeared, a feeling of incompleteness, a lack of wholeness. In addition to the genealogical sense of being cut off from one's roots, this incompleteness is often experienced in a physical sense of bodily incompleteness, a hurt from something missing. . . . Any injury to the basic goodness of Self interferes with healthy, phase-adequate ego development, resulting in premature ego development and a reluctance to trust others to "be there." While there is great merit in listening to what Verrier writes, it is important to remember that it is based on anecdotal rather than scientific research.

3 Definition from www.attach.org/faq.htm

4 Definition from specialchildren.about.com/od/gettingadiagnosis/g/fetalalcohol. htm

5 Definition from www.webmd.com/add-adhd/default.htm

6 Definition from science.education.nih.gov/supplements/nih3/hearing/other/ glossary.htm

7 Definition from specialchildren.about.com/od/gettingadiagnosis/g/Autism.htm

8 Definition from www.nimh.nih.gov/healthinformation/ptsdmenu.cfm

9 Definition from specialchildren.about.com/od/gettingadiagnosis/g/SID.htm

Index

Page numbers followed by "n" indicate notes.

AAAA. *See* American Academy of
	Adoption Attorneys
AAP. *See* American Academy of
	Pediatrics
abstract thinking, 122
Academy of Certified Social
	Workers, 278
accepting/acknowledging
	differences (AD), 96–97, 99,
	232, 503
Acker, Paula, 342
activism and politics, 502–7
AD. *See* Accepting/acknowledging
	differences
ADA. *See* Americans with
	Disabilities Act
adaptations. *See* Home
	environment
adjustment. *See also* Attachment
	adoptive versus non-adoptive
		families, 431
	birthparent relationships,
		464–66
	challenged attachment, 435–47
	dealing with reversals, 466–74
	developmental differences,
		455–64
	difficulties with, 109, 412

impact of prior experiences,
		434
	parenting challenges, 431–34
	post-adoption depression,
		453–55, 475–76
	of relationships between
		adults, 448–50
	resources, 475–77
	single parents, 450–52
adolescents. *See also* Older
		children
	artificial twinning and, 190
	communication with, 124–26
	connecting with birth
		families, 156
	identity issues, 121–22
	school issues, 140–41
	sex education and sexuality,
		146–47
adopt-a confusion, 489–94
Adopt USKids, 504
adoptees
	age considerations, 238–46
	availability of children, 226–
		27, 233, 252
	books for, 126–28, 135–36
	communicating with about
		adoption, 122–26

finding other children, 129–30
gains and losses, 90
gender selection, 227–29
health and abilities issues,
    229–32
learning about adoption,
    117–23
race and ethnicity, 232–38
rejection of differences
    behavior, 97–98
school issues, 137–41
sense of loss, 90, 93–94,
    119–20
terminology for, 485
Adopting after Cancer support
    group, 224
Adopting after Infertility (Johnston),
    352
*Adopting the Hurt Child and
    Parenting the Hurt Child*
    (Keck and Kupecky), 112
adoption
    as add on experience, 137
    child-centered nature of,
        161–62, 315
    compared to marriage,
        400–401
    competitive aspect of, 163–64
    historical perspective, 154,
        199–200, 226, 258–61,
        442–43
    images of, 488–96
    language and word choice,
        483–88
    motivations for, 84–85, 214
    myths about, 79–81, 496–501
    statistics, 78–79
    views of, 386, 482–83, 494–96
Adoption Agency Checklist, 310
Adoption Agency Research, 310
Adoption and Foster Care Analysis
    and Reporting System
    (AFCARS)

average ages of adoption, 246
birthparent rehabilitation and
    reunification, 245
foster care statistics, 78
singles adoptions, 204
Adoption and Safe Families Act of
    1997, 289
Adoption Community of New
    England (ACONE), 130
Adoption Council of Canada, 301
adoption counselors, 276–77
adoption educators, 281
adoption insurance, 222, 364
*Adoption Is a Family Affair: What
    Relatives and Friends Must
    Know* (Johnston), 39,
    496–501
Adoption Learning Partners, 132,
    133, 254, 255, 256
Adoption Policy Resource Center,
    255
Adoption Today magazine, 134, 394
adoption validation stage, 350, 351
Adoption.com, 255
adoptiondoctors.com, 399
Adoptions of Indiana, 407
Adoptive Breastfeeding Resources
    Website, 395
Adoptive Families magazine, 133–
    34, 157, 301, 394, 412
*Adoptive Kinship: A Modern
    Institution in Need of Reform*
    (Kirk), 96
adoptive nursing, 373–77
adoptive parents
    age considerations, 55–57, 65,
        80, 207, 239–40
    agency-client relationships,
        317–21
    characteristics of, 202–9, 431,
        450
    commitment requirement,
        181–84

declining a referral, 391–93,
    396
ethical responsibilities, 168–
    70, 175–77, 179–81
full disclosure by, 179–81
gains and losses, 90
physical conditioning, 358–59
psychological assessment,
    328–30
sense of loss, 89–93
sympathetic pregnancy,
    359–60
Adoptive Parents Committee of
    New York/New Jersey, 130
AdoptKorea, 255
An Adoptor's Advocate (Johnston),
    316
Adult Attachment Interview, 329,
    515
adult learning model, 101–2, 235
advertising and marketing
    emotional toll of, 54
    independent adoptions, 291,
        292, 334
    parent-initiated, 291, 292, 307
AFCARS. *See* Adoption and
    Foster Care Analysis and
    Reporting System
African Americans
    adoptions from foster care, 78
    children placed outside the
        U.S., 205
    lack of adoptive families, 205
    singles adoptions, 204
age considerations
    adoptive parents, 55–57, 65,
        239–40
    average ages of adoption, 246
    babies versus older children,
        238–46
    eligibility for adoption and,
        65, 80, 207
    life expectancies, 239–40

agencies. *See also* Professionals
    agency-client relationships,
        317–21
    approval requirements,
        312–14
    disclosure of health
        information, 328
    ethical practices and
        responsibilities,
        164–70
    for-profit versus not-for-profit,
        285–87
    licensing, 275, 282, 283
    number of, 275
    religiously connected
        agencies, 206, 282
    services provided, 282–84,
        287–88
    staff, 164
    types of adoptions handled,
        210, 273
alcohol-related neuro-
    developmental disease
    (ARND), 478
American Academy of Adoption
    Attorneys (AAAA), 275,
    279, 292, 504
American Academy of Pediatrics
    (AAP)
    International Adoption
        Guidelines, 370
    Section on Adoption and
        Foster Care (SOAFC),
        280
    umbilical cord blood storage,
        372
American Adoption Congress
    (AAC), 503, 504
American Fertility Association, 73
American Society for Reproductive
    Medicine, 73
Americans with Disabilities Act
    (ADA), 207, 224

Andringa, Robert, 287
Annie (musical), 488
Annie E. Casey Foundation, 504
anonymity. *See* Confidential
    adoptions
anticipation period. *See*
    Expectancy period
approval process
    criminal background checks,
        209, 330
    education and support, 331–35
    financial statements, 330–31
    health reports, 327–30
    home visits, 326–27
    homestudies, 272, 283, 312–
        14, 313, 315–16
    parent preparation, 314,
        316–17
    personal history, 322–24
    reasons for, 315
    references, providing, 324–26
*Are Those Kids Yours: American
    Families with Children
    Adopted from Other
    Countries* (Register), 236,
    461
Are You My Mother? (Eastman),
    127, 387
ARND. *See* Alcohol-related neuro-
    developmental disease
arousal-relaxation cycle, 106–7,
    423
artificial twinning
    ethical considerations, 183,
        184–89
    impact on children, 190–92
    professional view, 189–90
    strategies for parents, 192–94
Asian Americans
    children placed outside the
        U.S., 205
    international adoptions, 204–5

assessment
    criminal background checks,
        209, 330
    financial statements, 330–31
    health reports, 327–30
    home visits, 326–27
    homestudies, 272, 283, 312–
        14, 313, 315–16
    paperwork, 322
    personal history, 322–24
    references, providing, 324–26
Attaching in Adoption (Gray), 112
attachment. *See also* Claiming
    avoiding overstimulation, 412,
        413–14
    challenged attachment,
        435–47
    daycare and, 382
    infants and toddlers, 108–11,
        422–25, 444, 446–47
    insecure attachment,
        symptoms of, 422–24
    internationally adopted
        children, 109, 382, 412
    myths about, 104, 105
    need for education about,
        443–45
    obtaining information about
        previous care, 408–10
    older children, 112–13, 425–
        26, 444, 445–46
    overview, 105–8, 113, 410–14
    parental attachment history,
        108
    preschoolers, 111–12, 425–26,
        444
    reactive attachment disorder
        (RAD), 112
    reluctance to talk about
        problems, 109–11, 113,
        411, 445
    resources, 132, 427–28, 477

strategies for promoting,
    414–22
attention-deficit hyperactivity
    disorder (ADHD), 141,
    478–79
attorneys. *See also* American
    Academy of Adoption
    Attorneys
    as adoption intermediaries,
        276
    independent adoptions, 272,
        290, 292
    roles and responsibilities,
        278–79
auditory processing disorders, 479
auditory stimulation, 419–20
autism spectrum disorders, 460,
    479–80
autobiographies, 322

babbling, 460
Baby Blues, 453–55
baby books, 126
Bartels-Raab, Lisa, 461
Bartholet, Elizabeth, 233–34, 236
Bastard Nation, 504–5
bathing and swimming, 418
Beating the Adoption Game
    (Martin), 502
bedrooms. *See* Space
    considerations
Bernstein, Anne, 144–45
Berry, Marianne, 265
Bethany Christian Services, 206,
    225
Beyond Good Intentions: A
    Mother Reflects on Raising
    Internationally Adopted
    Children (Register), 237
bibliotherapy, 127
birthparents/birthfamilies. *See also*
    Open adoptions
    birthfathers' rights, 177–79

breast-feeding, 377–79
changes of heart, 163, 176–77,
    222, 390
clothing of, using during
    transition, 416
connecting with, 156–57, 261
counseling for, 175–76,
    295–96
gains and losses, 90
health reports, 328
learning and mental health
    issues, 141–44
open adoption relationships,
    153
open versus confidential
    adoptions, 265–68,
    464–66
rehabilitation and
    reunification, 245, 288
rejection of differences
    behavior, 97–98
relationships with, 464–66,
    480
resources, 159, 310
role in naming, 367
sense of loss, 90, 93
stages of pregnancy, 349–50
terminology for, 485
voluntary termination of
    rights, 175
blankets, 400, 410, 415–16, 417
Bombardieri, Merle, 36–37
Bond, June, 385
bonding. *See* Attachment
books
    for children, 126–28, 135–36,
        387
    resources, 135–36
Borya and the Burps, 387
breast-feeding
    adoptive nursing, 373–77
    benefits of, 372–73, 376
    by birthmothers, 377–79

by foster parents, 380
making decisions about,
    380–81
resources, 395
bribery, 172–73
Bridge Communications, 255
Brodzinsky, Anne Braff, 118
Brodzinsky, David
on acknowledging differences,
    99
on artificial twinning, 189
characteristics of adoptive
    parents, 431, 450
children's understanding of
    adoption, 118, 145, 490
losses experienced by
    adoptees, 119
Brown, Margaret Wise, 127

Cabbage Patch dolls, 215, 489
CAFFA. *See* Chicago Area Families
    for Adoption
Call, Justin, 455
Canada, 290
car seats, 364
caregivers, changes in, 439–40, 455
caseworkers. *See* Social workers
Casey National Center for Family
    Support (CNC), 219
Centers for Disease Control
    fetal alcohol syndrome, 478
    life expectancies, 239–40
Central America, 301
central auditory processing
    disorders, 479
ceremonies. *See* Rituals
Certified Social Workers (CSWs),
    278
CHADD. *See* Children and Adults
    with Attention Deficit/
    Hyperactivity Disorder
challenged attachment, 435–47
challenged family building. *See also*

Infertility
    communication strategies,
        34–37
    coping with stress of, 33–34
    family and friends, dealing
        with, 37–41
    losses accompanying, 20–26
    rituals, need for, 28–29
    victimhood, sense of, 26–28
changes of heart
    adoption insurance, 222, 364
    by adoptive parents, 391–93
    dealing with, 466–74
    grief associated with, 470–71
    grief of siblings, 474–75
    international adoptions,
        299–300, 390
    legal battles, 163, 176–77
    resources, 396
Chicago Area Families for
    Adoption (CAFFA), 130
child abuse or neglect, 141–42,
    370, 418–19
child distinction stage, 350, 351
child embodiment stage, 350, 351
Child Welfare Information
    Gateway web site, 58, 219,
    223
Child Welfare League of America
    (CWLA), 505
child welfare system, 213, 245,
    288–89
childfree living, 37, 70, 75
children. *See also* Adoptees;
    Siblings
    books for, 126–28, 135–36,
        387
    child-centered adoption,
        161–62, 315
    communicating with about
        adoption, 122–26
    learning about adoption,
        117–23

Children and Adults with
    Attention Deficit/
    Hyperactivity Disorder
    (CHADD), 479
Children's Home Society of
    Minnesota, 254, 346, 401
A Child's Journey through Placement
    (Fahlberg), 105, 399
Chile, 301
China
    adoption delays, 298
    health problems of adoptive
        parents, 208, 209
    number of adoptions from,
        301
    resources, 135, 225, 255
Chinese concept of crisis, 19, 29
Choosing Single Motherhood, 74
circling the wagons/cocooning,
    404–5
circumcision, 371
claiming. *See also* Attachment;
    Entitlement, building
    cultural issues, 147–52
    facilitating, 387–88, 404–5,
        405–8
    naming and, 366–68
classes
    parenting, 352, 356
    pre-approval education, 332
Cline, Foster, 429–30, 446
closed adoptions. *See* Confidential
    adoptions
clothing, 415–16, 417, 419
Cobb, Katherine, 408
cocooning process, 404–5
cognitive development, 113–17
Cohen, Maryanne, 93
collaborative reproduction, 65–67,
    74–75
Colombia, 301
comforting routines, 410, 418,
    420–21

commitment requirement, 181–84
communication
    with children about adoption,
        122–26
    gender-specific reactions,
        35–36
    openness, 257, 260
    resources, 72, 133
    role in stress reduction, 33
    strategies, 34–37
    Twenty Minute Rule, 36–37
communicative adoptions. *See*
    Open adoptions
compact officers, 273, 290
competition, in adoption, 163–64
Concerned Persons for Adoption in
    New Jersey, 130
Concerned United Birthparents
    (CUB), 503, 505
concrete operations stage of
    development, 115
conditioning. *See* Physical
    conditioning of adoptive
    parents
conferences
    as information sources, 58–59,
        130–31
    North American Council on
        Adoptable Children,
        246–47
confidential adoptions
    birthparents, feelings about,
        465–66
    compared to open adoptions,
        265–69
    historical perspective, 154,
        258, 260
    intercountry adoptions,
        153–54
    reasons for, 152–53, 264–65
    sealed records, 154, 155, 260
    terminology, 514
conflicts of interest, 272

conscious competence, 101–2
conscious incompetence, 101–2
consultants, 281, 284–85, 290
continuing education, 130–31,
    133–35. *See also* Education
control, loss of, 21–22, 317–18
cord blood storage, 371–72
costs. *See also* Fees
    of adoption, myths about,
        80–81, 496–97
    of parenting, 218, 362
    unexpected, 365
Council on Social Work Education,
    277
counseling
    adoption counselors, 276–77
    agency responsibilities, 283
    for birthparents, 175–76,
        295–96
    dealing with an impasse, 45
court system
    reluctance to terminate
        parental rights, 444
    views of adoption, 475
cradle care, 467. *See also* Foster
    care
credit cards, 221
criminal background checks, 209,
    330
crisis, Chinese concept of, 19, 29
crying behavior, 422–23, 424
CUB. *See* Concerned United
    Birthparents
cultural issues
    diversity, embracing, 128–29
    food preferences, 416–17
    names/naming, 366, 367
    overview, 147–52
    resources, 158–59
    samples of arts and crafts, 399
    transracial adoptions, 149–52,
        235–38

CWLA. *See* Child Welfare League
    of America

Darst, Shelia Steward, 394
Dave Thomas Foundation for
    Adoption, 219, 224, 505
daycare
    decisions about, 381–82
    expenses, 218
death of a child, 391, 511n2
DeBolt, Dorothy, 488
decision making. *See also* Planning
    adopting older children,
        246–49
    assessing resources, 52–57
    dealing with an impasse,
        44–45
    examples, 67–71
    information gathering, 57–59
    process, 42–44
    ranking and weighting
        system, 47, 49–50
    resources, 72–73, 75
    retreat weekend, 59–60
    self reflection, 46–48
    sharing with a partner, 48–51
depression, post-adoption, 453–55,
    475–76
designated adoptions, 290–91
development
    attachment, 106–12
    cognitive, 113–17
    first year of life, 430
    interrupted or unexperienced
        stages, 455–57
    motor skills, 457
    resources, 476
    speech/language delays,
        460–62
    stranger anxiety, 462–64
diapering, 371
differences

accepting/acknowledging
    (AD), 96–97, 99, 232,
    503
  insistence of (ID), 99
  rejection of (RD), 97–98, 99,
    295
directed agency adoptions, 290–91,
    314
disabilities, individuals with. *See
    also* Special needs adoptions
  acceptance or rejection of
    differences, 96–97
  adoptive parents, 207–8
  personal essay, 83–84
  subsidies, 213, 220–21, 249
  support groups, 130
disclosure of information, 143–44
dissolutions/disruptions, 194–95,
    513
diversity
  books for children
    emphasizing, 127–29
Dobrin, Arthur, 147
doctors. *See* Medical professionals;
    Pediatricians
Donley, Kay, 122, 137, 446
Donor Conception Network, 74
dossiers, 333–34
doulas, 404

Eastman, P.D., 127, 387
education
  continuing education, 130–31,
    133–35
  parenting classes, 352, 356
  pre-approval training, 331–33
  sex education, 146–47
egg donation, 65
emotional resources, assessing, 52,
    54
employee adoption benefits, 218,
    219, 220, 364

employment, preparing for changes
    in, 364–65, 421
entitlement, building
  others' reactions and, 100–103
  overview and examples,
    86–88, 102–3
  resources, 103
  sense of loss and, 88–95
  Shared Fate Theory, 95–99,
    260, 412
entrustment ceremonies, 400–402,
    426–27
Erickson, Eric, 25
Ethica: A Voice for Ethical
    Adoption, 505
ethical considerations
  artificial twinning, 183,
    184–94
  birthfathers' rights, 177–79
  commitment requirement,
    181–84
  competition, 163–64
  full disclosure, 179–81
  international adoptions,
    170–74
  practitioner responsibilities
    and practices, 164–70
  resources, 196
  termination of birthparent
    rights, 175–77
Ethiopia, 153, 301
Evan B. Donaldson Adoption
    Institute, 505–6
exercise and conditioning. *See*
    Physical conditioning of
    adoptive parents
expectancy period
  accepting parenthood, 345–48
  benefits of, 343
  emotional denial during,
    343–45
  financial readiness, 362–65

learning to parent, 348–49,
  356–57, 361–62
parallel expectancies, 389–90
physical conditioning, 357–59
preparing siblings, 382–84
psychological changes,
  349–52
schedules and routines, 355–
  56, 361
space planning, 352–55
timing and length of, 345
written records, keeping,
  340–42
expenses. *See* Costs; Fees
extended family. *See* Families
eye contact, 414, 421, 423, 425

facilitators, 276, 281, 284–85, 290
Fahlberg, Vera, 105, 112, 399, 446,
  464
false twinning. *See* Artificial
  twinning
families
  during child's transition
    period, 403–4
  claiming process, 403–8
  cocooning process and, 404–5
  communicating with children
    about adoption, 122–26
  concept of, 484
  connecting with other
    families, 129–30
  dealing with and preparing
    for adoption, 37–41,
    385–89
  impact on entitlement
    building, 100–103
  readjustment of relationships,
    448–50
  resources, 396
  statistical data, 199
  stereotyped assumptions, 100
Families for Russian and Ukrainian
  Adoption (FRUA), 134–35

Families Like Mine, 74
Families with Children from China
  (FCC), 135, 225, 255
Families with Children from
  Vietnam (FCVN), 135
*Family Bonds: Adoption, Infertility,
  and the New World of Child
  Production* (Bartholet), 234
fathers
  birthfathers' rights, 177–79
  breast-feeding and, 376, 381
  changing roles of, 448–49
  putative father registries, 178
FCC. *See* Families with Children
  from China
FCVN. *See* Families with Children
  from Vietnam
Federal Citizen Information
  Center, 219
federal laws
  Adoption and Safe Families
    Act of 1997, 289
  Hope for Children Act (PL
    107-16), 220
  Indian Child Welfare Act, 233
  Multi-Ethnic Placement Act,
    200, 204, 234
Federicci, Ronald, 169, 355–56
fees
  adoption fees, 209–10, 217–18,
    284
  allocation of, 210–11, 283–84
  conflicted feelings about,
    211–13, 214–17
  financial aid and incentives,
    219–22
  homestudy fees, 272
  independent adoptions, 291
  legal fees, 81
  reimbursement-for-service
    charges, 211
fetal alcohol syndrome (FAS), 478
fetal distinction stage, 349, 350
fetal embodiment stage, 349, 350

Filling in the Blanks: A Guided Look at Growing Up Adopted (Gabel), 121, 141

financial resources
  agency requirements, 218–19
  assessing, 52, 53–54
  financial aid and incentives, 219–22, 224–25, 255
  parenting costs, 218, 362
  preparing for changes, 362–65
  resources, 395
  statements, provision of, 330–31

finder's fees, 291

501c3 organizations, 285–87

flat affect, 422–23

flat fees, 291

Flight of the Stork: What Children Think (and When) about Sex and Family Building (Bernstein), 144–45

food preferences, 409–10, 416–17

foreign adoptions. *See* Intercountry adoptions

formal operations stage of development, 115–16

formula brands, 400, 416

foster care
  Adoption and Safe Families Act of 1997, 289
  adoptive parents' involvement in, 400
  breast-feeding, 380
  continuing education for foster parents, 331
  cradle care, 467
  foster-to-adopt families, 175, 289
  licensed foster parents, 213–14, 289
  rituals for transition from, 402
  statistics, 78
  support organizations, 230
  terminology for, 487

Fostering Families Today magazine, 134

frauds, 303–5. *See also* Scams

Free to be a Family (Thomas et al.), 129

Freud, Anna, 114–15

friends. *See also* Family
  during child's transition period, 403–4
  claiming process, 403–8
  cocooning process and, 404–5
  dealing with and preparing for adoption, 37–41, 385–89
  impact on entitlement building, 100–103
  resources, 396
  stereotyped assumptions, 100

FRUA. *See* Families for Russian and Ukrainian Adoption

fundraising ideas, 221

Gabel, Susan, 121, 141

Gallagher, Winifred, 375–76

gay couples
  adoption options, 241–42
  eligibility for adoption, 79, 205–6
  ethical considerations, 172
  resources, 74
  sense of loss of control, 22

gender considerations
  gender selection, 227–29
  singles adoptions, 204

genetic continuity, sense of loss of, 23, 227–28

genetic material, use of, 65–67

gestational carriers, 65–66

gestational multiples, 190–91

Gibran, Kalil, 485–86

The Giving Tree (Silverstein), 127

goals, setting, 60–62

Good Enough Baby, Search for, 253–54, 431

government subsidies, 213, 220–21, 249
grandparents
  claiming process, 387–88, 403–8
  wills, 363
Gray, Deborah, 111–12, 112, 399
grief. *See also* Loss
  adjustment problems and, 109, 412
  of birthparents, 465
  reaction to infertility, 511n2
  reversal of adoption, 470–71
  of siblings, 474–75
Gross, Gregory, 238
Grotevant, Harold, 154, 264, 265
Growing Child newsletter, 357, 456
guardianship, 363
Guatemala
  noncompliance with Hague Treaty, 299, 301
  number of adoptions from, 301
  resources, 135
  singles adoptions, 204
Guatemala Adoptive Families Network, 135
Guess How Much I Love You? (McBratney and Jeram), 127
Gurian, Michael, 117, 411

Hage, Deborah, 446
Hague Treaty
  overview and background, 173–74
  parent preparation rules, 316–17
  potential impact of, 301
  pre- and post-placement support, 331
  resources, 196–97
Hall, Beth, 236
Hall, Pat, 139

Hallenbeck, Carol, 350–51
Happily Childfree, 75
Hartzel, Mary, 117
health insurance, 221, 363
Health Insurance Portability and Accountability Act of 1996 (HIPAA), 327
health problems
  of adoptive parents, 55, 207–8
  changes of heart because of, 392–93
  considering children with, 229–32
  effect on attachment, 107
  resources, 224, 478–80
  testing for, 369–70
health reports, 327–30
hearing impairment, 460
Helping Children Cope with Separation (Jewett-Jarrett), 120
Hispanic children, 78
Holt, Bertha, 200
Holt, Henry, 200
Holt International Children's Services, 197, 200
home environment
  food preferences, 416–17
  scents and fragrance, 415–16
  schedules and routines, 355–56, 361, 420–22
  sounds, 419–20
  space considerations, 81, 352–55
  tactile sensations, 417–19
  visual cues, 414–15
home ownership, 81
home visits, 326–27
homestudies
  fees, 272
  independent adoptions, 293
  process, 272, 283, 313, 315–16
homosexuality. *See also* Gay

couples; Lesbians
    adolescent feelings about, 146
Honduras, 301
Hope for Children Act (PL 107-16), 220
Hopkins-Best, Mary, 415–16, 461
Horton Hatches an Egg (Seuss), 127, 387
How Can I Help? (Bombardieri and Clapp), 39
How to Make Adoption an Affordable Option, 219
How to Survive the Loss of a Love (Cosgrove et al.), 511n1 (chap. 2)
Hughes, Daniel, 112
Human Genome Project, 240
Humane Societies, 491

IAT. *See* Implicit Association Test
IChild, 135
ICWA. *See* Indian Child Welfare Act
I.D.: How Heredity and Experience Make You Who You Are (Gallagher), 375–76
identity issues, 121–22
immigration
    dossier preparation, 333–34
    Hague Treaty, 173–74, 301, 331
    statistics, 78
Implicit Association Test (IAT), 237
INCIID: International Council on Infertility Information Dissemination, 73
income
    eligibility for adoption and, 80
    preparing for changes in, 364–65
independent adoptions
    advertising and marketing, 334

attorney conflict of interest, 272
    compared to agency adoptions, 293–97, 315
    counseling for birthparents, 295–96
    danger of exploitation, 276, 293–94
    decision making considerations, 293–97
    legality of, 290–91, 292
    reasons for, 214, 294
    resources, 309
    types of adoptions handled, 273
India
    behavior of infants from, 424
    number of adoptions from, 301
Indian Child Welfare Act (ICWA), 233
Indianapolis Zoo, 492–93
infants. *See also* Preschoolers; Toddlers
    artificial twinning, 184–94
    attachment, 108–11, 422–25, 444, 446–47
    awareness during gestation, 104
    distress about changes in environment or caregivers, 455
    interrupted or unexperienced development, 455–57
    low birth weight, 458–60
    myths about adopting, 239, 252
    recognition of own name, 366
    time requirements, 55
infectious disease specialists, 232, 398
infertility
    communication strategies, 34–37

coping with stress of, 33–34
denial of impact, 89
family and friends, dealing
    with, 37–41
genetic material, use of, 65–67
grief reaction, 511n2
partner reactions to, 31–33
resources, 73
rituals, need for, 28–29
sense of loss associated with,
    21–26
victimhood and, 26–28
*Infertility: A Guide for the Childless
    Couple* (Menning), 511n2
Infertility Awareness Association of
    Canada, 73
insecure attachment, symptoms of,
    422–24
Inside Transracial Adoption
    (Steinberg and Hall), 236
insistence of differences (ID)
    behavior, 99
institutionalized children. *See*
    Orphanages, children from
insurance
    adoption insurance, 222, 364
    disability and life insurance,
        363–64
    health insurance, 221, 363
    while traveling, 399
intellectual development. *See*
    Cognitive development
intercountry adoptions. *See also*
    Orphanages, children from;
    Transracial/transcultural
    families
    agency selection, 302–3
    agency services, 287
    attachment issues, 109, 412
    average ages of adoption, 246
    challenges of, 301
    changes of heart, 299–300,
        390

concerns about, 297
confidentiality, 153–54, 299
countries allowing singles
    adoptions, 204
dossier preparation, 333–34
ethical considerations, 170–74,
    302–3
historical perspective, 171,
    298
immigration statistics, 78
misconceptions about, 167–
    68, 298–300
motivations for, 214, 298–300
Muslim families, 206, 258–59
naming considerations, 367
numbers of, 300–301
reasons for selecting
    particular countries,
    300
resources, 134–35, 256, 301–2,
    310
respecting laws and customs,
    170–74, 409
specialists in, 168
support groups, 130
transracial adoptions, 204–5
travel requirements, 55
travel tips, 397–98
U.S.-born children, 79
interim care, 400, 487. *See also*
    Foster care
intermediaries, 210, 276, 284–85,
    290
Internet
    chat groups, use of, 397–98
    as information source, 57–58
    scams, 306, 511n1 (chap. 1)
interstate adoptions, 273
Interstate Compact on the
    Placement of Children, 290
interviews, 322–24
intimacy surveys, 323–24
Islam, 206, 258–59

JCICS. *See* Joint Council on
International Children's Services
Jenista, Jeri, 168, 280
Jeram, Anita, 127
Jewett-Jarrett, Claudia, 120, 446
Jewish Social Services, 206
Johnson, Dana, 168, 280, 369–70
Joint Council on International
Children's Services (JCICS),
302, 506
journals, keeping, 340–42
judicial system. *See* Court system
Jusczyk, Peter, 366

kafala (Islam), 206, 258–59
Kazakhstan
number of adoptions from,
301
singles adoptions, 204
Keck, Greg, 112
Keller, Helen, 71
Kids Like Me in China, 387
Kingsley, Emily Perl, 83–84
kinship adoptions, 79
Kirk, H. David, 95–97, 232, 260,
503
Korea
birthfamily searches, 153
historical perspective, 171
number of adoptions from,
300–301
resources, 135, 255, 387
Korean Focus, 135
Kupecky, Regina, 112

La Leche League, 395
lactation. *See* Breast-feeding
Lamb, Michael, 104
language and terminology, 483–88
language delays, 460–62
Latina women, singles adoptions,
204
Launching a Baby's Adoption
(Johnston), 466

LBW. *See* Low birth weight babies
learning. *See also* Education
about parenting, 348–49,
356–57, 361–62
adult learning model, 101–2
cognitive development,
113–17
problems with, 141–44, 460
resources, 132–33
what children understand
about adoption, 117–23
legal fees, 81
legal issues
criminal background checks,
209, 330
gay or lesbian adoptive
parents, 205–6
racial differences, 200, 204
sealed records, 154, 155,
260–61
termination of parental rights,
178–79, 279
legislation. *See* Federal laws; State
laws
lesbians. *See also* Gay couples
adoption options, 241–42
eligibility for adoption, 205–6
Liberia, 301
Licensed Social Workers (LSWs),
278
licensing
agencies, 275
social workers, 278
life expectancies, 239–40
lifebooks, 126–27
lifestyle
financial considerations, 222
impact on children, 241
Lifton, Betty Jean, 260
lighting, 414, 415
loans, 221
loss. *See also* Grief
coping with, 19–21

entitlement building and,
88–95
reflecting on, 46–48
resources, 72
types of, 20, 21–26, 46
Love You Forever (Munche), 127,
387
Love You Like Crazy Cakes, 387
low birth weight (LBW) babies,
458–60
LSWs. *See* Licensed Social Workers

Maggio, Rosalie, 483
Mahoney, Jim, 101–2, 446
Main, Mary, 329
Maiser, Mary Anne, 346–47, 401,
467–68
marital history and status. *See also*
Singles
impact on adoptions, 203–4
resources, 223
marketing. *See* Advertising and
marketing
Martin, Cynthia, 502
master's in social work (MSW),
277
McBratney, Sam, 127
McDermott, Mark, 272
McRoy, Ruth, 154, 264, 265
mediators, 266
medical history, 328
medical professionals
as adoption specialists,
280–81
choosing, 231–32, 368–70
resources, 310
meetings. *See* Conferences
mental health issues
adoptees, 141–44, 251, 300
adoptive parents, 208–9,
328–30
birthparents, 141
mental retardation, 460
military subsidies, 221

*The Minds of Boys: Saving Our
Sons From Falling Behind in
School and Life* (Gurian),
117
mindsightedness, 117, 413
Minnesota Multiphasic Personality
Inventory (MMPI-2), 329
minority families, 79, 128–29, 205
*The Miracle Seekers: An Anthology
of Infertility* (Mason), 29
miscarriages, 391
Mitchell, Mary, 178–79
More, More, More! Said the Baby
(Williams), 129, 387
A Mother for Choco (Kasza), 387
motivations
for adopting, 84–85
for international adoptions,
214
motor skills development, 457
MSW. *See* Master's in social work
The Mulberry Bird (Brodzinsky),
387
Multi-Ethnic Placement Act
(MEPA), 200, 204, 234
multiculturalism. *See also* Cultural
issues; Transracial/
transcultural families
diversity, embracing, 128–29
resources, 158–59
multiple births, 190–91
Munche, Robert, 127, 129
music, 419, 420, 427
Muslim families, 206, 258–59
mutual consent registries, 260
myths
adopting infants, 239, 252
adoption, 79–81, 496–501
attachment, 104, 105
costs of adoption, 80–81,
496–97
homestudies, 313
mental health of adopted
children, 251

open adoption, 154–55,
    261–62
public adoption, 289
special needs adoptions, 250
transracial adoption, 232

NACAC. *See* North American
    Council on Adoptable
    Children
names/naming, 366–68
National Adoption Assistance
    Training Resource and
    Information Network
    Helpline, 225
National Adoption Center, 219
National Association of Black
    Social Workers, 233, 503
National Association of Social
    Workers, 278
National Center for PTSD, 480
National Child Welfare Resource
    Center for Adoption
    (NCWRCA), 507
National Coalition on Auditory
    Processing Disorders, 479
National Council for Adoption
    (NCFA), 503, 506
National Council for Single
    Adoptive Parents, 223
National Endowment for Financial
    Education, 219
National Institute on Deafness
    and Other Communication
    Disorders, 479
National Institutes of Mental
    Health, 480
National Organization on Fetal
    Alcohol Syndrome, 478
Native Americans, 233
NCFA. *See* National Council for
    Adoption
NCWRCA. *See* National Child
    Welfare Resource Center for
    Adoption

Nepal, 204
nesting behavior. *See* Expectancy
    period
newborns. *See* Infants
Nigeria, 511n1 (chap. 1)
Nine Months (film), 339
No Kidding, 75
nonagency service providers,
    210, 281–82, 314. *See also*
    Independent adoptions
North American Council on
    Adoptable Children
    (NACAC), 131, 134, 225,
    246–47, 255, 506
not-for-profit organizations,
    285–87
nursing. *See* Breast-feeding
*Nurture the Nature: Understanding
    and Supporting Your Child's
    Unique Core Personality*
    (Gurian), 117, 411
Nurturing Adoptions (Gray), 111–
    12, 112, 399

odors, 415–16
older children. *See also* Adolescents
    attachment, 112–13
    changing names of, 368
    decision making about,
        246–49
    definition of, 242
    negative stories about, 242
    non-agency intermediaries,
        210
    toddlers, 243–45
open adoptions
    advantages of, 464
    birthparents, relationships
        with, 153, 464–65
    compared to confidential
        adoptions, 265–69
    historical perspective, 258–61
    myths about, 261–62
    need for education and

ongoing support,
265–66
negative aspects of, 389–90
terminology, 514n2 (chap. 7)
trend toward, 154–57
types of, 262–64
openness, 257–58, 260. *See also*
Open adoptions
Organization of Parents through
Surrogacy (OPTS), 74
Orphan Train movement, 154, 259
Orphan Voyage, 260
orphanages, children from
adjustment suggestions, 354,
382, 415
challenges, 55
characteristics of, 422–23, 456
historical perspective, 259
misconceptions about, 300
*Our Child: Preparation for Parenting
in Adoption—Instructor's
Guide* (Hallenbeck), 350–51
OURS magazine, 109, 412
OURS of Northeastern Wisconsin,
130
overstimulation
avoiding, 356, 412, 413–14
susceptible ages for, 455

Pact: An Adoption Alliance, 134,
255–56
paperwork, 322, 330–31
parent-child relationships. *See*
Attachment
parent-initiated adoptions, 291–92
parent preparation process, 295,
316–17
parent support groups, 130, 230
parenting
annual costs, 218, 362
challenges of, 131–32, 157,
431–34
changes associated with, 162

commitment requirement,
181–84
learning to parent, 348–49,
356–57, 361–62
resources, 394–95, 476–77
sense of loss of, 25–26
Parenting from the Inside Out
(Hartzel), 117
parents. *See also* Adoptive parents;
Birthparents/birthfamilies
attachment history, 108
continuing education, 130–31,
352, 356
Pavao, Joyce Maguire, 139, 190
Peck, Cynthia Van Norden, 45,
450–52
pediatricians
as adoption specialists,
280–81
choosing, 231–32, 368–70
People (Spier), 129, 387
Personal Assessment Inventory,
329
personality traits of children, 91,
107, 117, 430, 463
Peru, 301
pervasive developmental disorders,
479–80
Peterson, Janelle, 446
Philippines, 301
photo albums, 127
physical conditioning of adoptive
parents, 358–59
physical resources, assessing, 52,
54–55
physicians. *See* Medical
professionals; Pediatricians
Piaget, Jean, 114, 145
Pinckney, Jerry, 129
PL 107-16. *See* Hope for Children
Act
planning. *See also* Decision making
applying resources, 63–65

evaluation, periodic, 67
examples, 67–71
financial readiness, 362–65
learning to parent, 348–49,
    356–57, 361–62
schedules and routines, 355–
    56, 361
setting goals, 60–62
space considerations, 352–55
strategizing, 63
poetry, 427
politics and activism, 502–7
Positive Adoption Language (PAL),
    483–84
post-adoption programs, 247, 293
post-arrival depression, 453–55,
    475–76
post placement reports, 173
post-traumatic stress, 141–42, 480
practitioners. See Agencies;
    Professionals
pre-logical/intuitive stage of
    development, 115
pre-term babies, 458, 459
preconceptual stage of
    development, 115
preferential adopters, 86, 89, 91
pregnancy
    definition of pregnant, 348
    emotional/psychological
        stages of, 349–51
    miscarriages, 391
    parallel expectancies, 389–90
    prenatal care, 141, 357–58,
        458
    psychological, 345–49,
        350–51
    sense of lost experiences,
        24–25
    sympathetic pregnancy,
        359–60
pregnancy validation stage, 349,
    350

prejudice, 150–52, 235–36, 498–
    500. See also Stereotypes
prenatal care, 141, 357–58, 458
preschoolers. See also Toddlers
    attachment, 111–12
    stranger anxiety, 462–64
Primal Wound theory, 515–16n2
    (chap. 15)
private adoptions. See Independent
    adoptions
private agencies
    adoption statistics, 78
    fees, 217–18
    services provided, 282–83,
        289–90
    types of adoptions handled,
        210, 214
professionals
    adoption counselors, 276–77
    agency-client relationships,
        317–21
    attorneys, 272, 276, 278–79,
        290, 292
    definitions, 275–76
    ethical practices and
        responsibilities,
        164–70
    pediatricians, 231–32, 280–81,
        368–70
    poor practices, examples of,
        439–40
    social workers, 276, 277–78,
        290
pseudo-twinning. See Artificial
    twinning
psychological assessment of
    adoptive parents, 328–30
psychological pregnancy. See also
    Expectancy period
    need for, 190
    stages of, 350–52
The Psychology of Adoption
    (Brodzinsky), 119

public agencies
    child welfare system, 213, 245,
        288–89
    fees, 217
    resources, 310
    services provided, 282,
        288–89
    types of adoptions handled,
        210
Pulaski, Mary Ann Spencer, 117
putative father registries, 178, 279

Quad A. *See* American Academy of
    Adoption Attorneys
quasi-adoption. *See* Genetic
    material, use of

Raabe, Mary Alice, 122–23
race/ethnicity. *See also* Transracial/
    transcultural families
    accepting or rejecting
        differences, 97
    challenges of interracial
        adoption, 235–38
    cultural issues, 147–52
    impact on adoptions, 204–5
    moving to a new
        neighborhood, 149–50
    Multi-Ethnic Placement Act,
        200, 204, 234
    race matching versus
        transracial placements,
        232–34
    racism, 150–52, 235–36,
        498–500
    resources, 158–59, 255–56
racism, 150–52, 235–36, 498–500
RAD. *See* Reactive attachment
    disorder
ranking and weighting system, 47,
    49–50
reactive attachment disorder
    (RAD), 112

readiness. *See* Expectancy period
Real Parents, Real Children (Van
        Gulden and Bartels-Raab),
        461
record keeping, 340–42
references, providing, 324–26
Register, Cheri, 236, 237, 461
registries
    mutual consent registries, 260
    putative father registries, 178
reimbursement-for-service charges,
    211
rejection of differences (RD),
    97–98, 99, 295
relatives. *See* Families;
    Grandparents
religious beliefs
    eligibility for adoption and,
        80, 206
    resources, 224
    transcultural adoptions,
        148–49
religiously oriented agencies, 206,
    282
*Residential Treatment: A Tapestry of
    Many Therapies* (Fahlberg),
    105
Resolve, Inc., 36, 39, 73
resources
    assessing, 52–57
    planning and applying, 63–65
respectful adoption language
    (RAL), 484–88
retreat weekends, 59–60
reunification, 245, 288
reversals. *See* Changes of heart;
        Dissolutions/disruptions
risks
    emotional risks during
        expectancy period, 344
    health problems, 226
    learning problems and mental
        health issues, 141–44

minimizing, 273–74
rituals
    entrustment ceremonies,
        400–402, 426–27
    during expectancy period, 352
    need for, 28–29
Rogu, George, 399
role transition stage
    pregnancy, 349, 350
    psychological pregnancy, 351,
        352
Romanchik, Brenda, 268, 344, 362,
    466
Romania, 300
Roots & Wings magazine, 412, 452
Roszia, Sharon Kaplan, 157, 359,
    416, 425
routines. *See* Schedules and
    routines
The Runaway Bunny (Brown), 127
Russia
    adoption delays, 298
    birthfamily searches, 153
    changes of heart, 299
    citizen priority, 299–300
    number of adoptions from,
        301
    resources, 134–35
    singles adoptions, 204

Say, Alan, 129
scams, 174, 305–7, 310–11, 511n1
    (chap. 1)
scents and fragrance, 415–16
Schecter, Marshall, 155
schedules and routines
    preparing for changes, 355–
        56, 361
    promoting attachment,
        420–22
school-aged children. *See* Older
    children
school issues, 137–41, 157–58
Schuler, Jennifer L, 508

scrapbooks, 342, 400
sealed records, 154, 155, 260–61
Search for the Good Enough Baby,
    253–54, 431
Sears, William, 413
second children, adopting, 253
second-parent adoptions, 205
self reflection, 46–48
sensory integration dysfunction,
    480
sensory/motor stage of
    development, 114–15
sensory processing disorders, 480
sensory sensitivities, 414–20
separation anxiety, 462–64
service providers. *See* Agencies;
    Nonagency service
    providers; Professionals
Seuss, Dr., 127
sex education, 144–47, 158
sexual orientation. *See also* Gay
    couples
    impact on adoptions, 205–6
    resources, 223–24
sexuality, interview questions
    about, 323–24
Shain, Merle, 29
Shared Fate (Kirk), 96
Shared Fate Theory, 95–99, 260,
    412
Shinyei, Marilyn, 465
siblings
    differing adoption styles for,
        384–85
    grief of, 474–75
    preparing for adoption,
        382–84
    resources, 396, 477
    sense of loss in adoption,
        94–95
Siegel, Daniel J., 117, 413
Silber, Kathleen, 268
Silverstein, Shel, 127
singles

adjustment issues, 450–52
adoption hurdles, 203–4
adoption options, 241–42
decision making, 45–46,
        67–68
eligibility for adoption, 79
resources, 74
sense of loss of control, 22
statistics, 199
sleeping arrangements, 409, 418
small for gestational age (SGA)
        babies, 458, 459
Smith, Jerome, 95
smokers, 208, 458
SOAFC. *See under* American
        Academy of Pediatrics
social workers, 276, 277–78, 290
Something Good (Munche), 129,
        387
sound stimulation, 419–20
South America, 153, 301
South Korea. *See also* Korea
        number of adoptions from,
        300–301
space considerations, 81, 352–55
Spaulding for Children, 506–7
special needs adoptions. *See also*
        Disabilities, individuals
        with
        conflicted feelings about,
        249–52
        older children, 246–49
        pressure tactics, 227, 251–52
        resources, 254–55, 395
speech/language delays, 460–62
Spencer, Marietta, 483–84
sperm donation, 65
Starr, Darilyn, 379
state laws
        attorney representation
        requirement, 272
        gay or lesbian adoptive
        parents, 205–6

independent adoptions, 290–
        91, 292
interstate adoptions, 273
sealed records, 154, 260–61
tax credits, 220
termination of parental rights,
        178–79, 279
Steinberg, Gail, 236
step-parent adoptions, 271
Steptoe, John, 129
stereotypes, 30–31, 100, 483
stranger anxiety, 462–64
stress, coping with, 33–34
subsidies, 213, 220–21, 249
substance abuse
        adoptive parents, 209
        birthparents, 141, 458
supplemental nursing systems
        (SNS), 374
support groups, 130, 230
surrogate mothers, 65–66
Suzuki method of teaching, 460
*Sweet Grapes: How to Stop Being
        Infertile and Start Living
        Again* (Carter and Carter),
        28–29, 37
swimming and bathing, 418
sympathetic pregnancy, 359–60
symposia. *See* Conferences

tactile sensations, 417–19
*Talking About People: A Guide to
        Fair and Accurate Language*
        (Maggio), 483
Tannen, Deborah, 35–36
taxes, 218, 219–20
teachers, views of adoption,
        494–95
teens. *See* Adolescents
*Tell Me Again about the Night I Was
        Born*, 387
termination of parental rights,
        178–79, 279

textures. *See* Tactile sensations
therapists, 276–77
ThinkAnxiety.org, 480
timing, assessing, 52, 55–57, 65
Toddler Adoption: The Weaver's Craft
        (Hopkins-Best), 415–16,
        461
toddlers
        adoption considerations,
                243–45
        attachment, 108–11
        stranger anxiety, 462–64
        time requirements, 55
traditional adopters, 86, 130
transition to new home. *See*
        also Expectancy period;
        Planning
        entrustment rituals, 400–402
        obtaining information about
                previous care, 408–10
        suggestions for, 399–400,
                403–4
transportation for children, 364
transracial/transcultural families.
        See also Cultural issues;
        Race/ethnicity
        challenges of, 235–38
        cultural issues, 147–52
        diversity and, 129
        moving to a new
                neighborhood, 149–50
        racism, 150–52, 235–36,
                498–500
travel
        requirements, 55
        resources, 426
        tips for, 397–98
Tremitiere, Barb, 446
Trout, Michael, 190
Twenty Minute Rule, 36–37
twinning. *See* Artificial twinning
2 Moms, 2 Dads, 74

Ukraine, 134–35, 301
umbilical cord blood storage,
        371–72
unconscious competence, 101–2
unconscious incompetence, 101–2,
        152, 235
*Understanding Infertility: Insights
        for Family and Friends*
        (Johnston), 39–40
United Kingdom, smokers as
        adoptive parents, 208
University of Minnesota, 280
U.S. Citizenship and Immigration
        Services
        dossier preparation, 333
        Hague Treaty, 331
U.S. Department of Agriculture,
        costs of parenting, 218, 362
U.S. Department of Health and
        Human Services, 199
U.S. State Department
        Hague Treaty, 196, 331
        website information, 196, 256,
                310

Van Gulden, Holly, 109, 424, 461
The Velveteen Rabbit (Williams),
        128, 387
Verny, Thomas, 104
victimhood, sense of, 26–28
Vietnam, 135, 204
virtual twinning. *See* Artificial
        twinning
visual cues, 414–15
vocabulary development, 460

waiting children. *See* Older
        children; Special needs
        adoptions
*What to Expect When You're
        Expecting,* 362
When You Were Born in Korea, 387
Williams, Margery, 128

Williams, Vera, 129
Williams, Wendy, 468–69, 470–74
wills, 363
*The Wonder of Girls: Understanding
    the Hidden Nature of Our
    Daughters* (Gurian), 117

word choices, 483–88
World Health Organization, growth
    charts, 370
*You Just Don't Understand: Women
and Men in Conversation* (Tannen),
35–36
Your Baby's Mind and How It Grows
    (Pulaski), 117

About the Author

For over 30 years Patricia Irwin Johnston, MS, has worked and volunteered in the fields of infertility and adoption—as an author and educator and trainer, as an advocate and organizational leader.

Over many years, her actively-involved volunteer leadership commitments to Resolve, INCIID, Adoptive Families of America, JCICS, Indiana's Adoption Education Coalition and more have resulted in several awards from NACAC, APC, Resolve, AFA and culminated in a 2007 Angel in Adoption award from the Congressional Coalition on Adoption.

Adopting: Sound Choices, Strong Families is Pat's eighth book. As publisher and senior editor for 25 years at Perspectives Press, Inc.: The Infertility and Adoption Publisher, she has edited many others.

Proud graduates of Butler University, Pat and her husband, Dave, parented three now grown children. They live in Indianapolis in an empty nest that needs to be downsized!

About the Publisher

Perspectives Press: The Infertility and Adoption Publisher
www.perspectivespress.com

Since 1982 Perspectives Press, Inc. has focused exclusively on infertility, adoption and related reproductive health and child welfare issues. Our purpose is to educate and support those experiencing these life situations, and to educate and sensitize professionals who work in these fields and to promote understanding of these issues to the public at large. Our titles are never duplicate of or competitive with good material already available through other publishers. Instead, we seek to find and fill empty niches.

Currently in print titles include

For adults

Nurturing Adoptions

Having Your Baby through Egg Donation

Adoption Is a Family Affair:
  What Relatives and Friends Must Know

Attaching in Adoption

Inside Transracial Adoption

PCOS: The Hidden Epidemic

Launching a Baby's Adoption

Toddler Adoption: The Weaver's Craft

Looking Back, Looking Forward

Sweet Grapes: How to Stop Being Infertile and Start Living Again

Taking Charge of Infertility

Flight of the Stork: What Children Think (and When)
  about Sex and Family Building

A Child's Journey through Placement

Understanding Infertility: Insights for Family and Friends

Perspectives on a Grafted Tree: Thoughts for Those Touched by Adoption

For Children

Borya and the Burps

Sam's Sister

The Mulberry Bird

Two Birthdays for Beth

Filling in the Blanks.

Is there a book for our audience in you?

Our writer's guidelines are on our website at
www.perspectivespress.com/writerguides.html